Applied Statistics (*Continued*)

DODGE and ROMIG · Sampling Inspection Tabl
FRYER · Elements of Statistics
GOLDBERGER · Econometric Theory
GOULDEN · Methods of Statistical Analysis, *Second Edition*
HALD · Statistical Tables and Formulas
HALD · Statistical Theory with Engineering Applications
HANSEN, HURWITZ, and MADOW · Sample Survey Methods and Theory, Volume I
HOEL · Elementary Statistics
KEMPTHORNE · An Introduction to Genetic Statistics
MEYER · Symposium on Monte Carlo Methods
MUDGETT · Index Numbers
RICE · Control Charts
ROMIG · 50–100 Binomial Tables
SARHAN and GREENBERG · Contributions to Order Statistics
TIPPETT · Technological Applications of Statistics
WILLIAMS · Regression Analysis
WOLD and JURÉEN · Demand Analysis
YOUDEN · Statistical Methods for Chemists

Books of Related Interest

ALLEN and ELY · International Trade Statistics
ARLEY and BUCH · Introduction to the Theory of Probability and Statistics
CHERNOFF and MOSES · Elementary Decision Theory
HAUSER and LEONARD · Government Statistics for Business Use, *Second Edition*
STEPHAN and McCARTHY · Sampling Opinions—An Analysis of Survey Procedures

Econometric Theory

A WILEY PUBLICATION IN APPLIED STATISTICS

Econometric Theory

ARTHUR S. GOLDBERGER

Professor, Department of Economics and Social Systems Research Institute, University of Wisconsin

John Wiley & Sons, Inc.
New York · London · Sydney

10 9 8 7 6

LIBRARY OF CONGRESS CATALOG CARD NUMBER: 64-10370

PRINTED IN THE UNITED STATES OF AMERICA

To Iefke

Preface

This book is intended as a text for a one-year course in econometrics at the graduate level. Its concern is with the methods of estimating and testing relationships among economic variables. Unity of treatment is provided by starting with the classical regression model and proceeding to weaken its several assumptions in turn. The resulting structure should make the book useful also as a reference for those engaged in empirical economic research.

The prerequisites appropriate to a course based on this book include a one-semester introduction to matrix algebra and a one-year introduction to mathematical statistics. Chapters 2 and 3 constitute a fairly comprehensive review of those courses. These chapters are designed to make the text reasonably self-contained: They serve as a convenient reference to many concepts and theorems used throughout the book, and they also permit some flexibility with respect to prerequisites. In addition, they include the elements of such topics as asymptotic sampling theory and stochastic processes which, while important in econometrics, are usually omitted in the introductory courses.

It is a pleasure to acknowledge my indebtedness to those who have contributed in various ways to the preparation of this book. A sequence of preliminary versions in the form of dittoed notes has been used in econometrics courses at Stanford University and at the University of Wisconsin. The questions and criticisms by students in these classes—Donald V. T. Bear, Charles Carr, and George C. Tiao in particular—have been extremely stimulating. Comments by John Hooper and Marc Nerlove on a draft chapter guided my thinking at an early stage. I am especially grateful to T. Kloek for a constructive critical reading of the major portion of the manuscript. The syllabi for the program of mathematical and managerial economics of the Netherlands School of Economics have clarified my views on many points, and I am deeply indebted to

H. Theil and his associates at the Econometric Institute for making these available to me. I have also benefited considerably from discussions on specific points with my colleagues Roger Miller, Guy Orcutt, and Arnold Zellner and with my former teacher Lawrence Klein. I can acknowledge, but hardly repay, my indebtedness to Roger Miller, whose painstaking assistance at the proof-reading stage went far beyond the call of fraternal duty.

Thanks also go to J. J. Johnston for access to a partial draft of his *Econometric Methods*; to R. L. Basmann, Peter de Janosi, James Tobin, and Arnold Zellner for permission to cite unpublished work; and to T. Kloek and L. B. M. Mennes for access to unpublished worksheets relating to computations reported in Chapter 7. For expert typing of difficult material I am grateful indeed to Mrs. Anna Campbell and Mrs. Alice Wilcox.

My work on this book has been substantially facilitated by my association with the Social Systems Research Institute of the University of Wisconsin. I am very happy to express my thanks to Guy Orcutt, Director of Research of the SSRI, for his sustained encouragement.

Madison, Wisconsin
October, 1963

ARTHUR S. GOLDBERGER

Contents

CHAPTER 1

Introduction

1. THE SCOPE OF ECONOMETRICS

Econometrics may be defined as the social science in which the tools of economic theory, mathematics, and statistical inference are applied to the analysis of economic phenomena. Its main objective is to give empirical content to economic theory; econometrics in fact encompasses a wide range of activities aimed at accomplishing this objective. First, there is continuing work on the mathematical formulation of economic theory—this is the field known as mathematical economics. Second, there is work on the development of appropriate techniques of statistical inference—this is the field we are calling econometric theory. And third, there is actual statistical inference from economic data—this is the field which may be termed empirical econometrics. On a somewhat broader interpretation econometrics has been taken to include such associated activities as the development of methods of collecting economic data, the collection of the data itself, and the application of empirical results to the problems of economic policy formation.

This suggests that a comprehensive program of training in econometrics involves the study of economic theory, mathematics, mathematical statistics, social accounting and survey methods, and empirical analyses. This book is concerned with econometric theory: Methods of statistical inference appropriate in economics are systematically developed, but economic theory and empirical econometrics are utilized only for illustrations. Although econometric theory draws heavily on the mainstream of mathematical statistics, it has a distinctive flavor which is attributable to characteristic features of economics. One feature is that as a rule observations on economic phenomena are not obtained by controlled experiments; consequently special methods for the analysis of nonexperimental data have to be devised. Another feature is that there is a rich body of theory of economic behavior; consequently special methods are devised to take advantage of this. It is not hard to see that to some extent economic theory can serve as a substitute for experimental control: factors whose influence can be ruled out on theoretical grounds need not be controlled.

2. RELATIONSHIPS AMONG ECONOMIC VARIABLES

Most of economic theory is concerned with *relationships among variables*. The quantity of a commodity demanded by an individual is related to his income and the price of the commodity; the cost of producing a commodity is related to the quantity produced and to the prices of the factors used in producing it; national consumption expenditure is related to national income; etc. Correspondingly, most of econometric theory is concerned with measuring relationships among variables—with methods of quantifying the relationships of economic theory.

Now it will be recognized that economic theory typically specifies *exact* functional relationships among its variables. On the other hand, even the most casual inspection of empirical economic data suffices to show that such exact functional relationships do not hold in reality. If, e.g., we plot annual personal consumption expenditures against disposable personal income for the United States for the years since 1929, we do not find all the points lying along a straight line—nor along some other smooth curve, for that matter. What follows is not that economic theory should be discarded as being worthless, but rather that it should be extended by the introduction of probabilistic elements. A main task of econometric theory, indeed, is to provide a bridge between the exact relationships of economic theory and the disturbed relationships of economic reality.

To illustrate, suppose that we are attempting to measure the familiar relationship $c = \alpha + \beta y$ where c is consumption expenditure and y is disposable income, and that for this purpose we have available observations on the consumption expenditures and disposable incomes of 3000 households in 1963. It is clear that this relationship will not hold exactly: All the households that have the same income will not have the same consumption, and the 3000 paired observations c_t, y_t ($t = 1, \ldots, 3000$) will not all satisfy $c_t = \alpha + \beta y_t$. Indeed the theoretical relationship does not really purport to describe the behavior of every individual household but rather to describe average behavior in some sense. This suggests that a probabilistic version of the economic theory might be $c = \alpha + \beta y + \epsilon$ where ϵ is a "disturbance term" which may take on positive or negative values but which is zero "on the average." This allows for individual variation from the exact relationship.

There are alternative interpretations or rationalizations of the disturbance term. First, we may say that consumption is in fact determined exactly as a function of income and other factors such as the number of persons in the household, their ages, their income expectations, their health, and their psychological makeups. On this interpretation, individual differences in consumption expenditure at a given level of income are simply attributable to differences in the values of these other variables. If all the other variables had been included, an exact relationship would have been observed; failing this, the disturbance term is introduced to represent the net effect of the omitted variables on consumption. Second, we may say that there is an inherent indeterminancy in human behavior so that even if all the other variables were introduced, individual differences would still be observed. On this interpretation, the disturbance term represents this inherent indeterminancy. Third, we may say that although there may really be an exact relationship among the variables considered in the economic theory, the observations we have are not exact measurements of those variables. On this interpretation, the disturbance term reflects these errors in the observations. It should be noted that these alternative interpretations are not mutually exclusive. Indeed, in practice, the distinction between the first and second evaporates because data limitations prevent us from including all the relevant variables.

Now the introduction of a disturbance term, although necessary, does not suffice to make an economic theory operational. After all, if we write $c = \alpha + \beta y + \epsilon$ and simply say that ϵ is an unobserved variable which takes on different values for different individuals, *any* pair of values for α and β—say a and b—will give us a "relationship" that fits the data: Simply take $\epsilon_t = c_t - (a + by_t)$ for each $t = 1, \ldots, 3000$. But such an "empirical relationship" is tautological and tells us nothing about economic behavior. What must be introduced is some specification of the stochastic properties of the disturbance term; e.g., that each ϵ_t is a random drawing from a probability distribution with mean zero and finite variance. For some purposes, in fact, an assumption about the form of the probability distribution—e.g., normal or rectangular—is needed. Such specifications—justified, of course, in the particular empirical context—are prerequisites for the development of rational methods of measuring relationships among economic variables. Their role is to translate the problems of measuring economic relationships into the problems of estimating the parameters of probability distributions.

In its probabilistic version, then, an economic theory will typically specify a functional relationship in which observed "independent variables" and unobserved "disturbances" determine an observed "dependent variable" and will also specify statistical properties of the disturbances. It is important to recognize that some specification of the mechanism generating the observed "independent variables" is also required. In much of mathematical statistics the specification is made that these are fixed, nonrandom variables. Generally speaking, this is appropriate for the analysis of experimental data where the values of the "independent variables" are controlled by the experimenter. For the analysis of the nonexperimental data of economics, however, this specification will often have to give way to alternatives which allow for an uncontrolled, stochastic determination of the observed "independent variables." Such alternative specifications—justified, of course, in the particular empirical contexts—will often have alternative implications for the choice of a method of measuring the economic relationship. For example, a method which is attractive when the disturbances are unrelated to the observed "independent variables" may lose its virtues when they are in fact related.

To sum up this introductory discussion, we may say that the models of econometric theory will have three basic components: a specification of the process by which certain observed "independent variables" are generated, a specification of the process by which unobserved "disturbances" are generated, and a specification of the relationship connecting these to observed "dependent variables." Taken together these components provide a model for the generation of economic observations, and implicitly, at least, they define a statistical population. A given body of economic observations may then be viewed as a sample from the population. A distinction commonly made is that between cross-section and time series samples: A cross-section sample consists of observations on many economic units—households, firms, countries, etc.—at a given point of time; a time series sample consists of observations at many points of time of a given economic unit—household, firm, country, etc. Broadly speaking, the same methods of analysis are applicable to these two types of data, but each has some distinctive features, as we shall see.

Once we have a specification of a parent population we may rely on the rules and criteria of statistical inference in order to develop a rational method of measuring a relationship of economic theory from a given sample of observations. In many cases we may rely also on previous theoretical or empirical knowledge about the value of parameters of the population: Such a priori information is a characteristic feature of econometric theory. In any event, it should be clear that the quantification of economic theory is not a mechanical task. In particular, it is not simply a matter of fitting curves to data, of "measurement without theory." The underlying theme of this book is that rational methods of measuring economic relationships must be grounded in a specification of the probabilistic mechanisms that link economic observations to economic theory.

3. THE PLAN OF THIS BOOK

The plan of this book is as follows. In Chapter 2 the basic concepts and results of matrix algebra are presented. In Chapter 3 the basic concepts and results of statistical inference are presented. These two chapters are not intended to replace textbooks in their respective fields. Rather, they serve as review material, provide a common vocabulary, and, most important, constitute a convenient reference source for the sequel. Then we turn to develop a series of models and estimation methods that appear fruitful for the measurement of economic relationships. In Chapter 4 the classical linear regression model is formulated, and appropriate methods of statistical inference are considered. This model, originally developed for the experimental sciences, still plays a central role in econometrics. Its assumptions are apparently quite restrictive, but it does serve as a starting point for the construction of more sophisticated models. Chapter 5 is devoted to indicating the flexibility of this classical model and to considering some of its elementary variants while retaining the specification that the "independent" variables are nonrandom. In Chapter 6 this specification is relaxed and models are developed in which the "independent" variables are themselves random. The implications of increasing degrees of complexity are explored. Finally, in Chapter 7 we consider in detail the statistical implications of *systems* of probabilistic economic relationships—of "econometric models" in the most familiar sense of the term.

A word on notation: The book is divided into Chapters 1–7, the chapters are divided into sections (numbered serially within each chapter), and some sections are divided into subsections (unnumbered). To refer to a section within its own chapter the section number is used; to refer to a section in another chapter the section number is preceded by the chapter number. When displayed, equations are identified by the section number followed by a period and a serial number, all in parentheses. To refer to an equation within its own chapter this pair of numbers is used; to refer to an equation in another chapter this pair of numbers is preceded by the chapter number.

Reference to the books and articles of the bibliography is by the author's name, followed by the year of publication in parentheses; on occasion, the year is followed by specific page or chapter numbers. The serious reader will want to supplement this book by consulting the standard textbooks of econometric theory—Tintner (1952), Klein (1953), and Johnston (1963)—and by exploring the literature of empirical econometrics—to which Klein (1962) is an instructive guide.

CHAPTER 2

Basic Concepts of Matrix Algebra

1. INTRODUCTION

In many areas of economics—consumer demand theory, interindustry analysis, general equilibrium models, and others—matrix algebra serves as a convenient and powerful notation. In mathematical statistics it is virtually a necessity. This chapter provides basic concepts and results on which we rely in our subsequent development of the theory of econometrics.

In Section 2 vectors, matrices, and operations on them are defined. In Section 3 the determinant of a square matrix is introduced. In Section 4 the concept of linear dependence of a set of vectors and the related concept of the rank of a matrix are defined and applied to investigate the solution to a system of simultaneous homogeneous linear equations. In Section 5 the inverse of a square matrix is introduced and applied to investigate the solution of a square system of simultaneous linear equations. This material constitutes the bare rudiments of matrix algebra and has wide applicability throughout economics. The remaining sections go somewhat deeper along lines that are particularly relevant for statistical theory. Section 6 is concerned with characteristic roots, diagonalization, orthogonal and idempotent matrices, and linear and quadratic forms. Section 7 develops the properties of definite matrices—positive, nonnegative, and others. Finally in Section 8 several basic concepts and results of the differential calculus are presented in matrix notation.

Our treatment hardly constitutes a rigorous introduction to matrix algebra. Nevertheless in many cases proofs are included to enhance understanding and to illustrate the power of this tool. For a more rigorous development see Hadley (1961).

2. VECTORS AND MATRICES

Column Vectors

We begin by defining an $m \times 1$ column vector, written $\mathbf{x}$, to be an ordered m-tuple of real numbers, arranged in a column;

$$\text{(2.1)} \qquad \mathbf{x} = \begin{pmatrix} x_1 \\ \cdot \\ \cdot \\ \cdot \\ x_m \end{pmatrix}.$$

The numbers x_i $(i = 1, \ldots, m)$ are called the elements (or components or coordinates) of the column vector. Two column vectors are equal if and only if they are equal element by element:

$$\text{(2.2)} \qquad \mathbf{x} = \mathbf{y} \text{ if and only if } x_i = y_i \quad (i = 1, \ldots, m).$$

We also have occasion to write $\mathbf{x} \leq \mathbf{y}$ to mean $x_i \leq y_i$ $(i = 1, \ldots, m)$ and $\mathbf{x} > \mathbf{y}$ to mean $x_i > y_i$ $(i = 1, \ldots, m)$. The fundamental operations on column vectors are addition, and multiplication by a scalar. To add two column vectors, add their corresponding elements; thus

$$\text{(2.3)} \qquad \mathbf{z} = \mathbf{x} + \mathbf{y} \text{ if and only if } z_i = x_i + y_i \quad (i = 1, \ldots, m).$$

Note that the sum of two column vectors is defined only if they have the same number of elements. To multiply a column vector by a scalar (i.e., a real number) multiply each element of the column vector by the scalar; thus

$$\text{(2.4)} \qquad \mathbf{y} = c\mathbf{x} \text{ if and only if } y_i = cx_i \quad (i = 1, \ldots, m).$$

Combining and extending these two operations defines a linear combination of a set of vectors:

$$\text{(2.5)} \qquad \begin{aligned} &\mathbf{y} = c_1\mathbf{x}^{(1)} + \cdots + c_n\mathbf{x}^{(n)} \text{ if and only if} \\ &y_i = c_1 x_i^{(1)} + \cdots + c_n x_i^{(n)} \quad (i = 1, \ldots, m) \end{aligned}$$

where $x_i^{(j)}$ is the ith element of the jth vector $\mathbf{x}^{(j)}$. For example,

$$\text{(2.6)} \qquad 3\begin{pmatrix} 4 \\ -2 \\ 1 \end{pmatrix} + 1\begin{pmatrix} -5 \\ 6 \\ 0 \end{pmatrix} = \begin{pmatrix} 3(4) + 1(-5) \\ 3(-2) + 1(6) \\ 3(1) + 1(0) \end{pmatrix} = \begin{pmatrix} 7 \\ 0 \\ 3 \end{pmatrix}.$$

Matrices

An $m \times n$ matrix is a rectangular array of mn real numbers arranged in m rows and n columns:

$$\mathbf{A} = \begin{pmatrix} a_{11} & a_{12} & \cdots & a_{1n} \\ a_{21} & a_{22} & \cdots & a_{2n} \\ \cdot & \cdot & & \cdot \\ \cdot & \cdot & & \cdot \\ \cdot & \cdot & & \cdot \\ a_{m1} & a_{m2} & \cdots & a_{mn} \end{pmatrix}. \tag{2.7}$$

The numbers a_{ij} $(i = 1, \ldots, m; j = 1, \ldots, n)$ are called the elements of the matrix $\mathbf{A}$. An $m \times n$ matrix is said to be of order $m \times n$. We sometimes write simply $\mathbf{A} = (a_{ij})$ meaning that $\mathbf{A}$ is the matrix whose typical element is a_{ij}. Two matrices are equal if and only if they are equal element by element:

$$\mathbf{A} = \mathbf{B} \text{ if and only if } a_{ij} = b_{ij} \quad (i = 1, \ldots, m; j = 1, \ldots, n). \tag{2.8}$$

Next we introduce the fundamental operations on matrices. To add two matrices, add their corresponding elements; thus

$$\mathbf{C} = \mathbf{A} + \mathbf{B} \text{ if and only if } c_{ij} = a_{ij} + b_{ij} \quad (i = 1, \ldots, m; j = 1, \ldots, n). \tag{2.9}$$

Note that the sum of two matrices is defined only if they are of the same order. To multiply a matrix by a scalar, multiply each element of the matrix by the scalar; thus

$$\mathbf{B} = c\mathbf{A} \text{ if and only if } b_{ij} = ca_{ij} \quad (i = 1, \ldots, m; j = 1, \ldots, n). \tag{2.10}$$

Combining and extending these two operations defines a linear combination of a set of matrices:

$$\mathbf{B} = c_1\mathbf{A}^{(1)} + \cdots + c_P\mathbf{A}^{(P)} \text{ if and only if } b_{ij} = c_1 a_{ij}^{(1)} + \cdots + c_P a_{ij}^{(P)} \quad (i = 1, \ldots, m; j = 1, \ldots, n). \tag{2.11}$$

where $a_{ij}^{(p)}$ is the i,j element of the pth $m \times n$ matrix $\mathbf{A}^{(p)}$. For example,

$$3\begin{pmatrix} 4 & -5 \\ -2 & 6 \\ 1 & 0 \end{pmatrix} + 2\begin{pmatrix} 2 & 3 \\ 3 & -6 \\ -5 & 13 \end{pmatrix} = \begin{pmatrix} 12 & -15 \\ -6 & 18 \\ 3 & 0 \end{pmatrix} + \begin{pmatrix} 4 & 6 \\ 6 & -12 \\ -10 & 26 \end{pmatrix} = \begin{pmatrix} 16 & -9 \\ 0 & 6 \\ -7 & 26 \end{pmatrix}. \tag{2.12}$$

From these definitions and the properties of real numbers it follows that

$$\mathbf{A} + \mathbf{B} = \mathbf{B} + \mathbf{A}, \tag{2.13}$$

$$(\mathbf{A} + \mathbf{B}) + \mathbf{C} = \mathbf{A} + (\mathbf{B} + \mathbf{C}) = \mathbf{A} + \mathbf{B} + \mathbf{C}, \tag{2.14}$$

$$c(\mathbf{A} + \mathbf{B}) = c\mathbf{A} + c\mathbf{B}, \tag{2.15}$$

$$(c + d)\mathbf{A} = c\mathbf{A} + d\mathbf{A}, \tag{2.16}$$

$$c(d\mathbf{A}) = (cd)\mathbf{A} = (dc)\mathbf{A} = d(c\mathbf{A}). \tag{2.17}$$

Comparing the definitions of the operations on matrices with those on column vectors, it will be seen that the definitions are consistent. That is, an $m \times 1$ column vector may be treated just like an $m \times 1$ matrix. Similarly, a $1 \times n$ matrix is often called a $1 \times n$ row vector.

The third fundamental operation is matrix multiplication. The product of an $m \times n$ matrix $\mathbf{A}$ times an $n \times p$ matrix $\mathbf{B}$ is an $m \times p$ matrix $\mathbf{C}$ whose i,j element is the sum of products of the elements in the ith row of $\mathbf{A}$ by the elements in the jth column of $\mathbf{B}$; thus

$$\mathbf{C} = \mathbf{AB} \text{ if and only if } c_{ij} = \sum_{k=1}^{n} a_{ik}b_{kj} \qquad (i = 1, \ldots, m;\ j = 1, \ldots, p). \tag{2.18}$$

For example, if $\mathbf{A}$ is 2×3 and $\mathbf{B}$ is 3×2,

$$\begin{pmatrix} a_{11} & a_{12} & a_{13} \\ a_{21} & a_{22} & a_{23} \end{pmatrix} \begin{pmatrix} b_{11} & b_{12} \\ b_{21} & b_{22} \\ b_{31} & b_{32} \end{pmatrix} = \begin{pmatrix} a_{11}b_{11} + a_{12}b_{21} + a_{13}b_{31} & a_{11}b_{12} + a_{12}b_{22} + a_{13}b_{32} \\ a_{21}b_{11} + a_{22}b_{21} + a_{23}b_{31} & a_{21}b_{12} + a_{22}b_{22} + a_{23}b_{32} \end{pmatrix}. \tag{2.19}$$

For a numerical example,

$$\mathbf{A} = \begin{pmatrix} 1 & 2 & 2 & 1 \\ 2 & -1 & -2 & 3 \\ 1 & 4 & 5 & 2 \end{pmatrix}, \qquad \mathbf{B} = \begin{pmatrix} 2 & 4 \\ 1 & -2 \\ 3 & 1 \\ 1 & 6 \end{pmatrix},$$

$$\mathbf{C} = \mathbf{AB} = \begin{pmatrix} 1(2) + 2(1) + 2(3) + 1(1) & 1(4) + 2(-2) + 2(1) + 1(6) \\ 2(2) + (-1)(1) + (-2)(3) + 3(1) & 2(4) + (-1)(-2) + (-2)(1) + 3(6) \\ 1(2) + 4(1) + 5(3) + 2(1) & 1(4) + 4(-2) + 5(1) + 2(6) \end{pmatrix} = \begin{pmatrix} 11 & 8 \\ 0 & 26 \\ 23 & 13 \end{pmatrix}. \tag{2.20}$$

In visual terms, the element in the ith row and jth column of $\mathbf{C} = \mathbf{AB}$ is obtained by "multiplying" the ith row of $\mathbf{A}$ into the jth column of $\mathbf{B}$. Alternatively, if we think of the columns of $\mathbf{A}$ and of $\mathbf{C}$ as $m \times 1$ vectors, we may interpret the jth column of $\mathbf{C}$, $\mathbf{C}_j$, as a linear combination of the columns of $\mathbf{A}$, $\mathbf{A}_1, \ldots, \mathbf{A}_n$, with the elements of the jth column of $\mathbf{B}$ as coefficients:

$$(2.21) \qquad \mathbf{C}_j = b_{1j}\mathbf{A}_1 + \cdots + b_{nj}\mathbf{A}_n.$$

Still another interpretation views the columns of $\mathbf{B}$ as $n \times 1$ vectors and considers the jth column of $\mathbf{C}$ as the matrix $\mathbf{A}$ times the jth column of $\mathbf{B}$:

$$(2.22) \qquad \mathbf{C}_j = \mathbf{AB}_j.$$

Note that for the product $\mathbf{C} = \mathbf{AB}$ to be defined, $\mathbf{B}$ must have as many rows as $\mathbf{A}$ has columns, and that then $\mathbf{C}$ has as many rows as $\mathbf{A}$ and as many columns as $\mathbf{B}$. If the product $\mathbf{AB}$ is defined, $\mathbf{A}$ and $\mathbf{B}$ are said to be conformable. When a product appears in this book it should be understood that the result holds only if the product is defined.

From these definitions and the properties of real numbers it follows that

$$(2.23) \qquad (\mathbf{AB})\mathbf{C} = \mathbf{A}(\mathbf{BC}) = \mathbf{ABC},$$

$$(2.24) \qquad \mathbf{A}(\mathbf{B} + \mathbf{C}) = \mathbf{AB} + \mathbf{AC},$$

$$(2.25) \qquad \mathbf{A}c\mathbf{B} = c\mathbf{AB}.$$

Matrix multiplication is not commutative, however; in general $\mathbf{BA}$ is not equal to $\mathbf{AB}$, because when $\mathbf{AB}$ is defined, $\mathbf{BA}$ may not be—see (2.20)—and even if it is—as in (2.19)—it will not necessarily equal $\mathbf{AB}$. Thus it is important to distinguish between pre- and postmultiplication by a matrix and to preserve the order of products of matrices.

The transpose of a matrix, denoted by a prime, is the matrix obtained by interchanging the rows with the columns; thus the transpose of the $m \times n$ matrix $\mathbf{A}$ of (2.7) is the $n \times m$ matrix.

$$(2.26) \qquad \mathbf{A}' = \begin{pmatrix} a_{11} & a_{21} & \cdots & a_{m1} \\ a_{12} & a_{22} & \cdots & a_{m2} \\ \cdot & \cdot & & \cdot \\ \cdot & \cdot & & \cdot \\ \cdot & \cdot & & \cdot \\ a_{1n} & a_{2n} & \cdots & a_{mn} \end{pmatrix}.$$

That is,

$$(2.27) \qquad \mathbf{B} = \mathbf{A}' \text{ if and only if } b_{ji} = a_{ij} \quad (i = 1, \ldots, m; j = 1, \ldots, n).$$

The following properties of transposition follow directly from the definitions of matrix operations and the properties of real numbers:

(2.28) $(\mathbf{A}')' = \mathbf{A},$

(2.29) $(\mathbf{A} + \mathbf{B})' = \mathbf{A}' + \mathbf{B}',$

(2.30) $(\mathbf{AB})' = \mathbf{B}'\mathbf{A}'.$

Thus, the transpose of a transpose is the original matrix; the transpose of a sum is the sum of the transposes; and the transpose of a product is the product of the transposes in the reverse order.

A matrix is called square if it has as many rows as it has columns, i.e., if $m = n$. The diagonal of a square matrix consists of the elements lying along the line running from northwest to southeast, i.e., the diagonal of the $n \times n$ matrix $\mathbf{A}$ consists of $a_{11}, a_{22}, \ldots, a_{nn}$. The trace of a square matrix is the sum of its diagonal elements:

(2.31) $$tr(\mathbf{A}) = a_{11} + \cdots + a_{nn} = \sum_{i=1}^{n} a_{ii}.$$

It follows directly that

(2.32) $tr(\mathbf{A} + \mathbf{B}) = tr(\mathbf{A}) + tr(\mathbf{B}),$

(2.33) $tr(\mathbf{A}') = tr(\mathbf{A}),$

(2.34) $tr(c\mathbf{A}) = c\, tr(\mathbf{A}),$

(2.35) $$tr(\mathbf{AB}) = tr(\mathbf{BA}) = \sum_{i=1}^{n} \sum_{j=1}^{n} a_{ij} b_{ji}.$$

A square matrix is said to be symmetric if it is equal to its transpose, i.e., if $a_{ij} = a_{ji}$ $(i = 1, \ldots, n;\ j = 1, \ldots, n)$.

A square matrix whose diagonal elements are all 1 and whose off-diagonal elements are all 0 is called the identity matrix and is written $\mathbf{I}$:

(2.36) $$\mathbf{I} = \begin{pmatrix} 1 & 0 & \cdots & 0 \\ 0 & 1 & \cdots & 0 \\ \cdot & \cdot & & \cdot \\ \cdot & \cdot & & \cdot \\ \cdot & \cdot & & \cdot \\ 0 & 0 & \cdots & 1 \end{pmatrix}.$$

Clearly, where $\mathbf{A}$ is any matrix, $\mathbf{IA} = \mathbf{A} = \mathbf{AI}$, so that the identity matrix plays the role that 1 plays in ordinary algebra. If the order of the $n \times n$ identity matrix is of interest we write it as $\mathbf{I}_n$. Note that

(2.37) $tr(\mathbf{I}_n) = n.$

A matrix, not necessarily square, whose elements are all zero, is called the zero matrix and is written $\mathbf{0}$. Clearly, where $\mathbf{A}$ is any matrix $\mathbf{0A} = \mathbf{0}$ and $\mathbf{A0} = \mathbf{0}$ and $\mathbf{A} + \mathbf{0} = \mathbf{A}$, so that the zero matrix plays the role that 0 plays in ordinary algebra. If the order of the zero matrix is of interest, we write it as $\mathbf{0}_{m,n}$, say; $\mathbf{0}_{m,1}$ may be called the zero (column) vector and $\mathbf{0}_{1,n}$ the zero (row) vector.

Partitioned Matrices

It is often convenient to partition a matrix into submatrices. Thus an $m \times n$ matrix $\mathbf{A}$ may be partitioned as

$$\mathbf{A} = (\mathbf{A}_1 \mid \mathbf{A}_2), \tag{2.38}$$

where $\mathbf{A}_1$ is $m \times n_1$, $\mathbf{A}_2$ is $m \times n_2$, and $n_1 + n_2 = n$. Doing this we see how the transpose of a partitioned matrix may be written in terms of the transposes of its submatrices; thus

$$\mathbf{A}' = (\mathbf{A}_1 \mid \mathbf{A}_2)' = \begin{pmatrix} \mathbf{A}_1' \\ \hline \mathbf{A}_2' \end{pmatrix}. \tag{2.39}$$

For example, the matrix $\mathbf{A}$ of (2.20) may be partitioned as

$$\mathbf{A} = (\mathbf{A}_1 \mid \mathbf{A}_2) = \left(\begin{array}{cc|cc} 1 & 2 & 2 & 1 \\ 2 & -1 & -2 & 3 \\ 1 & 4 & 5 & 2 \end{array}\right), \tag{2.40}$$

and its transpose is

$$\mathbf{A}' = \begin{pmatrix} \mathbf{A}_1' \\ \hline \mathbf{A}_2' \end{pmatrix} = \left(\begin{array}{ccc} 1 & 2 & 1 \\ 2 & -1 & 4 \\ \hline 2 & -2 & 5 \\ 1 & 3 & 2 \end{array}\right). \tag{2.41}$$

Note how the submatrices are treated as if they were scalars. This treatment extends to matrix multiplication as well. If the $m \times n$ matrix $\mathbf{A}$ is partitioned as $\mathbf{A} = (\mathbf{A}_1 \mid \mathbf{A}_2)$ where $\mathbf{A}_1$ is $m \times n_1$, $\mathbf{A}_2$ is $m \times n_2$, and $n_1 + n_2 = n$, and the $n \times p$ matrix $\mathbf{B}$ is partitioned as $\mathbf{B} = \begin{pmatrix} \mathbf{B}_1 \\ \hline \mathbf{B}_2 \end{pmatrix}$ where $\mathbf{B}_1$ is $n_1 \times p$ and $\mathbf{B}_2$ is $n_2 \times p$, then the product $\mathbf{C} = \mathbf{AB}$ may be expressed as

$$\mathbf{C} = \mathbf{AB} = (\mathbf{A}_1 \mid \mathbf{A}_2)\begin{pmatrix} \mathbf{B}_1 \\ \hline \mathbf{B}_2 \end{pmatrix} = (\mathbf{A}_1\mathbf{B}_1 + \mathbf{A}_2\mathbf{B}_2). \tag{2.42}$$

For example, let the **A** of (2.20) be partitioned as in (2.40) and the **B** of (2.20) be partitioned as

$$\mathbf{B} = \begin{pmatrix} \mathbf{B}_1 \\ \hdashline \mathbf{B}_2 \end{pmatrix} = \begin{pmatrix} 2 & 4 \\ 1 & -2 \\ \hdashline 3 & 1 \\ 1 & 6 \end{pmatrix}. \tag{2.43}$$

Then the product $\mathbf{C} = \mathbf{AB}$ may be computed as

$$\mathbf{C} = \mathbf{AB} = (\mathbf{A}_1 \mid \mathbf{A}_2)\begin{pmatrix} \mathbf{B}_1 \\ \hdashline \mathbf{B}_2 \end{pmatrix} = (\mathbf{A}_1\mathbf{B}_1 + \mathbf{A}_2\mathbf{B}_2) \tag{2.44}$$

$$= \begin{pmatrix} 1 & 2 \\ 2 & -1 \\ 1 & 4 \end{pmatrix}\begin{pmatrix} 2 & 4 \\ 1 & -2 \end{pmatrix} + \begin{pmatrix} 2 & 1 \\ -2 & 3 \\ 5 & 2 \end{pmatrix}\begin{pmatrix} 3 & 1 \\ 1 & 6 \end{pmatrix}$$

$$= \begin{pmatrix} 4 & 0 \\ 3 & 10 \\ 6 & -4 \end{pmatrix} + \begin{pmatrix} 7 & 8 \\ -3 & 16 \\ 17 & 17 \end{pmatrix} = \begin{pmatrix} 11 & 8 \\ 0 & 26 \\ 23 & 13 \end{pmatrix},$$

which is just the result of (2.20).

This device extends to finer partitionings. Thus an $m \times n$ matrix **A** may be partitioned as

$$\mathbf{A} = \begin{pmatrix} \mathbf{A}_{11} & \mathbf{A}_{12} \\ \mathbf{A}_{21} & \mathbf{A}_{22} \end{pmatrix}, \tag{2.45}$$

where $\mathbf{A}_{11}$ is $m_1 \times n_1$, $\mathbf{A}_{12}$ is $m_1 \times n_2$, $\mathbf{A}_{21}$ is $m_2 \times n_1$, $\mathbf{A}_{22}$ is $m_2 \times n_2$, $m_1 + m_2 = m$, and $n_1 + n_2 = n$. Its transpose may then be expressed as

$$\mathbf{A}' = \begin{pmatrix} \mathbf{A}_{11} & \mathbf{A}_{12} \\ \mathbf{A}_{21} & \mathbf{A}_{22} \end{pmatrix}' = \begin{pmatrix} \mathbf{A}'_{11} & \mathbf{A}'_{21} \\ \mathbf{A}'_{12} & \mathbf{A}'_{22} \end{pmatrix}. \tag{2.46}$$

If further the $n \times p$ matrix **B** is partitioned as

$$\mathbf{B} = \begin{pmatrix} \mathbf{B}_{11} & \mathbf{B}_{12} \\ \mathbf{B}_{21} & \mathbf{B}_{22} \end{pmatrix}, \tag{2.47}$$

where $\mathbf{B}_{11}$ is $n_1 \times p_1$, $\mathbf{B}_{12}$ is $n_1 \times p_2$, $\mathbf{B}_{21}$ is $n_2 \times p_1$, $\mathbf{B}_{22}$ is $n_2 \times p_2$, and $p_1 + p_2 = p$, then the product $\mathbf{C} = \mathbf{AB}$ may be computed in partitioned form as

$$\text{(2.48)} \qquad \mathbf{C} = \left(\begin{array}{c|c} \mathbf{C}_{11} & \mathbf{C}_{12} \\ \hline \mathbf{C}_{21} & \mathbf{C}_{22} \end{array}\right) = \left(\begin{array}{c|c} \mathbf{A}_{11} & \mathbf{A}_{12} \\ \hline \mathbf{A}_{21} & \mathbf{A}_{22} \end{array}\right)\left(\begin{array}{c|c} \mathbf{B}_{11} & \mathbf{B}_{12} \\ \hline \mathbf{B}_{21} & \mathbf{B}_{22} \end{array}\right)$$

$$= \left(\begin{array}{c|c} \mathbf{A}_{11}\mathbf{B}_{11} + \mathbf{A}_{12}\mathbf{B}_{21} & \mathbf{A}_{11}\mathbf{B}_{12} + \mathbf{A}_{12}\mathbf{B}_{22} \\ \hline \mathbf{A}_{21}\mathbf{B}_{11} + \mathbf{A}_{22}\mathbf{B}_{21} & \mathbf{A}_{21}\mathbf{B}_{12} + \mathbf{A}_{22}\mathbf{B}_{22} \end{array}\right)$$

where $\mathbf{C}_{11}$ is $m_1 \times p_1$, $\mathbf{C}_{12}$ is $m_1 \times p_2$, $\mathbf{C}_{21}$ is $m_2 \times p_1$, and $\mathbf{C}_{22}$ is $m_2 \times p_2$. For examples, let the **A** and **B** of (2.20) be partitioned as

$$\text{(2.49)} \qquad \mathbf{A} = \left(\begin{array}{cc|cc} 1 & 2 & 2 & 1 \\ 2 & -1 & -2 & 3 \\ \hline 1 & 4 & 5 & 2 \end{array}\right), \qquad \mathbf{B} = \left(\begin{array}{c|c} 2 & 4 \\ 1 & -2 \\ \hline 3 & 1 \\ 1 & 6 \end{array}\right).$$

Then

$$\text{(2.50)} \qquad \mathbf{A}' = \left(\begin{array}{c|c} \mathbf{A}'_{11} & \mathbf{A}'_{21} \\ \hline \mathbf{A}'_{12} & \mathbf{A}'_{22} \end{array}\right) = \left(\begin{array}{cc|c} 1 & 2 & 1 \\ 2 & -1 & 4 \\ \hline 2 & -2 & 5 \\ 1 & 3 & 2 \end{array}\right)$$

as before; and further

$$\mathbf{C}_{11} = \mathbf{A}_{11}\mathbf{B}_{11} + \mathbf{A}_{12}\mathbf{B}_{21} = \begin{pmatrix} 1 & 2 \\ 2 & -1 \end{pmatrix}\begin{pmatrix} 2 \\ 1 \end{pmatrix} + \begin{pmatrix} 2 & 1 \\ -2 & 3 \end{pmatrix}\begin{pmatrix} 3 \\ 1 \end{pmatrix}$$

$$= \begin{pmatrix} 4 \\ 3 \end{pmatrix} + \begin{pmatrix} 7 \\ -3 \end{pmatrix} = \begin{pmatrix} 11 \\ 0 \end{pmatrix},$$

$$\mathbf{C}_{12} = \mathbf{A}_{11}\mathbf{B}_{12} + \mathbf{A}_{12}\mathbf{B}_{22} = \begin{pmatrix} 1 & 2 \\ 2 & -1 \end{pmatrix}\begin{pmatrix} 4 \\ -2 \end{pmatrix} + \begin{pmatrix} 2 & 1 \\ -2 & 3 \end{pmatrix}\begin{pmatrix} 1 \\ 6 \end{pmatrix}$$

$$= \begin{pmatrix} 0 \\ 10 \end{pmatrix} + \begin{pmatrix} 8 \\ 16 \end{pmatrix} = \begin{pmatrix} 8 \\ 26 \end{pmatrix},$$

$$\mathbf{C}_{21} = \mathbf{A}_{21}\mathbf{B}_{11} + \mathbf{A}_{22}\mathbf{B}_{21} = (1 \quad 4)\begin{pmatrix} 2 \\ 1 \end{pmatrix} + (5 \quad 2)\begin{pmatrix} 3 \\ 1 \end{pmatrix}$$

$$= (6) + (17) = (23),$$

$$\mathbf{C}_{22} = \mathbf{A}_{21}\mathbf{B}_{12} + \mathbf{A}_{22}\mathbf{B}_{22} = (1 \quad 4)\begin{pmatrix} 4 \\ -2 \end{pmatrix} + (5 \quad 2)\begin{pmatrix} 1 \\ 6 \end{pmatrix}$$

$$= (-4) + (17) = (13),$$

so that

$$\mathbf{C} = \left(\begin{array}{c|c} \mathbf{C}_{11} & \mathbf{C}_{12} \\ \hline \mathbf{C}_{21} & \mathbf{C}_{22} \end{array}\right) = \left(\begin{array}{c|c} 11 & 8 \\ 0 & 26 \\ \hline 23 & 13 \end{array}\right) \tag{2.51}$$

as before. Still finer partitioning can be utilized. In viewing an $m \times n$ matrix as a set of column vectors we are effectively partitioning it into n $m \times 1$ submatrices. In the rest of this book the dashed partitioning lines are usually omitted.

Finally, a definition:

(2.52) Let $\mathbf{A}$ be an $m \times m$ matrix and $\mathbf{B}$ be an $n \times n$ matrix. Then the direct (or Kronecker) product of $\mathbf{A}$ and $\mathbf{B}$, written $\mathbf{A} \otimes \mathbf{B}$, is defined as the $mn \times mn$ matrix

$$\mathbf{C} = \mathbf{A} \otimes \mathbf{B} = \begin{pmatrix} a_{11}\mathbf{B} & \cdots & a_{1m}\mathbf{B} \\ \cdot & & \cdot \\ \cdot & & \cdot \\ \cdot & & \cdot \\ a_{m1}\mathbf{B} & \cdots & a_{mm}\mathbf{B} \end{pmatrix}.$$

3. DETERMINANTS

Associated with any square matrix $\mathbf{A}$ is a scalar function of its elements called the determinant of $\mathbf{A}$ and written $|\mathbf{A}|$. If $\mathbf{A}$ is $n \times n$, then $|\mathbf{A}|$ is said to be a determinant of order n. We define the determinant of an $n \times n$ matrix in recursive fashion. First, for $n = 1$,

(3.1) If $\mathbf{A} = (a)$, then $|\mathbf{A}| = a$,

and for $n = 2$,

$$\text{If } \mathbf{A} = \begin{pmatrix} a_{11} & a_{12} \\ a_{21} & a_{22} \end{pmatrix}, \text{ then } |\mathbf{A}| = a_{11}a_{22} - a_{12}a_{21}. \tag{3.2}$$

For $n \geq 2$, the determinant of an $n \times n$ matrix may be defined in terms of determinants of $(n - 1) \times (n - 1)$ submatrices as follows. The minor m_{ij} of an element a_{ij} in an $n \times n$ matrix $\mathbf{A}$ is the determinant of the $(n - 1) \times (n - 1)$ submatrix obtained by deletion of the ith row and jth column of $\mathbf{A}$. The cofactor c_{ij} of the element a_{ij} is its "signed" minor, $c_{ij} = (-1)^{i+j}m_{ij}$. Then the determinant of an $n \times n$ matrix may be defined as the sum of the products of the elements in any row of $\mathbf{A}$ by their cofactors:

$$\text{If } \mathbf{A} \text{ is } n \times n, \text{ then } |\mathbf{A}| = \sum_{k=1}^{n} a_{ik}c_{ik} \text{ for any } i = 1, \ldots, n. \tag{3.3}$$

For an example we take $n = 3$, and arrange the cofactors in a matrix:

(3.4a) $$\mathbf{A} = \begin{pmatrix} a_{11} & a_{12} & a_{13} \\ a_{21} & a_{22} & a_{23} \\ a_{31} & a_{32} & a_{33} \end{pmatrix},$$

(3.4b) $$\mathbf{C} = (c_{ij})$$
$$= \begin{pmatrix} (a_{22}a_{33}-a_{23}a_{32}) & -(a_{21}a_{33}-a_{23}a_{31}) & (a_{21}a_{32}-a_{22}a_{31}) \\ -(a_{12}a_{33}-a_{13}a_{32}) & (a_{11}a_{33}-a_{13}a_{31}) & -(a_{11}a_{32}-a_{12}a_{31}) \\ (a_{12}a_{23}-a_{13}a_{22}) & -(a_{11}a_{23}-a_{13}a_{21}) & (a_{11}a_{22}-a_{12}a_{21}) \end{pmatrix},$$

(3.4c) $$|\mathbf{A}| = \sum_{k=1}^{3} a_{1k}c_{1k} = a_{11}(a_{22}a_{33} - a_{23}a_{32}) - a_{12}(a_{21}a_{33} - a_{23}a_{31})$$
$$+ a_{13}(a_{21}a_{32} - a_{22}a_{31})$$
$$= \sum_{k=1}^{3} a_{2k}c_{2k} = -a_{21}(a_{12}a_{33} - a_{13}a_{32}) + a_{22}(a_{11}a_{33} - a_{13}a_{31})$$
$$- a_{23}(a_{11}a_{32} - a_{12}a_{31})$$
$$= \sum_{k=1}^{3} a_{3k}c_{3k} = a_{31}(a_{12}a_{23} - a_{13}a_{22}) - a_{32}(a_{11}a_{23} - a_{13}a_{21})$$
$$+ a_{33}(a_{11}a_{22} - a_{12}a_{21}).$$

For a numerical example,

(3.5a) $$\mathbf{A} = \begin{pmatrix} 1 & 2 & 3 \\ 1 & 3 & 5 \\ 1 & 5 & 12 \end{pmatrix},$$

(3.5b) $$\mathbf{C} = (c_{ij}) = \begin{pmatrix} 11 & -7 & 2 \\ -9 & 9 & -3 \\ 1 & -2 & 1 \end{pmatrix},$$

(3.5c) $$|\mathbf{A}| = 1(11) + 2(-7) + 3(2) = 1(-9) + 3(9) + 5(-3)$$
$$= 1(1) + 5(-2) + 12(1) = 3.$$

It follows from the definitions of the cofactors that the sum of products of the elements in any row of **A** by the cofactors of the elements of another row ("alien cofactors") is always zero; thus

(3.6) If $\mathbf{A}$ is $n \times n$, then $\sum_{k=1}^{n} a_{ik}c_{jk} = 0 \quad (i \neq j; i = 1, \ldots, n; j = 1, \ldots, n)$.

It follows from the definition of the determinant that

(3.7) $|\mathbf{A}| = |\mathbf{A}'|$,

(3.8) $|\mathbf{AB}| = |\mathbf{A}|\,|\mathbf{B}|$,

(3.9) If $\mathbf{A}$ is a diagonal matrix (i.e., $a_{ij} = 0$ if $i \neq j$), then

$$|\mathbf{A}| = a_{11} \cdots a_{nn},$$

and

(3.10) If $\mathbf{A}$ is an $n \times n$ matrix, then $|-\mathbf{A}| = (-1)^n\,|\mathbf{A}|$.

Finally, a definition:

(3.11) If $\mathbf{A}$ is an $n \times n$ matrix, then $\mathbf{A}$ is singular if and only if $|\mathbf{A}| = 0$, and $\mathbf{A}$ is nonsingular if and only if $|\mathbf{A}| \neq 0$.

4. LINEAR DEPENDENCE, RANK, AND HOMOGENEOUS EQUATION SYSTEMS

Linear Dependence

A set of vectors is said to be linearly dependent if there is a nontrivial linear combination of the vectors which is equal to the zero vector; thus

(4.1) The set of n $m \times 1$ vectors $\{\mathbf{x}^{(1)}, \ldots, \mathbf{x}^{(n)}\}$ is linearly dependent if and only if there exists a set of scalars $\{c_1, \ldots, c_n\}$ not all of which are zero, such that $c_1\mathbf{x}^{(1)} + \cdots + c_n\mathbf{x}^{(n)} = 0$.

If the set is not linearly dependent it is linearly independent. Thus a set is linearly independent if the only linear combination of the vectors which is equal to zero is the trivial one $0\mathbf{x}^{(1)} + \cdots + 0\mathbf{x}^{(n)} = 0$. Any set containing a zero vector is linearly dependent; if $\mathbf{x}^{(n)} = 0$, for example, then $0\mathbf{x}^{(1)} + \cdots + 0\mathbf{x}^{(n-1)} + 1\mathbf{x}^{(n)} = 0 + \cdots + 0 + 0 = 0$ shows a nontrivial linear combination equal to zero. Obviously,

(4.2) Any subset of a linearly independent set of vectors is linearly independent.

Without proof we note that

(4.3) If a set contains more than m $m \times 1$ vectors, it is linearly dependent.

Some of these points may be illustrated with the following vectors:

(4.4)
$$\mathbf{x}^{(1)} = \begin{pmatrix} 4 \\ -2 \\ 1 \end{pmatrix}, \quad \mathbf{x}^{(2)} = \begin{pmatrix} -5 \\ 6 \\ 0 \end{pmatrix}, \quad \mathbf{x}^{(3)} = \begin{pmatrix} 7 \\ 0 \\ 3 \end{pmatrix},$$
$$\mathbf{x}^{(4)} = \begin{pmatrix} 1 \\ 0 \\ 0 \end{pmatrix}, \quad \mathbf{x}^{(5)} = \begin{pmatrix} 0 \\ 1 \\ 0 \end{pmatrix}, \quad \mathbf{x}^{(6)} = \begin{pmatrix} 0 \\ 0 \\ 1 \end{pmatrix}.$$

The set $\{\mathbf{x}^{(1)}, \mathbf{x}^{(2)}, \mathbf{x}^{(3)}\}$ is linearly dependent since $3\mathbf{x}^{(1)} + 1\mathbf{x}^{(2)} - 1\mathbf{x}^{(3)} = 0$—see (2.6). The set $\{\mathbf{x}^{(4)}, \mathbf{x}^{(5)}, \mathbf{x}^{(6)}\}$ is linearly independent since

$$c_1 \begin{pmatrix} 1 \\ 0 \\ 0 \end{pmatrix} + c_2 \begin{pmatrix} 0 \\ 1 \\ 0 \end{pmatrix} + c_3 \begin{pmatrix} 0 \\ 0 \\ 1 \end{pmatrix} = \begin{pmatrix} c_1 \\ c_2 \\ c_3 \end{pmatrix}$$

is zero only if $c_1 = c_2 = c_3 = 0$; similarly, the sets $\{\mathbf{x}^{(4)}, \mathbf{x}^{(5)}\}$, $\{\mathbf{x}^{(4)}, \mathbf{x}^{(6)}\}$, and $\{\mathbf{x}^{(5)}, \mathbf{x}^{(6)}\}$ are each linearly independent. The set $\{\mathbf{x}^{(1)}, \mathbf{x}^{(2)}\}$ is also linearly independent. This is so because

$$c_1 \begin{pmatrix} 4 \\ -2 \\ 1 \end{pmatrix} + c_2 \begin{pmatrix} -5 \\ 6 \\ 0 \end{pmatrix} = \begin{pmatrix} 4c_1 - 5c_2 \\ -2c_1 + 6c_2 \\ 1c_1 + 0c_2 \end{pmatrix};$$

for the third element to be zero c_1 must be zero, and then for the first element to be zero c_2 must be zero. (In general a set containing two vectors will be linearly dependent if and only if one is a multiple of the other.) It will also be seen that any set of four or more of the 3×1 vectors of (4.4) is linearly dependent. Of course, it is not always so easy to find whether or not a set of vectors is linearly dependent.

Rank of a Matrix

The columns of an $m \times n$ matrix $\mathbf{A}$ may be viewed as a set of n $m \times 1$ column vectors $\mathbf{A}_1, \mathbf{A}_2, \ldots, \mathbf{A}_n$, where $\mathbf{A}_j$ is the jth column of $\mathbf{A}$. Taking this view, we define the rank of $\mathbf{A}$, written $r(\mathbf{A})$, as the maximum number of linearly independent vectors in the set $\mathbf{A}_1, \ldots, \mathbf{A}_n$; i.e., the number of vectors in the largest linearly independent set of vectors which can be constructed from the columns of **A**. For example,

$$r\begin{pmatrix} 4 & -5 & 7 \\ -2 & 6 & 0 \\ 1 & 0 & 3 \end{pmatrix} = 2 \tag{4.5}$$

since the first two columns form a linearly independent set, whereas the set containing all three columns is linearly dependent—see (4.4). Since any set of more than m $m \times 1$ vectors is linearly dependent it follows that where **A** is $m \times n$, $r(\mathbf{A}) \leq m$; and since there are only n columns, $r(\mathbf{A}) \leq n$; thus

(4.6) If **A** is an $m \times n$ matrix, $r(\mathbf{A}) \leq \min\{m, n\}$.

Without proof, we note the following very useful result:

(4.7) Consider all square submatrices of **A** whose determinants are nonzero. The rank of **A** is the order of the largest in order of these determinants.

Loosely speaking, the rank of **A** is the order of the largest-in-order nonzero subdeterminant of **A**. For example, let **A** be the matrix of (4.5); then

$$|\mathbf{A}| = \begin{vmatrix} 4 & -5 & 7 \\ -2 & 6 & 0 \\ 1 & 0 & 3 \end{vmatrix} \tag{4.8}$$

$$= 1[(-5)(0) - 7(6)] + 3[4(6) - (-5)(-2)]$$

$$= -42 + 42 = 0$$

so $r(\mathbf{A}) < 3$;

$$\begin{vmatrix} 4 & -5 \\ -2 & 6 \end{vmatrix} = 24 - 10 = 14 \neq 0,$$

so $r(\mathbf{A}) = 2$.

Incidentally, (4.7) provides a systematic method of testing for linear dependence. Given a set of n $m \times 1$ vectors $\{\mathbf{x}^{(1)}, \mathbf{x}^{(2)}, \ldots, \mathbf{x}^{(n)}\}$ with $n \leq m$, form the $m \times n$ matrix $\mathbf{X} = (\mathbf{x}^{(1)}\ \mathbf{x}^{(2)} \cdots \mathbf{x}^{(n)})$. [If $n > m$, the set is linearly dependent by (4.3).] If $n = m$, the set is linearly independent if and only if $r(\mathbf{X}) = n$, i.e., if the $n \times n$ determinant $|\mathbf{X}| \neq 0$; if $n < m$, the set is linearly independent if and only if **X** has a nonzero $n \times n$ subdeterminant.

The following results are straightforward. Since any set of column vectors that includes the zero vector is linearly dependent,

(4.9) $r(\mathbf{0}) = 0.$

Since the determinant of a diagonal matrix is the product of its diagonal elements,

(4.10) If $\mathbf{A}$ is diagonal, then $r(\mathbf{A})$ is the number of nonzero diagonal elements that $\mathbf{A}$ has.

Thus in particular

(4.11) $r(\mathbf{I}_n) = n.$

Since any submatrix of $\mathbf{A}'$ is the transpose of a submatrix of $\mathbf{A}$, and since $|\mathbf{B}| = |\mathbf{B}'|$.

(4.12) $r(\mathbf{A}') = r(\mathbf{A}).$

Furthermore, the rank of a product cannot exceed the smallest rank of the factors:

(4.13) $r(\mathbf{AB}) \leq \min \{r(\mathbf{A}), r(\mathbf{B})\}.$

The columns of $\mathbf{C} = \mathbf{AB}$ are linear combinations of the columns of $\mathbf{A}$, so that $\mathbf{C}$ cannot have more linearly independent columns than does $\mathbf{A}$; thus $r(\mathbf{C}) \leq r(\mathbf{A})$. Transposing $\mathbf{C} = \mathbf{AB}$ gives $\mathbf{C}' = \mathbf{B}'\mathbf{A}'$, in which the columns of $\mathbf{C}'$ are linear combinations of the columns of $\mathbf{B}'$ so that $\mathbf{C}'$ cannot have more linearly independent columns than does $\mathbf{B}'$; thus $r(\mathbf{C}') \leq r(\mathbf{B}')$. But $r(\mathbf{C}) = r(\mathbf{C}')$ and $r(\mathbf{B}) = r(\mathbf{B}')$; thus $r(\mathbf{C}) \leq r(\mathbf{B})$. Finally, recalling the definition of singularity,

(4.14) If $\mathbf{A}$ is an $n \times n$ matrix, then $r(\mathbf{A}) = n$ if and only if $\mathbf{A}$ is nonsingular; $r(\mathbf{A}) < n$ if and only if $\mathbf{A}$ is singular.

System of Simultaneous Homogeneous Linear Equations

The concept of rank is directly applicable to the investigation of the existence and uniqueness of solutions to a system of m simultaneous homogeneous linear equations in n unknowns:

$$
\begin{aligned}
a_{11}x_1 + \cdots + a_{1n}x_n &= 0 \\
\cdot \qquad\qquad & \cdot \\
\cdot \qquad\qquad & \cdot \qquad\qquad (4.15) \\
\cdot \qquad\qquad & \cdot \\
a_{m1}x_1 + \cdots + a_{mn}x_n &= 0.
\end{aligned}
$$

In view of the definition of matrix multiplication, the system may be compactly written as

(4.16) $\mathbf{Ax} = \mathbf{0}$

where

$$\mathbf{A} = \begin{pmatrix} a_{11} & \cdots & a_{1n} \\ \cdot & & \cdot \\ \cdot & & \cdot \\ \cdot & & \cdot \\ a_{m1} & \cdots & a_{mn} \end{pmatrix}, \quad \mathbf{x} = \begin{pmatrix} x_1 \\ \cdot \\ \cdot \\ \cdot \\ x_n \end{pmatrix}, \quad \mathbf{0} = \begin{pmatrix} 0 \\ \cdot \\ \cdot \\ \cdot \\ 0 \end{pmatrix}.$$

First, consider the existence of a nontrivial solution to the system, i.e., an $\mathbf{x} \neq \mathbf{0}$ such that $\mathbf{Ax} = \mathbf{0}$. Writing $\mathbf{Ax} = \mathbf{0}$ as $x_1\mathbf{A}_1 + \cdots + x_n\mathbf{A}_n = \mathbf{0}$, where the $\mathbf{A}_j$'s are the columns of $\mathbf{A}$, shows that the elements of a solution $\mathbf{x}$ may be interpreted as the coefficients of a linear combination of the columns of $\mathbf{A}$ which is equal to zero. Therefore

(4.17) A necessary and sufficient condition for the system of m simultaneous homogeneous linear equations in n unknowns, $\mathbf{Ax} = \mathbf{0}$, to have a nontrivial solution is $r(\mathbf{A}) < n$.

This is so because since $\mathbf{A}$ has n columns $r(\mathbf{A}) \leq n$. If $r(\mathbf{A}) = n$, the columns of $\mathbf{A}$ are linearly independent, the only linear combination of the columns which is equal to zero is the trivial one $0\mathbf{A}_1 + \cdots + 0\mathbf{A}_n$, and the only solution to $\mathbf{Ax} = \mathbf{0}$ is $\mathbf{x} = \mathbf{0}$. If, however, $r(\mathbf{A}) < n$, the columns of $\mathbf{A}$ are linearly dependent, there is a nontrivial linear combination of its columns which is equal to zero, $x_1\mathbf{A}_1 + \cdots + x_n\mathbf{A}_n = \mathbf{0}$ with not all the x_j's being zero, and the vector $\mathbf{x}$ made up of these x_j's is such that $\mathbf{x} \neq \mathbf{0}$ and $\mathbf{Ax} = \mathbf{0}$.

Second, consider the uniqueness of a nontrivial solution. If there is a nontrivial solution, there is an infinity of such solutions. If $\mathbf{x}$ is a nontrivial solution, $\mathbf{x} \neq \mathbf{0}$ and $\mathbf{Ax} = \mathbf{0}$, then $c\mathbf{x}$ where c is any nonzero scalar is also a nontrivial solution, because $c\mathbf{x} \neq \mathbf{0}$ and $\mathbf{A}(c\mathbf{x}) = c(\mathbf{Ax}) = c\mathbf{0} = \mathbf{0}$. Thus any multiple of a solution is also a solution. If all the solutions were multiples of one solution, the ratios of the elements of $\mathbf{x}$ would be uniquely determined, and the solution would be unique up to a factor of proportionality. It follows that

(4.18) A necessary and sufficient condition for the solution to a system of m simultaneous homogeneous linear equations in n unknowns, $\mathbf{Ax} = \mathbf{0}$, to be unique up to a factor of proportionality is $r(\mathbf{A}) = n - 1$.

We prove sufficiency first. Suppose $r(\mathbf{A}) = n - 1$, and without loss of generality suppose that it is the first $n - 1$ columns of $\mathbf{A}$ which form a linearly independent set. Let $\mathbf{x}^*$ be a nontrivial solution, i.e.,

$$x_1^*\mathbf{A}_1 + \cdots + x_n^*\mathbf{A}_n = \mathbf{0}. \tag{4.19}$$

Now $x_n^* \neq 0$; for if it were, then $x_1^*\,\mathbf{A}_1 + \cdots + x_{n-1}^*\,\mathbf{A}_{n-1} = \mathbf{0}$, which would contradict the assumption that $\mathbf{A}_1, \ldots, \mathbf{A}_{n-1}$ are linearly independent. Therefore we may divide (4.19) through by x_n^* and rearrange to find

$$\mathbf{A}_n = -\frac{x_1^*}{x_n^*}\mathbf{A}_1 - \cdots - \frac{x_{n-1}^*}{x_n^*}\mathbf{A}_{n-1}. \tag{4.20}$$

Let $\mathbf{x}^{**}$ be another nontrivial solution, i.e.,

$$x_1^{**}\mathbf{A}_1 + \cdots + x_n^{**}\mathbf{A}_n = \mathbf{0}. \tag{4.21}$$

Again, $x_n^{**} \neq 0$, so that we may divide (4.21) through by x_n^{**} and rearrange to find

$$\mathbf{A}_n = -\frac{x_1^{**}}{x_n^{**}}\mathbf{A}_1 - \cdots - \frac{x_{n-1}^{**}}{x_n^{**}}\mathbf{A}_{n-1}. \tag{4.22}$$

Subtracting (4.20) from (4.22) gives

$$\left(\frac{x_1^*}{x_n^*} - \frac{x_1^{**}}{x_n^{**}}\right)\mathbf{A}_1 + \cdots + \left(\frac{x_{n-1}^*}{x_n^*} - \frac{x_{n-1}^{**}}{x_n^{**}}\right)\mathbf{A}_{n-1} = \mathbf{0}. \tag{4.23}$$

Since the only linear combination of $\mathbf{A}_1, \ldots, \mathbf{A}_{n-1}$ that can be equal to zero is the trivial one, it must be true that $x_j^*/x_n^* = x_j^{**}/x_n^{**}$ $(j = 1, \ldots, n-1)$, i.e., $x_j^*/x_j^{**} = x_n^*/x_n^{**}$ $(j = 1, \ldots, n-1)$, so that the elements of $\mathbf{x}^{**}$ are indeed proportional to the elements of $\mathbf{x}^*$ as stated. Next we prove necessity. Suppose $r(\mathbf{A}) = n - 2$, and without loss of generality suppose that it is the first $n - 2$ columns of $\mathbf{A}$ which are linearly independent. Then $\mathbf{A}_{n-1}$ and $\mathbf{A}_n$ may each be expressed in terms of them, say

$$\mathbf{A}_{n-1} = x_1^*\mathbf{A}_1 + \cdots + x_{n-2}^*\mathbf{A}_{n-2} \tag{4.24}$$

and

$$\mathbf{A}_n = x_1^{**}\mathbf{A}_1 + \cdots + x_{n-2}^{**}\mathbf{A}_{n-2}. \tag{4.25}$$

Then we have two vectors satisfying $\mathbf{Ax} = \mathbf{0}$ whose elements are not proportional, namely,

$$\mathbf{x}^* = \begin{pmatrix} x_1^* \\ \cdot \\ \cdot \\ \cdot \\ x_{n-2}^* \\ -1 \\ 0 \end{pmatrix} \quad \text{and} \quad \mathbf{x}^{**} = \begin{pmatrix} x_1^{**} \\ \cdot \\ \cdot \\ \cdot \\ x_{n-2}^{**} \\ 0 \\ -1 \end{pmatrix}. \tag{4.26}$$

Similarly for $r(\mathbf{A}) < n - 2$.

Since $r(\mathbf{A}) \leq \min\{m, n\}$, a corollary of (4.18) is

(4.27) A necessary condition for the solution to a system of m simultaneous homogeneous linear equations in n unknowns, $\mathbf{Ax} = \mathbf{0}$, to be unique up to a factor of proportionality is $m \geq n - 1$.

Finally, as a corollary of (4.17) we have

(4.28) Let $\mathbf{A}$ be an $m \times n$ matrix of rank n, let $\mathbf{y}$ be an $n \times 1$ vector, and let $\mathbf{x} = \mathbf{Ay}$ be an $m \times 1$ vector. Then $\mathbf{x} = \mathbf{0}$ if and only if $\mathbf{y} = \mathbf{0}$.

This is so because if $\mathbf{y} = \mathbf{0}$ then $\mathbf{x} = \mathbf{A0} = \mathbf{0}$ and if $\mathbf{x} = \mathbf{0}$ then $\mathbf{Ay} = \mathbf{x}$ is a system of m homogeneous equations in n unknowns, and since $r(\mathbf{A}) = n$, the only solution is the trivial $\mathbf{y} = \mathbf{0}$.

5. THE INVERSE MATRIX AND SQUARE EQUATION SYSTEMS

Inverse Matrix

The inverse of an $n \times n$ matrix $\mathbf{A}$ is an $n \times n$ matrix that when pre- or postmultiplied into $\mathbf{A}$ yields the identity matrix. The inverse of $\mathbf{A}$ is written $\mathbf{A}^{-1}$; thus

(5.1) $\mathbf{B} = \mathbf{A}^{-1}$ if and only if $\mathbf{BA} = \mathbf{I} = \mathbf{AB}$.

For example,

$$\begin{pmatrix} 1 & 2 & 3 \\ 1 & 3 & 5 \\ 1 & 5 & 12 \end{pmatrix}^{-1} = \begin{pmatrix} 11/3 & -9/3 & 1/3 \\ -7/3 & 9/3 & -2/3 \\ 2/3 & -3/3 & 1/3 \end{pmatrix} \tag{5.2}$$

because

$$\begin{pmatrix} 11/3 & -9/3 & 1/3 \\ -7/3 & 9/3 & -2/3 \\ 2/3 & -3/3 & 1/3 \end{pmatrix}\begin{pmatrix} 1 & 2 & 3 \\ 1 & 3 & 5 \\ 1 & 5 & 12 \end{pmatrix} = \begin{pmatrix} 1 & 0 & 0 \\ 0 & 1 & 0 \\ 0 & 0 & 1 \end{pmatrix}$$

$$= \begin{pmatrix} 1 & 2 & 3 \\ 1 & 3 & 5 \\ 1 & 5 & 12 \end{pmatrix}\begin{pmatrix} 11/3 & -9/3 & 1/3 \\ -7/3 & 9/3 & -2/3 \\ 2/3 & -3/3 & 1/3 \end{pmatrix}.$$

The following result establishes the conditions under which a square matrix has an inverse and also indicates a method for obtaining if it does exist.

(5.3) Let **A** be an $n \times n$ matrix. Then **A** has an inverse if and only if $|\mathbf{A}| \neq 0$; i.e., if and only if $r(\mathbf{A}) = n$; i.e., if and only if **A** is nonsingular.

This may be demonstrated as follows. Suppose **A** has an inverse $\mathbf{A}^{-1}$. Then $|\mathbf{A}^{-1}|\,|\mathbf{A}| = |\mathbf{A}^{-1}\mathbf{A}| = |\mathbf{I}| = 1$ shows that $|\mathbf{A}| \neq 0$. Conversely, suppose $|\mathbf{A}| \neq 0$. If **A** is 1×1, $\mathbf{A} = (a)$ and the 1×1 matrix $\mathbf{B} = (a^{-1})$ satisfies $\mathbf{AB} = \mathbf{I} = \mathbf{BA}$ and is thus an inverse of **A**. If **A** is $n \times n$ with $n \geq 2$, consider the matrix $\mathbf{B} = (b_{ij})$ where $b_{ij} = |\mathbf{A}|^{-1} c_{ji}$ where c_{ji} is the cofactor of a_{ji}. The matrix **B** is well defined; the i,j element of **AB** is $\sum_{k=1}^{n} a_{ik}b_{kj} = |\mathbf{A}|^{-1} \sum_{k=1}^{n} a_{ik}c_{jk}$ which by (3.3) and (3.6) equals 1 if $i = j$ and equals 0 if $i \neq j$. Thus $\mathbf{AB} = \mathbf{I}$, and similarly it can be shown that $\mathbf{BA} = \mathbf{I}$, so that **B** is an inverse of **A**.

This theorem thus provides one method of computing the inverse of a nonsingular matrix:

(5.4) Let $\mathbf{A} = (a_{ij})$ be an $n \times n$ nonsingular matrix. Let the adjoint of **A**, written adj (**A**), be the $n \times n$ transposed matrix of cofactors of the elements of **A**; i.e., the element the ith row and jth column of adj (**A**) is c_{ji}, the cofactor of a_{ji}. Then $\mathbf{A}^{-1} = |\mathbf{A}|^{-1} \operatorname{adj}(\mathbf{A})$.

For example, consider the matrix **A** of (3.5):

$$\text{(5.5)} \qquad \operatorname{adj}(\mathbf{A}) = \mathbf{C}' = \begin{pmatrix} 11 & -9 & 1 \\ -7 & 9 & -2 \\ 2 & -3 & 1 \end{pmatrix}$$

and $|\mathbf{A}| = 3$ so that

$$\mathbf{A}^{-1} = \begin{pmatrix} 11/3 & -9/3 & 1/3 \\ -7/3 & 9/3 & -2/3 \\ 2/3 & -3/3 & 1/3 \end{pmatrix}$$

as in (5.2). Note that the determinant of **A** may be computed by "multiplying" the elements of any row of **A** by the elements in the corresponding column of adj (**A**) and summing. Note also that where **A** is $n \times n$, if $\mathbf{BA} = \mathbf{I}$, then $\mathbf{AB} = \mathbf{I}$.

The following properties of the inverse are straightforward. The inverse is unique:

(5.6) If $\mathbf{BA} = \mathbf{I}$ and $\mathbf{CA} = \mathbf{I}$ where $\mathbf{A}$, $\mathbf{B}$, and $\mathbf{C}$ are $n \times n$ matrices, then $\mathbf{B} = \mathbf{C}$.

This is so because $\mathbf{BAC} = (\mathbf{BA})\mathbf{C} = \mathbf{IC} = \mathbf{C}$ and $\mathbf{BAC} = \mathbf{B}(\mathbf{AC}) = \mathbf{BI} = \mathbf{B}$, so $\mathbf{C} = \mathbf{B}$. The inverse of an inverse is the original matrix:

(5.7) If $\mathbf{A}$ is nonsingular, then $\mathbf{A}^{-1}$ is nonsingular, $|\mathbf{A}^{-1}| = |\mathbf{A}|^{-1}$, and $(\mathbf{A}^{-1})^{-1} = \mathbf{A}$.

This is so because $|\mathbf{A}^{-1}|\,|\mathbf{A}| = |\mathbf{I}| = 1$ implies $|\mathbf{A}^{-1}| = |\mathbf{A}|^{-1} \neq 0$ and premultiplying $\mathbf{A}^{-1}\mathbf{A} = \mathbf{I}$ by $(\mathbf{A}^{-1})^{-1}$ gives $(\mathbf{A}^{-1})^{-1}\,\mathbf{A}^{-1}\mathbf{A} = (\mathbf{A}^{-1})^{-1}$, from which $\mathbf{A} = (\mathbf{A}^{-1})^{-1}$. The inverse of the transpose is the transpose of the inverse:

(5.8) $(\mathbf{A}')^{-1} = (\mathbf{A}^{-1})'$.

This is so because $|\mathbf{A}'| = |\mathbf{A}| \neq 0$ and transposing $\mathbf{A}'(\mathbf{A}')^{-1} = \mathbf{I}$ gives $[(\mathbf{A}')^{-1}]'\mathbf{A} = \mathbf{I}$, from which $[(\mathbf{A}')^{-1}]' = \mathbf{A}^{-1}$; transposing that gives $(\mathbf{A}')^{-1} = (\mathbf{A}^{-1})'$. It follows that

(5.9) If $\mathbf{A}$ is symmetric and nonsingular, then $\mathbf{A}^{-1}$ is symmetric.

Obviously the identity matrix is its own inverse:

(5.10) $\mathbf{I}^{-1} = \mathbf{I}$.

Finally, the inverse of a product is the product of the inverses in reverse order:

(5.11) If $\mathbf{A}$ and $\mathbf{B}$ are nonsingular, then $(\mathbf{AB})^{-1} = \mathbf{B}^{-1}\mathbf{A}^{-1}$.

This is so because $|\mathbf{AB}| = |\mathbf{A}|\,|\mathbf{B}| \neq 0$ if both $|\mathbf{A}| \neq 0$ and $|\mathbf{B}| \neq 0$, and then $(\mathbf{B}^{-1}\mathbf{A}^{-1})(\mathbf{AB}) = \mathbf{B}^{-1}(\mathbf{A}^{-1}\mathbf{A})\mathbf{B} = \mathbf{B}^{-1}\mathbf{IB} = \mathbf{B}^{-1}\mathbf{B} = \mathbf{I}$.

We can also show that the rank of a matrix is unaffected by pre- or postmultiplication by a nonsingular matrix:

(5.12) If $\mathbf{A}$ is $m \times n$, $\mathbf{P}$ is $m \times m$ and nonsingular, and $\mathbf{Q}$ is $n \times n$ and nonsingular, then $r(\mathbf{PAQ}) = r(\mathbf{A})$.

By (4.13), $r(\mathbf{PA}) \leq r(\mathbf{A})$. Let $\mathbf{B} = \mathbf{PA}$ so $\mathbf{A} = \mathbf{P}^{-1}\mathbf{B}$; then by (4.13) $r(\mathbf{A}) \leq r(\mathbf{B}) = r(\mathbf{PA})$. Hence $r(\mathbf{PA}) = r(\mathbf{A})$. Similarly $r(\mathbf{BQ}) \leq r(\mathbf{B})$. Let $\mathbf{BQ} = \mathbf{C}$ so $\mathbf{B} = \mathbf{CQ}^{-1}$; then $r(\mathbf{B}) \leq r(\mathbf{C}) = r(\mathbf{BQ})$. Hence $r(\mathbf{BQ}) = r(\mathbf{B})$. Thus $r(\mathbf{PAQ}) = r(\mathbf{BQ}) = r(\mathbf{B}) = r(\mathbf{PA}) = r(\mathbf{A})$.

Square System of Simultaneous Linear Equations

The inverse matrix is directly applicable to the investigation and computation of the solution to a system of n simultaneous equations in n

unknowns:

$$(5.13)\qquad \begin{array}{ccccc} a_{11}x_1 + \cdots + a_{1n}x_n = b_1 \\ \vdots \qquad\quad \vdots \quad\;\; \vdots \\ a_{n1}x_1 + \cdots + a_{nn}x_n = b_n. \end{array}$$

In view of the definition of matrix multiplication, the system may be compactly written as

$$(5.14)\qquad \mathbf{Ax} = \mathbf{b}$$

where

$$\mathbf{A} = \begin{pmatrix} a_{11} & \cdots & a_{1n} \\ \cdot & & \cdot \\ \cdot & & \cdot \\ \cdot & & \cdot \\ a_{n1} & \cdots & a_{nn} \end{pmatrix}, \quad \mathbf{x} = \begin{pmatrix} x_1 \\ \cdot \\ \cdot \\ \cdot \\ x_n \end{pmatrix}, \quad \mathbf{b} = \begin{pmatrix} b_1 \\ \cdot \\ \cdot \\ \cdot \\ b_n \end{pmatrix}.$$

It follows directly that

(5.15) If $\mathbf{A}$ is $n \times n$ and nonsingular and $\mathbf{x}$ and $\mathbf{b}$ are $n \times 1$, then $\mathbf{x} = \mathbf{A}^{-1}\mathbf{b}$ is the unique solution to the system of n simultaneous linear equations in n unknowns, $\mathbf{Ax} = \mathbf{b}$.

Clearly, $\mathbf{x} = \mathbf{A}^{-1}\mathbf{b}$ is a solution since $\mathbf{Ax} = \mathbf{A}(\mathbf{A}^{-1}\mathbf{b}) = (\mathbf{AA}^{-1})\mathbf{b} = \mathbf{Ib} = \mathbf{b}$. Suppose that $\mathbf{y}$ is another solution, $\mathbf{Ay} = \mathbf{b}$. Then $\mathbf{A}(\mathbf{y} - \mathbf{x}) = \mathbf{Ay} - \mathbf{Ax} = \mathbf{b} - \mathbf{b} = \mathbf{0}$. Since $r(\mathbf{A}) = n$, the only solution to the homogeneous system $\mathbf{A}(\mathbf{y} - \mathbf{x}) = 0$ is the trivial one $(\mathbf{y} - \mathbf{x}) = \mathbf{0}$. Thus if $\mathbf{y}$ is a solution, $\mathbf{y} = \mathbf{x}$. It may be noted without proof that if $\mathbf{A}$ is singular there will be a solution if and only if $r(\mathbf{A} \mid \mathbf{b}) = r(\mathbf{A})$.

The result of (5.15) provides a standard method for solving a square system of simultaneous linear equations: Find the inverse of the coefficient matrix and premultiply it into the right-hand vector. For example, using the $\mathbf{A}$ of (3.5), whose inverse was found in (5.2),

(5.16) The solution to $\begin{pmatrix} 1 & 2 & 3 \\ 1 & 3 & 5 \\ 1 & 5 & 12 \end{pmatrix}\begin{pmatrix} x_1 \\ x_2 \\ x_3 \end{pmatrix} = \begin{pmatrix} 2 \\ 3 \\ 2 \end{pmatrix}$ is

$$\begin{pmatrix} x_1 \\ x_2 \\ x_3 \end{pmatrix} = \begin{pmatrix} 11/3 & -9/3 & 1/3 \\ -7/3 & 9/3 & -2/3 \\ 2/3 & -3/3 & 1/3 \end{pmatrix}\begin{pmatrix} 2 \\ 3 \\ 2 \end{pmatrix} = \begin{pmatrix} -1 \\ 3 \\ -1 \end{pmatrix}.$$

There are alternative methods of solving a system of simultaneous linear equations. Many of them are based on the obvious:

(5.17) Let $\mathbf{A}$ be an $n \times n$ matrix and $\mathbf{x}$ and $\mathbf{b}$ be $n \times 1$ vectors. Suppose that $\mathbf{P}^{(1)}, \ldots, \mathbf{P}^{(n)}$ are a set of $n \times n$ matrices such that $\mathbf{P}^{(1)} \cdots \mathbf{P}^{(n)}\mathbf{A} = \mathbf{I}$. Then $\mathbf{P}^{(1)} \cdots \mathbf{P}^{(n)}\mathbf{b}$ is the solution to $\mathbf{Ax} = \mathbf{b}$ and $\mathbf{P}^{(1)} \cdots \mathbf{P}^{(n)} = \mathbf{A}^{-1}$.

Partitioned Inversion

It may sometimes be convenient to obtain the inverse of a matrix in partitioned form. The following result is then applicable.

(5.18) Let $\mathbf{A}$ be an $n \times n$ nonsingular matrix partitioned as

$$\mathbf{A} = \begin{pmatrix} \mathbf{E} & \mathbf{F} \\ \mathbf{G} & \mathbf{H} \end{pmatrix}$$

where $\mathbf{E}$ is $n_1 \times n_1$, $\mathbf{F}$ is $n_1 \times n_2$, $\mathbf{G}$ is $n_2 \times n_1$, $\mathbf{H}$ is $n_2 \times n_2$, and $n_1 + n_2 = n$, and suppose that $\mathbf{E}$ and $\mathbf{D} = \mathbf{H} - \mathbf{GE}^{-1}\mathbf{F}$ are nonsingular. Then

$$\mathbf{A}^{-1} = \begin{pmatrix} \mathbf{E}^{-1}(\mathbf{I} + \mathbf{FD}^{-1}\mathbf{GE}^{-1}) & -\mathbf{E}^{-1}\mathbf{FD}^{-1} \\ -\mathbf{D}^{-1}\mathbf{GE}^{-1} & \mathbf{D}^{-1} \end{pmatrix}.$$

The proof is direct. Multiplying the first "super-row" of $\mathbf{A}^{-1}$ into the first "super-column" of $\mathbf{A}$,

$$\mathbf{E}^{-1}(\mathbf{I} + \mathbf{FD}^{-1}\mathbf{GE}^{-1})\mathbf{E} - \mathbf{E}^{-1}\mathbf{FD}^{-1}\mathbf{G}$$
$$= \mathbf{E}^{-1}\mathbf{IE} + \mathbf{E}^{-1}\mathbf{FD}^{-1}\mathbf{G} - \mathbf{E}^{-1}\mathbf{FD}^{-1}\mathbf{G} = \mathbf{I};$$

multiplying the first "super-row" of $\mathbf{A}^{-1}$ into the second "super-column" of $\mathbf{A}$,

$$\begin{aligned} &\mathbf{E}^{-1}(\mathbf{I} + \mathbf{FD}^{-1}\mathbf{GE}^{-1})\mathbf{F} - \mathbf{E}^{-1}\mathbf{FD}^{-1}\mathbf{H} \\ &\quad = \mathbf{E}^{-1}\mathbf{IF} + \mathbf{E}^{-1}\mathbf{FD}^{-1}\mathbf{GE}^{-1}\mathbf{F} - \mathbf{E}^{-1}\mathbf{FD}^{-1}\mathbf{H} \\ &\quad = \mathbf{E}^{-1}\mathbf{F}(\mathbf{I} + \mathbf{D}^{-1}\mathbf{GE}^{-1}\mathbf{F} - \mathbf{D}^{-1}\mathbf{H}) \\ &\quad = \mathbf{E}^{-1}\mathbf{F}[\mathbf{I} + \mathbf{D}^{-1}(\mathbf{GE}^{-1}\mathbf{F} - \mathbf{H})] = \mathbf{E}^{-1}\mathbf{F}[\mathbf{I} + \mathbf{D}^{-1}(-\mathbf{D})] \\ &\quad = \mathbf{E}^{-1}\mathbf{F}(\mathbf{I} - \mathbf{I}) = \mathbf{E}^{-1}\mathbf{F0} = \mathbf{0}; \end{aligned}$$

multiplying the second "super-row" of $\mathbf{A}^{-1}$ into the first "super-column" of $\mathbf{A}$, $-\mathbf{D}^{-1}\mathbf{GE}^{-1}\mathbf{E} + \mathbf{D}^{-1}\mathbf{G} = -\mathbf{D}^{-1}\mathbf{G} + \mathbf{D}^{-1}\mathbf{G} = \mathbf{0}$; and multiplying the second "super-row" of $\mathbf{A}^{-1}$ into the second "super-column" of $\mathbf{A}$, $-\mathbf{D}^{-1}\mathbf{G}\mathbf{E}^{-1}\mathbf{F} + \mathbf{D}^{-1}\mathbf{H} = \mathbf{D}^{-1}(\mathbf{H} - \mathbf{G}\mathbf{E}^{-1}\mathbf{F}) = \mathbf{D}^{-1}\mathbf{D} = \mathbf{I}$. Thus

$$\mathbf{A}^{-1}\mathbf{A} = \begin{pmatrix} \mathbf{I} & \mathbf{0} \\ \mathbf{0} & \mathbf{I} \end{pmatrix} = \mathbf{I}$$

so that $\mathbf{A}^{-1}$ is indeed the inverse of $\mathbf{A}$.

6. CHARACTERISTIC ROOTS, DIAGONALIZATION OF A SYMMETRIC MATRIX, ORTHOGONAL AND IDEMPOTENT MATRICES, AND FORMS

Characteristic Roots of a Matrix

Associated with any $n \times n$ matrix $\mathbf{A}$ are n scalar functions of its elements called the characteristic roots (or eigenvalues) of $\mathbf{A}$ and written $\lambda_1, \ldots, \lambda_n$. The characteristic roots λ_i $(i = 1, \ldots, n)$ are defined by the property that $\mathbf{A}\mathbf{x}^{(i)} = \lambda_i \mathbf{x}^{(i)}$ for some nonzero vector $\mathbf{x}^{(i)}$ which is then called a characteristic vector (or eigenvector) of $\mathbf{A}$. Thus λ is a characteristic root of $\mathbf{A}$ if and only if $\mathbf{A}\mathbf{x} = \lambda\mathbf{x}$ for some $\mathbf{x} \neq \mathbf{0}$, i.e., if and only if $(\mathbf{A} - \lambda\mathbf{I})\mathbf{x} = \mathbf{0}$ for some $\mathbf{x} \neq \mathbf{0}$. Now for any choice of λ, $(\mathbf{A} - \lambda\mathbf{I})\mathbf{x} = \mathbf{0}$ is a system of n homogeneous linear equations in n unknowns; it has a nontrivial solution if and only if $r(\mathbf{A} - \lambda\mathbf{I}) < n$, i.e., if and only if $|\mathbf{A} - \lambda\mathbf{I}| = 0$. Thus

(6.1) Let $\mathbf{A}$ be an $n \times n$ matrix. Then the characteristic roots of $\mathbf{A}$ are the n roots, not necessarily distinct, of $|\mathbf{A} - \lambda\mathbf{I}| = 0$.

The polynomial $|\mathbf{A} - \lambda\mathbf{I}|$, which is of the nth degree in λ, is called the characteristic polynomial of $\mathbf{A}$, and the equation $|\mathbf{A} - \lambda\mathbf{I}| = 0$ is called the characteristic equation of $\mathbf{A}$. To illustrate,

$$\mathbf{A} = \begin{pmatrix} -3 & 2\sqrt{2} \\ 2\sqrt{2} & -1 \end{pmatrix}, \tag{6.2}$$

$$\mathbf{A} - \lambda\mathbf{I} = \begin{pmatrix} -3 & 2\sqrt{2} \\ 2\sqrt{2} & -1 \end{pmatrix} - \begin{pmatrix} \lambda & 0 \\ 0 & \lambda \end{pmatrix} = \begin{pmatrix} -3 - \lambda & 2\sqrt{2} \\ 2\sqrt{2} & -1 - \lambda \end{pmatrix},$$

$$\begin{aligned} |\mathbf{A} - \lambda\mathbf{I}| &= (-3 - \lambda)(-1 - \lambda) - (2\sqrt{2})(2\sqrt{2}) \\ &= \lambda^2 + 4\lambda - 5 = (\lambda + 5)(\lambda - 1). \end{aligned}$$

The characteristic roots of $\mathbf{A}$ are the roots of $(\lambda + 5)(\lambda - 1) = 0$, namely $\lambda_1 = -5$ and $\lambda_2 = 1$. Note

$$\begin{pmatrix} -3 & 2\sqrt{2} \\ 2\sqrt{2} & -1 \end{pmatrix}\begin{pmatrix} -4 \\ 2\sqrt{2} \end{pmatrix} = \begin{pmatrix} 20 \\ -10\sqrt{2} \end{pmatrix} = -5\begin{pmatrix} -4 \\ 2\sqrt{2} \end{pmatrix}$$

and

$$\begin{pmatrix} -3 & 2\sqrt{2} \\ 2\sqrt{2} & -1 \end{pmatrix}\begin{pmatrix} 2 \\ 2\sqrt{2} \end{pmatrix} = \begin{pmatrix} 2 \\ 2\sqrt{2} \end{pmatrix} = 1\begin{pmatrix} 2 \\ 2\sqrt{2} \end{pmatrix}.$$

The following results are straightforward.

(6.3) If $\mathbf{A}$ is an $n \times n$ matrix, $\mathbf{P}$ is an $n \times n$ nonsingular matrix, and $\mathbf{B} = \mathbf{PAP}^{-1}$, then the characteristic polynomial, characteristic roots, trace, and rank of $\mathbf{B}$ are identical with those of $\mathbf{A}$.

For $|\mathbf{B} - \lambda\mathbf{I}| = |\mathbf{PAP}^{-1} - \lambda\mathbf{I}| = |\mathbf{PAP}^{-1} - \lambda\mathbf{PP}^{-1}| = |\mathbf{P}(\mathbf{A} - \lambda\mathbf{I})\mathbf{P}^{-1}| = |\mathbf{P}|\,|\mathbf{A} - \lambda\mathbf{I}|\,|\mathbf{P}^{-1}| = |\mathbf{A} - \lambda\mathbf{I}|$ since $|\mathbf{P}|\,|\mathbf{P}^{-1}| = 1$, so that $\mathbf{B}$ has the same characteristic polynomial, and hence the same characteristic roots, as $\mathbf{A}$. Further, by (2.35) $tr(\mathbf{B}) = tr(\mathbf{PAP}^{-1}) = tr(\mathbf{P}^{-1}\mathbf{PA}) = tr(\mathbf{A})$. Finally, since $\mathbf{P}$ and $\mathbf{P}^{-1}$ are nonsingular, $r(\mathbf{B}) = r(\mathbf{PAP}^{-1}) = r(\mathbf{A})$ by (5.12).

(6.4) If $\mathbf{D}$ is a diagonal matrix, its characteristic roots are its diagonal elements.

If $\mathbf{D}$ is diagonal, then so is

$$\mathbf{D} - \lambda\mathbf{I} = \begin{pmatrix} d_{11} - \lambda & 0 & \cdots & 0 \\ 0 & d_{22} - \lambda & \cdots & 0 \\ \vdots & \vdots & & \vdots \\ 0 & 0 & \cdots & d_{nn} - \lambda \end{pmatrix}.$$

By (3.9) the determinant is $(d_{11} - \lambda) \cdots (d_{nn} - \lambda)$, which shows that the roots of $|\mathbf{D} - \lambda\mathbf{I}| = 0$ are just $d_{11}, \ldots, d_{nn}$.

(6.5) If λ is a characteristic root of $\mathbf{A}$ and p is a positive integer, then λ^p is a characteristic root of $\mathbf{A}^p$, and if in addition $\mathbf{A}$ is nonsingular, then λ^{-p} is a characteristic root of $\mathbf{A}^{-p}$.

If $\mathbf{Ax} = \lambda\mathbf{x}$, then $\mathbf{A}^2\mathbf{x} = \mathbf{A}(\mathbf{Ax}) = \mathbf{A}\lambda\mathbf{x} = \lambda(\mathbf{Ax}) = \lambda^2\mathbf{x}$, and similarly $\mathbf{A}^p\mathbf{x} = \lambda^p\mathbf{x}$; if $\mathbf{Ax} = \lambda\mathbf{x}$ and $\mathbf{A}$ is nonsingular, then $\lambda^{-1}\mathbf{A}^{-1}\mathbf{Ax} = \lambda^{-1}\mathbf{A}^{-1}\lambda\mathbf{x}$, from which $\lambda^{-1}\mathbf{x} = \mathbf{A}^{-1}\mathbf{x}$, and similarly $\lambda^{-p}\mathbf{x} = \mathbf{A}^{-p}\mathbf{x}$.

(6.6) If $(\mathbf{A} - \lambda_1\mathbf{I})\mathbf{x}_1 = \mathbf{0}$ and $(\mathbf{A} - \lambda_2\mathbf{I})\mathbf{x}_2 = \mathbf{0}$ where $\mathbf{A}$ is symmetric, $\lambda_1 \neq 0$, $\lambda_2 \neq 0$, and $\lambda_1 \neq \lambda_2$, then $\mathbf{x}_1'\mathbf{x}_2 = 0$.

This follows from the fact that $\mathbf{x}_2'(\mathbf{A} - \lambda_1\mathbf{I})\mathbf{x}_1 = \mathbf{x}_2'\mathbf{A}\mathbf{x}_1 - \lambda_1\mathbf{x}_2'\mathbf{x}_1 = 0$ so that $\lambda_1\mathbf{x}_2'\mathbf{x}_1 = \mathbf{x}_2'\mathbf{A}\mathbf{x}_1$; similarly $\lambda_2\mathbf{x}_1'\mathbf{x}_2 = \mathbf{x}_1'\mathbf{A}\mathbf{x}_2$. Since $\mathbf{x}_2'\mathbf{x}_1 = \mathbf{x}_1'\mathbf{x}_2$ and $\mathbf{x}_2'\mathbf{A}\mathbf{x}_1 = (\mathbf{x}_2'\mathbf{A}\mathbf{x}_1)' = \mathbf{x}_1'\mathbf{A}'\mathbf{x}_2 = \mathbf{x}_1'\mathbf{A}\mathbf{x}_2$, we find that $\lambda_1\mathbf{x}_1'\mathbf{x}_2 = \lambda_2\mathbf{x}_1'\mathbf{x}_2$ or $\mathbf{x}_1'\mathbf{x}_2 = (\lambda_2/\lambda_1)\mathbf{x}_1'\mathbf{x}_2$; since $\lambda_2 \neq \lambda_1$ this requires $\mathbf{x}_1'\mathbf{x}_2 = 0$. Extending, we have

(6.7) If $(\mathbf{B} - \lambda_1\mathbf{A})\mathbf{x}_1 = \mathbf{0}$ and $(\mathbf{B} - \lambda_2\mathbf{A})\mathbf{x}_2 = \mathbf{0}$ where $\mathbf{A}$ and $\mathbf{B}$ are symmetric, $\lambda_1 \neq 0$, $\lambda_2 \neq 0$, and $\lambda_1 \neq \lambda_2$, then $\mathbf{x}_1'\mathbf{A}\mathbf{x}_2 = 0$.

This is so because $\mathbf{x}_2'\mathbf{B}\mathbf{x}_1 = \lambda_1\mathbf{x}_2'\mathbf{A}\mathbf{x}_1$ and $\mathbf{x}_1'\mathbf{B}\mathbf{x}_2 = \lambda_2\mathbf{x}_1'\mathbf{A}\mathbf{x}_2$; therefore $\lambda_1\mathbf{x}_1'\mathbf{A}\mathbf{x}_2 = \lambda_2\mathbf{x}_1'\mathbf{A}\mathbf{x}_2$ or $\mathbf{x}_1'\mathbf{A}\mathbf{x}_2 = (\lambda_2/\lambda_1)\mathbf{x}_1'\mathbf{A}\mathbf{x}_2$; since $\lambda_2 \neq \lambda_1$, this requires $\mathbf{x}_1'\mathbf{A}\mathbf{x}_2 = 0$.

Orthogonal Matrix

A square matrix $\mathbf{C}$ is said to be orthogonal if and only if its transpose is its inverse; thus

(6.8) $\mathbf{C}$ is orthogonal if and only if $\mathbf{C}'\mathbf{C} = \mathbf{I}$.

Note that if $\mathbf{C}$ is orthogonal and if $\mathbf{C}_i$ and $\mathbf{C}_j$ are columns of $\mathbf{C}$ then $\mathbf{C}_i'\mathbf{C}_j$ equals 1 if $i = j$ and equals 0 if $i \neq j$. Moreover, if $\mathbf{C}$ is orthogonal, then $\mathbf{C}'$ is orthogonal. In addition,

(6.9) If $\mathbf{C}$ is orthogonal, then $|\mathbf{C}| = \pm 1$.

For $1 = |\mathbf{I}| = |\mathbf{C}'\mathbf{C}| = |\mathbf{C}'|\,|\mathbf{C}|$ and always $|\mathbf{C}'| = |\mathbf{C}|$. Examples of orthogonal matrices are the identity matrix ($\mathbf{I}'\mathbf{I} = \mathbf{I}\,\mathbf{I} = \mathbf{I}$) and

$$\text{(6.10)} \qquad \mathbf{C} = \begin{pmatrix} 1/\sqrt{3} & 2/\sqrt{6} & 0 \\ 1/\sqrt{3} & -1/\sqrt{6} & 1/\sqrt{2} \\ 1/\sqrt{3} & -1/\sqrt{6} & -1/\sqrt{2} \end{pmatrix}$$

since

$$\mathbf{C}'\mathbf{C} = \begin{pmatrix} 1/\sqrt{3} & 1/\sqrt{3} & 1/\sqrt{3} \\ 2/\sqrt{6} & -1/\sqrt{6} & -1/\sqrt{6} \\ 0 & 1/\sqrt{2} & -1/\sqrt{2} \end{pmatrix}$$

$$\times \begin{pmatrix} 1/\sqrt{3} & 2/\sqrt{6} & 0 \\ 1/\sqrt{3} & -1/\sqrt{6} & 1/\sqrt{2} \\ 1/\sqrt{3} & -1/\sqrt{6} & -1/\sqrt{2} \end{pmatrix} = \begin{pmatrix} 1 & 0 & 0 \\ 0 & 1 & 0 \\ 0 & 0 & 1 \end{pmatrix}.$$

Diagonalization of a Symmetric Matrix

Without proof we state the very useful diagonalization theorem:

(6.11) If $\mathbf{A}$ is an $n \times n$ symmetric matrix, there exists an $n \times n$ orthogonal matrix $\mathbf{C}$ such that $\mathbf{C'AC}$ is diagonal.

For a proof see Hadley (1961, pp. 242–249). Such a matrix $\mathbf{C}$ will be called an orthogonal matrix which diagonalizes $\mathbf{A}$. To illustrate the diagonalization process let $\mathbf{A}$ be the symmetric matrix of (6.2) and let

$$\mathbf{C} = \begin{pmatrix} 2/\sqrt{6} & \sqrt{2}/\sqrt{6} \\ -\sqrt{2}/\sqrt{6} & 2/\sqrt{6} \end{pmatrix}.$$

Then $\mathbf{C}$ is an orthogonal matrix that diagonalizes $\mathbf{A}$:

$$\begin{pmatrix} 2/\sqrt{6} & -\sqrt{2}/\sqrt{6} \\ \sqrt{2}/\sqrt{6} & 2/\sqrt{6} \end{pmatrix}\begin{pmatrix} 2/\sqrt{6} & \sqrt{2}/\sqrt{6} \\ -\sqrt{2}/\sqrt{6} & 2/\sqrt{6} \end{pmatrix} = \begin{pmatrix} 1 & 0 \\ 0 & 1 \end{pmatrix} \tag{6.12}$$

and

$$\begin{pmatrix} 2/\sqrt{6} & -\sqrt{2}/\sqrt{6} \\ \sqrt{2}/\sqrt{6} & 2/\sqrt{6} \end{pmatrix}\begin{pmatrix} -3 & 2\sqrt{2} \\ 2\sqrt{2} & -1 \end{pmatrix}\begin{pmatrix} 2/\sqrt{6} & \sqrt{2}/\sqrt{6} \\ -\sqrt{2}/\sqrt{6} & 2/\sqrt{6} \end{pmatrix} = \begin{pmatrix} -5 & 0 \\ 0 & 1 \end{pmatrix}.$$

It follows directly that

(6.13) Let $\mathbf{A}$ be a symmetric matrix and let $\mathbf{C}$ be an orthogonal matrix that diagonalizes $\mathbf{A}$. Then the characteristic roots of $\mathbf{A}$ are the diagonal elements of $\mathbf{\Lambda} = \mathbf{C'AC}$, and the rank of $\mathbf{A}$ is the number of nonzero diagonal elements of $\mathbf{\Lambda}$.

Since $\mathbf{\Lambda}$ is a diagonal matrix its characteristic roots are its diagonal elements by (6.4) and its rank is the number of nonzero elements on its diagonal, by (4.10). Since $\mathbf{C}$ is orthogonal, $(\mathbf{C'})^{-1} = \mathbf{C}$, so that $\mathbf{\Lambda} = \mathbf{C'AC} = \mathbf{C'A(C')}^{-1}$ has the same characteristic roots and rank as does $\mathbf{A}$ by (6.3). This result is illustrated in (6.12). It should be noted that the choice of an orthogonal matrix to diagonalize a symmetric matrix is not unique; however, the resulting diagonal matrices will all have the same diagonal elements, perhaps in a different order. We can always find an orthogonal matrix to diagonalize $\mathbf{A}$ into a matrix which has the diagonal elements in any specified order. Note also that since $|\mathbf{\Lambda}| = |\mathbf{C}'\mathbf{A}\mathbf{C}| = |\mathbf{C}|^2\,|\mathbf{A}| = |\mathbf{A}|$ by (6.9) and since $|\mathbf{\Lambda}|$ is the product of its diagonal elements by (3.9),

(6.14) The determinant of a symmetric matrix is the product of its characteristic roots.

Idempotent Matrix

A symmetric matrix that reproduces itself on multiplication by itself is said to be idempotent; thus

(6.15) $\mathbf{A}$ is idempotent if and only if $\mathbf{A}' = \mathbf{A}$ and $\mathbf{A}\mathbf{A} = \mathbf{A}$.

Examples of idempotent matrices are the identity matrix ($\mathbf{I}' = \mathbf{I}$ and $\mathbf{I}\,\mathbf{I} = \mathbf{I}$) and

(6.16) $$\mathbf{A} = \begin{pmatrix} \frac{1}{2} & -\frac{1}{2} \\ -\frac{1}{2} & \frac{1}{2} \end{pmatrix}$$

since

$$\mathbf{A}\mathbf{A} = \begin{pmatrix} \frac{1}{2} & -\frac{1}{2} \\ -\frac{1}{2} & \frac{1}{2} \end{pmatrix}\begin{pmatrix} \frac{1}{2} & -\frac{1}{2} \\ -\frac{1}{2} & \frac{1}{2} \end{pmatrix} = \begin{pmatrix} \frac{1}{2} & -\frac{1}{2} \\ -\frac{1}{2} & \frac{1}{2} \end{pmatrix}.$$

It follows that

(6.17) If $\mathbf{A}$ is idempotent, the characteristic roots of $\mathbf{A}$ are all either 1 or 0.

Let λ be a characteristic root of the idempotent matrix $\mathbf{A}$; then $\mathbf{A}\mathbf{x} = \lambda\mathbf{x}$ for some $\mathbf{x} \neq \mathbf{0}$. Premultiplying by $\mathbf{A}$ gives $\mathbf{A}(\mathbf{A}\mathbf{x}) = \mathbf{A}(\lambda\mathbf{x}) = \lambda(\mathbf{A}\mathbf{x}) = \lambda(\lambda\mathbf{x}) = \lambda^2\mathbf{x}$. But on the other hand $\mathbf{A}(\mathbf{A}\mathbf{x}) = (\mathbf{A}\mathbf{A})\mathbf{x} = \mathbf{A}\mathbf{x} = \lambda\mathbf{x}$. Thus $\lambda^2\mathbf{x} = \lambda\mathbf{x}$ for some nonzero $\mathbf{x}$, which requires that either $\lambda = 1$ or $\lambda = 0$.

An idempotent matrix may be diagonalized into a very simple form. Let $\mathbf{C}$ be an orthogonal matrix that diagonalizes the idempotent matrix $\mathbf{A}$. Then $\mathbf{\Lambda} = \mathbf{C}'\mathbf{A}\mathbf{C}$ displays the characteristic roots of $\mathbf{A}$ on its diagonal and has the same rank and trace as does $\mathbf{A}$. Since the characteristic roots of $\mathbf{A}$ are all either 1 or 0, and since the rank of a diagonal matrix is equal to the number of nonzero elements on its diagonal,

(6.18) Let $\mathbf{A}$ be an $n \times n$ idempotent matrix of rank r. Then there exists an orthogonal matrix $\mathbf{C}$ such that

$$\mathbf{\Lambda} = \mathbf{C}'\mathbf{A}\mathbf{C} = \begin{pmatrix} \mathbf{I}_r & \mathbf{0}_{r,n-r} \\ \mathbf{0}_{n-r,r} & \mathbf{0}_{n-r,n-r} \end{pmatrix}.$$

Finally, since $\mathbf{\Lambda}$ has the same trace as $\mathbf{A}$, and since $tr(\mathbf{\Lambda})$ is obviously r,

(6.19) If $\mathbf{A}$ is idempotent, then $r(\mathbf{A}) = tr(\mathbf{A})$.

For example, $r(\mathbf{I}_n) = n = tr(\mathbf{I}_n)$, and the trace of the matrix $\mathbf{A}$ of (6.16) is $\frac{1}{2} + \frac{1}{2} = 1$ and so is its rank (its determinant is zero, but $|\frac{1}{2}| \neq 0$).

Linear and Quadratic Forms

If $\mathbf{B}$ is an $m \times n$ matrix, then the $m \times 1$ vector $\mathbf{y} = \mathbf{Bx}$, which is defined for all $n \times 1$ vectors $\mathbf{x}$, is said to be a linear form in (the elements of) $\mathbf{x}$. Each element of $\mathbf{y}$ is indeed a homogeneous linear function of the elements of $\mathbf{x}$: $y_i = \Sigma_{j=1}^n b_{ij}x_j$ $(i = 1, \ldots, m)$. If $\mathbf{B}$ is an orthogonal matrix, then $\mathbf{y} = \mathbf{Bx}$ is said to be an orthogonal linear form in (the elements of) $\mathbf{x}$.

If $\mathbf{A}$ is an $n \times n$ symmetric matrix, the scalar $Q = \mathbf{x}'\mathbf{Ax}$, which is defined for all $n \times 1$ vectors $\mathbf{x}$, is said to be a quadratic form in (the elements of) $\mathbf{x}$. The scalar Q is indeed a homogeneous quadratic function of the elements of $\mathbf{x}$:

(6.20)
$$Q = (x_1 \quad \cdots \quad x_n)\begin{pmatrix} a_{11} & \cdots & a_{1n} \\ \cdot & & \cdot \\ \cdot & & \cdot \\ \cdot & & \cdot \\ a_{n1} & \cdots & a_{nn} \end{pmatrix}\begin{pmatrix} x_1 \\ \cdot \\ \cdot \\ \cdot \\ x_n \end{pmatrix}$$
$$= \mathbf{x}'\mathbf{Ax} = \sum_{i=1}^n \sum_{j=1}^n a_{ij}x_ix_j = \sum_{i=1}^n a_{ii}x_i^2 + \sum_{\substack{i=1 \\ i\neq j}}^n \sum_{j=1}^n a_{ij}x_ix_j.$$

If $r(\mathbf{A}) = r$, then $Q = \mathbf{x}'\mathbf{Ax}$ is said to be a quadratic form of rank r. If $\mathbf{A}$ is idempotent, then $Q = \mathbf{x}'\mathbf{Ax}$ is said to be an idempotent quadratic form.

The theory of the preceding subsection is directly applicable to show how an idempotent quadratic form can be written as a sum of squares:

(6.21) Let $Q = \mathbf{x}'\mathbf{Ax}$ be an idempotent quadratic form of rank r. Then $Q = \Sigma_{i=1}^r y_i^2 = \mathbf{y}_1'\mathbf{y}_1$, where

$$\begin{pmatrix} \mathbf{y}_1 \\ \mathbf{y}_2 \end{pmatrix} = \begin{pmatrix} y_1 \\ \cdot \\ \cdot \\ \cdot \\ y_r \\ y_{r+1} \\ \cdot \\ \cdot \\ \cdot \\ y_n \end{pmatrix} = \mathbf{y} = \mathbf{C}'\mathbf{x}$$

and $\mathbf{C}$ is orthogonal.

This may be shown as follows. Let $\mathbf{C}$ be the orthogonal matrix that diagonalizes $\mathbf{A}$ into the $\mathbf{\Lambda}$ of (6.18) and let $\mathbf{y} = \mathbf{C}'\mathbf{x}$ be partitioned as $\begin{pmatrix} \mathbf{y}_1 \\ \mathbf{y}_2 \end{pmatrix}$ where $\mathbf{y}_1$ is $r \times 1$ and $\mathbf{y}_2$ is $(n - r) \times 1$. Then

$$\begin{aligned} \mathbf{y}_1'\mathbf{y}_1 &= (\mathbf{y}_1' \quad \mathbf{y}_2')\begin{pmatrix} \mathbf{I} & \mathbf{0} \\ \mathbf{0} & \mathbf{0} \end{pmatrix}\begin{pmatrix} \mathbf{y}_1 \\ \mathbf{y}_2 \end{pmatrix} = \mathbf{y}'\mathbf{\Lambda}\mathbf{y} = (\mathbf{C}'\mathbf{x})'\mathbf{\Lambda}(\mathbf{C}'\mathbf{x}) \\ &= (\mathbf{x}'\mathbf{C})(\mathbf{C}'\mathbf{A}\mathbf{C})(\mathbf{C}'\mathbf{x}) = \mathbf{x}'(\mathbf{C}\mathbf{C}')\mathbf{A}(\mathbf{C}\mathbf{C}')\mathbf{x} \\ &= \mathbf{x}'\mathbf{I}\mathbf{A}\mathbf{I}\mathbf{x} = \mathbf{x}'\mathbf{A}\mathbf{x}. \end{aligned}$$

For example, let $\mathbf{A}$ be the idempotent matrix of (6.16); it is diagonalized by the orthogonal matrix

$$\mathbf{C} = \begin{pmatrix} -1/\sqrt{2} & -1/\sqrt{2} \\ 1/\sqrt{2} & -1/\sqrt{2} \end{pmatrix}.$$

Then let

$$\mathbf{y} = \mathbf{C}'\mathbf{x} = \begin{pmatrix} -1/\sqrt{2} & 1/\sqrt{2} \\ -1/\sqrt{2} & -1/\sqrt{2} \end{pmatrix}\begin{pmatrix} x_1 \\ x_2 \end{pmatrix};$$

i.e., $\mathbf{y}_1 = [-(1/\sqrt{2})](x_1 - x_2)$. Then

$$\mathbf{y}_1'\mathbf{y}_1 = \tfrac{1}{2}(x_1 - x_2)^2 = \tfrac{1}{2}x_1^2 + \tfrac{1}{2}x_2^2 - x_1x_2 = (x_1 \quad x_2)\begin{pmatrix} \frac{1}{2} & -\frac{1}{2} \\ -\frac{1}{2} & \frac{1}{2} \end{pmatrix} \times \begin{pmatrix} x_1 \\ x_2 \end{pmatrix} = \mathbf{x}'\mathbf{A}\mathbf{x}.$$

7. DEFINITE MATRICES

Positive Definite Matrix

Let $\mathbf{A}$ be an $n \times n$ symmetric matrix. Then $\mathbf{A}$ is said to be positive definite if and only if the quadratic form $\mathbf{x}'\mathbf{A}\mathbf{x}$ is positive for every non-zero $n \times 1$ vector $\mathbf{x}$; thus

(7.1) A symmetric matrix $\mathbf{A}$ is positive definite if and only if $\mathbf{x}'\mathbf{A}\mathbf{x} > 0$ for all $\mathbf{x} \neq \mathbf{0}$.

Many useful properties of positive definite matrices are readily established. First,

(7.2) A symmetric matrix $\mathbf{A}$ is positive definite if and only if all the characteristic roots of $\mathbf{A}$ are positive.

Let **C** be an orthogonal matrix that diagonalizes **A**; i.e., let

$$\mathbf{\Lambda} = \mathbf{C}'\mathbf{A}\mathbf{C} = \begin{pmatrix} \lambda_1 & 0 & \cdots & 0 \\ 0 & \lambda_2 & \cdots & 0 \\ \cdot & \cdot & & \cdot \\ \cdot & \cdot & & \cdot \\ \cdot & \cdot & & \cdot \\ 0 & 0 & \cdots & \lambda_n \end{pmatrix},$$

where the λ_i's are the characteristic roots of **A**. Let $\mathbf{y} = \mathbf{C}'\mathbf{x}$ so that $\mathbf{x} = (\mathbf{C}')^{-1}\mathbf{y} = \mathbf{C}\mathbf{y}$; then $\mathbf{x}'\mathbf{A}\mathbf{x} = (\mathbf{C}\mathbf{y})'\mathbf{A}(\mathbf{C}\mathbf{y}) = \mathbf{y}'\mathbf{C}'\mathbf{A}\mathbf{C}\mathbf{y} = \mathbf{y}'\mathbf{\Lambda}\mathbf{y} = \Sigma_{i=1}^{n} \lambda_i y_i^2$. If all $\lambda_i > 0$, then clearly $\mathbf{x}'\mathbf{A}\mathbf{x} = \mathbf{y}'\mathbf{\Lambda}\mathbf{y} \geq 0$ for all **y** with equality holding only when $\mathbf{y} = \mathbf{0}$, i.e., when $\mathbf{x} = \mathbf{C}\mathbf{y} = \mathbf{C}\mathbf{0} = \mathbf{0}$; thus **A** is positive definite. Conversely, let **A** be positive definite and suppose that a characteristic root of **A**, say λ_1, is not positive. Let $\mathbf{y}^*$ be the $n \times 1$ vector with first element 1 and remaining elements 0, and let $\mathbf{x}^* = \mathbf{C}\mathbf{y}^*$; then by (4.28) $\mathbf{x}^* \neq \mathbf{0}$. And then $\mathbf{x}^{*\prime}\mathbf{A}\mathbf{x}^* = \mathbf{y}^{*\prime}\mathbf{C}'\mathbf{A}\mathbf{C}\mathbf{y}^* = \mathbf{y}^{*\prime}\mathbf{\Lambda}\mathbf{y}^* = \Sigma_{i=1}^{n} \lambda_i y_i^{*2} = \lambda_1 \leq 0$ would contradict the assumption that **A** is positive definite. Next,

(7.3) If **A** is an $n \times n$ positive definite matrix, then $|\mathbf{A}| > 0$, $r(\mathbf{A}) = n$, and **A** is nonsingular.

Let $\lambda_1 \cdots \lambda_n$ be the characteristic roots of **A**. Then $|\mathbf{A}| = \lambda_1 \cdots \lambda_n$ by (6.14), and $\lambda_1 \cdots \lambda_n > 0$ by (7.2), whence $|\mathbf{A}| > 0$.

Another useful result is

(7.4) If **A** is an $n \times n$ positive definite matrix and **P** is an $n \times m$ matrix with $r(\mathbf{P}) = m$, then $\mathbf{P}'\mathbf{A}\mathbf{P}$ is positive definite.

For the $m \times m$ matrix $\mathbf{P}'\mathbf{A}\mathbf{P}$ is obviously symmetric. Let **y** be any nonzero $m \times 1$ vector. Then $\mathbf{y}'(\mathbf{P}'\mathbf{A}\mathbf{P})\mathbf{y} = \mathbf{x}'\mathbf{A}\mathbf{x}$ where $\mathbf{x} = \mathbf{P}\mathbf{y}$. Since **A** is positive definite and **x** is nonzero by (4.28), $\mathbf{x}'\mathbf{A}\mathbf{x} > 0$. But $\mathbf{y}'(\mathbf{P}'\mathbf{A}\mathbf{P})\mathbf{y} = \mathbf{x}'\mathbf{A}\mathbf{x}$. Hence $\mathbf{y}'(\mathbf{P}'\mathbf{A}\mathbf{P})\mathbf{y}$ is positive for all $\mathbf{y} \neq \mathbf{0}$. Several specializations of this theorem are important. If in (7.4) we take **P** to be an $n \times n$ nonsingular matrix, we find

(7.5) If **A** is positive definite and **P** is nonsingular, then $\mathbf{P}'\mathbf{A}\mathbf{P}$ is positive definite.

If in (7.4) we let $\mathbf{P} = \mathbf{A}^{-1}$, then $\mathbf{P}'\mathbf{A}\mathbf{P} = (\mathbf{A}^{-1})'\mathbf{A}\mathbf{A}^{-1} = (\mathbf{A}^{-1})' = \mathbf{A}^{-1}$ since **A** is symmetric; thus

(7.6) If **A** is positive definite, then $\mathbf{A}^{-1}$ is positive definite.

The identity matrix is positive definite, since $\mathbf{x}'\mathbf{I}\mathbf{x} = \Sigma_{i=1}^{n} x_i^2$ and a sum of squares is positive unless all the terms are zero. If, then, in (7.4) we take $\mathbf{A} = \mathbf{I}$, so that $\mathbf{P}'\mathbf{A}\mathbf{P} = \mathbf{P}'\mathbf{I}\mathbf{P} = \mathbf{P}'\mathbf{P}$, we find,

(7.7) If $\mathbf{P}$ is an $n \times m$ matrix with $r(\mathbf{P}) = m$, then $\mathbf{P}'\mathbf{P}$ is positive definite.

It is clear that if the matrix $\mathbf{A}^*$ is obtained from the matrix $\mathbf{A}$ by interchanging the ith and jth columns of $\mathbf{A}$ and interchanging the ith and jth rows of $\mathbf{A}$, then if $\mathbf{A}$ is positive definite, $\mathbf{A}^*$ will also be. For $\mathbf{A}^*$ will be symmetric and $\mathbf{x}^{*\prime}\mathbf{A}^*\mathbf{x}^* = \mathbf{x}'\mathbf{A}\mathbf{x}$ where $\mathbf{x}^*$ is any vector and $\mathbf{x}$ is obtained by interchanging the ith and jth elements of $\mathbf{x}^*$.

A principal submatrix of a square matrix is one obtained by deleting only corresponding rows and columns. Then

(7.8) If $\mathbf{A}$ is positive definite, every principal submatrix of $\mathbf{A}$ is positive definite.

Without loss of generality let $\mathbf{B}$ be the principal submatrix obtained by deleting the last $n - m$ rows and columns of $\mathbf{A}$. Then

$$\mathbf{B} = (\mathbf{I}_m \quad \mathbf{0}_{m,n-m}) \begin{pmatrix} \mathbf{A}_{11} & \mathbf{A}_{12} \\ \mathbf{A}_{21} & \mathbf{A}_{22} \end{pmatrix} \begin{pmatrix} \mathbf{I}_m \\ \mathbf{0}_{n-m,m} \end{pmatrix};$$

since $\begin{pmatrix} \mathbf{I}_m \\ \mathbf{0}_{n-m,m} \end{pmatrix}$ is an $n \times m$ matrix whose rank is clearly m, it may serve as the $\mathbf{P}$ of (7.4). A principal minor of a square matrix is the determinant of a principal submatrix. Then application of (7.3) and (7.8) shows that

(7.9) If $\mathbf{A}$ is positive definite, then every principal minor of $\mathbf{A}$ is positive;

in particular,

(7.10) If $\mathbf{A}$ is positive definite, then $a_{ii} > 0$, $a_{ii}a_{jj} - a_{ij}^2 > 0$, for all i and j.

Still another useful result is

(7.11) If $\mathbf{A}$ is positive definite, there exists a nonsingular matrix $\mathbf{P}$ such that $\mathbf{P}\mathbf{A}\mathbf{P}' = \mathbf{I}$ and $\mathbf{P}'\mathbf{P} = \mathbf{A}^{-1}$.

Let $\mathbf{C}$ be the orthogonal matrix such that

$$\mathbf{C}'\mathbf{A}\mathbf{C} = \mathbf{\Lambda} = \begin{pmatrix} \lambda_1 & \cdots & 0 \\ \cdot & & \cdot \\ \cdot & & \cdot \\ \cdot & & \cdot \\ 0 & \cdots & \lambda_n \end{pmatrix}$$

and let

$$\mathbf{D} = \begin{pmatrix} 1/\sqrt{\lambda_1} & \cdots & 0 \\ \cdot & & \cdot \\ \cdot & & \cdot \\ \cdot & & \cdot \\ 0 & \cdots & 1/\sqrt{\lambda_n} \end{pmatrix}.$$

Then $\mathbf{P} = \mathbf{D}'\mathbf{C}'$ is the required matrix, for $\mathbf{P}$, being the product of nonsingular matrices, is nonsingular, and $\mathbf{PAP}' = \mathbf{D}'\mathbf{C}'\mathbf{ACD} = \mathbf{D}'\mathbf{\Lambda D} = \mathbf{I}$. Further, if $\mathbf{PAP}' = \mathbf{I}$, then $\mathbf{P}'(\mathbf{PAP}')\mathbf{P} = \mathbf{P}'\mathbf{IP} = \mathbf{P}'\mathbf{P}$, from which $\mathbf{P}'\mathbf{PA} = \mathbf{I}$, from which $\mathbf{P}'\mathbf{P} = \mathbf{A}^{-1}$.

Nonnegative Definite Matrix

Let $\mathbf{A}$ be an $n \times n$ symmetric matrix. Then $\mathbf{A}$ is said to be nonnegative definite (or positive semidefinite) if and only if the quadratic form $\mathbf{x}'\mathbf{Ax}$ is nonnegative for every $n \times 1$ vector $\mathbf{x}$; thus

(7.12) A symmetric matrix $\mathbf{A}$ is nonnegative definite if and only if $\mathbf{x}'\mathbf{Ax} \geq 0$ for all $\mathbf{x}$.

Thus positive definiteness is a special case of nonnegative definiteness. The following implications of nonnegative definiteness may be derived by arguments parallel to those used in deriving the corresponding implications of positive definiteness.

(7.13) A symmetric matrix $\mathbf{A}$ is nonnegative definite if and only if all the characteristic roots of $\mathbf{A}$ are nonnegative,

(7.14) If $\mathbf{A}$ is nonnegative definite and $\mathbf{P}$ is any matrix, then $\mathbf{P}'\mathbf{AP}$ is nonnegative definite,

(7.15) If $\mathbf{P}$ is any matrix, then $\mathbf{P}'\mathbf{P}$ is nonnegative definite,

(7.16) If $\mathbf{A}$ is nonnegative definite, then any principal submatrix of $\mathbf{A}$ is nonnegative definite,

(7.17) If $\mathbf{A}$ is nonnegative definite, then every principal minor of $\mathbf{A}$ is nonnegative,

(7.18) If $\mathbf{A}$ is nonnegative definite, then $a_{ii} \geq 0$ and $a_{ii}a_{jj} - a_{ij}^2 \geq 0$ for all i and j.

It is readily seen that

(7.19) If $\mathbf{A}$ is nonnegative definite but not positive definite, then its smallest characteristic root is zero and $\mathbf{A}$ is singular.

All the characteristic roots of $\mathbf{A}$ are nonnegative, and if the *smallest* were positive then $\mathbf{A}$ would be positive definite by (7.2); then since $\mathbf{A}$ has at least one zero characteristic root and since $|\mathbf{A}|$ equals the product of these characteristic roots, $|\mathbf{A}| = 0$. Moreover, it follows that

(7.20) If $\mathbf{A}$ is positive definite and $\mathbf{B}$ is nonnegative definite but not positive definite, then the smallest root of the determinantal equation $|\mathbf{B} - \lambda\mathbf{A}| = 0$ is zero.

Let $\mathbf{Q} = \mathbf{PBP}'$ where $\mathbf{P}$ is a nonsingular matrix such that $\mathbf{PAP}' = \mathbf{I}$; then $\mathbf{Q}$ is nonnegative definite by (7.14) but not positive definite, since it is singular—$|\mathbf{Q}| = |\mathbf{P}|^2\,|\mathbf{B}| = 0$—so that its smallest characteristic root is zero by (7.19). Since $|\mathbf{Q} - \lambda\mathbf{I}| = |\mathbf{PBP}' - \lambda\mathbf{PAP}'| = |\mathbf{P}(\mathbf{B} - \lambda\mathbf{A})\mathbf{P}'| = |\mathbf{P}|^2\,|\mathbf{B} - \lambda\mathbf{A}|$, however, and since $|\mathbf{P}|^2 \neq 0$, the roots of $|\mathbf{B} - \lambda\mathbf{A}| = 0$ are the characteristic roots of $\mathbf{Q}$.

The following theorem gives meaning to the idea of one matrix being "more" positive definite than another:

(7.21) If $\mathbf{A} = \mathbf{B} + \mathbf{C}$ where $\mathbf{B}$ is positive definite and $\mathbf{C}$ is nonnegative definite, then (*a*) $\mathbf{A}$ is positive definite, (*b*) $|\mathbf{B}| \leq |\mathbf{A}|$, and (*c*) $\mathbf{B}^{-1} - \mathbf{A}^{-1}$ is nonnegative definite.

First, since for any $\mathbf{x} \neq \mathbf{0}$, $\mathbf{x}'\mathbf{Bx} > 0$ and $\mathbf{x}'\mathbf{Cx} \geq 0$, we have $\mathbf{x}'\mathbf{Ax} = \mathbf{x}'(\mathbf{B} + \mathbf{C})\mathbf{x} = \mathbf{x}'\mathbf{Bx} + \mathbf{x}'\mathbf{Cx} > 0$, establishing part (*a*). Next, let $\mathbf{P}$ be a nonsingular matrix such that $\mathbf{PAP}' = \mathbf{I}$ and $\mathbf{P}'\mathbf{P} = \mathbf{A}^{-1}$, and let $\mathbf{Q} = \mathbf{PBP}'$; then $(\mathbf{I} - \mathbf{Q}) = \mathbf{PAP}' - \mathbf{PBP}' = \mathbf{P}(\mathbf{A} - \mathbf{B})\mathbf{P}' = \mathbf{PCP}'$. Note that $\mathbf{Q}$ is positive definite by (7.5), $(\mathbf{I} - \mathbf{Q})$ is nonnegative definite by (7.14), and $|\mathbf{B}| = |\mathbf{Q}|\,|\mathbf{P}|^{-2} = |\mathbf{Q}|\,|\mathbf{A}|$. Let λ be a characteristic root of $\mathbf{Q}$; then $0 < \lambda$ since $\mathbf{Q}$ is positive definite. In addition, however, $0 \leq 1 - \lambda$ since $1 - \lambda$ must be a characteristic root of the nonnegative definite matrix $(\mathbf{I} - \mathbf{Q})$—because $|(\mathbf{I} - \mathbf{Q}) - (1 - \lambda)\mathbf{I}| = |-\mathbf{Q} + \lambda\mathbf{I}| = \pm\,|\mathbf{Q} - \lambda\mathbf{I}|$. Thus $0 < \lambda \leq 1$, which implies that $|\mathbf{Q}| \leq 1$ because $|\mathbf{Q}|$ is just the product of the characteristic roots of $\mathbf{Q}$; this establishes part (*b*). Finally, we may write $\mathbf{B}^{-1} - \mathbf{A}^{-1} = (\mathbf{P}^{-1}\mathbf{QP}'^{-1})^{-1} - \mathbf{P}'\mathbf{P} = \mathbf{P}'\mathbf{Q}^{-1}\mathbf{P} - \mathbf{P}'\mathbf{P} = \mathbf{P}'(\mathbf{Q}^{-1} - \mathbf{I})\mathbf{P}$, and recognize that by (7.14) $\mathbf{B}^{-1} - \mathbf{A}^{-1}$ is nonnegative definite if $\mathbf{Q}^{-1} - \mathbf{I}$ is. Now if μ is a characteristic root of $(\mathbf{Q}^{-1} - \mathbf{I})$, then $1 + \mu$ is a characteristic root of $\mathbf{Q}^{-1}$—because $|\mathbf{Q}^{-1} - (1 + \mu)\mathbf{I}| = |(\mathbf{Q}^{-1} - \mathbf{I}) - \mu\mathbf{I}|$—which in turn implies by (6.5) that $(1 + \mu)^{-1}$ is a characteristic root of $\mathbf{Q}$. The bounds we have established for the characteristic roots of $\mathbf{Q}$ show $0 < (1 + \mu)^{-1} \leq 1$, from which $0 \leq \mu$. Thus all of the characteristic roots of $(\mathbf{Q}^{-1} - \mathbf{I})$ are nonnegative, from which we see that $(\mathbf{Q}^{-1} - \mathbf{I})$ is nonnegative definite by (7.13); this establishes part (*c*).

Other Definite Matrices

Let **A** be an $n \times n$ symmetric matrix. Then **A** is said to be negative definite if and only if $-\mathbf{A}$ is positive definite; thus

(7.22) A symmetric matrix **A** is negative definite if and only if $\mathbf{x}'\mathbf{A}\mathbf{x} < 0$ for all $\mathbf{x} \neq \mathbf{0}$.

The implications of negative definiteness of **A** follow from the implications of the positive definiteness of $-\mathbf{A}$. We note explicitly only the following:

(7.23) If **A** is negative definite, the "nested" principal minors of **A** alternate in sign:

$$a_{ii} < 0, \qquad a_{ii}a_{jj} - a_{ij}^2 > 0, \qquad \ldots .$$

For completeness we may define the concept of nonpositive definiteness: The symmetric $n \times n$ matrix **A** is said to be nonpositive definite if and only if $-\mathbf{A}$ is nonnegative definite; thus

(7.24) A symmetric matrix **A** is nonpositive definite if and only if $\mathbf{x}'\mathbf{A}\mathbf{x} \leq 0$ for all **x**.

It should be recognized that a symmetric matrix need not be definite in any of these senses. For example,

$$(7.25) \qquad (x_1 \quad x_2)\begin{pmatrix} 1 & 2 \\ 2 & 1 \end{pmatrix}\begin{pmatrix} x_1 \\ x_2 \end{pmatrix} = x_1^2 + x_2^2 + 4x_1x_2$$

$$= \begin{cases} 6 & \text{if} \quad x_1 = 1, \quad x_2 = 1 \\ -2 & \text{if} \quad x_1 = 1, \quad x_2 = -1. \end{cases}$$

Finally, the concepts of definiteness are applied to quadratic forms as well as to their matrices. Thus the quadratic form $Q = \mathbf{x}'\mathbf{A}\mathbf{x}$ is said to be positive definite, nonnegative definite, negative definite, or nonpositive definite according as the matrix **A** is positive definite, nonnegative definite, negative definite, or nonpositive definite.

8. DIFFERENTIAL CALCULUS IN MATRIX NOTATION

Differentiation

If **x** is an $m \times 1$ vector and y is a scalar function of the elements of **x**—$y = f(x_1, \ldots, x_m)$—then $\partial y/\partial \mathbf{x}$ is defined to be the $m \times 1$ vector of partial derivatives $\partial y/\partial x_i$; thus

$$(8.1)\qquad \frac{\partial y}{\partial \mathbf{x}} = \begin{pmatrix} \partial y/\partial x_1 \\ \cdot \\ \cdot \\ \cdot \\ \partial y/\partial x_m \end{pmatrix}.$$

More generally, if $\mathbf{X}$ is an $m \times n$ matrix and y is a scalar function of the elements of $\mathbf{X}$—$y = f(x_{11}, \ldots, x_{1n}, \ldots, x_{m1}, \ldots, x_{mn})$—then $\partial y/\partial \mathbf{X}$ is defined to be the $m \times n$ matrix of partial derivatives $\partial y/\partial x_{ij}$; thus

$$(8.2)\qquad \frac{\partial y}{\partial \mathbf{X}} = \begin{pmatrix} \partial y/\partial x_{11} & \cdots & \partial y/\partial x_{1n} \\ \cdot & & \cdot \\ \cdot & & \cdot \\ \cdot & & \cdot \\ \partial y/\partial x_{m1} & \cdots & \partial y/\partial x_{mn} \end{pmatrix}.$$

If $\mathbf{x}$ is an $m \times 1$ vector and $\mathbf{y}$ is an $n \times 1$ vector each of whose elements is a scalar function of the elements of $\mathbf{x}$—$y_j = f_j(x_1, \ldots, x_m)$ $(j = 1, \ldots, n)$—then $\partial \mathbf{y}/\partial \mathbf{x}$ is defined to be the $m \times n$ matrix of partial derivatives $\partial y_j/\partial x_i$; thus

$$(8.3)\qquad \frac{\partial \mathbf{y}}{\partial \mathbf{x}} = \begin{pmatrix} \partial y_1/\partial x_1 & \cdots & \partial y_n/\partial x_1 \\ \cdot & & \cdot \\ \cdot & & \cdot \\ \cdot & & \cdot \\ \partial y_1/\partial x_m & \cdots & \partial y_n/\partial x_m \end{pmatrix} = \begin{pmatrix} \dfrac{\partial y_1}{\partial \mathbf{x}} & \cdots & \dfrac{\partial y_n}{\partial \mathbf{x}} \end{pmatrix}.$$

Then if $\mathbf{x}$ is an $m \times 1$ vector and $y = f(x_1, \ldots, x_m)$ is a scalar function of the elements of $\mathbf{x}$, $\partial^2 y/\partial \mathbf{x}^2$ is defined to be the $m \times m$ matrix of second partial derivatives $\partial^2 y/\partial x_i\, \partial x_j$; thus

$$(8.4)\qquad \frac{\partial^2 y}{\partial \mathbf{x}^2} = \begin{pmatrix} \partial^2 y/\partial x_1^2 & \cdots & \partial^2 y/(\partial x_m\, \partial x_1) \\ \cdot & & \cdot \\ \cdot & & \cdot \\ \cdot & & \cdot \\ \partial^2 y/(\partial x_1\, \partial x_m) & \cdots & \partial^2 y/\partial x_m^2 \end{pmatrix} = \frac{\partial(\partial y/\partial \mathbf{x})}{\partial \mathbf{x}}$$

$$= \left[\frac{\partial(\partial y/\partial x_1)}{\partial \mathbf{x}} \quad \cdots \quad \frac{\partial(\partial y/\partial x_m)}{\partial \mathbf{x}}\right].$$

It will be recognized that $\partial^2 y/\partial \mathbf{x}^2$ is symmetric under general conditions.

Consider the Taylor series expansion of the scalar $y = f(x_1, \ldots, x_m)$ about the point $\mathbf{x}^\circ = (x_1^\circ \cdots x_m^\circ)'$. The first two terms of the expansion have a convenient matrix representation:

$$y - y^\circ = \sum_{i=1}^{m} \frac{\partial y}{\partial x_i}(x_i - x_i^\circ) + \frac{1}{2}\sum_{i=1}^{m}\sum_{j=1}^{m} \frac{\partial^2 y}{\partial x_i \partial x_j}(x_i - x_i^\circ)(x_j - x_j^\circ) + \cdots = \mathbf{j}'(\mathbf{x} - \mathbf{x}^\circ) + \tfrac{1}{2}(\mathbf{x} - \mathbf{x}^\circ)'\mathbf{K}(\mathbf{x} - \mathbf{x}^\circ) + \cdots, \tag{8.5}$$

where $y^\circ = f(x_1^\circ, \ldots, x_m^\circ)$, and where $\mathbf{j} = \partial y/\partial \mathbf{x}$ and $\mathbf{K} = \partial^2 y/\partial \mathbf{x}^2$ are evaluated at $\mathbf{x}^\circ$. When $\mathbf{y}$ is an $n \times 1$ vector consider the sets of Taylor series expansions of the $y_j = f_j(x_1, \ldots, x_m)$ about the point $\mathbf{x}^\circ = (x_1^\circ \cdots x_m^\circ)'$. Since $y_j - y_j^\circ = \Sigma_{i=1}^m (\partial y_j/\partial x_i)(x_i - x_i^\circ) + \cdots$, the set of first terms of the expansions has a convenient matrix representation:

$$\mathbf{y} - \mathbf{y}^\circ = \mathbf{J}'(\mathbf{x} - \mathbf{x}^\circ) + \cdots, \tag{8.6}$$

where

$$\mathbf{y}^\circ = \begin{pmatrix} y_1^\circ \\ \cdot \\ \cdot \\ \cdot \\ y_n^\circ \end{pmatrix}$$

and $y_j^\circ = f_j(x_1^\circ, \ldots, x_m^\circ)$, and where $\mathbf{J} = \partial \mathbf{y}/\partial \mathbf{x}$ is evaluated at $\mathbf{x}^\circ$.

For some functions convenient formulas for differentiation with respect to a vector are available. A homogeneous linear function $y = \Sigma_{i=1}^m a_i x_i$ has $\partial y/\partial x_i = a_i$; hence if we define

$$\mathbf{x} = \begin{pmatrix} x_1 \\ \cdot \\ \cdot \\ \cdot \\ x_m \end{pmatrix} \quad \text{and} \quad \mathbf{a} = \begin{pmatrix} a_1 \\ \cdot \\ \cdot \\ \cdot \\ a_m \end{pmatrix},$$

then $y = \mathbf{x}'\mathbf{a}$ and by (8.1) we may write

$$\frac{\partial \mathbf{x}'\mathbf{a}}{\partial \mathbf{x}} = \mathbf{a}. \tag{8.7}$$

A set of homogeneous linear functions $y_j = \Sigma_{i=1}^m a_{ji}x_i$ $(j = 1, \ldots, n)$ has $\partial y_j/\partial x_i = a_{ji}$; hence if we define

$$\mathbf{y} = \begin{pmatrix} y_1 \\ \cdot \\ \cdot \\ \cdot \\ y_n \end{pmatrix}, \quad \mathbf{x} = \begin{pmatrix} x_1 \\ \cdot \\ \cdot \\ \cdot \\ x_m \end{pmatrix}, \quad \text{and} \quad \mathbf{A} = \begin{pmatrix} a_{11} & \cdots & a_{1m} \\ \cdot & & \cdot \\ \cdot & & \cdot \\ \cdot & & \cdot \\ a_{n1} & \cdots & a_{nm} \end{pmatrix},$$

then $\mathbf{y} = \mathbf{Ax}$, and by (8.3) we may write

$$\frac{\partial \mathbf{Ax}}{\partial \mathbf{x}} = \mathbf{A}'. \tag{8.8}$$

A quadratic form $y = \Sigma_{i=1}^m \Sigma_{j=1}^m a_{ij}x_ix_j$ with $a_{ij} = a_{ji}$ has $\partial y/\partial x_i = 2\Sigma_{j=1}^m a_{ij}x_j$; hence if we define

$$\mathbf{x} = \begin{pmatrix} x_1 \\ \cdot \\ \cdot \\ \cdot \\ x_m \end{pmatrix} \quad \text{and} \quad \mathbf{A} = \begin{pmatrix} a_{11} & \cdots & a_{1m} \\ \cdot & & \cdot \\ \cdot & & \cdot \\ \cdot & & \cdot \\ a_{m1} & \cdots & a_{mm} \end{pmatrix},$$

then $y = \mathbf{x}'\mathbf{Ax}$, and by (8.1) we may write

$$\frac{\partial \mathbf{x}'\mathbf{Ax}}{\partial \mathbf{x}} = 2\mathbf{Ax}. \tag{8.9}$$

The analogies of these matrix expressions to the conventional formulas should be noted.

It will also be useful to define the derivative of a matrix with respect to a scalar. If x is a scalar and if $\mathbf{Y}$ is an $m \times n$ matrix each element of which is a scalar function of x—$y_{ij} = f_{ij}(x)$ $(i = 1, \ldots, m; j = 1, \ldots, n)$—then $\partial \mathbf{Y}/\partial x$ is defined to be the $m \times n$ matrix of derivatives $\partial y_{ij}/\partial x$; thus

$$\frac{\partial \mathbf{Y}}{\partial x} = \begin{pmatrix} \partial y_{11}/\partial x & \cdots & \partial y_{1n}/\partial x \\ \cdot & & \cdot \\ \cdot & & \cdot \\ \cdot & & \cdot \\ \partial y_{m1}/\partial x & \cdots & \partial y_{mn}/\partial x \end{pmatrix}. \tag{8.10}$$

For some matrix functions convenient formulas for differentiation with respect to a scalar are available. If $\mathbf{A}$ and $\mathbf{B}$ are $n \times n$ matrices whose elements are functions of a scalar x and if $\mathbf{C} = \mathbf{AB}$, then since $c_{ij} = \Sigma_{k=1}^n a_{ik}b_{kj}$ implies

$$\frac{\partial c_{ij}}{\partial x} = \sum_{k=1}^{n} \left(a_{ik}\frac{\partial b_{kj}}{\partial x} + \frac{\partial a_{ik}}{\partial x} b_{kj} \right),$$

we have by (8.10)

$$\frac{\partial \mathbf{AB}}{\partial x} = \mathbf{A}\frac{\partial \mathbf{B}}{\partial x} + \frac{\partial \mathbf{A}}{\partial x}\mathbf{B}. \tag{8.11}$$

Suppose that $\mathbf{A}$ is an $n \times n$ nonsingular matrix whose elements are functions of a scalar x; then the elements of $\mathbf{A}^{-1}$ will also be functions of

x. Differentiating $\mathbf{A}\mathbf{A}^{-1} = \mathbf{I}$ gives $\mathbf{A}(\partial\mathbf{A}^{-1}/\partial x) + (\partial\mathbf{A}/\partial x)\mathbf{A}^{-1} = \partial\mathbf{I}/\partial x = \mathbf{0}$; premultiplying through by $\mathbf{A}^{-1}$ and rearranging gives

$$\text{(8.12)} \qquad \frac{\partial\mathbf{A}^{-1}}{\partial x} = -\mathbf{A}^{-1}\frac{\partial\mathbf{A}}{\partial x}\mathbf{A}^{-1}.$$

In particular, consider the derivative of $\mathbf{A}^{-1}$ with respect to an element a_{ij} of $\mathbf{A}$. With $x = a_{ij}$, $\partial\mathbf{A}/\partial x = \mathbf{E}_{ij} = \mathbf{e}_i\mathbf{e}_j'$ where $\mathbf{E}_{\mu\mu'}$ is the $n \times n$ matrix having 1 as its μ,μ' element and 0's elsewhere and $\mathbf{e}_\mu$ is the $n \times 1$ vector having 1 as its μth element and 0's elsewhere; (8.12) specializes to

$$\text{(8.13)} \qquad \frac{\partial\mathbf{A}^{-1}}{\partial a_{ij}} = -\mathbf{A}^{-1}\mathbf{E}_{ij}\mathbf{A}^{-1} = -(\mathbf{A}^{-1}\mathbf{e}_i)(\mathbf{e}_j'\mathbf{A}^{-1}) = -\mathbf{A}^i\mathbf{A}'^j$$

where $\mathbf{A}^i$ is the ith column of $\mathbf{A}^{-1}$ and $\mathbf{A}'^j$ is the jth row of $\mathbf{A}^{-1}$. In particular (8.13) means

$$\text{(8.14)} \qquad \frac{\partial a^{gh}}{\partial a_{ij}} = -a^{gi}a^{jh}$$

where $a^{\mu\mu'}$ is the μ,μ' element of $\mathbf{A}^{-1}$.

Finally, it is useful to record some results on differentiation of scalar functions of the elements of a matrix. Suppose that each element of an $n \times n$ matrix $\mathbf{Y}$ is a function of a scalar x—$y_{ij} = f_{ij}(x)$—and that $\mathbf{B}$ is an $n \times n$ constant matrix, i.e., the elements of $\mathbf{B}$ do not depend on x. Then since

$$tr(\mathbf{YB}) = \sum_{i=1}^{n}\sum_{j=1}^{n} y_{ij}b_{ji}$$

implies

$$\frac{\partial\, tr(\mathbf{YB})}{\partial x} = \sum_{i=1}^{n}\sum_{j=1}^{n}\frac{\partial y_{ij}}{\partial x}b_{ji},$$

by (8.10) we may write

$$\text{(8.15)} \qquad \frac{\partial\, tr(\mathbf{YB})}{\partial x} = tr\left(\frac{\partial\mathbf{Y}}{\partial x}\mathbf{B}\right).$$

Suppose that each element of an $n \times n$ matrix $\mathbf{A}$ is a function of a scalar x—$a_{ij} = f_{ij}(x)$. Then since $|\mathbf{A}| = \Sigma_{\mu'=1}^{n} a_{\mu\mu'}c_{\mu\mu'}$ implies $\partial\,|\mathbf{A}|/\partial a_{\mu\mu'} = c_{\mu\mu'}$ where $c_{\mu\mu'}$ is the cofactor of $a_{\mu\mu'}$, we have

$$\text{(8.16)} \qquad \frac{\partial\,|\mathbf{A}|}{\partial x} = \sum_{\mu=1}^{n}\sum_{\mu'=1}^{n}\frac{\partial\,|\mathbf{A}|}{\partial a_{\mu\mu'}}\frac{\partial a_{\mu\mu'}}{\partial x} = \sum_{\mu=1}^{n}\sum_{\mu'=1}^{n} c_{\mu\mu'}\frac{\partial a_{\mu\mu'}}{\partial x}.$$

In particular, suppose that $\mathbf{A}$ is symmetric and consider the partial derivative of $|\mathbf{A}|$ with respect to an element $a_{ij} = a_{ji}$ of $\mathbf{A}$. With $x = a_{ij} = a_{ji}$, $\partial a_{\mu\mu'}/\partial x = 1$ if $\mu = i$ and $\mu' = j$ or if $\mu = j$ and $\mu' = i$, and

$\partial a_{\mu\mu'}/\partial x = 0$ otherwise, (8.16) specializes to

(8.17) If $\mathbf{A}$ is symmetric, $$\frac{\partial |\mathbf{A}|}{\partial a_{ij}} = \begin{cases} c_{ii} & \text{if } i = j \\ 2c_{ij} & \text{if } i \neq j, \end{cases}$$

where we have used the fact that $c_{ji} = c_{ij}$ in a symmetric matrix. Further, since

$$\frac{\partial \log |\mathbf{A}|}{\partial a_{ij}} = \frac{\partial \log |\mathbf{A}|}{\partial |\mathbf{A}|} \frac{\partial |\mathbf{A}|}{\partial a_{ij}} = |\mathbf{A}|^{-1} \frac{\partial |\mathbf{A}|}{\partial a_{ij}}$$

and since $|\mathbf{A}|^{-1}c_{ji} = a^{ij}$, we have

(8.18) If $\mathbf{A}$ is symmetric, $$\frac{\partial \log |\mathbf{A}|}{\partial a_{ij}} = \begin{cases} a^{ii} & \text{if } i = j \\ 2a^{ij} & \text{if } i \neq j. \end{cases}$$

Unconstrained Extrema

The familiar rules for locating the extrema (minima or maxima) of a function of several variables are

(8.19) Let $y = f(x_1, \ldots, x_m)$. Then

(8.19*a*) *First-order condition:* For y to have an extremum at the point $(x_1^\circ, \ldots, x_m^\circ)$ it is necessary that $\partial y/\partial x_1 = \cdots = \partial y/\partial x_m = 0$; and

(8.19*b*) *Second-order condition:* Such a point will be a minimum if

$$\sum_{i=1}^{m} \sum_{j=1}^{m} \frac{\partial^2 y}{\partial x_i \, \partial x_j} \, dx_i \, dx_j > 0$$

for every set of dx's not all of which are zero; alternatively such a point will be a maximum if

$$\sum_{i=1}^{m} \sum_{j=1}^{m} \frac{\partial^2 y}{\partial x_i \, \partial x_j} \, dx_i \, dx_j < 0$$

for every set of dx's not all of which are zero; where all the derivatives are evaluated at $(x_1^\circ, \ldots, x_m^\circ)$.

A convenient matrix formulation is available if we use (8.1), (8.4), and the concepts of definite matrices:

(8.20) Let $\mathbf{x} = \begin{pmatrix} x_1 \\ \cdot \\ \cdot \\ \cdot \\ x_m \end{pmatrix}$ be an $m \times 1$ vector, let $y = f(x_1, \ldots, x_m)$ be a scalar function of the elements of **x**, and let $\mathbf{x}^\circ = \begin{pmatrix} x_1^\circ \\ \cdot \\ \cdot \\ \cdot \\ x_m^\circ \end{pmatrix}$

Then,

(8.20*a*) *First-order condition:* For y to have an extremum at $\mathbf{x}^\circ$ it is necessary that $\partial y/\partial \mathbf{x} = \mathbf{0}$; and

(8.20*b*) *Second-order condition:* Such a point will be a minimum if $\partial^2 y/\partial \mathbf{x}^2$ is positive definite; alternatively, such a point will be a maximum if $\partial^2 y/\partial \mathbf{x}^2$ is negative definite;

where all the derivatives are evaluated at $\mathbf{x}^\circ$.

To illustrate the application of the rules, suppose that $y = \mathbf{a} + \mathbf{x}'\mathbf{b} + \frac{1}{2}\mathbf{x}'\mathbf{C}\mathbf{x}$ is to be minimized where $\mathbf{x}$ is $m \times 1$, and where the 1×1 scalar $\mathbf{a}$, the $m \times 1$ vector $\mathbf{b}$, and the $m \times m$ positive definite matrix $\mathbf{C}$ are all constant. Then $\partial y/\partial \mathbf{x} = \mathbf{b} + \mathbf{C}\mathbf{x}$ and $\partial^2 y/\partial \mathbf{x}^2 = \mathbf{C}' = \mathbf{C}$. Setting $\partial y/\partial \mathbf{x} = \mathbf{0}$ gives $\mathbf{b} + \mathbf{C}\mathbf{x}^\circ = \mathbf{0}$, from which $\mathbf{x}^\circ = -\mathbf{C}^{-1}\mathbf{b}$ locates the extremum. Since $\partial^2 y/\partial \mathbf{x}^2$ is positive definite, $\mathbf{x}^\circ$ indeed locates the minimum.

Constrained Extrema

The familiar rules for locating the constrained extrema of a function of several variables are

(8.21) Let $y = f(x_1, \ldots, x_m)$ be subject to the $n < m$ constraints $g_1(x_1, \ldots, x_m) = 0, \ldots, g_n(x_1, \ldots, x_m) = 0$. Then

(8.21*a*) *First-order condition:* For y to have an extremum, subject to the constraints, at the point $(x_1^\circ, \ldots, x_m^\circ)$ it is necessary and sufficient that $z = y - \Sigma_{k=1}^n \lambda_k g_k$ have an extremum at the point $(x_1^\circ, \ldots, x_m^\circ, \lambda_1^\circ, \ldots, \lambda_n^\circ)$ where the λ's are Lagrange multipliers, and

(8.21*b*) *Second-order condition:* Such a point will be a (constrained) minimum if

$$\sum_{i=1}^m \sum_{j=1}^m \frac{\partial^2 y}{\partial x_i\, \partial x_j}\, dx_i\, dx_j > 0$$

for every set of dx's not all of which are zero which satisfy

$$\sum_{i=1}^m \frac{\partial g_1}{\partial x_i}\, dx_i = \cdots = \sum_{i=1}^m \frac{\partial g_n}{\partial x_i}\, dx_i = 0;$$

alternatively such a point will be a (constrained) maximum if

$$\sum_{i=1}^{m} \sum_{j=1}^{m} \frac{\partial^2 y}{\partial x_i \, \partial x_j} \, dx_i \, dx_j < 0$$

for every set of dx's not all of which are zero which satisfy

$$\sum_{i=1}^{m} \frac{\partial g_1}{\partial x_i} \, dx_i = \cdots = \sum_{i=1}^{m} \frac{\partial g_n}{\partial x_i} \, dx_i = 0;$$

where all the derivatives are evaluated at

$$(x_1^\circ, \ldots, x_m^\circ, \lambda_1^\circ, \ldots, \lambda_n^\circ).$$

A convenient matrix formulation of these rules is available if we use (8.1), (8.4), and the concepts of definite matrices:

(8.22) Let

$$\mathbf{x} = \begin{pmatrix} x_1 \\ \cdot \\ \cdot \\ \cdot \\ x_m \end{pmatrix}$$

be an $m \times 1$ vector, let $y = f(x_1, \ldots, x_m)$ be a scalar function of the elements of $\mathbf{x}$, and let

$$\mathbf{x}^\circ = \begin{pmatrix} x_1^\circ \\ \cdot \\ \cdot \\ \cdot \\ x_m^\circ \end{pmatrix}.$$

Further let

$$\mathbf{g} = \begin{pmatrix} g_1 \\ \cdot \\ \cdot \\ \cdot \\ g_n \end{pmatrix}$$

be an $n \times 1$ vector each element of which is a scalar function of the elements of $\mathbf{x}$. Further let

$$\boldsymbol{\lambda} = \begin{pmatrix} \lambda_1 \\ \cdot \\ \cdot \\ \cdot \\ \lambda_n \end{pmatrix}$$

be an $n \times 1$ vector of Lagrange multipliers, let $z = y - \boldsymbol{\lambda}'\mathbf{g}$, let

$$\mathbf{dx} = \begin{pmatrix} dx_1 \\ \cdot \\ \cdot \\ \cdot \\ dx_m \end{pmatrix},$$

and let

$$\boldsymbol{\lambda}^\circ = \begin{pmatrix} \lambda_1^\circ \\ \cdot \\ \cdot \\ \cdot \\ \lambda_n^\circ \end{pmatrix}.$$

Then

(8.22*a*) *First-order condition:* For y to have an extremum, subject to $\mathbf{g} = \mathbf{0}$, at $\mathbf{x}^\circ$, it is necessary that

$$\begin{pmatrix} \partial z/\partial \mathbf{x} \\ \partial z/\partial \boldsymbol{\lambda} \end{pmatrix} = \begin{pmatrix} \mathbf{0} \\ \mathbf{0} \end{pmatrix};$$

and

(8.22*b*) *Second-order condition:* Such a point will be a (constrained) minimum if $(\mathbf{dx})'(\partial^2 y/\partial \mathbf{x}^2)(\mathbf{dx}) > 0$ for every $\mathbf{dx} \neq \mathbf{0}$ satisfying $(\mathbf{dx})'(\partial \mathbf{g}/\partial \mathbf{x}) = \mathbf{0}$; alternatively, such a point will be a (constrained) maximum if $(\mathbf{dx})'(\partial^2 y/\partial \mathbf{x}^2)(\mathbf{dx}) < 0$ for every $\mathbf{dx} \neq \mathbf{0}$ satisfying $(\mathbf{dx})'(\partial \mathbf{g}/\partial \mathbf{x}) = \mathbf{0}$;

where all the derivatives are evaluated at $\begin{pmatrix} \mathbf{x}^\circ \\ \boldsymbol{\lambda}^\circ \end{pmatrix}$.

To illustrate the application of these rules, suppose that $y = \frac{1}{2}\mathbf{x}'\mathbf{A}\mathbf{x}$ is to be minimized subject to $\mathbf{B}\mathbf{x} - \mathbf{b} = \mathbf{0}$ where $\mathbf{x}$ is $m \times 1$, and where the $m \times m$ positive definite matrix $\mathbf{A}$, the $n \times m$ matrix $\mathbf{B}$ of rank n, and the $n \times 1$ vector $\mathbf{b}$ are all constant. Let $\boldsymbol{\lambda}$ be the $n \times 1$ Lagrange vector; then $\mathbf{g} = \mathbf{B}\mathbf{x} - \mathbf{b}$ and $z = \frac{1}{2}\mathbf{x}'\mathbf{A}\mathbf{x} - \boldsymbol{\lambda}'(\mathbf{B}\mathbf{x} - \mathbf{b})$. Then

$$\begin{pmatrix} \partial z/\partial \mathbf{x} \\ \partial z/\partial \boldsymbol{\lambda} \end{pmatrix} = \begin{pmatrix} \mathbf{A}\mathbf{x} - \mathbf{B}'\boldsymbol{\lambda} \\ \mathbf{B}\mathbf{x} - \mathbf{b} \end{pmatrix}, \quad \frac{\partial^2 y}{\partial \mathbf{x}^2} = \mathbf{A}' = \mathbf{A}, \quad \text{and} \quad \frac{\partial \mathbf{g}}{\partial \mathbf{x}} = \mathbf{B}'.$$

Setting the first derivative vector equal to zero gives $\mathbf{Ax}^\circ = \mathbf{B}'\boldsymbol{\lambda}^\circ$ and $\mathbf{Bx}^\circ = \mathbf{b}$. Thus $\mathbf{x}^\circ = \mathbf{A}^{-1}\mathbf{B}'\boldsymbol{\lambda}^\circ$; premultiplying by $\mathbf{B}$ and imposing $\mathbf{Bx}^\circ = \mathbf{b}$ gives $\mathbf{Bx}^\circ = \mathbf{BA}^{-1}\mathbf{B}'\boldsymbol{\lambda}^\circ = \mathbf{b}$, from which $\boldsymbol{\lambda}^\circ = (\mathbf{BA}^{-1}\mathbf{B}')^{-1}\mathbf{b}$. Inserting this into $\mathbf{x}^\circ = \mathbf{A}^{-1}\mathbf{B}'\boldsymbol{\lambda}^\circ$ then locates the (constrained) extremum at $\mathbf{x}^\circ = \mathbf{A}^{-1}\mathbf{B}'(\mathbf{BA}^{-1}\mathbf{B}')^{-1}\mathbf{b}$. Since $\partial^2 y/\partial \mathbf{x}^2$ is positive definite, $(\mathbf{dx})'(\partial^2 y/\partial \mathbf{x}^2)(\mathbf{dx}) > 0$ for all $\mathbf{dx} \neq \mathbf{0}$ including those $\mathbf{dx}$'s that satisfy $(\mathbf{dx})'\mathbf{B}' = \mathbf{0}$ so that $\mathbf{x}^\circ$ indeed locates the (constrained) minimum.

CHAPTER 3

Basic Concepts of Statistical Inference

1. INTRODUCTION

From one point of view econometrics is the specialized branch of mathematical statistics that treats statistical inference concerning the structure of an economic system. The techniques of econometrics are then adaptations of the standard techniques of statistical inference to fit special characteristics of economic phenomena. In this chapter we review the basic concepts of statistical inference to which we repeatedly refer in the development of the theory of econometrics.

First we review some rudiments of descriptive statistics, concerning empirical frequency distributions, in Section 2. In Section 3 we discuss random variables and probability distributions, which constitute the basic model of mathematical statistics. In Section 4 we consider random sampling and the distribution of sample statistics. Section 5 is devoted to the normal distribution and distributions associated with it. In Section 6 we treat the theory of sequences of random variables and apply this theory to the asymptotic distributions of sample statistics. Then in Section 7 we turn to the theory of statistical inference proper, developing criteria and techniques of drawing inferences from a sample about its parent population. Finally in Section 8 some rudimentary theory of stochastic processes is applied to the case where sampling is nonrandom.

For a more rigorous development of the material reviewed in this chapter, several excellent texts are available. Mood (1950) and Parzen (1960) are instructive introductions. Kendall and Stuart (1958, 1961) and Wilks (1962) are more advanced. Anderson (1958) emphasizes normal distribution theory but also provides a convenient general reference.

2. EMPIRICAL FREQUENCY DISTRIBUTIONS

Univariate Frequency Distribution

A set of T observations on a variable x may be organized and presented in the form of a frequency distribution. Let us suppose that there are $I \le T$ distinct values of x among the observations. The frequency distribution $f(x)$ gives for each value x_i $(i = 1, \ldots, I)$ the relative frequency $f(x_i)$ with which it occurs in the set of observations. It should be noted that since $f(x)$ is the relative frequency, $0 \le f(x) \le 1$ for any value of x, whereas, if we sum over all values of x, $\Sigma_{i=1}^{I} f(x_i) = 1$. (It is sometimes convenient to denote such summation over all values of x as $\Sigma_{x=-\infty}^{\infty}$ or simply Σ_x.) The distribution may be presented as a table, graph, or mathematical formula. Our illustrations are tabular. For an artificial example we take

(2.1)

x	$f(x)$
-1	0.25
1	0.75

When there are many distinct values of x occurring in the set of observations it may be convenient to present the frequency distribution in grouped form. The range of values of x is broken down into a set of exclusive and exhaustive classes, and the relative frequency with which values of x fall into each of these classes is given. For example, the distribution of incomes (in dollars) in the United States in 1956 may be presented as

(2.2)

x	$f(x)$
$-\infty$–1000	0.11
1001–3000	0.25
3001–5000	0.28
5001–∞	0.36

Bivariate Frequency Distribution

A set of T joint observations on two variables x and y may be organized and presented in the form of a joint frequency distribution. Let us suppose that there are $I \le T$ distinct values of x and $J \le T$ distinct values of y among the observations. The joint frequency distribution $f(x, y)$ gives for each pair of values (x_i, y_j) $(i = 1, \ldots, I; j = 1, \ldots, J)$ the relative frequency $f(x_i, y_j)$ with which it occurs in the set of observations. It should be noted that since $f(x, y)$ is the relative frequency, $0 \le f(x, y) \le 1$

for any pair of values (x, y), whereas, if we sum over all values of x and y, $\Sigma_{i=1}^{I} \Sigma_{j=1}^{J} f(x_i, y_j) = 1$. (Again it may be convenient to denote this summation by $\Sigma_{x=-\infty}^{\infty} \Sigma_{y=-\infty}^{\infty}$ or simply $\Sigma_x \Sigma_y$.) For an artificial example we take

(2.3)

	y		
x	-1	0	1
-1	0.04	0.01	0.20
1	0.12	0.03	0.60

Again, when there are many distinct values of x and y it may be convenient to present the joint frequency distribution in grouped form. The ranges of values of x and y are broken down into a set of exclusive and exhaustive cells, and the relative frequency with which pairs of values (x, y) fall into each of these cells is given. For example, the joint frequency distribution of incomes, x, and liquid assets, y (both in dollars), in the United States in 1956 may be presented as

(2.4)

	y				
x	0	1–500	501–2000	2001–5000	5001–∞
$-\infty$–1000	0.063	0.020	0.016	0.006	0.005
1001–3000	0.117	0.056	0.041	0.022	0.014
3001–5000	0.072	0.094	0.071	0.025	0.018
5001–∞	0.028	0.100	0.102	0.067	0.063

In the context of the joint distribution the univariate distribution of each of the variables is called its marginal distribution. Thus in the joint frequency distribution $f(x, y)$: the marginal frequency distribution of x, $f(x)$, simply gives for each x_i the relative frequency $f(x_i)$ with which it occurs, regardless of the values of y with which it may occur; the marginal frequency distribution of y, $f(y)$, simply gives for each y_j the relative frequency $f(y_j)$ with which it occurs, regardless of the values of x with which it may occur. Thus $f(x_i) = \Sigma_{j=1}^{J} f(x_i, y_j)$—or, equivalently, $f(x_i) = \Sigma_{y=-\infty}^{\infty} f(x_i, y_j) = \Sigma_y f(x_i, y_j)$; and $f(y_j) = \Sigma_{i=1}^{I} f(x_i, y_j)$—or, equivalently, $f(y_j) = \Sigma_{x=-\infty}^{\infty} f(x_i, y_j) = \Sigma_x f(x_i, y_j)$. The general definitions may then be written $f(x) = \Sigma_y f(x, y)$ and $f(y) = \Sigma_x f(x, y)$. Then in our artificial example we have the marginal distributions

(2.5)

x	$f(x)$
-1	0.25 (= 0.04 + 0.01 + 0.20)
1	0.75 (= 0.12 + 0.03 + 0.60)

y	$f(y)$
-1	0.16 (= 0.04 + 0.12)
0	0.04 (= 0.01 + 0.03)
1	0.80 (= 0.20 + 0.60)

Similarly in our income–liquid-assets example we have the marginal distributions

(2.6)

x	$f(x)$	y	$f(y)$
$-\infty$–1000	0.11	0	0.28
1001–3000	0.25	1–500	0.27
3001–5000	0.28	501–2000	0.23
5001–∞	0.36	2001–5000	0.12
		5001–∞	0.10

Note how the term marginal is suggestive of the way the distribution may be computed by summation across rows or columns of the joint distribution table. [The careful reader will have noted that we have used the same symbol, $f(\ )$, to refer to different functions. To economize on notation, this usage is continued throughout the book.]

A further concept in this context is that of the conditional distribution, which is a set of univariate frequency distributions of one of the variables conditional on particular values of the other. Thus in the joint distribution $f(x, y)$, the conditional frequency distribution of x given y_j, $f(x \mid y_j)$, gives for each x_i the relative frequency $f(x_i \mid y_j)$ with which it occurs in the subset of observations for which $y = y_j$; and the conditional frequency distribution of y given x_i, $f(y \mid x_i)$, gives for each y_j the relative frequency $f(y_j \mid x_i)$ with which it occurs in the subset of observations for which $x = x_i$. Clearly each conditional frequency is the ratio of a joint frequency to a marginal frequency:

$$(2.7) \qquad f(x_i \mid y_j) = \frac{f(x_i, y_j)}{f(y_j)} \quad \text{and} \quad f(y_j \mid x_i) = \frac{f(x_i, y_j)}{f(x_i)}$$

—provided that the denominators are nonzero—the general definitions being $f(x \mid y) = f(x, y)/f(y)$ and $f(y \mid x) = f(x, y)/f(x)$; thus $f(x, y) = f(x \mid y)f(y) = f(y \mid x)f(x)$. It should be noted that

$$\sum_x f(x \mid y_j) \equiv \sum_{x=-\infty}^{\infty} f(x_i \mid y_j) \equiv \sum_{i=1}^{I} f(x_i \mid y_j) = \sum_{i=1}^{I} \frac{f(x_i, y_j)}{f(y_j)}$$

$$= \frac{\sum_{i=1}^{I} f(x_i, y_j)}{f(y_j)} = \frac{f(y_j)}{f(y_j)} = 1$$

and similarly $\Sigma_y f(y \mid x_i) \equiv \Sigma_{y=-\infty}^{\infty} f(y_j \mid x_i) \equiv \Sigma_{j=1}^{J} f(y_j \mid x_i) = 1.$

For our artificial example we have the conditional distributions:

(2.8)

$f(x \mid y)$

x	$f(x \mid y = -1)$	$f(x \mid y = 0)$	$f(x \mid y = 1)$
-1	0.25 (= 0.04/0.16)	0.25 (= 0.01/0.04)	0.25 (= 0.20/0.80)
1	0.75 (= 0.12/0.16)	0.75 (= 0.03/0.04)	0.75 (= 0.60/0.80)

$f(y \mid x)$

y	$f(y \mid x = -1)$	$f(y \mid x = 1)$
-1	0.16 (= 0.04/0.25)	0.16 (= 0.12/0.75)
0	0.04 (= 0.01/0.25)	0.04 (= 0.03/0.75)
1	0.80 (= 0.20/0.25)	0.80 (= 0.60/0.75)

For our economic example we have the conditional distributions of income given liquid assets:

(2.9)

	y				
x	0	1–500	501–2000	2001–5000	5001–∞
$-\infty$–1000	0.22	0.07	0.07	0.05	0.05
1001–3000	0.42	0.21	0.18	0.18	0.14
3001–5000	0.26	0.35	0.31	0.21	0.18
5001–∞	0.10	0.37	0.44	0.56	0.63

and the conditional distributions of liquid assets given income:

(2.10)

	x			
y	$-\infty$–1000	1001–3000	3001–5000	5001–∞
0	0.57	0.47	0.26	0.08
1–500	0.18	0.22	0.34	0.28
501–2000	0.15	0.16	0.25	0.28
2001–5000	0.05	0.09	0.09	0.19
5001–∞	0.05	0.06	0.06	0.17

A crucial concept in this context is that of statistical independence. We say that y is distributed independently of x if and only if the conditional distributions of y are identical for all values of x. Now if each conditional distribution of y is identical with the marginal distribution of y, then all the conditional distributions are identical. On the other hand, suppose that $f(y_j \mid x_1) = \cdots = f(y_j \mid x_I) = f_j^*$; then $f(y_j) = \Sigma_{i=1}^I f(x_i, y_j) = \Sigma_{i=1}^I f(y_j \mid x_i) f(x_i) = f_j^* \ \Sigma_{i=1}^I f(x_i) = f_j^*$, so that if the conditional distributions are identical they are also identical to the marginal distribution. Similarly we say that x is distributed independently of y if and only if the conditional distributions of x are identical for all values of y; or, equivalently, if and only if each conditional distribution of x is identical with the marginal distribution of x. To summarize,

(2.11) y is distributed independently of x if and only if $f(y \mid x) = f(y)$—i.e., if and only if $f(y_j \mid x_i) = f(y_j)$ for all i and j; x is distributed independently of y if and only if $f(x \mid y) = f(x)$—i.e., if and only if $f(x_i \mid y_j) = f(x_i)$ for all i and j.

Now suppose that y is distributed independently of x; then $f(y) = f(y \mid x) = f(x, y)/f(x)$ so that $f(x, y) = f(y)f(x)$. But then $f(x \mid y) = f(x, y)/f(y) = f(x)f(y)/f(y) = f(x)$ so that x is distributed independently of y. Similarly, if we suppose that x is distributed independently of y, then it follows that y is distributed independently of x. Thus

(2.12) x is distributed independently of y if and only if y is distributed independently of x.

Then there is no ambiguity in saying that x and y are distributed independently; as we have seen,

(2.13) x and y are distributed independently if and only if $f(x, y) = f(x)f(y)$—i.e., if and only if $f(x_i, y_j) = f(x_i)f(y_j)$ for all i and j.

When x and y are distributed independently we may say that the distributions of x and y are independent or simply that x and y are independent.

Turning to our examples, for the artificial example of (2.3) it will be seen from (2.8) that the variables x and y are indeed independent; the property that each joint frequency is the product of two marginal frequencies is readily confirmed. On the other hand, from (2.9) or (2.10) it is seen that incomes and liquid assets are not independent, which should come as no surprise.

Multivariate Frequency Distribution

All these concepts extend to the case where we have a set of T joint observations on K variables. For simplicity we treat explicitly only $K = 3$; extensions to the general case are then straightforward.

Let us denote the three variables as x, y, and z. The joint frequency distribution $f(x, y, z)$ gives for each triplet of values the relative frequency with which it occurs in the set of observations. From the joint distribution we may derive the three marginal frequency distributions $f(x)$, $f(y)$, and $f(z)$ with, e.g., $f(x) = \Sigma_y \Sigma_z f(x, y, z)$; and also the three conditional frequency distributions $f(x \mid y, z)$, $f(y \mid x, z)$, and $f(z \mid x, y)$ with, e.g.,

$f(x \mid y, z) = f(x, y, z)/f(y, z)$. Other distributions may be derived; there are the marginal joint frequency distributions $f(x, y)$, $f(x, z)$, and $f(y, z)$ with, e.g., $f(x, y) = \Sigma_z f(x, y, z)$; and the conditional joint frequency distributions $f(x, y \mid z)$, $f(x, z \mid y)$, and $f(y, z \mid x)$ with, e.g., $f(x, y \mid z) = f(x, y, z)/f(z)$; and also conditional univariate frequency distributions $f(x \mid y)$, $f(x \mid z)$, $f(y \mid x)$, $f(y \mid z)$, $f(z \mid x)$, and $f(z \mid y)$ with, e.g.,

$$f(x \mid y) = \frac{f(x, y)}{f(y)} = \frac{\sum_z f(x, y, z)}{f(y)} = \sum_z \frac{f(x \mid y, z) f(y, z)}{f(y)}$$
$$= \sum_z f(x \mid y, z) f(z \mid y).$$

Again we say that two variables are independent if and only if the conditional distributions of one, given the other, are all identical with the marginal distribution of the first. Thus x and y are independent if and only if $f(x \mid y) = f(x)$—or equivalently $f(y \mid x) = f(y)$—or equivalently $f(x, y) = f(x)f(y)$. The concept of independence is extended to sets of variables. We say that two sets of variables are independent if and only if the conditional (joint) distributions of one set given the other are identical with the marginal (joint) distribution of the first set. Thus the set consisting of x and y and the set consisting of z are independent if and only if $f(x, y \mid z) = f(x, y)$. It will be seen that if $f(x, y \mid z) = f(x, y)$, then $f(x, y, z) = f(x, y \mid z)f(z) = f(x, y)f(z)$, and conversely. Further, if $f(x, y, z) = f(x, y)f(z)$, then $f(z \mid x, y) = f(x, y, z)/f(x, y) = f(x, y)f(z)/f(x, y) = f(z)$, and conversely. Note that if the two sets are independent any variable in the first set is independent of any variable in the second set. For if $f(x, y \mid z) = f(x, y)$, then

$$f(x \mid z) = \frac{f(x, z)}{f(z)} = \frac{\sum_y f(x, y, z)}{f(z)} = \sum_y \frac{f(x, y \mid z) f(z)}{f(z)}$$
$$= \sum_y f(x, y) = f(x)$$

and similarly $f(y \mid z) = f(y)$. The converse, however, is not true; we may have $f(x \mid z) = f(x)$ and $f(y \mid z) = f(y)$, and yet $f(x, y \mid z) \neq f(x, y)$, because equality of marginal distributions does not imply equality of joint distributions. The concept of independence is extended to more than two sets of variables as well. For example, the set consisting of x, the set consisting of y, and the set consisting of z are all independent—the variables x, y, and z are mutually independent—if and only if $f(x, y, z) = f(x)f(y)f(z)$. It is easy to see that mutual independence of all the variables implies that any pair of them are independent; if $f(x, y, z) = f(x)f(y)f(z)$, then $f(x, y) = \Sigma_z f(x, y, z) = f(x)f(y)\,\Sigma_z f(z) = f(x)f(y)$.

Again the converse is not true; we may have $f(x, y) = f(x)f(y)$, $f(x, z) = f(x)f(z)$, and $f(y, z) = f(y)f(z)$, and yet $f(x, y, z) \neq f(x)f(y)f(z)$. The following example may be used to illustrate this point. Suppose that the only four triplets (x, y, z) which occur are (1, 0, 0), (0, 1, 0), (0, 0, 1), and (1, 1, 1) and that each of these occurs with relative frequency $\frac{1}{4}$. It will be seen that each pair of variables are independent but that the three of them are not mutually independent, $f(x, y, z) \neq f(x)f(y)f(z)$. For future reference we note our general definition of mutual independence of a set of variables:

(2.14) The variables $x, y, \ldots, z$ are mutually independent if and only if $f(x, y, \ldots, z) = f(x)f(y) \cdots f(z)$.

We also note that regardless of independence a joint distribution can always be expressed as a product of conditional distributions, e.g., $f(x, y, z) = f(x \mid y, z)f(y \mid z)f(z)$ whether or not x, y, and z are independent.

Cumulative Distribution

Corresponding to each of the frequency distributions we have considered is a cumulative distribution. Thus the univariate cumulative frequency distribution $F(x)$ gives for each value x_i the relative frequency $F(x_i)$ with which it occurs or lesser values of x occur in the set of observations. The cumulative distribution is thus obtained by cumulating frequencies; $F(x_i) = \Sigma_{x=-\infty}^{x_i} f(x)$. (It is sometimes convenient to denote such a sum over all lesser values of x as $\Sigma_{x \le x_i}$.) It should be noted that $0 \le F(x) \le 1$ for any value of x, and also $F(-\infty) = 0$ and $F(\infty) = 1$. To illustrate for our artificial example (2.1),

(2.15)

x	$F(x)$
$-\infty$	0
-1	0.25
1	1.00
∞	1.00

for the income distribution of (2.2),

(2.16)

x	$F(x)$
$-\infty$	0
1000	0.11
3000	0.36
5000	0.64
∞	1.00

In similar fashion the joint cumulative distribution of x and y is defined by $F(x_i, y_j) = \Sigma_{x \le x_i} \Sigma_{y \le y_j} f(x, y)$, and the conditional cumulative distribution of x given y by $F(x_i \mid y_j) = \Sigma_{x \le x_i} f(x \mid y_j)$; the extensions to the general multivariate case are straightforward. Similarly the joint cumulative distribution of independent variables is expressible as the product of their marginal cumulative distributions; $F(x, y) = F(x)F(y)$ if and only if x and y are independent. For if $f(x, y) = f(x)f(y)$ for all values of x and y, then

$$F(x_i, y_j) = \sum_{x \le x_i} \sum_{y \le y_j} f(x)f(y) = \sum_{x \le x_i} f(x) \sum_{y \le y_j} f(y)$$
$$= F(x_i)F(y_j),$$

and conversely.

Summary Measures of Frequency Distributions

We first consider two summary measures for a univariate frequency distribution—the mean, which measures central tendency, and the variance, which measures variation about the mean.

Let the frequency distribution of x be $f(x)$. Then the mean of x is

$$(2.17) \qquad m = \sum_{i=1}^{I} x_i f(x_i) = \sum_x x f(x),$$

and the variance of x is

$$(2.18) \qquad v = \sum_{i=1}^{I} (x_i - m)^2 f(x_i) = \sum_x (x - m)^2 f(x),$$

or, equivalently,

$$(2.19) \qquad v = \sum_x (x - m)^2 f(x) = \sum_x (x^2 + m^2 - 2mx) f(x)$$
$$= \sum_x x^2 f(x) + m^2 \sum_x f(x) - 2m \sum_x x f(x)$$
$$= \sum_x x^2 f(x) - m^2,$$

since m is a constant, $\Sigma_x f(x) = 1$, and $\Sigma_x x f(x) = m$. The formula (2.19) is often used in practical computations since it avoids the tedious step of computing individual deviations from the mean. To illustrate for the distribution of (2.1),

$$(2.20a) \qquad m = (-1)(0.25) + 1(0.75) = 0.50 = \tfrac{1}{2}$$

$$(2.20b) \qquad v = (-1 - \tfrac{1}{2})^2(0.25) + (1 - \tfrac{1}{2})^2(0.75)$$
$$= (1.50)^2(0.25) + (0.50)^2(0.75) = 0.75 = \tfrac{3}{4}$$

or

$$v = (-1)^2(0.25) + 1^2(0.75) - (0.50)^2 = 0.75 = \tfrac{3}{4}.$$

When the frequency distribution is in grouped form we proceed as if all the observations in a class were concentrated at a single point in the class. For illustrative purposes, we assume that incomes in the four classes of our example were concentrated at 500, 2000, 4000, and 10,000, respectively, and compute

$$\begin{aligned}(2.21a)\qquad m &= 500(0.11) + 2000(0.25) + 4000(0.28) + 10{,}000(0.36)\\ &= 10^3[0.5(0.11) + 2.0(0.25) + 4.0(0.28) + 10.0(0.36)]\\ &= 5.275(10^3) = 5275\end{aligned}$$

and

$$\begin{aligned}(2.21b)\qquad v &= 10^6[(0.5)^2(0.11) + (2.0)^2(0.25) + (4.0)^2(0.28)\\ &\qquad + (10.0)^2(0.36) - 5.275^2]\\ &= 13.7(10^6).\end{aligned}$$

If we have simply an array of T observations we may say that each observation has relative frequency $1/T$, and the formulas specialize to the familiar

$$(2.22)\qquad m = \frac{\Sigma x}{T},$$

$$(2.23)\qquad v = \frac{\Sigma(x - m)^2}{T},$$

or

$$(2.24)\qquad v = \frac{\Sigma x^2}{T} - m^2;$$

the equivalent form

$$(2.25)\qquad v = T^{-2}[T\,\Sigma\, x^2 - (\Sigma\, x)^2]$$

may be computationally convenient. (In these expressions, summation is understood to be over all observations.) Finally we note that the square root of the variance is known as the standard deviation.

Turning to joint frequency distributions, we may define the mean and variance of any of the univariate distributions we have discussed. Thus in the bivariate case where x and y have joint frequency $f(x, y)$, there are the marginal means $m_x = \Sigma_x\, xf(x)$ and $m_y = \Sigma_y\, yf(y)$, and the marginal variances $v_x = \Sigma_x\,(x - m_x)^2 f(x)$ and $v_y = \Sigma_y\,(y - m_y)^2 f(y)$. In addition, for any given value of one variable there are the conditional mean and variance of the other; e.g., $m_{x|y_j} = \Sigma_x\, xf(x \mid y_j)$ and $v_{x|y_j} = \Sigma_x\,(x - m_{x|y_j})^2 f(x \mid y_j)$.

To illustrate with our artificial example, we have computed the marginal mean and variance of x in (2.20); similarly the marginal mean and variance of y may be found as

(2.26*a*) $m_y = 0.64,$

(2.26*b*) $v_y = 0.5504.$

Further we have seen that x and y are independent so that all conditional distributions are identical with the corresponding marginal distributions; it is readily confirmed that the conditional means and variance are equal to the corresponding marginal means and variances.

To illustrate with our economic example, we have computed the marginal mean and variance of income in (2.21); similarly the marginal mean and variance of liquid assets may be found as

(2.27*a*) $m_y = 1775$

(2.27*b*) $v_y = 8.7(10^6),$

if we assume that liquid assets in the five classes were concentrated at 0, 250, 1250, 3500, and 10,000 respectively. We have seen that income and liquid assets are not independent so that the conditional distributions are not identical with the corresponding marginal distributions. It is not surprising to find that the means and variances of these distributions are not identical. From the data of (2.9)—using our concentration assumptions—we compute the conditional means and variances of income for each of the liquid asset classes:

(2.28)

	y				
x	0	1–500	501–2000	2001–5000	5001–∞
Conditional mean	2990	5555	6035	6825	7325
Conditional variance	$7.0(10^6)$	$12.6(10^6)$	$13.3(10^6)$	$13.5(10^6)$	$12.8(10^6)$

Note that the conditional means and variances do differ, and that the pattern is not surprising—the conditional mean of income rises with liquid assets. Similarly from the data of (2.10)—using our concentration assumptions—we compute the conditional means and variances of liquid assets for each of the income classes:

(2.29)

	x			
y	$-\infty$–1000	1001–3000	3001–5000	5001–∞
Conditional mean	908	1170	1313	2785
Conditional variance	$5.0(10^6)$	$6.0(10^6)$	$5.8(10^6)$	$12.0(10^6)$

Again note that the conditional means and variances differ and that the conditional mean of liquid assets rises with income.

It may be noted that a marginal mean is a weighted average of the conditional means, the weights being the marginal frequencies of the respective conditions:

$$\begin{aligned} m_x &= \sum_x xf(x) = \sum_x x \sum_y f(x, y) = \sum_y \sum_x xf(x, y) \\ &= \sum_y \sum_x xf(x \mid y)f(y) = \sum_y f(y) \sum_x xf(x \mid y) = \sum_y f(y) m_{x|y} \\ &= \sum_y m_{x|y} f(y). \end{aligned}$$

Thus if the conditional mean of one variable is the same for all values of the other variable, it is equal to the marginal mean.

A new summary measure is available in a joint distribution; this is the covariance, which measures covariation about the means. Let x and y have the joint frequency distribution $f(x, y)$ and let m_x and m_y be their marginal means. Then the covariance of x and y is

$$\begin{aligned} \text{(2.30)} \qquad c &= \sum_{i=1}^{I} \sum_{j=1}^{J} (x_i - m_x)(y_j - m_y)f(x_i, y_j) \\ &= \sum_x \sum_y (x - m_x)(y - m_y)f(x, y), \end{aligned}$$

or equivalently,

$$\begin{aligned} \text{(2.31)} \qquad c &= \sum_x \sum_y (x - m_x)(y - m_y)f(x, y) \\ &= \sum_x \sum_y (xy + m_x m_y - m_x y - m_y x)f(x, y) \\ &= \sum_x \sum_y xyf(x, y) + m_x m_y \sum_x \sum_y f(x, y) - m_x \sum_y y \sum_x f(x, y) \\ &\quad - m_y \sum_x x \sum_y f(x, y) \\ &= \sum_x \sum_y xyf(x, y) - m_x m_y, \end{aligned}$$

since m_x and m_y are constants, $\Sigma_x \Sigma_y f(x, y) = 1$, $\Sigma_x f(x, y) = f(y)$, $\Sigma_y f(x, y) = f(x)$, $\Sigma_y yf(y) = m_y$, and $\Sigma_x xf(x) = m_x$. The formula (2.31) is often used in practical computations since it avoids the computing of individual deviations from the means. To illustrate with our artificial example, where $m_x = 0.5$ and $m_y = 0.64$,

$$\begin{aligned} \text{(2.32)} \qquad c &= (-1)(-1)(0.04) + (-1)(0)(0.01) + (-1)(1)(0.20) \\ &\quad + 1(-1)(0.12) + 1(0)(0.03) \\ &\quad + 1(1)(0.60) - (0.50)(0.64) \\ &= 0.04 - 0.20 - 0.12 + 0.60 - 0.32 = 0. \end{aligned}$$

Again when the distribution is in grouped form we proceed as if all the observations in a class were concentrated at a single point in the class. Thus from the data of (2.4)—using our concentration assumptions—we compute the covariance of income and liquid assets to be

$$c = 2.9(10^6). \tag{2.33}$$

If we simply have an array of T joint observations we may say that each joint observation has relative frequency $1/T$, and the formulas specialize to the familiar

$$c = \frac{\Sigma(x - m_x)(y - m_y)}{T} \tag{2.34}$$

or

$$c = \frac{\Sigma xy}{T} - m_x m_y. \tag{2.35}$$

The equivalent form

$$c = T^{-2}(T\,\Sigma xy - \Sigma x\,\Sigma y) \tag{2.36}$$

may be computationally convenient. (In these expressions, summation is understood to be over all observations.)

Turning to multivariate distributions involving more than two variables, we may define the covariance of any of the bivariate distributions we have discussed. Thus there are the marginal covariances between any pair of variables and also the conditional covariances between any pair of variables given some or all of the others.

The covariance of (2.31) may be written as

$$\begin{aligned} c &= \sum_x \sum_y xyf(y \mid x)f(x) - m_x m_y = \sum_x x \sum_y yf(y \mid x)f(x) - m_x m_y \\ &= \sum_x x m_{y|x} f(x) - m_x m_y. \end{aligned} \tag{2.37}$$

Doing so, we note that if $m_{y|x} = m_y$ for all x, the first term in the second line becomes $\Sigma_x\, x m_y f(x) = m_y m_x$, so that the covariance vanishes. Using the term uncorrelatedness to signify zero covariance, we see that

(2.38) If the conditional mean of y is the same for all values of x (or vice versa), then x and y are uncorrelated.

Although it is sufficient, constancy of the conditional mean is not necessary for uncorrelatedness, as the following counterexample shows. Suppose that the only three pairs (x, y) which occur are $(-1, 1)$, $(0, 0)$, and $(1, 1)$ and that each occurs with relative frequency $\frac{1}{3}$. Then $m_{y|-1} = 1$, $m_{y|0} = 0$, and $m_{y|1} = 1$, but $c = 0$. Finally note that if x and y are independent the premise of (2.38) is certainly satisfied; thus independent variables are uncorrelated—but uncorrelated variables need not be independent.

Moments of a Distribution

In concluding this section we note that means, variances, and covariances are specific examples of what are called the moments of a distribution. In a univariate distribution the rth raw moment (rth moment about zero) is defined as

$$(2.39) \qquad M'_r = \sum_x x^r f(x)$$

where r is any nonnegative integer; and the rth central moment (rth moment about the mean) is defined as

$$(2.40) \qquad M_r = \sum_x (x - m)^r f(x)$$

where r is any nonnegative integer. It is easy to see that $M'_0 = \Sigma_x x^0 f(x) = \Sigma_x f(x) = 1$, $M'_1 = \Sigma_x x^1 f(x) = m$, $M_1 = \Sigma_x (x - m)^1 f(x) = \Sigma_x x f(x) - m \Sigma_x f(x) = m - m = 0$, and $M_2 = \Sigma_x (x - m)^2 f(x) = v$. Similarly in a bivariate distribution we define the raw moments

$$(2.41) \qquad M'_{rs} = \sum_x \sum_y x^r y^s f(x, y),$$

and the central moments

$$(2.42) \qquad M_{rs} = \sum_x \sum_y (x - m_x)^r (y - m_y)^s f(x, y)$$

where r and s are any nonnegative integers. It is easy to see that

$$M'_{00} = \sum_x \sum_y x^0 y^0 f(x, y) = \sum_x \sum_y f(x, y) = 1;$$

$$M'_{10} = \sum_x \sum_y x^1 y^0 f(x, y) = \sum_x x \sum_y f(x, y) = \sum_x x f(x) = m_x;$$

$$M'_{01} = m_y; \qquad M_{10} = \sum_x \sum_y (x - m_x)^1 y^0 f(x, y) = \sum_x (x - m_x)$$

$$\times \sum_y f(x, y) = \sum_x (x - m_x) f(x) = 0; \qquad M_{01} = 0;$$

$$M_{11} = \sum_x \sum_y (x - m_x)^1 (y - m_y)^1 f(x, y) = c;$$

also $M_{20} = v_x$ and $M_{02} = v_y$.

All this extends to the general multivariate case. Thus if $x, y, \ldots, z$ have joint frequency $f(x, y, \ldots, z)$ we may define the raw moments $M'_{rs\cdots t} = \Sigma_x \Sigma_y \cdots \Sigma_z (x^r y^s \cdots z^t) f(x, y, \ldots, z)$ and the central moments $M_{rs\cdots t} = \Sigma_x \Sigma_y \cdots \Sigma_z (x - m_x)^r (y - m_y)^s \cdots (z - m_z)^t f(x, y, \ldots, z)$.

3. RANDOM VARIABLES AND PROBABILITY DISTRIBUTIONS

The Random-Variable–Probability-Distribution Model

The preceding section has dealt merely with statistical description—organizing, presenting, and summarizing a body of empirical data. Now we proceed to develop a general model of the generation of empirical phenomena.

We begin by considering an experiment and the set of its possible outcomes. We suppose that any outcome may be represented by a distinct point in n-dimensional Euclidean space; i.e., as a vector of real numbers. We call the function that maps the outcomes into points a random vector, written simply $\mathbf{x}$. A random vector is thus a function whose value is determined as the outcome of an experiment. A particular outcome—the result of a particular run of the experiment—is called an observation on the random vector.

The outcome space of the experiment, written S, is defined as the set of all possible outcomes of the experiment—i.e., as the range of the random vector. The space S may be the full n-dimensional Euclidean space (written R_n) or some subset thereof. Next, an event, written A, is defined to be a set of outcomes—i.e., a set of values of the random vector. An event is thus a subset of the outcome space; it may be a one-outcome set, or a two-outcome set, or any well-defined collection of outcomes. For example, when the outcome space is R_n, $\mathbf{x} \leq \mathbf{b}$, where $\mathbf{b}$ is some vector in R_n, is a well-defined event.

The ordinary concepts of set theory are applicable to events, and it is helpful to recall some of them at this point. An outcome which is contained in any event is called an element of that event. The outcome space S will be called the universal event, and the event containing no outcomes will be called the empty event and denoted by $\varnothing$. If A and B are events, their union, written $A \cup B$, is the event that contains just those outcomes which are elements of A or of B (or of both), and their intersection, written $A \cap B$, is the event that contains just those outcomes which are elements of both A and B. Extending these definitions, if A_i $(i = 1, 2, \ldots)$ is a sequence of events (finite or denumerably infinite in number) their union, written $\bigcup_i A_i$, is the event that contains just those outcomes which are elements of any of the events in the sequence, and their intersection, written $\bigcap_i A_i$, is the event that contains just those outcomes which are elements of all the events in the sequence. If A and B are events, their difference, written $A - B$, is the event that contains just those outcomes which are elements of A but not of B. If A is an event, its complement, written $\bar{A}$, is the event that contains just those outcomes which are in the universal event but not in A. Two or more events are said to be disjoint or mutually exclusive if they contain no outcomes in common, that is, if their intersection is the empty event.

Then we may note the following: $A \cup \bar{A} = S$, $\bar{A} = S - A$, $A \cup \varnothing = A$, $A \cap \varnothing = \varnothing$, and $A \cap (B - A) = \varnothing$. Furthermore, any event A may be expressed as the union of two disjoint events: $A = (A \cap B) \cup (A - A \cap B)$; and the union of any two events may be expressed as the union of two disjoint events: $A \cup B = A \cup (B - A \cap B)$. Note that any two one-outcome events are disjoint events.

We suppose that a Borel field of events is given for the outcome space. That is, a family of events $\mathbf{B}$ is specified with the following properties.

(3.1) The universal event is in $\mathbf{B}$: S is in $\mathbf{B}$;

(3.2) The complement of any event in $\mathbf{B}$ is also in $\mathbf{B}$: If A is in $\mathbf{B}$, then $\bar{A}$ is in $\mathbf{B}$;

(3.3) The union and intersection of any (finite or denumerably infinite) sequence of events in $\mathbf{B}$ is also in $\mathbf{B}$: If A_i $(i = 1, 2, \ldots)$ is in $\mathbf{B}$, then $\bigcup_i A_i$ is in $\mathbf{B}$ and $\bigcap_i A_i$ is in $\mathbf{B}$.

Furthermore, we suppose that a probability measure has been defined over the Borel field of events. That is, a function has been defined which assigns to every event A in $\mathbf{B}$ a number, called its probability and written $P(A)$, with the following properties:

(3.4) The probability of any event in $\mathbf{B}$ is nonnegative: If A is in $\mathbf{B}$, then $P(A) \geq 0$;

(3.5) The probability of the union of a sequence of disjoint events in $\mathbf{B}$ is the sum of their probabilities: If A_i $(i = 1, 2, \ldots)$ is in $\mathbf{B}$ and $A_i \cap A_j = \varnothing$ for all i and j, $i \neq j$, then $P(\bigcup_i A_i) = \Sigma_i P(A_i)$;

(3.6) The probability of the universal event is unity: $P(S) = 1$.

When a probability measure P has been defined over a Borel field $\mathbf{B}$ of events in an outcome space S we say that we have a probability distribution $(P, \mathbf{B}, S)$. The probability distribution—a set of elements that satisfy the axioms (3.1)–(3.6)—forms the underlying model in mathematical statistics. The requirement that probabilities be initially given for all events in the field $\mathbf{B}$ is only apparent since the probabilities of some events are immediate consequences of the probabilities of other events. Thus since $A \cup \bar{A} = S$, since $A \cap \bar{A} = \varnothing$, and since $P(S) = 1$, it follows that $P(\bar{A}) = 1 - P(A)$; from which, since $P(\bar{A}) \geq 0$, it follows that $P(A) \leq 1$. Moreover, for any two events, disjoint or not,

$$P(A \cup B) = P(A) + P(B) - P(A \cap B). \tag{3.7}$$

This is so because $P(A \cup B) = P(A) + P(B - A \cap B)$ and $P(B - A \cap B) = P(B) - P(A \cap B)$, since $P(B) = P(A \cap B) + P(B - A \cap B)$. Indeed, for two special types of probability distributions the probability of any event in the Borel field can be deduced from an ordinary function of the random vector $\mathbf{x}$. We restrict our attention to these "special" types, which in fact suffice to cover virtually all situations arising in econometrics.

First let us consider the discrete probability distribution. Here S contains only a finite or denumerably infinite number of outcomes, and $\boldsymbol{\beta}$ contains all the one-outcome events (and, of course, all those obtainable as unions or intersections of one-outcome events). Thus in the discrete case the range of the random vector $\mathbf{x}$ is confined to a finite or denumerable number of points which we may denote as $\mathbf{x}_1, \ldots, \mathbf{x}_i, \ldots$, and probabilities have been assigned to the one-outcome events $\{\mathbf{x}_1\}, \ldots, \{\mathbf{x}_i\}, \ldots$. We write these probabilities as

$$P(\{\mathbf{x}_i\}) = f(\mathbf{x}_i) \qquad (i = 1, 2, \ldots) \tag{3.8}$$

and call $f(\mathbf{x})$ the (probability) mass function of the discrete random vector $\mathbf{x}$. Now $\boldsymbol{\beta}$ will consist of all possible subsets of the outcomes in S. Each of these subsets can be expressed as the union of one-outcome events; since the one-outcome events are disjoint, the probability of any event in $\boldsymbol{\beta}$ is obtainable as the sum of the probabilities of its one-outcome constituents. These probabilities will satisfy the axioms (3.4)–(3.6). Thus the mass function (3.8) fully specifies a discrete probability distribution.

Next let us consider the continuous probability distribution. Here S is the full n-dimensional Euclidean space R_n, $\boldsymbol{\beta}$ contains all intervals of the form $\mathbf{x} \leq \mathbf{b}$ (where $\mathbf{b}$ is any vector in R_n), and the probability of any A in $\boldsymbol{\beta}$ is $P(A) = \int_A f(\mathbf{x})\, \mathbf{dx}$ $\left(\text{where } \int_A \text{ is shorthand for an } n\text{-dimensional integral and } \mathbf{dx} \text{ is shorthand for an } n\text{-dimensional volume element}\right)$ where $f(\mathbf{x})$ is a function with the following properties.

$$f(\mathbf{x}) \geq 0 \text{ for all } \mathbf{x} \text{ in } R_n, \tag{3.9}$$

$$\int_A f(\mathbf{x})\, \mathbf{dx} \text{ exists for all } A \text{ in } \boldsymbol{\beta}, \tag{3.10}$$

$$\int_{R_n} f(\mathbf{x})\, \mathbf{dx} = 1. \tag{3.11}$$

The function $f(\mathbf{x})$ is called the (probability) density function of the continuous random vector $\mathbf{x}$. Now $\boldsymbol{\beta}$ will contain all elementary geometric regions in R_n. For example, the event $\mathbf{a} < \mathbf{x} \leq \mathbf{b}$ where $\mathbf{a}$ and $\mathbf{b}$ are two vectors in R_n (with $\mathbf{a} < \mathbf{b}$) is in $\boldsymbol{\beta}$; for the event $\mathbf{a} < \mathbf{x} \leq \mathbf{b}$ is the intersection of the two events "$\mathbf{x} \leq \mathbf{b}$" and "$\mathbf{x} > \mathbf{a}$" which are both in $\boldsymbol{\beta}$. In addition, if $f(\mathbf{x})$ has the properties (3.9)–(3.11), then $P(A) = \int_A f(\mathbf{x})\, \mathbf{dx}$ will satisfy the probability axioms (3.4)–(3.6), for with $f(\mathbf{x}) \geq 0$, $\int_A f(\mathbf{x})\, \mathbf{dx} \geq 0$; with $\int_{R_n} f(\mathbf{x})\, \mathbf{dx} = 1$, $\int_S f(\mathbf{x})\, \mathbf{dx} = 1$; and $\int_{\bigcup_i A_i} f(\mathbf{x})\, \mathbf{dx} = \Sigma_i \int_{A_i} f(\mathbf{x})\, \mathbf{dx}$ where the A_i ($i = 1, 2, \ldots$) are disjoint. Thus the density function suffices to determine the probabilities of all events in the Borel field for a continuous probability distribution.

Let us illustrate some of these concepts. First, for the discrete case consider the experiment consisting of tossing a pair of dice, where the outcome is given by the 2×1 vector $\mathbf{x} = \begin{pmatrix} x_1 \\ x_2 \end{pmatrix}$ where x_1 gives the number of spots on the face of the first die when it lands and x_2 gives the number of spots on the face of the second die when it lands. There are 36 possible outcomes of the experiment—the random vector $\mathbf{x}$ can take only 36 different values $\begin{pmatrix} 1 \\ 1 \end{pmatrix}, \begin{pmatrix} 1 \\ 2 \end{pmatrix}, \ldots, \begin{pmatrix} 6 \\ 5 \end{pmatrix}, \begin{pmatrix} 6 \\ 6 \end{pmatrix}$—so that the outcome space is discrete. The Borel field for the outcome space contains the 36 one-outcome events along with events obtainable as unions of one-outcome events. For example, the event "the sum of the numbers of spots on the faces of the two dice is less than 4"— i.e., "$x_1 + x_2 < 4$"—is the union of the three events "$\mathbf{x} = \begin{pmatrix} 1 \\ 1 \end{pmatrix}$," "$\mathbf{x} = \begin{pmatrix} 1 \\ 2 \end{pmatrix}$," and "$\mathbf{x} = \begin{pmatrix} 2 \\ 1 \end{pmatrix}$." A probability distribution would be defined by the mass function

$$(3.12) \qquad f(\mathbf{x}) = \tfrac{1}{36} \quad \text{for} \quad \mathbf{x} = \begin{pmatrix} 1 \\ 1 \end{pmatrix}, \begin{pmatrix} 1 \\ 2 \end{pmatrix}, \ldots, \begin{pmatrix} 6 \\ 5 \end{pmatrix}, \begin{pmatrix} 6 \\ 6 \end{pmatrix}.$$

The probabilities of other events are deducible from the mass function; e.g., the probability of the event "$x_1 + x_2 < 4$," which we may denote as Prob $\{x_1 + x_2 < 4\}$ is then the sum of the probabilities of its three one-outcome constituent events, namely $\frac{3}{36}$.

Next, for the continuous case consider the experiment of spinning a pointer on a dial with a 10-inch circumference where the outcome is given by the scalar x = clockwise distance in inches from the origin of the pointer when it stops. There is a continuous infinity of possible outcomes, and we take the outcome space to be the full real line R_1. The Borel field for the outcome space will contain all half-lines of the form $x \leq b$ where b is any scalar, along with events obtainable as the union or intersection of half-lines. For example, the event "$1 < x \leq 5$" is the intersection of the two events "$x \leq 5$" and "$x > 1$." A probability distribution would be defined by the density function

$$(3.13) \qquad f(x) = \begin{cases} \frac{1}{10} & \text{for} \quad 0 \leq x < 10 \\ 0 & \text{otherwise.} \end{cases}$$

From this density function the probability of all events in the Borel field may be deduced. For example, the probability of the event "$1 < x \leq 5$," which we may denote as Prob $\{1 < x \leq 5\}$, is

$$\int_1^5 f(x)\,dx = \int_1^5 \tfrac{1}{10}\,dx = \tfrac{4}{10} = \text{Prob}\,\{x \leq 5\} - (1 - \text{Prob}\,\{x > 1\}).$$

We have now spelled out two axiom systems—the discrete probability distribution and the continuous probability distribution—that will serve as general models for the generation of empirical phenomena. That is, we shall interpret an empirical datum as an observation on a random vector, viewing the datum as the outcome of some experiment; also we shall take the empirical counterpart of the probability of an event to be the relative frequency of its occurrence in a long series of repeated trials. Given an initial assignment of probabilities, generally in the form of a mass or density function, we deduce the probabilities of other events. As we proceed in our work we develop specialized models to handle specific classes of empirical phenomena.

Economists are of course familiar with the idea of using a formal model in economic theory to represent some economic process. A set of assumptions are made, and deductions are drawn from them. The usefulness of the model is dependent on the success with which the assumptions capture the essential features of the process, and it is demonstrated by the success of the model in interpreting and predicting the development of the process. Mathematical statistics proceeds in similar fashion, with the random-vector–probability-distribution setup as its model. In this case the model, appropriately specialized, is intended to capture the essential features of a wide class of empirical processes, and deductions about the development of the processes are drawn. The usefulness of the random-vector–probability-distribution model has been amply demonstrated by its success in many fields of scientific research. Thus far we have treated the probability measure in abstract fashion: Any mass or density function is legitimate as long as it satisfies the requirements we have listed. In practice, of course, the success of the model when applied to a particular empirical process is dependent on an appropriate specification of the underlying probability distribution. It is to be emphasized that nothing in the model requires that equal probabilities be assigned to any set of outcomes, our examples to the contrary notwithstanding.

Finally, we present a few definitions. We have used the term random vector to emphasize that the outcome of an experiment is generally representable as a set of numbers rather than as a single number. An alternative term is "n-dimensional random variable" or simply "random variable," but in general we use the term "random variable" only when the vector contains just a single element. A random vector $\mathbf{x}$ can be considered as a set of random variables $x_1, \ldots, x_n$, each of which represents some aspect of the outcome of the experiment, and which jointly represent the outcome. The term "stochastic" is generally to be taken as synonymous with "probabilistic"—i.e., having a probability distribution. Nevertheless, a discrete random vector that has a degenerate probability distribution—i.e., one whose mass function is

$$f(\mathbf{x}) = \begin{cases} 1 & \text{for} \quad \mathbf{x}^* \\ 0 & \text{otherwise,} \end{cases}$$

where $\mathbf{x}^*$ is some fixed vector—will be called a nonstochastic random vector, or simply a constant. Such a distribution describes an experiment that has only one possible outcome.

A probability mass or density function $f(\mathbf{x})$ may be expressed in terms of certain parameters which we call the parameters of the distribution of the random vector $\mathbf{x}$. When the values of the parameters are left unspecified, a family of distributions is defined; when the values of the parameters are specified, a particular member of the family is defined. For a simple example,

$$(3.14) \qquad f(x) = \begin{cases} 1 - \mu & \text{for} \quad x = 0 \\ \mu & \text{for} \quad x = 1 \\ 0 & \text{otherwise,} \end{cases}$$

where $0 \leq \mu \leq 1$ is a parameter, defines a one-parameter family of discrete probability distributions, called the Bernoulli distribution and abbreviated $B(\mu)$. If the mass function of some random variable x is $B(\mu)$, we may say that x has the $B(\mu)$ distribution, or that x is distributed as $B(\mu)$, or simply that x is a $B(\mu)$ variable.

Probability Mass and Density Functions

Restricting our attention to the two "special" types of random vectors—discrete and continuous—we proceed to review some properties of the mass or density function and functions derived from them. These properties are in essence common to both discrete and continuous random vectors; we treat the two cases simultaneously, giving parallel results when necessary.

First consider the univariate case where the random vector **x** contains only a single element. Its mass or density function $f(x)$ has the properties $f(x) \geq 0$ for any value of x, while summation over all values of x in the outcome space gives $\Sigma_x f(x) = 1$ in the discrete case and $\int_{-\infty}^{\infty} f(x)\, dx = 1$ in the continuous case. Note that in the discrete case the probability of the event $x = x^*$ is given by $f(x^*) \geq 0$. In the continuous case, however, the probability assigned to any event of the form $x = x^*$ must be zero, because

$$\text{Prob}\,\{x^* < x \leq x^* + \Delta x\} = \int_{x^*}^{x^*+\Delta x} f(x)\, dx = f(x^* + \theta\Delta x)\Delta x$$

where $0 < \theta < 1$, by the mean value theorem, from which

$$\begin{aligned}\text{Prob}\,\{x = x^*\} &= \lim_{\Delta x \to 0} \text{Prob}\,\{x^* < x \leq x^* + \Delta x\} \\ &= \lim_{\Delta x \to 0} f(x^* + \theta\,\Delta x)\,\Delta x = f(x^*) \cdot 0 = 0.\end{aligned}$$

The fact that Prob $\{x = x^*\} = 0$ in the continuous case should not be interpreted by saying that the event $x = x^*$ is impossible; after all, in any run of the experiment some such event will be the outcome. We do have Prob $\{x^* < x \leq x^* + dx\} = f(x^*)\, dx$ so that $f(x^*)$ may be interpreted as the average probability of outcomes in the neighborhood of x^*.

Next consider the bivariate case where the random vector $\mathbf{x} = \begin{pmatrix} x_1 \\ x_2 \end{pmatrix}$ contains two elements. Its mass or density function $f(\mathbf{x})$ is often written as $f(x_1, x_2)$ and referred to as the joint mass or density function of the random variables x_1 and x_2. Again the joint mass or density function $f(x_1, x_2)$ has the properties $f(x_1, x_2) \geq 0$ for any pair of values x_1, x_2, whereas summation over all pairs of values in the outcome space gives $\Sigma_{x_1} \Sigma_{x_2} f(x_1, x_2) = 1$ in the discrete case and $\int_{-\infty}^{\infty} \int_{-\infty}^{\infty} f(x_1, x_2)\, dx_1\, dx_2 = 1$ in the continuous case.

Given the joint mass or density function $f(x_1, x_2)$ of the two random variables x_1 and x_2 we define the marginal mass or density function of each. [Recall that in this book the same symbol, $f(\ )$, may be used to denote several different functions.]

(3.15) Let the random variables x_1 and x_2 have the joint mass or density function $f(x_1, x_2)$. Then the marginal mass or density functions of x_1 and x_2 are defined as $f(x_1) = \Sigma_{x_2} f(x_1, x_2)$ and $f(x_2) = \Sigma_{x_1} f(x_1, x_2)$, respectively, in the discrete case; and as $f(x_1) = \int_{-\infty}^{\infty} f(x_1, x_2)\, dx_2$ and $f(x_2) = \int_{-\infty}^{\infty} f(x_1, x_2)\, dx_1$, respectively, in the continuous case.

First note that each marginal mass or density function has the properties required of a probability mass or density function: $f(x_1) = \Sigma_{x_2} f(x_1, x_2) \geq 0$ since $f(x_1, x_2) \geq 0$, and $\Sigma_{x_1} f(x_1) = \Sigma_{x_1} [\Sigma_{x_2} f(x_1, x_2)] = 1$ since $\Sigma_{x_1} \Sigma_{x_2} f(x_1, x_2) = 1$ in the discrete case; and $f(x_1) = \int_{-\infty}^{\infty} f(x_1, x_2)\, dx_2 \geq 0$ since $f(x_1, x_2) \geq 0$, and

$$\int_{-\infty}^{\infty} f(x_1)\, dx_1 = \int_{-\infty}^{\infty} \left[\int_{-\infty}^{\infty} f(x_1, x_2)\, dx_2\right] dx_1 = 1$$

since $\int_{-\infty}^{\infty} \int_{-\infty}^{\infty} f(x_1, x_2)\, dx_1\, dx_2 = 1$ in the continuous case; and similarly for $f(x_2)$. To interpret a marginal mass or density function consider the following: In the discrete case, consider the event "$x_1 = x_1^*$" where x_1^* is any value. It is the union of all the disjoint events of the form "$\mathbf{x} = \begin{pmatrix} x_1^* \\ x_2 \end{pmatrix}$;" hence its probability should be obtained as the sum of their probabilities, and this is precisely the assignment of probability defined by the marginal mass $f(x_1^*) = \Sigma_{x_2} f(x_1^*, x_2)$, which is the sum of the masses for all $\mathbf{x}$'s having $x_1 = x_1^*$. In the continuous case, consider the event "$x_1 \leq x_1^*$" where x_1^* is any value. It is the event "$\mathbf{x} \leq \begin{pmatrix} x_1^* \\ \infty \end{pmatrix}$," and hence its probability should be that of the latter event, and this is precisely the assignment of probability defined by the marginal density:

$$\int_{-\infty}^{x_1^*} f(x_1)\, dx_1 = \int_{-\infty}^{x_1^*} \left[\int_{-\infty}^{\infty} f(x_1, x_2)\, dx_2\right] dx_1$$

$$= \int_{-\infty}^{x_1^*} \int_{-\infty}^{\infty} f(x_1, x_2)\, dx_1\, dx_2$$

which is the integral of the densities for all $\mathbf{x}$'s having $x_1 \leq x_1^*$. Thus $f(x_1)$ is simply the probability mass or density function of the random variable x_1: It defines the probability measure over a new field of events; the events in the new field are either old events or unions of old events, and the new assignment of probabilities is consistent with the old one. The other marginal mass or density function $f(x_2)$ has the parallel interpretation.

Given the joint mass or density function $f(x_1, x_2)$ of the two random variables x_1 and x_2 we also define the conditional mass or density function of each one given the other.

(3.16) Let the random variables x_1 and x_2 have the joint mass or density function $f(x_1, x_2)$. Then the conditional mass or density function of x_1 given x_2 is defined as $f(x_1 \mid x_2) = f(x_1, x_2)/f(x_2)$ and the conditional mass or density function of x_2 given x_1 is defined as $f(x_2 \mid x_1) = f(x_1, x_2)/f(x_1)$.

First note that each conditional mass or density function has the properties required of a probability mass or density function: $f(x_1, x_2)/f(x_2) \geq 0$—provided that $f(x_2) \neq 0$—and $\Sigma_{x_1}[f(x_1, x_2)/f(x_2)] = \Sigma_{x_1} f(x_1, x_2)/f(x_2) = 1$ in the discrete case; and

$$\int_{-\infty}^{\infty} \left[\frac{f(x_1, x_2)}{f(x_2)}\right] dx_1 = \frac{\int_{-\infty}^{\infty} f(x_1, x_2)\, dx_1}{f(x_2)} = 1$$

in the continuous case; and similarly for $f(x_2 \mid x_1)$. To interpret a conditional mass or density function consider the following: Let A and B be any two events in the Borel field of the experiment with $P(B) \neq 0$. Then the conditional probability of the event A given the event B is defined as $P(A \mid B) = P(A \cap B)/P(B)$. It is readily verified that a conditional probability is a legitimate probability measure over a new outcome space. The new outcome space consists only of outcomes which are elements of the event B; a new event $A \mid B$ in the new outcome space corresponds to the event $A \cap B$ in the old outcome space. The conditional probability assigns to any events $A \mid B$ and $C \mid B$ in the new outcome space the same relative probabilities that the events $A \cap B$ and $C \cap B$ had in the old outcome space, and of course assigns probability 1 to the new certain event $P(B \mid B) = P(B \cap B)/P(B) = P(B)/P(B) = 1$.

A conditional mass or density function defines such an assignment of conditional probabilities. In the discrete case, take the event A to be "$x_1 = x_1^*$" and the event B to be "$x_2 = x_2^*$" where $f(x_2^*) \neq 0$; then the event $A \cap B$ is "$x_1 = x_1^*$ and $x_2 = x_2^*$" whose probability was given by the joint mass $f(x_1^*, x_2^*)$, whereas the probability of the event B was given by the marginal mass $f(x_2^*)$. Then the probability of the event "$x_1 = x_1^*$ given that $x_2 = x_2^*$" is given by the conditional mass $f(x_1^* \mid x_2^*) = f(x_1^*, x_2^*)/f(x_2^*)$. In the continuous case take the event A to be "$x_1 \leq x_1^*$" and the event B to be "$x_2^* < x_2 \leq x_2^* + dx_2$;" then the event $A \cap B$ is "$x_1 \leq x_1^*$ and $x_2^* < x_2 \leq x_2^* + dx_2$" whose probability was given by

$$\int_{-\infty}^{x_1^*} \int_{x_2^*}^{x_2^*+dx_2} f(x_1, x_2)\, dx_1\, dx_2 = dx_2 \int_{-\infty}^{x_1^*} f(x_1, x_2^*)\, dx_1$$

whereas the probability of the event "$x_2^* < x_2 \le x_2^* + dx_2$" was given by $\int_{x_2^*}^{x_2^*+dx_2} f(x_2)\,dx_2 = f(x_2^*)\,dx_2$. Then the probability of the event "$x_1 \le x_1^*$ given that $x_2^* < x_2 \le x_2^* + dx_2$"—which is effectively the event "$x_1 \le x_1^*$ and $x_2 = x_2^*$"—is given by

$$\int_{-\infty}^{x_1^*} f(x_1 \mid x_2^*)\,dx_1 = \int_{-\infty}^{x_1^*} \frac{f(x_1, x_2^*)}{f(x_2^*)}\,dx_1 = \frac{\int_{-\infty}^{x_1^*} f(x_1, x_2^*)\,dx_1}{f(x_2^*)}.$$

Thus $f(x_1 \mid x_2)$ is simply the probability density function of the "conditional random variable" $x_1 \mid x_2$: It defines the probability measure over a new outcome space, the outcomes in the new space all having the same value for x_2. It should be noted that in general x_2 will appear as a parameter in $f(x_1 \mid x_2)$. The other conditional density function $f(x_2 \mid x_1)$ has the parallel interpretation.

The numerical examples of Section 2 may serve as illustrations of these concepts if we interpret them as theoretical probability distributions rather than as empirical frequency distributions; this is possible since relative frequencies obviously have the properties of a probability measure —each relative frequency is nonnegative, and the sum of the relative frequencies over all observations is unity.

Finally, consider the general multivariate case where the random vector $\mathbf{x} = \begin{pmatrix} x_1 \\ \cdot \\ \cdot \\ \cdot \\ x_n \end{pmatrix}$ contains n elements. Its mass or density function $f(\mathbf{x})$ is often written as $f(x_1, \ldots, x_n)$ and referred to as the joint mass or density function of the random variables $x_1, \ldots, x_n$. Again the joint mass or density function has the properties $f(x_1, \ldots, x_n) \ge 0$ for any n-tuple of values $x_1, \ldots, x_n$, whereas summation over all n-tuples in the outcome space gives $\Sigma_{x_1} \cdots \Sigma_{x_n} f(x_1, \ldots, x_n) = 1$ in the discrete case and $\int_{-\infty}^{\infty} \cdots \int_{-\infty}^{\infty} f(x_1, \ldots, x_n)\,dx_1 \cdots dx_n = 1$ in the continuous case.

Given the joint mass or density function $f(x_1, \ldots, x_n)$ of the n random variables $x_1, \ldots, x_n$ we define the marginal mass or density function of any subset of them.

(3.17) Let the random variables $x_1, \ldots, x_n$ have the joint mass or density function $f(x_1, \ldots, x_n)$ and let $x_1, \ldots, x_m$ $(1 \le m < n)$ be any subset of them. Then the marginal mass or density function of $x_1, \ldots, x_m$ is

$$f(x_1, \ldots, x_m) = \Sigma_{x_{m+1}} \cdots \Sigma_{x_n} f(x_1, \ldots, x_n)$$

in the discrete case and

$$f(x_1, \ldots, x_m) = \int_{-\infty}^{\infty} \cdots \int_{-\infty}^{\infty} f(x_1, \ldots, x_n)\, dx_{m+1} \cdots dx_n$$

in the continuous case.

Once again a marginal mass or density function has the properties requisite of a probability mass or density function; and $f(x_1, \ldots, x_m)$ defines the probability measure over events that are obtained by uniting all events which differ only with respect to $x_{m+1}, \ldots, x_n$.

We also define the conditional mass or density function of any subset of the n random variables given the remaining ones:

(3.18) Let the random variables $x_1, \ldots, x_n$ have the joint mass or density function $f(x_1, \ldots, x_n)$ and let $x_1, \ldots, x_m (1 \leq m < n)$ be any subset of them. Then the conditional mass or density function of $x_1, \ldots, x_m$ given $x_{m+1}, \ldots, x_n$ is

$$f(x_1, \ldots, x_m \mid x_{m+1}, \ldots, x_n) = f(x_1, \ldots, x_n)/f(x_{m+1}, \ldots, x_n).$$

Once again a conditional mass or density function has the properties requisite of any probability mass or density function; and $f(x_1, \ldots, x_m \mid x_{m+1}, \ldots, x_n)$ defines the conditional probability measure over a new outcome space obtained by considering only outcomes which have specified values of $x_{m+1}, \ldots, x_n$. In general $x_{m+1}, \ldots, x_n$ will appear as parameters in $f(x_1, \ldots, x_m \mid x_{m+1}, \ldots, x_n)$. Still more conditional mass or density functions may be derived from the joint mass or density function $f(x_1, \ldots, x_n)$, because after having derived the marginal mass or density function $f(x_1, \ldots, x_m)$ with $1 < m < n$ we may define and derive the conditional mass or density function $f(x_1, \ldots, x_p \mid x_{p+1}, \ldots, x_m)$ for any $1 < p < m$. For $n = 3$ all such derived distributions were listed in Section 2 in our discussion of empirical frequency distributions.

Cumulative Probability Distributions

Corresponding to each of the mass and density functions we have considered is a cumulative function. For a univariate mass or density function $f(x)$, the cumulative function is defined by $F(x^*) = \Sigma_{x \leq x^*} f(x)$ in the discrete case and $F(x^*) = \int_{-\infty}^{x^*} f(x)\, dx$ in the continuous case. Thus the cumulative function defines the probability measure by giving for any value x^* the probability of the event "$x \leq x^*$." Similarly for a multivariate mass or density function $f(\mathbf{x}) = f(x_1, \ldots, x_n)$ the cumulative function is defined by $F(x_1^*, \ldots, x_n^*) = \Sigma_{x_1 \le x_1^*} \cdots \Sigma_{x_n \le x_n^*} f(x_1, \ldots, x_n)$—or more compactly $F(\mathbf{x}^*) = \Sigma_{\mathbf{x} \le \mathbf{x}^*} f(\mathbf{x})$—in the discrete case, and by $F(x_1^*, \ldots, x_n^*) = \int_{-\infty}^{x_1^*} \cdots \int_{-\infty}^{x_n^*} f(x_1, \ldots, x_n)\, dx_1 \cdots dx_n$—or more compactly $F(\mathbf{x}^*) = \int_{\mathbf{x} \le \mathbf{x}^*} f(\mathbf{x})\, \mathbf{dx}$—in the continuous case. Thus the cumulative function defines the probability measure by giving for any value $\mathbf{x}^*$ the probability of the event "$\mathbf{x} \le \mathbf{x}^*$." Note that we may have cumulative marginal and cumulative conditional functions as well as cumulative joint functions. The cumulative function provides an alternative method of defining the probability distribution; we employ it on occasion.

Stochastic Independence

A crucial concept in the model is that of stochastic independence. In terms of events the events A and B are said to be stochastically independent if $P(A \cap B) = P(A)P(B)$—which means that if two events are stochastically independent the conditional probability of either one given the other is equal to the unconditional probability of the first: e.g., $P(A \mid B) = P(A \cap B)/P(B)$ equals $P(A)P(B)/P(B) = P(A)$ if $P(A \cap B) = P(A)P(B)$. In terms of random variables we define, in the bivariate case,

(3.19) Let $\mathbf{x} = \begin{pmatrix} x_1 \\ x_2 \end{pmatrix}$ be a random vector; let $f(x_1, x_2)$ be the joint mass or density function and let $f(x_1)$ and $f(x_2)$ be the marginal mass or density functions. Then the random variables x_1 and x_2 are said to be stochastically independent—or, equivalently, independently distributed, or, equivalently, independent—if and only if $f(x_1, x_2) = f(x_1)f(x_2)$ for all values of x_1, x_2.

If x_1 and x_2 are independent, then $f(x_1 \mid x_2) = f(x_1, x_2)/f(x_2) = f(x_1)f(x_2)/f(x_2) = f(x_1)$ and similarly $f(x_2 \mid x_1) = f(x_2)$. Conversely, if $f(x_1 \mid x_2) = f(x_1)$, then $f(x_1, x_2) = f(x_1 \mid x_2)f(x_2) = f(x_1)f(x_2)$; similarly, if $f(x_2 \mid x_1) = f(x_2)$, then $f(x_1, x_2) = f(x_1)f(x_2)$. Thus we have

(3.20) The random variables x_1 and x_2 are independent if and only if $f(x_1 \mid x_2) = f(x_1)$—or equivalently if and only if $f(x_2 \mid x_1) = f(x_2)$—for all values of x_1, x_2.

If we interpret the artificial numerical example given in (2.3) as a theoretical probability distribution rather than as an empirical frequency distribution it may serve to illustrate the property of stochastic independence. Note also that if x_1 and x_2 are independent, $F(x_1, x_2) = F(x_1)F(x_2)$, the joint cumulative function is the product of the marginal cumulative functions.

Extending to the multivariate case, we define

(3.21) Let the $n \times 1$ random vector $\mathbf{x}$ be partitioned as $\mathbf{x} = \begin{pmatrix} \mathbf{x}_1 \\ \mathbf{x}_2 \end{pmatrix}$ where $\mathbf{x}_1 = \begin{pmatrix} x_1 \\ \cdot \\ \cdot \\ \cdot \\ x_m \end{pmatrix}$ and $\mathbf{x}_2 = \begin{pmatrix} x_{m+1} \\ \cdot \\ \cdot \\ \cdot \\ x_n \end{pmatrix}$ and let the joint mass or density function be $f(\mathbf{x}) = f(\mathbf{x}_1, \mathbf{x}_2) = f(x_1, \ldots, x_n)$ and the marginal mass or density functions be $f(\mathbf{x}_1) = f(x_1, \ldots, x_m)$ and $f(\mathbf{x}_2) = f(x_{m+1}, \ldots, x_n)$. Then the random vectors $\mathbf{x}_1$ and $\mathbf{x}_2$ are said to be stochastically independent—or independently distributed, or simply independent—if and only if $f(\mathbf{x}_1, \mathbf{x}_2) = f(\mathbf{x}_1)f(\mathbf{x}_2)$—for all values of $\mathbf{x}_1$, $\mathbf{x}_2$.

If $\mathbf{x}_1$ and $\mathbf{x}_2$ are independent, then $f(\mathbf{x}_1 \mid \mathbf{x}_2) = f(\mathbf{x}_1, \mathbf{x}_2)/f(\mathbf{x}_2) = f(\mathbf{x}_1)f(\mathbf{x}_2)/f(\mathbf{x}_2) = f(\mathbf{x}_1)$ and similarly $f(\mathbf{x}_2 \mid \mathbf{x}_1) = f(\mathbf{x}_2)$; the converse is again true. Thus we have

(3.22) The random vectors $\mathbf{x}_1$ and $\mathbf{x}_2$ are independent if and only if $f(\mathbf{x}_1 \mid \mathbf{x}_2) = f(\mathbf{x}_1)$—or equivalently, if and only if $f(\mathbf{x}_2 \mid \mathbf{x}_1) = f(\mathbf{x}_2)$—for all values of $\mathbf{x}_1$, $\mathbf{x}_2$.

Again, if $f(\mathbf{x}_1, \mathbf{x}_2) = f(\mathbf{x}_1)f(\mathbf{x}_2)$, then $F(\mathbf{x}_1, \mathbf{x}_2) = F(\mathbf{x}_1)F(\mathbf{x}_2)$. If $\mathbf{x}_1 = \begin{pmatrix} x_1 \\ \cdot \\ \cdot \\ \cdot \\ x_m \end{pmatrix}$ and $\mathbf{x}_2 = \begin{pmatrix} x_{m+1} \\ \cdot \\ \cdot \\ \cdot \\ x_n \end{pmatrix}$ are independent random vectors, we also describe this by saying that the two sets of random variables—the set $x_1, \ldots, x_m$ and the set $x_{m+1}, \ldots, x_n$—are independent. Of course this means that any random variable in the first set is independent of any random variable in the second set in the sense of (3.19). To see this we take x_1 and x_n for an example. We have

$$\begin{aligned} f(x_1, x_n) &= \sum_{x_2} \cdots \sum_{x_{n-1}} f(x_1, \ldots, x_n) \\ &= \sum_{x_2} \cdots \sum_{x_{n-1}} f(x_1, \ldots, x_m) f(x_{m+1}, \ldots, x_n) \\ &= \sum_{x_2} \cdots \sum_{x_m} f(x_1, \ldots, x_m) \\ &\quad \times \sum_{x_{m+1}} \cdots \sum_{x_{n-1}} f(x_{m+1}, \ldots, x_n) = f(x_1) f(x_n) \end{aligned}$$

in the discrete case; similarly in the continuous case. All this extends to finer partitioning; in particular we define

(3.23) Let $\mathbf{x} = \begin{pmatrix} x_1 \\ \cdot \\ \cdot \\ \cdot \\ x_n \end{pmatrix}$ be a random vector with joint mass or density function $f(x_1, \ldots, x_n)$ and marginal mass or density functions $f(x_1), \ldots, f(x_n)$. Then the n random variables $x_1, \ldots, x_n$ are said to be mutually stochastically independent if and only if $f(x_1, \ldots, x_n) = f(x_1) \cdots f(x_n)$ for all values of $x_1, \ldots, x_n$.

It follows that if $x_1, \ldots, x_n$ are mutually independent the conditional mass or density function of any subset of them, given any other subset of them, is the same for all values of the second subset and is identical with the marginal mass or density function of the first subset. Again if $f(x_1, \ldots, x_n) = f(x_1) \cdots f(x_n)$, then $F(x_1, \ldots, x_n) = F(x_1) \cdots F(x_n)$. If the random variables in a set are mutually independent, any pair of them are independent in the sense of (3.19); all pairs may be independent, however, without there being mutual independence; see the example above (2.14).

Clearly a nonstochastic random vector is independent of any other random vector—its sole possible value is the same for all values of other random vectors. Note that the statistical concept of stochastic independence should not be confused with the algebraic concept of linear independence. Finally, if $\mathbf{x}_1$ and $\mathbf{x}_2$ are independent, any event defined only by values of $\mathbf{x}_1$ is clearly independent of any event defined only by values of $\mathbf{x}_2$.

Functions of Random Variables

Suppose that $\mathbf{x}$ is a random vector with mass or density function $f(\mathbf{x})$, and let $\mathbf{y} = y(\mathbf{x})$ be a vector whose elements are single-valued functions of (the elements of) $\mathbf{x}$. Then $\mathbf{y}$ will also be a random vector: Its values are determined—"indirectly"—by the outcomes of the experiment. Indeed it is clear how the assignment of probabilities to events defined in terms of values of $\mathbf{y}$ may be derived from the original assignment of probabilities to events defined in terms of values of $\mathbf{x}$. The function $\mathbf{y} = y(\mathbf{x})$ associates with each value of $\mathbf{x}$ a value of $\mathbf{y}$—and thus represents each outcome by a value of $\mathbf{y}$. Suppose that B is an event defined in terms of values of $\mathbf{y}$ and let A be the event containing just the outcomes which have $\mathbf{x}$ such that $\mathbf{y} = y(\mathbf{x})$ is an element of B. Then $P(B) = P(A)$: The original assignment of probabilities to events defined in terms of $\mathbf{x}$ is transformed into an assignment of probabilities to events defined in terms of $\mathbf{y}$.

Under general conditions the new assignment of probabilities may be represented by a mass or density function $g(\mathbf{y})$. Suppose that $\mathbf{x}$ is a discrete random vector and let $\mathbf{y} = y(\mathbf{x})$ be a vector function of $\mathbf{x}$; then $\mathbf{y}$ will also be a discrete random vector. The probability $g(\mathbf{y}^*)$ that $\mathbf{y}$ takes on the value $\mathbf{y}^*$ is obtained by summing $f(\mathbf{x})$ over all $\mathbf{x}$'s such that $y(\mathbf{x}) = \mathbf{y}^*$. For example, suppose that the mass function of the random variable x is

$$f(x) = \begin{cases} \frac{1}{2} & \text{for} \quad x = -1 \\ \frac{1}{4} & \text{for} \quad x = 0 \\ \frac{1}{4} & \text{for} \quad x = 1 \end{cases}$$

and let $y = x^2$. Then the mass function of the random variable y is

$$g(y) = \begin{cases} \frac{1}{4} & \text{for} \quad y = 0 \\ \frac{3}{4} & \text{for} \quad y = 1. \end{cases}$$

Suppose that $\mathbf{x}$ is a continuous random vector and let $\mathbf{y} = y(\mathbf{x})$ be a vector function of $\mathbf{x}$; then $\mathbf{y}$ *may* be a discrete random vector. For example, suppose that x is a continuous random variable with density function $f(x)$ and let

$$y = \begin{cases} 0 & \text{if} \quad x \leq b \\ 1 & \text{if} \quad x > b \end{cases}$$

where b is some number. Then y is a discrete random variable and its mass function is given by

$$g(y) = \begin{cases} \int_{-\infty}^{b} f(x)\, dx & \text{for} \quad y = 0 \\ \int_{b}^{\infty} f(x)\, dx & \text{for} \quad y = 1. \end{cases}$$

Or suppose that $\mathbf{x}$ is a continuous random vector and let $\mathbf{y} = y(\mathbf{x})$ be a continuous vector function of $\mathbf{x}$; then $\mathbf{y}$ will be a continuous random vector whose density at $\mathbf{y}^*$ may be found by differentiating the cumulative function $G(\mathbf{y}^*) = \int_{y(\mathbf{x}) \leq \mathbf{y}^*} f(\mathbf{x})\, d\mathbf{x}$. For example, suppose that x is a continuous random variable with density function $f(x)$ and let $y = x^2$. Then

$$G(y^*) = \int_{-\sqrt{y^*}}^{\sqrt{y^*}} f(x)\, dx = \int_0^{\sqrt{y^*}} f(x)\, dx + \int_0^{\sqrt{y^*}} f(-x)\, dx$$

$$= \frac{1}{2} \int_0^{y^*} \frac{f(\sqrt{y}) + f(-\sqrt{y})}{\sqrt{y}}\, dy$$

for $y^* > 0$ and $G(y^*) = 0$ for $y^* \leq 0$; then the density function of y is given by

$$g(y) = \begin{cases} (1/2\sqrt{y})[f(\sqrt{y}) + f(-\sqrt{y})] & \text{for} \quad y > 0 \\ 0 & \text{for} \quad y \leq 0. \end{cases}$$

Although in our work we have little occasion to carry out such transformations, it is nevertheless important to appreciate how in principle the mass or density function of one random vector might be derived from that of another random vector to which the first is functionally related.

It is sometimes convenient to write "y is distributed as $c\,f(z)$"—where c is a constant—to mean "y/c is distributed as $f(z)$."

It is readily seen that functions of independent random vectors are also independent; more precisely,

(3.24) Let $\mathbf{x}_1$ and $\mathbf{x}_2$ be independent random vectors and let $\mathbf{y}_1 = y_1(\mathbf{x}_1)$ be a vector function of $\mathbf{x}_1$ and let $\mathbf{y}_2 = y_2(\mathbf{x}_2)$ be a vector function of $\mathbf{x}_2$. Then $\mathbf{y}_1$ and $\mathbf{y}_2$ are independent random vectors.

This is so because in the discrete case we may write the joint mass of the $\mathbf{y}$'s as the product of their marginal masses:

$$g(\mathbf{y}_1^*, \mathbf{y}_2^*) = \sum_{y_1(\mathbf{x}_1)=\mathbf{y}_1^*} \sum_{y_2(\mathbf{x}_2)=\mathbf{y}_2^*} f(\mathbf{x}_1, \mathbf{x}_2) = \sum_{y_1(\mathbf{x}_1)=\mathbf{y}_1^*} \sum_{y_2(\mathbf{x}_2)=\mathbf{y}_2^*} f(\mathbf{x}_1)f(\mathbf{x}_2)$$

$$= \sum_{y_1(\mathbf{x}_1)=\mathbf{y}_1^*} f(\mathbf{x}_1) \sum_{y_2(\mathbf{x}_2)=\mathbf{y}_2^*} f(\mathbf{x}_2) = g(\mathbf{y}_1^*)g(\mathbf{y}_2^*);$$

and similarly in the continuous case. Briefly, if $\mathbf{x}_1$ and $\mathbf{x}_2$ are independent and if A is an event defined in terms of $\mathbf{x}_1$ only and B is an event defined in terms of $\mathbf{x}_2$ only, then A and B must be independent events; (3.24) applies this to events defined by new random vectors.

Finally a definition: If $\mathbf{x} = \begin{pmatrix} x_1 \\ \cdot \\ \cdot \\ \cdot \\ x_n \end{pmatrix}$ is a random vector and there exists a constant vector $\mathbf{c} \neq \mathbf{0}$ such that $\mathbf{c}'\mathbf{x} = a$ is a degenerate (nonstochastic) random variable, the elements of $\mathbf{x}$ are said to be linearly dependent random variables. It will be seen that in this instance the value of at least one of the $x_1, \ldots, x_n$ is completely determined by the values of the others. If, say, $c_1 \neq 0$, then the conditional distribution of x_1 given $x_2, \ldots, x_n$ is degenerate:

$$f(x_1 \mid x_2, \ldots, x_n) = \begin{cases} 1 & \text{for} \quad x_1 = a - (c_2/c_1)x_2 - \cdots - (c_n/c_1)x_n \\ 0 & \text{otherwise.} \end{cases}$$

Moments of Probability Distribution

The moments of a probability distribution are defined in the same manner as were the moments of a frequency distribution and for the same purpose—to summarize certain properties of the distribution.

For a univariate distribution, where the random variable x has the mass or density function $f(x)$, the rth raw moment (rth moment about zero) is defined as $M'_r = \Sigma_x x^r f(x)$ in the discrete case and as $M'_r = \int_{-\infty}^{\infty} x^r f(x)\, dx$ in the continuous case where r is any nonnegative integer. The first raw moment is the mean of the distribution—or of the random variable—and is denoted by μ: $\mu = M'_1 = \Sigma_x xf(x)$ [or $\int_{-\infty}^{\infty} xf(x)\, dx$]. The rth central moment (rth moment about the mean) is defined as $M_r = \Sigma_x (x - \mu)^r f(x)$ in the discrete case and as $M_r = \int_{-\infty}^{\infty} (x - \mu)^r f(x)\, dx$ in the continuous case where r is any nonnegative integer. The second central moment is the variance of the distribution—or of the random variable—and is denoted by var (x) or by σ^2:

$$\sigma^2 = M_2 = \Sigma_x (x - \mu)^2 f(x) \quad [\text{or} \int_{-\infty}^{\infty} (x - \mu)^2 f(x)\, dx)].$$

The mean is a measure of central tendency; the variance is a measure of variability about the mean; the other moments describe other features of the distribution. Clearly a variance is nonnegative; if x is a constant, its mean is its sole value and its variance is zero.

The computation of moments may be illustrated with the $B(\mu)$ distribution. Suppose then that x is a discrete random variable with mass function

$$f(x) = \begin{cases} 1 - \mu & \text{for} \quad x = 0 \\ \mu & \text{for} \quad x = 1 \end{cases}$$

where $0 \leq \mu \leq 1$. Then the following are readily confirmed:

$$M'_1 = 0(1 - \mu) + 1(\mu) = \mu \qquad = 0^r(1 - \mu) + 1^r(\mu) = M'_r \quad (r = 2, 3, \ldots);$$

(3.25)
$$M_2 = (0 - \mu)^2(1 - \mu) + (1 - \mu)^2\mu = \mu(1 - \mu)$$

$$M_3 = (0 - \mu)^3(1 - \mu) + (1 - \mu)^3\mu = \mu(1 - \mu) \times [-\mu^2 + (1 - \mu)^2]$$

$$M_4 = (0 - \mu)^4(1 - \mu) + (1 - \mu)^4\mu = \mu(1 - \mu) \times [\mu^3 + (1 - \mu)^3].$$

It should be noted that the moments of a distribution may not exist—i.e., they may not be finite. The Cauchy distribution $f(x) = (1/\pi)[\alpha/(\alpha^2 + x^2)]$ provides an example; although $\int_{-\infty}^{\infty} (1/\pi)[\alpha/(\alpha^2 + x^2)]\,dx = 1$, the expression $\int_{-\infty}^{\infty} (1/\pi)[\alpha x/(\alpha^2 + x^2)]\,dx$ has no finite value. In our work, however, we assume implicitly that the moments of the relevant distributions exist; thus in all our results the restriction "provided that the necessary moments exist" is to be understood.

The following important theorem shows how the variance of a distribution can be used to set an upper bound on the probability of large deviations from the mean.

(3.26) ***Chebyshev's inequality.*** Let x be a random variable with mean μ and variance σ^2. Then for any $\delta > 0$,

$$\text{(3.26a)} \qquad \text{Prob}\,\{|x - \mu| \geq \delta\sigma\} \leq \frac{1}{\delta^2};$$

or equivalently for any $\epsilon > 0$,

$$\text{(3.26b)} \qquad \text{Prob}\,\{|x - \mu| \geq \epsilon\} \leq \frac{\sigma^2}{\epsilon^2}.$$

Suppose that x is a continuous random variable with density function $f(x)$; then

$$\text{(3.27)} \qquad \sigma^2 = \int_{-\infty}^{\infty} (x - \mu)^2 f(x)\,dx$$

$$= \int_{-\infty}^{\mu-\delta\sigma} (x - \mu)^2 f(x)\,dx + \int_{\mu-\delta\sigma}^{\mu+\delta\sigma} (x - \mu)^2 f(x)\,dx$$

$$+ \int_{\mu+\delta\sigma}^{\infty} (x - \mu)^2 f(x)\,dx,$$

from which, since the second term on the right is nonnegative,

$$\text{(3.28)} \qquad \sigma^2 \geq \int_{-\infty}^{\mu-\delta\sigma} (x - \mu)^2 f(x)\,dx + \int_{\mu+\delta\sigma}^{\infty} (x - \mu)^2 f(x)\,dx.$$

Now when $x \leq \mu - \delta\sigma$, $(x - \mu)^2 \geq \delta^2\sigma^2$ and when $x \geq \mu + \delta\sigma$, $(x - \mu)^2 \geq \delta^2\sigma^2$; thus

$$\text{(3.29)} \qquad \sigma^2 \geq \int_{-\infty}^{\mu-\delta\sigma} \delta^2\sigma^2 f(x)\,dx + \int_{\mu+\delta\sigma}^{\infty} \delta^2\sigma^2 f(x)\,dx$$

$$\geq \delta^2\sigma^2\left[\int_{-\infty}^{\mu-\delta\sigma} f(x)\,dx + \int_{\mu+\delta\sigma}^{\infty} f(x)\,dx\right]$$

$$\geq \delta^2\sigma^2(\text{Prob}\,\{|x - \mu| \geq \delta\sigma\}),$$

which after division by $\delta^2\sigma^2$ gives (3.26*a*). Then taking $\delta = \epsilon/\sigma$ gives (3.26*b*). A similar argument holds in the discrete case.

Proceeding to the multivariate case where the random variables $x_1, \ldots, x_n$ have the joint mass or density function $f(x_1, \ldots, x_n)$ we may define raw moments by $M'_{r \cdots s} = \Sigma_{x_1} \cdots \Sigma_{x_n} x_1^r \cdots x_n^s f(x_1, \ldots, x_n)$ in the discrete case and similarly in the continuous case and similarly for central moments. For almost all of our purposes, however, we need only the means $\mu_{x_i} = \mu_i = \Sigma_{x_i} x_i f(x_i)$ $\left[\text{or} \int_{-\infty}^{\infty} x_i f(x_i)\, dx_i\right]$, the variances var (x_i) $= \sigma_{ii} = \sigma_i^2 = \Sigma_{x_i} (x_i - \mu_i)^2 f(x_i)$ $\left[\text{or} \int_{-\infty}^{\infty} (x_i - \mu_i)^2 f(x_i)\, dx_i\right]$, and the covariances cov $(x_i, x_j) = \sigma_{ij} = \Sigma_{x_i} \Sigma_{x_j} (x_i - \mu_i)(x_j - \mu_j) f(x_i, x_j)$ $\left[\text{or} \int_{-\infty}^{\infty} \int_{-\infty}^{\infty} (x_i - \mu_i)(x_j - \mu_j) f(x_i, x_j)\, dx_i\, dx_j\right]$ for $i, j = 1, \ldots, n$. Note that $\sigma_{ij} = \text{cov}\,(x_i, x_j) = \text{cov}\,(x_j, x_i) = \sigma_{ji}$. For many purposes it will be useful to have these moments arranged together; thus we define

(3.30) Let $\mathbf{x} = \begin{pmatrix} x_1 \\ \cdot \\ \cdot \\ \cdot \\ x_n \end{pmatrix}$ be a random vector. Then its mean (vector) is defined as $\boldsymbol{\mu} = \begin{pmatrix} \mu_1 \\ \cdot \\ \cdot \\ \cdot \\ \mu_n \end{pmatrix}$ and its covariance matrix is defined as

$$\boldsymbol{\Sigma} = \begin{pmatrix} \sigma_{11} & \cdots & \sigma_{1n} \\ \cdot & & \cdot \\ \cdot & & \cdot \\ \cdot & & \cdot \\ \sigma_{n1} & \cdots & \sigma_{nn} \end{pmatrix}$$

where μ_i is the mean of x_i, σ_{ii} is the variance of x_i, and $\sigma_{ij} = \sigma_{ji}$ is the covariance of x_i and x_j.

The covariance matrix is sometimes called the variance-covariance matrix. It should be noted that

(3.31) If x_i and x_j are independent random variables, cov $(x_i, x_j) = 0$; but uncorrelated random variables need not be independent.

If $f(x_i, x_j) = f(x_i)f(x_j)$, then

$$\begin{aligned}\operatorname{cov}(x_i, x_j) &= \sum_{x_i}\sum_{x_j}(x_i - \mu_i)(x_j - \mu_j)f(x_i, x_j)\\ &= \sum_{x_i}\sum_{x_j}(x_i - \mu_i)(x_j - \mu_j)f(x_i)f(x_j)\\ &= \sum_{x_i}(x_i - \mu_i)f(x_i)\sum_{x_j}(x_j - \mu_j)f(x_j) = 0\end{aligned}$$

since

$$\sum_{x_j}(x_j - \mu_j)f(x_j) = \sum_{x_j} x_j f(x_j) - \mu_j \sum_{x_j} f(x_j) = \mu_j - \mu_j = 0,$$

and similarly in the continuous case. A counterexample to the converse may be found after (2.38). Again cov $(x_i, x_j) = 0$ simply if the conditional mean of x_j is the same for all values of x_i.

Calculus of Expectations

The definition and manipulation of moments—in particular the derivation of the moments of a function of a random vector in terms of the moments of the latter random vector—is greatly facilitated by the use of the so-called calculus of expectations. We make extensive use of this machinery in the sequel. First for the univariate case we define:

(3.32) Let x be a random variable with mass or density function $f(x)$, and let $y = y(x)$ be a scalar single-valued function of x. Then the expectation—or expected value—of y is defined as $Ey = \Sigma_x\, y(x)f(x)$ in the discrete case and as $Ey = \int_{-\infty}^{\infty} y(x)f(x)\, dx$ in the continuous case.

The expression Ey should be read as "E of y" and not as "E times y;" E is an operator and not a quantity. Taking $y(x) = x$ we see that the expectation of x is simply the mean of x:

$$Ex = \begin{Bmatrix} \sum_x xf(x) \quad \text{or} \\ \int_{-\infty}^{\infty} xf(x)\, dx \end{Bmatrix} = \mu;$$

taking $y(x) = (x - \mu)^2$ we see that the expectation of $(x - \mu)^2$ is simply the variance of x:

$$E(x - \mu)^2 = \begin{Bmatrix} \sum_x (x - \mu)^2 f(x) \quad \text{or} \\ \int_{-\infty}^{\infty} (x - \mu)^2 f(x)\, dx \end{Bmatrix} = \sigma^2$$

Indeed Ex^r is simply the rth raw moment of x and $E(x - \mu)^r$ is simply the rth central moment of x.

Extending to the multivariate case we define:

(3.33) Let $\mathbf{x}$ be a random vector with mass or density function $f(\mathbf{x})$ and let $y = y(\mathbf{x})$ be a scalar single-valued function of (the elements of) $\mathbf{x}$. Then the expectation—or expected value—of y is defined as $Ey = \Sigma_{\mathbf{x}}\, y(\mathbf{x})f(\mathbf{x})$ in the discrete case and as $Ey = \int_{\mathbf{x}} y(\mathbf{x})f(\mathbf{x})\, d\mathbf{x}$ in the continuous case.

Taking $y(\mathbf{x}) = (x_i - \mu_i)(x_j - \mu_j)$ we see that the expectation of $(x_i - \mu_i)(x_j - \mu_j)$ is simply the covariance of x_i and x_j:

$$E(x_i - \mu_i)(x_j - \mu_j) = \sum_{x_1} \cdots \sum_{x_n} (x_i - \mu_i)(x_j - \mu_j) f(x_1, \ldots, x_n)$$

$$= \sum_{x_i} \sum_{x_j} (x_i - \mu_i)(x_j - \mu_j) f(x_i, x_j) = \sigma_{ij}$$

in the discrete case and similarly in the continuous case.

It is convenient to use the expectation operator on vectors as well as on scalars; thus we define the expectation of a random vector to be the vector of the expectations of its elements:

(3.34) $$\text{If } \mathbf{x} = \begin{pmatrix} x_1 \\ \cdot \\ \cdot \\ \cdot \\ x_n \end{pmatrix}, \text{ then } E\mathbf{x} = \begin{pmatrix} Ex_1 \\ \cdot \\ \cdot \\ \cdot \\ Ex_n \end{pmatrix}.$$

Further, a set of random variables will sometimes be arranged as a matrix—a "random matrix"—and the expectation of a random matrix is defined to be the matrix of the expectations of its elements:

(3.35) If

$$\mathbf{X} = \begin{pmatrix} x_{11} & \cdots & x_{1n} \\ \cdot & & \cdot \\ \cdot & & \cdot \\ \cdot & & \cdot \\ x_{m1} & \cdots & x_{mn} \end{pmatrix}, \text{ then } E\mathbf{X} = \begin{pmatrix} Ex_{11} & \cdots & Ex_{1n} \\ \cdot & & \cdot \\ \cdot & & \cdot \\ \cdot & & \cdot \\ Ex_{m1} & \cdots & Ex_{mn} \end{pmatrix}.$$

With these definitions we see that if $\mathbf{x}$ is a random vector, then $E\mathbf{x}$ is its mean vector and $E(\mathbf{x} - \boldsymbol{\mu})(\mathbf{x} - \boldsymbol{\mu})'$ is its covariance matrix:

(3.36) If $\mathbf{x}$ is a random vector with mean (vector) $\boldsymbol{\mu}$ and covariance matrix $\boldsymbol{\Sigma}$, then $\boldsymbol{\mu} = E\mathbf{x}$ and $\boldsymbol{\Sigma} = E(\mathbf{x} - \boldsymbol{\mu})(\mathbf{x} - \boldsymbol{\mu})'$.

This is so because

$$E\mathbf{x} = \begin{pmatrix} Ex_1 \\ \cdot \\ \cdot \\ \cdot \\ Ex_n \end{pmatrix} = \begin{pmatrix} \mu_1 \\ \cdot \\ \cdot \\ \cdot \\ \mu_n \end{pmatrix} = \boldsymbol{\mu}$$

and

$$\begin{aligned} &E(\mathbf{x} - \boldsymbol{\mu})(\mathbf{x} - \boldsymbol{\mu})' \\ &= E\left[\begin{pmatrix} x_1 - \mu_1 \\ \cdot \\ \cdot \\ \cdot \\ x_n - \mu_n \end{pmatrix} (x_1 - \mu_1 \quad \cdots \quad x_n - \mu_n)\right] \\ &= \begin{pmatrix} E(x_1 - \mu_1)^2 & \cdots & E(x_1 - \mu_1)(x_n - \mu_n) \\ \cdot & & \cdot \\ \cdot & & \cdot \\ \cdot & & \cdot \\ E(x_n - \mu_n)(x_1 - \mu_1) & \cdots & E(x_n - \mu_n)^2 \end{pmatrix} \\ &= \begin{pmatrix} \sigma_{11} & \cdots & \sigma_{1n} \\ \cdot & & \cdot \\ \cdot & & \cdot \\ \cdot & & \cdot \\ \sigma_{n1} & \cdots & \sigma_{nn} \end{pmatrix} = \boldsymbol{\Sigma}. \end{aligned}$$

The point of introducing the concept and notation of expectation is that E is a linear operator. First in algebraic notation we note

(3.37) If a is a constant, then $Ea = a$;

(3.38) If a is a constant and x is a random variable, then $Eax = aEx$;

(3.39) If x and y are random variables, then $E(x + y) = Ex + Ey$.

Statement (3.37) simply says that the mean of a constant is its sole value. Then $Eax = \Sigma_x axf(x) = a\, \Sigma_x xf(x) = aEx$ in the discrete case or $Eax = \int_{-\infty}^{\infty} axf(x)\, dx = a \int_{-\infty}^{\infty} xf(x)\, dx = aEx$ in the continuous case. Then

$$\begin{aligned} E(x+y) &= \sum_x \sum_y (x+y) f(x,y) = \sum_x \sum_y x f(x,y) + \sum_x \sum_y y f(x,y) \\ &= \sum_x x \sum_y f(x,y) + \sum_y y \sum_x f(x,y) = \sum_x x f(x) + \sum_y y f(y) \\ &= Ex + Ey \end{aligned}$$

in the discrete case and similarly in the continuous case. Combining and extending (3.37)–(3.39) we have for a linear function of random variables

(3.40) If $a_0, a_1, \ldots, a_n$ are constants and $x_1, \ldots, x_n$ are random variables, then $E(a_0 + a_1x_1 + \cdots + a_nx_n) = a_0 + a_1Ex_1 + \cdots + a_nEx_n$—briefly, $E \Sigma ax = \Sigma aEx$.

Thus the expectation of a linear function of random variables is the linear function of their expectations—whether or not the random variables are independent. For nonlinear functions this result does not hold, i.e., in general, $Ey(x) \neq y(Ex)$, as the following counterexample shows.

$$(3.41) \qquad f(x) = \begin{cases} \frac{1}{2} & \text{for} \quad x = 2 \\ \frac{1}{2} & \text{for} \quad x = 3; \end{cases}$$

$$Ex = 2(\tfrac{1}{2}) + 3(\tfrac{1}{2}) = \tfrac{5}{2},$$
$$Ex^2 = 4(\tfrac{1}{2}) + 9(\tfrac{1}{2}) = \tfrac{13}{2} \neq (\tfrac{5}{2})^2.$$

In (6.31) and (6.32) below we do present approximate formulas for the expectation of a nonlinear function.

It is clear that the variance can be expressed simply in terms of expectations:

$$\begin{aligned} (3.42) \qquad \text{var}(x) = E(x - Ex)^2 &= E[x^2 + (Ex)^2 - 2(Ex)x] \\ &= Ex^2 + E(Ex)^2 - E[2(Ex)x] \\ &= Ex^2 + (Ex)^2 - 2(Ex)(Ex) \\ &= Ex^2 - (Ex)^2, \end{aligned}$$

since Ex is a constant, and similarly for the covariance:

$$(3.43) \qquad \text{cov}(x, y) = E(x - Ex)(y - Ey) = Exy - ExEy.$$

Independence implies that joint moments factor; in particular

(3.44) If x and y are independent random variables, then $Exy = ExEy$,

for independence implies $\text{cov}(x, y) = Exy - ExEy = 0$.

Continuing we have

(3.45) If a is a constant, then $\text{var}(a) = 0$;

(3.46) If a is a constant and x is a random variable, then $\text{var}(ax) = a^2 \text{var}(x)$;

(3.47) If x and y are random variables, then $\text{var}(x + y) = \text{var}(x) + \text{var}(y) + 2\,\text{cov}(x, y)$ and $\text{var}(x - y) = \text{var}(x) + \text{var}(y) - 2\,\text{cov}(x, y)$;

(3.48) If $a_0, a_1, \ldots, a_n$ are constants and $x_1, \ldots, x_n$ are random variables, then

$$\text{var}(a_0 + a_1 x_1 + \cdots + a_n x_n) = \sum_{i=1}^{n} a_i^2 \text{var}(x_i) + \sum_{\substack{i=1 \\ i \neq j}}^{n} \sum_{j=1}^{n} a_i a_j \text{cov}(x_i, x_j).$$

Statement (3.45) simply repeats that the variance of a constant is zero. Then

$$\begin{aligned} \text{var}(ax) &= E(ax - Eax)^2 = E[a(x - Ex)]^2 = a^2 E(x - Ex)^2 \\ &= a^2 \text{var}(x) \end{aligned}$$

and

$$\begin{aligned} \text{var}(x + y) &= E[(x + y) - E(x + y)]^2 \\ &= E[(x - Ex) + (y - Ey)]^2 \\ &= E(x - Ex)^2 + E(y - Ey)^2 + 2E(x - Ex)(y - Ey) \\ &= \text{var}(x) + \text{var}(y) + 2\,\text{cov}(x, y) \end{aligned}$$

and similarly for the remaining results. Since independence implies that the covariance vanishes, it follows that

(3.49) If x and y are independent, then $\text{var}(x + y) = \text{var}(x) + \text{var}(y)$ and $\text{var}(x - y) = \text{var}(x) + \text{var}(y)$;

(3.50) If $a_0, a_1, \ldots, a_n$ are constants and $x_1, \ldots, x_n$ are mutually independent random variables, then $\text{var}(a_0 + a_1 x_1 + \cdots + a_n x_n) = a_1^2 \text{var}(x_1) + \cdots + a_n^2 \text{var}(x_n)$.

It will be convenient to have matrix formulations of some of these results; thus

(3.51) If $\mathbf{A}$ is a constant matrix, then $E\mathbf{A} = \mathbf{A}$,

(3.52) If $\mathbf{A}$ is a constant matrix and $\mathbf{X}$ is a random matrix, then $E\mathbf{AX} = \mathbf{A}E\mathbf{X}$,

(3.53) If $\mathbf{X}$ and $\mathbf{Y}$ are independent random matrices—i.e., if the set of random variables in $\mathbf{X}$ is independent of the set of random variables in $\mathbf{Y}$—then $E\mathbf{XY} = E\mathbf{X}E\mathbf{Y}$,

(3.54) Let $\mathbf{x}$ be a random vector with $E\mathbf{x} = \boldsymbol{\mu}$ and $E(\mathbf{x} - \boldsymbol{\mu})(\mathbf{x} - \boldsymbol{\mu})' = \boldsymbol{\Sigma}$ and let $\mathbf{y} = \mathbf{Ax}$, where $\mathbf{A}$ is a constant matrix; then $E\mathbf{y} = \mathbf{A}\boldsymbol{\mu}$ and $E(\mathbf{y} - E\mathbf{y})(\mathbf{y} - E\mathbf{y})' = \mathbf{A}\boldsymbol{\Sigma}\mathbf{A}'$.

The first three results are readily confirmed from the preceding algebraic expressions; and then $E\mathbf{Ax} = \mathbf{A}E\mathbf{x} = \mathbf{A}\boldsymbol{\mu}$ and $E(\mathbf{y} - E\mathbf{y})(\mathbf{y} - E\mathbf{y})' = E[\mathbf{A}(\mathbf{x} - E\mathbf{x})][\mathbf{A}(\mathbf{x} - E\mathbf{x})]' = \mathbf{A}E(\mathbf{x} - E\mathbf{x})(\mathbf{x} - E\mathbf{x})'\mathbf{A}' = \mathbf{A}\boldsymbol{\Sigma}\mathbf{A}'$.

Next we note

(3.55) If $\mathbf{x}$ is a random vector and if $\boldsymbol{\Sigma} = E(\mathbf{x} - \boldsymbol{\mu})(\mathbf{x} - \boldsymbol{\mu})'$ is its covariance matrix, then $\boldsymbol{\Sigma}$ is nonnegative definite; further $\boldsymbol{\Sigma}$ is positive definite if and only if the elements of $\mathbf{x}$ are not linearly dependent random variables.

First, $\boldsymbol{\Sigma}$ is symmetric, since $\sigma_{ij} = \sigma_{ji}$. Then, supposing $\mathbf{x}$ is an $n \times 1$ random vector, let $\mathbf{c} \neq \mathbf{0}$ be any $n \times 1$ constant vector. Then $\mathbf{c}'\boldsymbol{\Sigma}\mathbf{c} = \mathbf{c}'E(\mathbf{x} - \boldsymbol{\mu})(\mathbf{x} - \boldsymbol{\mu})'\mathbf{c} = E\mathbf{c}'(\mathbf{x} - \boldsymbol{\mu})(\mathbf{x} - \boldsymbol{\mu})'\mathbf{c} = E[\mathbf{c}'(\mathbf{x} - \boldsymbol{\mu})]^2$ since $\mathbf{c}'(\mathbf{x} - \boldsymbol{\mu})$ is a scalar. Now $E[\mathbf{c}'(\mathbf{x} - \boldsymbol{\mu})]^2$ is seen to be the variance of the random variable $\mathbf{c}'\mathbf{x}$ since $E(\mathbf{c}'\mathbf{x}) = \mathbf{c}'E\mathbf{x} = \mathbf{c}'\boldsymbol{\mu}$ and $\operatorname{var}(\mathbf{c}'\mathbf{x}) = E[\mathbf{c}'\mathbf{x} - E\mathbf{c}'\mathbf{x}]^2 = E[\mathbf{c}'(\mathbf{x} - \boldsymbol{\mu})]^2$. Since any variance must be nonnegative it follows that $\mathbf{c}'\boldsymbol{\Sigma}\mathbf{c} = E[\mathbf{c}'(\mathbf{x} - \boldsymbol{\mu})]^2 \geq 0$ for any $\mathbf{c} \neq \mathbf{0}$ so that $\boldsymbol{\Sigma}$ is nonnegative definite. Further, if $\boldsymbol{\Sigma}$ is not positive definite, then $\mathbf{c}'\boldsymbol{\Sigma}\mathbf{c} = 0$ for some $\mathbf{c} \neq \mathbf{0}$, say $\mathbf{c}^*$, so that $\operatorname{var}(\mathbf{c}^{*\prime}\mathbf{x}) = 0$, from which $\mathbf{c}^{*\prime}\mathbf{x}$ is a degenerate random variable, and the elements of $\mathbf{x}$ are linearly dependent random variables. Conversely, if the elements of $\mathbf{x}$ are linearly dependent, then $\mathbf{c}^{*\prime}\mathbf{x}$ is a degenerate random variable for some $\mathbf{c}^* \neq \mathbf{0}$ so that $\mathbf{c}^{*\prime}\boldsymbol{\Sigma}\mathbf{c}^* = \operatorname{var}(\mathbf{c}^{*\prime}\mathbf{x}) = 0$, whence $\boldsymbol{\Sigma}$ is not positive definite.

We note that the conditional expectation of a random vector $\mathbf{x}_1$ given the random vector $\mathbf{x}_2$, written $E(\mathbf{x}_1 \mid \mathbf{x}_2)$, is simply the expectation of the conditional distribution of $\mathbf{x}_1$ given $\mathbf{x}_2$. It is readily confirmed that a marginal expectation may be written as a weighted average of conditional expectations, the weights being the masses or densities of the respective conditions: $E\mathbf{x}_1 = \Sigma_{x_2} E(\mathbf{x}_1 \mid \mathbf{x}_2)f(\mathbf{x}_2)$ for

$$\begin{aligned} E\mathbf{x}_1 &= \sum_{\mathbf{x}_1} \mathbf{x}_1 f(\mathbf{x}_1) = \sum_{\mathbf{x}_1} \mathbf{x}_1 \sum_{\mathbf{x}_2} f(\mathbf{x}_1, \mathbf{x}_2) = \sum_{\mathbf{x}_2}\sum_{\mathbf{x}_1} \mathbf{x}_1 f(\mathbf{x}_1, \mathbf{x}_2) \\ &= \sum_{\mathbf{x}_2}\sum_{\mathbf{x}_1} \mathbf{x}_1 f(\mathbf{x}_1 \mid \mathbf{x}_2) f(\mathbf{x}_2) = \sum_{\mathbf{x}_2} E(\mathbf{x}_1 \mid \mathbf{x}_2) f(\mathbf{x}_2) = EE(\mathbf{x}_1 \mid \mathbf{x}_2) \end{aligned}$$

and similarly in the continuous case. Of course if $\mathbf{x}_1$ and $\mathbf{x}_2$ are independent, the conditional expectation of $\mathbf{x}_1$ is the same for all values of $\mathbf{x}_2$ and identical with its marginal expectation.

Finally, a definition:

(3.56) If $\mathbf{x}$ is a random vector with covariance matrix $\boldsymbol{\Sigma}$, then the scalar $|\boldsymbol{\Sigma}|$ is called the generalized variance of $\mathbf{x}$.

4. SAMPLING THEORY

Random Sampling

Suppose that x is a random variable with probability mass or density distribution $f(x)$—i.e., the value taken on by x is the outcome of an experiment and the probabilities of various outcomes are defined by the function $f(x)$. Suppose that we repeat the experiment T times, each time independently of the others, recording the outcomes as $x_1, \ldots, x_T$. Then we say that we have drawn a random sample of size T from the population $f(x)$. Thus a random sample of size T consists of observations on T mutually independent and identically distributed random variables, x_t $(t = 1, \ldots, T)$. The two senses of the adjective random should be distinguished: A random variable is simply a variable whose values are given according to a probability distribution, whereas a random sample is a set of T independent drawings from a probability distribution.

Of course we may think of a sample of size T as a $T \times 1$ random vector; the value of the vector is determined by a (compound) experiment. This random vector has a probability mass or density function which we may write as $f(x_1, \ldots, x_T)$. The crucial property of a random sample is that the elements $x_1, \ldots, x_T$ are mutually independent as well as identically distributed so that the joint mass or density is in fact equal to the product of their common individual masses or densities:

$$f(x_1, \ldots, x_T) = f(x_1) \cdots f(x_T) = \prod_{t=1}^{T} f(x_t).$$

The obvious purpose of sampling is to learn something about the population distribution; i.e., to engage in statistical inference. Before considering statistical inference, however, it is necessary to consider statistical deduction. We first investigate what the population distribution implies about the random sample observations that are drawn from it; in particular what it implies about the probability distributions of certain functions of random sample observations. This will be our concern in the present section and in the two succeeding ones; after which we consider statistical inference proper. In Section 8 we consider nonrandom sampling, where the joint mass or density of the observations is not expressible as the product of common individual masses or densities.

We have spoken of drawing the sample from the population; we may also describe this by saying that the population generates the sample. Another verbalization refers to the population as the parent and to the sample observations as its offspring. In statistical deduction we deduce properties of all of the offspring from those of the parent; in statistical inference we attempt to infer properties of the parent from those of some of its offspring.

Likelihood Function

Suppose that the random variable x has the probability mass or density distribution $f(x)$. Then the probability mass or density of the random sample $x_1, \ldots, x_T$—the joint mass or density $f(x_1, \ldots, x_T)$—is simply the product of the individual masses or densities: $f(x_1, \ldots, x_T) = f(x_1) \cdots f(x_T)$. We call this joint mass or density the likelihood of the sample and denote it by $\mathscr{L}$; thus

(4.1) Let x be a random variable with probability mass or density distribution $f(x)$. Then the likelihood of the random sample $x_1, \ldots, x_T$ is the product of the individual masses or densities:

$$\mathscr{L}(x_1, \ldots, x_T) = f(x_1, \ldots, x_T) = f(x_1) \cdots f(x_T) = \prod_{t=1}^{T} f(x_t).$$

For example, suppose that the random variable x has the probability mass distribution

$$(4.2) \qquad f(x) = \begin{cases} \frac{2}{3} & \text{for} \quad x = 0 \\ \frac{1}{3} & \text{for} \quad x = 1 \\ 0 & \text{otherwise.} \end{cases}$$

Then the likelihood of the random sample (1, 0, 1) is

$$\mathscr{L}(1, 0, 1) = f(1)f(0)f(1) = (\tfrac{1}{3})(\tfrac{2}{3})(\tfrac{1}{3}) = \tfrac{2}{27}.$$

Now suppose that the probability mass or density distribution of x is given as a function of the parameters $\theta_1, \ldots, \theta_K$; then we may write the probability mass or density of x as $f(x \mid \theta_1, \ldots, \theta_K)$. The probability mass or density of the random sample $x_1, \ldots, x_T$ will again be the product of the individual masses or densities:

$$\begin{aligned} \mathscr{L}(x_1, \ldots, x_T \mid \theta_1, \ldots, \theta_K) &= f(x_1, \ldots, x_T \mid \theta_1, \ldots, \theta_K) \\ &= f(x_1 \mid \theta_1, \ldots, \theta_K) \cdots f(x_T \mid \theta_1, \ldots, \theta_K) \\ &= \prod_{t=1}^{T} f(x_t \mid \theta_1, \ldots, \theta_K). \end{aligned}$$

The likelihood $\mathscr{L}(x_1, \ldots, x_T \mid \theta_1, \ldots, \theta_T)$ *considered as a function of the parameters* for given $x_1, \ldots, x_T$ is called the likelihood function (of the sample); thus

(4.3) Let x be a random variable with probability mass or density distribution $f(x \mid \theta_1, \ldots, \theta_K)$ where $\theta_1, \ldots, \theta_K$ are parameters. Then the likelihood function of the random sample $x_1, \ldots, x_T$

is the product of the individual masses or densities considered as functions of the parameters:

$$\begin{aligned}\mathscr{L}(x_1, \ldots, x_T \mid \theta_1, \ldots, \theta_K) &= f(x_1, \ldots, x_T \mid \theta_1, \ldots, \theta_K) \\ &= f(x_1 \mid \theta_1, \ldots, \theta_K) \cdots f(x_T \mid \theta_1, \ldots, \theta_K) \\ &= \prod_{t=1}^{T} f(x_t \mid \theta_1, \ldots, \theta_K).\end{aligned}$$

For example, suppose that the random variable x has the $B(\mu)$ distribution; i.e., the probability mass of x is the following function of the parameter μ;

$$(4.4) \qquad f(x \mid \mu) = \begin{cases} 1 - \mu & \text{for } \; x = 0 \\ \mu & \text{for } \; x = 1 \\ 0 & \text{otherwise.} \end{cases}$$

Then the likelihood function of the random sample (0, 1, 0) is

$$\begin{aligned}\mathscr{L}(0, 1, 0 \mid \mu) &= f(0 \mid \mu)f(1 \mid \mu)f(0 \mid \mu) = (1 - \mu)\mu(1 - \mu) \\ &= \mu(1 - \mu)^2.\end{aligned}$$

Note that a likelihood function is not a probability distribution; it is a function of the parameters, not of the random variables.

It is easy to write down the likelihood function for any random sample from a $B(\mu)$ population. The likelihood of a random sample of size T from such a population, which contains R 1's and hence $T - R$ 0's in a specified order, is obviously $\mu^R(1 - \mu)^{T-R}$. Given T and R this is a function of μ.

Sampling Distributions

Suppose that the random variable x has the probability mass or density distribution $f(x)$ and consider drawing random samples of size T from this population. Let $g(x_1, \ldots, x_T)$ denote a function of the sample observations; we call such a function a sample statistic. Examples of sample statistics are the sample sum $\Sigma_{t=1}^{T} x_t$, the sample mean $\bar{x} = \Sigma_{t=1}^{T} x_t/T$, the sample variance $s^2 = \Sigma_{t=1}^{T} (x_t - \bar{x})^2/T$, and the sample maximum $u = \max\{x_1, \ldots, x_T\}$. Being a function of the random variables that constitute the sample, a sample statistic is a random variable, and its probability distribution may be derived from their probability distribution. More specifically, we may consider all the distinct random samples of a given size T that can be drawn from the population and for each one compute the value of the sample statistic. Then the probability mass or density of each value of the sample statistic is obtained by summing the likelihoods of all of the distinct samples in which the sample statistic takes on that value. (This is simply an application of the rule for computing the probability of an event as the sum of the probabilities of its mutually exclusive and exhaustive components.)

We call the probability distribution of a sample statistic the sampling distribution of the statistic; e.g., we speak of the sampling distribution of the sample mean and the sampling distribution of the sample variance. We proceed to illustrate, quite explicitly, how the sampling distributions of several sample statistics may be derived from a population distribution.

Let x be a random variable that is distributed $B(\frac{1}{3})$—this probability mass is given in (4.2)—and consider random samples of size 3. There are just 8 distinct samples of size 3, and the following tabulation of their likelihoods is readily confirmed:

(4.5) ***Likelihoods: sample size 3; $B(\frac{1}{3})$ population***

Sample (x_1, x_2, x_3)	Likelihood $\mathscr{L}(x_1, x_2, x_3)$
0,0,0	$\frac{8}{27}$
0,1,0	$\frac{4}{27}$
0,1,1	$\frac{2}{27}$
0,0,1	$\frac{4}{27}$
1,0,0	$\frac{4}{27}$
1,1,0	$\frac{2}{27}$
1,1,1	$\frac{1}{27}$
1,0,1	$\frac{2}{27}$

We consider three sample statistics: the sample mean $\bar{x}$, the sample variance s^2, and the sample maximum u. We may compute the value of these statistics in each of the 8 distinct samples. Thus consider the sample (1, 0, 1); the frequency distribution of the variable x in this sample is

$$f_*(x) = \begin{cases} \frac{1}{3} & \text{for } x = 0 \\ \frac{2}{3} & \text{for } x = 1 \\ 0 & \text{otherwise,} \end{cases}$$

where we have used $f_*(x)$ to distinguish the frequency distribution of a set of sample observations from the population probability distribution of the random variable x, $f(x)$. In this sample we have the mean $\bar{x} = \Sigma_x x f_*(x) = 0(\frac{1}{3}) + 1(\frac{2}{3}) = \frac{2}{3}$, the variance $s^2 = \Sigma_x x^2 f_*(x) - \bar{x}^2 = 0^2(\frac{1}{3}) + 1^2(\frac{2}{3}) - (\frac{2}{3})^2 = \frac{2}{9}$, and the maximum $u = \max\{1, 0, 1\} = 1$. The remainder of the following tabulation—in which the likelihoods of (4.5) have been repeated—is readily confirmed.

(4.6) ***Likelihoods and sample statistics: sample size 3; $B(\frac{1}{3})$ population***

Sample	Likelihood	$\bar{x}$	s^2	u
0,0,0	$\frac{8}{27}$	0	0	0
0,1,0	$\frac{4}{27}$	$\frac{1}{3}$	$\frac{2}{9}$	1
0,1,1	$\frac{2}{27}$	$\frac{2}{3}$	$\frac{2}{9}$	1
0,0,1	$\frac{4}{27}$	$\frac{1}{3}$	$\frac{2}{9}$	1
1,0,0	$\frac{4}{27}$	$\frac{1}{3}$	$\frac{2}{9}$	1
1,1,0	$\frac{2}{27}$	$\frac{2}{3}$	$\frac{2}{9}$	1
1,1,1	$\frac{1}{27}$	1	0	1
1,0,1	$\frac{2}{27}$	$\frac{2}{3}$	$\frac{2}{9}$	1

Now we may derive the sampling distribution of each of these sample statistics. For example, consider the sample mean $\bar{x}$; it takes on the values 0, $\frac{1}{3}$, $\frac{2}{3}$, and 1. Its value is 0 only in a sample that has $(x_1, x_2, x_3) = (0, 0, 0)$, and the likelihood of such a sample is $\frac{8}{27}$; hence $f(\bar{x} = 0) = \frac{8}{27}$. Its value is $\frac{1}{3}$ in samples which have $(x_1, x_2, x_3) = (0, 1, 0)$ or $(1, 0, 0)$ or $(0, 0, 1)$ and the likelihood of such samples is $\frac{4}{27} + \frac{4}{27} + \frac{4}{27} = \frac{12}{27}$; hence $f(\bar{x} = \frac{1}{3}) = \frac{12}{27}$. Similarly we find $f(\bar{x} = \frac{2}{3}) = \frac{6}{27}$ and $f(\bar{x} = 1) = \frac{1}{27}$ so that the sampling distribution of $\bar{x}$ is:

(4.7) ***Sampling distribution of $\bar{x}$: sample size 3; $B(\frac{1}{3})$ population***

$\bar{x}$	$f(\bar{x})$
0	$\frac{8}{27}$
$\frac{1}{3}$	$\frac{12}{27}$
$\frac{2}{3}$	$\frac{6}{27}$
1	$\frac{1}{27}$

In similar fashion we derive the sampling distribution of s^2:

(4.8) ***Sampling distribution of s^2: sample size 3; $B(\frac{1}{3})$ population***

s^2	$f(s^2)$
0	$\frac{1}{3}$
$\frac{2}{9}$	$\frac{2}{3}$

and the sampling distribution of u:

(4.9) ***Sampling distribution of u: sample size 3; $B(\frac{1}{3})$ population***

u	$f(u)$
0	$\frac{8}{27}$
1	$\frac{19}{27}$

We may also derive the joint sampling distribution of two or more sample statistics. Thus the following is readily confirmed:

(4.10) ***Joint sampling distribution of $\bar{x}$ and s^2: sample size 3; $B(\frac{1}{3})$ population***

$\bar{x}$ \ s^2	0	$\frac{2}{9}$
0	$\frac{8}{27}$	0
$\frac{1}{3}$	0	$\frac{12}{27}$
$\frac{2}{3}$	0	$\frac{6}{27}$
1	$\frac{1}{27}$	0

If we considered random samples of size 2 rather than 3 from our $B(\frac{1}{3})$ population we could readily derive the following tabulations:

(4.11) ***Likelihoods and sample statistics: sample size 2; $B(\frac{1}{3})$ population***

Sample	Likelihood	$\bar{x}$	s^2	u
0,0	$\frac{4}{9}$	0	0	0
0,1	$\frac{2}{9}$	$\frac{1}{2}$	$\frac{1}{4}$	1
1,0	$\frac{2}{9}$	$\frac{1}{2}$	$\frac{1}{4}$	1
1,1	$\frac{1}{9}$	1	0	1

(4.12) ***Sampling distributions of $\bar{x}$, s^2, and u: sample size 2; $B(\frac{1}{3})$ population***

$\bar{x}$	$f(\bar{x})$	s^2	$f(s^2)$	u	$f(u)$
0	$\frac{4}{9}$	0	$\frac{5}{9}$	0	$\frac{4}{9}$
$\frac{1}{2}$	$\frac{4}{9}$	$\frac{1}{4}$	$\frac{4}{9}$	1	$\frac{5}{9}$
1	$\frac{1}{9}$				

It will be noted that the sampling distribution of a sample statistic depends on the size of sample being considered. Of course it also depends on the population distribution. For example, suppose that x has the $B(\frac{2}{3})$ distribution; i.e., suppose that the probability mass distribution of x is

$$(4.13) \qquad f(x) = \begin{cases} \frac{1}{3} & \text{for } x = 0 \\ \frac{2}{3} & \text{for } x = 1 \\ 0 & \text{otherwise.} \end{cases}$$

Then the following tabulations are readily confirmed:

(4.14) ***Likelihoods and sample statistics: sample size 3, $B(\frac{2}{3})$ population***

Sample	Likelihood	$\bar{x}$	s^2	u
0,0,0	$\frac{1}{27}$	0	0	0
0,1,0	$\frac{2}{27}$	$\frac{1}{3}$	$\frac{2}{9}$	1
0,1,1	$\frac{4}{27}$	$\frac{2}{3}$	$\frac{2}{9}$	1
0,0,1	$\frac{2}{27}$	$\frac{1}{3}$	$\frac{2}{9}$	1
1,0,0	$\frac{2}{27}$	$\frac{1}{3}$	$\frac{2}{9}$	1
1,1,0	$\frac{4}{27}$	$\frac{2}{3}$	$\frac{2}{9}$	1
1,1,1	$\frac{8}{27}$	1	0	1
1,0,1	$\frac{4}{27}$	$\frac{2}{3}$	$\frac{2}{9}$	1

(4.15) ***Sampling distributions of $\bar{x}$, s^2, and u: sample size 3; $B(\frac{2}{3})$ population***

$\bar{x}$	$f(\bar{x})$
0	$\frac{1}{27}$
$\frac{1}{3}$	$\frac{6}{27}$
$\frac{2}{3}$	$\frac{12}{27}$
1	$\frac{8}{27}$

s^2	$f(s^2)$
0	$\frac{1}{3}$
$\frac{2}{9}$	$\frac{2}{3}$

u	$f(u)$
0	$\frac{1}{27}$
1	$\frac{26}{27}$

Comparing (4.14) with (4.6) we see that different populations can generate the same sample but that they may do so with different probabilities. Consequently, as a comparison of (4.15) with (4.7)–(4.9) indicates, different populations can produce the same value of a sample statistic, but they may do so with different probabilities.

These elementary examples should serve to illustrate how the sampling distribution of any sample statistic may be derived for random sampling with any given sample size from any given population. Of course the derivation will typically be analytical rather than numerical—certainly if the random variable is continuous rather than discrete as in our examples. Indeed it is easy to derive a general result for the sampling distribution of the sample mean for any sample size T from any $B(\mu)$ population. We have seen that from such a population, the likelihood of a random sample which contains R 1's and $T - R$ 0's in a specified order is $\mu^R(1 - \mu)^{T-R}$. In samples of size T from a Bernoulli population the sample mean $\bar{x}$ can take on only the values $0, 1/T, 2/T, \ldots, 1$. The probability $f(R/T)$ that $\bar{x}$ takes on the value R/T is obtained by summing the likelihood of all samples which have $\bar{x} = R/T$; i.e., of all samples which have $\Sigma\, x = T\bar{x} = R$. As it happens, all such samples have the same likelihood, namely $\mu^R(1 - \mu)^{T-R}$, so that the sum may be evaluated by multiplying that likelihood by the number of distinct samples having $\Sigma\, x = R$. The number of such samples is clearly the number of permutations of R 1's and $T - R$ 0's, which is $T!/[R!\,(T - R)!]$. Thus we have for the sampling distribution of the sample mean for sample size T from a $B(\mu)$ population:

$$(4.16) \qquad f(\bar{x}) = \begin{cases} \dfrac{T!}{R!(T - R!)}\,\mu^R(1 - \mu)^{T-R} & \text{for } \bar{x} = R/T, \\ & (R = 0, 1, \ldots, T), \\ 0 & \text{otherwise,} \end{cases}$$

a result which may be checked out in our examples.

Parameters of Sampling Distributions

This discussion has suggested how the sampling distribution of a sample statistic can be deduced from the population distribution when the sampling is random. The sampling distribution is seen to be related to the population distribution—to its form and its parameters—and to the sample size. It is useful to recognize that the relation of parameters of the sampling distribution of a sample statistic to parameters of the population distribution—and to the sample size—may not depend on the form of the population distribution. Such relations may often be derived in a straightforward manner by use of the calculus of expectations.

We consider random samples of size T—$x_1, \ldots, x_T$—from any population where the random variable x has mean μ and variance σ^2. First note that

$$(4.17) \qquad Ex_t = \mu \qquad (t = 1, \ldots, T)$$

$$(4.18) \qquad E(x_t - \mu)(x_s - \mu) = \begin{cases} \sigma^2 & \text{if } t = s \\ 0 & \text{if } t \neq s \end{cases} \qquad (t, s = 1, \ldots, T)$$

since each x_t has mean μ and variance σ^2 and since random sampling implies that the sample observations are mutually independent random variables so that all their covariances are zero.

Now consider the sample mean $\bar{x} = T^{-1}\,\Sigma_{t=1}^T\, x_t$. We find for the mean of the sampling distribution of $\bar{x}$

$$(4.19) \qquad E\bar{x} = ET^{-1}\sum_{t=1}^{T} x_t = T^{-1}\sum_{t=1}^{T} Ex_t = T^{-1}\sum_{t=1}^{T} \mu = T^{-1}T\mu = \mu,$$

and for the variance of this sampling distribution

$$(4.20)\qquad E(\bar{x} - E\bar{x})^2 = E(\bar{x} - \mu)^2 = E\left[T^{-1}\sum_{t=1}^{T} x_t - \mu\right]^2$$

$$= T^{-2}E\left[\sum_{t=1}^{T}(x_t - \mu)\right]^2$$

$$= T^{-2}E\left[\sum_{t=1}^{T}(x_t - \mu)^2 + \sum_{\substack{t=1\\t\neq s}}^{T}\sum_{s=1}^{T}(x_t - \mu)(x_s - \mu)\right]$$

$$= T^{-2}\left[\sum_{t=1}^{T} E(x_t - \mu)^2 + \sum_{\substack{t=1\\t\neq s}}^{T}\sum_{s=1}^{T} E(x_t - \mu)(x_s - \mu)\right]$$

$$= T^{-2}\left[\sum_{t=1}^{T}\sigma^2 + \sum_{\substack{t=1\\t\neq s}}^{T}\sum_{s=1}^{T} 0\right] = T^{-2}T\sigma^2$$

$$= T^{-1}\sigma^2.$$

Thus we have the powerful general result

(4.21) For random sampling with sample size T from any population with $Ex = \mu$ and $E(x - \mu)^2 = \sigma^2$ the sample mean is distributed with mean $E\bar{x} = \mu$ and variance $E(\bar{x} - \mu)^2 = \sigma^2/T$.

Then let us add the specification that the fourth central moment of the population distribution is $\mu_4 = E(x - \mu)^4$ so that in addition to (4.17) and (4.18) we have

$$(4.22)\qquad E(x_t - \mu)(x_s - \mu)(x_r - \mu)(x_q - \mu)$$

$$= \begin{cases} \mu_4 & \text{if } t = s = r = q \\ \sigma^4 & \text{if 2 pairs of subscripts, but not all 4 subscripts, are equal} \\ 0 & \text{otherwise} \end{cases}$$

$$(t, s, r, q = 1, \ldots, T).$$

If $t = s = r = q$, then the expression on the left is $E(x_t - \mu)^4 = \mu_4$ since each x_t has the same fourth central moment; if two pairs of subscripts—but not all four subscripts—are equal, the expression on the left is of the form $E(x_t - \mu)^2(x_s - \mu)^2 = E(x_t - \mu)^2E(x_s - \mu)^2 = (\sigma^2)^2 = \sigma^4$ since x_t and x_s are independent if $t \neq s$ and since each x_t has the same variance; otherwise the expression on the left is of the form

$$E(x_t - \mu)E(x_s - \mu)(x_r - \mu)(x_q - \mu) = 0$$

since x_t is independent of x_s, x_r, and x_q if $t \neq s$, $t \neq r$, and $t \neq q$ and since each $E(x_t - \mu) = 0$.

Now consider the sample variance $s^2 = T^{-1} \sum_{t=1}^{T} (x_t - \bar{x})^2$. Since

$$(4.23) \qquad \sum_{t=1}^{T} (x_t - \bar{x})^2 = \sum_{t=1}^{T} [(x_t - \mu) - (\bar{x} - \mu)]^2$$

$$= \sum_{t=1}^{T} (x_t - \mu)^2 + \sum_{t=1}^{T} (\bar{x} - \mu)^2 - 2(\bar{x} - \mu) \sum_{t=1}^{T} (x_t - \mu)$$

$$= \sum_{t=1}^{T} (x_t - \mu)^2 + T(\bar{x} - \mu)^2 - 2(\bar{x} - \mu)T(\bar{x} - \mu)$$

$$= \sum_{t=1}^{T} (x_t - \mu)^2 - T(\bar{x} - \mu)^2,$$

we may write the sample variance as

$$(4.24) \qquad s^2 = T^{-1} \sum_{t=1}^{T} (x_t - \mu)^2 - (\bar{x} - \mu)^2.$$

Let us then treat s^2 as a linear function of

$$(4.25a) \qquad y = \sum_{t=1}^{T} (x_t - \mu)^2$$

and

$$(4.25b) \qquad z = (\bar{x} - \mu)^2 = \left[T^{-1} \sum_{t=1}^{T} (x_t - \mu) \right]^2.$$

Since $s^2 = T^{-1}y - z$ we have, by (3.40),

$$(4.26) \qquad Es^2 = T^{-1}Ey - Ez$$

and by (3.48),

$$(4.27) \qquad E(s^2 - Es^2)^2 = \mathrm{var}\,(s^2)$$

$$= T^{-2} \mathrm{var}\,(y) + \mathrm{var}\,(z) - 2T^{-1} \mathrm{cov}\,(y, z).$$

Now $Ey = \sum_{t=1}^{T} E(x_t - \mu)^2 = T\sigma^2$ by (4.18) and $Ez = E(\bar{x} - \mu)^2 = T^{-1}\sigma^2$ by (4.20); inserting these in (4.26) gives

$$(4.28) \qquad Es^2 = T^{-1}T\sigma^2 - T^{-1}\sigma^2 = T^{-1}(T - 1)\sigma^2$$

for the mean of the sampling distribution of s^2. The derivation of the variance of this distribution is more tedious. First

$$(4.29) \qquad \mathrm{var}\,(y) = Ey^2 - (Ey)^2 = E\left[\sum_{t=1}^{T} (x_t - \mu)^2 \right]^2 - (T\sigma^2)^2$$

$$= \sum_{t=1}^{T} E(x_t - \mu)^4 + \sum_{\substack{t=1 \\ t \neq s}}^{T} \sum_{s=1}^{T} E(x_t - \mu)^2(x_s - \mu)^2 - T^2\sigma^4$$

$$= T\mu_4 + T(T - 1)\sigma^2\sigma^2 - T^2\sigma^4 = T(\mu_4 - \sigma^4).$$

Next

(4.30)
$$\begin{aligned}\operatorname{var}(z) = Ez^2 - (Ez)^2 &= E\left[T^{-1}\sum_{t=1}^{T}(x_t - \mu)\right]^4 - (T^{-1}\sigma^2)^2 \\ &= T^{-4}E\left[\sum_{t=1}^{T}(x_t - \mu)\right]^4 - T^{-2}\sigma^4 \\ &= T^{-4}\sum_{t=1}^{T}\sum_{s=1}^{T}\sum_{r=1}^{T}\sum_{q=1}^{T}E(x_t - \mu)(x_s - \mu)(x_r - \mu)(x_q - \mu) \\ &\quad - T^{-2}\sigma^4 \\ &= T^{-4}[T\mu_4 + 3T(T-1)\sigma^4] - T^{-2}\sigma^4 \\ &= T^{-3}(\mu_4 - 3\sigma^4) + 2T^{-2}\sigma^4\end{aligned}$$

using (4.22) and the fact that in the quadruple sum all four subscripts are equal T times and two pairs of subscripts—but not all four—are equal $3T(T-1)$ times. Next

(4.31)
$$\begin{aligned}\operatorname{cov}(z, y) &= Ezy - EzEy \\ &= E\left[T^{-1}\sum_{t=1}^{T}(x_t - \mu)\right]^2\sum_{t=1}^{T}(x_t - \mu)^2 - (T^{-1}\sigma^2)(T\sigma^2) \\ &= T^{-2}E\left[\sum_{t=1}^{T}(x_t - \mu)\right]^2\sum_{t=1}^{T}(x_t - \mu)^2 - \sigma^4 \\ &= T^{-2}E\left[\sum_{t=1}^{T}(x_t - \mu)^2 + \sum_{\substack{s=1\\ s\neq r}}^{T}\sum_{r=1}^{T}(x_s - \mu)(x_r - \mu)\right]\sum_{t=1}^{T}(x_t - \mu)^2 - \sigma^4 \\ &= T^{-2}E\left[\sum_{t=1}^{T}(x_t - \mu)^2\right]^2 + T^{-2}\sum_{t=1}^{T}\sum_{\substack{s=1\\ s\neq r}}^{T}\sum_{r=1}^{T}E(x_r - \mu)(x_s - \mu)(x_t - \mu)^2 \\ &\quad - \sigma^4 \\ &= T^{-2}[T\mu_4 + T(T-1)\sigma^4] - \sigma^4 = T^{-1}(\mu_4 - \sigma^4)\end{aligned}$$

using (4.29), (4.22), and the fact that in the triple sum one subscript is always different from the others. Finally, inserting (4.29)–(4.31) into (4.27) we have for the variance of the sample variance

(4.32)
$$\begin{aligned}E(s^2 - Es^2)^2 &= T^{-2}T(\mu_4 - \sigma^4) + T^{-3}(\mu_4 - 3\sigma^4) \\ &\quad + 2T^{-2}\sigma^4 - 2T^{-1}T^{-1}(\mu_4 - \sigma^4) \\ &= T^{-1}(\mu_4 - \sigma^4) - 2T^{-2}(\mu_4 - 2\sigma^4) \\ &\quad + T^{-3}(\mu_4 - 3\sigma^4).\end{aligned}$$

Thus we have the powerful general result

(4.33) For random sampling with sample size T from any population with $Ex = \mu$, $E(x - \mu)^2 = \sigma^2$, and $E(x - \mu)^4 = \mu_4$, the sample variance is distributed with mean $Es^2 = T^{-1}(T - 1)\sigma^2$ and variance

$$E(s^2 - Es^2)^2 = T^{-1}(\mu_4 - \sigma^4) - 2T^{-2}(\mu_4 - 2\sigma^4) + T^{-3}(\mu_4 - 3\sigma^4).$$

It is to be emphasized that these results connecting the mean and variance of the sample mean and the sample variance with the mean, variance, and fourth central moment of the population hold regardless of the specific structure of the population distribution. We may of course check them out in our previous numerical examples. In so doing we recall that if x is distributed $B(\mu)$, then $Ex = \mu$, $E(x - \mu)^2 = \mu(1 - \mu)$, and $E(x - \mu)^4 = \mu(1 - \mu)[\mu^3 + (1 - \mu)^3]$. Then, e.g., consider the distribution of $\bar{x}$ for $T = 3$ from a $B(\frac{1}{3})$ population, given in (4.7). We compute the mean of this sampling distribution to be

$$E\bar{x} = \sum_x \bar{x}f(\bar{x}) = 0\left(\frac{8}{27}\right) + \frac{1}{3}\left(\frac{12}{27}\right) + \frac{2}{3}\left(\frac{6}{27}\right) + 1\left(\frac{1}{27}\right)$$
$$= \frac{27}{3(27)} = \frac{1}{3}$$

and the variance to be

$$E(\bar{x} - E\bar{x})^2 = \sum_x \bar{x}^2 f(\bar{x}) - (E\bar{x})^2 = (0)^2\left(\frac{8}{27}\right) + \left(\frac{1}{3}\right)^2\left(\frac{12}{27}\right)$$
$$+ \left(\frac{2}{3}\right)^2\left(\frac{6}{27}\right) + (1)^2\left(\frac{1}{27}\right) - \left(\frac{1}{3}\right)^2 = \frac{45}{(9)(27)}$$
$$- \frac{27}{(9)(27)} = \frac{2}{27};$$

which checks out (4.21) since $\frac{1}{3} = \mu$ and $\frac{2}{27} = \frac{2}{9}/3 = \sigma^2/T$.

For future reference we note that if we define the sample statistic $s_*^2 = \Sigma_{t=1}^T(x_t - \mu)^2/T$, then $s_*^2 = T^{-1}y$ [where y was defined in (4.25a)], so that $Es_*^2 = T^{-1}Ey = T^{-1}T\sigma^2 = \sigma^2$ and $E(s_*^2 - \sigma^2)^2 = \text{var}(s_*^2) = T^{-2}\,\text{var}(y) = T^{-2}T(\mu_4 - \sigma^4) = T^{-1}(\mu_4 - \sigma^4)$, by (4.29).

Multivariate Sampling

Although our discussion has been confined to sampling from a univariate population, the extensions to the multivariate case are straightforward.

Consider then the random vector $\mathbf{x} = \begin{pmatrix} x_1 \\ \cdot \\ \cdot \\ \cdot \\ x_K \end{pmatrix}$ with probability mass or density function $f(\mathbf{x})$. A random sample of size T from this population will consist of T joint observations, $\mathbf{x}_t = \begin{pmatrix} x_{t1} \\ \cdot \\ \cdot \\ \cdot \\ x_{tK} \end{pmatrix}$ $(t = 1, \ldots, T)$; the likelihood of the random sample will be the product of the individual masses or densities, $\mathscr{L}(\mathbf{x}_1, \ldots, \mathbf{x}_T) = \prod_{t=1}^{T} f(\mathbf{x}_t)$; and the likelihood function of a random sample will be the likelihood considered as a function of the population parameters. Sample statistics—functions of the sample observations—may be defined and their sampling distributions deduced from the population distribution. The distribution of a sample statistic will be determined by the form and parameters of the population distribution and by the sample size. We may be able to find simple relations between parameters of a sampling distribution and parameters of the population distribution by application of the calculus of expectations.

Here we establish a few such relations. Let the $K \times 1$ random vector $\mathbf{x}$ have mean vector $\boldsymbol{\mu}$ and covariance matrix $\boldsymbol{\Sigma}$. Then for random samples of size T—$\mathbf{x}_1, \ldots, \mathbf{x}_T$—we have

$$(4.34) \qquad E\mathbf{x}_t = \boldsymbol{\mu} \qquad (t = 1, \ldots, T)$$

$$(4.35) \qquad E(\mathbf{x}_t - \boldsymbol{\mu})(\mathbf{x}_s - \boldsymbol{\mu})' = \begin{cases} \boldsymbol{\Sigma} & \text{if } t = s \\ \mathbf{0} & \text{if } t \neq s \end{cases} \qquad (t, s = 1, \ldots, T).$$

Now the sample mean vector is defined by

$$(4.36) \qquad \bar{\mathbf{x}} = \begin{pmatrix} \bar{x}_1 \\ \cdot \\ \cdot \\ \cdot \\ \bar{x}_K \end{pmatrix} = T^{-1} \sum_{t=1}^{T} \mathbf{x}_t$$

where $\bar{x}_i = T^{-1} \sum_{t=1}^{T} x_{ti}$ is the sample mean of the variable x_i; and the sample covariance matrix is defined by

$$(4.37) \qquad \mathbf{S} = \begin{pmatrix} s_{11} & \cdots & s_{1K} \\ \cdot & & \cdot \\ \cdot & & \cdot \\ \cdot & & \cdot \\ s_{K1} & \cdots & s_{KK} \end{pmatrix} = T^{-1} \sum_{t=1}^{T} (\mathbf{x}_t - \bar{\mathbf{x}})(\mathbf{x}_t - \bar{\mathbf{x}})'.$$

where $s_{ij} = T^{-1} \sum_{t=1}^{T}(x_{ti} - \bar{x}_i)(x_{tj} - \bar{x}_j)$ is the sample covariance of the variables x_i and x_j, or sample variance for $i = j$. Then for the sample mean vector we find

$$E\bar{\mathbf{x}} = ET^{-1}\sum_{t=1}^{T}\mathbf{x}_t = T^{-1}\sum_{t=1}^{T}E\mathbf{x}_t = T^{-1}T\boldsymbol{\mu} = \boldsymbol{\mu}, \tag{4.38}$$

and writing $\bar{\mathbf{x}} - \boldsymbol{\mu} = T^{-1}\sum_{t=1}^{T}\mathbf{x}_t - \boldsymbol{\mu} = T^{-1}\sum_{t=1}^{T}(\mathbf{x}_t - \boldsymbol{\mu})$,

$$\begin{aligned} E(\bar{\mathbf{x}} - \boldsymbol{\mu})(\bar{\mathbf{x}} - \boldsymbol{\mu})' &= T^{-2}E\sum_{t=1}^{T}(\mathbf{x}_t - \boldsymbol{\mu})\sum_{s=1}^{T}(\mathbf{x}_s - \boldsymbol{\mu})' \\ &= T^{-2}\sum_{t=1}^{T}\sum_{s=1}^{T}E(\mathbf{x}_t - \boldsymbol{\mu})(\mathbf{x}_s - \boldsymbol{\mu})' \\ &= T^{-2}T\boldsymbol{\Sigma} = T^{-1}\boldsymbol{\Sigma}. \end{aligned} \tag{4.39}$$

Writing

$$\begin{aligned} \mathbf{S} &= T^{-1}\sum_{t=1}^{T}(\mathbf{x}_t - \bar{\mathbf{x}})(\mathbf{x}_t - \bar{\mathbf{x}})' \\ &= T^{-1}\sum_{t=1}^{T}[(\mathbf{x}_t - \boldsymbol{\mu}) - (\bar{\mathbf{x}} - \boldsymbol{\mu})][(\mathbf{x}_t - \boldsymbol{\mu}) - (\bar{\mathbf{x}} - \boldsymbol{\mu})]' \\ &= T^{-1}\sum_{t=1}^{T}[(\mathbf{x}_t - \boldsymbol{\mu})(\mathbf{x}_t - \boldsymbol{\mu})' + (\bar{\mathbf{x}} - \boldsymbol{\mu})(\bar{\mathbf{x}} - \boldsymbol{\mu})' \\ &\qquad - (\mathbf{x}_t - \boldsymbol{\mu})(\bar{\mathbf{x}} - \boldsymbol{\mu})' - (\bar{\mathbf{x}} - \boldsymbol{\mu})(\mathbf{x}_t - \boldsymbol{\mu})'] \\ &= T^{-1}\sum_{t=1}^{T}(\mathbf{x}_t - \boldsymbol{\mu})(\mathbf{x}_t - \boldsymbol{\mu})' - (\bar{\mathbf{x}} - \boldsymbol{\mu})(\bar{\mathbf{x}} - \boldsymbol{\mu})', \end{aligned} \tag{4.40}$$

we find for the sample covariance matrix

$$\begin{aligned} E\mathbf{S} &= T^{-1}\sum_{t=1}^{T}E(\mathbf{x}_t - \boldsymbol{\mu})(\mathbf{x}_t - \boldsymbol{\mu})' - E(\bar{\mathbf{x}} - \boldsymbol{\mu})(\bar{\mathbf{x}} - \boldsymbol{\mu})' \\ &= T^{-1}T\boldsymbol{\Sigma} - T^{-1}\boldsymbol{\Sigma} = T^{-1}(T - 1)\boldsymbol{\Sigma}. \end{aligned} \tag{4.41}$$

These results are clearly direct generalizations of those we found in the univariate case. To summarize:

(4.42) For random sampling with sample size T from any population with $E\mathbf{x} = \boldsymbol{\mu}$ and $E(\mathbf{x} - \boldsymbol{\mu})(\mathbf{x} - \boldsymbol{\mu})' = \boldsymbol{\Sigma}$, the sample mean vector is distributed with mean vector $E\bar{\mathbf{x}} = \boldsymbol{\mu}$ and covariance matrix $E(\bar{\mathbf{x}} - \boldsymbol{\mu})(\bar{\mathbf{x}} - \boldsymbol{\mu})' = T^{-1}\boldsymbol{\Sigma}$, and the sample covariance matrix is distributed with mean matrix $E\mathbf{S} = T^{-1}(T - 1)\boldsymbol{\Sigma}$.

A matrix formulation is sometimes convenient. The sample observations may be collected in the $T \times K$ matrix

$$(4.43) \qquad \mathbf{X} = \begin{pmatrix} x_{11} & \cdots & x_{1K} \\ \cdot & & \cdot \\ \cdot & & \cdot \\ \cdot & & \cdot \\ x_{T1} & \cdots & x_{TK} \end{pmatrix},$$

in which each *row* gives one observation on the random vector; it is readily confirmed that the sample mean vector is given by

$$(4.44) \qquad \bar{\mathbf{x}} = T^{-1}\mathbf{X}'\boldsymbol{\iota}$$

where $\boldsymbol{\iota}$ is the $T \times 1$ vector of 1's, and the sample covariance matrix is given by

$$(4.45) \qquad \mathbf{S} = T^{-1}\mathbf{X}'\mathbf{X} - \bar{\mathbf{x}}\bar{\mathbf{x}}' = T^{-1}\mathbf{X}'\mathbf{M}\mathbf{X}$$

where $\mathbf{M} = \mathbf{I} - T^{-1}\boldsymbol{\iota\iota}'$. The sample second-moment matrix may be defined as $T^{-1}\mathbf{X}'\mathbf{X} = \mathbf{S} + \bar{\mathbf{x}}\bar{\mathbf{x}}'$; clearly

$$(4.46) \qquad \begin{aligned} ET^{-1}\mathbf{X}'\mathbf{X} &= E\mathbf{S} + E\bar{\mathbf{x}}\bar{\mathbf{x}}' \\ &= T^{-1}(T-1)\boldsymbol{\Sigma} + (T^{-1}\boldsymbol{\Sigma} + \boldsymbol{\mu\mu}') \\ &= \boldsymbol{\Sigma} + \boldsymbol{\mu\mu}' = E\mathbf{x}\mathbf{x}'. \end{aligned}$$

Finally, we note that the determinant of the sample covariance matrix, $|\mathbf{S}|$, is called the generalized sample variance.

5. NORMAL DISTRIBUTION AND ASSOCIATED DISTRIBUTIONS

Univariate Normal Distribution

A random variable is said to be normally distributed, or to have the normal distribution, or, simply, to be a normal variable if its density function is

$$(5.1) \qquad f(x) = \frac{1}{\sqrt{2\pi\sigma^2}} e^{-(x-\mu)^2/2\sigma^2} = (2\pi\sigma^2)^{-\frac{1}{2}} \exp\{-(2\sigma^2)^{-1}(x-\mu)^2\}$$

where e is the base of natural logarithms, $\exp\{y\}$ denotes e^y, and μ and σ^2 are parameters. The density function defines a two-parameter family of distributions; a specific member of the family is identified by specifying the values of μ and σ^2. As a shorthand notation we often use the expression "x is distributed $\mathcal{N}(\mu, \sigma^2)$" to mean that x is normally distributed with parameters μ and σ^2. For example, "x is distributed $\mathcal{N}(0, 1)$" means that $f(x) = (2\pi \cdot 1^2)^{-\frac{1}{2}} e^{-(2\cdot 1^2)^{-1}(x-0)^2} = (2\pi)^{-\frac{1}{2}} e^{-\frac{1}{2}x^2}$. If x is distributed $\mathcal{N}(0, 1)$, we say that x has the standard normal distribution or, equivalently, that x is a standard normal variable.

As the notation suggests, and as can be shown, if x is distributed $\mathcal{N}(\mu, \sigma^2)$, then $Ex = \mu$ and $E(x - \mu)^2 = \sigma^2$; thus the distribution of a normally distributed variable is fully specified if its mean and variance are known. It can be shown that a normal distribution is symmetric about μ, that all its odd central moments are zero, and that the fourth central moment equals thrice the squared variance; thus

(5.2) If x is distributed $\mathcal{N}(\mu, \sigma^2)$, then $E(x - \mu)^r = 0$ for all odd integers r and $E(x - \mu)^4 = 3\sigma^4$.

A useful theorem is

(5.3) If x is distributed $\mathcal{N}(\mu, \sigma^2)$ and if $y = B(x - b)$ where $B \neq 0$ and b are constants, then y is distributed $\mathcal{N}(B(\mu - b), B^2\sigma^2)$.

We do not prove the heart of the theorem, which states that a linear function of a normal variable is also a normal variable. The rest of the result is straightforward; since $y = B(x - b)$, $Ey = EB(x - b) = BE(x - b) = B(\mu - b)$, whence $y - Ey = B(x - b) - B(\mu - b) = B(x - \mu)$ and $E(y - Ey)^2 = E[B(x - \mu)]^2 = B^2E(x - \mu)^2 = B^2\sigma^2$. Then it is clear from (5.1) that

(5.4) If x is distributed $\mathcal{N}(\mu, \sigma^2)$, then $(x - \mu)/\sigma$ is distributed $\mathcal{N}(0, 1)$.

To see this, let $B = 1/\sigma$ and $b = \mu$ in (5.3); then $(1/\sigma)(\mu - \mu) = 0$ and $(1/\sigma)^2\sigma^2 = 1$. Thus a normal variable can be transformed into a standard normal variable by subtracting its mean and dividing by its standard deviation. A standard normal variable has zero mean and unit variance.

The cumulative normal distribution obtained by integrating the density distribution of (5.1) is

(5.5) $$F(x) = (2\pi\sigma^2)^{-\frac{1}{2}} \int_{-\infty}^{x} e^{-(2\sigma^2)^{-1}(x-\mu)^2}\, dx;$$

in particular, if x is distributed $\mathcal{N}(0, 1)$, then

$$F(x) = (2\pi)^{-\frac{1}{2}} \int_{-\infty}^{x} e^{-\frac{1}{2}x^2}\, dx.$$

The symmetry of the distribution is again reflected in the fact that $F(-x) = 1 - F(x)$. A partial tabulation of the cumulative standard normal distribution is:

(5.6) ***Cumulative standard normal table***

x	$F(x)$
-3	0.001
-2	0.023
-1	0.159
0	0.500
1	0.841
2	0.977
3	0.999

In view of (5.4) this tabulation may be applied to any normal distribution. For example, suppose that y is normally distributed with mean 5000 and variance 1,000,000. Then $x = (y - 5000)/1000$ is a standard normal variable, and

$$\begin{aligned}\text{Prob}\,\{y \leq 7000\} &= \text{Prob}\left\{\frac{y - 5000}{1000} \leq \frac{7000 - 5000}{1000}\right\}\\ &= \text{Prob}\,\{x \leq 2\} = 0.977\end{aligned}$$

from the table. More complete tabulations are found in most statistics textbooks.

Multivariate Normal Distribution

An $n \times 1$ random vector

$$\mathbf{x} = \begin{pmatrix} x_1 \\ \cdot \\ \cdot \\ \cdot \\ x_n \end{pmatrix}$$

is said to be (multivariate) normally distributed, or, equivalently, to have the (multivariate) normal distribution, or, equivalently, to be a normal vector, if its density function is

$$f(\mathbf{x}) = (2\pi)^{-(n/2)}\, |\boldsymbol{\Sigma}|^{-1/2} \exp\{-\tfrac{1}{2}(\mathbf{x} - \boldsymbol{\mu})'\, \boldsymbol{\Sigma}^{-1}(\mathbf{x} - \boldsymbol{\mu})\} \tag{5.7}$$

where

$$\boldsymbol{\mu} = \begin{pmatrix} \mu_1 \\ \cdot \\ \cdot \\ \cdot \\ \mu_n \end{pmatrix}$$

and the positive definite matrix

$$\boldsymbol{\Sigma} = \begin{pmatrix} \sigma_{11} & \cdots & \sigma_{1n} \\ \cdot & & \cdot \\ \cdot & & \cdot \\ \cdot & & \cdot \\ \sigma_{n1} & \cdots & \sigma_{nn} \end{pmatrix}$$

are parameters. The density function defines an $n + \frac{1}{2}n(n + 1)$-parameter family of distributions; a specific member of the family is identified by specifying the n elements of $\boldsymbol{\mu}$ and the $n + \frac{1}{2}n(n - 1)$ distinct elements of $\boldsymbol{\Sigma}$. As a shorthand notation we often use the expression "$\mathbf{x}$ is distributed $\mathcal{N}(\boldsymbol{\mu}, \boldsymbol{\Sigma})$" to mean that $\mathbf{x}$ is normally distributed with parameters $\boldsymbol{\mu}$ and $\boldsymbol{\Sigma}$. For example, "$\mathbf{x}$ is distributed $\mathcal{N}(\mathbf{0}, \mathbf{I})$" means that

$$\begin{aligned} f(\mathbf{x}) &= (2\pi)^{-(n/2)} \, |\mathbf{I}|^{-\frac{1}{2}} \exp\{-\tfrac{1}{2}(\mathbf{x} - \mathbf{0})'\mathbf{I}^{-1}(\mathbf{x} - \mathbf{0})\} \\ &= (2\pi)^{-(n/2)} \exp\{-\tfrac{1}{2}\mathbf{x}'\mathbf{x}\}. \end{aligned}$$

If $\mathbf{x}$ is distributed $\mathcal{N}(\mathbf{0}, \mathbf{I})$, we say that $\mathbf{x}$ has the standard (multivariate) normal distribution, or, equivalently, that $\mathbf{x}$ is a standard normal vector. For another example, "$\mathbf{x}$ is distributed $\mathcal{N}(\mathbf{0}, \sigma^2\mathbf{I})$" means that

$$\begin{aligned} f(\mathbf{x}) &= (2\pi)^{-(n/2)} |\sigma^2\mathbf{I}|^{-\frac{1}{2}} \exp\{-\tfrac{1}{2}(\mathbf{x} - \mathbf{0})'(\sigma^2\mathbf{I})^{-1}(\mathbf{x} - \mathbf{0})\} \\ &= (2\pi)^{-(n/2)}\sigma^{-n} \exp\left\{-\frac{1}{2\sigma^2}\mathbf{x}'\mathbf{x}\right\}. \end{aligned}$$

If $\mathbf{x}$ is distributed $\mathcal{N}(\mathbf{0}, \sigma^2\mathbf{I})$, we say that $\mathbf{x}$ has the spherical (multivariate) normal distribution, or, equivalently, that $\mathbf{x}$ is a spherical normal vector. [Some authors use the term spherical normal distribution to refer to $\mathcal{N}(\boldsymbol{\mu}, \sigma^2\mathbf{I})$ without requiring $\boldsymbol{\mu} = \mathbf{0}$.]

As the notation suggests, and as can be shown, if $\mathbf{x}$ is distributed $\mathcal{N}(\boldsymbol{\mu}, \boldsymbol{\Sigma})$, then $E\mathbf{x} = \boldsymbol{\mu}$ and $E(\mathbf{x} - \boldsymbol{\mu})(\mathbf{x} - \boldsymbol{\mu})' = \boldsymbol{\Sigma}$; thus the distribution of a normally distributed vector is fully specified if its mean vector and covariance matrix are known. In particular, $Ex_i = \mu_i$, $E(x_i - \mu_i)^2 = \sigma_{ii}$, and $E(x_i - \mu_i)(x_j - \mu_j) = \sigma_{ij} = \sigma_{ji}$.

A useful theorem is

(5.8) If the $n \times 1$ vector $\mathbf{x}$ is distributed $\mathcal{N}(\boldsymbol{\mu}, \boldsymbol{\Sigma})$ and if $\mathbf{y} = \mathbf{B}(\mathbf{x} - \mathbf{b})$ where $\mathbf{B}$ is an $m \times n$ matrix of rank m and $\mathbf{b}$ is an $n \times 1$ vector and $\mathbf{B}$ and $\mathbf{b}$ are constant, then $\mathbf{y}$ is distributed $\mathcal{N}(\mathbf{B}(\boldsymbol{\mu} - \mathbf{b}), \mathbf{B\Sigma B}')$.

We do not prove the heart of the theorem, which states that a linear form in a normal vector is also a normal vector. [The condition $r(\mathbf{B}) = m$ is needed to ensure that $\mathbf{B\Sigma B}'$ is positive definite.] For a proof see Anderson (1958, pp. 19–27). The rest of the result is straightforward; since $\mathbf{y} = \mathbf{B}(\mathbf{x} - \mathbf{b})$, $E\mathbf{y} = E\mathbf{B}(\mathbf{x} - \mathbf{b}) = \mathbf{B}E(\mathbf{x} - \mathbf{b}) = \mathbf{B}(\boldsymbol{\mu} - \mathbf{b})$, whence $\mathbf{y} - E\mathbf{y} = \mathbf{B}(\mathbf{x} - \mathbf{b}) - \mathbf{B}(\boldsymbol{\mu} - \mathbf{b}) = \mathbf{B}(\mathbf{x} - \boldsymbol{\mu})$, and $E(\mathbf{y} - E\mathbf{y})(\mathbf{y} - E\mathbf{y})' = E\mathbf{B}(\mathbf{x} - \boldsymbol{\mu})(\mathbf{x} - \boldsymbol{\mu})'\mathbf{B}' = \mathbf{B}E(\mathbf{x} - \boldsymbol{\mu})(\mathbf{x} - \boldsymbol{\mu})'\mathbf{B}' = \mathbf{B\Sigma B}'$. Then it is clear from (5.7) that

(5.9) If $\mathbf{x}$ is distributed $\mathcal{N}(\boldsymbol{\mu}, \boldsymbol{\Sigma})$, then $\mathbf{P}(\mathbf{x} - \boldsymbol{\mu})$ is distributed $\mathcal{N}(\mathbf{0}, \mathbf{I})$ where $\mathbf{P}$ is a nonsingular matrix such that $\mathbf{P}'\mathbf{P} = \boldsymbol{\Sigma}^{-1}$.

To see this, let $\mathbf{B} = \mathbf{P}$ and $\mathbf{b} = \boldsymbol{\mu}$ in (5.8); then $\mathbf{P}(\boldsymbol{\mu} - \boldsymbol{\mu}) = \mathbf{0}$ and $\mathbf{P\Sigma P}' = [(\mathbf{P}')^{-1}\boldsymbol{\Sigma}^{-1}\mathbf{P}^{-1}]^{-1} = [(\mathbf{P}')^{-1}\mathbf{P}'\mathbf{P}\mathbf{P}^{-1}]^{-1} = (\mathbf{I}\,\mathbf{I})^{-1} = \mathbf{I}$ since $\mathbf{P}'\mathbf{P} = \boldsymbol{\Sigma}^{-1}$. Thus a normal vector can be transformed into a standard normal vector by subtracting out its mean vector and applying a certain nonsingular transformation. The elements of a standard normal vector have zero means, unit variances, and zero covariances. The elements of a spherical normal vector have zero means, a common variance, and zero covariances. A standard normal vector is a spherical normal vector with common variance unity.

The cumulative multivariate normal distribution obtained by integrating the density function of (5.7) is

(5.10)
$$F(\mathbf{x}) = (2\pi)^{-(n/2)}\,|\boldsymbol{\Sigma}|^{-1/2}\int_{-\infty}^{x_1}\cdots\int_{-\infty}^{x_n}\exp\{-\tfrac{1}{2}(\mathbf{x} - \boldsymbol{\mu})'\boldsymbol{\Sigma}^{-1}(\mathbf{x} - \boldsymbol{\mu})\} \times dx_1\cdots dx_n.$$

Note that for $n = 1$ the formulas of this subsection reduce to the corresponding ones of the preceding subsection; the univariate normal distribution is a special case of the multivariate normal distribution.

It is easily seen that a subvector of a normal vector is also normal:

(5.11) Let $\mathbf{x}$ be distributed $\mathcal{N}(\boldsymbol{\mu}, \boldsymbol{\Sigma})$; let $\mathbf{x}$ be partitioned as

$$\begin{pmatrix} \mathbf{x}_1 \\ \mathbf{x}_2 \end{pmatrix}$$

and let $\boldsymbol{\mu}$ and $\boldsymbol{\Sigma}$ be correspondingly partitioned as

$$\begin{pmatrix} \boldsymbol{\mu}_1 \\ \boldsymbol{\mu}_2 \end{pmatrix} \quad \text{and} \quad \begin{pmatrix} \boldsymbol{\Sigma}_{11} & \boldsymbol{\Sigma}_{12} \\ \boldsymbol{\Sigma}_{21} & \boldsymbol{\Sigma}_{22} \end{pmatrix}$$

Then $\mathbf{x}_1$ is distributed $\mathcal{N}(\boldsymbol{\mu}_1, \boldsymbol{\Sigma}_{11})$ and $\mathbf{x}_2$ is distributed $\mathcal{N}(\boldsymbol{\mu}_2, \boldsymbol{\Sigma}_{22})$.

This is so because we may write $\mathbf{x}_1 = (\mathbf{I} \quad \mathbf{0})\mathbf{x}$ and apply (5.8); similarly for $\mathbf{x}_2$. This extends to finer partitioning; in particular, if $\mathbf{x}$ is distributed $\mathcal{N}(\boldsymbol{\mu}, \boldsymbol{\Sigma})$, then the marginal distribution of any element x_i is $\mathcal{N}(\mu_i, \sigma_{ii})$. It can also be shown that the conditional distribution of a subvector of a normal vector, given the remaining subvector, is normal with an expectation linear in the conditioning subvector:

(5.12) Let $\mathbf{x}$ be distributed $\mathcal{N}(\boldsymbol{\mu}, \boldsymbol{\Sigma})$; let $\mathbf{x}$ be partitioned as

$$\begin{pmatrix} \mathbf{x}_1 \\ \mathbf{x}_2 \end{pmatrix}$$

and let $\boldsymbol{\mu}$ and $\boldsymbol{\Sigma}$ be correspondingly partitioned as

$$\begin{pmatrix} \boldsymbol{\mu}_1 \\ \boldsymbol{\mu}_2 \end{pmatrix} \quad \text{and} \quad \begin{pmatrix} \boldsymbol{\Sigma}_{11} & \boldsymbol{\Sigma}_{12} \\ \boldsymbol{\Sigma}_{21} & \boldsymbol{\Sigma}_{22} \end{pmatrix}$$

Then the conditional distribution of $\mathbf{x}_2$, given $\mathbf{x}_1$, is

$$\mathcal{N}[\boldsymbol{\mu}_2 + \boldsymbol{\Sigma}_{21} \boldsymbol{\Sigma}_{11}^{-1}(\mathbf{x}_1 - \boldsymbol{\mu}_1),\ \boldsymbol{\Sigma}_{22} - \boldsymbol{\Sigma}_{21} \boldsymbol{\Sigma}_{11}^{-1} \boldsymbol{\Sigma}_{12}].$$

For a proof see Anderson (1958, pp. 27–30).

It will be recalled that for any joint distribution independence implies uncorrelatedness. For the normal distribution the converse is true; thus

(5.13) Let $\mathbf{x}$ be distributed $\mathcal{N}(\boldsymbol{\mu}, \boldsymbol{\Sigma})$ where

$$\mathbf{x} = \begin{pmatrix} \mathbf{x}_1 \\ \mathbf{x}_2 \end{pmatrix}, \quad \boldsymbol{\mu} = \begin{pmatrix} \boldsymbol{\mu}_1 \\ \boldsymbol{\mu}_2 \end{pmatrix}, \quad \text{and} \quad \boldsymbol{\Sigma} = \begin{pmatrix} \boldsymbol{\Sigma}_{11} & \boldsymbol{\Sigma}_{12} \\ \boldsymbol{\Sigma}_{21} & \boldsymbol{\Sigma}_{22} \end{pmatrix}.$$

If $\boldsymbol{\Sigma}_{12} = \mathbf{0}(=\boldsymbol{\Sigma}_{21}')$, then $\mathbf{x}_1$ is independent of $\mathbf{x}_2$.

This extends to finer partitioning; in particular, if $\mathbf{x}$ is distributed $\mathcal{N}(\boldsymbol{\mu}, \boldsymbol{\Sigma})$ and if $\sigma_{ij} = 0 = \sigma_{ji}$, then x_i is independent of x_j. In addition, if the covariance matrix of a normal vector is diagonal, all the elements of the vector are mutually independent and the joint density (5.7) may be written

$$f(\mathbf{x}) = \prod_{i=1}^{n} f(x_i) = (2\pi)^{-(n/2)}(\sigma_{11} \cdots \sigma_{nn})^{-\frac{1}{2}}$$

$$\times \exp\left\{-\frac{1}{2}\sum_{i=1}^{n}\frac{(x_i - \mu_i)^2}{\sigma_{ii}}\right\}.$$

Distributions Associated with the Normal Distribution

Without proof we specify the distributions of certain functions of normally distributed variables. First, the chi-square distribution:

(5.14) Let $x_1, \ldots, x_k$ be independent $\mathcal{N}(0, 1)$ variables and let $w = \Sigma_{i=1}^{k} x_i^2$. Then w has the χ_k^2 distribution; i.e., the sum of squares of k independent standard normal variables has the chi-square distribution with k "degrees of freedom."

Such a variable will be said to be distributed as χ_k^2 or simply to be a χ_k^2 variable. We do not give the formula for the chi-square distribution; the cumulative chi-square distribution is tabulated in most statistics textbooks. We note that the chi-square distribution is in fact a one-parameter family of distributions; the parameter, k, is called the "degrees of freedom" of the distribution. We also note that $E\chi_k^2 = k$ and $E(\chi_k^2 - E\chi_k^2)^2 = 2k$.

Next, the Student t distribution:

(5.15) Let x be distributed $\mathcal{N}(0, 1)$ and let w be distributed χ_k^2, and suppose that x and w are independent. Then $x/\sqrt{w/k}$ has the t_k distribution; i.e., the ratio of a standard normal variable to the square root of an independent chi-square variable divided by its degrees of freedom has the t distribution with those degrees of freedom.

A variable that has the t_k distribution is said to be distributed as t_k or simply to be a t_k variable. We do not give the formula for the t distribution; the cumulative t distribution is tabulated in most statistics textbooks. We note that the t distribution is in fact a one-parameter family of distributions; the parameter k is called the "degrees of freedom" of the distribution. We also note that the t distribution is symmetric, that $Et_k = 0$ and $E(t_k - Et_k)^2 = k/(k - 2)$, and that as $k \to \infty$ the t_k distribution approaches the standard normal distribution $\mathcal{N}(0, 1)$.

Third, the Snedecor F distribution:

(5.16) Let w_1 be distributed $\chi^2_{k_1}$, let w_2 be distributed $\chi^2_{k_2}$, and suppose that w_1 and w_2 are independent. Then $(w_1/k_1)/(w_2/k_2)$ has the $F^{k_1}_{k_2}$ distribution; i.e., the ratio of two independent chi-square variables, each divided by its degrees of freedom, has the F distribution with those degrees of freedom.

A variable that has the $F^{k_1}_{k_2}$ distribution is said to be distributed as $F^{k_1}_{k_2}$ or simply to be an $F^{k_1}_{k_2}$ variable. We do not give the formula for the F distribution; the cumulative F distribution is tabulated in most statistics textbooks. We note that the F distribution is in fact a two-parameter family of distributions; the parameters k_1 and k_2 are called the numerator degrees of freedom and the denominator degrees of freedom respectively. We also note that $EF^{k_1}_{k_2} = k_2/(k_2 - 2)$ and that the square of a t_k variable is an F^1_k variable; to justify this last recognize that the square of an $\mathcal{N}(0, 1)$ variable is a χ^2_1 variable.

Linear and Quadratic Forms in Normal Vectors

We may now establish the distributions of certain linear and quadratic forms in normally distributed vectors. First we consider orthogonal linear forms.

(5.17) Let the $n \times 1$ vector $\mathbf{x}$ be distributed $\mathcal{N}(\boldsymbol{\mu}, \sigma^2\mathbf{I})$ and let the $n \times n$ matrix $\mathbf{C}'$ be orthogonal. Then the $n \times 1$ vector $\mathbf{y} = \mathbf{C}'\mathbf{x}$ is distributed $\mathcal{N}(\mathbf{C}'\boldsymbol{\mu}, \sigma^2\mathbf{I})$; i.e., orthogonal linear functions of independent normally distributed variables with a common variance are also independent normally distributed variables with the same common variance.

This is so because by (5.8) $\mathbf{y}$ is distributed $\mathcal{N}(\mathbf{C}'\boldsymbol{\mu}, \sigma^2\mathbf{C}'\mathbf{I}\mathbf{C})$, and since $\mathbf{C}'$ is orthogonal, $\mathbf{C}'\mathbf{I}\mathbf{C} = \mathbf{C}'\mathbf{C} = \mathbf{I}$. A special case is obtained by letting $\boldsymbol{\mu} = \mathbf{0}$ in (5.17):

(5.18) Let the $n \times 1$ vector $\mathbf{x}$ be distributed $\mathcal{N}(\mathbf{0}, \sigma^2\mathbf{I})$ and let the $n \times n$ matrix $\mathbf{C}'$ be orthogonal. Then the $n \times 1$ vector $\mathbf{y} = \mathbf{C}'\mathbf{x}$ is also distributed $\mathcal{N}(\mathbf{0}, \sigma^2\mathbf{I})$; i.e., an orthogonal linear form in a spherical normal vector is also a spherical normal vector.

A still more special case is obtained by letting $\sigma^2 = 1$ in (5.18):

(5.19) Let the $n \times 1$ vector $\mathbf{x}$ be distributed $\mathcal{N}(\mathbf{0}, \mathbf{I})$ and let the $n \times n$ matrix $\mathbf{C}'$ be orthogonal. Then the $n \times 1$ vector $\mathbf{y} = \mathbf{C}'\mathbf{x}$ is also distributed $\mathcal{N}(\mathbf{0}, \mathbf{I})$; i.e., an orthogonal linear form in a standard normal vector is also a standard normal vector.

Second we consider idempotent quadratic forms.

(5.20) Let the $n \times 1$ vector $\mathbf{x}$ be distributed $\mathscr{N}(\mathbf{0}, \mathbf{I})$. Then $\mathbf{x}'\mathbf{x}$ is distributed as χ^2_n.

This is so because $\mathbf{x}'\mathbf{x} = \Sigma_{i=1}^n x_i^2$, which, since $x_1, \ldots, x_n$ are independent standard normal variables, is distributed as χ^2_n. More interesting cases follow from (5.20).

(5.21) Let the $n \times 1$ vector $\mathbf{x}$ be distributed $\mathscr{N}(\mathbf{0}, \mathbf{I})$ and let the $n \times n$ matrix $\mathbf{A}$ be idempotent of rank r. Then $\mathbf{x}'\mathbf{A}\mathbf{x}$ is distributed as χ^2_r; i.e., an idempotent quadratic form of rank r in a standard normal vector is distributed as the sum of squares of r independent standard normal variables.

To see this, let $\mathbf{C}$ be the orthogonal matrix that diagonalizes $\mathbf{A}$ into

$$\mathbf{\Lambda} = \begin{pmatrix} \mathbf{I} & \mathbf{0} \\ \mathbf{0} & \mathbf{0} \end{pmatrix}$$

as in (2.6.18), let $\mathbf{y} = \mathbf{C}'\mathbf{x}$, and let $\mathbf{y}$ be partitioned as

$$\mathbf{y} = \begin{pmatrix} \mathbf{y}_1 \\ \mathbf{y}_2 \end{pmatrix} = \begin{pmatrix} y_1 \\ \cdot \\ \cdot \\ \cdot \\ y_r \\ y_{r+1} \\ \cdot \\ \cdot \\ \cdot \\ y_n \end{pmatrix}.$$

By (5.19) $\mathbf{y}$ is a standard normal vector; in particular, its $r \times 1$ subvector $\mathbf{y}_1$ is a standard normal vector. Then $\mathbf{y}_1'\mathbf{y}_1$ is distributed as χ^2_r by (5.20). Since $\mathbf{C}\mathbf{C}' = \mathbf{C}'\mathbf{C} = \mathbf{I}$, however,

$$\mathbf{x}'\mathbf{A}\mathbf{x} = \mathbf{x}'(\mathbf{C}\mathbf{C}')\mathbf{A}(\mathbf{C}\mathbf{C}')\mathbf{x} = \mathbf{x}'\mathbf{C}(\mathbf{C}'\mathbf{A}\mathbf{C})\mathbf{C}'\mathbf{x} = \mathbf{y}'\mathbf{\Lambda}\mathbf{y}$$

$$= (\mathbf{y}_1' \quad \mathbf{y}_2')\begin{pmatrix} \mathbf{I} & \mathbf{0} \\ \mathbf{0} & \mathbf{0} \end{pmatrix}\begin{pmatrix} \mathbf{y}_1 \\ \mathbf{y}_2 \end{pmatrix} = \mathbf{y}_1'\mathbf{y}_1.$$

Thus an idempotent quadratic form of rank r in n standard normal variables is in fact equivalent to the sum of squares of only r standard normal variables. Generalizing somewhat,

(5.22) Let the $n \times 1$ vector $\mathbf{x}$ be distributed $\mathcal{N}(\mathbf{0}, \sigma^2\mathbf{I})$ and let the $n \times n$ matrix $\mathbf{A}$ be idempotent of rank r. Then $\mathbf{x}'\mathbf{A}\mathbf{x}$ is distributed as $\sigma^2\chi_r^2$, i.e., an idempotent quadratic form of rank r in a spherical normal vector is distributed as $\sigma^2\chi_r^2$.

To see this, let $\mathbf{x}^* = (1/\sigma)\mathbf{x}$. Then

$$E\mathbf{x}^* = (1/\sigma)E\mathbf{x} = \mathbf{0} \quad \text{and} \quad E\mathbf{x}^*\mathbf{x}^{*\prime} = (1/\sigma^2)\sigma^2\mathbf{I} = \mathbf{I}$$

so that $\mathbf{x}^*$ is a standard normal vector, and (5.21) is applicable to $\mathbf{x}^{*\prime}\mathbf{A}\mathbf{x}^*$. But $\mathbf{x}'\mathbf{A}\mathbf{x} = \sigma^2\mathbf{x}^{*\prime}\mathbf{A}\mathbf{x}^*$.

Next we turn to the independence of linear and quadratic forms.

(5.23) Let the $n \times 1$ vector $\mathbf{x}$ be distributed $\mathcal{N}(\mathbf{0}, \mathbf{I})$, let $\mathbf{A}$ be an $n \times n$ idempotent matrix of rank r, let $\mathbf{B}$ be an $m \times n$ matrix, and suppose that $\mathbf{BA} = \mathbf{0}$. Then the linear form $\mathbf{Bx}$ is distributed independently of the quadratic form $\mathbf{x}'\mathbf{A}\mathbf{x}$.

To see this, let $\mathbf{C}$ again be the orthogonal matrix that diagonalizes $\mathbf{A}$ into $\boldsymbol{\Lambda} = \begin{pmatrix} \mathbf{I} & \mathbf{0} \\ \mathbf{0} & \mathbf{0} \end{pmatrix}$ and let $\mathbf{y} = \mathbf{C}'\mathbf{x}$ again be partitioned into $\begin{pmatrix} \mathbf{y}_1 \\ \mathbf{y}_2 \end{pmatrix}$. Then as under (5.21), $\mathbf{x}'\mathbf{A}\mathbf{x} = \mathbf{y}_1'\mathbf{y}_1$, so that the quadratic form is expressed in terms of the first r elements of the standard normal vector $\mathbf{y}$. Next define $\mathbf{F} = \mathbf{BC}$; then $\mathbf{F}\boldsymbol{\Lambda} = \mathbf{BCC}'\mathbf{AC} = \mathbf{BAC} = \mathbf{0C} = \mathbf{0}$ since $\mathbf{BA} = \mathbf{0}$. Partitioning $\mathbf{F}$ as $(\mathbf{F}_1 \quad \mathbf{F}_2)$ where $\mathbf{F}_1$ is $m \times r$ and $\mathbf{F}_2$ is $m \times (n - r)$,

$$(\mathbf{F}_1 \quad \mathbf{F}_2)\begin{pmatrix} \mathbf{I} & \mathbf{0} \\ \mathbf{0} & \mathbf{0} \end{pmatrix} = (\mathbf{F}_1 \quad \mathbf{0}) = (\mathbf{0} \quad \mathbf{0})$$

whence $\mathbf{F}_1 = \mathbf{0}$. Then the linear form

$$\mathbf{Bx} = \mathbf{BCC}'\mathbf{x} = \mathbf{Fy} = (\mathbf{0} \quad \mathbf{F}_2)\begin{pmatrix} \mathbf{y}_1 \\ \mathbf{y}_2 \end{pmatrix} = \mathbf{F}_2\mathbf{y}_2$$

is expressed in terms of the last $n - r$ elements of the standard normal vector $\mathbf{y}$. Since all the elements of $\mathbf{y}$ are independent, two functions of $\mathbf{y}$ that have none of these elements in common are independent. Generalizing somewhat,

(5.24) Let the $n \times 1$ vector $\mathbf{x}$ be distributed $\mathcal{N}(\mathbf{0}, \sigma^2\mathbf{I})$, let $\mathbf{A}$ be an $n \times n$ idempotent matrix, let $\mathbf{B}$ be an $m \times n$ matrix, and suppose that $\mathbf{BA} = \mathbf{0}$. Then the linear form $\mathbf{Bx}$ is distributed independently of the quadratic form $\mathbf{x}'\mathbf{A}\mathbf{x}$.

To see this, let $\mathbf{x}^* = (1/\sigma)\mathbf{x}$, and apply (5.23) to show that $\mathbf{Bx}^*$ is independent of $\mathbf{x}^{*\prime}\mathbf{Ax}^*$. Since σ and σ^2 are constants, $\mathbf{Bx} = \sigma\mathbf{Bx}^*$ is then independent of $\mathbf{x}'\mathbf{Ax} = \sigma^2\mathbf{x}^{*\prime}\mathbf{Ax}^*$.

Next we turn to the independence of quadratic forms.

(5.25) Let the $n \times 1$ vector $\mathbf{x}$ be distributed $\mathcal{N}(\mathbf{0}, \mathbf{I})$, let $\mathbf{A}$ be an $n \times n$ idempotent matrix of rank r, let $\mathbf{B}$ be an $n \times n$ idempotent matrix of rank s, and suppose that $\mathbf{BA} = \mathbf{0}$. Then the quadratic form $\mathbf{x}'\mathbf{Ax}$ is distributed independently of the quadratic form $\mathbf{x}'\mathbf{Bx}$.

To see this, let $\mathbf{C}$ again be the orthogonal matrix that diagonalizes $\mathbf{A}$ into $\mathbf{\Lambda} = \begin{pmatrix} \mathbf{I} & \mathbf{0} \\ \mathbf{0} & \mathbf{0} \end{pmatrix}$ and let $\mathbf{y} = \mathbf{C}'\mathbf{x}$ again be partitioned into $\begin{pmatrix} \mathbf{y}_1 \\ \mathbf{y}_2 \end{pmatrix}$. Then $\mathbf{x}'\mathbf{Ax} = \mathbf{y}_1'\mathbf{y}_1$ so that the first quadratic form is expressed in terms of the first r elements of the standard normal vector $\mathbf{y}$. Next define $\mathbf{G} = \mathbf{C}'\mathbf{BC}$; then $\mathbf{G}$ is symmetric since $\mathbf{C}'\mathbf{B}'\mathbf{C} = \mathbf{C}'\mathbf{BC}$, and $\mathbf{G\Lambda} = \mathbf{C}'\mathbf{BCC}'\mathbf{AC} = \mathbf{C}'\mathbf{BAC} = \mathbf{0}$ since $\mathbf{BA} = \mathbf{0}$. That is, partitioning $\mathbf{G}$ as $\begin{pmatrix} \mathbf{G}_1 & \mathbf{G}_2 \\ \mathbf{G}_2' & \mathbf{G}_3 \end{pmatrix}$ where $\mathbf{G}_1$ is $r \times r$, $\mathbf{G}_2$ is $r \times (n - r)$, and $\mathbf{G}_3$ is $(n - r) \times (n - r)$,

$$\mathbf{G\Lambda} = \begin{pmatrix} \mathbf{G}_1 & \mathbf{G}_2 \\ \mathbf{G}_2' & \mathbf{G}_3 \end{pmatrix}\begin{pmatrix} \mathbf{I} & \mathbf{0} \\ \mathbf{0} & \mathbf{0} \end{pmatrix} = \begin{pmatrix} \mathbf{G}_1 & \mathbf{0} \\ \mathbf{G}_2' & \mathbf{0} \end{pmatrix} = \begin{pmatrix} \mathbf{0} & \mathbf{0} \\ \mathbf{0} & \mathbf{0} \end{pmatrix}$$

whence $\mathbf{G}_1 = \mathbf{0}$, $\mathbf{G}_2' = \mathbf{0}$, and hence $\mathbf{G}_2 = \mathbf{0}$. Then the second quadratic form

$$\mathbf{x}'\mathbf{Bx} = \mathbf{x}'\mathbf{CC}'\mathbf{BCC}'\mathbf{x} = \mathbf{y}'\mathbf{Gy} = (\mathbf{y}_1' \quad \mathbf{y}_2')\begin{pmatrix} \mathbf{0} & \mathbf{0} \\ \mathbf{0} & \mathbf{G}_3 \end{pmatrix}\begin{pmatrix} \mathbf{y}_1 \\ \mathbf{y}_2 \end{pmatrix} = \mathbf{y}_2'\mathbf{G}_3\mathbf{y}_2$$

is expressed in terms of the last $n - r$ elements of the standard normal vector $\mathbf{y}$. Since all of the elements of $\mathbf{y}$ are independent, two functions of $\mathbf{y}$ that have none of these elements in common are independent. Generalizing somewhat,

(5.26) Let the $n \times 1$ vector $\mathbf{x}$ be distributed $\mathcal{N}(\mathbf{0}, \sigma^2\mathbf{I})$, let $\mathbf{A}$ be an $n \times n$ idempotent matrix of rank r, let $\mathbf{B}$ be an $n \times n$ idempotent matrix of rank s, and suppose that $\mathbf{BA} = \mathbf{0}$. Then the quadratic form $\mathbf{x}'\mathbf{Ax}$ is distributed independently of the quadratic form $\mathbf{x}'\mathbf{Bx}$.

To see this, let $\mathbf{x}^* = (1/\sigma)\mathbf{x}$ and apply (5.25) to show that $\mathbf{x}^{*\prime}\mathbf{Ax}^*$ is independent of $\mathbf{x}^{*\prime}\mathbf{Bx}^*$. Since σ^2 is a constant, $\mathbf{x}'\mathbf{Ax} = \sigma^2\mathbf{x}^{*\prime}\mathbf{Ax}^*$ is then independent of $\mathbf{x}'\mathbf{Bx} = \sigma^2\mathbf{x}^{*\prime}\mathbf{Bx}^*$.

As an important corollary we have

(5.27) Let the $n \times 1$ vector $\mathbf{x}$ be distributed $\mathcal{N}(\mathbf{0}, \sigma^2\mathbf{I})$, let $\mathbf{A}$ be an $n \times n$ idempotent matrix of rank r, let $\mathbf{B}$ be an $n \times n$ idempotent matrix of rank s, and suppose that $\mathbf{BA} = \mathbf{0}$. Then the ratio of the two quadratic forms each divided by its rank, $(\mathbf{x}'\mathbf{A}\mathbf{x}/r)/(\mathbf{x}'\mathbf{B}\mathbf{x}/s)$, is distributed as F^r_s.

By (5.22) $\mathbf{x}'\mathbf{A}\mathbf{x}$ is distributed as $\sigma^2\chi^2_r$ and $\mathbf{x}'\mathbf{B}\mathbf{x}$ is distributed as $\sigma^2\chi^2_s$, and by (5.26) $\mathbf{x}'\mathbf{A}\mathbf{x}$ and $\mathbf{x}'\mathbf{B}\mathbf{x}$ are independent. Therefore by (5.16)

$$\frac{\dfrac{\mathbf{x}'\mathbf{A}\mathbf{x}}{\sigma^2}\Big/ r}{\dfrac{\mathbf{x}'\mathbf{B}\mathbf{x}}{\sigma^2}\Big/ s}$$

is distributed as F^r_s. Canceling out the σ^2's gives the result.

Distribution of Sample Statistics from Normal Population

The preceding results find direct application in deriving the distribution of the sample mean and sample variance when random samples are drawn from a normal population. First,

(5.28) Let $x_1, \ldots, x_T$ be a random sample from a normal population with mean μ and variance σ^2. Then the sample mean $\bar{x}$ is distributed $\mathcal{N}(\mu, \sigma^2/T)$ and the sample variance s^2 is distributed as $(1/T)\sigma^2\chi^2_{T-1}$; or, equivalently, $\sqrt{T}(\bar{x} - \mu)/\sigma$ is distributed $\mathcal{N}(0, 1)$ and $\sqrt{T}\, s/\sigma\sqrt{T-1}$ is distributed $\sqrt{\chi^2_{T-1}/(T-1)}$.

To see this, let $\mathbf{x} = \begin{pmatrix} x_1 \\ \cdot \\ \cdot \\ \cdot \\ x_T \end{pmatrix}$ be the vector of sample observations. Since each element of $\mathbf{x}$ comes from the same $\mathcal{N}(\mu, \sigma^2)$ population and since all the elements are independent, the $T \times 1$ vector $\mathbf{x}$ is distributed $\mathcal{N}(\boldsymbol{\mu}, \sigma^2\mathbf{I})$ where $\boldsymbol{\mu} = \begin{pmatrix} \mu \\ \cdot \\ \cdot \\ \cdot \\ \mu \end{pmatrix}$, or, equivalently, $\mathbf{x} - \boldsymbol{\mu}$ is distributed $\mathcal{N}(\mathbf{0}, \sigma^2\mathbf{I})$, it is a spherical normal vector. Now define the $1 \times T$ vector $\mathbf{m}' = T^{-1}\boldsymbol{\iota}'$ where $\boldsymbol{\iota}' = (1 \cdots 1)$ is the $1 \times T$ vector all of whose elements are 1. Note that $\mathbf{m}'\mathbf{x} = T^{-1}\boldsymbol{\iota}'\mathbf{x} = \bar{x}$, $\mathbf{m}'\boldsymbol{\mu} = T^{-1}\boldsymbol{\iota}'\boldsymbol{\mu} = T^{-1}T\mu = \mu$, and $\mathbf{m}'\mathbf{I}\mathbf{m} = \mathbf{m}'\mathbf{m} = T^{-1}\boldsymbol{\iota}'\boldsymbol{\iota}T^{-1} = T^{-1}$. Since

$$\bar{x} - \mu = T^{-1}\sum_{t=1}^{T} x_t - \mu = T^{-1}\boldsymbol{\iota}'\mathbf{x} - \mu = \mathbf{m}'(\mathbf{x} - \boldsymbol{\mu})$$

is a linear form in the $\mathcal{N}(\mathbf{0}, \sigma^2\mathbf{I})$ vector $\mathbf{x} - \boldsymbol{\mu}$, it follows from (5.8) that $\bar{x} - \mu$ is distributed $\mathcal{N}(\mathbf{m}'\mathbf{0}, \sigma^2\mathbf{m}'\mathbf{I}\mathbf{m})$. In view of the properties of $\mathbf{m}'$ this means that $\bar{x} - \mu$ is distributed $\mathcal{N}(0, \sigma^2/T)$; equivalently $\bar{x}$ is distributed $\mathcal{N}(\mu, \sigma^2/T)$; equivalently $\sqrt{T}(\bar{x} - \mu)/\sigma$ is distributed $\mathcal{N}(0, 1)$. Note that as is true in random sampling from *any* population with mean μ and variance σ^2, $E\bar{x} = \mu$ and $E(\bar{x} - \mu)^2 = \sigma^2/T$.

Next define the $T \times T$ matrix $\mathbf{M} = \mathbf{I} - T^{-1}\boldsymbol{\iota}\boldsymbol{\iota}'$. Note that $\mathbf{M}\mathbf{x} = (\mathbf{I} - T^{-1}\boldsymbol{\iota}\boldsymbol{\iota}')\mathbf{x} = \mathbf{x} - T^{-1}\boldsymbol{\iota}'\mathbf{x}\boldsymbol{\iota} = \mathbf{x} - \bar{x}\boldsymbol{\iota}$ so that $\mathbf{M}\mathbf{x}$ is the vector of deviations from the sample means; $\mathbf{M}\boldsymbol{\mu} = (\mathbf{I} - T^{-1}\boldsymbol{\iota}\boldsymbol{\iota}')\boldsymbol{\mu} = \boldsymbol{\mu} - T^{-1}\boldsymbol{\iota}T\mu = \boldsymbol{\mu} - \boldsymbol{\mu} = \mathbf{0}$, so that $\mathbf{M}(\mathbf{x} - \boldsymbol{\mu}) = \mathbf{M}\mathbf{x} - \mathbf{M}\boldsymbol{\mu} = \mathbf{M}\mathbf{x} - \mathbf{0} = \mathbf{M}\mathbf{x}$ is also the vector of deviations from the sample means. Further, $\mathbf{M}' = \mathbf{M}$,

$$\begin{aligned}\mathbf{M}\mathbf{M} &= (\mathbf{I} - T^{-1}\boldsymbol{\iota}\boldsymbol{\iota}')(\mathbf{I} - T^{-1}\boldsymbol{\iota}\boldsymbol{\iota}')\\ &= \mathbf{I} + T^{-2}\boldsymbol{\iota}\boldsymbol{\iota}'\boldsymbol{\iota}\boldsymbol{\iota}' - T^{-1}\boldsymbol{\iota}\boldsymbol{\iota}' - T^{-1}\boldsymbol{\iota}\boldsymbol{\iota}'\\ &= \mathbf{I} - T^{-1}\boldsymbol{\iota}\boldsymbol{\iota}' = \mathbf{M}\end{aligned}$$

so that $\mathbf{M}$ is idempotent; and $tr(\mathbf{M}) = tr(\mathbf{I}) - T^{-1}\, tr(\boldsymbol{\iota}\boldsymbol{\iota}') = T - T^{-1}T = T - 1$, so that $\mathbf{M}$ is idempotent of rank $T - 1$. Since

$$\begin{aligned}Ts^2 &= \sum_{t=1}^{T}(x_t - \bar{x})^2 = [\mathbf{M}(\mathbf{x} - \boldsymbol{\mu})]'[\mathbf{M}(\mathbf{x} - \boldsymbol{\mu})]\\ &= (\mathbf{x} - \boldsymbol{\mu})'\mathbf{M}'\mathbf{M}(\mathbf{x} - \boldsymbol{\mu}) = (\mathbf{x} - \boldsymbol{\mu})'\mathbf{M}(\mathbf{x} - \boldsymbol{\mu})\end{aligned}$$

is an idempotent quadratic form of rank $T - 1$ in the spherical normal vector $\mathbf{x} - \boldsymbol{\mu}$, it follows from (5.22) that Ts^2 is distributed $\sigma^2\chi^2_{T-1}$; equivalently, that Ts^2/σ^2 is distributed χ^2_{T-1}; equivalently, that $\sqrt{T}\,s/\sigma\sqrt{T-1}$ is distributed $\sqrt{\chi^2_{T-1}/(T-1)}$. Note that, as is true in random sampling from *any* population with variance σ^2, $Es^2 = T^{-1}(T - 1)\sigma^2$.

As an immediate corollary we have

(5.29) In random sampling from a normal population the sample mean $\bar{x}$ is distributed independently of the sample variance s^2.

For continuing the previous argument, $Ts^2 = (\mathbf{x} - \boldsymbol{\mu})'\mathbf{M}(\mathbf{x} - \boldsymbol{\mu})$ is an idempotent quadratic form, and $\bar{x} - \mu = \mathbf{m}'(\mathbf{x} - \boldsymbol{\mu})$ a linear form, in the spherical normal vector $\mathbf{x} - \boldsymbol{\mu}$; and

$$\begin{aligned}\mathbf{m}'\mathbf{M} &= T^{-1}\boldsymbol{\iota}'(\mathbf{I} - T^{-1}\boldsymbol{\iota}\boldsymbol{\iota}') = T^{-1}(\boldsymbol{\iota}'\mathbf{I} - T^{-1}\boldsymbol{\iota}'\boldsymbol{\iota}\boldsymbol{\iota}')\\ &= T^{-1}(\boldsymbol{\iota}' - \boldsymbol{\iota}') = \mathbf{0}.\end{aligned}$$

Therefore by (5.24) $\bar{x} - \mu$ and Ts^2 are independently distributed; which, since μ and T are constants, implies that $\bar{x}$ and s^2 are independently distributed. And finally

(5.30) Let $x_1, \ldots, x_T$ be a random sample from a normal population with mean μ and variance σ^2. Then the statistic $(\bar{x} - \mu)/(s/\sqrt{T-1})$ is distributed as t_{T-1}.

This is so because

$$\frac{\bar{x} - \mu}{s/\sqrt{T-1}} = \frac{\sqrt{T}(\bar{x} - \mu)/\sigma}{\sqrt{T}\, s/\sigma\sqrt{T-1}};$$

$\sqrt{T}(\bar{x} - \mu)/\sigma$ is distributed $\mathcal{N}(0, 1)$ and $\sqrt{T}\, s/\sigma\sqrt{T-1}$ is distributed $\sqrt{\chi^2_{T-1}/(T-1)}$ by (5.28); and they are independently distributed by (5.29). Therefore by (5.15) $[\sqrt{T}(\bar{x} - \mu)/\sigma]/[\sqrt{T}\, s/\sigma\sqrt{T-1}]$ is distributed as t_{T-1}.

6. ASYMPTOTIC DISTRIBUTION THEORY

Sequence of Random Variables

Consider a sequence of random variables $\{x^{(n)}\} = x^{(1)}, \ldots, x^{(n)}, \ldots$ each of which has its own distribution, expectation, and variance. For example, $x^{(n)}$ might be the sample mean from size n samples drawn from a given population; the sequence would then consist of the sample means drawn from successively larger samples; for each sample size there is a distribution, expectation, and variance of the sample means. In any event it may be the case that as the sequence index n goes to infinity the distributions converge to a certain distribution. If so, this is called the limiting, or asymptotic, distribution of the sequence. For many purposes we are interested only in certain characteristics of the asymptotic distribution; much of the material in this section is concerned with the first and second moments of the asymptotic distribution. The concept of a sequence of random variables extends directly to a sequence of random vectors.

Asymptotic Expectation and Variance

We begin with definitions.

(6.1) Let $\{x^{(n)}\} = x^{(1)}, \ldots, x^{(n)}, \ldots$ be a sequence of random variables and let $\{Ex^{(n)}\} = Ex^{(1)}, \ldots, Ex^{(n)}, \ldots$ be the sequence of their expectations. Suppose that $\lim_{n\to\infty} Ex^{(n)} = \mu$ where μ is a finite constant. Then μ is said to be the asymptotic expectation of the sequence $\{x^{(n)}\}$, and we write $\bar{E}x^{(n)} = \mu$ or simply $\bar{E}x = \mu$.

Suppose that each item in the sequence has the same expectation; then the asymptotic expectation is just that common expectation, for if $Ex^{(n)} = \mu$ for all n, then $\bar{E}x = \lim_{n\to\infty} Ex^{(n)} = \lim_{n\to\infty} \mu = \mu$. Alternatively, suppose that $Ex^{(n)} = \mu + n^{-1}c_1 + n^{-2}c_2 + \cdots$ where the c's are finite constants; then $\bar{E}x = \lim_{n\to\infty} Ex^{(n)} = \lim_{n\to\infty} (\mu + n^{-1}c_1 + n^{-2}c_2 + \cdots) = \mu$. Thus if the expectation of $x^{(n)}$ is expressible as a power series in $n^0, n^{-1}, n^{-2}, \ldots$, the asymptotic expectation of $x^{(n)}$ is the leading term of this power series; as n goes to infinity the terms of "higher order of smallness" in n vanish.

(6.2) Let $\{x^{(n)}\} = x^{(1)}, \ldots, x^{(n)}, \ldots$ be a sequence of random variables; let $\{Ex^{(n)}\} = Ex^{(1)}, \ldots, Ex^{(n)}, \ldots$ be the sequence of their expectations; and let $\{E(x^{(n)} - Ex^{(n)})^2\} = E(x^{(1)} - Ex^{(1)})^2, \ldots, E(x^{(n)} - Ex^{(n)})^2, \ldots$ be the sequence of their variances. Suppose that the asymptotic expectation of the sequence exists, $\bar{E}x^{(n)} = \bar{E}x$. Suppose further that $\lim_{n\to\infty} E[\sqrt{n}(x^{(n)} - Ex^{(n)})]^2 = v$ where v is a finite constant. Then $\sigma^2 = v/n$ is said to be the asymptotic variance of the sequence $\{x^{(n)}\}$, and we write $\bar{E}(x^{(n)} - Ex^{(n)})^2 = \sigma^2$ or simply $\bar{E}(x - \bar{E}x)^2 = \sigma^2$.

Suppose that each item in the sequence has the variance v/n; then the asymptotic variance is just that common variance, for if $E(x^{(n)} - Ex^{(n)})^2 = v/n$ for all n, then $\bar{E}(x - \bar{E}x)^2 = n^{-1} \lim_{n\to\infty} E[\sqrt{n}(x^{(n)} - Ex^{(n)})]^2 = n^{-1} \times \lim_{n\to\infty} (nv)/n = v/n$. Alternatively, suppose that $E(x^{(n)} - Ex^{(n)})^2 = n^{-1}v + n^{-2}c_2 + n^{-3}c_3 + \cdots$ where the c's are finite constants; then

$$
\begin{aligned}
\bar{E}(x - \bar{E}x)^2 &= n^{-1} \lim_{n\to\infty} E[\sqrt{n}(x^{(n)} - Ex^{(n)})]^2 \\
&= n^{-1} \lim_{n\to\infty} [nE(x^{(n)} - Ex^{(n)})^2] \\
&= n^{-1} \lim_{n\to\infty} (v + n^{-1}c_2 + n^{-2}c_3 + \cdots) = n^{-1}v.
\end{aligned}
$$

Thus if the variance of each $x^{(n)}$ is expressible as a power series in n^{-1}, $n^{-2}, \ldots$, the asymptotic variance of $x^{(n)}$ is the leading term of this power series; as n goes to infinity the terms of "higher order of smallness" in n vanish. In many applications we deal with sequences where the expectations are expressible as power series in $n^0, n^{-1}, n^{-2}, \ldots$, and the variances are expressible as power series in $n^{-1}, n^{-2}, \ldots$. Of course the asymptotic moments may be used as approximations to the moments for any n. It may also be noted that the asymptotic variance of the sequence $\{x^{(n)}\}$ is just n^{-1} times the asymptotic expectation of the sequence $\{[\sqrt{n}(x^{(n)} - Ex^{(n)})]^2\}$.

These concepts extend directly to sequences of random vectors; i.e., sequences in which each item is a vector of random variables. The joint distributions may converge to an asymptotic distribution; again we concentrate on the first and second asymptotic moments.

(6.3) Let $\{\mathbf{x}^{(n)}\} = \mathbf{x}^{(1)}, \ldots, \mathbf{x}^{(n)}, \ldots$ be a sequence of random vectors and let $\{E\mathbf{x}^{(n)}\} = E\mathbf{x}^{(1)}, \ldots, E\mathbf{x}^{(n)}, \ldots$ be the sequence of their expectation vectors. Suppose that $\lim_{n\to\infty} E\mathbf{x}^{(n)} = \boldsymbol{\mu}$ where $\boldsymbol{\mu}$ is a vector of finite constants. Then $\boldsymbol{\mu}$ is said to be the asymptotic expectation of the sequence $\mathbf{x}^{(n)}$ and we write $\bar{E}\mathbf{x}^{(n)} = \boldsymbol{\mu}$ or simply $\bar{E}\mathbf{x} = \boldsymbol{\mu}$.

Thus the asymptotic expectation of a vector is simply the vector of asymptotic expectations of the random variables that are the elements of the vector.

(6.4) Let $\{\mathbf{x}^{(n)}\} = \mathbf{x}^{(1)}, \ldots, \mathbf{x}^{(n)}, \ldots$ be a sequence of random vectors; let $\{E\mathbf{x}^{(n)}\} = E\mathbf{x}^{(1)}, \ldots, E\mathbf{x}^{(n)}, \ldots$ be the sequence of their expectation vectors; and let

$$\begin{aligned}\{E(\mathbf{x}^{(n)} - E\mathbf{x}^{(n)})(\mathbf{x}^{(n)} - E\mathbf{x}^{(n)})'\} \\ = E(\mathbf{x}^{(1)} - E\mathbf{x}^{(1)})(\mathbf{x}^{(1)} - E\mathbf{x}^{(1)})', \ldots, \\ E(\mathbf{x}^{(n)} - E\mathbf{x}^{(n)})(\mathbf{x}^{(n)} - E\mathbf{x}^{(n)})', \ldots\end{aligned}$$

be the sequence of their covariance matrices. Suppose that the asymptotic expectation of the sequence exists, $\bar{E}\mathbf{x}^{(n)} = \bar{E}\mathbf{x}$. Suppose further that $\lim_{n\to\infty} E[\sqrt{n}(\mathbf{x}^{(n)} - E\mathbf{x}^{(n)})][\sqrt{n}(\mathbf{x}^{(n)} - E\mathbf{x}^{(n)})]' = \mathbf{V}$ where $\mathbf{V}$ is a matrix of finite constants. Then $\boldsymbol{\Sigma} = n^{-1}\mathbf{V}$ is said to be the asymptotic covariance matrix of the sequence $\mathbf{x}^{(n)}$, and we write $\bar{E}(\mathbf{x}^{(n)} - E\mathbf{x}^{(n)})(\mathbf{x}^{(n)} - E\mathbf{x}^{(n)})' = \boldsymbol{\Sigma}$, or simply $\bar{E}(\mathbf{x} - \bar{E}\mathbf{x})(\mathbf{x} - \bar{E}\mathbf{x})' = \boldsymbol{\Sigma}$.

Thus the asymptotic covariance matrix of a random vector is simply the matrix of asymptotic variances and covariances of the random variables that are the elements of the vector.

Extending a bit further we may define the asymptotic expectation of a sequence of random matrices as the matrix of asymptotic expectations of the random variables that are the elements of the matrix.

Probability Limit

Again consider the sequence of random variables $\{x^{(n)}\}$. It may be that as n goes to infinity the mass or density function becomes entirely concentrated on some point x^*. If so, the sequence is said to converge in probability to x^*; equivalently x^* is said to be the probability limit of the sequence. Thus

(6.5) Let $\{x^{(n)}\} = x^{(1)}, \ldots, x^{(n)}, \ldots$ be a sequence of random variables. Suppose that $\lim_{n\to\infty} \text{Prob}\,\{|x^{(n)} - x^*| \geq \delta\} = 0$ for every $\delta > 0$, where x^* is a finite constant. Then x^* is said to be the probability limit of the sequence $\{x^{(n)}\}$, and we write $\text{plim}\, x^{(n)} = x^*$ or simply $\text{plim}\, x = x^*$.

Clearly if the entire distribution collapses on a point that point must be the asymptotic expectation; thus

(6.6) If $\text{plim}\, x = x^*$, then $\bar{E}x = x^*$.

Of course the converse is not true, for the expectation can approach a constant without the distribution collapsing. If the variance goes to zero, however, the distribution will collapse; thus

(6.7) If $\bar{E}x = x^*$ and $\lim_{n\to\infty} \bar{E}(x - \bar{E}x)^2 = 0$, then $\text{plim}\, x = x^*$.

Taking limits in Chebyshev's inequality,

$$\lim_{n\to\infty} \text{Prob}\,\{|x^{(n)} - Ex^{(n)}| \geq \epsilon\} \leq \lim_{n\to\infty} \frac{E(x^{(n)} - Ex^{(n)})^2}{\epsilon^2}$$

for every $\epsilon > 0$. Now as n goes to infinity $Ex^{(n)}$ goes to $\bar{E}x = x^*$ and $E(x^{(n)} - Ex^{(n)})^2$ goes to $\bar{E}(x - \bar{E}x)^2$. If in fact $\bar{E}(x - \bar{E}x)^2$ goes to zero, the limit on the right-hand side is zero, so that the limit on the left-hand side is also zero. Then by (6.5) $\text{plim}\, x = x^*$. For example, suppose $\bar{E}x = x^*$ exists and $\bar{E}(x - \bar{E}x)^2 = v/n$ where v is a finite constant; then $\lim_{n\to\infty} v/n = 0$ so that $\text{plim}\, x = x^*$.

It is clear that the probability limit of a constant is just the constant:

(6.8) If c is a constant, then $\text{plim}\, c = c$.

An important property of probability limits is that the probability limit of a continuous function is the function of the probability limits; thus

(6.9) If $\text{plim}\, x = x^*$ and if $g(x)$ is a continuous function, then $\text{plim}\, g(x) = g(x^*)$.

This theorem is due to Slutsky; for a proof see Wilks (1962, pp. 102–103). Note that the corresponding theorem for expectations is not true; $Eg(x) \neq g(Ex)$, in general.

These concepts extend directly to sequences of random vectors.

(6.10) Let $\{\mathbf{x}^{(n)}\} = \mathbf{x}^{(1)}, \ldots, \mathbf{x}^{(n)}, \ldots$ be a sequence of random vectors. Suppose that $\lim_{n\to\infty} \text{Prob}\,\{|\mathbf{x}^{(n)} - \mathbf{x}^*| \geq \boldsymbol{\delta}\} = 0$ for every vector $\boldsymbol{\delta} > \mathbf{0}$, however small its elements, where $\mathbf{x}^*$ is a vector of finite constants. Then $\mathbf{x}^*$ is said to be the probability limit of the sequence $\{\mathbf{x}^{(n)}\}$, and we write $\text{plim}\,\mathbf{x}^{(n)} = \mathbf{x}^*$ or simply $\text{plim}\,\mathbf{x} = \mathbf{x}^*$.

Thus the probability limit of a random vector is simply the vector of probability limits of the random variables composing the vector. It will be convenient to record the extensions of (6.6)–(6.9):

(6.11) If $\text{plim}\,\mathbf{x} = \mathbf{x}^*$, then $\bar{E}\mathbf{x} = \mathbf{x}^*$;

and

(6.12) If $\bar{E}\mathbf{x} = \mathbf{x}^*$ and $\lim_{n\to\infty} \bar{E}(\mathbf{x} - \bar{E}\mathbf{x})(\mathbf{x} - \bar{E}\mathbf{x})' = \mathbf{0}$, then $\text{plim}\,\mathbf{x} = \mathbf{x}^*$.

For example, suppose that $\bar{E}\mathbf{x} = \mathbf{x}^*$ and $\bar{E}(\mathbf{x} - \bar{E}\mathbf{x})(\mathbf{x} - \bar{E}\mathbf{x})' = n^{-1}\mathbf{V}$ where $\mathbf{V}$ is a matrix of finite constants; since $\lim_{n\to\infty} n^{-1}\mathbf{V} = \mathbf{0}$ it will be true that $\text{plim}\,\mathbf{x} = \mathbf{x}^*$. Continuing,

(6.13) If $\mathbf{c}$ is a constant vector, then $\text{plim}\,\mathbf{c} = \mathbf{c}$;

and Slutsky's theorem extends to

(6.14) If $\text{plim}\,\mathbf{x} = \mathbf{x}^*$ and if $\mathbf{y}$ is a random vector, whose elements $y_i = g_i(\mathbf{x})$ are continuous functions of the elements of $\mathbf{x}$, then $\text{plim}\,\mathbf{y} = \mathbf{y}^*$ where $y_i^* = g_i(\mathbf{x}^*)$.

The concepts extend further to sequences of random matrices. Thus the probability limit of a random matrix is the matrix of probability limits of the random variables that are the elements of the matrix; the probability limit of a matrix is also its asymptotic expectation; if the matrix is constant, its probability limit is itself. It is convenient to record two important applications of Slutsky's theorem applied to matrices. Since the elements of a product matrix are continuous functions of the elements of the component matrices,

(6.15) $\text{plim}\,(\mathbf{AB}) = (\text{plim}\,\mathbf{A})(\text{plim}\,\mathbf{B})$.

Since the elements of an inverse matrix are continuous functions of the elements of the original matrix,

(6.16) $\text{plim}\,(\mathbf{A}^{-1}) = (\text{plim}\,\mathbf{A})^{-1}$.

In both cases, of course, we assume that the probability limits on the right-hand side exist.

Finally we note a useful result, which follows from the remark that the asymptotic variance of the sequence $\{x^{(n)}\}$ is just n^{-1} times the asymptotic expectation of the sequence $\{[\sqrt{n}(x^{(n)} - Ex^{(n)})]^2\}$:

(6.17) If $\text{plim}\ [\sqrt{n}(\mathbf{x}^{(n)} - E\mathbf{x}^{(n)})][\sqrt{n}(\mathbf{x}^{(n)} - E\mathbf{x}^{(n)})]' = \mathbf{V}$, then $\bar{E}(\mathbf{x} - \bar{E}\mathbf{x})(\mathbf{x} - \bar{E}\mathbf{x})' = n^{-1}\mathbf{V}$.

Asymptotic Distribution of Sample Statistics

The leading application of the theory of sequences of random variables and asymptotic distributions is to sample statistics. Given a parent population and a function of the sample observations we can consider the distribution of this function for sample size 1, sample size 2, . . . , sample size T, ... The functions for the successive sample sizes constitute a sequence of random variables. The distribution of the function typically varies systematically with the sample size, and in important cases converges to a limiting distribution as the sample size T goes to infinity. This limiting distribution is of interest, particularly since it may be used as an approximation for the distributions for finite sample sizes, which are often difficult to derive. In fact we are often interested only in moments of the limiting distribution such as the asymptotic mean and asymptotic variance, and in the probability limit.

We have used the superscript n for general sequences of random variables; in its stead we use the subscript T in our discussion of sample statistics.

Consider random sampling from a population with mean μ and variance σ^2 and fourth central moment μ_4. For sample size T the sample mean $\bar{x} = T^{-1} \sum_{t=1}^{T} x_t$, and we have seen that $E\bar{x} = \mu$ and $E(\bar{x} - \mu)^2 = T^{-1}\sigma^2$. It follows that $\bar{E}\bar{x} = \lim_{T\to\infty} E\bar{x} = \mu$ and $\bar{E}(\bar{x} - \mu)^2 = T^{-1} \lim_{T\to\infty} E[\sqrt{T}(\bar{x} - \mu)]^2 = T^{-1} \lim_{T\to\infty} TT^{-1}\sigma^2 = T^{-1}\sigma^2$; further, since $\lim_{T\to\infty} T^{-1}\sigma^2 = 0$, it follows that $\text{plim}\ \bar{x} = \mu$. Thus the asymptotic expectation and probability limit of $\bar{x}$ is μ, and its asymptotic variance is $T^{-1}\sigma^2$. For sample size T the sample variance $s^2 = T^{-1} \sum_{t=1}^{T} (x_t - \bar{x})^2$, and we have seen that $Es^2 = (T - 1)T^{-1}\sigma^2$ and $E(s^2 - Es^2)^2 = T^{-1}(\mu_4 - \sigma^4) - 2T^{-2}(\mu_4 - 2\sigma^4) + T^{-3}(\mu_4 - 3\sigma^4)$. It follows that $\bar{E}s^2 = \lim_{T\to\infty} (T - 1)T^{-1}\sigma^2 = \sigma^2$ and

$$\begin{aligned}\bar{E}(s^2 - \sigma^2)^2 &= T^{-1} \lim_{T\to\infty} E[\sqrt{T}(s^2 - Es^2)]^2 \\ &= T^{-1} \lim_{T\to\infty} \{T[T^{-1}(\mu_4 - \sigma^4) - 2T^{-2}(\mu_4 - 2\sigma^4) \\ &\quad + T^{-3}(\mu_4 - 3\sigma^4)]\} = T^{-1}(\mu_4 - \sigma^4);\end{aligned}$$

further, since $\lim_{T\to\infty} T^{-1}(\mu_4 - \sigma^4) = 0$, it follows that $\text{plim}\ s^2 = \sigma^2$. Thus the asymptotic expectation and probability limit of s^2 is σ^2, and its asymptotic variance is $T^{-1}(\mu_4 - \sigma^4)$. An instructive alternative derivation of plim $s^2 = \sigma^2$ is based on the fact that $s^2 = s_*^2 - (\bar{x} - \mu)^2$ where $s_*^2 = T^{-1} \Sigma (x_t - \mu)^2$. We have seen that $Es_*^2 = \sigma^2$ and

$$E(s_*^2 - \sigma^2)^2 = T^{-1}(\mu_4 - \sigma^4);$$

hence $\bar{E}s_*^2 = \sigma^2$, $\bar{E}(s_*^2 - \sigma^2)^2 = T^{-1}(\mu_4 - \sigma^4)$, and plim $s_*^2 = \sigma^2$. Then, applying Slutsky's theorem, plim s^2 = plim s_*^2 + plim $[(\bar{x} - \mu)^2]$ = plim s_*^2 + [plim $(\bar{x} - \mu)]^2 = \sigma^2$, since plim $(\bar{x} - \mu)$ = plim $\bar{x}$ − plim μ = $\mu - \mu = 0$. Summarizing,

(6.18) For random sampling from a population with mean μ, variance σ^2, and fourth central moment μ_4,

(6.18*a*) $\bar{E}\bar{x} = \mu$, $\bar{E}(\bar{x} - \mu)^2 = \sigma^2/T$, plim $\bar{x} = \mu$,

(6.18*b*) $\bar{E}s^2 = \sigma^2$, $\bar{E}(s^2 - \sigma^2)^2 = (\mu_4 - \sigma^4)/T$, plim $s^2 = \sigma^2$.

Thus the distributions of these sample statistics become entirely concentrated on the corresponding population parameters as the sample size grows indefinitely large. The result plim $\bar{x} = \mu$ is known as the weak law of large numbers.

The multivariate extension of some of these results is straightforward; we record the following:

(6.19) Let $\mathbf{x}$ be a random vector with mean vector $\boldsymbol{\mu}$ and covariance matrix $\boldsymbol{\Sigma}$; let $\bar{\mathbf{x}}$ be the sample mean vector and $\mathbf{S}$ be the sample covariance matrix. Then for random sampling

(6.19*a*) $\bar{E}\bar{\mathbf{x}} = \boldsymbol{\mu}$, $\bar{E}(\bar{\mathbf{x}} - \boldsymbol{\mu})(\bar{\mathbf{x}} - \boldsymbol{\mu})' = T^{-1}\boldsymbol{\Sigma}$, plim $\bar{\mathbf{x}} = \boldsymbol{\mu}$,

(6.19*b*) $\bar{E}\mathbf{S} = \boldsymbol{\Sigma}$, plim $\mathbf{S} = \boldsymbol{\Sigma}$.

In fact we can say much more about the limiting distribution of the sequence of sample means:

(6.20) For random sampling from a population x with mean μ and variance σ^2 the distribution of $\bar{x}$ converges to $\mathcal{N}(\mu, \sigma^2/T)$ as T goes to infinity.

For a proof see Wilks (1962, pp. 256–257). We have already seen that if the parent population is $\mathcal{N}(\mu, \sigma^2)$ then the sample mean is distributed $\mathcal{N}(\mu, \sigma^2/T)$ for *all* sample sizes. The remarkable point of (6.20) is that regardless of the shape of the parent distribution the distribution of sample means approaches $\mathcal{N}(\mu, \sigma^2/T)$ as T becomes large—provided that the population mean and variance are finite. In many cases this approach is so rapid that the normal distribution provides an adequate approximation for quite small sample sizes.

Indeed, (6.20) is a special case of a very important result which we formulate as

(6.21) ***Central limit theorem.*** Let $\{x^{(n)}\} = x^{(1)}, \ldots, x^{(n)}, \ldots$ be a sequence of independent random variables; let $\{Ex^{(n)}\} = \mu^{(1)}, \ldots, \mu^{(n)}, \ldots$ be the sequence of their expectations; and let $\{E(x^{(n)} - Ex^{(n)})^2\} = \sigma^{2(1)}, \ldots, \sigma^{2(n)}, \ldots$ be the sequence of their variances. In addition, let $x_n = \Sigma_{i=1}^n x^{(i)}$, $\mu_n = Ex_n = \Sigma_{i=1}^n \mu^{(i)}$, and $\sigma_n^2 = E(x_n - Ex_n)^2 = \Sigma_{i=1}^n \sigma^{2(i)}$. Then under general conditions x_n converges to $\mathcal{N}(\mu_n, \sigma_n^2)$ as n goes to infinity.

For discussion of proofs see Wilks (1962, pp. 257–259). We note the "general conditions" involve the requirement that none of the individual items $x^{(i)}$ dominate the sum as far as its variance is concerned; i.e., that $\lim_{n\to\infty} (\sigma^{2(i)}/\sigma_n^2) = 0$ for all i. Verbally, the central limit theorem states that the distribution of the sum of a large number of independent random variables tends to be normally distributed, almost regardless of the shape of the original distributions. Note also that the mean of these variables will also tend to be normally distributed: If x_n is $\mathcal{N}(\mu_n, \sigma_n^2)$, then $\bar{x}_n = x_n/n$ is $\mathcal{N}(\bar{\mu}_n, \bar{\sigma}_n^2)$, where $\bar{\mu}_n = \mu_n/n$ and $\bar{\sigma}_n^2 = \sigma_n^2/n^2$. It is the central limit theorem that accounts for the central role of the normal distribution in mathematical statistics; although individual variables are not necessarily normally distributed, the sum or mean of a large number of such variables does tend to be normally distributed.

One consequence of the central limit theorem is that the distributions of sample statistics—(5.28) and (5.30)—derived in the preceding section under the assumption of a normal parent are often valid as approximations for large samples even when the parent is not normal.

Asymptotic Mean and Variance for Functions of Random Variables

In (3.40) and (3.48) we obtained exact formulas for the means and variances of linear functions of random variables. Using the concepts of this section we proceed to obtain corresponding approximate formulas for nonlinear functions.

We deal with a sequence of random vectors $\{\mathbf{x}^{(n)}\} = \mathbf{x}^{(1)}, \ldots, \mathbf{x}^{(n)}, \ldots$

where $\mathbf{x}^{(n)} = \begin{pmatrix} x_1^{(n)} \\ \cdot \\ \cdot \\ \cdot \\ x_m^{(n)} \end{pmatrix}$ with $\bar{E}\mathbf{x}^{(n)} = \boldsymbol{\mu} = \begin{pmatrix} \mu_1 \\ \cdot \\ \cdot \\ \cdot \\ \mu_m \end{pmatrix}$ and

$$\bar{E}(\mathbf{x}^{(n)} - \bar{E}\mathbf{x}^{(n)})(\mathbf{x}^{(n)} - \bar{E}\mathbf{x}^{(n)})' = \boldsymbol{\Sigma} = \begin{pmatrix} \sigma_{11} & \cdots & \sigma_{1m} \\ \cdot & & \cdot \\ \cdot & & \cdot \\ \cdot & & \cdot \\ \sigma_{m1} & \cdots & \sigma_{mm} \end{pmatrix}.$$

Now let y be a differentiable scalar function of $\mathbf{x}$, $y = y(\mathbf{x})$; then we have a sequence of random variables $\{y^{(n)}\} = y^{(1)}, \ldots, y^{(n)}, \ldots$ where $y^{(i)} = y(\mathbf{x}^{(i)})$. For simplicity the superscript index is generally omitted. Expanding y in a Taylor series around the point $\boldsymbol{\mu}$,

$$(6.22) \qquad y = y(\boldsymbol{\mu}) + \sum_{i=1}^{m} \frac{\partial y}{\partial x_i}(x_i - \mu_i) + \frac{1}{2}\sum_{i=1}^{m}\sum_{j=1}^{m} \frac{\partial^2 y}{\partial x_i\,\partial x_j}(x_i - \mu_i)(x_j - \mu_j) + \cdots$$

where the derivatives are evaluated at $\boldsymbol{\mu}$. Taking expectations,

$$(6.23) \qquad Ey = y(\boldsymbol{\mu}) + \sum_{i=1}^{m} \frac{\partial y}{\partial x_i}E(x_i - \mu_i) + \frac{1}{2}\sum_{i=1}^{m}\sum_{j=1}^{m} \frac{\partial^2 y}{\partial x_i\,\partial x_j}E(x_i - \mu_i)(x_j - \mu_j) + \cdots.$$

Taking limits as n goes to infinity,

$$(6.24) \qquad \bar{E}y = \lim_{n\to\infty} Ey = y(\boldsymbol{\mu}) + \sum_{i=1}^{m} \frac{\partial y}{\partial x_i}\lim_{n\to\infty} E(x_i - \mu_i) + \frac{1}{2}\sum_{i=1}^{m}\sum_{j=1}^{m} \frac{\partial^2 y}{\partial x_i\,\partial x_j}\lim_{n\to\infty} E(x_i - \mu_i)(x_j - \mu_j) + \cdots$$

$$= y(\boldsymbol{\mu}) + \frac{1}{2}\sum_{i=1}^{m}\sum_{j=1}^{m} \frac{\partial^2 y}{\partial x_i\,\partial x_j}\lim_{n\to\infty}\sigma_{ij} + \cdots$$

since as n goes to infinity Ex_i goes to $\bar{E}x_i = \mu_i$ and $E(x_i - \mu_i)(x_j - \mu_j)$ goes to $\bar{E}(x_i - \mu_i)(x_j - \mu_j) = \sigma_{ij}$. Thus the asymptotic expectation of y is expressed in terms of the asymptotic expectations, variances and covariances, and higher moments of the elements of $\mathbf{x}$. Suppose in fact that $\boldsymbol{\Sigma} = n^{-1}\mathbf{V}$ where $\mathbf{V} = (v_{ij})$ is a constant matrix; then $\lim_{n\to\infty}\sigma_{ij} = 0$ for all i and j (and the higher order moments also go to zero). Then

$$(6.25) \qquad \bar{E}y = y(\boldsymbol{\mu})$$

so that in this case the asymptotic expectation of the function will be the function of the asymptotic expectations, despite the nonlinearity of the function. Further, subtracting (6.25) from (6.22),

(6.26)
$$y - \bar{E}y = \sum_{i=1}^{m} \frac{\partial y}{\partial x_i}(x_i - \mu_i) + \frac{1}{2}\sum_{i=1}^{m}\sum_{j=1}^{m} \frac{\partial^2 y}{\partial x_i\,\partial x_j}(x_i - \mu_i)(x_j - \mu_j) + \cdots;$$

multiplying through by $\sqrt{n}$ and squaring,

(6.27)
$$[\sqrt{n}(y - \bar{E}y)]^2 = \left[\sum_{i=1}^{m} \frac{\partial y}{\partial x_i}\sqrt{n}(x_i - \mu_i)\right]^2 + \left[\frac{1}{2}\sum_{i=1}^{m}\sum_{j=1}^{m} \frac{\partial^2 y}{\partial x_i\,\partial x_j}\sqrt{n}(x_i - \mu_i)(x_j - \mu_j)\right]^2 + \cdots$$

and taking expectations,

(6.28)
$$E[\sqrt{n}(y - \bar{E}y)]^2 = \sum_{i=1}^{m}\sum_{j=1}^{m} \frac{\partial y}{\partial x_i}\frac{\partial y}{\partial x_j} E[\sqrt{n}(x_i - \mu_i)\sqrt{n}(x_j - \mu_j)] + \cdots.$$

Then taking limits as n goes to infinity,

(6.29)
$$\lim_{n\to\infty} E[\sqrt{n}(y - \bar{E}y)]^2 = \sum_{i=1}^{m}\sum_{j=1}^{m} \frac{\partial y}{\partial x_i}\frac{\partial y}{\partial x_j} \lim_{n\to\infty} E[\sqrt{n}(x_i - \mu_i)\sqrt{n}(x_j - \mu_j)]$$

since the higher-order terms go to zero. Thus

(6.30)
$$\bar{E}(y - \bar{E}y)^2 = n^{-1}\lim_{n\to\infty} E[\sqrt{n}(y - \bar{E}y)]^2 = n^{-1}\sum_{i=1}^{m}\sum_{j=1}^{m} \frac{\partial y}{\partial x_i}\frac{\partial y}{\partial x_j} v_{ij} = \sum_{i=1}^{m}\sum_{j=1}^{m} \frac{\partial y}{\partial x_i}\frac{\partial y}{\partial x_j} \sigma_{ij}$$

since $\sigma_{ij} = n^{-1}v_{ij}$. Thus in this case the asymptotic variance of the function y will be expressed in terms of the variances and covariances of the elements of $\mathbf{x}$.

Summarizing and using a convenient matrix notation, we have

(6.31) Let $\mathbf{x}$ be the typical item in a sequence of random vectors and let $y = y(\mathbf{x})$ be a differentiable scalar function of $\mathbf{x}$. Suppose that $\bar{E}\mathbf{x} = \boldsymbol{\mu}$ and $\bar{E}(\mathbf{x} - \bar{E}\mathbf{x})(\mathbf{x} - \bar{E}\mathbf{x})' = \boldsymbol{\Sigma} = n^{-1}\mathbf{V}$ where $\mathbf{V}$ is a matrix of finite constants. Then $\bar{E}y = y(\boldsymbol{\mu})$ and $\bar{E}(y - \bar{E}y)^2 = \mathbf{j}'\boldsymbol{\Sigma}\mathbf{j}$ where $\mathbf{j} = \partial y/\partial\mathbf{x}$ is evaluated at $\boldsymbol{\mu}$.

This useful result extends to the multivariate case in a straightforward way. Thus

(6.32) Let $\mathbf{x}$ be the typical item in a sequence of random vectors and let $\mathbf{y} = y(\mathbf{x})$ be a vector whose elements are differentiable functions of $\mathbf{x}$. Suppose that $\bar{E}\mathbf{x} = \boldsymbol{\mu}$ and $\bar{E}(\mathbf{x} - \bar{E}\mathbf{x})(\mathbf{x} - \bar{E}\mathbf{x})' = \boldsymbol{\Sigma} = n^{-1}\mathbf{V}$, where $\mathbf{V}$ is a matrix of finite constants. Then $\bar{E}\mathbf{y} = y(\boldsymbol{\mu})$ and $\bar{E}(\mathbf{y} - \bar{E}\mathbf{y})(\mathbf{y} - \bar{E}\mathbf{y})' = \mathbf{J}'\boldsymbol{\Sigma}\mathbf{J}$ where $\mathbf{J} = \partial\mathbf{y}/\partial\mathbf{x}$ is evaluated at $\boldsymbol{\mu}$.

It is easily seen that these asymptotic results—which may be used as approximations for finite n—hold exactly for finite n when the functions are in fact linear.

7. STATISTICAL INFERENCE

Statistical Inference

We now turn to the problem of statistical inference proper: Given a sample, what can be inferred about the population from which it was drawn? We have seen that a population can generate different samples and that different populations can generate the same sample, so that we cannot expect to identify with certainty the population from which a given sample was drawn. Nevertheless reasonable rules of statistical inference can be developed.

Often we have, or are willing to assume, partial a priori knowledge of the parent population; e.g., we may know the functional form of the population distribution but not the values of its parameters. Then our interest is in utilizing the information contained in the sample to narrow the gaps in our knowledge; e.g., to ascertain the value of some parameter of the population distribution. Although we do not always assume that the functional form of the population distribution is known, in this book we do confine our attention to statistical inference about population parameters. The discussion follows the classical theory of statistical inference, distinguishing among point estimation, interval estimation, and hypothesis testing.

Point Estimation

In the theory of point estimation we seek to select a function of the sample observations whose value in a given sample will be acceptable as a "good estimate" of a parameter of the parent population. A function used to provide estimates of a parameter θ is called an estimator and written $\hat{\theta} = \hat{\theta}(x_1, \ldots, x_T)$, or if we wish to emphasize the sample size,

$\hat{\theta}_T = \hat{\theta}_T(x_1, \ldots, x_T)$. The value taken by an estimator when a specific set of sample observations are inserted in the function is called an estimate. Since the sample observations are random variables the estimator is also a random variable: Its values, the estimates, are sample statistics and vary from sample to sample drawn from the same population. Hence we cannot expect to find an estimator that always produces the true value of the population parameter. The sampling error of an estimator in a sample is the difference between its value in the sample and the true value of the parameter, $\hat{\theta} - \theta$. Of course we would like to have an estimator whose sampling errors tend to be small; i.e., one whose sampling distribution is in some sense concentrated about the parameter. Suppose that $\hat{\theta}$ were a function of the sample observations such that, for any positive numbers c_1 and c_2 and any other function of the sample observations $\tilde{\theta}$, Prob $\{\theta - c_1 < \hat{\theta} < \theta + c_2\} \geq$ Prob $\{\theta - c_1 < \tilde{\theta} < \theta + c_2\}$. Then there is no question that $\hat{\theta}$ would be the best estimator of θ.

Such unquestionably best estimators are available, however, only in trivial circumstances. Statisticians have come to list more modest desirable properties of an estimator, most of which refer to the mean and variance of the sampling distribution of the estimator. In any particular problem one utilizes these properties—or, rather, such of them as are attainable—as criteria for selection of an estimator from the infinite set of functions of the sample observations. It should be noted that opinion as to which criteria should dominate is not always unanimous.

We proceed to consider some traditional desirable properties that may serve as criteria for selecting an estimator. First, several properties often called "small-sample" properties that relate to samples of any size:

(7.1) $\hat{\theta}$ is an unbiased estimator of θ if $E\hat{\theta} = \theta$,

(7.2) $\hat{\theta}$ is a minimum variance estimator of θ if $E(\hat{\theta} - E\hat{\theta})^2 \leq E(\tilde{\theta} - E\tilde{\theta})^2$ where $\tilde{\theta}$ is any other estimator of θ,

(7.3) $\hat{\theta}$ is a best unbiased (or efficient) estimator of θ if $\hat{\theta}$ is unbiased and $E(\hat{\theta} - \theta)^2 \leq E(\tilde{\theta} - \theta)^2$ where $\tilde{\theta}$ is any other unbiased estimator of θ,

(7.4) $\hat{\theta}$ is a minimum second moment (or minimum mean square error) estimator of θ if $E(\hat{\theta} - \theta)^2 \leq E(\tilde{\theta} - \theta)^2$ where $\tilde{\theta}$ is any other estimator of θ.

The bias of an estimator is the expected value of its sampling error; i.e., the difference between its expectation and the parameter, $E(\hat{\theta} - \theta) = E\hat{\theta} - \theta$. An unbiased estimator is one whose bias is zero; i.e., one that "on the average" gives the true value of the parameter. In interpreting the criteria (7.2)–(7.4) note that the second moment of an estimator about a parameter equals the sum of the variance of the estimator (around its expectation) and the squared bias of the estimator:

(7.5) $$E(\hat{\theta} - \theta)^2 = E[(\hat{\theta} - E\hat{\theta}) + (E\hat{\theta} - \theta)]^2$$
$$= E(\hat{\theta} - E\hat{\theta})^2 + (E\hat{\theta} - \theta)^2 + 2(E\hat{\theta} - \theta)E(\hat{\theta} - E\hat{\theta})$$
$$= E(\hat{\theta} - E\hat{\theta})^2 + (E\hat{\theta} - \theta)^2 = \text{var}(\hat{\theta}) + \text{bias}^2(\hat{\theta}).$$

Note further that the property of minimum variance (concentrated distribution) is not particularly desirable in itself. After all, the trivial estimator $\hat{\theta} = c$ where c is any constant will have a zero variance, but its estimates will not be connected with the parameter, and its bias may be enormous. Taken together with unbiasedness, however, minimum variance is clearly desirable. On the other hand, unbiasedness is not sacred; it may well be reasonable to prefer an estimator that has a small bias and a small variance to one that has no bias but a large variance. This point underlies the minimum second moment (or "minimum mean square error") criterion, which selects a biased estimator if its variance is small enough to compensate for its bias. (In practice a minimum second moment estimator often involves the value of the parameter so that the criterion may not be operational.) The best unbiased or efficient estimator is the minimum variance (and minimum second moment) estimator within the class of unbiased estimators. The term "best" is now to be taken in this technical sense and not to mean "unquestionably most desirable." It is sometimes convenient to use efficiency in a relative sense: $\hat{\theta}$ is more efficient than $\tilde{\theta}$ if $\hat{\theta}$ and $\tilde{\theta}$ are unbiased and $\hat{\theta}$ has a smaller variance than $\tilde{\theta}$.

It is difficult to consider all the possible functions of the sample observations in order to choose the preferred one. We may well be willing to confine our attention to a limited class of functions and to choose within this class. In particular a traditional criterion is given by

(7.6) $\hat{\theta}$ is a best linear unbiased estimator (or BLUE) of θ if $\hat{\theta}$ is a linear estimator (i.e., a linear function of the sample observations), unbiased, and has the minimum variance within the class of linear unbiased estimators of θ.

Since a wide class of functions may be approximated by a linear function, we may not be sacrificing much in confining our attention to the class of linear functions. An analogous criterion is best quadratic unbiasedness.

Next we consider several properties that relate to the limiting distribution of an estimator as the sample size approaches infinity, often called "asymptotic" or "large-sample" properties:

(7.7) $\hat{\theta}$ is an asymptotically unbiased estimator of θ if $\bar{E}\hat{\theta} = \theta$,

(7.8) $\hat{\theta}$ is a consistent estimator of θ if $\text{plim } \hat{\theta} = \theta$,

(7.9) $\hat{\theta}$ is an asymptotically efficient estimator of θ if it is consistent and $\bar{E}(\hat{\theta} - \theta)^2 \leq \bar{E}(\tilde{\theta} - \theta)^2$ where $\tilde{\theta}$ is any other consistent estimator of θ.

The asymptotic bias of an estimator is the difference between its asymptotic expectation and the parameter, $\bar{E}(\hat{\theta} - \theta) = \bar{E}\hat{\theta} - \theta$. Thus, loosely speaking, an asymptotically unbiased estimator is one whose bias vanishes when the sample size is sufficiently large. In interpreting the criteria (7.7)–(7.9) note that an unbiased estimator is asymptotically unbiased but not conversely. A consistent estimator is one whose distribution collapses on the parameter as the sample size gets sufficiently large. A consistent estimator is asymptotically unbiased but the converse is not true; the mean of a distribution can approach a constant without the distribution collapsing on that constant. If the asymptotic variance of an asymptotically unbiased estimator is of the form $n^{-1}v$, however, where v is a constant, then the distribution will collapse and the estimator will be consistent. Although the variance of any consistent estimator goes to zero as the sample size grows infinite, it is still reasonable to prefer the one that goes fastest in the sense that its asymptotic variance—which serves as an approximation to the variance for large finite samples—is smallest. This preference is captured in the criterion of asymptotic efficiency. Asymptotic efficiency is also used in a relative sense. Also in view of Slutsky's theorem we have

(7.10) If $\hat{\theta}$ is a consistent estimator of θ, and if $\psi = g(\theta)$ is a continuous function of θ, then $\hat{\psi} = g(\hat{\theta})$ is a consistent estimator of ψ.

These concepts extend to the case of joint estimation of several parameters of the population distribution. Arranging the parameters in a vector $\boldsymbol{\theta} = \begin{pmatrix} \theta_1 \\ \cdot \\ \cdot \\ \cdot \\ \theta_K \end{pmatrix}$ we seek to choose an estimator vector $\hat{\boldsymbol{\theta}} = \begin{pmatrix} \hat{\theta}_1 \\ \cdot \\ \cdot \\ \cdot \\ \hat{\theta}_K \end{pmatrix}$ each element of which is a function of the sample observations used to estimate the corresponding element of the parameter vector. The traditional desirable properties in this case include:

(7.11) $\hat{\boldsymbol{\theta}}$ is an unbiased estimator of $\boldsymbol{\theta}$ if $E\hat{\boldsymbol{\theta}} = \boldsymbol{\theta}$,

(7.12) $\hat{\boldsymbol{\theta}}$ is a minimum variance estimator of $\boldsymbol{\theta}$ if $E(\tilde{\boldsymbol{\theta}} - E\tilde{\boldsymbol{\theta}})(\tilde{\boldsymbol{\theta}} - E\tilde{\boldsymbol{\theta}})' - E(\hat{\boldsymbol{\theta}} - E\hat{\boldsymbol{\theta}})(\hat{\boldsymbol{\theta}} - E\hat{\boldsymbol{\theta}})'$ is nonnegative definite where $\tilde{\boldsymbol{\theta}}$ is any other estimator of $\boldsymbol{\theta}$,

(7.13) $\hat{\boldsymbol{\theta}}$ is a best unbiased (or efficient) estimator of $\boldsymbol{\theta}$ if $\hat{\boldsymbol{\theta}}$ is unbiased and $E(\tilde{\boldsymbol{\theta}} - \boldsymbol{\theta})(\tilde{\boldsymbol{\theta}} - \boldsymbol{\theta})' - E(\hat{\boldsymbol{\theta}} - \boldsymbol{\theta})(\hat{\boldsymbol{\theta}} - \boldsymbol{\theta})'$ is nonnegative definite where $\tilde{\boldsymbol{\theta}}$ is any other unbiased estimator of $\boldsymbol{\theta}$,

(7.14) $\hat{\boldsymbol{\theta}}$ is a minimum second moment estimator of $\boldsymbol{\theta}$ if

$$E(\tilde{\boldsymbol{\theta}} - \boldsymbol{\theta})(\tilde{\boldsymbol{\theta}} - \boldsymbol{\theta})' - E(\hat{\boldsymbol{\theta}} - \boldsymbol{\theta})(\hat{\boldsymbol{\theta}} - \boldsymbol{\theta})'$$

is nonnegative definite where $\tilde{\boldsymbol{\theta}}$ is any other estimator of $\boldsymbol{\theta}$,

(7.15) $\hat{\boldsymbol{\theta}}$ is a best linear unbiased estimator (or BLUE) of $\boldsymbol{\theta}$ if $\hat{\boldsymbol{\theta}}$ is a linear estimator (i.e., a linear form in the sample observations), unbiased, and is the minimum variance estimator within the class of linear unbiased estimators of $\boldsymbol{\theta}$,

(7.16) $\hat{\boldsymbol{\theta}}$ is an asymptotically unbiased estimator of $\boldsymbol{\theta}$ if $\bar{E}\hat{\boldsymbol{\theta}} = \boldsymbol{\theta}$,

(7.17) $\hat{\boldsymbol{\theta}}$ is a consistent estimator of $\boldsymbol{\theta}$ if $\operatorname{plim} \hat{\boldsymbol{\theta}} = \boldsymbol{\theta}$,

(7.18) $\hat{\boldsymbol{\theta}}$ is an asymptotically efficient estimator of $\boldsymbol{\theta}$ if $\hat{\boldsymbol{\theta}}$ is consistent and $\bar{E}(\tilde{\boldsymbol{\theta}} - \boldsymbol{\theta})(\tilde{\boldsymbol{\theta}} - \boldsymbol{\theta})' - \bar{E}(\hat{\boldsymbol{\theta}} - \boldsymbol{\theta})(\hat{\boldsymbol{\theta}} - \boldsymbol{\theta})'$ is nonnegative definite where $\tilde{\boldsymbol{\theta}}$ is any other consistent estimator of $\boldsymbol{\theta}$.

To interpret these criteria recall that the expectation of a vector is the vector of expectations, the probability limit of a vector is the vector of probability limits, the kth diagonal element of a covariance matrix is the variance of the kth element of the vector, and each diagonal element of a nonnegative definite matrix is greater than or equal to zero. Thus when a vector estimator has a certain desirable property each of its elements has that property.

The decomposition of (7.5) generalizes to

(7.19)
$$\begin{aligned} E(\hat{\boldsymbol{\theta}} - \boldsymbol{\theta})(\hat{\boldsymbol{\theta}} - \boldsymbol{\theta})' &= E\{[(\hat{\boldsymbol{\theta}} - E\hat{\boldsymbol{\theta}}) + (E\hat{\boldsymbol{\theta}} - \boldsymbol{\theta})][(\hat{\boldsymbol{\theta}} - E\hat{\boldsymbol{\theta}}) + (E\hat{\boldsymbol{\theta}} - \boldsymbol{\theta})]'\} \\ &= E(\hat{\boldsymbol{\theta}} - E\hat{\boldsymbol{\theta}})(\hat{\boldsymbol{\theta}} - E\hat{\boldsymbol{\theta}})' + (E\hat{\boldsymbol{\theta}} - \boldsymbol{\theta})(E\hat{\boldsymbol{\theta}} - \boldsymbol{\theta})' \\ &\quad + E(\hat{\boldsymbol{\theta}} - E\hat{\boldsymbol{\theta}})(E\hat{\boldsymbol{\theta}} - \boldsymbol{\theta})' + (E\hat{\boldsymbol{\theta}} - \boldsymbol{\theta})E(\hat{\boldsymbol{\theta}} - E\hat{\boldsymbol{\theta}})' \\ &= E(\hat{\boldsymbol{\theta}} - E\hat{\boldsymbol{\theta}})(\hat{\boldsymbol{\theta}} - E\hat{\boldsymbol{\theta}})' + (E\hat{\boldsymbol{\theta}} - \boldsymbol{\theta})(E\hat{\boldsymbol{\theta}} - \boldsymbol{\theta})' \\ &= \text{covariance matrix} + (\text{bias vector})(\text{bias vector})'. \end{aligned}$$

The invariance property of (7.10) generalizes to

(7.20) If $\hat{\boldsymbol{\theta}}$ is a consistent estimator of $\boldsymbol{\theta}$, and if $\boldsymbol{\psi} = g(\boldsymbol{\theta})$ is a vector of continuous functions of $\boldsymbol{\theta}$, then $\hat{\boldsymbol{\psi}} = g(\hat{\boldsymbol{\theta}})$ is a consistent estimator of $\boldsymbol{\psi}$.

Note also that a best unbiased estimator minimizes the generalized variance within the class of unbiased estimators: If $\hat{\boldsymbol{\theta}}$, with covariance matrix $\boldsymbol{\Sigma}_{\hat{\theta}\hat{\theta}}$, is the best unbiased estimator of $\boldsymbol{\theta}$, and if $\tilde{\boldsymbol{\theta}}$, with covariance matrix $\boldsymbol{\Sigma}_{\tilde{\theta}\tilde{\theta}}$, is any other unbiased estimator, then since $\boldsymbol{\Sigma}_{\tilde{\theta}\tilde{\theta}} - \boldsymbol{\Sigma}_{\hat{\theta}\hat{\theta}}$ is nonnegative definite, $|\boldsymbol{\Sigma}_{\hat{\theta}\hat{\theta}}| \leq |\boldsymbol{\Sigma}_{\tilde{\theta}\tilde{\theta}}|$ by (2.7.21).

Occasionally it is convenient to arrange the set of parameters in a matrix; the desirable properties are readily extended in that event.

Once we have decided which desirable properties we want an estimator to have it is still necessary to locate an estimator having those properties. This is not a trivial problem in general, and therefore it is useful to note a method that under general conditions leads to an estimator with at least desirable asymptotic properties. We have defined the likelihood function of a sample drawn from a population with parameter vector $\boldsymbol{\theta}$ as the probability of the sample expressed as a function of the parameter vector. Thus the likelihood function of the sample $x_1, \ldots, x_T$ is $\mathscr{L} = \mathscr{L}(x_1, \ldots, x_T \mid \theta_1, \ldots, \theta_K)$ or compactly $\mathscr{L} = \mathscr{L}(\mathbf{x} \mid \boldsymbol{\theta})$. Given the sample observation vector $\mathbf{x}$ we may evaluate its likelihood as a function of the unknown parameter vector $\boldsymbol{\theta}$ and, often in a straightforward manner, find the value $\hat{\boldsymbol{\theta}}$ that maximizes this function. Thus

(7.21) Let the likelihood function of a given sample be $\mathscr{L}(\mathbf{x} \mid \boldsymbol{\theta})$ where $\mathbf{x}$ is the vector of sample observations and $\boldsymbol{\theta}$ is the vector of unknown parameters. Then the maximum likelihood estimator of $\boldsymbol{\theta}$ is the vector $\hat{\boldsymbol{\theta}}$ such that $\mathscr{L}(\mathbf{x} \mid \hat{\boldsymbol{\theta}}) \geq \mathscr{L}(\mathbf{x} \mid \tilde{\boldsymbol{\theta}})$ where $\tilde{\boldsymbol{\theta}}$ is any other value of $\boldsymbol{\theta}$.

Thus the hypothetical population with parameter $\boldsymbol{\theta} = \hat{\boldsymbol{\theta}}$ would generate the given sample with a higher probability than would a population with any other value for $\boldsymbol{\theta}$. This should not be paraphrased as "the population with parameter $\hat{\boldsymbol{\theta}}$ is most likely to be the true one" nor as "the sample is most likely to have come from the population with parameter $\hat{\boldsymbol{\theta}}$."

When the sampling is random the observations are independent so that the likelihood function may be written as the product of the individual density functions; $\mathscr{L}(\mathbf{x} \mid \boldsymbol{\theta}) = f(x_1 \mid \boldsymbol{\theta}) \cdots f(x_T \mid \boldsymbol{\theta}) = \Pi_{t=1}^{T} f(x_t \mid \boldsymbol{\theta})$. Further, the logarithm of a function increases monotonically with the function, so that the logarithm attains a maximum at the same point that the function attains a maximum. Hence the maximum likelihood estimator may be obtained by maximizing the logarithmic likelihood $L = \log \mathscr{L}$ (or indeed by maximizing cL where c is any positive constant).

This feature will be useful when the sampling is random, for then the logarithmic likelihood will be, conveniently, a sum of terms.

Although the maximum likelihood method has some intuitive appeal, its value lies in the fact that it generates estimators with desirable asymptotic properties:

(7.22) Under very general conditions a maximum likelihood estimator is consistent, asymptotically unbiased, and asymptotically efficient.

For a specification of the general conditions (which are concerned with regularity of the likelihood function) and a proof of this important theorem, see Wilks (1962, pp. 358–365, 379–381) and Kendall and Stuart (1961, pp. 35–46, 51–60), where it is also shown that

(7.23) Under very general conditions the asymptotic covariance matrix of a maximum likelihood estimator $\hat{\boldsymbol{\theta}}$ is given by $\boldsymbol{\Sigma} = [-(\partial^2 L/\partial \boldsymbol{\theta}^2)]^{-1}$, where the derivatives are evaluated at $\hat{\boldsymbol{\theta}} = \boldsymbol{\theta}$, and the asymptotic distribution of $\hat{\boldsymbol{\theta}}$ is $\mathcal{N}(\boldsymbol{\theta}, \boldsymbol{\Sigma})$,

and that maximum likelihood estimators possess a useful invariance property:

(7.24) If $\hat{\boldsymbol{\theta}}$ is a maximum likelihood estimator of $\boldsymbol{\theta}$ and if $\boldsymbol{\psi} = g(\boldsymbol{\theta})$ is a vector of single-valued functions of $\boldsymbol{\theta}$, then $\hat{\boldsymbol{\psi}} = g(\hat{\boldsymbol{\theta}})$ is a maximum likelihood estimator of $\boldsymbol{\psi}$.

In assessing the value of this fruitful method it is important to recognize that its application demands knowledge of the functional form of the population distribution and also that maximum likelihood estimators need not have any desirable "small-sample" properties.

We now illustrate the use of these criteria in particular problems. We consider a random sample drawn from a population with unknown mean μ and unknown variance σ^2. We do not assume knowledge of the functional form of the population distribution at this point.

Consider the problem of estimating μ. An obvious estimator is the sample mean $\bar{x} = T^{-1} \sum_{t=1}^{T} x_t$. In (4.21) and (6.18) we have seen that $E\bar{x} = \bar{E}\bar{x} = \text{plim}\, \bar{x} = \mu$, so that $\bar{x}$ indeed has desirable properties as an estimator of μ. We now show that $\bar{x}$ also has a desirable minimum variance property. Let $\hat{\theta} = \sum_{t=1}^{T} a_t x_t$ be any linear estimator of μ, where the a_t's are constants. Then $E\hat{\theta} = \sum_{t=1}^{T} a_t E x_t = \mu \sum_{t=1}^{T} a_t$ since $Ex_t = \mu$. Thus

(7.25) $\hat{\theta} = \Sigma\, ax$ is an unbiased estimator of μ (for every μ) if and only if $\Sigma\, a = 1$.

Using the unbiasedness condition (which implies $\Sigma\, a\mu = \mu$),

$$E(\hat{\theta} - \mu)^2 = E\left[\sum_{t=1}^{T} a_t x_t - \mu\right]^2 = E\left[\sum_{t=1}^{T} a_t(x_t - \mu)\right]^2$$

$$= \sum_{t=1}^{T}\sum_{s=1}^{T} a_t a_s E(x_t - \mu)(x_s - \mu) = \sum_{t=1}^{T} a_t^2\sigma^2$$

since

$$E(x_t - \mu)(x_s - \mu) = \begin{cases} \sigma^2 & \text{if } \; s = t \\ 0 & \text{if } \; s \neq t\,. \end{cases}$$

Thus

(7.26) If $\hat{\theta} = \Sigma\, ax$ is an unbiased estimator of μ (for every μ) then $E(\hat{\theta} - \mu)^2 = \sigma^2\, \Sigma\, a^2$.

Now the sample mean is the linear estimator that has each $a_t = T^{-1}$; $\bar{x} = T^{-1}\,\Sigma_{t=1}^T\, x_t = \Sigma_{t=1}^T\, T^{-1} x_t$. Since it has $\Sigma_{t=1}^T\, a_t = \Sigma_{t=1}^T\, T^{-1} = TT^{-1} = 1$, it is unbiased by (7.25); since it has $\Sigma_{t=1}^T\, a_t^2 = \Sigma_{t=1}^T\, T^{-2} = TT^{-2} = T^{-1}$ its variance is $T^{-1}\sigma^2$ by (7.26). [We already had these results in (4.21)]. Now without loss of generality any linear estimator $\hat{\theta} = \Sigma_{t=1}^T\, a_t x_t$ may be written as $\hat{\theta} = \Sigma_{t=1}^T\, (T^{-1} + b_t)x_t$ where $b_t = a_t - T^{-1}$. Then $\Sigma_{t=1}^T\, a_t = \Sigma_{t=1}^T\, (T^{-1} + b_t) = 1 + \Sigma_{t=1}^T\, b_t$ so that the unbiasedness requirement becomes $\Sigma b = 0$, and the variance may be written

$$\sigma^2 \sum_{t=1}^{T} a_t^2 = \sigma^2 \sum_{t=1}^{T} (T^{-1} + b_t)^2$$

$$= \sigma^2\left(\sum_{t=1}^{T} T^{-2} + \sum_{t=1}^{T} b_t^2 + 2\sum_{t=1}^{T} T^{-1} b_t\right)$$

$$= \sigma^2\left(T^{-1} + \sum_{t=1}^{T} b_t^2\right).$$

To minimize the variance (given T and σ^2) we must take $\Sigma_{t=1}^T\, b_t^2 = 0$. This requires, however, that each $b_t = 0$; i.e., that each $a_t = T^{-1}$; i.e., that we take $\bar{x}$ as our estimator. Summarizing these results we have

(7.27) For random sampling from any population the sample mean is an unbiased, best linear unbiased, asymptotically unbiased, and consistent estimator of the population mean.

It is interesting to note that the sample mean has a "least-squares" property. Suppose that we want to "fit" the sample observations $x_1, \ldots, x_T$ by a single number x^*, and that our criterion of goodness of fit is the least-squares criterion: the best fitting number is that which minimizes the sum of squared deviations $S = \Sigma_{t=1}^T\, (x_t - x^*)^2$. Then setting $\partial S/\partial x^* = -2\,\Sigma_{t=1}^T\, (x_t - x^*)$ equal to zero gives $\Sigma_{t=1}^T\, x_t = T\hat{x}^*$ or $\hat{x}^* = \bar{x}$ for the least-squares value of x^*. Thus the purely descriptive criterion of least squares gives a function of the observations that turns out to be a desirable estimator of a population parameter under certain assumptions about the origin of the observations. This phenomenon recurs frequently in the sequel.

Now consider the problem of estimating σ^2. An obvious estimator is the sample variance $s^2 = T^{-1}\Sigma_{t=1}^T(x_t - \bar{x})^2$. In (4.33) and (6.18) we have seen that $Es^2 = (T-1)T^{-1}\sigma^2$, $\bar{E}s^2 = \text{plim } s^2 = \sigma^2$ so that

(7.28) For random sampling from any population the sample variance is a biased but asymptotically unbiased and consistent estimator of the population variance.

Although s^2 is biased we can easily obtain an unbiased estimator. Let $s'^2 = T(T-1)^{-1}s^2$ be the "adjusted sample variance." Then $Es'^2 = T(T-1)^{-1}Es^2 = \sigma^2$ so that s'^2 is unbiased; obviously, it is also asymptotically unbiased and consistent. (Indeed, it can be shown that for normal distributions s'^2 is the best quadratic unbiased estimator of σ^2). The multivariate extensions of (7.27) and (7.28) are straightforward.

In deriving these results we have not used knowledge of the parent population. If we know, or are willing to assume, the functional form of the parent population distribution, we may also consider applying the maximum likelihood method. Two examples will suffice.

In the first example we consider random sampling from a Bernoulli population with unknown mean μ. We have seen that the likelihood of a sample consisting of R 1's and $T - R$ 0's in a specified order is $\mathscr{L}(\mathbf{x} \mid \mu) = \mu^R(1-\mu)^{T-R}$. To maximize $\mathscr{L}$ we maximize $L = \log \mathscr{L} = R \log \mu + (T-R)\log(1-\mu)$. Differentiating,

$$\frac{\partial L}{\partial \mu} = R\frac{\partial \log \mu}{\partial \mu} + (T-R)\frac{\partial \log(1-\mu)}{\partial(1-\mu)}\frac{\partial(1-\mu)}{\partial \mu}$$

$$= \frac{R}{\mu} - \frac{T-R}{1-\mu}.$$

Setting the derivative equal to zero gives $R/\hat{\mu} = (T-R)/(1-\hat{\mu})$, whence $\hat{\mu} = R/T$. But for a sample of size T consisting of R 1's and $T - R$ 0's, $R/T = \bar{x}$. Thus

(7.29) For random sampling from a Bernoulli population the sample mean is the maximum likelihood estimator of the population mean.

Thus by (7.22) the sample mean will have asymptotic efficiency, when the parent distribution is Bernoulli, as well as the properties it has for any population. In addition, by the invariance rule of (7.24), $s^2 = \bar{x}(1 - \bar{x})$ will be the maximum likelihood estimator of $\mu(1 - \mu) = \sigma^2$. It is also instructive to apply the general formula for the asymptotic variance of the maximum likelihood estimator. We have

$$\frac{\partial^2 L}{\partial \mu^2} = \frac{\partial(\partial L/\partial \mu)}{\partial \mu} = -\frac{R}{\mu^2} - \frac{T - R}{(1 - \mu)^2},$$

which evaluated at $\mu = \hat{\mu} = R/T$ is

$$\frac{\partial^2 L}{\partial \mu^2} = -\frac{T\mu}{\mu^2} - \frac{T(1 - \mu)}{(1 - \mu)^2} = -\frac{T}{\mu(1 - \mu)}.$$

Then by (7.23) the asymptotic variance of $\hat{\mu}$ is

$$[T/\mu(1 - \mu)]^{-1} = \mu(1 - \mu)/T.$$

Since $\sigma^2 = \mu(1 - \mu)$ in a Bernoulli distribution, this result conforms to the general result for the asymptotic variance of a sample mean, (6.18*a*).

In the second example we consider random sampling from a $\mathcal{N}(\mu, \sigma^2)$ population. Since the likelihood function of a random sample is the product of the individual density functions, we have

$$\mathscr{L}(\mathbf{x} \mid \mu, \sigma^2) = (2\pi\sigma^2)^{-(T/2)} \exp\{-(2\sigma^2)^{-1} \Sigma_{t=1}^{T} (x_t - \mu)^2\}.$$

To maximize $\mathscr{L}$ we maximize

$$L = \log \mathscr{L} = -T2^{-1} \log 2\pi - T2^{-1} \log \sigma^2 - (2\sigma^2)^{-1} \Sigma_{t=1}^{T} (x_t - \mu)^2.$$

Differentiating,

$$\frac{\partial L}{\partial \boldsymbol{\theta}} = \begin{pmatrix} \partial L/\partial \mu \\ \partial L/\partial \sigma^2 \end{pmatrix} = \begin{pmatrix} (2\sigma^2)^{-1} 2 \Sigma (x - \mu) \\ -T(2\sigma^2)^{-1} + 2^{-1}(\sigma^2)^{-2} \Sigma (x - \mu)^2 \end{pmatrix}. \tag{7.30}$$

Setting the derivatives equal to zero gives

$$\Sigma(x - \hat{\mu}) = 0 \quad \text{and} \quad T^{-1} \Sigma (x - \hat{\mu})^2 = \hat{\sigma}^2,$$

whence $\hat{\mu} = \bar{x}$ and $\hat{\sigma}^2 = s^2$. Thus

(7.31) For random sampling from a $\mathcal{N}(\mu, \sigma^2)$ population the sample mean and sample variance are the maximum likelihood estimators of the population mean and population variance respectively.

Thus, again, the sample mean—and the sample variance—will have asymptotic efficiency when the parent distribution is normal, in addition to the properties they have for any population. It is also instructive to apply the general formula for the asymptotic covariance matrix of the maximum likelihood estimator. We have

$$\frac{\partial^2 L}{\partial \boldsymbol{\theta}^2} = \frac{\partial(\partial L/\partial \boldsymbol{\theta})}{\partial \boldsymbol{\theta}}$$
$$= \begin{pmatrix} -T(\sigma^2)^{-1} & -(\sigma^2)^{-2}\Sigma\,(x-\mu) \\ -(\sigma^2)^{-2}\Sigma\,(x-\mu) & 2^{-1}T(\sigma^2)^{-2} - (\sigma^2)^{-3}\Sigma\,(x-\mu)^2 \end{pmatrix},$$

which evaluated at $\Sigma(x-\mu) = 0$ and $\Sigma(x-\mu)^2 = T\sigma^2$ is

$$\frac{\partial^2 L}{\partial \boldsymbol{\theta}^2} = \begin{pmatrix} -T(\sigma^2)^{-1} & 0 \\ 0 & -2^{-1}T(\sigma^2)^{-2} \end{pmatrix}.$$

Then by (7.23) the asymptotic covariance matrix of $\begin{pmatrix} \hat{\mu} \\ \hat{\sigma}^2 \end{pmatrix}$ is

$$\boldsymbol{\Sigma} = \left(-\frac{\partial^2 L}{\partial \boldsymbol{\theta}^2}\right)^{-1} = \begin{pmatrix} T^{-1}\sigma^2 & 0 \\ 0 & T^{-1}2\sigma^4 \end{pmatrix}.$$

Since $\mu_4 = 3\sigma^4$ in a normal distribution this result conforms to the general result for the asymptotic variance of a sample mean, (6.18*a*), and a sample variance, (6.18*b*). Moreover, the zero asymptotic covariance of $\bar{x}$ and s^2 is a consequence of their independence for any sample size when the parent is normal, (5.29).

Finally we note that the standard deviation of the sampling distribution of an estimator is called the standard error of the estimator. Thus if the variance of an unbiased estimator $\hat{\theta}$ is σ_{θ}^2, then σ_{θ} is the standard error of $\hat{\theta}$. In addition if the asymptotic variance of a consistent estimator $\hat{\theta}$ is σ_{θ}^2, then σ_{θ} is called the asymptotic standard error of $\hat{\theta}$. Clearly the standard error gives some indication of the precision of the estimator. In practical situations the variance of an estimator—and hence its standard error—will be a function of unknown parameters and hence unknown. For example, the variance of the sample mean is $\sigma_{\bar{x}}^2 = \sigma^2/T$; its standard error is then $\sigma_{\bar{x}} = \sigma/\sqrt{T}$, which will be unknown if σ^2 is unknown. It will generally be possible, however, to obtain an estimate of the variance—and hence of the standard error. For example, let $s_{\bar{x}}^2 = s^2/(T-1)$; then $Es_{\bar{x}}^2 = Es^2/(T-1) = \sigma^2/T = \sigma_{\bar{x}}^2$ so that $s_{\bar{x}}^2$ is an unbiased estimator of $\sigma_{\bar{x}}^2$. Then $s_{\bar{x}} = s/\sqrt{T-1}$ will serve as an estimated standard error of the sample mean. Frequently the estimated standard error is presented in parentheses below the point estimator: $\underset{(\hat{\sigma}_{\theta})}{\hat{\theta}}$.

Interval Estimation

A more systematic method of indicating the precision of a point estimate is to construct an interval estimate for the population parameter. In the theory of interval estimation we seek to select a pair of functions of the sample observations whose values in a given sample will provide the end points of an interval within which the population parameter may be said to lie. Since the sample observations are random variables the end points will also be random variables; the interval they define will vary from sample to sample drawn from the same population. Hence we cannot expect to find an interval estimator that always covers the true value of the population parameter. We are, however, able to make well-defined probabilistic statements. Rather than discuss the theory of interval estimation in general terms we illustrate its application in several leading cases.

Consider random sampling from a population that is distributed $\mathcal{N}(\mu, \sigma^2)$ where μ is unknown but σ^2 is known. Let $1 - \alpha$ $(0 < \alpha < 1)$ be a preassigned "confidence coefficient"; let n_β^* be the value of a standard normal variable which is exceeded $100\beta\%$ of the time—i.e., $1 - F(n_\beta^*) = F(-n_\beta^*) = \beta$ where F is the cumulative standard normal distribution function; and let $\bar{x}$ be the observed sample mean. Now we know that $\sqrt{T}(\bar{x} - \mu)/\sigma$ is distributed $\mathcal{N}(0, 1)$ so that the statement

$$-n_{\alpha/2}^* \leq \frac{\sqrt{T}(\bar{x} - \mu)}{\sigma} \leq n_{\alpha/2}^* \tag{7.32}$$

will be true for $100(1 - \alpha)\%$ of the samples drawn. But (7.32) is identical with

$$\bar{x} - n_{\alpha/2}^* \frac{\sigma}{\sqrt{T}} \leq \mu \leq \bar{x} + n_{\alpha/2}^* \frac{\sigma}{\sqrt{T}}. \tag{7.33}$$

so that

$$\text{Prob}\left\{\bar{x} - n_{\alpha/2}^* \frac{\sigma}{\sqrt{T}} \leq \mu \leq \bar{x} + n_{\alpha/2}^* \frac{\sigma}{\sqrt{T}}\right\} = 1 - \alpha. \tag{7.34}$$

Then we call $\bar{x} \pm n_{\alpha/2}^* (\sigma/\sqrt{T})$ a $100(1 - \alpha)\%$ confidence interval for the parameter μ [with endpoints $\bar{x} - n_{\alpha/2}^*(\sigma/\sqrt{T})$, $\bar{x} + n_{\alpha/2}^*(\sigma/\sqrt{T})$]. In any given sample the interval $\bar{x} \pm n_{\alpha/2}^*(\sigma/\sqrt{T})$ may not cover μ; but it will do so in $100(1 - \alpha)\%$ of the samples. For a numerical example suppose that we wish to construct a 95% confidence interval for the μ of a population which is distributed $\mathcal{N}(\mu, 425)$. We have drawn from this population a sample of size 17 with mean 10. Thus $\alpha = 0.05$ so $n_{\alpha/2}^* = 1.96$ from the tabulated standard normal distribution [for $1 - F(1.96) = 0.025 = F(-1.96)$]; also $\sigma/\sqrt{T} = \sqrt{425}/\sqrt{17} = 5$. Then $10 \pm 1.96(5) = 10 \pm 9.8$ constitutes a 95% confidence interval for μ; i.e., the statement $0.2 \leq \mu \leq 19.8$ may be made with 95% confidence. A difficulty of this procedure is that it requires knowledge of σ^2, which is lacking in most practical cases.

Consider then random sampling from a population that is $\mathcal{N}(\mu, \sigma^2)$ where both μ and σ^2 are unknown. We know that $\sqrt{T-1}\,(\bar{x}-\mu)/s$ is distributed t_{T-1}. Therefore the statement

$$(7.35)\qquad -t^*_{T-1,\,\alpha/2} \le \frac{\sqrt{T-1}(\bar{x}-\mu)}{s} \le t^*_{T-1,\,\alpha/2}$$

and its equivalent

$$(7.36)\qquad \bar{x} - t^*_{T-1,\,\alpha/2}\frac{s}{\sqrt{T-1}} \le \mu \le \bar{x} + t^*_{T-1,\,\alpha/2}\frac{s}{\sqrt{T-1}}$$

will be true for $100(1-\alpha)\%$ of the samples drawn, where $t^*_{k,\beta}$ is the value of a t_k variable that is exceeded $100\beta\,\%$ of the time—i.e., $1 - F(t^*_{k,\beta}) = F(-t^*_{k,\beta}) = \beta$ where F is the cumulative t_k distribution. Thus

$$(7.37)\qquad \text{Prob}\left\{\bar{x} - t^*_{T-1,\,\alpha/2}\frac{s}{\sqrt{T-1}} \le \mu \le \bar{x} + t^*_{T-1,\,\alpha/2}\frac{s}{\sqrt{T-1}}\right\} = 1-\alpha$$

and $\bar{x} \pm t^*_{T-1,\alpha/2}(s/\sqrt{T-1})$ is a $100(1-\alpha)\%$ confidence interval for the parameter μ. For a numerical example, suppose that we wish to construct a 95% confidence interval for the μ of a population which is distributed $\mathcal{N}(\mu, \sigma^2)$. We have drawn from this population a sample of size 17 with mean 10 and variance 400. Thus $\alpha = 0.05$ so $t^*_{T-1,\,\alpha/2} = 2.12$ from the tabulated t_{16} distribution [for $1 - F(2.12) = 0.025 = F(-2.12)$]; also $s/\sqrt{T-1} = \sqrt{400}/\sqrt{16} = 5$. Then $10 \pm 2.12(5) = 10 \pm 10.6$ constitutes a 95% confidence interval for μ; i.e., the statement $-0.6 \le \mu \le 20.6$ may be made with 95% confidence. Clearly this procedure does not require knowledge of σ^2 and hence is operational in practical cases.

These two examples serve to illustrate the application of the theory of interval estimation. The sampling distribution of a sample statistic is known to involve the population parameter in a specific way; this knowledge is exploited to make a probabilistic statement about the parameter based on the value of the statistic in a specific sample. [Thus a confidence interval for the σ^2 of a $\mathcal{N}(\mu, \sigma^2)$ population would exploit the fact that Ts^2/σ^2 has the χ^2_{T-1} distribution.] Conventional confidence coefficients are 0.90, 0.95, and 0.99. There are of course many sample statistics whose distribution involves a certain population parameter. Moreover, given a confidence coefficient and a sample statistic there are alternative methods of constructing confidence intervals. For example, $1 - F(1.658) = 0.0488$ and $F(-3.000) = 0.0012$ so that

$[\bar{x} - 3.000(\sigma/\sqrt{T}),\ \bar{x} + 1.658(\sigma/\sqrt{T})]$ also provides a 95% confidence interval for the μ of a $\mathcal{N}(\mu, \sigma^2)$ population. The general theory of interval estimation develops criteria for choice among alternatives, quite analogously to the theory of point estimation; e.g., "narrow width" is an obvious desirable property of an interval estimator. We do not pursue this here; we do note that the intervals $\bar{x} \pm n^*_{\alpha/2}(\sigma/\sqrt{T})$ and $\bar{x} \pm t^*_{T-1,\alpha/2}(s/\sqrt{T-1})$ possess desirable properties for random sampling from a normal parent.

It may also be noted that in view of the central limit theorem many point estimators are asymptotically normally distributed so that $\hat{\theta} \pm n^*_{\alpha/2}\sigma_{\hat{\theta}}$ (or even $\hat{\theta} \pm n^*_{\alpha/2}\hat{\sigma}_{\hat{\theta}}$) in many cases provides a $100(1 - \alpha)\%$ "asymptotic confidence interval" for θ—i.e., when the sample size is large, such an interval covers θ with probability approximately $1 - \alpha$. This emphasizes the value of the practice noted at the end of the previous subsection of providing the standard error of a point estimator along with the point estimate itself.

Finally we note that a theory of confidence regions has been developed to cover the case where there are several unknown parameters.

Hypothesis Testing

In the theory of hypothesis testing we seek to select a function of the sample observations, called a test statistic, and a prespecified region of values, called a critical region, such that if for a given sample the value of the test statistic lies in the critical region it will be reasonable to reject a specified hypothesis about a parameter of the parent population.

Consider a random variable x whose distribution function $f(x \mid \theta)$ involves the unknown parameter θ. Suppose that we are interested in testing the hypothesis that $\theta = \theta_0$ where θ_0 is prespecified; the hypothesis $\theta = \theta_0$ is called the null hypothesis. We also suppose that it is known that θ certainly lies in some set Ω where Ω is prespecified; the specification θ in Ω is called the maintained hypothesis. The set Ω contains θ_0 and all admissible alternatives $\theta \neq \theta_0$. At one extreme Ω may consist of all conceivable values of θ; at the other it may consist of a unique alternative hypothesis θ_1. Now let $\tau = \tau(x_1, \ldots, x_T)$ be a function of the sample observations and let R be a prespecified critical region of values of τ. Then the test will proceed as follows: Given a random sample from the population the test statistic is evaluated. If its value lies in the critical region, we reject the null hypothesis; if its value does not lie in the critical region, we accept it. Since the sample observations are random variables, the test statistic will also be a random variable; the decision it leads to will vary from sample to sample drawn from the same population. Hence we cannot expect to find a test procedure that always leads to a correct decision.

Indeed it is clear that there are two sources of erroneous decisions in such a test procedure. If the null hypothesis is true, τ may still fall in R and we will erroneously reject the null hypothesis. This is known as Type I error; its probability $P(\text{I})$, say, equals $P(\tau \text{ in } R \mid \theta = \theta_0)$. On the other hand, if the null hypothesis is false, τ may still not fall in R and we will erroneously accept the null hypothesis. This is known as Type II error; its probability $P(\text{II})$, say, equals $1 - P(\tau \text{ in } R \mid \theta \neq \theta_0)$. Clearly a good test procedure—one that makes the probability of both errors small—will specify a critical region that contains those values of τ which are unlikely to occur when the null hypothesis is true but which are likely to occur when it is false. It is also clear, however, that if we reduce the size of R in order to reduce $P(\text{I})$ we will tend to increase $P(\text{II})$.

The classical theory of hypothesis testing incorporates the following compromise. The probability of Type I error is fixed at some value α (often 0.10, 0.05, or 0.01); $100\alpha\%$ is called the level of significance. Then a test procedure—a function τ and a critical region R—is sought such that $P(\text{II})$ is small, given $P(\text{I})$. It is clear that $P(\text{II})$ will depend on the true value of θ, and hence that our choice among alternative test procedures having the same $P(\text{I})$ will depend on the admissible alternatives to θ_0. Let us call $1 - P(\text{II}) = P(\tau \text{ in } R \mid \theta \neq \theta_0)$ the power of the test; it is clearly a function of θ. The theory of hypothesis testing utilizes the power function as a criterion for choosing among alternative tests. In some cases, a "uniformly most powerful test" can be found, which, for a given level of significance, minimizes $P(\text{II})$ for all admissible values of $\theta \neq \theta_0$. In most cases, however, no uniformly most powerful test is available, and tests that possess more modest desirable properties are sought. Rather than discuss the theory of hypothesis testing in general terms we illustrate its application in several leading cases.

Consider random sampling from a population that is distributed $\mathcal{N}(\mu, \sigma^2)$ where μ is unknown but σ^2 is known. Let the null hypothesis be $\mu = \mu_0$ where μ_0 is some prespecified number, and let the maintained hypothesis be simply $-\infty < \mu < \infty$. Let $100\alpha\%$ $(0 < \alpha < 1)$ be the prespecified level of significance, and again let n_β^* be the value of the standard normal variable for which $1 - F(n_\beta^*) = \beta$. Now $\sqrt{T}(\bar{x} - \mu)/\sigma$ is distributed $\mathcal{N}(0, 1)$; in particular, on the null hypothesis—i.e., if $\mu = \mu_0$—$\sqrt{T}(\bar{x} - \mu_0)/\sigma$ is distributed $\mathcal{N}(0, 1)$. Thus on the null hypothesis Prob $\{-n_{\alpha/2}^* \leq \sqrt{T}(\bar{x} - \mu_0)/\sigma \leq n_{\alpha/2}^*\} = 1 - \alpha$. Taking $\tau = \sqrt{T}(\bar{x} - \mu_0)/\sigma$ and R as the "two-tailed" critical region $\tau < -n_{\alpha/2}^*$ and $\tau > n_{\alpha/2}^*$ thus provides a test with level of significance $100\alpha\%$:

$$P(\mathrm{I}) = P(\tau \text{ in } R|\mu = \mu_0) = 1 - \mathrm{Prob}\left\{-n^*_{\alpha/2} \leq \frac{\sqrt{T}(\bar{x} - \mu_0)}{\sigma} \leq n^*_{\alpha/2}\right\}$$
$$= 1 - (1 - \alpha) = \alpha.$$

This indeed is a traditional test procedure for a hypothesis about the mean of a normal population when the variance is known. For a numerical example suppose that we wish to test at the 5% level of significance the hypothesis that the μ of a $\mathcal{N}(\mu, 425)$ population is $\mu_0 = 30$; the maintained hypothesis is simply $-\infty < \mu < \infty$. We have drawn a sample of size 17 with mean 10. Using the test procedure just described, we compute $\tau = \sqrt{T}(\bar{x} - \mu_0)/\sigma = \sqrt{17}(10 - 30)/\sqrt{425} = -4$. Since $-4 < -1.96 = -n^*_{.025}$ we reject the null hypothesis. A difficulty of this procedure is that it requires knowledge of σ^2. When σ^2 is unknown the analogous test using the t distribution is available. Thus we would use

$$\tau = \sqrt{T-1}(\bar{x} - \mu_0)/s$$

and R as the two-tailed critical region $\tau < -t^*_{T-1,\alpha/2}$ and $\tau > t^*_{T-1,\alpha/2}$ giving a test with level of significance 100α %. A connection between these two-tailed tests and interval estimation is apparent. At the 100α % level of significance the tests will reject any null hypothesis $\mu = \mu_0$ for which μ_0 does not lie in the $100(1 - \alpha)$% confidence interval for μ. The two-tailed test will reject a μ_0 that is "too far" away from $\bar{x}$ in either direction.

Again consider random sampling from a population that is $\mathcal{N}(\mu, \sigma^2)$ where μ is unknown but σ^2 is known. Let the null hypothesis again be $\mu = \mu_0$ where μ_0 is some prespecified number, but now let the maintained hypothesis be $\mu_0 \leq \mu < \infty$. Thus it is known with certainty that μ is not less than μ_0; and it would clearly be foolish to reject the null hypothesis $\mu = \mu_0$ if $\bar{x}$ was less than μ_0. Comparing the test that uses

$$\tau = \sqrt{T}(\bar{x} - \mu_0)/\sigma$$

and the critical region $\tau > n^*_\alpha$ with the test that uses the same τ but the critical region $\tau > n^*_{\alpha/2}$ and $\tau < -n^*_{\alpha/2}$, we see that they have the same significance level, 100α %. However, the former one-tailed test is more powerful against any admissible alternative $\mu > \mu_0$ and hence will be preferred when it is known that $\mu \geq \mu_0$. Similarly if the maintained hypothesis is $-\infty < \mu \leq \mu_0$, the one-tailed test with critical region $\tau < -n^*_\alpha$ will be preferred. Again when σ^2 is unknown one-tailed tests using $\tau = \sqrt{T-1}(\bar{x} - \mu_0)/s$ and rejection region $\tau > t^*_{T-1,\alpha}$ or $\tau < -t^*_{T-1,\alpha}$ are available.

These examples serve to illustrate the methods of hypothesis testing. The sampling distribution of a sample statistic is known to involve the population parameter in a specific way; this knowledge is exploited to reject or accept an hypothesis about the parameter, based on the value of a statistic in a specific sample. It may be noted again that many point estimators are asymptotically normally distributed, so that the two-tailed regions $|(\hat{\theta} - \theta_0)/\sigma_{\hat{\theta}}| > n^*_{\alpha/2}$ [or $|(\hat{\theta} - \theta_0)/\hat{\sigma}_{\hat{\theta}}| > n^*_{\alpha/2}$] or their one-tailed counterparts in many cases provide 100α % level-of-significance critical regions for testing $\theta = \theta_0$, when the sample size is large. Again, the value of providing the standard error along with the point estimate is apparent.

Finally we note that our discussion has been restricted to the case of simple null hypotheses, those of the form $\theta = \theta_0$. The theory of hypothesis testing extends to cover the more general case of composite null hypotheses, those of the form "θ lies in ω" where ω is a subset of Ω containing more than a single point.

Conclusions

The basic concepts of the classical theory of statistical inference have been surveyed in this section. We have seen how specifications about the parent population and about the process by which a sample is generated are needed to permit reasonable inferences about the population. On the basis of the a priori information the distribution of functions of the sample observations is deduced; this derived information, taken together with certain criteria, leads us to reasonable inference procedures.

In many cases only a limited amount of a priori information is needed to establish the desirability of a technique of inference; thus the sample mean is the BLUE of the population mean regardless of the form of the population distribution, provided the sample is random. It is clear, however, that additional a priori information leads to better inference; as an extreme case if we know the population mean, we can "infer" it exactly. One implication of this is that our results on the efficiency of certain estimators are conditional on the amount of a priori information available. If, e.g., we know a priori that the parameter vector lies in a certain region, the estimator obtained by maximizing the likelihood subject to that constraint will be more efficient than the unconstrained maximum likelihood estimator; see Kendall and Stuart (1961, pp. 57–60).

As we shall see, a priori information—particularly restrictions on the values of population parameters—plays an important role in econometrics. On the one hand the econometric investigator often has small samples which he cannot extend or reproduce so that the opportunity for increasing efficiency by increasing the sample size or repeating the experiment is not available. On the other hand there is a large body of economic theory on which he can draw for restrictions to increase the reliability of his inferences.

In recent years there has been a revival of interest in the Bayesian approach to statistical inference as opposed to the classical approach taken here. The former approach puts heavy stress on a priori information about population parameters, formulating this knowledge as an a priori probability distribution *of the parameters*. It views statistical inference as a method of combining this a priori distribution with the sample information to arrive at an a posteriori probability distribution of the parameters. Such an approach has many attractive features. Our treatment will proceed, however, within the classical framework, which is flexible enough to incorporate important types of a priori information about population parameters.

8. STOCHASTIC PROCESSES

Stationary Stochastic Processes

In many economic contexts successive observations are not independent so that a model which specifies that a given body of observations is a random sample from some population is inappropriate. This may well be the case with most time series. A more general model is provided by the theory of stochastic processes. For our purpose a stochastic process is defined as a family of random variables $\{x_t\}$ where $t = \ldots, -2, -1, 0, 1, 2, \ldots$ denotes time, such that for every finite set of choices of t, e.g., $t_1, \ldots, t_n$, a joint probability distribution is defined for the random variables $x_{t_1}, \ldots, x_{t_n}$. A stationary stochastic process is one in which the joint probability distributions are invariant under translations along the time axis, so that the joint probability distribution of any finite set $x_{t_1}, \ldots, x_{t_n}$ is the same as the joint probability distribution of the set $x_{t_1+\tau}, \ldots, x_{t_n+\tau}$ for any $\tau = \ldots, -2, -1, 0, 1, 2, \ldots$.

We confine our attention to stationary stochastic processes, and we assume that the relevant moments exist. Then since the univariate distribution of x_t is the same for all values of t, and since the bivariate distribution of x_t and $x_{t+\tau}$ depends only on τ, we may define the following moments:

$$(8.1) \qquad Ex_t = \mu, \qquad E(x_t - \mu)^2 = \sigma^2, \qquad E(x_t - \mu)^4 = \mu_4;$$

$$(8.2) \qquad E(x_t - \mu)(x_{t+\tau} - \mu) = \gamma_\tau, \qquad E(x_t - \mu)^2(x_{t+\tau} - \mu)^2 = \delta_\tau.$$

The covariance γ_τ considered as a function of the "lag" τ is called the autocovariance function of the stationary stochastic process $\{x_t\}$.

By a sample of size T of the stationary stochastic process $\{x_t\}$ we mean a joint drawing $x_1, \ldots, x_T$ from the joint distribution of T consecutive x_t's, where with no loss of generality $t = 1, \ldots, T$. (The term realization is used to denote an infinite sample $\ldots, x_{-2}, x_{-1}, x_0, x_1, x_2, \ldots$). It will be seen that a random sample is a sample of a special stationary stochastic process; i.e., one in which the random variables are mutually independent. In general, however, the random variables of a stationary stochastic process, although identically distributed, are not independent. Viewing a set of observations as a sample of a stationary stochastic process thus provides a more general model and one that may well be appropriate for economic time series. Loosely speaking, we now have a model for non-random sampling from a univariate probability distribution. For detailed discussions of the theory of stationary stochastic processes see Yaglom (1962) and Hannan (1960).

It may be helpful to have a matrix representation of the first and second moments of sample observations of a stationary stochastic process. If we let $\mathbf{x}$ be the $T \times 1$ vector of outcomes $x_1, \ldots, x_T$ of the stationary stochastic process, then using (8.1) and (8.2) we have

$$(8.3) \qquad E\mathbf{x} = \boldsymbol{\mu} = \begin{pmatrix} \mu \\ \cdot \\ \cdot \\ \cdot \\ \mu \end{pmatrix},$$

$$E(\mathbf{x} - \boldsymbol{\mu})(\mathbf{x} - \boldsymbol{\mu})' = \boldsymbol{\Sigma} = \begin{pmatrix} \sigma^2 & \gamma_1 & \cdots & \gamma_{T-1} \\ \gamma_1 & \sigma^2 & \cdots & \gamma_{T-2} \\ \cdot & \cdot & & \cdot \\ \cdot & \cdot & & \cdot \\ \cdot & \cdot & & \cdot \\ \gamma_{T-1} & \gamma_{T-2} & \cdots & \sigma^2 \end{pmatrix}.$$

Estimation of Parameters

We now consider statistical inference concerning some of the parameters of (8.1) and (8.2) of the stationary stochastic process $\{x_t\}$. Given a sample $x_1, \ldots, x_T$ of this process we may of course compute the sample mean $\bar{x} = T^{-1} \sum_{t=1}^{T} x_t$, the sample variance $s^2 = T^{-1} \sum_{t=1}^{T} (x_t - \bar{x})^2$, and also the sample autocovariances $c_\tau = (T - \tau)^{-1} \sum_{t=1}^{T-\tau} (x_t - \bar{x})(x_{t+\tau} - \bar{x})$ for $\tau = 1, \ldots, T - 1$. Since a sample is one drawing from a joint probability distribution, these sample statistics are random variables whose values vary across samples. We now consider the properties of these statistics as estimators of the corresponding population parameters.

For the sample mean $\bar{x}$ we find

$$(8.4)\qquad E\bar{x} = ET^{-1}\sum_{t=1}^{T} x_t = T^{-1}\sum_{t=1}^{T} Ex_t = T^{-1}T\mu = \mu,$$

and

$$(8.5)\qquad E(\bar{x}-\mu)^2 = E\left[T^{-1}\sum_{t=1}^{T} x_t - \mu\right]^2 = T^{-2}E\left[\sum_{t=1}^{T}(x_t-\mu)\right]^2$$

$$= T^{-2}E\left[\sum_{t=1}^{T}(x_t-\mu)^2 + \sum_{\substack{t=1\\t\neq s}}^{T}\sum_{s=1}^{T}(x_t-\mu)(x_s-\mu)\right]$$

$$= T^{-2}\left[\sum_{t=1}^{T}E(x_t-\mu)^2 + 2\sum_{t=1}^{T}\sum_{\substack{s=2\\s>t}}^{T}E(x_t-\mu)(x_s-\mu)\right]$$

$$= T^{-2}\left[\sum_{t=1}^{T}E(x_t-\mu)^2 + 2\sum_{t=1}^{T}\sum_{\tau=1}^{T-t}E(x_t-\mu)(x_{t+\tau}-\mu)\right]$$

$$= T^{-2}\left[T\sigma^2 + 2\sum_{t=1}^{T}\sum_{\tau=1}^{T-t}\gamma_\tau\right]$$

$$= T^{-2}\left[T\sigma^2 + 2\sum_{\tau=1}^{T-1}(T-\tau)\gamma_\tau\right],$$

using

$$\sum_{t=1}^{T}\sum_{\tau=1}^{T-t}\gamma_\tau = (\gamma_1+\cdots+\gamma_{T-1}) + (\gamma_1+\cdots+\gamma_{T-2}) + \cdots$$

$$+ (\gamma_1+\gamma_2) + \gamma_1 = \sum_{\tau=1}^{T-1}(T-\tau)\gamma_\tau.$$

Thus the sample mean $\bar{x}$ is still an unbiased estimator of μ but its variance is now given by (8.5) rather than by $T^{-1}\sigma^2$ as in random sampling—see (4.20). Note that (8.5) reduces to $T^{-1}\sigma^2$ if $\gamma_\tau = 0$ for all $\tau > 0$; this is the case in random sampling, for there the variables are independent; indeed, it is the case if the variables are merely uncorrelated. It will be recalled that an unbiased estimator is consistent if its variance goes to zero as the sample size goes to infinity. A sufficient condition for (8.5) to go to zero as T goes to infinity is that the covariance between x_t and $x_{t+\tau}$ declines so strongly as τ increases that $\lim_{\tau\to\infty}\gamma_\tau = 0$. This is so because (8.5) may be written as

$$(8.6)\qquad E(\bar{x}-\mu)^2 = T^{-1}\sigma^2 + 2T^{-1}\sum_{\tau=1}^{T-1}\gamma_\tau - 2T^{-2}\sum_{\tau=1}^{T-1}\tau\gamma_\tau$$

and $\lim_{\tau\to\infty} \gamma_\tau = 0$ implies $\lim_{T\to\infty} T^{-1} \sum_{\tau=1}^{T-1} \gamma_\tau = 0$ and $\lim_{T\to\infty} T^{-2} \sum_{\tau=1}^{T-1} \tau\gamma_\tau = 0$; recall that γ_τ is bounded because it is a covariance between two variables which have the same variance so that $|\gamma_\tau| \leq \sigma^2$ for all $\tau > 0$. In many circumstances the dependence between distant values of x wears off rapidly as the distance increases so that the condition $\lim_{\tau\to\infty} \gamma_\tau = 0$ will be met. Thus under general conditions $\text{plim}\, \bar{x} = \mu$ even though the sampling is nonrandom.

The sample variance s^2 may be written as

$$(8.7) \qquad s^2 = T^{-1} \sum_{t=1}^{T} (x_t - \mu)^2 - (\bar{x} - \mu)^2,$$

whence

$$(8.8) \qquad Es^2 = T^{-1} \sum_{t=1}^{T} E(x_t - \mu)^2 - E(\bar{x} - \mu)^2$$

$$= T^{-1} T\sigma^2 - E(\bar{x} - \mu)^2 = \sigma^2 - E(\bar{x} - \mu)^2$$

where $E(\bar{x} - \mu)^2$ was given in (8.5). Thus the sample variance s^2 is a biased estimator of σ^2 but is asymptotically unbiased if $\lim_{T\to\infty} E(\bar{x} - \mu)^2 = 0$. Note that if the variables are independent or even merely uncorrelated (8.8) reduces to $\sigma^2 - T^{-1}\sigma^2 = T^{-1}(T - 1)\sigma^2$, which is the random sampling result—see (4.28). To investigate the consistency of s^2 we consider

$$(8.9) \qquad s_*^2 = T^{-1} \sum_{t=1}^{T} (x_t - \mu)^2.$$

We have

$$(8.10) \qquad Es_*^2 = \sigma^2,$$

$$(8.11) \qquad Es_*^4 = T^{-2} E\left[\sum_{t=1}^{T} (x_t - \mu)^2\right]^2$$

$$= T^{-2} E\left[\sum_{t=1}^{T} (x_t - \mu)^4 + \sum_{\substack{t=1 \\ t\neq s}}^{T} \sum_{s=1}^{T} (x_t - \mu)^2 (x_s - \mu)^2\right]$$

$$= T^{-2}\left[\sum_{t=1}^{T} E(x_t - \mu)^4 + 2 \sum_{t=1}^{T} \sum_{\tau=1}^{T-t} E(x_t - \mu)^2 (x_{t+\tau} - \mu)^2\right]$$

$$= T^{-2}\left[T\mu_4 + 2 \sum_{t=1}^{T} \sum_{\tau=1}^{T-t} \delta_\tau\right] = T^{-2}\left[T\mu_4 + 2 \sum_{\tau=1}^{T-1} (T - \tau)\delta_\tau\right].$$

Thus the variance of s_*^2 is

$$(8.12)\qquad E(s_*^2 - \sigma^2)^2 = Es_*^4 - \sigma^4 = T^{-2}\left[T\mu_4 + 2\sum_{\tau=1}^{T-1}(T-\tau)\delta_\tau\right] - \sigma^4$$

$$= T^{-2}\left[T\mu_4 + 2\sum_{\tau=1}^{T-1}(T-\tau)(\delta_\tau - \sigma^4) + 2\sum_{\tau=1}^{T-1}(T-\tau)\sigma^4\right] - \sigma^4$$

$$= T^{-2}\left[T\mu_4 + 2\sum_{\tau=1}^{T-1}(T-\tau)(\delta_\tau - \sigma^4) + T(T-1)\sigma^4\right] - \sigma^4$$

$$= T^{-2}\left[T(\mu_4 - \sigma^4) + 2\sum_{\tau=1}^{T-1}(T-\tau)(\delta_\tau - \sigma^4)\right]$$

using

$$\sum_{\tau=1}^{T-1}(T-\tau)\sigma^4 = \sigma^4\sum_{\tau'=1}^{T-1}\tau' = \sigma^4\,\frac{T(T-1)}{2}$$

where $\tau' = T - \tau$. Again s_*^2 will be a consistent estimator if its variance goes to zero as the sample size goes to infinity. A sufficient condition for (8.12) to go to zero as T goes to infinity is $\lim_{\tau\to\infty}(\delta_\tau - \sigma^4) = 0$; note that (8.12) has the same form as does (8.5). Now

$$\delta_\tau - \sigma^4 = E(x_t - \mu)^2(x_{t+\tau} - \mu)^2 - E(x_t - \mu)^2E(x_{t+\tau} - \mu)^2$$

is the covariance between $(x_t - \mu)^2$ and $(x_{t+\tau} - \mu)^2$. In many cases the dependence between distant values of x wears off so rapidly as the distance increases that the condition $\lim_{\tau\to\infty}(\delta_\tau - \sigma^4) = 0$ will be met. Thus under general conditions $\text{plim}\, s_*^2 = \sigma^2$ even though the sampling is nonrandom. Returning to the sample variance itself, (8.7) implies $\text{plim}\, s^2 = \text{plim}\, s_*^2 - [\text{plim}\,(\bar{x} - \mu)]^2$ so that s^2 will be a consistent estimator of σ^2 if $\text{plim}\, s_*^2 = \sigma^2$ and $\text{plim}\, \bar{x} = \mu$. Thus under general conditions—where the dependence between distant values of x wears off so rapidly that $\lim_{\tau\to\infty}\gamma_\tau = 0$ and $\lim_{\tau\to\infty}(\delta_\tau - \sigma^4) = 0$—$\text{plim}\, s^2 = \sigma^2$ even though the sampling is nonrandom.

Finally, consider the first sample autocovariance

$$(8.13)\qquad c_1 = (T-1)^{-1}\sum_{t=1}^{T-1}(x_t-\bar{x})(x_{t+1}-\bar{x})$$

$$= (T-1)^{-1}\sum_{t=1}^{T-1}(x_t-\mu)(x_{t+1}-\mu) + (\bar{x}-\mu)^2$$

$$- (T-1)^{-1}(\bar{x}-\mu)\left[\sum_{t=1}^{T-1}(x_t-\mu)+\sum_{t=1}^{T-1}(x_{t+1}-\mu)\right]$$

$$= (T-1)^{-1}\sum_{t=1}^{T-1}(x_t-\mu)(x_{t+1}-\mu) - (\bar{x}-\mu)^2$$

$$- (T-1)^{-1}(\bar{x}-\mu)[2(\bar{x}-\mu)-(x_1-\mu)-(x_T-\mu)],$$

using

$$\sum_{t=1}^{T-1}(x_t-\mu)+\sum_{t=1}^{T-1}(x_{t+1}-\mu) = 2\sum_{t=1}^{T}(x_t-\mu)-(x_1-\mu)-(x_T-\mu)$$

$$= 2T(\bar{x}-\mu)-(x_1-\mu)-(x_T-\mu).$$

Then

$$(8.14)\qquad Ec_1 = (T-1)^{-1}(T-1)\gamma_1 - E(\bar{x}-\mu)^2$$

$$-(T-1)^{-1}E(\bar{x}-\mu)[2(\bar{x}-\mu)-(x_1-\mu)-(x_T-\mu)]$$

$$= \gamma_1 - E(\bar{x}-\mu)^2 - 2(T-1)^{-1}T^{-2}\left[\sum_{\tau=1}^{T-1}(T-\tau)\gamma_\tau - \sum_{\tau=1}^{T-1}\tau\gamma_\tau\right],$$

using

$$E(\bar{x}-\mu)(x_1-\mu) = T^{-1}E\sum_{t=1}^{T}(x_t-\mu)(x_1-\mu)$$

$$= T^{-1}\left(\sigma^2+\sum_{\tau=1}^{T-1}\gamma_\tau\right) = E(\bar{x}-\mu)(x_T-\mu)$$

along with the formula (8.5) for $E(\bar{x}-\mu)^2$. Thus the first sample autocovariance c_1 is a biased estimator of γ_1 but is asymptotically unbiased if $\lim_{\tau\to\infty}\gamma_\tau = 0$ (for then $\lim_{T\to\infty}E(\bar{x}-\mu)^2 = 0$ also). To investigate the consistency of c_1 we consider

$$(8.15)\qquad c_{1*} = (T-1)^{-1}\sum_{t=1}^{T-1}(x_t-\mu)(x_{t+1}-\mu).$$

We have

$$(8.16)\qquad Ec_{1*} = \gamma_1$$

$$(8.17)\qquad Ec_{1*}^2 = (T-1)^{-2}E\left[\sum_{t=1}^{T-1}(x_t-\mu)(x_{t+1}-\mu)\right]^2$$

$$= (T-1)^{-2}E\left[\sum_{t=1}^{T-1}(x_t-\mu)^2(x_{t+1}-\mu)^2\right.$$

$$\left.+\sum_{\substack{t=1\\t\neq s}}^{T-1}\sum_{s=1}^{T-1}(x_t-\mu)(x_{t+1}-\mu)(x_s-\mu)(x_{s+1}-\mu)\right]$$

$$= (T-1)^{-2}\left[\sum_{t=1}^{T-1}E(x_t-\mu)^2(x_{t+1}-\mu)^2\right.$$

$$\left.+2\sum_{t=1}^{T-1}\sum_{\tau=1}^{T-t-1}E(x_t-\mu)(x_{t+1}-\mu)(x_{t+\tau}-\mu)(x_{t+\tau+1}-\mu)\right]$$

$$= (T-1)^{-2}\left[(T-1)\delta_1 + 2\sum_{\tau=1}^{T-2}(T-\tau-1)\eta_\tau\right],$$

where $\eta_\tau = E(x_t-\mu)(x_{t+1}-\mu)(x_{t+\tau}-\mu)(x_{t+\tau+1}-\mu)$. Thus the variance of c_{1*} is

$$(8.18)\qquad E(c_{1*}-\gamma_1)^2 = Ec_{1*}^2-\gamma_1^2 = (T-1)^{-2}\left[(T-1)\delta_1\right.$$

$$\left.+2\sum_{\tau=1}^{T-2}(T-\tau-1)\eta_\tau\right]-\gamma_1^2$$

$$= (T-1)^{-2}\left[(T-1)(\delta_1-\gamma_1^2)\right.$$

$$\left.+2\sum_{\tau=1}^{T-2}(T-\tau-1)(\eta_\tau-\gamma_1^2)\right].$$

Now

$$\eta_\tau-\gamma_1^2 = E[(x_t-\mu)(x_{t+1}-\mu)][(x_{t+\tau}-\mu)(x_{t+\tau+1}-\mu)]$$
$$-E[(x_t-\mu)(x_{t+1}-\mu)]E[(x_{t+\tau}-\mu)(x_{t+\tau+1}-\mu)]$$

is the covariance between $(x_t-\mu)(x_{t+1}-\mu)$ and $(x_{t+\tau}-\mu)(x_{t+\tau+1}-\mu)$. In many cases the dependence between distant values of x wears off so rapidly as the distance increases that the condition $\lim_{\tau\to\infty}(\eta_\tau-\gamma_1^2)=0$ will be met. Thus under general conditions plim $c_{1*}=\gamma_1$ despite the nonrandom sampling. Returning to the first sample autocovariance itself, from (8.13) we see that plim c_1 = plim c_{1*} if plim $\bar{x}=\mu$, so that c_1 will be a consistent estimator of γ_1 if plim $c_{1*}=\gamma_1$. Thus under general conditions—where the dependence between distant values of x wears off so rapidly that $\lim_{\tau\to\infty}\gamma_\tau=0$ and $\lim_{\tau\to\infty}(\eta_\tau-\gamma_1^2)=0$—plim $c_1=\gamma_1$.

In similar fashion it can be shown that the higher-order sample autocovariances, although biased, are consistent estimators of the corresponding population parameters under general conditions, i.e., when the dependence between distant values of x is not too strong.

Autoregressive Processes

As an important example of a stationary stochastic process we consider the first-order autoregressive process. Let u_t $(t = \ldots, -2, -1, 0, 1, 2, \ldots)$ be independent, identically distributed random variables with

$$(8.19) \qquad Eu_t = 0, \qquad Eu_t^2 = \sigma_u^2, \qquad Eu_t^4 = \mu_{4u},$$

and let x_t be a random variable defined by

$$(8.20) \qquad x_t - \mu = \rho(x_{t-1} - \mu) + u_t$$

where $-1 < \rho < 1$ is some constant. By repeated lagging and substitution into (8.20) we find

$$(8.21) \qquad x_t - \mu = \sum_{s=0}^{\infty} \rho^s u_{t-s}.$$

It is clear that the family of random variables $\ldots, x_{-2}, x_{-1}, x_0, x_1, x_2, \ldots$ constitutes a stationary stochastic process. This is so because, e.g., $x_{t+\tau} - \mu = \Sigma_{s=0}^{\infty} \rho^s u_{t+\tau-s} = \Sigma_{s=0}^{\infty} \rho^s u_{t-s}'$ (where $u_t' = u_{t+\tau}$) is the same function of identical random variables as is x_t, so that x_t and $x_{t+\tau}$ have identical univariate distributions; similarly the multivariate distributions are invariant under translations along the time axis. It is also clear that x_t and $x_{t+\tau}$ are not independently distributed—they have $\ldots, u_{t-1}, u_t$ in common. Thus (8.20) provides an example of a nontrivial stationary stochastic process; it is known as the first-order autoregressive process.

Parameters of the stochastic process $\{x_t\}$ may be expressed in terms of parameters of the process $\{u_t\}$. Thus from (8.19) and (8.21),

$$(8.22) \qquad Ex_t = \mu + \sum_{s=0}^{\infty} \rho^s Eu_{t-s} = \mu,$$

$$(8.23) \qquad E(x_t - \mu)^2 = E\left(\sum_{s=0}^{\infty} \rho^s u_{t-s}\right)^2 = \sum_{s=0}^{\infty} \sum_{r=0}^{\infty} \rho^{s+r} Eu_{t-s}u_{t-r}$$

$$= \sigma_u^2 \sum_{s=0}^{\infty} \rho^{2s} = \sigma_u^2(1 - \rho^2)^{-1} = \sigma^2,$$

say; for in the double sum the expectation is zero unless the two subscripts are equal, in which case it is σ_u^2. Further,

$$(8.24) \qquad E(x_t - \mu)^4 = E\left(\sum_{s=0}^{\infty} \rho^s u_{t-s}\right)^4$$

$$= \sum_{s=0}^{\infty}\sum_{r=0}^{\infty}\sum_{q=0}^{\infty}\sum_{p=0}^{\infty} \rho^{s+r+q+p} E u_{t-s} u_{t-r} u_{t-q} u_{t-p}$$

$$= \mu_{4u} \sum_{s=0}^{\infty} \rho^{4s} + \sigma_u^4 \sum_{s=0}^{\infty} \sum_{\substack{q=0 \\ q \neq s}}^{\infty} \rho^{2s+2q} + \sigma_u^4 \sum_{s=0}^{\infty} \sum_{\substack{r=0 \\ r \neq s}}^{\infty} \rho^{2s+2r}$$

$$+ \sigma_u^4 \sum_{s=0}^{\infty} \sum_{\substack{p=0 \\ p \neq s}}^{\infty} \rho^{2s+2p}$$

$$= \mu_{4u} \sum_{s=0}^{\infty} \rho^{4s} + 3\sigma_u^4 \sum_{s=0}^{\infty} \sum_{\substack{q=0 \\ q \neq s}}^{\infty} \rho^{2s+2q}$$

$$= \mu_{4u} \sum_{s=0}^{\infty} \rho^{4s} + 3\sigma_u^4 \sum_{s=0}^{\infty} \rho^{2s} \sum_{\substack{q=0 \\ q \neq s}}^{\infty} \rho^{2q}$$

$$= \mu_{4u}(1 - \rho^4)^{-1} + 3\sigma_u^4 \sum_{s=0}^{\infty} \rho^{2s}[(1 - \rho^2)^{-1} - \rho^{2s}]$$

$$= 3\sigma_u^4(1 - \rho^2)^{-2} + (\mu_{4u} - 3\sigma_u^4)(1 - \rho^4)^{-1} = \mu_4,$$

say; for in the quadruple sum the expectation is zero unless the subscripts are pairwise equal in which case it is μ_{4u} if all four are equal or $(\sigma_u^2)^2$ if not.

Turning to the bivariate moments we note that x_t—which depends only on $\ldots, u_{t-1}, u_t$—is independent of all u_{t+s} for $s > 0$; and that by repeated leading and substitution in (8.20) we may write

$$(8.25) \qquad x_{t+\tau} - \mu = \rho^\tau(x_t - \mu) + \sum_{s=1}^{\tau} \rho^{\tau-s} u_{t+s}.$$

Multiplying (8.25) by $x_t - \mu$ and taking expectations we find for the autocovariance function of $\{x_t\}$

$$(8.26) \qquad \gamma_\tau = E(x_t - \mu)(x_{t+\tau} - \mu) = \rho^\tau E(x_t - \mu)^2 + \sum_{s=1}^{\tau} \rho^{\tau-s} E(x_t - \mu) u_{t+s}$$

$$= \rho^\tau \sigma^2.$$

Since $|\rho| < 1$, it is apparent that the covariance between x_t and $x_{t+\tau}$ declines as τ increases in such a manner that $\lim_{\tau\to\infty} \gamma_\tau = 0$. It may be helpful to note that the matrix representation of (8.3) specializes to

$$(8.27)\qquad E\mathbf{x} = \boldsymbol{\mu} = \begin{pmatrix} \mu \\ \cdot \\ \cdot \\ \cdot \\ \mu \end{pmatrix},$$

$$E(\mathbf{x} - \boldsymbol{\mu})(\mathbf{x} - \boldsymbol{\mu})' = \boldsymbol{\Sigma}$$

$$= \sigma^2 \begin{pmatrix} 1 & \rho & \rho^2 & \cdots & \rho^{T-1} \\ \rho & 1 & \rho & \cdots & \rho^{T-2} \\ \cdot & \cdot & \cdot & & \cdot \\ \cdot & \cdot & \cdot & & \cdot \\ \cdot & \cdot & \cdot & & \cdot \\ \rho^{T-1} & \rho^{T-2} & \rho^{T-3} & \cdots & 1 \end{pmatrix}$$

It may be noted that in obtaining (8.22), (8.23), (8.26), and (8.27) the only properties of the u_t that have in fact been used are $Eu_t = 0$, $Eu_t^2 = \sigma_u^2$, and $Eu_su_t = 0$ for $s \neq t$. Squaring (8.25), multiplying by $(x_t - \mu)^2$, and taking expectations we find

$$(8.28)\qquad \delta_\tau = E(x_t - \mu)^2(x_{t+\tau} - \mu)^2$$

$$= \rho^{2\tau}E(x_t - \mu)^4 + E(x_t - \mu)^2\left(\sum_{s=1}^{\tau} \rho^{\tau-s}u_{t+s}\right)^2$$

$$+ 2\rho^\tau E(x_t - \mu)^3 \sum_{s=1}^{\tau} \rho^{\tau-s}u_{t+s}$$

$$= \rho^{2\tau}\mu_4 + \sigma^2 \sum_{s=1}^{\tau}\sum_{r=1}^{\tau} \rho^{2\tau-s-r}Eu_{t+s}u_{t+r}$$

$$= \rho^{2\tau}\mu_4 + \sigma^2\sigma_u^2 \sum_{s=1}^{\tau} \rho^{2(\tau-s)}$$

$$= \rho^{2\tau}\mu_4 + \sigma^4(1 - \rho^2)(1 - \rho^2)^{-1}(1 - \rho^{2\tau})$$

$$= \rho^{2\tau}(\mu_4 - \sigma^4) + \sigma^4.$$

Again since $|\rho| < 1$, it is apparent that $\delta_\tau - \sigma^4$, the covariance between $(x_t - \mu)^2$ and $(x_{t+\tau} - \mu)^2$, declines as τ increases in such a manner that

$\lim_{\tau\to\infty}(\delta_\tau - \sigma^4) = 0$. Finally, for $\tau > 0$,

(8.29)
$$\begin{aligned}\eta_\tau &= E(x_t - \mu)(x_{t+1} - \mu)(x_{t+\tau} - \mu)(x_{t+\tau+1} - \mu)\\ &= E[\rho(x_t - \mu)^2 + (x_t - \mu)u_{t+1}][\rho(x_{t+\tau} - \mu)^2 + (x_{t+\tau} - \mu)u_{t+\tau+1}]\\ &= \rho^2 E(x_t - \mu)^2(x_{t+\tau} - \mu)^2 + \rho E(x_t - \mu)(x_{t+\tau} - \mu)^2 u_{t+1}\\ &= \rho^2\delta_\tau + \rho E\Bigg[\rho^{2\tau}(x_t - \mu)^3 u_{t+1} + (x_t - \mu)u_{t+1}\Big(\sum_{s=1}^{\tau}\rho^{\tau-s}u_{t+s}\Big)^2\\ &\qquad + 2\rho^\tau(x_t - \mu)^2 u_{t+1}\sum_{s=1}^{\tau}\rho^{\tau-s}u_{t+s}\Bigg]\\ &= \rho^2\delta_\tau + 2\rho^{\tau+1}\sigma^2\rho^{\tau-1}Eu_{t+1}^2 = \rho^2\delta_\tau + 2\rho^{2\tau}\sigma^2\sigma_u^2\\ &= \rho^2\delta_\tau + 2\rho^{2\tau}\sigma^4(1 - \rho^2)\\ &= \rho^2[\rho^{2\tau}(\mu_4 - \sigma^4) + \sigma^4] + 2\rho^{2\tau}\sigma^4(1 - \rho^2)\\ &= \rho^{2\tau}[\rho^2(\mu_4 - 3\sigma^4) + 2\sigma^4] + \gamma_1^2\end{aligned}$$

using (8.25), (8.26), and (8.28). Again since $|\rho| < 1$ it is apparent that $\eta_\tau - \gamma_1^2$, the covariance between $(x_t - \mu)(x_{t+1} - \mu)$ and $(x_{t+\tau} - \mu) \times (x_{t+\tau+1} - \mu)$, declines as τ increases in such a manner that $\lim_{\tau\to\infty}(\eta_\tau - \gamma_1^2) = 0$.

This analysis implies that where the x_t's are generated by a first-order autoregressive process the sample mean, variance, and first autocovariance are consistent estimators of the corresponding population parameters. More generally it can be shown that where the x_t's are generated by a Kth-order autoregressive process

(8.30)
$$x_t - \mu = \rho_1(x_{t-1} - \mu) + \cdots + \rho_K(x_{t-K} - \mu) + u_t$$

the sample mean, variance, and autocovariances are consistent estimators of the corresponding population parameters provided that the u_t's are independent and identically distributed and that all roots of

(8.31)
$$\rho_K + \rho_{K-1}\lambda + \rho_{K-2}\lambda^2 + \cdots + \rho_1\lambda^{K-1} - \lambda^K = 0$$

are less than 1 in absolute value. This second "stability" condition—which reduces to $|\rho| < 1$ for the first-order process—is required to ensure that $E(x_t - \mu)^2$ does not increase with t.

Our results for the parameters of the first-order autoregressive process may be inserted in the general formulas of the preceding subsection to obtain explicitly the exact means and variances of sample statistics in our special case. We illustrate with the variance of the sample mean. Using (8.26) in (8.5) we find

(8.32)
$$\begin{aligned}E(\bar{x} - \mu)^2 &= T^{-2}\Big[T\sigma^2 + 2\sigma^2\sum_{\tau=1}^{T-1}(T - \tau)\rho^\tau\Big]\\ &= T^{-2}[T\sigma^2 + 2T\sigma^2\rho(1 - \rho)^{-1} - 2\sigma^2\rho(1 - \rho^T)(1 - \rho)^{-2}]\\ &= T^{-1}\sigma^2(1 + \rho)(1 - \rho)^{-1} - 2T^{-2}\sigma^2\rho(1 - \rho^T)(1 - \rho)^{-2},\end{aligned}$$

using

$$(8.33)\qquad (1-\rho)\sum_{\tau=1}^{T-1}(T-\tau)\rho^{\tau} = \sum_{\tau=1}^{T-1}(T-\tau)\rho^{\tau} - \sum_{\tau=1}^{T-1}(T-\tau)\rho^{\tau+1}$$

$$= \sum_{\tau=1}^{T-1}(T-\tau)\rho^{\tau} - \sum_{\tau'=2}^{T}(T-\tau'+1)\rho^{\tau'}$$

$$= (T-1)\rho - \sum_{\tau=2}^{T-1}\rho^{\tau} - \rho^{T} = T\rho - \sum_{\tau=1}^{T}\rho^{\tau}$$

$$= T\rho - \rho(1-\rho^{T})(1-\rho)^{-1}.$$

In the last line of (8.32) the first term on the right is the asymptotic variance of $\bar{x}$. Clearly when the x_t's are "positively autocorrelated" so that $\rho > 0$—as may well be true of most economic time series—this asymptotic variance exceeds the classical $T^{-1}\sigma^2$.

Stationary Multivariate Stochastic Processes

A direct multivariate generalization of a stochastic process is available. A multivariate stochastic process is a family of random $K \times 1$ vectors $\{\mathbf{x}_t\}$ where

$$\mathbf{x}_t = \begin{pmatrix} x_{t1} \\ \cdot \\ \cdot \\ \cdot \\ x_{tK} \end{pmatrix}$$

such that for every finite set of choices of t, say $t_1, \ldots, t_n$, a joint probability distribution is defined for the random vectors $\mathbf{x}_{t_1}, \ldots, \mathbf{x}_{t_n}$—i.e., for the random variables $x_{t_11}, \ldots, x_{t_1K}, \ldots, x_{t_n1}, \ldots, x_{t_nK}$. Again a stationary multivariate stochastic process is one in which these distributions are invariant under translations along the time axis.

Confining our attention to the stationary case and assuming the relevant moments exist we may define

$$(8.34)\qquad E\mathbf{x}_t = \boldsymbol{\mu} = \begin{pmatrix} \mu_1 \\ \cdot \\ \cdot \\ \cdot \\ \mu_K \end{pmatrix},$$

$$E(\mathbf{x}_t - \boldsymbol{\mu})(\mathbf{x}_t - \boldsymbol{\mu})' = \boldsymbol{\Sigma} = \begin{pmatrix} \sigma_{11} & \cdots & \sigma_{1K} \\ \cdot & & \cdot \\ \cdot & & \cdot \\ \cdot & & \cdot \\ \sigma_{K1} & \cdots & \sigma_{KK} \end{pmatrix},$$

$$E(\mathbf{x}_t - \boldsymbol{\mu})(\mathbf{x}_{t+\tau} - \boldsymbol{\mu})' = \boldsymbol{\Gamma}_\tau = \begin{pmatrix} \gamma_{\tau 11} & \cdots & \gamma_{\tau 1K} \\ \cdot & & \cdot \\ \cdot & & \cdot \\ \cdot & & \cdot \\ \gamma_{\tau K1} & \cdots & \gamma_{\tau KK} \end{pmatrix},$$

where $\mu_i = Ex_{ti}$ is the mean of the random variable x_i; $\sigma_{ij} = E(x_{ti} - \mu_i)(x_{tj} - \mu_j)$ is the contemporaneous covariance between the random variables x_i and x_j—or simply variance for $i = j$; and $\gamma_{\tau ij} = E(x_{ti} - \mu_i) \times (x_{t+\tau,j} - \mu_j)$ is the lag-τ crosscovariance between x_i and x_j—or simply τth autocovariance for $i = j$.

Each component $\{x_{ti}\}$ $(i = 1, \ldots, K)$ of the multivariate stochastic process $\{\mathbf{x}_t\}$ is clearly a univariate stochastic process and is stationary if the multivariate process is stationary. Two stationary processes $\{x_{ti}\}$ and $\{x_{tj}\}$ will be said to be independent if the conditional distribution of every finite set $x_{t_1i}, \ldots, x_{t_ni}$ is the same for all values of $x_{t_1j}, \ldots, x_{t_nj}$; if so, then clearly $\sigma_{ij} = 0$ and $\gamma_{\tau ij} = 0$. A weaker condition is contemporaneous uncorrelatedness: Two stationary processes $\{x_{ti}\}$ and $\{x_{tj}\}$ will be said to be contemporaneously uncorrelated if $\sigma_{ij} = 0$.

By a sample of size T of the stationary multivariate stochastic process $\{\mathbf{x}_t\}$ we mean a joint drawing $\mathbf{x}_1, \ldots, \mathbf{x}_T$ from the joint distribution of T consecutive $\mathbf{x}_t$'s. Viewing a set of observations as a sample from a stationary multivariate stochastic process provides a rather general model for the generation of economic data; loosely speaking, we now have a model for nonrandom sampling from a multivariate probability distribution.

Given such a sample we may compute the sample means $\bar{x}_i = T^{-1} \sum_{t=1}^T x_{ti}$ and the sample variances and contemporaneous covariances $s_{ij} = T^{-1} \sum_{t=1}^T (x_{ti} - \bar{x}_i)(x_{tj} - \bar{x}_j)$ and consider using these as estimates of the corresponding population parameters. A matrix representation is helpful; the sample observations may be arranged in the $T \times K$ matrix as in Section 4:

$$\mathbf{X} = \begin{pmatrix} x_{11} & \cdots & x_{1K} \\ \cdot & & \cdot \\ \cdot & & \cdot \\ \cdot & & \cdot \\ x_{T1} & \cdots & x_{TK} \end{pmatrix} \tag{8.35}$$

where each row gives one observation on the random vector $\mathbf{x}_t$. Again the sample mean vector is

$$(8.36) \qquad \bar{\mathbf{x}} = \begin{pmatrix} \bar{x}_1 \\ \cdot \\ \cdot \\ \cdot \\ \bar{x}_K \end{pmatrix} = T^{-1}\mathbf{X}'\boldsymbol{\iota}$$

where $\boldsymbol{\iota}$ is the $T \times 1$ vector of 1's and the sample contemporaneous covariance matrix is

$$(8.37) \qquad \mathbf{S} = \begin{pmatrix} s_{11} & \cdots & s_{1K} \\ \cdot & & \cdot \\ \cdot & & \cdot \\ \cdot & & \cdot \\ s_{K1} & \cdots & s_{KK} \end{pmatrix} = T^{-1}\mathbf{X}'\mathbf{X} - \bar{\mathbf{x}}\bar{\mathbf{x}}' = T^{-1}\mathbf{X}'\mathbf{M}\mathbf{X}$$

where $\mathbf{M} = \mathbf{I} - T^{-1}\boldsymbol{\iota}\boldsymbol{\iota}'$.

Now under general conditions corresponding to those in the univariate case, these sample statistics are consistent estimators of the corresponding population parameters $\boldsymbol{\mu}$ and $\boldsymbol{\Sigma}$. This consistency is obvious when the stationary process consists of independent random vectors; it remains true in the presence of dependence provided that the dependence between $\mathbf{x}_t$ and $\mathbf{x}_{t+\tau}$ decreases sufficiently fast as τ increases. We state these results in the form of a theorem.

(8.38) Let the $T \times K$ matrix $\mathbf{X}$ be a sample of the stationary multivariate stochastic process with mean vector $\boldsymbol{\mu}$ and contemporaneous covariance matrix $\boldsymbol{\Sigma}$. Then under general conditions, $\text{plim}\ \bar{\mathbf{x}} = \boldsymbol{\mu}$ and $\text{plim}\ \mathbf{S} = \boldsymbol{\Sigma}$ where $\bar{\mathbf{x}}$ is the sample mean vector $T^{-1}\mathbf{X}'\boldsymbol{\iota}$ and $\mathbf{S}$ is the sample contemporaneous covariance matrix $T^{-1}\mathbf{X}'\mathbf{X} - \bar{\mathbf{x}}\bar{\mathbf{x}}'$.

For future reference we note that under these general conditions the sample second moment matrix $T^{-1}\mathbf{X}'\mathbf{X}$ also has a probability limit: $\text{plim}\ T^{-1}\mathbf{X}'\mathbf{X} = \text{plim}\ (\mathbf{S} + \bar{\mathbf{x}}\bar{\mathbf{x}}') = \text{plim}\ \mathbf{S} + (\text{plim}\ \bar{\mathbf{x}})(\text{plim}\ \bar{\mathbf{x}})' = \boldsymbol{\Sigma} + \boldsymbol{\mu}\boldsymbol{\mu}' = E\mathbf{x}_t\mathbf{x}_t'$.

CHAPTER 4

Classical Linear Regression

1. INTRODUCTION

Most of economic theory is concerned with relationships among variables, and correspondingly most of this book is concerned with statistical methods for investigating relationships among economic variables. In this chapter we develop the classical linear regression model in which the value of one observable random variable is expressed as a linear function of several observable nonstochastic variables and an additive nonobservable disturbance. This model is the basic stochastic model for relationships among variables; in the succeeding chapters more flexible models are obtained by relaxing its assumptions.

Linear regression is treated simply as a descriptive device in Section 2. We specify the assumptions of the classical linear regression model in Section 3 and treat statistical inference in this model in Sections 4 and 5. In Section 6 we add the assumption that the disturbance is normally distributed and then proceed to obtain further results on statistical inference in Sections 7 and 8. Section 9 is devoted to computational techniques. In Section 10 we treat several special problems of linear regression. Finally, Section 11 extends the analysis to sets of linear regressions.

From the start, our discussion proceeds in terms of the general case of *multiple regression*—where there are several "independent" variables—and, correspondingly, in terms of matrix algebra. The reader will find it instructive to specialize the results to the case of *simple* regression—where there is only one "independent" variable. For analyses of simple regression see Mood (1950, Ch. 13) and Johnston (1963, Ch. 1). The reader will also find it instructive to specialize the results to the case where there are just two "independent" variables; see Johnston (1963, pp. 52–62).

2. DESCRIPTIVE LINEAR REGRESSION

Given a set of T joint observations on the $1 + K$ variables $y, x_1, \ldots, x_K$,

$$
\begin{array}{ccccccc}
y_1 & x_{11} & \cdots & x_{1k} & \cdots & x_{1K} \\
\cdot & \cdot & & \cdot & & \cdot \\
\cdot & \cdot & & \cdot & & \cdot \\
\cdot & \cdot & & \cdot & & \cdot \\
y_t & x_{t1} & \cdots & x_{tk} & \cdots & x_{tK} \\
\cdot & \cdot & & \cdot & & \cdot \\
\cdot & \cdot & & \cdot & & \cdot \\
\cdot & \cdot & & \cdot & & \cdot \\
y_T & x_{T1} & \cdots & x_{Tk} & \cdots & x_{TK}
\end{array}
\tag{2.1}
$$

we may wish to summarize the pattern of the observations by fitting a hyperplane of the form $y = \alpha + \beta_1 x_1 + \cdots + \beta_K x_K$. A conventional basis for choosing the best-fitting hyperplane is the least-squares criterion. Let

$$
y_t = \beta_0 x_{t0} + \beta_1 x_{t1} + \cdots + \beta_K x_{tK} + e_t \qquad (t = 1, \ldots, T), \tag{2.2}
$$

where $x_{t0} \equiv 1$ so that β_0 is the intercept α. Then the least-squares hyperplane is that for which $S = \Sigma_{t=1}^{T} e_t^2$, the sum of squared deviations from the hyperplane, is minimized. Adopting this criterion we seek the coefficients of the least-squares hyperplane.

A matrix formulation is desirable. The T equations (2.2) are written

$$
\begin{pmatrix} y_1 \\ \cdot \\ \cdot \\ \cdot \\ y_T \end{pmatrix} = \begin{pmatrix} x_{10} & \cdots & x_{1K} \\ \cdot & & \cdot \\ \cdot & & \cdot \\ \cdot & & \cdot \\ x_{T0} & \cdots & x_{TK} \end{pmatrix} \begin{pmatrix} \beta_0 \\ \cdot \\ \cdot \\ \cdot \\ \beta_K \end{pmatrix} + \begin{pmatrix} e_1 \\ \cdot \\ \cdot \\ \cdot \\ e_T \end{pmatrix} \tag{2.3}
$$

or

$$
\mathbf{y} = \mathbf{X}\boldsymbol{\beta} + \mathbf{e} \tag{2.4}
$$

where $\mathbf{y}$ is the $T \times 1$ vector of observations on the regressand,
$\mathbf{X}$ is the $T \times (1 + K)$ matrix of observations on the regressors,
$\boldsymbol{\beta}$ is the $(1 + K) \times 1$ vector of coefficients, and
$\mathbf{e}$ is the $T \times 1$ vector of residuals.

The quantity to be minimized is the scalar

$$(2.5)\qquad \begin{aligned} S = \mathbf{e}'\mathbf{e} &= (\mathbf{y} - \mathbf{X}\boldsymbol{\beta})'(\mathbf{y} - \mathbf{X}\boldsymbol{\beta}) && \text{[by (2.4)]} \\ &= \mathbf{y}'\mathbf{y} - \mathbf{y}'\mathbf{X}\boldsymbol{\beta} - \boldsymbol{\beta}'\mathbf{X}'\mathbf{y} + \boldsymbol{\beta}'\mathbf{X}'\mathbf{X}\boldsymbol{\beta} \\ &= \mathbf{y}'\mathbf{y} - 2\boldsymbol{\beta}'\mathbf{X}'\mathbf{y} + \boldsymbol{\beta}'\mathbf{X}'\mathbf{X}\boldsymbol{\beta} && [\mathbf{y}'\mathbf{X}\boldsymbol{\beta} \text{ is } 1 \times 1]. \end{aligned}$$

Differentiating with respect to $\boldsymbol{\beta}$ gives

$$(2.6)\qquad \frac{\partial S}{\partial \boldsymbol{\beta}} = -2\mathbf{X}'\mathbf{y} + 2\mathbf{X}'\mathbf{X}\boldsymbol{\beta},$$

which set equal to $\mathbf{0}$ gives the "normal equations"

$$(2.7)\qquad \mathbf{X}'\mathbf{X}\mathbf{b} = \mathbf{X}'\mathbf{y},$$

where $\mathbf{X}'\mathbf{X}$ is the moment matrix of regressors, $\mathbf{X}'\mathbf{y}$ is the moment matrix of regressand by regressors, and $\mathbf{b}$ is the coefficient vector of the least-squares hyperplane. The solution of (2.7) is

$$(2.8)\qquad \mathbf{b} = (\mathbf{X}'\mathbf{X})^{-1}\mathbf{X}'\mathbf{y}$$

which defines the least-squares hyperplane. Written more explicitly, the normal equations are

$$(2.9)\qquad \begin{pmatrix} T & \Sigma x_1 & \cdots & \Sigma x_K \\ \Sigma x_1 & \Sigma x_1^2 & \cdots & \Sigma x_1 x_K \\ \cdot & \cdot & & \cdot \\ \cdot & \cdot & & \cdot \\ \cdot & \cdot & & \cdot \\ \Sigma x_K & \Sigma x_K x_1 & \cdots & \Sigma x_K^2 \end{pmatrix} \begin{pmatrix} b_0 \\ b_1 \\ \cdot \\ \cdot \\ \cdot \\ b_K \end{pmatrix} = \begin{pmatrix} \Sigma y \\ \Sigma x_1 y \\ \cdot \\ \cdot \\ \cdot \\ \Sigma x_K y \end{pmatrix},$$

where the summation runs over $t = 1, \ldots, T$ and where we have used $x_{t0} \equiv 1$. We have assumed that $r(\mathbf{X}) = 1 + K$, whence $\mathbf{X}'\mathbf{X}$ is positive definite by (2.7.7). By (2.7.3) this ensures that $(\mathbf{X}'\mathbf{X})^{-1}$ exists and by (2.8.20*b*) it ensures that $\mathbf{b}$ defines a minimum—for $\partial^2 S/\partial\boldsymbol{\beta}^2 = 2\mathbf{X}'\mathbf{X}$.

The vector of "calculated values of y," $\hat{\mathbf{y}}$, may be computed as

$$(2.10)\qquad \hat{\mathbf{y}} = \mathbf{X}\mathbf{b},$$

and then the vector of residuals, $\hat{\mathbf{e}}$, may be computed as

$$(2.11)\qquad \hat{\mathbf{e}} = \mathbf{y} - \mathbf{X}\mathbf{b} = \mathbf{y} - \hat{\mathbf{y}}.$$

As may be seen in (2.9) the first normal equation says

(2.12) $\boldsymbol{\iota}'\mathbf{X}\mathbf{b} = \boldsymbol{\iota}'\mathbf{y},$

where $\boldsymbol{\iota}$ is the $T \times 1$ vector all of whose elements are unity.

Some properties of the least-squares hyperplane are easily derived:

(2.13) $\boldsymbol{\iota}'\hat{\mathbf{y}} = \boldsymbol{\iota}'\mathbf{X}\mathbf{b} = \boldsymbol{\iota}'\mathbf{y}$ [by (2.10), (2.12)]

the sum of calculated y_t's equals the sum of observed y_t's;

(2.14) $\boldsymbol{\iota}'\hat{\mathbf{e}} = \boldsymbol{\iota}'\mathbf{y} - \boldsymbol{\iota}'\hat{\mathbf{y}} = 0$ [by (2.11), (2.13)]

the sum of residuals is zero;

(2.15) $\mathbf{X}'\hat{\mathbf{e}} = \mathbf{X}'\mathbf{y} - \mathbf{X}'\mathbf{X}\mathbf{b} = \mathbf{0}$ [by (2.11), (2.7)]

the sum of cross products of each regressor and the residuals is zero; and

(2.16) $\hat{\mathbf{y}}'\hat{\mathbf{e}} = \mathbf{b}'\mathbf{X}'\hat{\mathbf{e}} = 0$ [by (2.10), (2.15)]

the sum of cross products of the calculated y_t's and the residuals is zero.

Having found the best-fitting hyperplane we may measure how well it does fit. With this objective we find the sum of squared residuals $\hat{S} = \Sigma_{t=1}^{T} \hat{e}_t^2$ to be

(2.17)
$$\begin{aligned}\hat{S} &= \hat{\mathbf{e}}'\hat{\mathbf{e}} = (\mathbf{y} - \mathbf{X}\mathbf{b})'(\mathbf{y} - \mathbf{X}\mathbf{b}) && \text{[by (2.11)]}\\ &= \mathbf{y}'\mathbf{y} - \mathbf{y}'\mathbf{X}\mathbf{b} - \mathbf{b}'\mathbf{X}'\mathbf{y} + \mathbf{b}'\mathbf{X}'\mathbf{X}\mathbf{b}\\ &= \mathbf{y}'\mathbf{y} - 2\mathbf{b}'\mathbf{X}'\mathbf{y} + \mathbf{b}'\mathbf{X}'\mathbf{X}(\mathbf{X}'\mathbf{X})^{-1}\mathbf{X}'\mathbf{y} && \text{[by (2.8)]}\\ &= \mathbf{y}'\mathbf{y} - \mathbf{b}'\mathbf{X}'\mathbf{y}.\end{aligned}$$

Also by (2.10) we find

(2.18) $\hat{\mathbf{y}}'\hat{\mathbf{y}} = (\mathbf{X}\mathbf{b})'(\mathbf{X}\mathbf{b}) = \mathbf{b}'\mathbf{X}'\mathbf{X}\mathbf{b} = \mathbf{b}'\mathbf{X}'\mathbf{y}.$

The last two equations enable us to write

(2.19) $\mathbf{y}'\mathbf{y} = \hat{\mathbf{y}}'\hat{\mathbf{y}} + \hat{\mathbf{e}}'\hat{\mathbf{e}},$

which decomposes the total $\Sigma\, y_t^2$ into $\Sigma\, \hat{y}_t^2$ plus $\Sigma\, \hat{e}_t^2$. A more interesting decomposition is that of the variation about the mean. Of course $\Sigma(y_t - \bar{y})^2 = \Sigma\, y_t^2 - (\Sigma\, y_t)^2/T$ and $\Sigma(\hat{y}_t - \bar{\hat{y}})^2 = \Sigma\, \hat{y}_t^2 - (\Sigma\, \hat{y}_t)^2/T$. Further from (2.13) we have $\bar{\hat{y}} = \bar{y}$. Subtracting $(\Sigma\, y_t)^2/T$ from both sides of (2.19) we have

(2.20) $\Sigma(y - \bar{y})^2 = \Sigma(\hat{y} - \bar{\hat{y}})^2 + \Sigma\, \hat{e}^2,$

in which the variation of the observed y's is broken down into the variations of the calculated y's plus the variation of the residuals, all variations being measured as the sum of squared deviations about the respective means. For obvious reasons this is termed the decomposition of variance.

A natural measure of goodness of fit is the coefficient of determination

$$R^2 = 1 - \frac{\Sigma \hat{e}^2}{\Sigma (y - \bar{y})^2} = \frac{\Sigma (\hat{y} - \bar{\hat{y}})^2}{\Sigma (y - \bar{y})^2}, \tag{2.21}$$

which lies between 0 and 1. When the fit is perfect, the least-squares plane passes through every observed y, every $\hat{e} = 0$, so $R^2 = 1$. At the other extreme $b_1 = \cdots = b_K = 0$, $b_0 = \bar{y}$, the plane is horizontal at $\bar{y}$, every $\hat{e} = y - \bar{y}$, so $R^2 = 0$. Example 2.1 provides a numerical illustration of fitting a least-squares hyperplane.

Example 2.1. Illustration of descriptive linear regression.

Computation of **b**:

$$\underset{\mathbf{X}}{\begin{pmatrix} 1 & -1 & 0 \\ 1 & 0 & 1 \\ 1 & 1 & 0 \\ 1 & 2 & 1 \\ 1 & 0 & -1 \\ 1 & 0 & 0 \end{pmatrix}} \quad \underset{\mathbf{y}}{\begin{pmatrix} 0 \\ 2 \\ 1 \\ 2 \\ -1 \\ 1 \end{pmatrix}} \quad \underset{\mathbf{X}'\mathbf{X}}{\begin{pmatrix} 6 & 2 & 1 \\ 2 & 6 & 2 \\ 1 & 2 & 3 \end{pmatrix}} \quad \underset{\mathbf{X}'\mathbf{y}}{\begin{pmatrix} 5 \\ 5 \\ 5 \end{pmatrix}} \quad \underset{\mathbf{y}'\mathbf{y}}{(11)}$$

$$\underset{\text{adj}(\mathbf{X}'\mathbf{X})}{\begin{pmatrix} 14 & -4 & -2 \\ -4 & 17 & -10 \\ -2 & -10 & 32 \end{pmatrix}} \quad \underset{(\mathbf{X}'\mathbf{X})^{-1}}{\begin{pmatrix} 14/74 & -4/74 & -2/74 \\ -4/74 & 17/74 & -10/74 \\ -2/74 & -10/74 & 32/74 \end{pmatrix}} \quad \underset{\mathbf{X}'\mathbf{y}}{\begin{pmatrix} 5 \\ 5 \\ 5 \end{pmatrix}} \quad \underset{\mathbf{b}}{\begin{pmatrix} 40/74 \\ 15/74 \\ 100/74 \end{pmatrix}}$$

$|\mathbf{X}'\mathbf{X}| = 74$

Confirmation of properties:

$$\underset{\hat{\mathbf{y}}}{\begin{pmatrix} 25/74 \\ 140/74 \\ 55/74 \\ 170/74 \\ -60/74 \\ 40/74 \end{pmatrix}} \quad \underset{\hat{\mathbf{e}}}{\begin{pmatrix} -25/74 \\ 8/74 \\ 19/74 \\ -22/74 \\ -14/74 \\ 34/74 \end{pmatrix}}$$

$\boldsymbol{\iota}'\mathbf{y} = 5$

$\boldsymbol{\iota}'\hat{\mathbf{y}} = 5$

$\boldsymbol{\iota}'\hat{\mathbf{e}} = 0$

$\hat{\mathbf{y}}'\hat{\mathbf{e}} = 0$

$$\mathbf{X}'\hat{\mathbf{e}} = \begin{pmatrix} 0 \\ 0 \\ 0 \end{pmatrix}$$

Decomposition of variance:

$$\Sigma(y - \bar{y})^2 = \mathbf{y}'\mathbf{y} - (\boldsymbol{\iota}'\mathbf{y})^2/T = 11 - 5^2/6 = 1517/222$$

$$\Sigma(\hat{y} - \bar{\hat{y}})^2 = \mathbf{b}'\mathbf{X}'\mathbf{y} - (\boldsymbol{\iota}'\mathbf{y})^2/T = 775/74 - 5^2/6 = 1400/222$$

$$\Sigma e^2 = \Sigma(y - \bar{y})^2 - \Sigma(\hat{y} - \bar{\hat{y}})^2 = 117/222$$

$$R^2 = \Sigma(\hat{y} - \bar{\hat{y}})^2/\Sigma(y - \bar{y})^2 = 1400/1517 = 0.92.$$

3. CLASSICAL LINEAR REGRESSION MODEL

The preceding discussion was entirely in terms of descriptive statistics. To place the fitting of linear relationships among many variables in the framework of statistical inference, we must have a theory or model of how the observations are generated. In this chapter we develop the classical linear regression model. In this model, the body of T joint observations constitutes a sample drawn from a population in which there is a conditional distribution of y for every set of values of $x_1, \ldots, x_K$. The mean of the conditional distribution is a linear function of $x_1, \ldots, x_K$; the variance of the conditional distribution is constant. Each joint observation is in fact a given set of values of the x's together with a drawing of y from the appropriate conditional distribution. Successive drawings of the y's are uncorrelated. The T sets of regressor values are fixed in repeated samples.

A convenient alternative formulation is: There are T populations of random disturbances; each has mean zero, all have the same variance. Each joint observation is a given set of values of the x's together with a value of y determined as a constant linear function of the x's plus a drawing from a disturbance population. Successive drawings of the disturbance are uncorrelated. The T sets of regressor values are fixed in repeated samples.

We formalize the model using the matrix notation of the previous section but write $\boldsymbol{\epsilon}$ for the $T \times 1$ vector of disturbances:

$$\boldsymbol{\epsilon} = \begin{pmatrix} \epsilon_1 \\ \cdot \\ \cdot \\ \cdot \\ \epsilon_t \\ \cdot \\ \cdot \\ \cdot \\ \epsilon_T \end{pmatrix}.$$

Classical linear regression model

(3.1) $\mathbf{y} = \mathbf{X}\boldsymbol{\beta} + \boldsymbol{\epsilon}$,

(3.2) $E\boldsymbol{\epsilon} = \mathbf{0}$,

(3.3) $E\boldsymbol{\epsilon}\boldsymbol{\epsilon}' = \sigma^2\mathbf{I}$,

(3.4) $\mathbf{X}$ is a $T \times (1 + K)$ matrix which is fixed in repeated samples,

(3.5) Rank of $\mathbf{X} = 1 + K \leq T$.

Assumption (3.1) states that each observation y_t is a linear function of the observations x_{tk} plus the disturbance ϵ_t. Assumption (3.2) states that each disturbance has expectation zero. Assumption (3.3) states first that $E\epsilon_t^2 = \sigma^2$ for all t, which embodies the constant-variance specification; and also that $E\epsilon_s\epsilon_t = 0$ for all $s \neq t$, which embodies the uncorrelated disturbance assumption. Assumption (3.4) states that the regressors are nonstochastic, which of course implies that $\mathbf{X}$ and $\boldsymbol{\epsilon}$ are independent. Thus

(3.6) $E(\boldsymbol{\epsilon} \mid \mathbf{X}) = E\boldsymbol{\epsilon} = \mathbf{0}$,

(3.7) $E\mathbf{X}'\boldsymbol{\epsilon} = \mathbf{X}'E\boldsymbol{\epsilon} = \mathbf{0}$,

and

(3.8) $E(\boldsymbol{\epsilon}\boldsymbol{\epsilon}' \mid \mathbf{X}) = E\boldsymbol{\epsilon}\boldsymbol{\epsilon}' = \sigma^2\mathbf{I}$.

Assumption (3.5) states that there are no exact linear relationships among the regressors; as will become clear this is a necessary precondition for estimation.

From (3.1) and (3.6) we may confirm

(3.9) $E(\mathbf{y} \mid \mathbf{X}) = \mathbf{X}\boldsymbol{\beta} + E(\boldsymbol{\epsilon} \mid \mathbf{X}) = \mathbf{X}\boldsymbol{\beta}$,

i.e., $E(y_t \mid x_{t1}, \ldots, x_{tK}) = \beta_0 x_{t0} + \beta_1 x_{t1} + \cdots + \beta_K x_{tK}$, the conditional expectation of y is a linear function of the x's. From (3.1), (3.8), and (3.9) we may confirm

(3.10) $E[(\mathbf{y} - E\mathbf{y})(\mathbf{y} - E\mathbf{y})' \mid \mathbf{X}] = E(\boldsymbol{\epsilon}\boldsymbol{\epsilon}' \mid \mathbf{X}) = \sigma^2\mathbf{I}$,

so that $E[(y_t - Ey_t)'(y_t - Ey_t) \mid x_{t1}, \ldots, x_{tK}] = \sigma^2$, the conditional variance of y is the same for all observations.

On the assumption that the classical linear regression model correctly specifies the generation of our observations, we proceed to consider inferences that may be made about the values of $\boldsymbol{\beta}$, σ^2, and related parameters.

4. STATISTICAL INFERENCE IN CLASSICAL LINEAR REGRESSION: BASIC RESULTS

Estimator of $\boldsymbol{\beta}$

We adopt the criterion of best linear unbiasedness and seek the BLUE of $\boldsymbol{\beta}$; i.e., the vector whose elements are BLUE's of the corresponding elements of $\boldsymbol{\beta}$. Let $\hat{\boldsymbol{\beta}}$ be a linear estimator of $\boldsymbol{\beta}$:

$$\hat{\boldsymbol{\beta}} = \mathbf{C}'\mathbf{y} \tag{4.1}$$

where $\mathbf{C}'$ is a $(1 + K) \times T$ nonstochastic matrix. Substitute (3.1) into (4.1) to find

$$\hat{\boldsymbol{\beta}} = \mathbf{C}'(\mathbf{X}\boldsymbol{\beta} + \boldsymbol{\epsilon}) = \mathbf{C}'\mathbf{X}\boldsymbol{\beta} + \mathbf{C}'\boldsymbol{\epsilon}, \tag{4.2}$$

the expected value of which is

$$E\hat{\boldsymbol{\beta}} = \mathbf{C}'\mathbf{X}\boldsymbol{\beta} + E\mathbf{C}'\boldsymbol{\epsilon} = \mathbf{C}'\mathbf{X}\boldsymbol{\beta}, \tag{4.3}$$

since $\mathbf{C}'$ is nonstochastic and $E\boldsymbol{\epsilon} = \mathbf{0}$. Thus for $\hat{\boldsymbol{\beta}}$ to be an unbiased estimator of $\boldsymbol{\beta}$, whatever $\boldsymbol{\beta}$ may be, $\mathbf{C}'$ must satisfy

$$\mathbf{C}'\mathbf{X} = \mathbf{I}. \tag{4.4}$$

In such a case we see from (4.2) and (4.3) that

$$\hat{\boldsymbol{\beta}} - \boldsymbol{\beta} = \hat{\boldsymbol{\beta}} - E\hat{\boldsymbol{\beta}} = \mathbf{C}'\boldsymbol{\epsilon}, \tag{4.5}$$

the sampling error vector is a linear function of the disturbance vector. Multiplying and taking expectations we find for the covariance matrix of $\hat{\boldsymbol{\beta}}$:

$$\begin{aligned} \boldsymbol{\Sigma}_{\hat{\beta}\hat{\beta}} &= E[(\hat{\boldsymbol{\beta}} - \boldsymbol{\beta})(\hat{\boldsymbol{\beta}} - \boldsymbol{\beta})'] = E[(\mathbf{C}'\boldsymbol{\epsilon})(\mathbf{C}'\boldsymbol{\epsilon})'] = E(\mathbf{C}'\boldsymbol{\epsilon}\boldsymbol{\epsilon}'\mathbf{C}) \\ &= \mathbf{C}'(E\boldsymbol{\epsilon}\boldsymbol{\epsilon}')\mathbf{C} = \mathbf{C}'\sigma^2\mathbf{I}\mathbf{C} \qquad \text{[by (3.3)]} \\ &= \sigma^2\mathbf{C}'\mathbf{C}. \end{aligned} \tag{4.6}$$

Now consider the least-squares coefficient vector of the preceding section,

$$\mathbf{b} = (\mathbf{X}'\mathbf{X})^{-1}\mathbf{X}'\mathbf{y}. \tag{4.7}$$

It is in fact a linear estimator, $\mathbf{b} = \hat{\mathbf{C}}'\mathbf{y}$ with

$$\hat{\mathbf{C}}' = (\mathbf{X}'\mathbf{X})^{-1}\mathbf{X}'; \tag{4.8}$$

it is unbiased by (4.4) since

$$\hat{\mathbf{C}}'\mathbf{X} = (\mathbf{X}'\mathbf{X})^{-1}\mathbf{X}' \cdot \mathbf{X} = \mathbf{I}; \tag{4.9}$$

thus by (4.5) its sampling error is

(4.10) $$\mathbf{b} - \boldsymbol{\beta} = \hat{\mathbf{C}}'\boldsymbol{\epsilon} = (\mathbf{X}'\mathbf{X})^{-1}\mathbf{X}'\boldsymbol{\epsilon},$$

and by (4.6) its covariance matrix is

(4.11) $$\boldsymbol{\Sigma}_{\mathbf{bb}} = \sigma^2\hat{\mathbf{C}}'\hat{\mathbf{C}} = \sigma^2(\mathbf{X}'\mathbf{X})^{-1}\mathbf{X}' \cdot \mathbf{X}(\mathbf{X}'\mathbf{X})^{-1} = \sigma^2(\mathbf{X}'\mathbf{X})^{-1}.$$

Without loss of generality we may express the $\mathbf{C}'$ of any linear estimator $\hat{\boldsymbol{\beta}}$ as

(4.12) $$\mathbf{C}' = \hat{\mathbf{C}}' + \mathbf{D}' = (\mathbf{X}'\mathbf{X})^{-1}\mathbf{X}' + \mathbf{D}'$$

where $\mathbf{D}'$ is a $(1 + K) \times T$ nonstochastic matrix. For $\hat{\boldsymbol{\beta}}$ to be unbiased it is required that $\mathbf{C}'\mathbf{X} = \mathbf{I} + \mathbf{D}'\mathbf{X} = \mathbf{I}$, i.e.,

(4.13) $$\mathbf{D}'\mathbf{X} = \mathbf{0},$$

in which case its covariance matrix is

(4.14) $$\begin{aligned}\boldsymbol{\Sigma}_{\hat{\boldsymbol{\beta}}\hat{\boldsymbol{\beta}}} &= \sigma^2\{[(\mathbf{X}'\mathbf{X})^{-1}\mathbf{X}' + \mathbf{D}'][(\mathbf{X}'\mathbf{X})^{-1}\mathbf{X}' + \mathbf{D}']'\}\\ &= \sigma^2[(\mathbf{X}'\mathbf{X})^{-1} + \mathbf{D}'\mathbf{X}(\mathbf{X}'\mathbf{X})^{-1} + (\mathbf{X}'\mathbf{X})^{-1}\mathbf{X}'\mathbf{D} + \mathbf{D}'\mathbf{D}]\\ &= \sigma^2[(\mathbf{X}'\mathbf{X})^{-1} + \mathbf{D}'\mathbf{D}] = \boldsymbol{\Sigma}_{\mathbf{bb}} + \sigma^2\mathbf{D}'\mathbf{D}.\end{aligned}$$

Since $\mathbf{D}'\mathbf{D}$ is nonnegative definite by (2.7.15) we see that the following theorem is established:

(4.15) ***Gauss-Markov least-squares theorem.*** In the classical linear regression model the best linear unbiased estimator of $\boldsymbol{\beta}$ is the least-squares vector

(4.15*a*) $$\mathbf{b} = (\mathbf{X}'\mathbf{X})^{-1}\mathbf{X}'\mathbf{y},$$

whose covariance matrix is

(4.15*b*) $$\boldsymbol{\Sigma}_{\mathbf{bb}} = \sigma^2(\mathbf{X}'\mathbf{X})^{-1}.$$

The relevance of assumption (3.5) is now apparent. Were $r(\mathbf{X}) < 1 + K$, then $\mathbf{X}'\mathbf{X}$ would be singular by (2.4.13), and the least-squares estimator would not be uniquely defined. When $r(\mathbf{X}) < 1 + K$ the columns of $\mathbf{X}$ form a linearly dependent set, and it is easy to see why no reasonable estimation procedure exists: Without loss of generality let x_K be linearly dependent on $x_0, x_1, \ldots, x_{K-1}$:

(4.16) $$x_{tK} = \sum_{k=0}^{K-1} a_k x_{tk} \quad \text{for} \quad \text{all } t = 1, \ldots, T.$$

Then insertion of (4.16) into the conditional expectation of y will lead to a distinct alternative expression. Thus

$$(4.17) \quad \sum_{k=0}^{K} \beta_k x_{tk} = \sum_{k=0}^{K-1} \beta_k x_{tk} + \beta_K x_{tK} = \sum_{k=0}^{K-1} \beta_k x_{tk} + \delta\beta_K x_{tK} + (1-\delta)\beta_K x_{tK}$$

$$= \sum_{k=0}^{K-1} \beta_k x_{tk} + \delta\beta_K \sum_{k=0}^{K-1} a_k x_{tk} + (1-\delta)\beta_K x_{tK}$$

$$= \sum_{k=0}^{K-1} (\beta_k + \delta\beta_K a_k) x_{tk} + (1-\delta)\beta_K x_{tK}$$

$$= \sum_{k=0}^{K} \beta_k^* x_{tk} \quad \text{for} \quad \text{all } t = 1, \ldots, T,$$

where $\beta_k^* = \beta_k + \delta\beta_K a_k$ for $k = 0, 1, \ldots, K-1$; $\beta_K^* = (1-\delta)\beta_K$; and δ is an arbitrary number within the interval (0, 1). It is clear that either side of (4.17) would give the conditional expectation of y_t given $x_{t0}, \ldots, x_{tK}$. Thus the vector $\boldsymbol{\beta}$ that we seek to estimate would not be well defined.

A further property of the least-squares estimator may be noted. Recalling that a best unbiased estimator minimizes the generalized variance, we have:

(4.18) In the classical linear regression model the least-squares estimator $\mathbf{b}$ has the minimum generalized variance within the class of linear unbiased estimators of $\boldsymbol{\beta}$.

Decomposition of Variance

Since the best linear unbiased estimator of $\boldsymbol{\beta}$ in the classical linear regression model is just the least-squares coefficient vector $\mathbf{b}$, the results of Section 2 carry over. The calculated value of $\mathbf{y}$ is again

$$(4.19) \quad \hat{\mathbf{y}} = \mathbf{Xb},$$

and now we write

$$(4.20) \quad \hat{\boldsymbol{\epsilon}} = \mathbf{y} - \hat{\mathbf{y}} = \mathbf{y} - \mathbf{Xb}$$

to emphasize that each residual $\hat{\epsilon}_t$ is an estimator of the corresponding disturbance ϵ_t. The standard terminology for the decomposition of variance is

(4.21)

SST: Total sum of squares $= \Sigma(y - \bar{y})^2 = \mathbf{y}'\mathbf{y} - (\boldsymbol{\iota}'\mathbf{y})^2/T$,

SSR: Regression sum of squares $= \Sigma(\hat{y} - \bar{\hat{y}})^2 = \mathbf{b}'\mathbf{X}'\mathbf{y} - (\boldsymbol{\iota}'\mathbf{y})^2/T$,

SSE: Error sum of squares $= \Sigma\hat{\epsilon}_t^2 = SST - SSR$.

With this notation the coefficient of determination may be written

(4.22) $$R^2 = SSR/SST = 1 - SSE/SST.$$

Estimator of σ^2

An estimator of the disturbance variance σ^2 will naturally be based on the error sum of squares $\Sigma\hat{\epsilon}_t^2$. Inserting (3.1) and (4.10) into (4.20) we obtain

(4.23) $$\begin{aligned}\hat{\boldsymbol{\epsilon}} = \mathbf{y} - \hat{\mathbf{y}} &= (\mathbf{X}\boldsymbol{\beta} + \boldsymbol{\epsilon}) - \mathbf{X}\mathbf{b} = \mathbf{X}\boldsymbol{\beta} + \boldsymbol{\epsilon} - \mathbf{X}[\boldsymbol{\beta} + (\mathbf{X}'\mathbf{X})^{-1}\mathbf{X}'\boldsymbol{\epsilon}] \\ &= \boldsymbol{\epsilon} - \mathbf{X}(\mathbf{X}'\mathbf{X})^{-1}\mathbf{X}'\boldsymbol{\epsilon} = [\mathbf{I} - \mathbf{X}(\mathbf{X}'\mathbf{X})^{-1}\mathbf{X}']\boldsymbol{\epsilon} = \mathbf{M}\boldsymbol{\epsilon},\end{aligned}$$

where

(4.24) $$\mathbf{M} = \mathbf{I} - \mathbf{X}(\mathbf{X}'\mathbf{X})^{-1}\mathbf{X}'.$$

Direct computation shows that $\mathbf{M}$ is idempotent:

(4.25) $$\mathbf{M} = \mathbf{M}' \quad \text{and} \quad \mathbf{M}^2 = \mathbf{M},$$

whence the error sum of squares is

(4.26) $$\hat{\boldsymbol{\epsilon}}'\hat{\boldsymbol{\epsilon}} = \boldsymbol{\epsilon}'\mathbf{M}'\mathbf{M}\boldsymbol{\epsilon} = \boldsymbol{\epsilon}'\mathbf{M}^2\boldsymbol{\epsilon} = \boldsymbol{\epsilon}'\mathbf{M}\boldsymbol{\epsilon}.$$

Taking expectations,

(4.27) $$\begin{aligned} E\hat{\boldsymbol{\epsilon}}'\hat{\boldsymbol{\epsilon}} &= E\boldsymbol{\epsilon}'\mathbf{M}\boldsymbol{\epsilon} \\ &= E\, tr(\boldsymbol{\epsilon}'\mathbf{M}\boldsymbol{\epsilon}) && [\boldsymbol{\epsilon}'\mathbf{M}\boldsymbol{\epsilon} \text{ is a scalar}] \\ &= E\, tr(\mathbf{M}\boldsymbol{\epsilon}\boldsymbol{\epsilon}') && [\text{for } tr(\mathbf{AB}) = tr(\mathbf{BA})] \\ &= tr\ E(\mathbf{M}\boldsymbol{\epsilon}\boldsymbol{\epsilon}') && [\text{for trace is linear function}] \\ &= tr(\mathbf{M} \cdot E\boldsymbol{\epsilon}\boldsymbol{\epsilon}') && [\text{for } \mathbf{M} \text{ is nonstochastic}] \\ &= tr(\mathbf{M}\sigma^2\mathbf{I}) && [\text{by (3.3)}] \\ &= \sigma^2\, tr\, \mathbf{M} && [\text{for } tr(c\mathbf{A}) = c\, tr(\mathbf{A})]. \end{aligned}$$

Further, where $\mathbf{I}_n$ denotes the $n \times n$ identity matrix,

(4.28) $$\begin{aligned} tr\,\mathbf{M} &= tr(\mathbf{I}_T) - tr[\mathbf{X}(\mathbf{X}'\mathbf{X})^{-1}\mathbf{X}'] && [\text{for } tr(\mathbf{A} + \mathbf{B}) = tr(\mathbf{A}) + tr(\mathbf{B})] \\ &= tr(\mathbf{I}_T) - tr[\mathbf{X}'\mathbf{X}(\mathbf{X}'\mathbf{X})^{-1}] && [\text{for } tr(\mathbf{AB}) = tr(\mathbf{BA})] \\ &= tr(\mathbf{I}_T) - tr(\mathbf{I}_{1+K}) \\ &= T - (1 + K) && [\text{for } tr(\mathbf{I}_n) = n]. \end{aligned}$$

Thus we have found for the expectation of the error sum of squares

(4.29) $$E\hat{\boldsymbol{\epsilon}}'\hat{\boldsymbol{\epsilon}} = \sigma^2(T - K - 1),$$

from which we see that an unbiased estimator of the disturbance variance is obtainable by dividing the error sum of squares by $T - K - 1$:

(4.30) In the classical linear regression model an unbiased estimator of σ^2 is

(4.30a) $$s^2 = \frac{SSE}{T - K - 1}.$$

Estimator of $E(\mathbf{b} - \boldsymbol{\beta})(\mathbf{b} - \boldsymbol{\beta})'$

Since $(\mathbf{X}'\mathbf{X})^{-1}$ is nonstochastic, it follows that an unbiased estimator of the covariance matrix of the coefficient estimator $\mathbf{b}$ is obtainable by using s^2 for σ^2; $E[s^2(\mathbf{X}'\mathbf{X})^{-1}] = (Es^2) \cdot (\mathbf{X}'\mathbf{X})^{-1} = \sigma^2(\mathbf{X}'\mathbf{X})^{-1}$. Thus

(4.31) In the classical linear regression model an unbiased estimator of $\boldsymbol{\Sigma}_{\mathbf{bb}}$ is

(4.31a) $$\mathbf{S}_{\mathbf{bb}} = s^2(\mathbf{X}'\mathbf{X})^{-1}.$$

For a comment on the asymptotic properties of least-squares estimation in the classical linear regression model, see the final paragraph of Section 6.2, p. 272.

5. STATISTICAL INFERENCE IN CLASSICAL LINEAR REGRESSION: FURTHER RESULTS

Estimator of Linear Function of $\boldsymbol{\beta}$

Consider the problem of estimating a scalar linear function of $\boldsymbol{\beta}$

(5.1) $$\pi = \boldsymbol{\delta}'\boldsymbol{\beta}$$

where $\boldsymbol{\delta}$ is a $(1 + K) \times 1$ vector of known numbers. An estimator of π is obtained by replacing $\boldsymbol{\beta}$ in (5.1) by its least-squares estimator $\mathbf{b}$. Indeed, we may establish that

(5.2) In the classical linear regression model, the BLUE of $\pi = \boldsymbol{\delta}'\boldsymbol{\beta}$ is the least-squares estimator

(5.2a) $$p = \boldsymbol{\delta}'\mathbf{b},$$

the variance of which is

(5.2b) $$\sigma_p^2 = \sigma^2\boldsymbol{\delta}'(\mathbf{X}'\mathbf{X})^{-1}\boldsymbol{\delta} = \boldsymbol{\delta}'\boldsymbol{\Sigma}_{\mathbf{bb}}\boldsymbol{\delta}.$$

To establish this consider any linear estimator of π

(5.3) $$\hat{\pi} = \mathbf{c}'\mathbf{y}$$

where $\mathbf{c}$ is a $T \times 1$ nonstochastic vector; without loss of generality we may write

$$(5.4) \qquad \mathbf{c}' = \boldsymbol{\delta}'(\mathbf{X}'\mathbf{X})^{-1}\mathbf{X}' + \mathbf{d}'$$

where $\mathbf{d}$ is a $T \times 1$ nonstochastic vector. Inserting (3.1) in (5.3) we find $\hat{\pi} = \mathbf{c}'\mathbf{X}\boldsymbol{\beta} + \mathbf{c}'\boldsymbol{\epsilon}$, whence for $\hat{\pi}$ to be an unbiased estimator of π, whatever π may be, it is necessary and sufficient that

$$(5.5) \qquad \mathbf{c}'\mathbf{X} = \boldsymbol{\delta}'$$

which, since $\boldsymbol{\delta}'(\mathbf{X}'\mathbf{X})^{-1}\mathbf{X}' \cdot \mathbf{X} = \boldsymbol{\delta}'$, is equivalent to

$$(5.6) \qquad \mathbf{d}'\mathbf{X} = \mathbf{0}.$$

In such a case we have

$$(5.7) \qquad \hat{\pi} - \pi = \mathbf{c}'\mathbf{X}\boldsymbol{\beta} + \mathbf{c}'\boldsymbol{\epsilon} - \boldsymbol{\delta}'\boldsymbol{\beta} = \boldsymbol{\delta}'\boldsymbol{\beta} + \mathbf{c}'\boldsymbol{\epsilon} - \boldsymbol{\delta}'\boldsymbol{\beta} = \mathbf{c}'\boldsymbol{\epsilon}$$

and

$$(5.8) \qquad \begin{aligned} \text{var}(\hat{\pi}) &= E(\hat{\pi} - \pi)(\hat{\pi} - \pi)' = E\mathbf{c}'\boldsymbol{\epsilon}\boldsymbol{\epsilon}'\mathbf{c} = \mathbf{c}'E\boldsymbol{\epsilon}\boldsymbol{\epsilon}'\mathbf{c} = \sigma^2\mathbf{c}'\mathbf{c} \\ &= \sigma^2[\boldsymbol{\delta}'(\mathbf{X}'\mathbf{X})^{-1}\mathbf{X}' + \mathbf{d}'][\mathbf{X}(\mathbf{X}'\mathbf{X})^{-1}\boldsymbol{\delta} + \mathbf{d}] \\ &= \sigma^2[\boldsymbol{\delta}'(\mathbf{X}'\mathbf{X})^{-1}\boldsymbol{\delta} + \mathbf{d}'\mathbf{d}] \qquad \text{[by (5.6)].} \end{aligned}$$

Since $\mathbf{d}'\mathbf{d} \geq 0$, the variance is minimized by choosing $\mathbf{d}'\mathbf{d} = 0$, which requires $\mathbf{d} = \mathbf{0}$. Thus the BLUE of π is the one obtained by choosing $\hat{\mathbf{c}}' = \boldsymbol{\delta}'(\mathbf{X}'\mathbf{X})^{-1}\mathbf{X}'$, namely $\hat{\pi} = \hat{\mathbf{c}}'\mathbf{y} = \boldsymbol{\delta}'(\mathbf{X}'\mathbf{X})^{-1}\mathbf{X}'\mathbf{y}$, but this is precisely the least-squares estimator $p = \boldsymbol{\delta}'\mathbf{b}$. The variance of p follows from (5.8). It is clear that an unbiased estimator of this variance is given by

$$(5.9) \qquad s_p^2 = s^2\boldsymbol{\delta}'(\mathbf{X}'\mathbf{X})^{-1}\boldsymbol{\delta} = \boldsymbol{\delta}'\mathbf{S}_{\mathbf{bb}}\boldsymbol{\delta}.$$

As an economic example, consider the aggregate consumption function $y = \beta_0 + \beta_1 x_1 + \beta_2 x_2 + \epsilon$, where y is consumption, x_1 is labor income, and x_2 is nonlabor income. Then interest attaches to the difference between the marginal propensities to consume out of the two income shares. This difference is a linear function of the β's, i.e., $0\beta_0 + 1\beta_1 - 1\beta_2$.

Estimator of Conditional Expectation of y

It is clear that in obtaining an estimator of $\boldsymbol{\beta}$ we have effectively obtained an estimator of the conditional expectation of y for any given set of x's. For the set of x's contained in the $(1 + K) \times 1$ vector $\mathbf{X}_*$, the first element being $x_{*0} = 1$, the conditional expectation of y is

$$(5.10) \qquad E(y \mid \mathbf{X}'_*) = \mathbf{X}'_*\boldsymbol{\beta},$$

the least-squares estimator of which is

$$(5.11) \qquad \hat{y}_* = \mathbf{X}'_*\mathbf{b}.$$

As (5.10) shows, the conditional expectation is in fact a linear function of $\boldsymbol{\beta}$, so that (5.2) is applicable; i.e.,

(5.12) In the classical linear regression model, the BLUE of $E(y \mid \mathbf{X}'_*)$ is the least-squares estimator

(5.12*a*) $$\hat{y}_* = \mathbf{X}'_*\mathbf{b},$$

the variance of which is

(5.12*b*) $$\sigma^2_{\hat{y}_*} = \sigma^2\mathbf{X}'_*(\mathbf{X}'\mathbf{X})^{-1}\mathbf{X}_* = \mathbf{X}'_*\boldsymbol{\Sigma}_{\mathbf{bb}}\mathbf{X}_*.$$

It is clear that an unbiased estimator of this variance is given by

(5.13) $$s^2_{\hat{y}_*} = s^2\mathbf{X}'_*(\mathbf{X}'\mathbf{X})^{-1}\mathbf{X}_* = \mathbf{X}'_*\mathbf{S}_{\mathbf{bb}}\mathbf{X}_*.$$

Forecast

Since $\hat{y}_*$ estimates the mean of the conditional distribution of y given $\mathbf{X}_*$ it may also be used to "forecast" a single random drawing from this conditional distribution. The actual drawing will be

(5.14) $$y_* = \mathbf{X}'_*\boldsymbol{\beta} + \epsilon_*$$

where ϵ_* is the disturbance. This disturbance is assumed to be an independent drawing from the same kind of distribution that provided the sample disturbances; thus

(5.15) $$E\epsilon_* = 0,$$

(5.16) $$E\epsilon^2_* = \sigma^2,$$

and

(5.17) $$E\boldsymbol{\epsilon}\epsilon_* = \mathbf{0}.$$

If we forecast y_* by

(5.18) $$\hat{y}_* = \mathbf{X}'_*\mathbf{b},$$

the forecast error will be

(5.19) $$f = y_* - \hat{y}_* = \mathbf{X}'_*(\boldsymbol{\beta} - \mathbf{b}) + \epsilon_*.$$

The expectation of the forecast error will be

(5.20) $$Ef = \mathbf{X}'_*E(\boldsymbol{\beta} - \mathbf{b}) + E\epsilon_* = 0$$

and its variance will be

(5.21) $$\begin{aligned}\sigma^2_f = Ef^2 &= \mathbf{X}'_*E(\mathbf{b} - \boldsymbol{\beta})(\mathbf{b} - \boldsymbol{\beta})'\mathbf{X}_* + E\epsilon^2_* = \mathbf{X}'_*\boldsymbol{\Sigma}_{\mathbf{bb}}\mathbf{X}_* + \sigma^2 \\ &= \sigma^2_{\hat{y}_*} + \sigma^2 \qquad \text{[by (5.12}b\text{)]},\end{aligned}$$

where we have used the fact that $E(\mathbf{b} - \boldsymbol{\beta})\epsilon_* = E(\mathbf{X}'\mathbf{X})^{-1}\mathbf{X}'\boldsymbol{\epsilon}\epsilon_* = (\mathbf{X}'\mathbf{X})^{-1}\mathbf{X}'E\boldsymbol{\epsilon}\epsilon_* = \mathbf{0}$ by (5.17). Note the interpretation of (5.21). The error made in forecasting an individual drawing is the sum of two uncorrelated errors: the error in estimating the expectation of the distribution from which the drawing comes and the deviation of the drawing from its expectation. The variance of the forecast error is then the sum of the two corresponding variances.

We define the best linear unbiased forecast of y_* to be the linear function of $\mathbf{y}$, $\tilde{y}_*$, which minimizes $E(y_* - \tilde{y}_*)^2$ subject to $E(y_* - \tilde{y}_*) = 0$. Then an argument parallel to that of the preceding subsections shows that this is $\hat{y}_*$. Thus

(5.22) In the classical linear regression model, the best linear unbiased forecast of y_* is the least-squares forecast

(5.22a) $\hat{y}_* = \mathbf{X}'_*\mathbf{b},$

the forecast variance of which is

(5.22b) $\sigma_f^2 = \sigma_{\hat{y}_*}^2 + \sigma^2.$

It is clear that an unbiased estimator of this variance is provided by

(5.23) $s_f^2 = s_{\hat{y}_*}^2 + s^2.$

It is important to note that our results do not refer to the distribution of forecast errors generated by repeated forecasting from a regression hyperplane estimated from a single sample; then $\mathbf{b}$ and $\hat{y}_*$ would be constants. Rather we have been considering the distribution of forecast errors generated when each forecast is constructed from a fresh sample regression.

Numerical Illustration

Assuming that the classical linear regression model is appropriate to the data of Example 2.1, we illustrate the results of Sections 4 and 5 by computations on those data.

Example 5.1. From Example 2.1 we have

$$\mathbf{b} = \begin{pmatrix} 40/74 \\ 15/74 \\ 100/74 \end{pmatrix}, \qquad SSE = 117/222,$$

$$(\mathbf{X}'\mathbf{X})^{-1} = \begin{pmatrix} 14/74 & -4/74 & -2/74 \\ -4/74 & 17/74 & -10/74 \\ -2/74 & -10/74 & 32/74 \end{pmatrix}.$$

Computation of s^2:

$$s^2 = \frac{SSE}{T - K - 1} = \frac{117/222}{3} = \frac{13}{74}.$$

Computation of $\mathbf{S_{bb}}$:

$$\mathbf{S_{bb}} = s^2(\mathbf{X'X})^{-1} = \begin{pmatrix} 13(14)/74^2 & 13(-4)/74^2 & 13(-2)/74^2 \\ 13(-4)/74^2 & 13(17)/74^2 & 13(-10)/74^2 \\ 13(-2)/74^2 & 13(-10)/74^2 & 13(32)/74^2 \end{pmatrix}.$$

Computation of $\hat{y}_*$ for $\mathbf{X}'_* = (1 \quad 1 \quad 1)$:

$$\hat{y}_* = \mathbf{X}'_*\mathbf{b} = (1 \quad 1 \quad 1)\begin{pmatrix} 40/74 \\ 15/74 \\ 100/74 \end{pmatrix} = 155/74.$$

Computation of $s^2_{\hat{y}*}$ for $\mathbf{X}'_* = (1 \quad 1 \quad 1)$:

$$\begin{aligned} s^2_{\hat{y}*} &= \mathbf{X}'_*\mathbf{S_{bb}}\mathbf{X}_* \\ &= (1 \quad 1 \quad 1)\begin{pmatrix} 13(14)/74^2 & 13(-4)/74^2 & 13(-2)/74^2 \\ 13(-4)/74^2 & 13(17)/74^2 & 13(-10)/74^2 \\ 13(-2)/74^2 & 13(-10)/74^2 & 13(32)/74^2 \end{pmatrix}\begin{pmatrix} 1 \\ 1 \\ 1 \end{pmatrix} \\ &= (13/74)(31/74) = 13(31)/74^2. \end{aligned}$$

Computation of s^2_f for $\mathbf{X}'_* = (1 \quad 1 \quad 1)$:

$$s^2_f = s^2_{\hat{y}*} + s^2 = 13(31)/74^2 + 13/74 = 13(105)/74^2.$$

6. CLASSICAL NORMAL LINEAR REGRESSION MODEL

We have come this far without specification of the form of the distribution of the disturbance. In many cases it is reasonable to assume that this distribution is in fact normal; or, equivalently, that the conditional distribution of each y is normal. Where the disturbance is interpreted as the net effect of a large number of independent random variables, this assumption is supported by the central limit theorem (3.6.21).

The classical normal linear regression model comprises the assumptions (3.1)–(3.5) together with

(6.1) $\quad \boldsymbol{\epsilon}$ is normally distributed.

Assumptions (3.2), (3.3), and (6.1) together imply that

(6.2) $\quad \boldsymbol{\epsilon}$ is a spherical normal vector with $E\boldsymbol{\epsilon} = \mathbf{0}$ and $E\boldsymbol{\epsilon\epsilon}' = \sigma^2\mathbf{I}$,

i.e., the ϵ_t ($t = 1, \ldots, T$) are a set of mutually independent normally distributed variables with common expectation zero and common variance σ^2.

All the results established for the classical linear regression model carry over, but now further important results obtain. As (4.10) shows, $\mathbf{b} - \boldsymbol{\beta} = (\mathbf{X}'\mathbf{X})^{-1}\mathbf{X}'\boldsymbol{\epsilon}$ is now a linear form in a normally distributed vector, and hence by (3.5.8) is itself normally distributed. In particular, since $E\mathbf{b} = \boldsymbol{\beta}$ and $E(\mathbf{b} - \boldsymbol{\beta})(\mathbf{b} - \boldsymbol{\beta})' = \sigma^2(\mathbf{X}'\mathbf{X})^{-1}$,

$$(6.3) \qquad \frac{b_k - \beta_k}{\sigma_{b_k}} \text{ is } \mathcal{N}(0, 1) \qquad (k = 0, \ldots, K),$$

where σ_{b_k} is the square root of the kth diagonal element of $\boldsymbol{\Sigma}_{\mathbf{bb}} = \sigma^2(\mathbf{X}'\mathbf{X})^{-1}$. Were σ^2 known, interval estimation and hypothesis testing for $\boldsymbol{\beta}$ could be developed by exploiting the normality of $\mathbf{b}$. In the absence of such knowledge operational procedures are still available and are developed in the next section.

7. STATISTICAL INFERENCE IN CLASSICAL NORMAL LINEAR REGRESSION: BASIC RESULTS

Single Coefficient

From (4.23)–(4.28) we see that

$$(7.1) \qquad SSE = \hat{\boldsymbol{\epsilon}}'\hat{\boldsymbol{\epsilon}} = \boldsymbol{\epsilon}'\mathbf{M}\boldsymbol{\epsilon}$$

where $\mathbf{M} = \mathbf{I} - \mathbf{X}(\mathbf{X}'\mathbf{X})^{-1}\mathbf{X}'$ is an idempotent matrix of rank $T - K - 1$ (since the rank of an idempotent matrix is equal to its trace). Since in classical normal linear regression $\boldsymbol{\epsilon}$ is spherical normal SSE is now an idempotent quadratic form of rank $T - K - 1$ in spherical normal variables, and hence by (3.5.22)

$$(7.2) \qquad SSE \text{ is distributed as } \sigma^2\chi^2_{T-K-1}$$

and with $s^2 = SSE/(T - K - 1)$,

$$(7.3) \qquad \frac{s^2}{\sigma^2} \text{ is distributed as } \frac{\chi^2_{T-K-1}}{T - K - 1}.$$

Consider then the ratio

$$(7.4) \qquad \frac{b_k - \beta_k}{s_{b_k}} = \frac{(b_k - \beta_k)/\sigma_{b_k}}{s_{b_k}/\sigma_{b_k}}$$

where s_{b_k} is the estimated standard error of b_k, i.e., $s_{b_k} = s\sqrt{s^{kk}}$ where $\sqrt{s^{kk}}$ is the square root of the kth diagonal element of $(\mathbf{X}'\mathbf{X})^{-1}$. In the right-hand side of (7.4) the numerator is a standard normal variable by (6.3), and the denominator equals s/σ, which by (7.3) is the square root of a $\chi^2_{T-K-1}/(T - K - 1)$ variable. Furthermore, since $\mathbf{M}'\mathbf{X}(\mathbf{X}'\mathbf{X})^{-1} = \mathbf{0}$, the linear form $\mathbf{b} - \boldsymbol{\beta} = (\mathbf{X}'\mathbf{X})^{-1}\mathbf{X}'\boldsymbol{\epsilon}$ is independent of the quadratic form

$SSE = \boldsymbol{\epsilon}'\mathbf{M}\boldsymbol{\epsilon}$ and thus of $s/\sigma = \sqrt{SSE}/\sigma\sqrt{T-K-1}$ by (3.5.24). We conclude from (3.5.15) that

(7.5) $\dfrac{b_k - \beta_k}{s_{b_k}}$ is distributed as t_{T-K-1}.

This result permits us to construct a confidence interval for β_k or to test the hypothesis that $\beta_k = \beta_k^*$ by exploiting the t distribution just as was done for the mean of a normal distribution in Section 3.7. Indeed, β_k *is* the mean of the normally distributed b_k. In particular, the verbal hypothesis that "y does not vary with x_k" translates into the hypothesis that the conditional expectation of y does not involve x_k, which is in turn the hypothesis $\beta_k = 0$. The so-called "t-ratio," b_k/s_{b_k}, is the test statistic appropriate to this hypothesis.

Set of Coefficients

Next consider a hypothesis on the entire vector $\boldsymbol{\beta}$, i.e., $\boldsymbol{\beta} = \boldsymbol{\beta}^*$. Clearly a test of this hypothesis will be based on $\mathbf{b} - \boldsymbol{\beta}^*$. Now, on the hypothesis that $\boldsymbol{\beta} = \boldsymbol{\beta}^*$, it will be true that $\mathbf{b} - \boldsymbol{\beta}^* = \mathbf{b} - \boldsymbol{\beta} = (\mathbf{X}'\mathbf{X})^{-1}\mathbf{X}'\boldsymbol{\epsilon}$. Then consider the statistic $Q = (\mathbf{b} - \boldsymbol{\beta}^*)'\mathbf{X}'\mathbf{X}(\mathbf{b} - \boldsymbol{\beta}^*)$. On the hypothesis $\boldsymbol{\beta} = \boldsymbol{\beta}^*$, we see that

(7.6) $$\begin{aligned} Q &= \boldsymbol{\epsilon}'\mathbf{X}(\mathbf{X}'\mathbf{X})^{-1} \cdot \mathbf{X}'\mathbf{X} \cdot (\mathbf{X}'\mathbf{X})^{-1}\mathbf{X}'\boldsymbol{\epsilon} = \boldsymbol{\epsilon}'\mathbf{X}(\mathbf{X}'\mathbf{X})^{-1}\mathbf{X}'\boldsymbol{\epsilon} \\ &= \boldsymbol{\epsilon}'(\mathbf{I} - \mathbf{M})\boldsymbol{\epsilon}, \end{aligned}$$

where again $\mathbf{M} = \mathbf{I} - \mathbf{X}(\mathbf{X}'\mathbf{X})^{-1}\mathbf{X}'$. Now it is readily seen that $(\mathbf{I} - \mathbf{M})$ is idempotent and that

$$\begin{aligned} r(\mathbf{I} - \mathbf{M}) &= tr(\mathbf{I} - \mathbf{M}) = tr(\mathbf{I}) - tr(\mathbf{M}) = T - (T - K - 1) \\ &= 1 + K \end{aligned}$$

so that Q is then an idempotent quadratic form of rank $1 + K$ in spherical normal variables. All this is on the null hypothesis; thus by (3.5.22) we conclude:

(7.7) On the hypothesis $\boldsymbol{\beta} = \boldsymbol{\beta}^*$,
$(\mathbf{b} - \boldsymbol{\beta}^*)'\mathbf{X}'\mathbf{X}(\mathbf{b} - \boldsymbol{\beta}^*)$ is distributed as $\sigma^2\chi^2_{1+K}$.

Further note that since $\mathbf{M}(\mathbf{I} - \mathbf{M}) = \mathbf{M} - \mathbf{M}^2 = \mathbf{M} - \mathbf{M} = \mathbf{0}$, the quadratic forms Q and SSE are in fact independent by (3.5.26), whence by (3.5.16),

(7.8) On the hypothesis $\boldsymbol{\beta} = \boldsymbol{\beta}^*$, the ratio

$$\frac{Q/(1 + K)}{SSE/(T - K - 1)}$$

is distributed as F^{1+K}_{T-K-1}.

This provides the basis for testing the hypothesis $\boldsymbol{\beta} = \boldsymbol{\beta}^*$ by exploiting the

F distribution. It is clear that a one-tailed test is appropriate; the rejection region should consist of high values of

$$\frac{Q/(1+K)}{SSE/(T-K-1)}$$

since these correspond to high values of Q, i.e., to large deviations of $\mathbf{b}$ from $\boldsymbol{\beta}^*$.

In practice we are rarely interested in testing a hypothesis on the full vector $\boldsymbol{\beta}$. Instead we are concerned either with an hypothesis on the set $\beta_1, \ldots, \beta_K$ (with no hypothesis on the "constant" term β_0) or with an hypothesis on a subset $\beta_{H+1}, \ldots, \beta_K$ (with no hypothesis on $\beta_0, \beta_1, \ldots, \beta_H$). Let us therefore partition the relationship $\mathbf{y} = \mathbf{X}\boldsymbol{\beta} + \boldsymbol{\epsilon}$ as

$$\text{(7.9)} \qquad \mathbf{y} = \mathbf{X}_1\boldsymbol{\beta}_1 + \mathbf{X}_2\boldsymbol{\beta}_2 + \boldsymbol{\epsilon},$$

where $\mathbf{X}_1$ is $T \times (1 + H)$ and $\boldsymbol{\beta}_1$ is $(1 + H) \times 1$, and $\mathbf{X}_2$ is $T \times (K - H)$ and $\boldsymbol{\beta}_2$ is $(K - H) \times 1$. Note that for $H = 0$ we have the first alternative. In terms of (7.9), then, we wish to consider the hypothesis that $\boldsymbol{\beta}_2 = \boldsymbol{\beta}_2^*$. Clearly a test of this hypothesis will be based on $\mathbf{b}_2 - \boldsymbol{\beta}_2^*$, where $\mathbf{b}_2$ is the corresponding subvector of the estimator $\mathbf{b}$. Now on the hypothesis that $\boldsymbol{\beta}_2 = \boldsymbol{\beta}_2^*$, it will be true that $\mathbf{b}_2 - \boldsymbol{\beta}_2^* = \mathbf{b}_2 - \boldsymbol{\beta}_2$. We require an expression for the latter in terms of $\boldsymbol{\epsilon}$; to obtain it, we resort to inversion of partitioned matrices.

With $\mathbf{X}$ partitioned as $(\mathbf{X}_1 \quad \mathbf{X}_2)$ the formula $\mathbf{b} = (\mathbf{X}'\mathbf{X})^{-1}\mathbf{X}'\mathbf{y}$ reads

$$\text{(7.10)} \qquad \begin{pmatrix} \mathbf{b}_1 \\ \mathbf{b}_2 \end{pmatrix} = \begin{pmatrix} \mathbf{X}_1'\mathbf{X}_1 & \mathbf{X}_1'\mathbf{X}_2 \\ \mathbf{X}_2'\mathbf{X}_1 & \mathbf{X}_2'\mathbf{X}_2 \end{pmatrix}^{-1} \begin{pmatrix} \mathbf{X}_1'\mathbf{y} \\ \mathbf{X}_2'\mathbf{y} \end{pmatrix}.$$

Letting

$$\text{(7.11)} \qquad \mathbf{M}_1 = \mathbf{I} - \mathbf{X}_1(\mathbf{X}_1'\mathbf{X}_1)^{-1}\mathbf{X}_1'$$

and

$$\text{(7.12)} \qquad \mathbf{D} = \mathbf{X}_2'\mathbf{X}_2 - \mathbf{X}_2'\mathbf{X}_1(\mathbf{X}_1'\mathbf{X}_1)^{-1}\mathbf{X}_1'\mathbf{X}_2 = \mathbf{X}_2'\mathbf{M}_1\mathbf{X}_2$$

and applying the partitioned inversion rule (2.5.18) yields

$$\begin{pmatrix} (\mathbf{X}_1'\mathbf{X}_1)^{-1}[\mathbf{I} + \mathbf{X}_1'\mathbf{X}_2\mathbf{D}^{-1}\mathbf{X}_2'\mathbf{X}_1(\mathbf{X}_1'\mathbf{X}_1)^{-1}] & -(\mathbf{X}_1'\mathbf{X}_1)^{-1}\mathbf{X}_1'\mathbf{X}_2\mathbf{D}^{-1} \\ -\mathbf{D}^{-1}\mathbf{X}_2'\mathbf{X}_1(\mathbf{X}_1'\mathbf{X}_1)^{-1} & \mathbf{D}^{-1} \end{pmatrix} \begin{pmatrix} \mathbf{X}_1'\mathbf{y} \\ \mathbf{X}_2'\mathbf{y} \end{pmatrix},$$

$$\text{(7.13)} \qquad \begin{pmatrix} \mathbf{b}_1 \\ \mathbf{b}_2 \end{pmatrix} = \begin{pmatrix} (\mathbf{X}_1'\mathbf{X}_1)^{-1}\mathbf{X}_1'\mathbf{y} - (\mathbf{X}_1'\mathbf{X}_1)^{-1}\mathbf{X}_1'\mathbf{X}_2\mathbf{D}^{-1}\mathbf{X}_2'\mathbf{M}_1\mathbf{y} \\ \mathbf{D}^{-1}\mathbf{X}_2'\mathbf{M}_1\mathbf{y} \end{pmatrix}.$$

From the second "row" of (7.13) we see that

(7.14) $$\mathbf{b}_2 = \mathbf{D}^{-1}\mathbf{X}_2'\mathbf{M}_1\mathbf{y} = \mathbf{D}^{-1}\mathbf{X}_2'\mathbf{M}_1(\mathbf{X}_1\boldsymbol{\beta}_1 + \mathbf{X}_2\boldsymbol{\beta}_2 + \boldsymbol{\epsilon}) = \boldsymbol{\beta}_2 + \mathbf{D}^{-1}\mathbf{X}_2'\mathbf{M}_1\boldsymbol{\epsilon}$$

where we have used the facts that $\mathbf{M}_1\mathbf{X}_1 = \mathbf{X}_1 - \mathbf{X}_1(\mathbf{X}_1'\mathbf{X}_1)^{-1}\mathbf{X}_1'\mathbf{X}_1 = \mathbf{0}$ and that $\mathbf{D}^{-1}\mathbf{X}_2'\mathbf{M}_1\mathbf{X}_2 = \mathbf{D}^{-1}\mathbf{D} = \mathbf{I}$. Thus we have the desired expression

(7.15) $$\mathbf{b}_2 - \boldsymbol{\beta}_2 = \mathbf{D}^{-1}\mathbf{X}_2'\mathbf{M}_1\boldsymbol{\epsilon}.$$

Consider then the statistic $Q_2 = (\mathbf{b}_2 - \boldsymbol{\beta}_2^*)'\mathbf{D}(\mathbf{b}_2 - \boldsymbol{\beta}_2^*)$. We see that on the hypothesis that $\boldsymbol{\beta}_2 = \boldsymbol{\beta}_2^*$,

(7.16) $$Q_2 = \boldsymbol{\epsilon}'\mathbf{M}_1\mathbf{X}_2\mathbf{D}^{-1}\cdot\mathbf{D}\cdot\mathbf{D}^{-1}\mathbf{X}_2'\mathbf{M}_1\boldsymbol{\epsilon} = \boldsymbol{\epsilon}'\mathbf{M}_1\mathbf{X}_2\mathbf{D}^{-1}\mathbf{X}_2'\mathbf{M}_1\boldsymbol{\epsilon} = \boldsymbol{\epsilon}'\mathbf{P}\boldsymbol{\epsilon},$$

where

(7.17) $$\mathbf{P} = \mathbf{M}_1\mathbf{X}_2\mathbf{D}^{-1}\mathbf{X}_2'\mathbf{M}_1.$$

Now it is readily seen that $\mathbf{P}$ is idempotent and that

$$r(\mathbf{P}) = tr(\mathbf{D}^{-1}\mathbf{X}_2'\mathbf{M}_1\mathbf{M}_1\mathbf{X}_2) = tr(\mathbf{D}^{-1}\mathbf{X}_2'\mathbf{M}_1\mathbf{X}_2) = tr(\mathbf{D}^{-1}\mathbf{D}) = tr(\mathbf{I}_{K-H}) = K - H,$$

so that Q_2 is then an idempotent quadratic form of rank $K - H$ in spherical normal variables. All this is on the null hypothesis; thus by (3.5.22) we conclude that

(7.18) On the hypothesis $\boldsymbol{\beta}_2 = \boldsymbol{\beta}_2^*$,
$(\mathbf{b}_2 - \boldsymbol{\beta}_2^*)'\mathbf{D}(\mathbf{b}_2 - \boldsymbol{\beta}_2^*)$ is distributed as $\sigma^2\chi^2_{K-H}$.

Further it may be seen that $\mathbf{PM}_1 = \mathbf{P}$ and $\mathbf{M} = \mathbf{M}_1 - \mathbf{P}$ so that

$$\mathbf{PM} = \mathbf{P}(\mathbf{M}_1 - \mathbf{P}) = \mathbf{P} - \mathbf{P} = \mathbf{0},$$

whence Q_2 and SSE are independent idempotent quadratic forms in spherical normal variables by (3.5.26), whence by (3.5.16),

(7.19) On the hypothesis that $\boldsymbol{\beta}_2 = \boldsymbol{\beta}_2^*$, the ratio

$$\frac{Q_2/(K - H)}{SSE/(T - K - 1)}$$

is distributed as F^{K-H}_{T-K-1}.

This provides the basis for testing the hypothesis $\boldsymbol{\beta}_2 = \boldsymbol{\beta}_2^*$ by exploiting the F distribution. Again, it is clear that a one-tailed test is appropriate; the rejection region should consist of high values of

$$\frac{Q_2/(K - H)}{SSE/(T - K - 1)}$$

since these correspond to high values of Q_2, i.e., to large deviations of $\mathbf{b}_2$ from $\boldsymbol{\beta}_2^*$.

Standard Cases

With this general result in hand we turn to the standard hypotheses which specify that some elements of $\boldsymbol{\beta}$ are zero. Now if the hypothesis is in fact $\boldsymbol{\beta}_2^* = \mathbf{0}$, then $\mathbf{b}_2 - \boldsymbol{\beta}_2^* = \mathbf{b}_2$, so that the test statistic is simply $Q_2 = \mathbf{b}_2'\mathbf{D}\mathbf{b}_2$, which in view of (7.13) we may write as

(7.20) When the hypothesis is $\boldsymbol{\beta}_2 = \mathbf{0}$, then

$$Q_2 = \mathbf{y}'\mathbf{M}_1\mathbf{X}_2\mathbf{D}^{-1} \cdot \mathbf{D} \cdot \mathbf{D}^{-1}\mathbf{X}_2'\mathbf{M}_1\mathbf{y},$$

$$\text{i.e., } Q_2 = \mathbf{y}'\mathbf{M}_1\mathbf{X}_2\mathbf{D}^{-1}\mathbf{X}_2'\mathbf{M}_1\mathbf{y}.$$

From (4.21) we have $SSR + (\Sigma y)^2/T = \mathbf{y}'\mathbf{X}\mathbf{b} = \mathbf{y}'\mathbf{X}_1\mathbf{b}_1 + \mathbf{y}'\mathbf{X}_2\mathbf{b}_2$. Then using (7.13) we see

$$(7.21) \qquad SSR + \frac{(\Sigma y)^2}{T} = \mathbf{y}'\mathbf{X}_1 \cdot (\mathbf{X}_1'\mathbf{X}_1)^{-1}\mathbf{X}_1'\mathbf{y} - \mathbf{y}'\mathbf{X}_1(\mathbf{X}_1'\mathbf{X}_1)^{-1}\mathbf{X}_1'\mathbf{X}_2\mathbf{D}^{-1}\mathbf{X}_2'\mathbf{M}_1\mathbf{y} + \mathbf{y}'\mathbf{X}_2\mathbf{D}^{-1}\mathbf{X}_2'\mathbf{M}_1\mathbf{y}$$
$$= \mathbf{y}'\mathbf{X}_1(\mathbf{X}_1'\mathbf{X}_1)^{-1}\mathbf{X}_1'\mathbf{y} + \mathbf{y}'\mathbf{M}_1\mathbf{X}_2\mathbf{D}^{-1}\mathbf{X}_2'\mathbf{M}_1\mathbf{y}.$$

Now consider the case where the partitioning has $H = 0$, i.e., where $\mathbf{X}_1$ contains only the "constant" term. Then

(7.22) $\mathbf{X}_1 = \boldsymbol{\iota}$,

where $\boldsymbol{\iota}$ denotes the $T \times 1$ vector of ones. Then

$$(7.23) \qquad \mathbf{y}'\mathbf{X}_1(\mathbf{X}_1'\mathbf{X}_1)^{-1}\mathbf{X}_1'\mathbf{y} = \mathbf{y}'\boldsymbol{\iota}(\boldsymbol{\iota}'\boldsymbol{\iota})^{-1}\boldsymbol{\iota}'\mathbf{y} = (\Sigma y)T^{-1}(\Sigma y) = \frac{(\Sigma y)^2}{T}.$$

It follows then by subtraction from both sides of (7.21) that SSR is just the second term on the right of (7.21), which is after all Q_2 in the present case. Thus in view of (7.19)

(7.24) On the hypothesis that $\beta_1 = \cdots = \beta_K = 0$,

$$\frac{SSR/K}{SSE/(T - K - 1)}$$

is distributed as F^K_{T-K-1}.

The verbal hypothesis that "y does not depend on $x_1, \ldots, x_K$" translates into the hypothesis that the conditional expectation of y does not involve these x's, which in turn is the null hypothesis that $\beta_1 = \cdots = \beta_K = 0$. Then the test statistic of (7.24) is appropriate; the F distribution is exploited with high values of F leading to rejection. It is quite natural that rejection of the null hypothesis occurs when SSR is high relative to SSE, i.e., when R^2 is high.

Finally let us consider the general partitioning case, $H \neq 0$. If we had used only $\mathbf{X}_1$ in the regression, we would have estimated $\boldsymbol{\beta}_1$ to be

$$\text{(7.25)} \qquad \tilde{\mathbf{b}}_1 = (\mathbf{X}_1'\mathbf{X}_1)^{-1}\mathbf{X}_1'\mathbf{y}$$

and would have computed the regression sum of squares from

$$\text{(7.26)} \qquad (SSR)_{\sim} + \frac{(\Sigma y)^2}{T} = \tilde{\mathbf{b}}_1{}'\mathbf{X}_1'\mathbf{y} = \mathbf{y}'\mathbf{X}_1(\mathbf{X}_1'\mathbf{X}_1)^{-1}\mathbf{X}_1'\mathbf{y}.$$

Subtracting this from (7.21) we find that the additional regression sum of squares attributable to using $\mathbf{X}_2$ along with $\mathbf{X}_1$ is

$$\text{(7.27)} \qquad \Delta SSR = SSR - (SSR)_{\sim} = \mathbf{y}'\mathbf{M}_1\mathbf{X}_2\mathbf{D}^{-1}\mathbf{X}_2'\mathbf{M}_1\mathbf{y}.$$

Thus in view of (7.19)

(7.28) On the hypothesis that $\beta_{H+1} = \ldots = \beta_K = 0$,

$$\frac{\Delta SSR/(K - H)}{SSE/(T - K - 1)} \text{ is distributed as } F^{K-H}_{T-K-1}.$$

The verbal hypothesis that "y does not depend on $x_{H+1}, \ldots, x_K$" translates into the hypothesis that the conditional expectation of y does not involve these x's, which in turn is the null hypothesis that $\beta_{H+1} = \cdots = \beta_K = 0$. The test statistic of (7.28) is appropriate; the F distribution is exploited with high values of F leading to rejection. It is quite natural that rejection of the null hypothesis occurs when inclusion of $x_{H+1}, \ldots, x_K$ raises SSR substantially relative to SSE.

For computational purposes note that in view of the second "row" of (7.13), (7.27) may be written

$$\text{(7.29)} \qquad \Delta SSR = \mathbf{b}_2'\mathbf{D}\mathbf{b}_2$$

and that $\mathbf{D}^{-1}$ is the submatrix of $(\mathbf{X}'\mathbf{X})^{-1}$ corresponding to $\mathbf{X}_2$. It is therefore unnecessary to recompute the regression omitting a subset of x's if we are interested in finding the increase in regression sum of squares attributable to introducing them. For

(7.30) Let $(\mathbf{X}'\mathbf{X})^{-1}_{\circ\circ}$ be the submatrix of $(\mathbf{X}'\mathbf{X})^{-1}$ and $\mathbf{b}_\circ$ the subvector of $\mathbf{b}$ corresponding to any subset of the x's. Then $\Delta SSR = \mathbf{b}_\circ'[(\mathbf{X}'\mathbf{X})^{-1}_{\circ\circ}]^{-1}\mathbf{b}_\circ$, where ΔSSR is the increase in the regression sum of squares attributable to using that subset of the x's in addition to all the others.

Confidence Regions

The intimate connection between hypothesis testing and interval estimation may be exploited to construct a confidence region for a set of regression coefficients. The development leading up to (7.19) in fact shows that the statistic

$$\frac{(\mathbf{b}_2 - \boldsymbol{\beta}_2)'\mathbf{D}(\mathbf{b}_2 - \boldsymbol{\beta}_2)/(K - H)}{SSE/(T - K - 1)}$$

is distributed as F^{K-H}_{T-K-1} where $\boldsymbol{\beta}_2$ is the true value of the coefficient subvector. That is,

$$\text{(7.31)} \qquad \text{Prob}\left\{\frac{(\mathbf{b}_2 - \boldsymbol{\beta}_2)'\mathbf{D}(\mathbf{b}_2 - \boldsymbol{\beta}_2)/(K - H)}{SSE/(T - K - 1)} \leq F^*_\alpha\right\} = 1 - \alpha,$$

where F^*_α is the value of an F^{K-H}_{T-K-1} variable which is exceeded $100\alpha\%$ of the time. Now (7.31) may be written as

$$\text{(7.32)} \qquad \text{Prob}\,\{(\mathbf{b}_2 - \boldsymbol{\beta}_2)'\mathbf{D}(\mathbf{b}_2 - \boldsymbol{\beta}_2) \leq (K - H)s^2F^*_\alpha\} = 1 - \alpha$$

from which it is clear that the region in $(K - H)$-space enclosed by the hypersurface $(\mathbf{b}_2 - \boldsymbol{\beta}_2)'\mathbf{D}(\mathbf{b}_2 - \boldsymbol{\beta}_2) = (K - H)s^2F^*_\alpha$ is a $100(1 - \alpha)\%$ confidence region for $\boldsymbol{\beta}_2$. This hypersurface is in fact an ellipsoid with center at the point $\mathbf{b}_2$; for further details see Scheffé (1959, pp. 406–408).

8. STATISTICAL INFERENCE IN CLASSICAL NORMAL LINEAR REGRESSION: FURTHER RESULTS

Derived Estimators

The results of Section 5 are similarly extended when the normality assumption is made. Thus $p = \boldsymbol{\delta}'\mathbf{b}$, the least-squares estimator of the linear function of $\boldsymbol{\beta}$, $\pi = \boldsymbol{\delta}'\boldsymbol{\beta}$, with $p - \pi = \boldsymbol{\delta}'(\mathbf{b} - \boldsymbol{\beta}) = \boldsymbol{\delta}'(\mathbf{X}'\mathbf{X})^{-1}\mathbf{X}'\boldsymbol{\epsilon}$, is now a linear function of normally distributed variables. Indeed

$$\text{(8.1)} \qquad \frac{p - \pi}{\sigma_p} \text{ is distributed as } \mathcal{N}(0, 1);$$

whence by an argument parallel to that underlying (7.5),

$$\text{(8.2)} \qquad \frac{p - \pi}{s_p} \text{ is distributed as } t_{T-K-1}.$$

Confidence intervals and hypothesis tests on π are obtainable by exploitation of the t distribution.

As a special case we have for $\hat{y}_* = \mathbf{X}'_*\mathbf{b}$, the estimator of $E(y \mid \mathbf{X}'_*)$:

(8.3) $$\frac{\hat{y}_* - E(y \mid \mathbf{X}'_*)}{\sigma_{\hat{y}_*}} \text{ is distributed as } \mathcal{N}(0, 1);$$

and

(8.4) $$\frac{\hat{y}_* - E(y \mid \mathbf{X}'_*)}{s_{\hat{y}_*}} \text{ is distributed as } t_{T-K-1}.$$

Confidence intervals and hypothesis tests on $E(y \mid \mathbf{X}'_*)$ are obtainable by exploitation of the t distribution.

Similarly the forecast error $f = y_* - \hat{y}_* = \epsilon_* - \mathbf{X}'_*(\mathbf{b} - \boldsymbol{\beta})$ is now a linear function of normally distributed variables, so that

(8.5) $$\frac{y_* - \hat{y}_*}{\sigma_f} \text{ is distributed as } \mathcal{N}(0, 1);$$

and

(8.6) $$\frac{y_* - \hat{y}_*}{s_f} \text{ is distributed as } t_{T-K-1}.$$

The t distribution may be exploited to construct a confidence interval for y_*, commonly known as the "forecast interval." Note that the standard error of forecast, s_f, and hence the width of the forecast interval, will depend on $\mathbf{X}_*$.

Maximum Likelihood Estimation

Since the form of the distribution is specified in the classical normal linear regression model, the maximum likelihood principle may be applied to estimate $\boldsymbol{\beta}$. The likelihood of the sample $\epsilon_1, \ldots, \epsilon_T$ in this model is in accordance with (3.4.1) and (3.5.1)

(8.7) $$\mathscr{L} = (2\pi\sigma^2)^{-T/2} e^{-(2\sigma^2)^{-1}\epsilon'\epsilon},$$

whence the logarithmic likelihood is

(8.8) $$L = -\frac{T}{2}\log(2\pi\sigma^2) - (2\sigma^2)^{-1}\boldsymbol{\epsilon}'\boldsymbol{\epsilon}.$$

Replacing $\boldsymbol{\epsilon}$ by $\mathbf{y} - \mathbf{X}\boldsymbol{\beta}$ we obtain the logarithmic likelihood expressed in terms of the observations $\mathbf{y}$ and $\mathbf{X}$ and the parameters $\boldsymbol{\beta}$ and σ^2:

(8.9) $$L = -\frac{T}{2}\log(2\pi\sigma^2) - (2\sigma^2)^{-1}(\mathbf{y} - \mathbf{X}\boldsymbol{\beta})'(\mathbf{y} - \mathbf{X}\boldsymbol{\beta}).$$

Differentiating,

$$(8.10)\qquad \frac{\partial L}{\partial \boldsymbol{\beta}} = (2\sigma^2)^{-1}2\mathbf{X}'(\mathbf{y} - \mathbf{X}\boldsymbol{\beta}),$$

$$(8.11)\qquad \frac{\partial L}{\partial \sigma^2} = -\frac{T}{2}(\sigma^2)^{-1} + \tfrac{1}{2}(\sigma^2)^{-2}(\mathbf{y} - \mathbf{X}\boldsymbol{\beta})'(\mathbf{y} - \mathbf{X}\boldsymbol{\beta});$$

setting the derivatives equal to zero and solving gives the equations determining the maximum likelihood estimators $\hat{\boldsymbol{\beta}}$ and $\hat{\sigma}^2$:

$$(8.12)\qquad \hat{\boldsymbol{\beta}} = (\mathbf{X}'\mathbf{X})^{-1}\mathbf{X}'\mathbf{y},$$

$$(8.13)\qquad \hat{\sigma}^2 = T^{-1}(\mathbf{y} - \mathbf{X}\hat{\boldsymbol{\beta}})'(\mathbf{y} - \mathbf{X}\hat{\boldsymbol{\beta}}).$$

That these indeed determine a maximum is confirmed, e.g., by the fact that $\partial^2 L/\partial\boldsymbol{\beta}^2 = -(\sigma^2)^{-1}\mathbf{X}'\mathbf{X}$ is negative definite. Thus

(8.14) In the classical normal linear regression model, the maximum likelihood estimator of $\boldsymbol{\beta}$ is the least-squares estimator $\mathbf{b}$, and the maximum likelihood estimator of σ^2 is SSE/T.

The least-squares estimator of $\boldsymbol{\beta}$, which is the BLUE regardless of the shape of the disturbance distribution, will then be consistent and asymptotically efficient when the distribution is normal.

Numerical Illustration

Assuming that the classical normal linear regression model is appropriate to the data of Examples 2.1 and 5.1, we illustrate the results of Sections 6 and 7 by further computations on those data.

Example 8.1. Illustration of classical normal linear regression.

Construction of confidence interval for β_0:
From Examples 2.1 and 5.1 we have $b_0 = 40/74$ and

$$s_{b_0} = \sqrt{(13)(14)/74^2} \doteq 13/74,$$

and from tables $t_{3,.025} = 3.18$. Then a 95% confidence interval for β_0 is $b_0 \pm t_{3,.025}s_{b_0} = 40/74 \pm 3.18(13/74)$.

Test of hypothesis that $\beta_2 = 1$:
From Examples 2.1 and 5.1 we have $b_2 = 100/74$ and $s_{b_2} = \sqrt{(13)(32)/74^2} \doteq 20/74$, and from tables $t_{3,.025} = 3.18$. Then since

$$\left|\frac{b_2 - \beta_2^*}{s_{b_2}}\right| = \left|\frac{100/74 - 74/74}{20/74}\right| = \frac{26}{20} < 3.18,$$

accept the hypothesis $\beta_2 = 1$ at the 5% level of significance.

Test of hypothesis that $\beta_1 = \beta_2 = 0$:

From Examples 2.1 and 5.1 we have $SSR = 1400/222 = 1400/(3)(74)$ and $SSE/(T - K - 1) = 13/74$, and from tables, $F^2_{3,.05} = 9.55$. Then since

$$\frac{SSR/K}{SSE/(T - K - 1)} = \frac{1400/(3)(74)(2)}{13/74} = \frac{1400}{78} \doteq 18 > 9.55$$

reject the hypothesis $\beta_1 = \beta_2 = 0$ at the 5% level of significance.

Test of hypothesis that $\beta_1 = 0$:

For illustrative purposes we use the "subset" procedure of (7.28). We first compute $(SSR)_\sim$ by regressing y on x_0 and x_2 alone. From Example 2.1 we derive for this "short" regression:

$\mathbf{X}'\mathbf{X}$	$(\mathbf{X}'\mathbf{X})^{-1}$	$\mathbf{X}'\mathbf{y}$	$\mathbf{b}$
$\begin{pmatrix} 6 & 1 \\ 1 & 3 \end{pmatrix}$	$\begin{pmatrix} 3/17 & -1/17 \\ -1/17 & 6/17 \end{pmatrix}$	$\begin{pmatrix} 5 \\ 5 \end{pmatrix}$	$\begin{pmatrix} 10/17 \\ 25/17 \end{pmatrix}$

$$\mathbf{b}'\mathbf{X}'\mathbf{y} = 175/17$$

$$(SSR)_\sim = \mathbf{b}'\mathbf{X}'\mathbf{y} - (\Sigma y)^2/T = 175/17 - 5^2/6 = 625/102$$

Then

$$\Delta(SSR) = SSR - (SSR)_\sim = 1400/222 - 625/102 = 225/(17)(74).$$

We also have $SSE/(T - K - 1) = 13/74$, and from tables, $F^1_{3,.05} = 10.13$. Then since

$$\frac{\Delta(SSR)/(K - H)}{SSE/(T - K - 1)} = \frac{[225/(17)(74)]/1}{13/74} = \frac{225}{221} < 10.13,$$

accept the hypothesis $\beta_1 = 0$ at the 5% level of significance.

Note that we might have tested $\beta_1 = 0$ by the t test procedure of (7.5). This is, however, an equivalent procedure. Firstly, $(t_{v,\alpha/2})^2 = F^1_{v,\alpha}$; and secondly

$$\left(\frac{b_k}{s_{b_k}}\right)^2 = \frac{\Delta(SSR)_k}{SSE/(T - K - 1)}$$

where $\Delta(SSR)_k$ is the addition to the regression sum of squares due to adding x_k to all the other regressors. To see the second point, specialize (7.30) to the case $H = 1$. Then we find $\Delta(SSR)_k = b_k^2/s^{kk}$ where s^{kk} is the kth diagonal element of $(\mathbf{X}'\mathbf{X})^{-1}$, so that

$$\frac{\Delta(SSR)_k}{SSE/(T - K - 1)} = \frac{b_k^2/s^{kk}}{s^2} = \frac{b_k^2}{s^2 s^{kk}} = \frac{b_k^2}{s^2_{b_k}} = \left(\frac{b_k}{s_{b_k}}\right)^2.$$

For instance in our example, first, $(3.18)^2 = 10.13$ and second, from Examples 2.1 and 5.1

$$b_1 = 15/74 \text{ and } s_{b_1} = \sqrt{(13)(17)/74^2} \text{ so that}$$

$$\left(\frac{b_1}{s_{b_1}}\right)^2 = \frac{(15/74)^2}{(13)(17)/(74)^2} = \frac{225}{221} = \frac{\Delta(SSR)_1/1}{SSE/(T - K - 1)}.$$

9. COMPUTATIONAL PROCEDURE IN LINEAR REGRESSION

The purpose of this section is to establish and illustrate an efficient computational formulary for linear regression. Recall that the partitioned inversion development of (7.10)–(7.13) was algebraic and did not depend on normality of $\boldsymbol{\epsilon}$.

Variables as Deviations from Means

Let us partition the observation matrix $\mathbf{X}$ as

$$\text{(9.1)} \qquad \mathbf{X} = (\boldsymbol{\iota} \quad \mathbf{Z})$$

where $\boldsymbol{\iota}$ is the observation vector on x_0, and $\mathbf{Z}$ is the observation matrix on $x_1, \ldots, x_K$. Correspondingly let us partition $\boldsymbol{\beta} = \begin{pmatrix} \beta_0 \\ \boldsymbol{\beta}_z \end{pmatrix}$ and $\mathbf{b} = \begin{pmatrix} b_0 \\ \mathbf{b}_z \end{pmatrix}$. Thus $\boldsymbol{\beta}_z$ and its estimator $\mathbf{b}_z$ is just the coefficient vector of the nonconstant regressors. Then the regressor moment matrix is partitioned as

$$\text{(9.2)} \qquad \mathbf{X}'\mathbf{X} = \begin{pmatrix} \boldsymbol{\iota}' \\ \mathbf{Z}' \end{pmatrix} (\boldsymbol{\iota} \quad \mathbf{Z}) = \begin{pmatrix} \boldsymbol{\iota}'\boldsymbol{\iota} & \boldsymbol{\iota}'\mathbf{Z} \\ \mathbf{Z}'\boldsymbol{\iota} & \mathbf{Z}'\mathbf{Z} \end{pmatrix} = \begin{pmatrix} T & \boldsymbol{\iota}'\mathbf{Z} \\ \mathbf{Z}'\boldsymbol{\iota} & \mathbf{Z}'\mathbf{Z} \end{pmatrix}.$$

Now let us define for this section $\mathbf{M}$:

$$\text{(9.3)} \qquad \mathbf{M} = \mathbf{I} - \frac{\boldsymbol{\iota}\boldsymbol{\iota}'}{T}.$$

Now apply the partitioned inversion rule of (2.5.18) with $\mathbf{E} = T$, $\mathbf{F} = \boldsymbol{\iota}'\mathbf{Z}$, $\mathbf{G} = \mathbf{Z}'\boldsymbol{\iota}$, $\mathbf{H} = \mathbf{Z}'\mathbf{Z}$, and $\mathbf{D} = \mathbf{H} - \mathbf{G}\mathbf{E}^{-1}\mathbf{F} = \mathbf{Z}'\mathbf{Z} - \mathbf{Z}'\boldsymbol{\iota}T^{-1}\boldsymbol{\iota}'\mathbf{Z} = \mathbf{Z}'(\mathbf{I} - \boldsymbol{\iota}\boldsymbol{\iota}'/T)\mathbf{Z} = \mathbf{Z}'\mathbf{M}\mathbf{Z}$, to find

$$\text{(9.4)} \qquad (\mathbf{X}'\mathbf{X})^{-1} = \begin{pmatrix} T^{-1}[\mathbf{I} + \boldsymbol{\iota}'\mathbf{Z}(\mathbf{Z}'\mathbf{M}\mathbf{Z})^{-1}\mathbf{Z}'\boldsymbol{\iota}T^{-1}] & -T^{-1}\boldsymbol{\iota}'\mathbf{Z}(\mathbf{Z}'\mathbf{M}\mathbf{Z})^{-1} \\ -(\mathbf{Z}'\mathbf{M}\mathbf{Z})^{-1}\mathbf{Z}'\boldsymbol{\iota}T^{-1} & (\mathbf{Z}'\mathbf{M}\mathbf{Z})^{-1} \end{pmatrix}.$$

Thus the least-squares solution $\mathbf{b} = (\mathbf{X}'\mathbf{X})^{-1}\mathbf{X}'\mathbf{y}$ is expressible as

$$\text{(9.5)} \qquad \begin{pmatrix} b_0 \\ \mathbf{b}_z \end{pmatrix} = \begin{pmatrix} T^{-1}[\mathbf{I} + \boldsymbol{\iota}'\mathbf{Z}(\mathbf{Z}'\mathbf{M}\mathbf{Z})^{-1}\mathbf{Z}'\boldsymbol{\iota}T^{-1}]\boldsymbol{\iota}'\mathbf{y} - T^{-1}\boldsymbol{\iota}'\mathbf{Z}(\mathbf{Z}'\mathbf{M}\mathbf{Z})^{-1}\mathbf{Z}'\mathbf{y} \\ -(\mathbf{Z}'\mathbf{M}\mathbf{Z})^{-1}\mathbf{Z}'\boldsymbol{\iota}T^{-1}\boldsymbol{\iota}'\mathbf{y} + (\mathbf{Z}'\mathbf{M}\mathbf{Z})^{-1}\mathbf{Z}'\mathbf{y} \end{pmatrix}$$

$$= \begin{pmatrix} T^{-1}[\boldsymbol{\iota}'\mathbf{y} - \boldsymbol{\iota}'\mathbf{Z}(\mathbf{Z}'\mathbf{M}\mathbf{Z})^{-1}(\mathbf{Z}'\mathbf{M}\mathbf{y})] \\ (\mathbf{Z}'\mathbf{M}\mathbf{Z})^{-1}(\mathbf{Z}'\mathbf{M}\mathbf{y}) \end{pmatrix}.$$

Thus the solution for $\mathbf{b}$ may always be broken down into two pieces. First solve the $K \times K$ system

$$\text{(9.6)} \qquad (\mathbf{Z}'\mathbf{M}\mathbf{Z})\mathbf{b}_z = (\mathbf{Z}'\mathbf{M}\mathbf{y})$$

to obtain the estimates $b_1, \ldots, b_K$ and then use this solution in the single equation for b_0:

$$(9.7) \qquad b_0 = T^{-1}[\boldsymbol{\iota}'\mathbf{y} - \boldsymbol{\iota}'\mathbf{Z}(\mathbf{Z}'\mathbf{M}\mathbf{Z})^{-1}(\mathbf{Z}'\mathbf{M}\mathbf{y})] = T^{-1}(\boldsymbol{\iota}'\mathbf{y} - \boldsymbol{\iota}'\mathbf{Z}\mathbf{b}_z)$$
$$= T^{-1}\Big[\sum_t y_t - \sum_k \Big(b_k \sum_t x_{kt}\Big)\Big].$$

The interesting point about this breakdown is that it can be interpreted in terms of the variables expressed as deviations from their (sample) means. For

$$(9.8) \qquad \mathbf{MZ} = \begin{pmatrix} x_{11} - \bar{x}_1 & \cdots & x_{1K} - \bar{x}_K \\ \cdot & & \cdot \\ \cdot & & \cdot \\ \cdot & & \cdot \\ x_{T1} - \bar{x}_1 & \cdots & x_{TK} - \bar{x}_K \end{pmatrix} \quad \text{and } \mathbf{My} = \begin{pmatrix} y_1 - \bar{y} \\ \cdot \\ \cdot \\ \cdot \\ y_T - \bar{y} \end{pmatrix}$$

and since $\mathbf{M}'\mathbf{M} = \mathbf{M}$, we see that the matrices of (9.6):

$$(9.9) \qquad \mathbf{Z}'\mathbf{M}\mathbf{Z} = \mathbf{Z}'\mathbf{M}'\mathbf{M}\mathbf{Z} = (\mathbf{MZ})'(\mathbf{MZ}) \quad \text{and}$$
$$\mathbf{Z}'\mathbf{M}\mathbf{y} = \mathbf{Z}'\mathbf{M}'\mathbf{M}\mathbf{y} = (\mathbf{MZ})'(\mathbf{My})$$

are the moment matrices of the variables expressed as deviations about means. Hence, instead of computing "raw moments" of the original variables and solving the $(1 + K) \times (1 + K)$ system $(\mathbf{X}'\mathbf{X})\mathbf{b} = \mathbf{X}'\mathbf{y}$, we may express the variables as deviations from their respective means, solve the $K \times K$ system $(\mathbf{Z}'\mathbf{M}'\mathbf{M}\mathbf{Z})\mathbf{b}_z = \mathbf{Z}'\mathbf{M}'\mathbf{M}\mathbf{y}$, where the matrices contain the so-called "moments about the mean," and then obtain the constant term from (9.7).

When moments about the mean are used, the other statistics are also readily computable. It is directly seen that

$$(9.10) \qquad SST = \mathbf{y}'\mathbf{M}\mathbf{y},$$

$$(9.11) \qquad SSR = \mathbf{b}_z'(\mathbf{Z}'\mathbf{M}\mathbf{y}).$$

For the covariance matrix we see first that

$$(9.12) \qquad \mathbf{S}_{\mathbf{b}_z\mathbf{b}_z} = s^2(\mathbf{Z}'\mathbf{M}\mathbf{Z})^{-1}$$

because the matrix $(\mathbf{Z}'\mathbf{M}\mathbf{Z})^{-1}$ is the submatrix of $(\mathbf{X}'\mathbf{X})^{-1}$ corresponding to $\mathbf{b}_z$. Then from the first row of (9.4) we have for the $1 \times K$ vector of estimated covariances of b_0 with $\mathbf{b}_z$

$$(9.13) \qquad \mathbf{s}_{0z}' = -s^2T^{-1}\boldsymbol{\iota}'\mathbf{Z}(\mathbf{Z}'\mathbf{M}\mathbf{Z})^{-1} = -T^{-1}\boldsymbol{\iota}'\mathbf{Z}\mathbf{S}_{\mathbf{b}_z\mathbf{b}_z}$$

and for the estimated variance of b_0

$$(9.14) \qquad s_{00} = s^2T^{-1} + s^2T^{-1}\boldsymbol{\iota}'\mathbf{Z}(\mathbf{Z}'\mathbf{M}\mathbf{Z})^{-1}\mathbf{Z}'\boldsymbol{\iota}T^{-1}$$
$$= s^2T^{-1} - T^{-1}\mathbf{s}_{0z}'\mathbf{Z}'\boldsymbol{\iota}.$$

The procedure of this subsection, which is due to Kloek (1961), is not intended as a practical computational one, because deviations from means are tedious to compute. Rather, our analysis provides the basis for the efficient computational procedure of the following subsection. In addition, we have a powerful analytical result. The *slope* estimates $b_1, \ldots, b_K$ depend only on the deviations from the means and not on the levels of the means. In future discussion it is often useful to reduce the order of the problem by thinking of the variables as being expressed as deviations about their means from the start, and to ignore β_0.

Augmented Moments about the Means

We have seen that the j, k element of $\mathbf{Z}'\mathbf{MZ}$ is $\Sigma(x_j - \bar{x}_j)(x_k - \bar{x}_k)$ and that the jth element of $\mathbf{Z}'\mathbf{My}$ is $\Sigma(x_j - \bar{x})(y - \bar{y})$. Consider then the $K \times K$ matrix

$$\text{(9.15)} \qquad \mathbf{M}_{xx} = \begin{pmatrix} m_{11} & \cdots & m_{1K} \\ \cdot & & \cdot \\ \cdot & & \cdot \\ \cdot & & \cdot \\ m_{K1} & \cdots & m_{KK} \end{pmatrix},$$

the typical element of which is the "augmented moment about the mean"

$$\text{(9.16)} \qquad m_{jk} = T\Sigma x_j x_k - \Sigma x_j \Sigma x_k = T\Sigma(x_j - \bar{x}_j)(x_k - \bar{x}_k),$$

and also the $K \times 1$ vector

$$\text{(9.17)} \qquad \mathbf{M}_{xy} = \begin{pmatrix} m_{1y} \\ \cdot \\ \cdot \\ \cdot \\ m_{Ky} \end{pmatrix},$$

the typical element of which is the augmented moment about the mean

$$\text{(9.18)} \qquad m_{jy} = T\Sigma x_j y - \Sigma x_j \Sigma y = T\Sigma(x_j - \bar{x}_j)(y - \bar{y}).$$

In virtue of their definitions we see that

$$\text{(9.19)} \qquad \mathbf{M}_{xx} = T(\mathbf{Z}'\mathbf{MZ}),$$

$$\text{(9.20)} \qquad \mathbf{M}_{xy} = T(\mathbf{Z}'\mathbf{My});$$

thus if we multiply the normal equations (9.6) through by T, we find

$$\text{(9.21)} \qquad \mathbf{M}_{xx}\mathbf{b}_z = \mathbf{M}_{xy}$$

so that

$$\text{(9.22)} \qquad \mathbf{b}_z = \mathbf{M}_{xx}^{-1}\mathbf{M}_{xy},$$

which is efficient to compute.

Further defining the scalar

$$(9.23) \qquad M_{yy} = T\Sigma y^2 - (\Sigma y)^2 = T\Sigma(y - \bar{y})^2,$$

we have the decomposition of (augmented) variances from (9.10) and (9.11):

$$(9.24) \qquad T\,SST = M_{yy},$$

$$(9.25) \qquad T\,SSR = \mathbf{b}_z'\mathbf{M}_{xy},$$

$$(9.26) \qquad T\,SSE = T\,SST - T\,SSR.$$

Continuing our formulary,

$$(9.27) \qquad Ts^2 = \frac{T\,SSE}{T - K - 1},$$

$$(9.28) \qquad R^2 = \frac{T\,SSR}{T\,SST}.$$

Moreover, since $\mathbf{M}_{xx} = T(\mathbf{Z}'\mathbf{M}\mathbf{Z})$ implies $\mathbf{M}_{xx}^{-1} = T^{-1}(\mathbf{Z}'\mathbf{M}\mathbf{Z})^{-1}$, we have from (9.12)–(9.14):

$$(9.29) \qquad \mathbf{S}_{\mathbf{b}_z\mathbf{b}_z} = (Ts^2)\mathbf{M}_{xx}^{-1},$$

and again

$$(9.30) \qquad \mathbf{s}_{0z}' = -T^{-1}(\boldsymbol{\iota}'\mathbf{Z})\mathbf{S}_{\mathbf{b}_z\mathbf{b}_z}$$

and

$$(9.31) \qquad s_{00} = T^{-1}\left[\frac{Ts^2}{T} - \mathbf{s}_{0z}'(\mathbf{Z}'\boldsymbol{\iota})\right].$$

Finally, for computation of ΔSSR for any subset of the regressors, we have from (7.30),

(9.32) Let $(\mathbf{M}_{xx})_{\circ\circ}^{-1}$ be the submatrix of $\mathbf{M}_{xx}^{-1}$ and $\mathbf{b}_\circ$ the subvector of $\mathbf{b}$ corresponding to any subset of the x's. Then $T\,\Delta SSR = \mathbf{b}_\circ'[(\mathbf{M}_{xx})_{\circ\circ}^{-1}]^{-1}\mathbf{b}_\circ$ where ΔSSR is the increase in the regression sum of squares attributable to using that subset of the x's in addition to all the others.

A useful exercise would be to recompute the results of Examples 2.1, 5.1, and 8.1 by the methods of this subsection.

Scaling of Variables

It is often convenient to carry out computations in units other than those in which the variables are originally measured. It is then necessary to translate the computational results back into those appropriate to the original units. Suppose that the original observations are $x_{t0}, \ldots, x_{tk}, \ldots, x_{tK}, y_t$ $(t = 1, \ldots, T)$ and we wish to undertake computations in terms of the scaled observations $x_{t0}^* = p_0 x_{t0}, \ldots, x_{tk}^* = p_k x_{tk}, \ldots, x_{tK}^* = p_K x_{tK}$, $y_t^* = p y_t$ $(t = 1, \ldots, T)$ where the p's are the scale factors. It is easily seen that the scaled observations are expressed in terms of the original ones by

$$\text{(9.33)} \qquad \mathbf{X}^* = \mathbf{X}\mathbf{P}, \qquad y^* = \mathbf{y}p$$

where $\mathbf{P}$ is the $(1 + K) \times (1 + K)$ diagonal matrix with p_k's $(k = 0, \ldots, K)$ on the diagonal and zeroes elsewhere. Thus $\mathbf{X} = \mathbf{X}^*\mathbf{P}^{-1}$ and $\mathbf{y} = \mathbf{y}^*p^{-1}$.

Then in turn the following relations between the results in original units and the results in scaled units (starred) are readily confirmed; note that $\mathbf{P}$ is symmetric and p is scalar:

$$\text{(9.34)} \qquad (\mathbf{X}'\mathbf{X})^{-1} = [(\mathbf{X}^*\mathbf{P}^{-1})'(\mathbf{X}^*\mathbf{P}^{-1})]^{-1} = (\mathbf{P}^{-1}\mathbf{X}^{*\prime}\mathbf{X}^*\mathbf{P}^{-1})^{-1}$$
$$= \mathbf{P}(\mathbf{X}^{*\prime}\mathbf{X}^*)^{-1}\mathbf{P},$$

$$\text{(9.35)} \qquad \mathbf{X}'\mathbf{y} = (\mathbf{X}^*\mathbf{P}^{-1})'(\mathbf{y}^*p^{-1}) = \mathbf{P}^{-1}\mathbf{X}^{*\prime}\mathbf{y}^*p^{-1},$$

$$\text{(9.36)} \qquad \mathbf{b} = (\mathbf{X}'\mathbf{X})^{-1}\mathbf{X}'\mathbf{y} = \mathbf{P}(\mathbf{X}^{*\prime}\mathbf{X}^*)^{-1}\mathbf{P}\mathbf{P}^{-1}\mathbf{X}^{*\prime}\mathbf{y}^*p^{-1}$$
$$= \mathbf{P}(\mathbf{X}^{*\prime}\mathbf{X}^*)^{-1}\mathbf{X}^{*\prime}\mathbf{y}^*p^{-1} = p^{-1}\mathbf{P}\mathbf{b}^*,$$

$$\text{(9.37)} \qquad \mathbf{y}'\mathbf{y} = (\mathbf{y}^*p^{-1})'(\mathbf{y}^*p^{-1}) = p^{-2}\mathbf{y}^{*\prime}\mathbf{y}^*,$$

$$\text{(9.38)} \qquad \mathbf{b}'\mathbf{X}'\mathbf{y} = p^{-1}\mathbf{b}^{*\prime}\mathbf{P}\mathbf{P}^{-1}\mathbf{X}^{*\prime}\mathbf{y}^*p^{-1} = p^{-2}\mathbf{b}^{*\prime}\mathbf{X}^{*\prime}\mathbf{y}^*,$$

$$\text{(9.39)} \qquad \frac{(\Sigma y)^2}{T} = \frac{(\Sigma p^{-1}y^*)^2}{T} = p^{-2}\frac{(\Sigma y^*)^2}{T},$$

$$\text{(9.40)} \qquad SST = p^{-2}SST^*, \qquad SSR = p^{-2}SSR^*, \qquad SSE = p^{-2}SSE^*,$$
$$R^2 = R^{2*},$$

$$\text{(9.41)} \qquad s^2 = p^{-2}s^{2*},$$

$$\text{(9.42)} \qquad \mathbf{S}_{\mathbf{bb}} = s^2(\mathbf{X}'\mathbf{X})^{-1} = p^{-2}s^{2*}\mathbf{P}(\mathbf{X}^{*\prime}\mathbf{X}^*)^{-1}\mathbf{P} = p^{-2}\mathbf{P}\mathbf{S}_{\mathbf{b}^*\mathbf{b}^*}\mathbf{P},$$

and similarly for other statistics.

In applying these translation formulas it is helpful to take advantage of the diagonality of $\mathbf{P}$; thus (9.36) simply says $b_k = p^{-1}p_k b_k^*$, and taking square roots of the diagonal elements (9.42) simply says $s_{b_k} = p^{-1}p_k s_{b_k}^*$. It is common to use powers of 10 as the scaling factors—i.e., to change units by shifting the decimal points in the observations. We see that in that event, the regression coefficients and their standard errors are translated back into those corresponding to the original units by mere shifts of decimal points. It is reassuring that R^2 and hypothesis tests are unaffected by such changes of units.

Computational Layout

A computational layout for desk calculator work is presented here. For our example we take a macroeconomic production function:

$$y_t = \beta_0 x_{t0} + \beta_1 x_{t1} + \beta_2 x_{t2} + \beta_3 x_{t3} + \epsilon_t \tag{9.43}$$

where y is real gross national product in billions of dollars, $x_0 = 1$, x_1 is labor inputs in millions of man-years, x_2 is real capital in billions of dollars, measured from an arbitrary origin, and x_3 is the time in years measured from 1929 = 1. The sample consists of 23 annual observations for the United States 1929–1941 and 1946–1955. The observations are as follows, with the check-sum column $S_t = x_{t0} + x_{t1} + x_{t2} + x_{t3} + y_t$ added.

(9.44) ***Observation matrix* (X y S)**

1	47	54	1	142	245
1	43	59	2	127	232
1	39	57	3	113	218
1	34	48	4	98	185
1	34	36	5	94	170
1	36	24	6	102	169
1	38	19	7	116	181
1	41	18	8	128	196
1	42	22	9	140	214
1	37	24	10	131	203
1	40	23	11	143	218
1	42	27	12	157	239
1	47	36	13	182	279
1	51	9	18	209	288
1	53	25	19	214	312
1	53	39	20	225	338
1	50	51	21	221	344
1	52	62	22	243	380
1	54	75	23	257	410
1	54	94	24	265	438
1	55	108	25	276	465
1	52	118	26	271	468
1	54	124	27	291	497

From the observation matrix we obtain the raw moments $\mathbf{X}'\mathbf{X}$, $\mathbf{X}'\mathbf{y}$, and $\mathbf{y}'\mathbf{y}$, recording only the upper half—in view of symmetry—and checking that the sum of *all* (25) elements equals ΣS^2, and that the sum of the first row equals ΣS.

(9.45) ***Raw moment matrix*** $\begin{pmatrix} \mathbf{X'X} & \mathbf{X'y} \\ & \mathbf{y'y} \end{pmatrix}$

23	1048	1152	316	4150	$\Sigma S = 6689\surd$
	48918	55559	15571	198974	
		82218	19568	241633	
			5964	68842	
				842448	$\Sigma S^2 = 2193197\surd$

From the raw moments we derive the augmented moments about the mean, omitting redundant symmetric elements and checking that the sum of *all* (16) elements equals $M_{ss} = N\Sigma S^2 - (\Sigma S)^2$.

(9.46) ***Augmented moment-about-the-mean matrix*** $\begin{pmatrix} \mathbf{M}_{xx} & \mathbf{M}_{xy} \\ & M_{yy} \end{pmatrix}$

26810	70561	26965	227202	
	563910	86032	776759	
		37316	271966	
			2153804	$M_{ss} = 5700810\surd$

Next these moments are scaled by even powers of 10 to put the diagonal elements of the augmented moment-about-the-mean matrix in the range 0.1 to 10. This implicitly scales the observations into starred variables. The appropriate scale factors are listed, and the sums of the starred variables as well, for future use. (The check-sum is dropped).

(9.47) ***Scaling***

$x_1^* = 10^{-2}x_1$	$x_2^* = 10^{-3}x_2$	$x_3^* = 10^{-2}x_3$	$y^* = 10^{-3}y$
$\Sigma x_1^* = 10.48$	$\Sigma x_2^* = 1.152$	$\Sigma x_3^* = 3.16$	$\Sigma y^* = 4.150$

This makes sense if the off-diagonal moments are scaled consistently, as in the following. Note how zeros are added to present a uniform number of decimal places. We work in terms of the scaled variables but omit the stars for simplicity *from here until p. 191.*

(9.48) ***(Scaled) Augmented moment-about-the-mean matrix***

2.681000	0.705610	2.696500	2.272020
	0.563910	0.860320	0.776759
		3.731600	2.719660
			2.153804

To avoid unnecessary copying of numbers, it is desirable not to write out (9.48) but just to pencil in carets to show where the decimal point belongs, in (9.46).

Now we are ready to proceed with the solution of $\mathbf{M}_{xx}\mathbf{b}_z = \mathbf{M}_{xy}$ and the obtaining of $\mathbf{M}_{xx}^{-1}$, which are done together. The worksheet of (9.49) is generated row by row. First we write in rows R_1–R_3, which consist of $\mathbf{M}_{xx}$, $\mathbf{M}_{xy}$, $\mathbf{I}_3$ (a 3×3 identity matrix), and a *new* check-sum column S, the elements of which are obtained as the sum of all the elements in the row, including the "invisible" lower off-diagonal of $\mathbf{M}_{xx}$. All operations performed on the "real" columns are performed on this column also, and the check, performed on each row *as it is generated,* is that the sum of all other elements in the row equals the element in the check-sum column.

The successive rows of the worksheet are generated as follows:

(4) A_{1j}, the element in row A_1, column $j = R_{1j}$, the element in row R_1, column j; i.e., copy row R_1.

(5) $B_{1j} = A_{1j}/A_{11}$; i.e., divide preceding row by its leading element. Check that the row sum equals B_{18}; similarly in the sequel.

(6) $A_{2j} = R_{2j} - A_{12}B_{1j}$. Compute as a unit, without intermediate copying out; similarly in the sequel. There is no need to compute A_{21}, which is guaranteed to equal zero; similarly with lower off-diagonal elements in the sequel. The "pivot" A_{12} is underlined; similarly in the sequel.

(7) $B_{2j} = A_{2j}/A_{22}$.

(8) $A_{3j} = R_{3j} - A_{13}B_{1j} - A_{23}B_{2j}$.

(9) $B_{3j} = A_{3j}/A_{33}$.

This completes the "forward solution." The check-sum is no longer used.

Next, the estimates b_1, b_2, and b_3 are computed *in reverse order* in row C_0:

$$C_{03} = B_{34}.$$

(10) $$C_{02} = B_{24} - B_{23}C_{03}.$$

$$C_{01} = B_{14} - B_{13}C_{03} - B_{12}C_{02}.$$

To check these see that they satisfy the last normal equation; i.e., check that $R_{13}C_{01} + R_{23}C_{02} + R_{33}C_{03} = R_{34}$.

The inverse matrix $\mathbf{M}_{xx}^{-1}$ is then produced in rows C_1–C_3, columns 6–8:

(11) $C_{1j} = A_{15}B_{1j} + A_{25}B_{2j} + A_{35}B_{3j}$.

(12) $C_{2j} = \qquad A_{26}B_{2j} + A_{36}B_{3j}$.

(13) $C_{3j} = \qquad\qquad B_{3j}$.

To check these, first note symmetry, then check the elements of $\mathbf{M}_{xx}^{-1}\mathbf{M}_{xx} = \mathbf{I}$.

(9.49) ***Worksheet***

	1	2	3	4	5	6	7	8	9
R_1	2.681000	0.705610	2.696500	2.272020	1.000000	0.000000	0.000000	9.355130	
R_2		0.563910	0.860320	0.776759	0.000000	1.000000	0.000000	3.906599	
R_3			3.731600	2.719660	0.000000	0.000000	1.000000	11.008080	
(4) A_1	2.681000	0.705610	2.696500	2.272020	1.000000	0.000000	0.000000	9.355130	√
(5) B_1	1.000000	0.263189	1.005781	0.847452	0.372995	0.000000	0.000000	3.489418	√
(6) A_2		0.378201	0.150631	0.178788	−0.263189	1.000000	0.000000	1.444431	√
(7) B_2		1.000000	0.398282	0.472733	−0.695897	2.644096	0.000000	3.819212	√
(8) A_3			0.959517	0.363296	−0.900958	−0.398282	1.000000	1.023574	√
(9) B_3			1.000000	0.378624	−0.938970	−0.415086	1.042191	1.066759	√
(10) C_0	0.381910	0.321934	0.378624						
(11) C_1					1.402120	−0.321922	−0.938970		
(12) C_2					−0.321922	2.809417	−0.415086		
(13) C_3					−0.938970	−0.415086	1.042191		
(14) C_4				2.147500 = $T\,SSR$		$R^2 = .997$			
				2.153804 = $T\,SST$					
				0.006304 = $T\,SSE$		$Ts^2 = 0.000332$			
C_5	0.000466	−0.000107	−0.000312						
C_6	−0.000107	0.000933	−0.000138						
C_7	−0.000312	−0.000138	0.000346						
C_8	0.021587	0.030545	0.018601						

1	2	3	
(4.150)			$= \boldsymbol{\iota}'\mathbf{y}$
(10.480	1.152	3.160)	$= \boldsymbol{\iota}'\mathbf{Z}$
−0.061728			$= b_0$
(0.003775	−0.000483	−0.002335)	$= -(\boldsymbol{\iota}'\mathbf{Z})\mathbf{S}_{\mathbf{b}_z\mathbf{b}_z}$
(−0.000164	0.000021	0.000102)	$= \mathbf{s}_{0_z}'$
		0.001372	$= -\mathbf{s}_{0_z}'(\mathbf{Z}'\boldsymbol{\iota})$
		0.000014	$= Ts^2/T$
		0.001386	
		0.000060	$= s_{00}$
		0.007746	$= s_{b_0}$

$$\underset{(0.007746)}{y^* = -0.061728} + \underset{(0.021587)}{0.381910x_1^*} + \underset{(0.030545)}{0.321934x_2^*} + \underset{(0.018601)}{0.378624x_3^*}$$

$$10^{-3}y = -0.061728 + 0.381910(10^{-2})x_1 + 0.321934(10^{-3})x_2 + 0.378624(10^{-2})x_3$$

$$y = -0.061728(10^3) + 0.381910(10^1)x_1 + 0.321934(10^0)x_2 + 0.378624(10^1)x_3$$

$$y = \underset{(7.746)}{-61.728} + \underset{(0.21587)}{3.81910x_1} + \underset{(0.030545)}{0.321934x_2} + \underset{(0.18601)}{3.78624x_3}$$

Then the (augmented) regression sum of squares $T\,SSR$ is computed in

(14) $$C_{44} = A_{14}B_{14} + A_{24}B_{24} + A_{34}B_{34}.$$

To check, obtain $T\,SSR$ in the alternative way: $\mathbf{b}_z'\mathbf{M}_{xy} = C_{01}R_{14} + C_{02}R_{24} + C_{03}R_{34}$. A side calculation, using M_{yy} and T, which are in the moment tables, gives Ts^2 and R^2. The covariance matrix $\mathbf{S}_{\mathbf{b}_z\mathbf{b}_z} = (Ts^2)\mathbf{M}_{xx}^{-1}$ is obtained element by element, entered in rows C_5–C_7, columns 1–3; the square roots of the diagonal elements are computed and entered in row C_8, columns 1–3. Side calculations using the scaled sums in (9.47) give b_0, the vector of its covariances with the slopes, its variance, and the square root of the variance as well.

The presentation of the estimated equation follows, *with the stars reintroduced*, and estimated standard errors in parentheses below the coefficients. Then to descale, substitute the expressions of (9.47) into the scaled equation; multiply through to clear out the power of 10 on the left (in this case multiply by 10^3); if any powers of 10 besides 10^0 remain, use them to adjust the coefficient, leaving the original variables. To descale the standard errors, shift each by the same number of places as the corresponding coefficient was shifted in its descaling. The final equation is the presentation in terms of the original variables with estimated standard errors in parentheses below the coefficients. All this is in accord with the discussion of the preceding subsection. Tests are carried out in the usual fashion. Either formulate the hypothesis in terms of the scaled variables, in which case all the data in the worksheet are directly usable; or formulate it in terms of the original variables, in which case the worksheet data must be descaled.

The solution process, known as the Gauss-Doolittle method, may be viewed as a systematic method of solving a simultaneous equation system by substitution and elimination. Alternatively, it can be justified by reference to partitioned inversion. Or, the operations can be shown to be equivalent to a series of matrix multiplications applied to $\mathbf{M}_{xx}$ and $\mathbf{I}$ which transform the former into an identity matrix and thus the latter into $\mathbf{M}_{xx}^{-1}$; since $\mathbf{PA} = \mathbf{I}$, $\mathbf{PI} = \mathbf{A}^{-1}$. For further details on this and other methods of solution see Dwyer (1951).

For a variety of purposes it may be useful to calculate the individual calculated values $\hat{y}_t$ and residuals $\hat{\epsilon}_t$. This is done by way of

(9.50) $$\hat{\mathbf{y}} = \mathbf{Xb}$$

and

(9.51) $$\hat{\boldsymbol{\epsilon}} = \mathbf{y} - \hat{\mathbf{y}}.$$

10. SPECIAL PROBLEMS IN LINEAR REGRESSION

Multicollinearity

One assumption of the classical linear regression model is that there are no exact linear relations holding among the observed values of the regressors. If there are, then as we have seen in Section 4, the parameter vector $\boldsymbol{\beta}$ is not estimable. For an explicit example of how the least-squares estimation procedure breaks down, consider the case $K = 2$, and with no loss of generality suppose the variables are already measured as deviations about means. Now if there is an exact linear relation between the regressors,

$$(10.1) \qquad x_{t2} = ax_{t1} \quad \text{for} \quad \text{all } t$$

where a is some constant; then

$$(10.2) \qquad \Sigma x_{t2}^2 = \Sigma(ax_{t1})^2 = a^2 \Sigma x_{t1}^2 \quad \text{and} \quad \Sigma x_{t1}x_{t2} = \Sigma(x_{t1}ax_{t1}) = a\,\Sigma x_{t1}^2,$$

so that the moment matrix $\mathbf{X'X}$ is

$$(10.3) \qquad \mathbf{X'X} = \begin{pmatrix} \Sigma x_{t1}^2 & a\,\Sigma x_{t1}^2 \\ a\,\Sigma x_{t1}^2 & a^2\Sigma x_{t1}^2 \end{pmatrix}$$

which has as its determinant

$$(10.4) \qquad |\mathbf{X'X}| = (\Sigma x_1^2)(a^2\,\Sigma x_1^2) - (a\,\Sigma x_1^2)(a\,\Sigma x_1^2)$$
$$= a^2(\Sigma x_1^2)^2 - a^2(\Sigma x_1^2)^2 = 0.$$

That is, the matrix would be singular, so that it would have no inverse. (In the cofactor method, we would be asked to divide the adjoint by 0, which is impossible; in the Gauss-Doolittle solution, an A_{ii} would be zero, and we could not divide by it as called for.)

In practice an exact linear relationship is highly improbable, but the general interdependence of economic phenomena may easily result in the appearance of approximate linear relationships in time series of regressors. This phenomenon is known as multicollinearity or intercorrelation. Consider, e.g., the time paths of wage income and nonwage income in the United States 1929–1960 and the possibility of using them as separate regressors to explain consumption. To see the effect of approximate linear relationships, suppose (10.1) holds only approximately: Add u_t assumed small and such that $\Sigma x_{t1}u_t = 0$. Then $|\mathbf{X'X}| = \Sigma u_t^2 \Sigma x_{t1}^2$, which will be small also. Division of adj $(\mathbf{X'X})$ by this small number will give an inverse $(\mathbf{X'X})^{-1}$ with very large elements, and hence the elements of the covariance matrix $\boldsymbol{\Sigma}_{\mathbf{bb}}$ may be very large.

This generalizes to $K > 2$. If the columns of $\mathbf{X}$ are not independent, then $r(\mathbf{X}) < 1 + K$ and $r(\mathbf{X}'\mathbf{X}) < 1 + K$, so that $\mathbf{X}'\mathbf{X}$ is singular. An approximate linear relationship among the columns of $\mathbf{X}$ can result in $(\mathbf{X}'\mathbf{X})^{-1}$, and hence $\mathbf{\Sigma}_{\mathbf{bb}}$, having large diagonal elements.

That is, multicollinearity may produce large standard errors of the coefficients; we will be very uncertain of their population values; we will be unable to reject very diverse hypotheses concerning them. Note that it is entirely possible to have a relationship that fits very well—R^2 can be very high—while no coefficient tests to be significantly different from zero. (Suppose a simple correlation on x_1 gives a high R^2, and consider what will happen when a multiple regression is taken on x_1 and x_2, where x_2 is virtually a constant multiple of x_1. The R^2 cannot fall, of course, but the standard errors will explode.) The prevalence of multicollinearity is to be emphasized, as is the inherent obstacle it introduces; reliable estimates of the coefficients may not be made from the sample itself. The sample is poor in terms of independent movement of the regressors, and we should not expect to obtain estimates of their independent effects from that sample. Outside, "extraneous" information may help.

If the ratio of two coefficients is known a priori, the two variables may be combined into one whose coefficients may be estimated from the sample. Suppose we know that $\beta_2 = \frac{1}{2}\beta_1$ in

$$(10.5) \qquad y = \beta_1 x_1 + \beta_2 x_2 + \epsilon;$$

then we may rewrite this as

$$(10.6) \qquad y = \beta_1 x_1 + \tfrac{1}{2}\beta_1 x_2 + \epsilon = \beta_1(x_1 + \tfrac{1}{2}x_2) + \epsilon = \beta_1 x + \epsilon$$

where $x = x_1 + \frac{1}{2}x_2$, and take the regression of y on x to estimate β_1, finally multiplying that estimate by $\frac{1}{2}$ to estimate β_2. A variant has often been used in consumer demand relations. Attempts to estimate both price and income elasticities of demand from time series are often futile because prices and incomes move so closely together. To estimate the demand relationship

$$(10.7) \qquad q = \beta_1 y + \beta_2 p + \epsilon$$

a combination of cross-section and time series data has been used. The income coefficient β_1 is estimated as b_1 from a cross section. Then the adjusted demand time series $q^* = q - b_1 y$ is constructed, and the time series regression of q^* on p estimates β_2. The use of extraneous information is considered more systematically in Section 5.6.

Although multicollinearity is associated with time series, it rears its ugly head in cross-section studies as well. If a sample of households is such that high incomes and high assets go together, the separate influences of income and assets will be hard to estimate reliably. The econometrician relies on experiments performed by nature, and these are unlikely to have the controlled—i.e., independent variation—properties of laboratory experiments.

Changing the List of Regressors

In practice we do not formulate a relationship, estimate it, test a few hypotheses, and stop. It is common to explore a range of alternative formulations. Thus after estimating a linear regression we are often interested in investigating the effect of adding—or of dropping—one or more regressors.

We have already developed the test of significance for dropping a set of regressors—this is the subset hypothesis $\beta_{H+1} = \cdots = \beta_K = 0$ (which, for a single regressor, reduces to a t test). It may well be worthwhile to drop out regressors whose coefficients are not significantly different from zero and reestimate the relation. If the discarded variables are at the end of the list of regressors, the forward solution of the Gauss-Doolittle program may be preserved. If we consider adding regressors, we may do so by adding them to the end of the list and reestimating the extended regression; clearly, the entire original forward solution may be utilized again.

Stepwise Regression

As a device for investigating proposed additional regressors it is common to regress the residuals from the original regression on the candidates. That is, suppose the relationship $\mathbf{y} = \mathbf{X}\boldsymbol{\beta} + \boldsymbol{\epsilon}$ is partitioned as

$$\mathbf{y} = \mathbf{X}_1\boldsymbol{\beta}_1 + \mathbf{X}_2\boldsymbol{\beta}_2 + \boldsymbol{\epsilon} \tag{10.8}$$

where $\mathbf{X}_1$ includes H regressors and $\mathbf{X}_2$ includes $K - H$ regressors (we assume all the regressors have zero means). Then

$$\mathbf{y} - \mathbf{X}_1\boldsymbol{\beta}_1 = \mathbf{X}_2\boldsymbol{\beta}_2 + \boldsymbol{\epsilon}, \tag{10.9}$$

which suggests that an estimate of $\boldsymbol{\beta}_2$ could be obtained by regressing the residuals from the regression of $\mathbf{y}$ on $\mathbf{X}_1$—which apparently estimate the left-hand side of (10.9)—on $\mathbf{X}_2$.

Now the results of the full regression of $\mathbf{y}$ on $\mathbf{X}_1$ and $\mathbf{X}_2$ together are, from (7.13),

$$\mathbf{b}_1 = (\mathbf{X}_1'\mathbf{X}_1)^{-1}\mathbf{X}_1'\mathbf{y} - (\mathbf{X}_1'\mathbf{X}_1)^{-1}\mathbf{X}_1'\mathbf{X}_2\mathbf{D}^{-1}\mathbf{X}_2'\mathbf{M}_1\mathbf{y}, \tag{10.10}$$

$$\mathbf{b}_2 = \mathbf{D}^{-1}(\mathbf{X}_2'\mathbf{M}_1\mathbf{y}) = (\mathbf{X}_2'\mathbf{M}_1\mathbf{X}_2)^{-1}(\mathbf{X}_2'\mathbf{M}_1\mathbf{y}), \tag{10.11}$$

where

(10.12) $\mathbf{D} = \mathbf{X}_2'\mathbf{X}_2 - \mathbf{X}_2'\mathbf{X}_1(\mathbf{X}_1'\mathbf{X}_1)^{-1}\mathbf{X}_1'\mathbf{X}_2 = \mathbf{X}_2'\mathbf{M}_1\mathbf{X}_2,$

(10.13) $\mathbf{M}_1 = \mathbf{I} - \mathbf{X}_1(\mathbf{X}_1'\mathbf{X}_1)^{-1}\mathbf{X}_1'.$

On the other hand, in the "stepwise regression" procedure we first regress $\mathbf{y}$ on $\mathbf{X}_1$ alone, estimating $\boldsymbol{\beta}_1$ as

(10.14) $\tilde{\mathbf{b}}_1 = (\mathbf{X}_1'\mathbf{X}_1)^{-1}\mathbf{X}_1'\mathbf{y},$

Then we compute the residuals from that regression

(10.15) $\tilde{\mathbf{y}} = \mathbf{y} - \mathbf{X}_1\tilde{\mathbf{b}}_1 = \mathbf{y} - \mathbf{X}_1(\mathbf{X}_1'\mathbf{X}_1)^{-1}\mathbf{X}_1'\mathbf{y} = \mathbf{M}_1\mathbf{y}$

and regress them on $\mathbf{X}_2$, estimating $\boldsymbol{\beta}_2$ as

(10.16) $\tilde{\mathbf{b}}_2 = (\mathbf{X}_2'\mathbf{X}_2)^{-1}\mathbf{X}_2'\tilde{\mathbf{y}} = (\mathbf{X}_2'\mathbf{X}_2)^{-1}\mathbf{X}_2'\mathbf{M}_1\mathbf{y}.$

Comparison of (10.16) with (10.11) shows that

(10.17) $$\begin{aligned}\tilde{\mathbf{b}}_2 &= (\mathbf{X}_2'\mathbf{X}_2)^{-1}(\mathbf{X}_2'\mathbf{M}_1\mathbf{X}_2)\mathbf{b}_2\\ &= [\mathbf{I} - (\mathbf{X}_2'\mathbf{X}_2)^{-1}\mathbf{X}_2'\mathbf{X}_1(\mathbf{X}_1'\mathbf{X}_1)^{-1}\mathbf{X}_1'\mathbf{X}_2]\mathbf{b}_2.\end{aligned}$$

Thus $\tilde{\mathbf{b}}_2 \neq \mathbf{b}_2$ unless $\mathbf{X}_1'\mathbf{X}_2 = \mathbf{0}$ or $\mathbf{b}_2 = \mathbf{0}$. In the special case where $K - H = 1$—so that $\mathbf{b}_2$ and $\tilde{\mathbf{b}}_2$ are scalars—it is simple to indicate the qualitative relation between the stepwise regression estimate and the full regression estimate of $\boldsymbol{\beta}_2$. For in that case the quantity in brackets on the right of (10.17) is in fact $[1 - R_{21}^2]$—where R_{21}^2 is the coefficient of determination of $\mathbf{X}_2$ on the set $\mathbf{X}_1$—which must lie between zero and one.

It is also clear that the estimator of $\boldsymbol{\beta}_1$ obtained in the first step will in general not coincide with that obtained in the full regression, for substitution of (10.11) and (10.10) into (10.14) gives

(10.18) $\tilde{\mathbf{b}}_1 = \mathbf{b}_1 + (\mathbf{X}_1'\mathbf{X}_1)^{-1}\mathbf{X}_1'\mathbf{X}_2\mathbf{b}_2 = \mathbf{b}_1 + \mathbf{B}\mathbf{b}_2,$

where

(10.19) $\mathbf{B} = (\mathbf{X}_1'\mathbf{X}_1)^{-1}\mathbf{X}_1'\mathbf{X}_2$

will be recognized as the $H \times (K - H)$ matrix of coefficients in a set of "auxiliary regressions" of each variable in $\mathbf{X}_2$ on the set $\mathbf{X}_1$—the jth column of $\mathbf{B}$ is indeed $(\mathbf{X}_1'\mathbf{X}_1)^{-1}\mathbf{X}_1'\mathbf{X}_j$ where $\mathbf{X}_j$ is the jth column of $\mathbf{X}_2$. From (10.18) we see $\tilde{\mathbf{b}}_1 \neq \mathbf{b}_1$ unless $\mathbf{X}_1'\mathbf{X}_2 = \mathbf{0}$ or $\mathbf{b}_2 = \mathbf{0}$.

Further insight into the full regression and its relationship to stepwise regression is available. The residuals from the auxiliary regressions are given in the $T \times (K - H)$ matrix

(10.20) $\tilde{\mathbf{X}}_2 = \mathbf{X}_2 - \mathbf{X}_1\mathbf{B} = \mathbf{X}_2 - \mathbf{X}_1(\mathbf{X}_1'\mathbf{X}_1)^{-1}\mathbf{X}_1'\mathbf{X}_2 = \mathbf{M}_1\mathbf{X}_2$

—the jth column of $\tilde{\mathbf{X}}_2$ is indeed $\mathbf{X}_j - \mathbf{X}_1\mathbf{B}_j$ where $\mathbf{B}_j$ is the jth column of $\mathbf{B}$.

Now if we regressed $\tilde{\mathbf{y}}$ on $\tilde{\mathbf{X}}_2$ or even $\mathbf{y}$ on $\tilde{\mathbf{X}}_2$ we would obtain the full regression's estimate of $\boldsymbol{\beta}_2$:

$$(10.21)\qquad (\tilde{\mathbf{X}}_2'\tilde{\mathbf{X}}_2)^{-1}\tilde{\mathbf{X}}_2'\tilde{\mathbf{y}} = (\mathbf{X}_2'\mathbf{M}_1\mathbf{M}_1\mathbf{X}_2)^{-1}\mathbf{X}_2'\mathbf{M}_1\mathbf{M}_1\mathbf{y}$$
$$= (\mathbf{X}_2'\mathbf{M}_1\mathbf{X}_2)^{-1}\mathbf{X}_2'\mathbf{M}_1\mathbf{y} = \mathbf{b}_2$$

and also

$$(10.22)\qquad (\tilde{\mathbf{X}}_2'\tilde{\mathbf{X}}_2)^{-1}\tilde{\mathbf{X}}_2'\mathbf{y} = (\mathbf{X}_2'\mathbf{M}_1\mathbf{X}_2)^{-1}\mathbf{X}_2'\mathbf{M}_1\mathbf{y} = \mathbf{b}_2;$$

however, as we have seen, regressing $\tilde{\mathbf{y}}$ on $\mathbf{X}_2$ gives a result which is in general different:

$$(10.23)\qquad (\mathbf{X}_2'\mathbf{X}_2)^{-1}\mathbf{X}_2'\tilde{\mathbf{y}} = (\mathbf{X}_2'\mathbf{X}_2)^{-1}\mathbf{X}_2'\mathbf{M}_1\mathbf{y} = \tilde{\mathbf{b}}_2.$$

We may verbalize (10.22) by saying that regressing $\mathbf{y}$ on $\mathbf{X}_2$ and $\mathbf{X}_1$ together is equivalent to regressing $\mathbf{y}$ on $\mathbf{X}_2$ corrected for $\mathbf{X}_1$, in the sense that it gives the same coefficient vector $\mathbf{b}_2$ for the regressors in $\mathbf{X}_2$.

Specification Error

Although the results of the preceding subsection refer to least-squares plane fitting in general, they may be placed within the context of our classical linear regression model and considered from the point of view of specification error. We suppose that the classical linear regression model is applicable to the full relationship $\mathbf{y} = \mathbf{X}_1\boldsymbol{\beta}_1 + \mathbf{X}_2\boldsymbol{\beta}_2 + \boldsymbol{\epsilon}$ so that $E\mathbf{b}_1 = \boldsymbol{\beta}_1$ and $E\mathbf{b}_2 = \boldsymbol{\beta}_2$. Now the stepwise estimator $\tilde{\mathbf{b}}_1$ may be viewed as the classical estimator of $\boldsymbol{\beta}_1$ in the relation

$$(10.24)\qquad \mathbf{y} = \mathbf{X}_1\boldsymbol{\beta}_1 + \boldsymbol{\epsilon}^*,$$

obtained from the full relationship by taking $\boldsymbol{\epsilon}^* = \mathbf{X}_2\boldsymbol{\beta}_2 + \boldsymbol{\epsilon}$. From (10.18) we see that the expectation of the stepwise estimator is

$$(10.25)\qquad E\tilde{\mathbf{b}}_1 = E\mathbf{b}_1 + \mathbf{B}E\mathbf{b}_2 = \boldsymbol{\beta}_1 + \mathbf{B}\boldsymbol{\beta}_2$$

so that the estimator is biased in general. This bias is attributable to the fact that there is a "specification error"; the classical model is not appropriate to (10.24) because the "disturbance" $\boldsymbol{\epsilon}^*$ does not have a zero expectation:

$$(10.26)\qquad E\boldsymbol{\epsilon}^* = \mathbf{X}_2\boldsymbol{\beta}_2 + E\boldsymbol{\epsilon} = \mathbf{X}_2\boldsymbol{\beta}_2.$$

Similarly the stepwise estimator $\tilde{\mathbf{b}}_2$ may be viewed as the classical estimator of $\boldsymbol{\beta}_2$ in the relation

$$(10.27)\qquad \tilde{\mathbf{y}} = \mathbf{X}_2\boldsymbol{\beta}_2 + \boldsymbol{\epsilon}^{**},$$

obtained from the full relationship by taking $\tilde{\mathbf{y}} = \mathbf{y} - \mathbf{X}_1\tilde{\mathbf{b}}_1$ and $\boldsymbol{\epsilon}^{**} = -\mathbf{X}_1(\tilde{\mathbf{b}}_1 - \boldsymbol{\beta}_1) + \boldsymbol{\epsilon}$. From (10.17) we see that

$$(10.28)\qquad E\tilde{\mathbf{b}}_2 = [\mathbf{I} - (\mathbf{X}_2'\mathbf{X}_2)^{-1}\mathbf{X}_2'\mathbf{X}_1(\mathbf{X}_1'\mathbf{X}_1)^{-1}\mathbf{X}_1'\mathbf{X}_2]E\mathbf{b}_2$$
$$= \boldsymbol{\beta}_2 - (\mathbf{X}_2'\mathbf{X}_2)^{-1}\mathbf{X}_2'\mathbf{X}_1\mathbf{B}\boldsymbol{\beta}_2$$

so that the estimator is biased in general. This bias is attributable to the fact that there is a specification error; the classical model is not appropriate to (10.27) since the "disturbance" $\boldsymbol{\epsilon}^{**}$ does not have a zero expectation:

$$(10.29)\qquad E\boldsymbol{\epsilon}^{**} = -\mathbf{X}_1 E(\tilde{\mathbf{b}}_1 - \boldsymbol{\beta}_1) + E\boldsymbol{\epsilon} = -\mathbf{X}_1\mathbf{B}\boldsymbol{\beta}_2,$$

using (10.25).

Note that if in fact $\boldsymbol{\beta}_2 = \mathbf{0}$, the "disturbances" have zero expectations, the previously indicated specification errors are absent, and both stepwise estimators are unbiased. Also if $\mathbf{X}_1'\mathbf{X}_2 = \mathbf{0}$ so that $\mathbf{B} = \mathbf{0}$, then $\boldsymbol{\epsilon}^{**}$ has zero expectation, the previously indicated specification error is absent from (10.27), and the stepwise estimator $\tilde{\mathbf{b}}_2$ is unbiased. Finally if $\mathbf{X}_1'\mathbf{X}_2 = \mathbf{0}$, while $\boldsymbol{\epsilon}^*$ still has a nonzero expectation and there is a specification error in (10.24), the stepwise estimator $\tilde{\mathbf{b}}_1$ is nevertheless unbiased. This last result reflects the fact that the assumptions of the classical linear regression model constitute a set of sufficient, not necessary, conditions for the unbiasedness of the least-squares estimators. Back in (4.10) we found $\mathbf{b} - \boldsymbol{\beta} = (\mathbf{X}'\mathbf{X})^{-1}\mathbf{X}'\boldsymbol{\epsilon}$; with $\mathbf{X}$ fixed this implies $E(\mathbf{b} - \boldsymbol{\beta}) = (\mathbf{X}'\mathbf{X})^{-1}E(\mathbf{X}'\boldsymbol{\epsilon})$. If in fact the disturbance $\boldsymbol{\epsilon} = \mathbf{z} + \mathbf{u}$ where $\mathbf{z}$ is fixed and $\mathbf{u}$ is random with zero expectation, then $E(\mathbf{b} - \boldsymbol{\beta}) = (\mathbf{X}'\mathbf{X})^{-1}\mathbf{X}'\mathbf{z}$, which will be zero if simply $\mathbf{X}'\mathbf{z} = \mathbf{0}$, i.e., if the regressors are uncorrelated with the fixed component of the disturbance. That is, indeed, the situation in (10.24) if $\mathbf{X}_1'\mathbf{X}_2 = \mathbf{0}$.

Individual Contributions to Explanation

A common although not always well-defined problem is to measure the importance of the individual regressors by their individual contributions to (the calculated value of) y. The simple determination coefficient of y on x_j, R^2_{jy}, is clearly inadequate. The sheer size of the coefficient b_j is no measure of importance, since the size can be changed at will by changing the units of measurement of the variable. We may think of using the effect on y of a typical or "equally likely" change in each variable as a measure of importance: If Δ_j is the typical change in x_j, then $b_j\,\Delta_j$ is the typical effect on y induced by x_j, and we may like to say that x_j is more important than x_k if $b_j\,\Delta_j > b_k\,\Delta_k$.

Now variation in the sample does provide an objective measure of typical changes in the form of the sample standard deviation. This is used in the so-called "beta coefficients":

$$(10.30)\qquad \beta_j = b_j \frac{s_{jj}}{s_{yy}}$$

where $s_{jj} = \sqrt{\Sigma(x_{tj} - \bar{x}_j)^2} = \sqrt{T}$ times the standard deviation of x_j, and similarly for s_{yy}. (Beta coefficients should not be confused with the elements of the population coefficient vector $\boldsymbol{\beta}$!)

Note that in matrix form (10.30) may be written as

$$(10.31) \qquad \boldsymbol{\beta} = \mathbf{S}\mathbf{b}s_y^{-1}$$

where s_y is the scalar s_{yy}; $\mathbf{S}$ is the $K \times K$ matrix with s_{jj}'s on the diagonal and zeroes elsewhere. For simplicity let us restrict our attention to variables with zero mean. Then the "standardized" value of the variable x_j is $x_j^* = x_j/s_{jj}$, and the standardized value of the variable y is $y^* = y/s_{yy}$. Putting these definitions in matrix form we have

$$(10.32) \qquad \mathbf{X}_* = \mathbf{X}\mathbf{S}^{-1} \quad \text{and} \quad \mathbf{y}_* = \mathbf{y}s_y^{-1}.$$

Now note that the moments of the standardized variables are in fact correlation coefficients of the original variables: The j,k element of $\mathbf{X}_*'\mathbf{X}_*$ is $\Sigma x_j x_k/\sqrt{\Sigma x_j^2}\sqrt{\Sigma x_k^2}$, the square root of the determination coefficient R_{jk}^2. Thus the matrices $\mathbf{X}_*'\mathbf{X}_*$ and $\mathbf{X}_*'\mathbf{y}_*$ are sometimes called correlation matrices. Now the beta coefficients may be interpreted as ordinary regression coefficients for the standardized variables. That this is so can be shown as follows: Take the normal equations $\mathbf{X}'\mathbf{X}\mathbf{b} = \mathbf{X}'\mathbf{y}$, premultiply by $\mathbf{S}^{-1}$, postmultiply by s_y^{-1}, and insert $\mathbf{S}^{-1}\mathbf{S} = \mathbf{I}$:

$$(10.33) \qquad \mathbf{S}^{-1}\mathbf{X}'\mathbf{X}\mathbf{S}^{-1}\mathbf{S}\mathbf{b}s_y^{-1} = \mathbf{S}^{-1}\mathbf{X}'\mathbf{y}s_y^{-1}.$$

In view of (10.32) and the symmetry of $\mathbf{S}^{-1}$, this is simply

$$(10.34) \qquad \mathbf{X}_*'\mathbf{X}_*(\mathbf{S}\mathbf{b}s_y^{-1}) = \mathbf{X}_*'\mathbf{y}_*.$$

Comparison of (10.34) with (10.31) identifies the beta coefficients as the straightforward regression coefficients of the standardized variables. Although they are extensively used in psychological statistics, standardized variables and beta coefficients are rarely used in econometrics.

Another measure of importance is the marginal contribution of a regressor to the explanation of y *given all the other regressors.* This is ΔSSR, given all the others; an obvious disadvantage of this measure is that the sum of the ΔSSR's does not equal SSR. In the literature this concept appears as the partial correlation coefficient, or its square, the partial determination coefficient, $R^2_{yj.1,\ldots,j-1,j+1,\ldots,K}$. The partial determination coefficient of y and a regressor x_j is defined to be the ordinary determination coefficient between them after allowing for the influence of the other regressors. More precisely, let $\tilde{y}$ be the residuals from the regression of y on $x_1, \ldots, x_{j-1}, x_{j+1}, \ldots, x_K$ and let $\tilde{x}_j$ be the residuals from the regression of x_j on the same variables; without loss of generality we take all the variables to have zero means. Then the partial determination coefficient of y and x_j is the ordinary determination coefficient of $\tilde{y}$ and $\tilde{x}_j$, namely $R^2_{\tilde{y}\tilde{x}_j} = (\Sigma\tilde{y}\tilde{x}_j)^2/(\Sigma\tilde{x}_j^2)(\Sigma\tilde{y}^2)$. It is readily seen that in the notation used previously in this section this is

$$R^2_{\tilde{y}\tilde{x}_j} = (\mathbf{y}'\mathbf{M}_1\mathbf{X}_2)^2/(\mathbf{X}_2'\mathbf{M}_1\mathbf{X}_2)(\mathbf{y}'\mathbf{M}_1\mathbf{y})$$

where x_j is the only variable in the set $\mathbf{X}_2$ and the remaining regressors constitute the set $\mathbf{X}_1$. Referring back to (7.27) we see that

$$(\mathbf{y}'\mathbf{M}_1\mathbf{X}_2)^2/(\mathbf{X}_2'\mathbf{M}_1\mathbf{X}_2) = \Delta SSR,$$

the increase in regression sum of squares attributable to introducing $\mathbf{X}_2$ after $\mathbf{X}_1$ has been included, and it is also clear that $\mathbf{y}'\mathbf{M}_1\mathbf{y}$ is the error sum of squares with $\mathbf{X}_1$ but not $\mathbf{X}_2$ included—i.e., $SSE + \Delta SSR$—so that the partial determination coefficient may be written as

$$R^2_{\tilde{y}\tilde{x}_j} = \Delta SSR/(SSE + \Delta SSR).$$

Thus the partial determination coefficient measures the proportion of the variation in y remaining after all the other regressors have been used which is accounted for by x_j. Further manipulation, using the connection between the t and F statistics discussed in Example 8.1, shows that

$$(10.35) \qquad R^2_{\tilde{y}\tilde{x}_j} = \frac{(b_j/s_{b_j})^2}{(b_j/s_{b_j})^2 + (T - K - 1)}.$$

It is to be emphasized that the sum of the partial determination coefficients $R^2_{\tilde{y}\tilde{x}_j}$ $(j = 1, \ldots, K)$ is not in general equal to the R^2 of the original regression.

Alternatively, we might think of decomposing the total regression sum of squares into contributions of the individual regressors. One such decomposition is by marginal contributions, given all preceding regressors:

$$(10.36) \quad T\,SSR = (T\,SSR)_1 + (T\,\Delta SSR)_{2.1} + \cdots + (T\,\Delta SSR)_{K.1,\ldots,K-1}$$

these terms being readily obtainable in the Gauss-Doolittle scheme as $A_{1,K+1}B_{1,K+1}, \ldots, A_{K,K+1}B_{K,K+1}$, respectively. These measures obviously depend on the order in which the regressors are listed and hence are not unambiguous measures of contribution to explanation or importance. A second decomposition is

$$(10.37) \qquad T\,SSR = b_1 m_{1y} + \cdots + b_K m_{Ky}$$

in which the terms do not depend on the order of the list of regressors. In the literature, this concept appears as the separate determination coefficient

$$(10.38)\qquad d_{yj}^2 = b_j \frac{m_{jy}}{m_{yy}}$$

but is not widely used either.

Orthogonal Regressors

In conclusion let us consider the situation at the opposite end of the spectrum from multicollinearity. Let $\mathbf{y} = \mathbf{X}\boldsymbol{\beta} + \boldsymbol{\epsilon}$ be partitioned as $\mathbf{y} = \mathbf{X}_1\boldsymbol{\beta}_1 + \mathbf{X}_2\boldsymbol{\beta}_2 + \boldsymbol{\epsilon}$ and suppose that it is the case that $\mathbf{X}_1'\mathbf{X}_2 = \mathbf{0}$; i.e., for all x_j in the subset $\mathbf{X}_1$ and all x_k in the subset $\mathbf{X}_2$, it is the case that $\Sigma x_j x_k = 0$. (Supposing that variables are already measured as deviations from the sample mean, what we are assuming is that x_j and x_k are uncorrelated.) Then the least-squares estimate of $\boldsymbol{\beta}$ is

$$(10.39)\qquad \begin{pmatrix}\mathbf{b}_1\\ \mathbf{b}_2\end{pmatrix} = \begin{pmatrix}\mathbf{X}_1'\mathbf{X}_1 & \mathbf{0}\\ \mathbf{0} & \mathbf{X}_2'\mathbf{X}_2\end{pmatrix}^{-1}\begin{pmatrix}\mathbf{X}_1'\mathbf{y}\\ \mathbf{X}_2'\mathbf{y}\end{pmatrix}$$

$$= \begin{pmatrix}(\mathbf{X}_1'\mathbf{X}_1)^{-1} & \mathbf{0}\\ \mathbf{0} & (\mathbf{X}_2'\mathbf{X}_2)^{-1}\end{pmatrix}\begin{pmatrix}\mathbf{X}_1'\mathbf{y}\\ \mathbf{X}_2'\mathbf{y}\end{pmatrix}$$

$$= \begin{pmatrix}(\mathbf{X}_1'\mathbf{X}_1)^{-1}\mathbf{X}_1'\mathbf{y}\\ (\mathbf{X}_2'\mathbf{X}_2)^{-1}\mathbf{X}_2'\mathbf{y}\end{pmatrix}.$$

Thus when the subset $\mathbf{X}_1$ is *orthogonal* to $\mathbf{X}_2$ (i.e., when $\mathbf{X}_1'\mathbf{X}_2 = \mathbf{0}$), the least-squares estimate of $\boldsymbol{\beta}$ might just as well have been obtained in two separate regressions of $\mathbf{y}$ on $\mathbf{X}_1$ and of $\mathbf{y}$ on $\mathbf{X}_2$. Further, referring to (7.27) we find that the increase in *SSR* attributable to introducing $\mathbf{X}_2$ in addition to $\mathbf{X}_1$ is now equal to the *SSR* attained by using $\mathbf{X}_2$ alone:

$$\Delta SSR = \mathbf{y}'\mathbf{M}_1\mathbf{X}_2\mathbf{D}^{-1}\mathbf{X}_2'\mathbf{M}_1\mathbf{y} = \mathbf{b}_2'\mathbf{X}_2'\mathbf{y},$$

where we used the facts that $\mathbf{b}_2' = \mathbf{y}'\mathbf{M}_1\mathbf{X}_2\mathbf{D}^{-1}$ by (7.13), and

$$\mathbf{X}_2'\mathbf{M}_1 = \mathbf{X}_2'[\mathbf{I} - \mathbf{X}_1(\mathbf{X}_1'\mathbf{X}_1)^{-1}\mathbf{X}_1'] = \mathbf{X}_2'$$

since $\mathbf{X}_2'\mathbf{X}_1 = \mathbf{0}$. Notice how all computations and hypothesis testing are simplified in case $\mathbf{X}_1'\mathbf{X}_2 = \mathbf{0}$.

This idea extends in the obvious way when there are more than two orthogonal sets. Thus when $\mathbf{y} = \mathbf{X}\boldsymbol{\beta} + \boldsymbol{\epsilon}$ is partitioned as

$$\mathbf{y} = \mathbf{X}_1\boldsymbol{\beta}_1 + \cdots + \mathbf{X}_p\boldsymbol{\beta}_p + \cdots + \mathbf{X}_P\boldsymbol{\beta}_P + \boldsymbol{\epsilon}$$

and where $\mathbf{X}_p'\mathbf{X}_{p'} = \mathbf{0}$ for all $p \neq p'$, the least-squares estimate of each $\boldsymbol{\beta}_p$ is simply $\mathbf{b}_p = (\mathbf{X}_p'\mathbf{X}_p)^{-1}\mathbf{X}_p'\mathbf{y}$; i.e., it is obtainable from the regression of $\mathbf{y}$ on $\mathbf{X}_p$ alone.

The extreme case of this will be found when each subset $\mathbf{X}_p$ contains only a single regressor. Then we say that the regressors form an orthogonal set, and then each coefficient estimate can be obtained by a *simple* regression of y on the corresponding regressor. It is also easy to see that the coefficient estimates will have zero covariances: cov $(b_j, b_k) = 0$, for all $j \neq k$; that the decomposition of (10.36) is not dependent on the order of the list of regressors; and that the total *SSR* is just the sum of the *SSR*'s of all the simple regressions.

Note that orthogonality is not a property of the model, but rather of the sample observations on $\mathbf{X}$. Where the researcher has control over these observations—e.g., in "controlled" laboratory experiments—he will try to achieve orthogonality by varying each regressor independently of the others. This is part of the theory of "design of experiments." Econometric researchers are rarely if ever in this fortunate situation; they have to accept the experiments performed by nature, and these experiments are likely to feature multicollinearity, as we have seen, rather than orthogonality. Indeed, the whole point of *multiple* regression as contrasted with simple regression is to *try* to isolate the effects of the individual regressors, by "controlling" on the others. Still, when orthogonality is absent the concept of the contribution of an individual regressor remains inherently ambiguous.

11. SETS OF LINEAR REGRESSION RELATIONS

At this point we extend our discussion to cover sets of linear regression relations. This straightforward extension will be particularly useful as background when we come to consider systems of simultaneous linear relationships in Chapter 7.

Least-Squares Fitting

Suppose that we are given a set of T joint observations on each of M variables $y_1, \ldots, y_M$ and on each of K variables $x_1, \ldots, x_K$. (For convenience we use K rather than $1 + K$.) We may wish to summarize the pattern of the observations by fitting, for each y variable, a hyperplane of the form

$$(11.1) \qquad y_{tm} = \beta_{1m}x_{t1} + \cdots + \beta_{Km}x_{tK} + e_{tm} \qquad (t = 1, \ldots, T).$$

It is useful to develop a matrix formulation for all the M relations together.

Thus we define the $T \times M$ regressand observation matrix $\mathbf{Y}$

$$(11.2)\qquad \mathbf{Y} = (\mathbf{y}_1 \ \cdots \ \mathbf{y}_m \ \cdots \ \mathbf{y}_M) = \begin{pmatrix} y_{11} & \cdots & y_{1m} & \cdots & y_{1M} \\ \cdot & & \cdot & & \cdot \\ \cdot & & \cdot & & \cdot \\ \cdot & & \cdot & & \cdot \\ y_{t1} & \cdots & y_{tm} & \cdots & y_{tM} \\ \cdot & & \cdot & & \cdot \\ \cdot & & \cdot & & \cdot \\ \cdot & & \cdot & & \cdot \\ y_{T1} & \cdots & y_{Tm} & \cdots & y_{TM} \end{pmatrix},$$

the $T \times K$ regressor observation matrix $\mathbf{X}$

$$(11.3)\qquad \mathbf{X} = (\mathbf{x}_1 \ \cdots \ \mathbf{x}_k \ \cdots \ \mathbf{x}_K) = \begin{pmatrix} x_{11} & \cdots & x_{1k} & \cdots & x_{1K} \\ \cdot & & \cdot & & \cdot \\ \cdot & & \cdot & & \cdot \\ \cdot & & \cdot & & \cdot \\ x_{t1} & \cdots & x_{tk} & \cdots & x_{tK} \\ \cdot & & \cdot & & \cdot \\ \cdot & & \cdot & & \cdot \\ \cdot & & \cdot & & \cdot \\ x_{T1} & \cdots & x_{Tk} & \cdots & x_{TK} \end{pmatrix},$$

the $K \times M$ coefficient matrix $\boldsymbol{\beta}$

$$(11.4)\qquad \boldsymbol{\beta} = (\boldsymbol{\beta}_1 \ \cdots \ \boldsymbol{\beta}_m \ \cdots \ \boldsymbol{\beta}_M) = \begin{pmatrix} \beta_{11} & \cdots & \beta_{1m} & \cdots & \beta_{1M} \\ \cdot & & \cdot & & \cdot \\ \cdot & & \cdot & & \cdot \\ \cdot & & \cdot & & \cdot \\ \beta_{k1} & \cdots & \beta_{km} & \cdots & \beta_{kM} \\ \cdot & & \cdot & & \cdot \\ \cdot & & \cdot & & \cdot \\ \cdot & & \cdot & & \cdot \\ \beta_{K1} & \cdots & \beta_{Km} & \cdots & \beta_{KM} \end{pmatrix},$$

and the $T \times M$ residual matrix **E**

$$(11.5)\qquad \mathbf{E} = (\mathbf{e}_1 \quad \cdots \quad \mathbf{e}_m \quad \cdots \quad \mathbf{e}_M) = \begin{pmatrix} e_{11} & \cdots & e_{1m} & \cdots & e_{1M} \\ \cdot & & \cdot & & \cdot \\ \cdot & & \cdot & & \cdot \\ \cdot & & \cdot & & \cdot \\ e_{t1} & \cdots & e_{tm} & \cdots & e_{tM} \\ \cdot & & \cdot & & \cdot \\ \cdot & & \cdot & & \cdot \\ \cdot & & \cdot & & \cdot \\ e_{T1} & \cdots & e_{Tm} & \cdots & e_{TM} \end{pmatrix}.$$

The MT equations (11.1) may then be written compactly as

$$(11.6)\qquad \mathbf{Y} = \mathbf{X}\boldsymbol{\beta} + \mathbf{E},$$

in which each column refers to one of the M relations.

Let us again fit each of the relations by the least-squares criterion. That is, for each m we minimize $w_{mm} = \Sigma_{t=1}^{T} e_{tm}^2 = \mathbf{e}_m'\mathbf{e}_m$. This again leads to $\mathbf{b}_m = (\mathbf{X}'\mathbf{X})^{-1}\mathbf{X}'\mathbf{y}_m$ as the coefficient vector of the mth hyperplane, assuming $r(\mathbf{X}) = K$. And again the $T \times 1$ vector of calculated values for the mth hyperplane is defined by $\hat{\mathbf{y}}_m = \mathbf{X}\mathbf{b}_m$ and the $T \times 1$ vector of residuals from the mth fitted hyperplane is defined by $\hat{\mathbf{e}}_m = \mathbf{y}_m - \hat{\mathbf{y}}_m$. It is useful to develop a matrix formulation for all the m fitted relations together. Thus we define the $K \times M$ coefficient matrix **B**

$$(11.7)\qquad \mathbf{B} = (\mathbf{b}_1 \quad \cdots \quad \mathbf{b}_m \quad \cdots \quad \mathbf{b}_M) = \begin{pmatrix} b_{11} & \cdots & b_{1m} & \cdots & b_{1M} \\ \cdot & & \cdot & & \cdot \\ \cdot & & \cdot & & \cdot \\ \cdot & & \cdot & & \cdot \\ b_{k1} & \cdots & b_{km} & \cdots & b_{kM} \\ \cdot & & \cdot & & \cdot \\ \cdot & & \cdot & & \cdot \\ \cdot & & \cdot & & \cdot \\ b_{K1} & \cdots & b_{Km} & \cdots & b_{KM} \end{pmatrix},$$

the $T \times M$ calculated value matrix $\hat{\mathbf{Y}}$

$$(11.8)\qquad \hat{\mathbf{Y}} = (\hat{\mathbf{y}}_1 \;\cdots\; \hat{\mathbf{y}}_m \;\cdots\; \hat{\mathbf{y}}_M) = \begin{pmatrix} \hat{y}_{11} & \cdots & \hat{y}_{1m} & \cdots & \hat{y}_{1M} \\ \cdot & & \cdot & & \cdot \\ \cdot & & \cdot & & \cdot \\ \cdot & & \cdot & & \cdot \\ \hat{y}_{t1} & \cdots & \hat{y}_{tm} & \cdots & \hat{y}_{tM} \\ \cdot & & \cdot & & \cdot \\ \cdot & & \cdot & & \cdot \\ \cdot & & \cdot & & \cdot \\ \hat{y}_{T1} & \cdots & \hat{y}_{Tm} & \cdots & \hat{y}_{TM} \end{pmatrix},$$

and the $T \times M$ residual matrix $\hat{\mathbf{E}}$

$$(11.9)\qquad \hat{\mathbf{E}} = (\hat{\mathbf{e}}_1 \;\cdots\; \hat{\mathbf{e}}_m \;\cdots\; \hat{\mathbf{e}}_M) = \begin{pmatrix} \hat{e}_{11} & \cdots & \hat{e}_{1m} & \cdots & \hat{e}_{1M} \\ \cdot & & \cdot & & \cdot \\ \cdot & & \cdot & & \cdot \\ \cdot & & \cdot & & \cdot \\ \hat{e}_{t1} & \cdots & \hat{e}_{tm} & \cdots & \hat{e}_{tM} \\ \cdot & & \cdot & & \cdot \\ \cdot & & \cdot & & \cdot \\ \cdot & & \cdot & & \cdot \\ \hat{e}_{T1} & \cdots & \hat{e}_{Tm} & \cdots & \hat{e}_{TM} \end{pmatrix}.$$

Then the results of the M least-squares fits may be written compactly as

$$(11.10)\qquad \mathbf{B} = (\mathbf{X}'\mathbf{X})^{-1}\mathbf{X}'\mathbf{Y},$$

$$(11.11)\qquad \hat{\mathbf{Y}} = \mathbf{X}\mathbf{B},$$

$$(11.12)\qquad \hat{\mathbf{E}} = \mathbf{Y} - \hat{\mathbf{Y}}.$$

The following generalizations of results of Section 2 may be noted

$$(11.13)\qquad \mathbf{X}'\hat{\mathbf{E}} = \mathbf{X}'\mathbf{Y} - \mathbf{X}'\hat{\mathbf{Y}} = \mathbf{X}'\mathbf{Y} - \mathbf{X}'\mathbf{X}(\mathbf{X}'\mathbf{X})^{-1}\mathbf{X}'\mathbf{Y} = \mathbf{0},$$

$$(11.14)\qquad \hat{\mathbf{Y}}'\hat{\mathbf{E}} = \mathbf{B}'\mathbf{X}'\hat{\mathbf{E}} = \mathbf{B}'\mathbf{0} = \mathbf{0},$$

$$(11.15)\qquad \mathbf{Y}'\mathbf{Y} = (\hat{\mathbf{Y}} + \hat{\mathbf{E}})'(\hat{\mathbf{Y}} + \hat{\mathbf{E}}) = \hat{\mathbf{Y}}'\hat{\mathbf{Y}} + \hat{\mathbf{E}}'\hat{\mathbf{E}} + \hat{\mathbf{Y}}'\hat{\mathbf{E}} + \hat{\mathbf{E}}'\hat{\mathbf{Y}}$$

$$= \hat{\mathbf{Y}}'\hat{\mathbf{Y}} + \hat{\mathbf{E}}'\hat{\mathbf{E}}.$$

In (11.15) the matrix of sums of squares and cross products of the y's is "analyzed" into the matrix of sums of squares and cross products of the calculated y's plus the matrix of sums of squares and cross products of their residuals. Also note that

$$\text{(11.16)} \quad \begin{aligned} \hat{\mathbf{Y}}'\hat{\mathbf{Y}} &= \mathbf{B}'\mathbf{X}'\mathbf{X}\mathbf{B} = \mathbf{Y}'\mathbf{X}(\mathbf{X}'\mathbf{X})^{-1}\mathbf{X}'\mathbf{X}(\mathbf{X}'\mathbf{X})^{-1}\mathbf{X}'\mathbf{Y} \\ &= \mathbf{Y}'\mathbf{X}(\mathbf{X}'\mathbf{X})^{-1}\mathbf{X}'\mathbf{Y} \end{aligned}$$

and

$$\text{(11.17)} \quad \begin{aligned} \hat{\mathbf{E}}'\hat{\mathbf{E}} &= \mathbf{Y}'\mathbf{Y} - \hat{\mathbf{Y}}'\hat{\mathbf{Y}} = \mathbf{Y}'\mathbf{I}\mathbf{Y} - \mathbf{Y}'\mathbf{X}(\mathbf{X}'\mathbf{X})^{-1}\mathbf{X}'\mathbf{Y} \\ &= \mathbf{Y}'[\mathbf{I} - \mathbf{X}(\mathbf{X}'\mathbf{X})^{-1}\mathbf{X}']\mathbf{Y}. \end{aligned}$$

Let us define the $M \times M$ symmetric residual moment matrix $\mathbf{W}$

$$\text{(11.18)} \quad \mathbf{W} = \mathbf{E}'\mathbf{E} = \begin{pmatrix} w_{11} & \cdots & w_{1M} \\ \cdot & & \cdot \\ \cdot & w_{\mu\mu'} & \cdot \\ \cdot & & \cdot \\ w_{M1} & \cdots & w_{MM} \end{pmatrix} = \begin{pmatrix} \mathbf{e}_1'\mathbf{e}_1 & \cdots & \mathbf{e}_1'\mathbf{e}_M \\ \cdot & & \cdot \\ \cdot & \mathbf{e}_\mu'\mathbf{e}_{\mu'} & \cdot \\ \cdot & & \cdot \\ \mathbf{e}_M'\mathbf{e}_1 & \cdots & \mathbf{e}_M'\mathbf{e}_M \end{pmatrix}.$$

The least-squares hyperplanes, which were chosen to minimize individually the diagonal elements of $\mathbf{W}$, in fact also minimize $\log |\mathbf{W}|$, hence $|\mathbf{W}|$, and hence $|T^{-1}\mathbf{W}|$, the generalized residual variance. To see this, we first note that by (2.8.18),

$$\text{(11.19)} \quad \frac{\partial \log |\mathbf{W}|}{\partial \beta_{km}} = \sum_{\mu=1}^{M} \sum_{\mu'=1}^{M} \frac{\partial \log |\mathbf{W}|}{\partial w_{\mu\mu'}} \frac{\partial w_{\mu\mu'}}{\partial \beta_{km}} = \sum_{\mu=1}^{M} \sum_{\mu'=1}^{M} w^{\mu\mu'} \frac{\partial w_{\mu\mu'}}{\partial \beta_{km}}$$

where $w^{\mu\mu'}$ is the element in the μth row and μ'th column of $\mathbf{W}^{-1}$ and by definition

$$\text{(11.20)} \quad w_{\mu\mu'} = \sum_{t=1}^{T} e_{t\mu} e_{t\mu'}.$$

Then

$$\text{(11.21)} \quad \frac{\partial w_{\mu\mu'}}{\partial \beta_{km}} = \sum_{t=1}^{T} \left(e_{t\mu} \frac{\partial e_{t\mu'}}{\partial \beta_{km}} + e_{t\mu'} \frac{\partial e_{t\mu}}{\partial \beta_{km}} \right),$$

and since

$$\text{(11.22)} \quad e_{t\mu} = y_{t\mu} - \sum_{\kappa=1}^{K} x_{t\kappa} \beta_{\kappa\mu}$$

implies

$$\text{(11.23)} \quad \frac{\partial e_{t\mu}}{\partial \beta_{km}} = \begin{cases} -x_{tk} & \text{if } \mu = m \\ 0 & \text{if } \mu \neq m, \end{cases}$$

it follows that (11.21) is zero if both $\mu \neq m$ and $\mu' \neq m$, and

$$(11.24) \qquad \frac{\partial w_{\mu\mu'}}{\partial \beta_{km}} = \begin{cases} -\sum_{t=1}^{T} e_{t\mu'} x_{tk} & \text{if } \mu = m, \mu' \neq m \\ -\sum_{t=1}^{T} e_{t\mu} x_{tk} & \text{if } \mu' = m, \mu \neq m \\ -2\sum_{t=1}^{T} e_{t\mu} x_{tk} & \text{if } \mu = \mu' = m. \end{cases}$$

Inserting (11.22) and (11.24) into (11.19) gives, in view of the symmetry of $\mathbf{W}$,

$$(11.25) \qquad \begin{aligned} \frac{\partial \log |\mathbf{W}|}{\partial \beta_{km}} &= -2 \sum_{\mu'=1}^{M} w^{\mu' m} \sum_{t=1}^{T} e_{t\mu'} x_{tk} \\ &= -2 \sum_{\mu'=1}^{M} w^{\mu' m} \sum_{t=1}^{T} \left(y_{t\mu'} - \sum_{\kappa=1}^{K} x_{t\kappa} \beta_{\kappa\mu'} \right) (x_{tk}) \\ &= -2 \sum_{\mu'=1}^{M} w^{\mu' m} \sum_{t=1}^{T} \left(x_{tk} y_{t\mu'} - \sum_{\kappa=1}^{K} x_{t\kappa} x_{tk} \beta_{\kappa\mu'} \right). \end{aligned}$$

Now these derivatives may be collected into the $K \times M$ matrix

$$\frac{\partial \log |\mathbf{W}|}{\partial \boldsymbol{\beta}} = \begin{pmatrix} \frac{\partial \log |\mathbf{W}|}{\partial \beta_{11}} & \cdots & \frac{\partial \log |\mathbf{W}|}{\partial \beta_{1M}} \\ \cdot & & \cdot \\ \cdot & \frac{\partial \log |\mathbf{W}|}{\partial \beta_{km}} & \cdot \\ \cdot & & \cdot \\ \frac{\partial \log |\mathbf{W}|}{\partial \beta_{K1}} & \cdots & \frac{\partial \log |\mathbf{W}|}{\partial \beta_{KM}} \end{pmatrix}$$

and (11.25) may be written

$$(11.26) \qquad \frac{\partial \log |\mathbf{W}|}{\partial \boldsymbol{\beta}} = -2(\mathbf{X}'\mathbf{Y} - \mathbf{X}'\mathbf{X}\boldsymbol{\beta})\mathbf{W}^{-1}.$$

The value of $\boldsymbol{\beta}$ that minimizes $\log |\mathbf{W}|$ is then defined by setting all the derivatives equal to zero, i.e., by

$$(11.27) \qquad (\mathbf{X}'\mathbf{Y} - \mathbf{X}'\mathbf{X}\hat{\boldsymbol{\beta}})\mathbf{W}^{-1} = \mathbf{0}.$$

Postmultiplying by $\mathbf{W}$ gives

$$(11.28) \qquad \mathbf{X}'\mathbf{Y} = \mathbf{X}'\mathbf{X}\hat{\boldsymbol{\beta}},$$

the solution to which is indeed the least-squares coefficient matrix $\mathbf{B} = (\mathbf{X}'\mathbf{X})^{-1}\mathbf{X}'\mathbf{Y}$.

Multivariate Classical Linear Regression Model

Now suppose that the classical linear regression model is applicable to each of the M relationships, i.e., suppose

$$(11.29) \qquad \mathbf{y}_m = \mathbf{X}\boldsymbol{\beta}_m + \boldsymbol{\epsilon}_m \qquad (m = 1, \ldots, M),$$

$$(11.30) \qquad E\boldsymbol{\epsilon}_m = \mathbf{0} \qquad (m = 1, \ldots, M),$$

$$(11.31) \qquad E\boldsymbol{\epsilon}_m\boldsymbol{\epsilon}'_m = \omega_{mm}\mathbf{I} \qquad (m = 1, \ldots, M),$$

(11.32) $\mathbf{X}$ is a $T \times K$ matrix which is fixed in repeated samples,

(11.33) Rank of $\mathbf{X} = K \leq T$.

We shall also allow the disturbances in different relationships to be correlated with one another for the same t:

$$(11.34) \qquad E\boldsymbol{\epsilon}_m\boldsymbol{\epsilon}'_{m'} = \omega_{mm'}\mathbf{I} \qquad (m, m' = 1, \ldots, M;\ m \neq m').$$

The specifications (11.29)–(11.34) define the multivariate classical linear regression model. To collect the specifications for all M relationships we may define the $T \times M$ disturbance matrix

$$(11.35) \qquad \boldsymbol{\mathcal{E}} = (\boldsymbol{\epsilon}_1 \ \cdots \ \boldsymbol{\epsilon}_M) = \begin{pmatrix} \boldsymbol{\epsilon}'(1) \\ \cdot \\ \cdot \\ \cdot \\ \boldsymbol{\epsilon}'(t) \\ \cdot \\ \cdot \\ \cdot \\ \boldsymbol{\epsilon}'(T) \end{pmatrix} = \begin{pmatrix} \epsilon_{11} & \cdots & \epsilon_{1m} & \cdots & \epsilon_{1M} \\ \cdot & & \cdot & & \cdot \\ \cdot & & \cdot & & \cdot \\ \cdot & & \cdot & & \cdot \\ \epsilon_{t1} & \cdots & \epsilon_{tm} & \cdots & \epsilon_{tM} \\ \cdot & & \cdot & & \cdot \\ \cdot & & \cdot & & \cdot \\ \cdot & & \cdot & & \cdot \\ \epsilon_{T1} & \cdots & \epsilon_{Tm} & \cdots & \epsilon_{TM} \end{pmatrix},$$

in which $\boldsymbol{\epsilon}'(t)$ is the $1 \times M$ row vector of disturbances in all equations at observation t; and the $M \times M$ disturbance contemporaneous covariance matrix

$$(11.36) \qquad \boldsymbol{\Omega} = E\boldsymbol{\epsilon}(t)\boldsymbol{\epsilon}'(t) = \begin{pmatrix} \omega_{11} & \cdots & \omega_{1M} \\ \cdot & & \cdot \\ \cdot & \omega_{\mu\mu'} & \cdot \\ \cdot & & \cdot \\ \omega_{M1} & \cdots & \omega_{MM} \end{pmatrix}.$$

Then (11.29)–(11.34), which specify the multivariate classical linear regression model, may be written

(11.37) $\mathbf{Y} = \mathbf{X}\boldsymbol{\beta} + \boldsymbol{\mathcal{E}},$

(11.38) $E\boldsymbol{\mathcal{E}} = \mathbf{0},$

(11.39) $E\boldsymbol{\epsilon}(t)\boldsymbol{\epsilon}'(t') = \begin{cases} \boldsymbol{\Omega} & \text{if} \quad t = t' \\ \mathbf{0} & \text{if} \quad t \neq t', \end{cases}$

(11.40) $\mathbf{X}$ is a $T \times K$ matrix which is fixed in repeated samples,

(11.41) Rank of $\mathbf{X} = K \leq T.$

Clearly in this model the least-squares coefficient matrix $\mathbf{B}$ provides unbiased estimators of the coefficient matrix $\boldsymbol{\beta}$:

(11.42) $\mathbf{B} = (\mathbf{X}'\mathbf{X})^{-1}\mathbf{X}'\mathbf{Y} = (\mathbf{X}'\mathbf{X})^{-1}\mathbf{X}'(\mathbf{X}\boldsymbol{\beta} + \boldsymbol{\mathcal{E}}) = \boldsymbol{\beta} + (\mathbf{X}'\mathbf{X})^{-1}\mathbf{X}'\boldsymbol{\mathcal{E}},$

whence

(11.43) $E\mathbf{B} = \boldsymbol{\beta} + (\mathbf{X}'\mathbf{X})^{-1}\mathbf{X}'E\boldsymbol{\mathcal{E}} = \boldsymbol{\beta}.$

To derive the variances and covariances of the $\mathbf{b}_m$ we note

(11.44) $\mathbf{b}_m = (\mathbf{X}'\mathbf{X})^{-1}\mathbf{X}'\mathbf{y}_m = \boldsymbol{\beta}_m + (\mathbf{X}'\mathbf{X})^{-1}\mathbf{X}'\boldsymbol{\epsilon}_m,$

whence

(11.45) $\mathbf{b}_m - \boldsymbol{\beta}_m = (\mathbf{X}'\mathbf{X})^{-1}\mathbf{X}'\boldsymbol{\epsilon}_m,$

so that the variances and covariances of the coefficients in the mth relation are given by

(11.46) $$\begin{aligned} \boldsymbol{\Sigma}_{\mathbf{b}_m\mathbf{b}_m} &= E(\mathbf{b}_m - \boldsymbol{\beta}_m)(\mathbf{b}_m - \boldsymbol{\beta}_m)' = (\mathbf{X}'\mathbf{X})^{-1}\mathbf{X}'E\boldsymbol{\epsilon}_m\boldsymbol{\epsilon}'_m\mathbf{X}(\mathbf{X}'\mathbf{X})^{-1} \\ &= \omega_{mm}(\mathbf{X}'\mathbf{X})^{-1}, \end{aligned}$$

and also the covariances of coefficients in the mth relation with coefficients in the m'th relation are given by

(11.47) $$\begin{aligned} \boldsymbol{\Sigma}_{\mathbf{b}_m\mathbf{b}_{m'}} &= E(\mathbf{b}_m - \boldsymbol{\beta}_m)(\mathbf{b}_{m'} - \boldsymbol{\beta}_{m'})' = (\mathbf{X}'\mathbf{X})^{-1}\mathbf{X}'E\boldsymbol{\epsilon}_m\boldsymbol{\epsilon}'_{m'}\mathbf{X}(\mathbf{X}'\mathbf{X})^{-1} \\ &= \omega_{mm'}(\mathbf{X}'\mathbf{X})^{-1}. \end{aligned}$$

All these variances and covariances may be collected together if we define the $MK \times 1$ vectors of coefficients and coefficient estimators

$$(11.48)\qquad \boldsymbol{\beta} = \begin{pmatrix} \boldsymbol{\beta}_1 \\ \cdot \\ \cdot \\ \cdot \\ \boldsymbol{\beta}_m \\ \cdot \\ \cdot \\ \cdot \\ \boldsymbol{\beta}_M \end{pmatrix}, \qquad \mathbf{b} = \begin{pmatrix} \mathbf{b}_1 \\ \cdot \\ \cdot \\ \cdot \\ \mathbf{b}_m \\ \cdot \\ \cdot \\ \cdot \\ \mathbf{b}_M \end{pmatrix}.$$

Then

$$(11.49)\qquad E(\mathbf{b} - \boldsymbol{\beta})(\mathbf{b} - \boldsymbol{\beta})' = \begin{pmatrix} \omega_{11}(\mathbf{X}'\mathbf{X})^{-1} & \cdots & \omega_{1M}(\mathbf{X}'\mathbf{X})^{-1} \\ \cdot & & \cdot \\ \cdot & \omega_{mm'}(\mathbf{X}'\mathbf{X})^{-1} & \cdot \\ \cdot & & \cdot \\ \omega_{M1}(\mathbf{X}'\mathbf{X})^{-1} & \cdots & \omega_{MM}(\mathbf{X}'\mathbf{X})^{-1} \end{pmatrix} = \boldsymbol{\Omega} \otimes (\mathbf{X}'\mathbf{X})^{-1}.$$

That **B** is the BLUE of $\boldsymbol{\beta}$ will be shown in Section 5.4. (At the present stage it might be thought that each $\boldsymbol{\beta}_m$ might be estimated more efficiently by a function of all the $\mathbf{y}_m$'s than by a function of $\mathbf{y}_m$ only.)

The residual covariance matrix provides unbiased estimates of the disturbance covariance matrix as follows. For the residual vector from the mth fitted relation we have

$$(11.50)\qquad \hat{\boldsymbol{\epsilon}}_m = \mathbf{y}_m - \mathbf{X}\mathbf{b}_m = \mathbf{X}\boldsymbol{\beta}_m + \boldsymbol{\epsilon}_m - \mathbf{X}[\boldsymbol{\beta}_m + (\mathbf{X}'\mathbf{X})^{-1}\mathbf{X}'\boldsymbol{\epsilon}_m] = [\mathbf{I} - \mathbf{X}(\mathbf{X}'\mathbf{X})^{-1}\mathbf{X}']\boldsymbol{\epsilon}_m;$$

whence, paralleling the argument of (4.23)–(4.29),

$$(11.51)\qquad E\hat{\boldsymbol{\epsilon}}_m'\hat{\boldsymbol{\epsilon}}_{m'} = \omega_{mm'}(T - K).$$

(Note that in the present section we are using K rather than $1 + K$ regressors.) Therefore if we define

$$(11.52)\qquad \bar{w}_{mm'} = (T - K)^{-1}\hat{\boldsymbol{\epsilon}}_m'\hat{\boldsymbol{\epsilon}}_{m'},$$

we have $E\bar{w}_{mm'} = \omega_{mm'}$. Further if we define

$$(11.53)\qquad \mathbf{S}_{\mathbf{b}_m\mathbf{b}_{m'}} = \bar{w}_{mm'}(\mathbf{X}'\mathbf{X})^{-1},$$

we have $E\mathbf{S}_{\mathbf{b}_m\mathbf{b}_{m'}} = \boldsymbol{\Sigma}_{\mathbf{b}_m\mathbf{b}_{m'}}$.

For a given set of values of the x's the calculated values of the least-squares hyperplanes again provide unbiased estimators of the conditional expectations of the y's and also unbiased forecasts. Let $\mathbf{X}_*$ be a $K \times 1$ vector of values of the x's; then the $1 \times M$ row vector of calculated values of the y's is

$$\text{(11.54)} \qquad \hat{\mathbf{y}}'_* = \mathbf{X}'_*\mathbf{B} = \mathbf{b}'\mathbf{F},$$

where $\mathbf{F}$ is the $MK \times M$ matrix

$$\text{(11.55)} \qquad \mathbf{F} = \begin{pmatrix} \mathbf{X}_* & \mathbf{0} & \cdots & \mathbf{0} \\ \mathbf{0} & \mathbf{X}_* & \cdots & \mathbf{0} \\ \cdot & \cdot & & \cdot \\ \cdot & \cdot & & \cdot \\ \cdot & \cdot & & \cdot \\ \mathbf{0} & \mathbf{0} & \cdots & \mathbf{X}_* \end{pmatrix}.$$

The $1 \times M$ row vector of conditional expectations is

$$\text{(11.56)} \qquad E(\mathbf{y} \mid \mathbf{X}'_*)' = \mathbf{X}'_*\boldsymbol{\beta} = \boldsymbol{\beta}'\mathbf{F},$$

so that

$$\text{(11.57)} \qquad \hat{\mathbf{y}}_* - E(\mathbf{y} \mid \mathbf{X}'_*) = (\mathbf{B} - \boldsymbol{\beta})'\mathbf{X}_* = \mathbf{F}'(\mathbf{b} - \boldsymbol{\beta}).$$

Then

$$\text{(11.58)} \qquad E[\hat{\mathbf{y}}_* - E(\mathbf{y} \mid \mathbf{X}'_*)] = \mathbf{F}'E(\mathbf{b} - \boldsymbol{\beta}) = \mathbf{0}$$

and

$$\text{(11.59)} \qquad E[\hat{\mathbf{y}}_* - E(\mathbf{y} \mid \mathbf{X}'_*)][\hat{\mathbf{y}}_* - E(\mathbf{y} \mid \mathbf{X}'_*)]' = \mathbf{F}'E(\mathbf{b} - \boldsymbol{\beta})(\mathbf{b} - \boldsymbol{\beta})'\mathbf{F}$$
$$= \mathbf{F}'[\boldsymbol{\Omega} \otimes (\mathbf{X}'\mathbf{X})^{-1}]\mathbf{F}.$$

Further let $\boldsymbol{\epsilon}'_*$ be the $1 \times M$ vector of disturbances for a forecast period with

$$\text{(11.60)} \qquad E\boldsymbol{\epsilon}_* = \mathbf{0}, \qquad E\boldsymbol{\epsilon}_*\boldsymbol{\epsilon}'_* = \boldsymbol{\Omega}, \qquad E\boldsymbol{\epsilon}_*\boldsymbol{\epsilon}'_m = \mathbf{0} \quad \text{for all } m;$$

the actual values of the y's will be

$$\text{(11.61)} \qquad \mathbf{y}'_* = \mathbf{X}'_*\boldsymbol{\beta} + \boldsymbol{\epsilon}'_* = \boldsymbol{\beta}'\mathbf{F} + \boldsymbol{\epsilon}'_*.$$

The $M \times 1$ vector of forecast errors will be

$$\text{(11.62)} \qquad \mathbf{f} = \mathbf{y}_* - \hat{\mathbf{y}}_* = \mathbf{F}'(\boldsymbol{\beta} - \mathbf{b}) + \boldsymbol{\epsilon}_*.$$

Then

(11.63) $$E\mathbf{f} = \mathbf{F}'E(\boldsymbol{\beta} - \mathbf{b}) + E\boldsymbol{\epsilon}_* = \mathbf{0},$$

and the forecast covariance matrix will be

(11.64) $$\begin{aligned} E\mathbf{f}\mathbf{f}' &= \mathbf{F}'E(\boldsymbol{\beta} - \mathbf{b})(\boldsymbol{\beta} - \mathbf{b})'\mathbf{F} + E\boldsymbol{\epsilon}_*\boldsymbol{\epsilon}_*' + \mathbf{F}'E(\boldsymbol{\beta} - \mathbf{b})\boldsymbol{\epsilon}_*' \\ &\quad + E\boldsymbol{\epsilon}_*(\boldsymbol{\beta} - \mathbf{b})'\mathbf{F} \\ &= \mathbf{F}'[\boldsymbol{\Omega} \otimes (\mathbf{X}'\mathbf{X})^{-1}]\mathbf{F} + \boldsymbol{\Omega}, \end{aligned}$$

since $E(\mathbf{b}_m - \boldsymbol{\beta}_m)\boldsymbol{\epsilon}_*' = E(\mathbf{X}'\mathbf{X})^{-1}\mathbf{X}'\boldsymbol{\epsilon}_m\boldsymbol{\epsilon}_*' = (\mathbf{X}'\mathbf{X})^{-1}\mathbf{X}'E\boldsymbol{\epsilon}_m\boldsymbol{\epsilon}_*' = \mathbf{0}$ for all m.

Multivariate Classical Normal Linear Regression Model

If we add to the multivariate classical linear regression model the specification that the disturbances are jointly normally distributed, we have the multivariate classical normal linear regression model. We may consider estimating the coefficient matrix $\boldsymbol{\beta}$ by the maximum likelihood method. Now we have that $\boldsymbol{\epsilon}(t)$ is $\mathcal{N}(\mathbf{0}, \boldsymbol{\Omega})$ for $t = 1, \ldots, T$, so that the density of each $\boldsymbol{\epsilon}(t)$ is

(11.65) $$f[\boldsymbol{\epsilon}(t)] = (2\pi)^{-M/2}\,|\boldsymbol{\Omega}|^{-\frac{1}{2}}\exp\{-\tfrac{1}{2}\boldsymbol{\epsilon}'(t)\boldsymbol{\Omega}^{-1}\boldsymbol{\epsilon}(t)\},$$

and since the $\boldsymbol{\epsilon}(t)$'s are independent the likelihood of the sample is

(11.66) $$\mathcal{L} = \prod_{t=1}^{T} f[\boldsymbol{\epsilon}(t)] = (2\pi)^{-MT/2}|\boldsymbol{\Omega}|^{-T/2}\exp\left\{-\frac{1}{2}\sum_{t=1}^{T}\boldsymbol{\epsilon}'(t)\boldsymbol{\Omega}^{-1}\boldsymbol{\epsilon}(t)\right\}.$$

To maximize $\mathcal{L}$ we may as well maximize

(11.67) $$\begin{aligned} L^* &= 2T^{-1}\log\mathcal{L} + M\log 2\pi \\ &= \log|\boldsymbol{\Omega}^{-1}| - T^{-1}\sum_{t=1}^{T}\boldsymbol{\epsilon}'(t)\boldsymbol{\Omega}^{-1}\boldsymbol{\epsilon}(t). \end{aligned}$$

It is readily confirmed that

(11.68) $$\sum_{t=1}^{T}\boldsymbol{\epsilon}'(t)\boldsymbol{\Omega}^{-1}\boldsymbol{\epsilon}(t) = tr\,\boldsymbol{\mathcal{E}}\boldsymbol{\Omega}^{-1}\boldsymbol{\mathcal{E}}' = tr\,\boldsymbol{\mathcal{E}}'\boldsymbol{\mathcal{E}}\boldsymbol{\Omega}^{-1};$$

and, since $\boldsymbol{\mathcal{E}} = \mathbf{Y} - \mathbf{X}\boldsymbol{\beta}$, the function to be maximized in terms of the parameters is

(11.69) $$\begin{aligned} L^* = \log|\boldsymbol{\Omega}^{-1}| - T^{-1}\,tr\,[(&\mathbf{Y}'\mathbf{Y} - \mathbf{Y}'\mathbf{X}\boldsymbol{\beta} - \boldsymbol{\beta}'\mathbf{X}'\mathbf{Y} \\ &+ \boldsymbol{\beta}'\mathbf{X}'\mathbf{X}\boldsymbol{\beta})\boldsymbol{\Omega}^{-1}]. \end{aligned}$$

Using (2.8.15) for each $\partial L^*/\partial\beta_{km}$, we can write

(11.70) $$\frac{\partial L^*}{\partial\boldsymbol{\beta}} = -2T^{-1}(-\mathbf{X}'\mathbf{Y} + \mathbf{X}'\mathbf{X}\boldsymbol{\beta})\boldsymbol{\Omega}^{-1}.$$

The maximum likelihood estimator is obtained by setting $\partial L^*/\partial \boldsymbol{\beta}$ equal to zero, which after postmultiplication by $\boldsymbol{\Omega}$ and multiplication by $\frac{1}{2}T$ gives

$$\text{(11.71)} \qquad \mathbf{X}'\mathbf{X}\hat{\boldsymbol{\beta}} = \mathbf{X}'\mathbf{Y},$$

the solution to which is the least-squares coefficient matrix $\mathbf{B} = (\mathbf{X}'\mathbf{X})^{-1}\mathbf{X}'\mathbf{Y}$. Similarly by (2.8.15) and (2.8.18) we find that

$$\text{(11.72)} \qquad \frac{\partial L^*}{\partial \boldsymbol{\Omega}^{-1}} = \boldsymbol{\Omega} - T^{-1}\boldsymbol{\varepsilon}'\boldsymbol{\varepsilon},$$

whence the maximum likelihood estimator of $\boldsymbol{\Omega}$ is $\hat{\boldsymbol{\Omega}} = T^{-1}\hat{\mathbf{E}}'\hat{\mathbf{E}} = T^{-1}\mathbf{W} = \overline{\mathbf{W}}$, say, where $\overline{\mathbf{W}}$ is the covariance matrix of the residuals from the least-squares hyperplanes. Thus the least-squares hyperplanes are asymptotically efficient when the disturbances are normally distributed in addition to the desirable properties they have without that specification.

Hypothesis testing and interval estimation are carried out by direct generalization of our results in the univariate model. For a detailed presentation, see Anderson (1958, Ch. 8).

CHAPTER 5

Extensions of Linear Regression

1. INTRODUCTION

The strict assumptions of the classical linear regression model, which have justified the use of least-squares estimation, may be untenable in many economic situations. This chapter is devoted to a variety of adaptations and modifications of the model and of the estimation procedure that have been developed to handle specific problems of econometric research. In Section 2 we consider how nonlinear relationships may be handled. Section 3 explores the connections between the classical linear regression model and the testing procedure known as the analysis of variance.

Economic disturbances may not be "spherical"—they may be interdependent and/or have different variances; in Section 4, we investigate this situation, where $E\boldsymbol{\epsilon\epsilon}' \neq \sigma^2\mathbf{I}$. In Section 5 we consider special cases that arise when the range of variation of the regressand is inherently limited. Finally, in Section 6 we consider methods for exploiting outside information in estimation from a sample.

The remaining assumption of the classical model is that the regressors are fixed in repeated samples, and hence independent of the disturbances. Economic regressors are themselves, however, often generated stochastically so that the independence assumption may be inappropriate. This important problem is reserved for Chapters 6 and 7.

2. FUNCTIONAL FORMS

Conventional Curvilinear Forms

The classical linear regression model includes the assumption that the (expected value of the) regressand y is a linear function of the regressors $x_1, \ldots, x_K$. Now this is much less restrictive than it might appear, because it does not prevent the (expected value of) y from being nonlinear in some "natural" explanatory variables. Thus it is perfectly in keeping with the model to have income squared, or the logarithm of income, or the cosine of income among the regressors. Hence considerable flexibility in the form of the function is available.

In our analysis it will be helpful to distinguish between the natural variables and the variables that actually appear in the relationship. Thus we want to make a distinction between an *explanatory variable* and the *regressor(s)* that represent it in the relationship. For example, if we consider consumption y to be a function of income x, and write $y = \alpha + \beta x + \gamma x^2$, then income is the explanatory variable while the regressors are income and income squared. What the classical model requires is that (the expected value of) y be a linear function of the *regressors*.

To be sure, the economic theory that proposes that y is a function of x rarely specifies the exact functional form. Still, sometimes the theory does include some propositions about the qualitative behavior of the slope or elasticity (e.g., marginal cost falls and then rises as output increases), or about behavior at the extremes (e.g., the production function goes through the origin). When this is the case, it is well to adopt a functional form that incorporates or allows for the specified behavior. The following table illustrates the point by tabulating the properties of several simple functions that have been found to be useful in Engel curve studies. Here y is the expenditure on a particular commodity, x is income, the slope is dy/dx, the elasticity is $(x\ dy)/(y\ dx)$, $y(\infty)$ is the value approached by y as x approaches ∞, $x(0)$ is the value of x at which $y = 0$, and β and γ are taken as positive.

(2.1) ***Alternative functional forms***

Name	Form	Slope	Elasticity	$y(\infty)$	$x(0)$
Linear	$y = \alpha + \beta x$	β	$\beta x/y$	∞	$-\alpha/\beta$
Semilog	$y = \alpha + \beta \log x$	β/x	β/y	∞	antilog $(-\alpha/\beta)$
Hyperbola	$y = \alpha - \beta/x$	β/x^2	β/xy	α	β/α

As is well known, any of a wide range of functions can be closely approximated by a polynomial in accordance with Taylor's theorem. Thus using several powers of the explanatory variable as separate regressors may suffice to express a hypothesized nonlinear function. When the sample size is small, however, and when the range of variation of the explanatory variable is narrow, the reliability of the separate coefficients is likely to be low. A high-order polynomial has many parameters to be estimated, and this is expensive in terms of degrees of freedom, which leads to large standard errors. (The unbiased variance estimator $s^2 = SSE/(T - K - 1)$ will rise rapidly with K when T is small.) In addition, over narrow ranges of variation, the successive powers of x may be multicollinear; x^2, for example, is approximately a linear function of x over any narrow range. We have already seen how multicollinearity may lead to large standard errors. This argues for using a specific nonlinear form —like those of (2.1)—to economize on degrees of freedom.

Within the classical model further flexibility is attainable by transforming y; e.g., using the logarithm of expenditure instead of expenditure as the regressand. Now it is useful to distinguish between the *dependent variable* and the *regressand* that represents it in the relationship. We may continue our illustration of functional forms useful for Engel curve analysis with (2.2).

(2.2) ***Alternative functional forms {continued}***

Name	Form	Slope	Elasticity	$y(\infty)$	$x(0)$
Doublelog	$\log y = \alpha + \beta \log x$	$\beta y/x$	β	∞	0
Loghyperbola	$\log y = \alpha - \beta/x$	$\beta y/x^2$	β/x	antilog α	0

The doublelog form, which incorporates a constant elasticity, is very common in econometric work. The nonlinear relationship

(2.3) $$y = \beta_0 x^{\beta_1}$$

may be written as

(2.4) $$\log y = \log \beta_0 + \beta_1 \log x,$$

which is the linear relationship

(2.5) $$y^* = \beta_0^* + \beta_1^* x^*,$$

where $y^* = \log y$, $x^* = \log x$, $\beta_0^* = \log \beta_0$, and $\beta_1^* = \beta_1$. If the classical linear regression model is to be appropriate for (2.5), a special assumption about the disturbance term of (2.3) is required. We assume that the disturbance in (2.3) is multiplicative,

(2.6) $$y = \beta_0 x^{\beta_1} \epsilon,$$

and then (2.5) will have the required additive disturbance:

(2.7) $$y^* = \beta_0^* + \beta_1^* x^* + \epsilon^*$$

where $\epsilon^* = \log \epsilon$. Further specification of the distribution of ϵ is needed to give $E\epsilon^* = 0$ and $E\epsilon^{*2} = \sigma^2$. For example, if ϵ^* is to be distributed $\mathcal{N}(0, \sigma^2)$, then ϵ must be log-normally distributed with mean $e^{\sigma^2/2}$ and variance $e^{\sigma^2}(e^{\sigma^2} - 1)$. A variable is said to be log-normally distributed if and only if its logarithm is normally distributed. To justify the assumption of log-normality of the distribution of the disturbance ϵ, we may call on the

(2.8) ***Multiplicative central limit theorem:*** The distribution of the product of N independent random variables tends to log-normality as $N \to \infty$, under very general conditions.

Thus if we think of ϵ as representing the net effect of a large number of independent multiplicative factors, it is reasonable to assume that it is indeed log-normally distributed. Incidentally, it is easy to deduce this multiplicative central limit theorem from the earlier (additive) central limit theorem. For if $X = (X_1) \cdots (X_N)$, then $Y = \log X = \log X_1 + \cdots + \log X_N = Y_1 + \cdots + Y_N$, where $Y_i = \log X_i$. Then when Y, a sum of random variables, tends to normality by the earlier theorem, $X =$ antilog Y tends to log-normality. On all this, see Aitchison and Brown (1957, Chapter 2).

We have been discussing nonlinearity in the effect of a single explanatory variable on the (expected value of) y, where dy/dx varies with x. A distinct situation is nonadditivity, where the effect of one explanatory variable depends on the value of another one, i.e., where $\partial y/\partial x$ varies with z, another explanatory variable. For example, it may be held that the marginal propensity to spend on food varies with family size. The classical linear regression model is flexible enough to handle such non-additivities or "interactions" by the use of compound regressors which are products or other functions of the natural explanatory variables. For example, let $w = xz$; then in

$$y = \alpha x + \beta z + \gamma w, \tag{2.9}$$

we have $\partial y/\partial x = \alpha + \gamma z$ and $\partial y/\partial z = \beta + \gamma x$. Nonlinearities and non-additivities may both be incorporated, as in this savings function adapted from Klein (1951):

$$s = \alpha y + \beta(y \log y) + \gamma(y \log n) + \delta a + \pi(ay), \tag{2.10}$$

where $s =$ savings, $y =$ income, $n =$ family size, and $a =$ liquid assets. Note that

$$\frac{\partial s}{\partial y} = (\alpha + \beta) + \beta \log y + \gamma \log n + \pi a, \tag{2.11}$$

$$\frac{\partial s}{\partial n} = \frac{\gamma y}{n}, \tag{2.12}$$

$$\frac{\partial s}{\partial a} = \delta + \pi y. \tag{2.13}$$

It is important to realize that when an explanatory variable is represented by several regressors the hypothesis that the explanatory variable does not influence (the expected value of) y is formulated as the hypothesis that the coefficients of all its regressors are jointly zero [the F test of (4.7.28)].

In practice, the choice among alternative functional forms involves a compromise among several criteria including economic theory, goodness of fit, and simplicity. According to Occam's razor the simpler hypothesis is to be preferred to the more complicated one. It is not always obvious which of two forms is the simpler; but it is reasonable to assert that the smaller the number of parameters, the simpler the function. It is conventional to pay homage to this by comparing functions on the basis of the *corrected* coefficient of determination defined by

$$\bar{R}^2 = 1 - (1 - R^2)\frac{T-1}{T-K-1} = R^2 - \frac{K}{T-K-1}(1 - R^2) \tag{2.14}$$

which clearly penalizes functions having a higher K. It should be noted that where the regressand has been transformed the determination coefficient may be misleading as a measure of goodness of fit. Thus if a doublelog form has been fit, the R^2 measures the proportion of the variation of the logarithm of y that has been accounted for, which is not the same thing as the proportion of the variation of y. To put such an equation on a comparable footing with one that simply has y as regressand, we should take antilogs of calculated values of log y and find their determination coefficient with the observed values of y. Barten (1962) treats R^2, $\bar{R}^2$, and other variants as estimators of a population parameter and investigates their sampling distributions.

A final comment on transformations of relationships to put them in the form for which the classical model is appropriate: The BLUE properties of least squares hold for the transformed relationship. Thus, the estimators of the (possibly) transformed parameters are best unbiased within the class of linear functions of the (possibly) transformed regressand. Thus b_0^*, the least-squares estimator of β_0^* in (2.7), is the best unbiased estimator of $\log \beta_0$ within the class of linear functions of $\log y$. Now it is natural to estimate β_0 as $\tilde{b}_0 = \text{antilog}\, b_0^*$. But $\tilde{b}_0$ is certainly not the BLUE of β_0. It is not a linear function of y nor of $\log y$; nor is it unbiased, for the expectation of a nonlinear function is in general not the nonlinear function of the expectation. The sampling properties of nonlinear functions of BLUE's remain to be established in individual cases. In the present case we may show that $E\tilde{b}_0 > \beta_0$. We proceed in general terms. Suppose $Y = \text{antilog}\, X$; then expanding in Taylor series about EX and dropping high-order terms gives

$$\text{(2.15)} \qquad \operatorname{antilog} X = \operatorname{antilog} EX + (X - EX)(\operatorname{antilog} X)|_{X=EX} + \frac{(X - EX)^2}{2}(\operatorname{antilog} X)\Big|_{X=EX}$$

$$= \operatorname{antilog} EX + (X - EX) \operatorname{antilog} EX + \frac{(X - EX)^2}{2} \times \operatorname{antilog} EX.$$

Since $E(X - EX) = 0$, and writing $E(X - EX)^2 = \sigma^2$, we have

$$\text{(2.16)} \qquad E(\operatorname{antilog} X) = (\operatorname{antilog} EX)\left(1 + \frac{\sigma^2}{2}\right),$$

which indicates a positive bias since $\sigma^2 > 0$. It is of course true that maximum likelihood properties do carry over; this is the invariance property noted in (3.7.24). Thus if the classical normal linear regression model were appropriate in (2.7), $\tilde{b}_0$ would be the maximum likelihood estimator of β_0.

Step Functions

Suppose that the relationship between the (expected value of) y and the explanatory variable x is known to be a step function of the form illustrated in the accompanying figure, with the breakpoints x^* and x^{**} known.

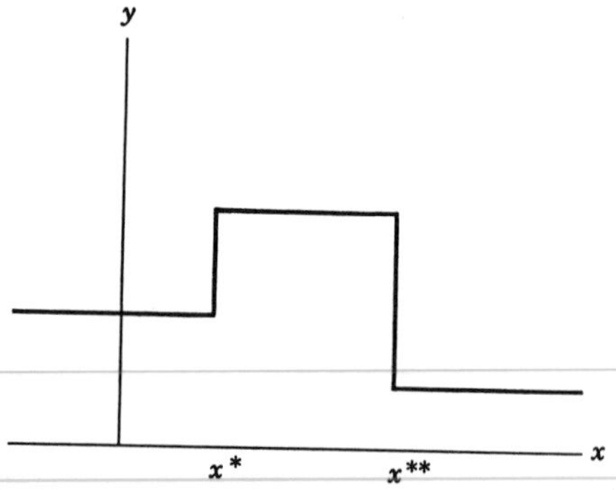

Although it is possible to approximate this by a high-order polynomial, a more natural approach is to represent the explanatory variable x by a set of "dummy variable" regressors. Let us define the regressors

$$x_1 = \begin{cases} 1 & \text{if } x \leq x^* \\ 0 & \text{otherwise,} \end{cases}$$

$$(2.17) \qquad x_2 = \begin{cases} 1 & \text{if } x^* < x \leq x^{**} \\ 0 & \text{otherwise,} \end{cases}$$

$$x_3 = \begin{cases} 1 & \text{if } x > x^{**} \\ 0 & \text{otherwise,} \end{cases}$$

and designate the observations for which $x \leq x^*$ as group A, those for which $x^* < x \leq x^{**}$ as group B, and those for which $x > x^{**}$ as group C. Then it is clear that the expected value of y may be written as

$$(2.18) \qquad E(y \mid x) = \beta_1 x_1 + \beta_2 x_2 + \beta_3 x_3,$$

because the expected value of y for $x \leq x^*$ is $\beta_1(1) + \beta_2(0) + \beta_3(0) = \beta_1$, since $x_1 = 1$ and $x_2 = x_3 = 0$ in group A. Similarly for the other groups. Thus

$$(2.19) \qquad E(y \mid A) = \beta_1, \qquad E(y \mid B) = \beta_2, \qquad E(y \mid C) = \beta_3,$$

which precisely captures the specified step function.

Making the classical assumptions on ϵ, we may proceed to least-squares estimation of

$$(2.20) \qquad y = \beta_1 x_1 + \beta_2 x_2 + \beta_3 x_3 + \epsilon.$$

It is not hard to find what the least-squares estimators will be; the typical individual observations will look as follows:

(2.21)

Group	x_1	x_2	x_3	y
A	1	0	0	y_{iA}
B	0	1	0	y_{jB}
C	0	0	1	y_{kC}

with the first subscript of y denoting the individual and the second the group. Then it is easy to see that the moment matrices will be

$$(2.22) \qquad \mathbf{X'X} = \begin{pmatrix} T_A & 0 & 0 \\ 0 & T_B & 0 \\ 0 & 0 & T_C \end{pmatrix}, \qquad \mathbf{X'y} = \begin{pmatrix} y_{.A} \\ y_{.B} \\ y_{.C} \end{pmatrix}$$

where T_A = the number of observations in group A, etc., and $y_{.A} = \sum_i y_{iA}$ = the sum of the y's for those in group A, etc. Then we find for the least-squares coefficient vector

$$(2.23)\qquad \begin{pmatrix} b_1 \\ b_2 \\ b_3 \end{pmatrix} = (\mathbf{X}'\mathbf{X})^{-1}\mathbf{X}'\mathbf{y} = \begin{pmatrix} 1/T_A & 0 & 0 \\ 0 & 1/T_B & 0 \\ 0 & 0 & 1/T_C \end{pmatrix} \begin{pmatrix} y_{.A} \\ y_{.B} \\ y_{.C} \end{pmatrix} = \begin{pmatrix} \bar{y}_{.A} \\ \bar{y}_{.B} \\ \bar{y}_{.C} \end{pmatrix},$$

where $\bar{y}_{.A} = y_{.A}/T_A$ = the mean y for those in group A, etc. Thus the estimates of the expected value in each group are just the corresponding observed means, which is not surprising.

In the present formulation there is no room for a constant term. Had we also included a variable $x_0 = 1$ for all observations, then $x_0 = x_1 + x_2 + x_3$ for all observations, so that there would be an exact linear relation among the columns of $\mathbf{X}$ which would preclude estimation. In brief, it takes only three variables to represent a trichotomy. Of course, our formulation is not unique. Instead of the regressors of (2.17) we might have chosen the following:

$$(2.24)\qquad \begin{aligned} z_1 &= 1 \quad \text{for all observations,} \\ z_2 &= \begin{cases} 1 & \text{if } \ x^* < x \leq x^{**} \quad \text{(i.e., for group } B) \\ 0 & \text{otherwise,} \end{cases} \\ z_3 &= \begin{cases} 1 & \text{if } \ x > x^{**} \quad \text{(i.e., for group } C) \\ 0 & \text{otherwise,} \end{cases} \end{aligned}$$

and estimated

$$(2.25)\qquad y = \gamma_1 z_1 + \gamma_2 z_2 + \gamma_3 z_3 + \epsilon.$$

Then the typical individual observations would look as follows:

(2.26)

Group	z_1	z_2	z_3	y
A	1	0	0	y_{iA}
B	1	1	0	y_{jB}
C	1	0	1	y_{kC}

To find the least-squares estimators in this formulation, we may argue as follows. Comparison of (2.26) with (2.21) shows that the new regressor observation matrix $\mathbf{Z}$ is related to the old regressor observation matrix $\mathbf{X}$ by $\mathbf{Z} = \mathbf{XP}$ where

$$(2.27)\qquad \mathbf{P} = \begin{pmatrix} 1 & 0 & 0 \\ 1 & 1 & 0 \\ 1 & 0 & 1 \end{pmatrix}.$$

Thus we may find the new coefficient estimator in terms of the old one:

$$(2.28) \qquad \mathbf{c} = (\mathbf{Z}'\mathbf{Z})^{-1}\mathbf{Z}'\mathbf{y} = (\mathbf{P}'\mathbf{X}'\mathbf{X}\mathbf{P})^{-1}\mathbf{P}'\mathbf{X}'\mathbf{y}$$
$$= \mathbf{P}^{-1}(\mathbf{X}'\mathbf{X})^{-1}\mathbf{P}'^{-1}\mathbf{P}'\mathbf{X}'\mathbf{y} = \mathbf{P}^{-1}\mathbf{b},$$

or more explicitly,

$$(2.29) \qquad \begin{pmatrix} c_1 \\ c_2 \\ c_3 \end{pmatrix} = \begin{pmatrix} 1 & 0 & 0 \\ -1 & 1 & 0 \\ -1 & 0 & 1 \end{pmatrix} \begin{pmatrix} \bar{y}_{.A} \\ \bar{y}_{.B} \\ \bar{y}_{.C} \end{pmatrix} = \begin{pmatrix} \bar{y}_{.A} \\ \bar{y}_{.B} - \bar{y}_{.A} \\ \bar{y}_{.C} - \bar{y}_{.A} \end{pmatrix} = \begin{pmatrix} b_1 \\ b_2 - b_1 \\ b_3 - b_1 \end{pmatrix}.$$

The new coefficient vector differs from the old one, but there is no cause for alarm; after all, the parameters being estimated are different. What should remain invariant are the calculated values of y—the estimates of the conditional expectation of y—and they do. In view of (2.24) the conditional expectations in (2.25) are

$$(2.30) \qquad E(y \mid A) = \gamma_1, \qquad E(y \mid B) = \gamma_2 + \gamma_1, \qquad E(y \mid C) = \gamma_3 + \gamma_1;$$

from (2.29) we estimate these as

$$(2.31) \qquad \hat{y}_A = c_1 = \bar{y}_{.A}, \qquad \hat{y}_B = c_2 + c_1 = \bar{y}_{.B} - \bar{y}_{.A} + \bar{y}_{.A} = \bar{y}_{.B},$$
$$\hat{y}_C = c_3 + c_1 = \bar{y}_{.C} - \bar{y}_{.A} + \bar{y}_{.A} = \bar{y}_{.C},$$

which is just as in (2.23). The alternative formulation of the regressors makes no essential difference. The estimates differ because they are estimates of different things: In the first case the b's estimate group expected values, in the second case the latter two c's estimate differences between the expected values of the latter two groups and the expected value of the first group. When translated into estimates of the same parameters, the two sets of results are identical. Similarly for any other alternative formulation of the regressors expressible as linear functions of the original regressors. Further, since the calculated values of y are identical, the SSR's obtained under alternative representations of the regressors will also be identical.

An interesting expression for SSR is obtainable as follows from the result of (2.23). Write T for the total number of observations, $T = T_A + T_B + T_C$; $y_{..}$ for the overall sum of the y's, $y_{..} = \Sigma\, y = y_{.A} + y_{.B} + y_{.C}$, and $\bar{y}_{..}$ for the overall mean of the y's: $\bar{y}_{..} = \Sigma\, y/T = y_{..}/T$. Then

$$(2.32) \qquad SSR = \mathbf{b}'\mathbf{X}'\mathbf{y} - \frac{(\Sigma y)^2}{T} = \bar{y}_{.A}y_{.A} + \bar{y}_{.B}y_{.B} + \bar{y}_{.C}y_{.C} - \bar{y}_{..}y_{..}$$
$$= T_A\bar{y}^2_{.A} + T_B\bar{y}^2_{.B} + T_C\bar{y}^2_{.C} - T\bar{y}^2_{..}$$
$$= T_A(\bar{y}^2_{.A} - \bar{y}^2_{..}) + T_B(\bar{y}^2_{.B} - \bar{y}^2_{..}) + T_C(\bar{y}^2_{.C} - \bar{y}^2_{..})$$
$$= T_A(\bar{y}_{.A} - \bar{y}_{..})^2 + T_B(\bar{y}_{.B} - \bar{y}_{..})^2 + T_C(\bar{y}_{.C} - \bar{y}_{..})^2,$$

where the last line is obtained from the preceding one by the addition of $-2\bar{y}_{..}[T_A(\bar{y}_{.A} - \bar{y}_{..}) + T_B(\bar{y}_{.B} - \bar{y}_{..}) + T_C(\bar{y}_{.C} - \bar{y}_{..})] = 0$. In (2.32) the regression sum of squares is seen to be the weighted sum of squared deviations of group means from the overall mean of y. Thus the SSR will be large if the group means are substantially different from each other and hence from the overall mean. On the other hand, the error sum of squares is simply the sum of squared deviations of observations about their respective group means, since the calculated value of y for any observation is the group mean. Thus we see that R^2 will be large when the between-group variation of y is large relative to the within-group variation.

Of course, economic theory rarely specifies a step function. As contrasted with a linear or conventional curvilinear form, however, the step function is very free in form: The path of the expectation of y is free to vary in complex ways as the explanatory variables vary. The basic restriction is that the function remains flat over ranges of the explanatory variable; another limitation is that the dummy variables are expensive in terms of degrees of freedom.

The dummy variable approach extends to a step function with any number of levels. Moreover, each additional explanatory variable may be represented by its own set of dummy variables, so that the classical linear regression model may be applied to quite general functions of the form

$$y = \beta_0 + F_1(W_1) + F_2(W_2) + \cdots + F_R(W_R) + \epsilon, \tag{2.33}$$

where each F_r is a step function of the explanatory variable W_r, each W_r being represented by a set of dummy variables one less in number than the number of levels of the function. Suppose, e.g., that there are three groups in W_1 and two groups in W_2. Then we formulate the regression relationship as

$$y = \beta_0 x_0 + \beta_1 x_1 + \beta_2 x_2 + \beta_3 x_3 + \epsilon, \tag{2.34}$$

with the definition of the regressors deducible from the following tabulation of their typical observations:

(2.35)

Group					
W_1	W_2	x_0	x_1	x_2	x_3
A	A	1	0	0	0
A	B	1	0	0	1
B	A	1	1	0	0
B	B	1	1	0	1
C	A	1	0	1	0
C	B	1	0	1	1

We may then tabulate the group expected values as

(2.36)

		W_2: A	W_2: B
W_1	A	β_0	$\beta_0 + \beta_3$
	B	$\beta_0 + \beta_1$	$\beta_0 + \beta_1 + \beta_3$
	C	$\beta_0 + \beta_2$	$\beta_0 + \beta_2 + \beta_3$

It is seen that β_3 measures the differential effect of being in group B (relative to group A) of W_2, whereas β_1 and β_2 measure the differential effect of being in group B and C respectively (relative to group A) of W_1.

Although (2.33) is a quite free functional form, it is restrictive in that the effects of the separate explanatory variables are additive. Thus in our illustration the effect of W_1 is independent of the level of W_2 and vice versa. The dummy variable formulation can be extended to allow for nonadditivities in a manner parallel to the use of compound variables in the conventional curvilinear forms. To illustrate this, consider extending (2.34) to

$$y = \beta_0 x_0 + \beta_1 x_1 + \beta_2 x_2 + \beta_3 x_3 + \beta_4 x_4 + \epsilon, \tag{2.37}$$

where the new regressor x_4 distinguishes those in the "cell" (B, B):

$$x_4 = \begin{cases} 1 & \text{if both } W_1 = B \text{ and } W_2 = B \\ 0 & \text{otherwise.} \end{cases} \tag{2.38}$$

Now the tabulation of the group expected values is

(2.39)

		W_2: A	W_2: B
W_1	A	β_0	$\beta_0 + \beta_3$
	B	$\beta_0 + \beta_1$	$\beta_0 + \beta_1 + \beta_3 + \beta_4$
	C	$\beta_0 + \beta_2$	$\beta_0 + \beta_2 + \beta_3$

It is seen that now the effect of being in group B rather than group A of W_2 depends on the level of W_1. For those in group A of W_1 this differential effect is $(\beta_0 + \beta_3) - \beta_0 = \beta_3$; for those in group B of W_1 it is $(\beta_0 + \beta_1 + \beta_3 + \beta_4) - (\beta_0 + \beta_1) = \beta_3 + \beta_4$. Similarly it will be seen here that the effect of W_1 depends on the level of W_2. Note, incidentally, that x_4 could be defined as $x_1 x_3$.

Even this formulation is not fully general, because the differential effect of being in group B rather than group A of W_2 is the same for those in groups A and C of W_1; $(\beta_0 + \beta_2 + \beta_3) - (\beta_0 + \beta_2) = \beta_3$ also. We might consider extending once again to

$$y = \beta_0 x_0 + \beta_1 x_1 + \beta_2 x_2 + \beta_3 x_3 + \beta_4 x_4 + \beta_5 x_5 + \epsilon, \tag{2.40}$$

where the new regressor x_5 distinguishes those in the "cell" (C, B):

$$x_5 = \begin{cases} 1 & \text{if both } W_1 = C \text{ and } W_2 = B \\ 0 & \text{otherwise.} \end{cases} \tag{2.41}$$

Then the tabulation of the group expected values is

(2.42)

		W_2	
		A	B
W_1	A	β_0	$\beta_0 + \beta_3$
	B	$\beta_0 + \beta_1$	$\beta_0 + \beta_1 + \beta_3 + \beta_4$
	C	$\beta_0 + \beta_2$	$\beta_0 + \beta_2 + \beta_3 + \beta_5$

It is then seen that in all cases the effect of W_1 depends on the level of W_2 and vice versa. For example, the differential effect of being in group B rather than group A of W_2 is β_3 for those in group A of W_1, $\beta_3 + \beta_4$ for those in group B of W_1, and $\beta_3 + \beta_5$ for those in group C of W_1.

If we want this level of generality, however, there is no point in treating the full sample as a unit. If the effect of W_2 is completely different at the different levels of W_1, we might just as well estimate three separate relationships of y on W_2, one for those in group A of W_1, another for those in group B of W_1, and another for those in group C of W_1. In fact, least-squares estimation of (2.40) for the full sample will reduce to doing just that, as study of the normal equations will show. What this suggests is another way of introducing an explanatory variable, i.e., as a classification device. If the level of one explanatory variable W_r influences the effects of the other explanatory variables in an unspecified way, the sample should be broken into subsamples by classification on W_r.

Qualitative Regressors

By now it should be clear how qualitative "attribute" explanatory variables such as region, occupation, and sex may be handled within the classical linear regression framework. Suppose that we are interested in investigating the variation of personal income over the four regions of the United States; we may estimate the relation

$$y = \beta_0 x_0 + \beta_1 x_1 + \beta_2 x_2 + \beta_3 x_3 + \epsilon \tag{2.43}$$

with the definitions of the regressors deducible from the following tabulation of their typical observations:

(2.44)

Group	x_0	x_1	x_2	x_3
Northeast	1	1	0	0
Northwest	1	0	1	0
Southeast	1	0	0	1
Southwest	1	0	0	0

The slope coefficients will then represent the regional effects relative to the Southwest.

Several attributes can be included, each with its own set of dummy variables, and interaction terms may be introduced as well. It has long been common in econometrics to use dummy variables to represent dichotomous variables that are not directly observable. For example, to capture the impact of the war on consumption behavior the following consumption function has been fit to annual time series, 1929–1960:

$$C = \beta_0 + \beta_1 Y + \beta_2 W + \epsilon, \tag{2.45}$$

where $C =$ consumption, $Y =$ income, and $W = 1$ for 1941–1945, $= 0$ otherwise. This gives $E(C \mid \text{peace}) = \beta_0 + \beta_1 Y$ and $E(C \mid \text{war}) = \beta_0 + \beta_2 + \beta_1 Y$, so that the impact of the war is taken to be a parallel shift in the consumption function with no change in the marginal propensity to consume. Alternatively, to capture the hypothesis that the MPC changed while the intercept did not, we should fit

$$C = \gamma_0 + \gamma_1 Y + \gamma_2 Z + \epsilon, \tag{2.46}$$

where $Z = WY$, i.e., $Z = Y$ for 1941–1945 and $= 0$ otherwise. Suppose the specification was that the impact of the war was to change both the level and the slope of the consumption function. Then we might formulate this as

$$C = \delta_0 + \delta_1 W + \delta_2 Y + \delta_3 Z + \epsilon. \tag{2.47}$$

But this would be equivalent to breaking the sample into a peace sample and a war sample and estimating two separate regressions, as the following shows: The typical observations would be tabulated as

(2.48)

	1	W	Y	Z	C
War	1	1	Y_{iW}	Y_{iW}	C_{iW}
Peace	1	0	Y_{jP}	0	C_{jP}

with the first subscript denoting the year and the second the period. Accordingly, the normal equations $\mathbf{X'Xd} = \mathbf{X'y}$ would be

$$(2.49)\qquad \begin{pmatrix} T & T_W & \Sigma Y & \Sigma Y_W \\ T_W & T_W & \Sigma Y_W & \Sigma Y_W \\ \Sigma Y & \Sigma Y_W & \Sigma Y^2 & \Sigma Y_W^2 \\ \Sigma Y_W & \Sigma Y_W & \Sigma Y_W^2 & \Sigma Y_W^2 \end{pmatrix} \begin{pmatrix} d_0 \\ d_1 \\ d_2 \\ d_3 \end{pmatrix} = \begin{pmatrix} \Sigma C \\ \Sigma C_W \\ \Sigma CY \\ \Sigma C_W Y_W \end{pmatrix},$$

where T_W is the number of war observations and the summation runs over the period indicated by the subscript, if any. Now the second and fourth lines involve only the war observations; they may be written as

$$(2.50)\qquad \begin{pmatrix} T_W & \Sigma Y_W \\ \Sigma Y_W & \Sigma Y_W^2 \end{pmatrix} \begin{pmatrix} f_0 \\ f_1 \end{pmatrix} = \begin{pmatrix} \Sigma C_W \\ \Sigma C_W Y_W \end{pmatrix}$$

(where $f_0 = d_0 + d_1$ and $f_1 = d_2 + d_3$), which is just the set of normal equations for least-squares regression for the war years. In addition, if we subtract the second line from the first and the fourth from the third we are left with the normal equations for least-squares regression for the peace years:

$$(2.51)\qquad \begin{pmatrix} T_P & \Sigma Y_P \\ \Sigma Y_P & \Sigma Y_P^2 \end{pmatrix} \begin{pmatrix} g_0 \\ g_1 \end{pmatrix} = \begin{pmatrix} \Sigma C_P \\ \Sigma C_P Y_P \end{pmatrix}$$

(where $g_0 = d_0$ and $g_1 = d_2$, using $T_P = T - T_W$, $\Sigma\, Y_P = \Sigma\, Y - \Sigma\, Y_W$, and $\Sigma\, Y_P^2 = \Sigma\, Y^2 - \Sigma\, Y_W^2$. Note that we can obtain d_0 as g_0, d_1 as $f_0 - g_0$, d_2 as g_1, and d_3 as $f_1 - g_1$. Thus, once again, where the level of an explanatory variable influences all the effects of the other explanatory variables in an unspecified way, the sample can be broken into subsamples.

We may conclude this discussion of functional forms by presenting, as an illustration, a relation for cost of house purchased drawn from a study by Tong Hun Lee (1963):

$$(2.52)\qquad \begin{aligned} y = 3715 &+ \underset{(0.65)}{2.10x_1} - \underset{(0.000022)}{0.000046x_2} - \underset{(487)}{142x_3} + \underset{(5.7)}{4.5x_4} \\ &- \underset{(3994)}{3487x_5} - \underset{(4831)}{496x_6} + \underset{(3118)}{4119x_7} + \underset{(2948)}{556x_8} - \underset{(4740)}{953x_9} \\ &+ \underset{(2147)}{1116x_{10}} + \underset{(2881)}{463x_{11}} + \underset{(4507)}{928x_{12}} - \underset{(5733)}{830x_{13}} - \underset{(2497)}{728x_{14}} \\ &- \underset{(2434)}{2668x_{15}} - \underset{(2711)}{4798x_{16}} - \underset{(2619)}{2703x_{17}} - \underset{(2185)}{4345x_{18}} - \underset{(1972)}{37x_{19}} \end{aligned}$$

where y = cost of house purchased in dollars;
x_1 = income in dollars;
$x_2 = x_1^2$
x_3 = age in years,
$x_4 = x_3^2$
x_5 = 1 if unmarried, 0 otherwise;
x_6 = 1 if married less than 1 year, 0 otherwise ($x_5 = x_6 = 0$ if married more than 1 year);
x_7 = 1 if manager, 0 otherwise;
x_8 = 1 if clerk, 0 otherwise;
x_9 = 1 if laborer, 0 otherwise ($x_7 = x_8 = x_9 = 0$ if unemployed or retired);
x_{10} = 1 if has high-school degree, 0 otherwise;
x_{11} = 1 if has college degree, 0 otherwise ($x_{10} = x_{11} = 0$ if education stopped before high-school degree);
x_{12} = 1 if white, 0 if nonwhite;
x_{13} = 1 if female, 0 if male;
x_{14} = 1 if in northcentral states, 0 otherwise;
x_{15} = 1 if in southern states, 0 otherwise;
x_{16} = 1 if in western states, 0 otherwise ($x_{14} = x_{15} = x_{16} = 0$ if in northeastern states);
x_{17} = 1 if no income change over previous year, 0 otherwise;
x_{18} = 1 if income increase over previous year, 0 otherwise ($x_{17} = x_{18} = 0$ if income decrease over previous year);
x_{19} = 1 if owned house at beginning of year, 0 if not.

The sample consisted of 117 households who bought houses in 1957, and the demographic characteristics refer to the head of the household. Note how both conventional curvilinear forms and dummy variable formulations are used, and note that an explanatory variable with three categories is represented by two dummy variables, etc. Also note that when a dummy variable formulation is used the coefficients represent differential effects relative to the "basis" category. Thus, e.g., the expected value of the house cost is \$3487 lower for an unmarried household than for those married more than 1 year, if all other variables are identical. Finally note that if we want to test the hypothesis that, e.g., marital status does not influence the house cost, we should test the *joint* hypothesis that $\beta_5 = \beta_6 = 0$.

3. ANALYSIS OF VARIANCE

"Analysis of variance" is a very rich classical procedure for testing the "relevance," i.e., significance, of a classification. Our discussion here serves as the very barest introduction and is included to indicate the connection with dummy variable regression. For a comprehensive discussion see Scheffé (1959).

Suppose that we have a set of T observations on a variable y, and that these observations are classified on some criterion into $1 + K$ groups. The observations are y_{tk} with $k = 0, 1, \ldots, K$ and t running to T_k in the kth group; note that $T = \Sigma_{k=0}^{K} T_k$. Let us denote the sum of the

y's in the kth group as $y_{.k}$ and the mean of the y's in the kth group as

$$\bar{y}_{.k} = \frac{y_{.k}}{T_k}. \tag{3.1}$$

Further let us denote the sum of the y's over all groups as $y_{..}$ and the corresponding overall mean of the y's as

$$\bar{y}_{..} = \frac{y_{..}}{T} = \frac{\sum_k T_k \bar{y}_{.k}}{T}. \tag{3.2}$$

Now consider the sum of squared deviations of the y's in the kth group about the overall mean: $\Sigma_t(y_{tk} - \bar{y}_{..})^2$. It maybe decomposed ("analyzed") into

$$\begin{aligned} \sum_t (y_{tk} - \bar{y}_{..})^2 &= \sum_t [(y_{tk} - \bar{y}_{.k}) + (\bar{y}_{.k} - \bar{y}_{..})]^2 \\ &= \sum_t (y_{tk} - \bar{y}_{.k})^2 + T_k(\bar{y}_{.k} - \bar{y}_{..})^2 \\ &\quad + 2(\bar{y}_{.k} - \bar{y}_{..}) \sum_t (y_{tk} - \bar{y}_{.k}) \\ &= \sum_t (y_{tk} - \bar{y}_{.k})^2 + T_k(\bar{y}_{.k} - \bar{y}_{..})^2, \end{aligned} \tag{3.3}$$

since $\Sigma_t(y_{tk} - \bar{y}_{.k}) = 0$. Then summing over all the groups we find

$$\sum_k \sum_t (y_{tk} - \bar{y}_{..})^2 = \sum_k \sum_t (y_{tk} - \bar{y}_{.k})^2 + \sum_k T_k(\bar{y}_{.k} - \bar{y}_{..})^2. \tag{3.4}$$

Thus the total variation of the y's (sum of squared deviations about the overall mean) is decomposed into the within-group variation (sum of squared deviations about the respective group means) plus the between-group variation (weighted sum of squared deviations of the group means about the overall mean).

Intuitively the classification is relevant if the group means differ substantially from one another (and hence from the overall mean); i.e., if the conditional mean of y varies across the groups. A standard of comparison is provided by the variation of the y's about their group means. This suggests that a test of the null hypothesis that the classification is irrelevant might be based on the following ratio of mean squared deviations:

$$F = \frac{\sum_k T_k(\bar{y}_{.k} - \bar{y}_{..})^2/K}{\sum_t \sum_k (y_{tk} - \bar{y}_{.k})^2/(T - K - 1)}. \tag{3.5}$$

When this ratio is large the classification would seem to be relevant, in the sense that the group means differ substantially from one another as compared with the variation of the observations within these groups.

To develop an actual test procedure, we require a formal model. Suppose that the y's are generated by the following scheme:

(3.6) $$y_{tk} = \mu + \alpha_k + \epsilon_{tk},$$

with $\Sigma_k \alpha_k = 0$, where the disturbance is spherical normal:

(3.7) $$\epsilon_{tk} \text{ is } \mathcal{N}(0, \sigma^2) \text{ and } E\epsilon_{tk}\epsilon_{t'k'} = 0 \text{ for all } t, k, t', k', t \neq t'.$$

This gives the conditional expectation of y in group k as $\mu + \alpha_k$, so that the hypothesis that the classification is irrelevant may be formulated as

(3.8) $$\alpha_0 = \cdots = \alpha_K = 0.$$

Now on this null hypothesis we have $y_{tk} = \mu + \epsilon_{tk}$, whence with obvious notation $\bar{y}_{.k} = \mu + \bar{\epsilon}_{.k}$ and $\bar{y}_{..} = \mu + \bar{\epsilon}_{..}$. This gives $(\bar{y}_{.k} - \bar{y}_{..}) = (\bar{\epsilon}_{.k} - \bar{\epsilon}_{..})$ and $(y_{tk} - \bar{y}_{.k}) = (\epsilon_{tk} - \bar{\epsilon}_{.k})$. Then by application of our results on quadratic forms in spherically normal variables it is easy to show that the ratio of (3.5) has the F^K_{T-K-1} distribution on the null hypothesis, thus providing a test.

The connection with the dummy variable regression formulation should be clear. We might have formulated the present model as

(3.9) $$y = \beta_0 x_0 + \beta_1 x_1 + \cdots + \beta_K x_K + \epsilon,$$

where $x_0 = 1$ for all observations, where

(3.10) $$x_k = \begin{cases} 1 & \text{for those in group } k \\ 0 & \text{otherwise,} \end{cases} \qquad (k = 1, \ldots, K)$$

and where the disturbance satisfies the classical normal assumptions. In the regression framework, the hypothesis that (the expected value of) y does not vary with the x's—i.e., that the classification is irrelevant—would be formulated as $\beta_1 = \cdots = \beta_K = 0$. In accordance with (4.7.24) the appropriate test procedure is based on the F^K_{T-K-1} distribution of

(3.11) $$\frac{SSR/K}{SSE/(T - K - 1)}.$$

But from (2.32) we can see that the sum of squares in the numerator of (3.5) is just SSR, and that the sum of squares in the denominator of (3.5) (being the difference between the total sum of squares and the regression sum of squares) is just SSE. Thus we see that the classical analysis of variance can be carried out within the framework of linear regression.

The analysis of variance extends to cross-classifications. Suppose that our observations on y are cross-classified by two criteria; that there are J categories on the first criterion ("rows") and K categories on the second criterion ("columns"). Further suppose that there are S observations in each of the JK cells, and that the y's in cell (j, k) are generated by the following scheme:

$$y_{tjk} = \mu + \alpha_j + \beta_k + \gamma_{jk} + \epsilon_{tjk} \tag{3.12}$$

with $\Sigma_j \alpha_j = \Sigma_k \beta_k = \Sigma_j \gamma_{jk} = \Sigma_k \gamma_{jk} = 0$, where the disturbances are spherical normal. By an extension of the manipulation of (3.3) and (3.4) the total sum of squared deviations of the y's about their overall mean may be decomposed as in the following table,

(3.13)

Source	Sum of Squares
Row	$SK\sum_j (\bar{y}_{.j.} - \bar{y}_{...})^2$
Column	$SJ\sum_k (\bar{y}_{..k} - \bar{y}_{..})^2$
Interaction	$S\sum_j\sum_k (\bar{y}_{.jk} - \bar{y}_{.j.} - \bar{y}_{..k} + \bar{y}_{...})^2$
Error	$\sum_t\sum_j\sum_k (y_{tjk} - \bar{y}_{.jk})^2$
Total	$\sum_t\sum_j\sum_k (y_{tjk} - \bar{y}_{...})^2$

where $\bar{y}_{.jk}$ is the mean in the (j, k) cell, $\bar{y}_{.j.}$ is the mean in the jth "row," $\bar{y}_{..k}$ is the mean in the kth "column," and $\bar{y}_{...}$ is the mean over all.

Intuitively, when the first criterion is relevant, the row means will differ substantially so that the row sum of squares will be large; when the second criterion is relevant, the column means will differ substantially so that the column sum of squares will be large. The interaction sum of squares will be large when the cell means differ substantially from what they would be if the row and column effects were simply additive. In all cases a standard of comparison is provided by the error sum of squares—the sum of squared deviations of the observations about their respective cell means. This suggests that hypothesis tests may be based on the ratio of the row, column, or interaction sum of squares to the error sum of squares. This is indeed the case, as may be shown by direct application of the theory of quadratic forms in spherical normal variables. Alternatively, a dummy variable regression formulation leads to the same tests.

The connection between analysis of variance and regression should now be clear; from the point of view of hypothesis testing they are equivalent. If we are interested only in testing whether an explanatory variable is relevant for (the expected value of) y, and in what form it is relevant, the analysis of variance approach often provides a computationally efficient way of getting to the test statistic without matrix inversion. For multiple cross-classifications with unequal numbers of observations in the cells, however, the regression formulation is in order, since a simple partitioning of the sum of squares is no longer possible. In either event, the regression approach is in order if we are interested in estimating the parameters of the relation between the explanatory variable and (the expected value of) y.

Finally we mention the analysis of covariance model, exemplified by

$$y_{tk} = \mu + \alpha_k + \beta x_{tk} + \epsilon_{tk}, \tag{3.14}$$

where x_{tk} is a nonstochastic variable. This corresponds to a linear regression model of y on x in which the constant term varies with a qualitative variable—see our discussion of war and peace consumption functions in Section 2.

4. NONSPHERICAL DISTURBANCES

Assumption (4.3.3) of the classical linear regression model requires that

$$E\boldsymbol{\epsilon\epsilon}' = \sigma^2\mathbf{I}, \tag{4.1}$$

i.e., that both

$$E\epsilon_t^2 = \sigma^2 \quad \text{for} \quad \text{all } t, \tag{4.2}$$

and

$$E\epsilon_s\epsilon_t = 0 \quad \text{for} \quad \text{all } s \neq t. \tag{4.3}$$

If (4.2) does not hold, the disturbances are said to be heteroskedastic; if (4.3) does not hold, the disturbances are said to be interdependent. Failure to satisfy (4.1) on either count may be described as nonsphericalness. Both heteroskedasticity and interdependence of disturbances are common in economic behavior. For example, high-income families show much greater variability in their savings behavior than do low-income families, so that the assumption of common disturbance variance would be inappropriate for a cross-section savings-income relationship. For another example, in time series analysis a disturbance is likely to persist over several periods so that the assumption of independently drawn disturbances may be inappropriate. Thus it is in order to develop a less restrictive statistical framework.

Generalized Linear Regression Model

If we replace the $\mathbf{I}$ matrix of (4.1) by $\boldsymbol{\Omega}$, a $T \times T$ positive definite matrix, then we allow for both heteroskedasticity (differing diagonal elements of

$\mathbf{\Omega}$) and interdependence (nonzero off-diagonal elements of $\mathbf{\Omega}$). Let us then consider the following model:

Generalized linear regression model

$$\mathbf{y} = \mathbf{X}\boldsymbol{\beta} + \boldsymbol{\epsilon}, \tag{4.4}$$

$$E\boldsymbol{\epsilon} = \mathbf{0}, \tag{4.5}$$

$$E\boldsymbol{\epsilon}\boldsymbol{\epsilon}' = \sigma^2\mathbf{\Omega} \text{ where } \mathbf{\Omega} \text{ is positive definite}, \tag{4.6}$$

$$\mathbf{X} \text{ is a } T \times (1 + K) \text{ matrix which is fixed in repeated samples}, \tag{4.7}$$

$$\text{Rank of } \mathbf{X} = 1 + K \leq T. \tag{4.8}$$

Since σ^2 plays the role of a scale factor we may assume that $\mathbf{\Omega}$ is "normalized" so that its diagonal elements sum to T, with no loss of generality.

In this model the best linear unbiased estimator of $\boldsymbol{\beta}$ may be readily derived. Let $\hat{\boldsymbol{\beta}} = \mathbf{C}'\mathbf{y}$ be a linear estimator of $\boldsymbol{\beta}$. Then $\hat{\boldsymbol{\beta}} = \mathbf{C}'\mathbf{X}\boldsymbol{\beta} + \mathbf{C}'\boldsymbol{\epsilon}$, so that $E\hat{\boldsymbol{\beta}} = \mathbf{C}'\mathbf{X}\boldsymbol{\beta}$, whence unbiasedness, whatever $\boldsymbol{\beta}$ may be, requires

$$\mathbf{C}'\mathbf{X} = \mathbf{I}. \tag{4.9}$$

If $\hat{\boldsymbol{\beta}}$ is unbiased, its sampling error is

$$\hat{\boldsymbol{\beta}} - \boldsymbol{\beta} = \boldsymbol{\beta} + \mathbf{C}'\boldsymbol{\epsilon} - \boldsymbol{\beta} = \mathbf{C}'\boldsymbol{\epsilon}, \tag{4.10}$$

whence its covariance matrix is

$$\mathbf{\Sigma}_{\hat{\beta}\hat{\beta}} = E(\hat{\boldsymbol{\beta}} - \boldsymbol{\beta})(\hat{\boldsymbol{\beta}} - \boldsymbol{\beta})' = E\mathbf{C}'\boldsymbol{\epsilon}\boldsymbol{\epsilon}'\mathbf{C} = \sigma^2\mathbf{C}'\mathbf{\Omega}\mathbf{C}. \tag{4.11}$$

Now consider the estimator

$$\tilde{\mathbf{b}} = (\mathbf{X}'\mathbf{\Omega}^{-1}\mathbf{X})^{-1}\mathbf{X}'\mathbf{\Omega}^{-1}\mathbf{y}, \tag{4.12}$$

the nonsingularity of $\mathbf{X}'\mathbf{\Omega}^{-1}\mathbf{X}$ being assured by (4.6), (4.8), and (2.7.4). It is in fact a linear estimator, $\tilde{\mathbf{b}} = \tilde{\mathbf{C}}'\mathbf{y}$ with

$$\tilde{\mathbf{C}}' = (\mathbf{X}'\mathbf{\Omega}^{-1}\mathbf{X})^{-1}\mathbf{X}'\mathbf{\Omega}^{-1}; \tag{4.13}$$

it is unbiased since

$$\tilde{\mathbf{C}}'\mathbf{X} = (\mathbf{X}'\mathbf{\Omega}^{-1}\mathbf{X})^{-1}\mathbf{X}'\mathbf{\Omega}^{-1}\mathbf{X} = \mathbf{I}; \tag{4.14}$$

and its covariance matrix is given by

$$\begin{aligned}\mathbf{\Sigma}_{\tilde{b}\tilde{b}} &= \sigma^2\tilde{\mathbf{C}}'\mathbf{\Omega}\tilde{\mathbf{C}} = \sigma^2(\mathbf{X}'\mathbf{\Omega}^{-1}\mathbf{X})^{-1}\mathbf{X}'\mathbf{\Omega}^{-1}\cdot\mathbf{\Omega}\cdot\mathbf{\Omega}^{-1}\mathbf{X}(\mathbf{X}'\mathbf{\Omega}^{-1}\mathbf{X})^{-1}\\ &= \sigma^2(\mathbf{X}'\mathbf{\Omega}^{-1}\mathbf{X})^{-1}.\end{aligned} \tag{4.15}$$

Without loss of generality we may express the $\mathbf{C}'$ of any linear estimator as

$$\mathbf{C}' = \tilde{\mathbf{C}}' + \mathbf{D}', \tag{4.16}$$

where $\mathbf{D}'$ like $\tilde{\mathbf{C}}'$ is a $(1 + K) \times T$ nonstochastic matrix. The unbiasedness condition is then $\mathbf{D}'\mathbf{X} = \mathbf{0}$, so that the covariance matrix is

$$(4.17) \qquad \begin{aligned} \mathbf{\Sigma}_{\hat{\boldsymbol{\beta}}\hat{\boldsymbol{\beta}}} &= \sigma^2[(\tilde{\mathbf{C}}' + \mathbf{D}')\mathbf{\Omega}(\tilde{\mathbf{C}} + \mathbf{D})] \\ &= \sigma^2[\tilde{\mathbf{C}}'\mathbf{\Omega}\tilde{\mathbf{C}} + \mathbf{D}'\mathbf{\Omega}\mathbf{D} + \tilde{\mathbf{C}}'\mathbf{\Omega}\mathbf{D} + \mathbf{D}'\mathbf{\Omega}\tilde{\mathbf{C}}] \\ &= \sigma^2[\tilde{\mathbf{C}}'\mathbf{\Omega}\tilde{\mathbf{C}} + \mathbf{D}'\mathbf{\Omega}\mathbf{D}] \\ &= \sigma^2[(\mathbf{X}'\mathbf{\Omega}^{-1}\mathbf{X})^{-1} + \mathbf{D}'\mathbf{\Omega}\mathbf{D}] = \mathbf{\Sigma}_{\tilde{\mathbf{b}}\tilde{\mathbf{b}}} + \sigma^2\mathbf{D}'\mathbf{\Omega}\mathbf{D} \end{aligned}$$

since $\tilde{\mathbf{C}}'\mathbf{\Omega}\mathbf{D} = (\mathbf{X}'\mathbf{\Omega}^{-1}\mathbf{X})^{-1}\mathbf{X}'\mathbf{\Omega}^{-1} \cdot \mathbf{\Omega}\mathbf{D} = (\mathbf{X}'\mathbf{\Omega}^{-1}\mathbf{X})^{-1}\mathbf{X}'\mathbf{D} = \mathbf{0}$ in view of unbiasedness and similarly $\mathbf{D}'\mathbf{\Omega}\tilde{\mathbf{C}} = \mathbf{0}$. Since, in view of (2.7.14), $\mathbf{D}'\mathbf{\Omega}\mathbf{D}$ is nonnegative definite we see that $\tilde{\mathbf{b}}$ is the BLUE of $\boldsymbol{\beta}$ in our model.

Note that $\tilde{\mathbf{b}}$ is a kind of least-squares estimator; consider the "generalized sum of squared deviations," i.e., the quadratic form

$$(4.18) \qquad \begin{aligned} S &= \mathbf{e}'\mathbf{\Omega}^{-1}\mathbf{e} = (\mathbf{y} - \mathbf{X}\boldsymbol{\beta})'\mathbf{\Omega}^{-1}(\mathbf{y} - \mathbf{X}\boldsymbol{\beta}) \\ &= \mathbf{y}'\mathbf{\Omega}^{-1}\mathbf{y} + \boldsymbol{\beta}'\mathbf{X}'\mathbf{\Omega}^{-1}\mathbf{X}\boldsymbol{\beta} - 2\boldsymbol{\beta}'\mathbf{X}'\mathbf{\Omega}^{-1}\mathbf{y}. \end{aligned}$$

Differentiating with respect to $\boldsymbol{\beta}$ gives

$$(4.19) \qquad \partial S/\partial\boldsymbol{\beta} = 2\mathbf{X}'\mathbf{\Omega}^{-1}\mathbf{X}\boldsymbol{\beta} - 2\mathbf{X}'\mathbf{\Omega}^{-1}\mathbf{y},$$

which set equal to $\mathbf{0}$ gives the normal equations

$$(4.20) \qquad \mathbf{X}'\mathbf{\Omega}^{-1}\mathbf{X}\hat{\boldsymbol{\beta}} = \mathbf{X}'\mathbf{\Omega}^{-1}\mathbf{y}$$

with solution

$$(4.21) \qquad \hat{\boldsymbol{\beta}} = (\mathbf{X}'\mathbf{\Omega}^{-1}\mathbf{X})^{-1}\mathbf{X}'\mathbf{\Omega}^{-1}\mathbf{y} = \tilde{\mathbf{b}}.$$

This then establishes Aitken's generalization of the Gauss-Markov theorem.

(4.22) ***Aitken's generalized Gauss-Markov least-squares theorem.*** In the generalized linear regression model the BLUE of $\boldsymbol{\beta}$ is the generalized least-squares vector

$$(4.22a) \qquad \tilde{\mathbf{b}} = (\mathbf{X}'\mathbf{\Omega}^{-1}\mathbf{X})^{-1}(\mathbf{X}'\mathbf{\Omega}^{-1}\mathbf{y})$$

whose covariance matrix is

$$(4.22b) \qquad \mathbf{\Sigma}_{\tilde{\mathbf{b}}\tilde{\mathbf{b}}} = \sigma^2(\mathbf{X}'\mathbf{\Omega}^{-1}\mathbf{X})^{-1}.$$

Further, an unbiased estimator of σ^2 is obtainable by an argument parallel to that used in the classical case. Thus where $\tilde{\mathbf{y}} = \mathbf{X}\tilde{\mathbf{b}}$,

$$(4.23) \qquad \begin{aligned} \tilde{\boldsymbol{\epsilon}} &= \mathbf{y} - \tilde{\mathbf{y}} = \mathbf{X}\boldsymbol{\beta} + \boldsymbol{\epsilon} - \mathbf{X}\tilde{\mathbf{b}} \\ &= \mathbf{X}\boldsymbol{\beta} + \boldsymbol{\epsilon} - \mathbf{X}[\boldsymbol{\beta} + (\mathbf{X}'\mathbf{\Omega}^{-1}\mathbf{X})^{-1}\mathbf{X}'\mathbf{\Omega}^{-1}\boldsymbol{\epsilon}] \\ &= \boldsymbol{\epsilon} - \mathbf{X}(\mathbf{X}'\mathbf{\Omega}^{-1}\mathbf{X})^{-1}\mathbf{X}'\mathbf{\Omega}^{-1}\boldsymbol{\epsilon} \\ &= [\mathbf{I} - \mathbf{X}(\mathbf{X}'\mathbf{\Omega}^{-1}\mathbf{X})^{-1}\mathbf{X}'\mathbf{\Omega}^{-1}]\boldsymbol{\epsilon} \\ &= \mathbf{M}\boldsymbol{\epsilon}, \end{aligned}$$

say, where

$$\text{(4.24)} \qquad \mathbf{M} = \mathbf{I} - \mathbf{X}(\mathbf{X}'\mathbf{\Omega}^{-1}\mathbf{X})^{-1}\mathbf{X}'\mathbf{\Omega}^{-1}.$$

Direct computation shows that $\mathbf{M}'\mathbf{\Omega}^{-1}\mathbf{M} = \mathbf{\Omega}^{-1}\mathbf{M}$ and that $tr(\mathbf{M}) = tr(\mathbf{I}_T) - tr(\mathbf{I}_{1+K}) = T - (1 + K)$. Then it follows that

$$\tilde{\boldsymbol{\epsilon}}'\mathbf{\Omega}^{-1}\tilde{\boldsymbol{\epsilon}} = \boldsymbol{\epsilon}'\mathbf{M}'\mathbf{\Omega}^{-1}\mathbf{M}\boldsymbol{\epsilon} = \boldsymbol{\epsilon}'\mathbf{\Omega}^{-1}\mathbf{M}\boldsymbol{\epsilon}$$

so that

$$\begin{aligned}\text{(4.25)} \qquad E(\tilde{\boldsymbol{\epsilon}}'\mathbf{\Omega}^{-1}\tilde{\boldsymbol{\epsilon}}) &= E(\boldsymbol{\epsilon}'\mathbf{\Omega}^{-1}\mathbf{M}\boldsymbol{\epsilon}) = E\, tr(\boldsymbol{\epsilon}'\mathbf{\Omega}^{-1}\mathbf{M}\boldsymbol{\epsilon}) \\ &= E\, tr(\mathbf{M}\boldsymbol{\epsilon}\boldsymbol{\epsilon}'\mathbf{\Omega}^{-1}) = tr\, E(\mathbf{M}\boldsymbol{\epsilon}\boldsymbol{\epsilon}'\mathbf{\Omega}^{-1}) \\ &= \sigma^2\, tr(\mathbf{M}) \\ &= \sigma^2(T - K - 1).\end{aligned}$$

Thus an unbiased estimator of σ^2 is

$$\text{(4.26)} \qquad \tilde{s}^2 = \frac{\tilde{\boldsymbol{\epsilon}}'\mathbf{\Omega}^{-1}\tilde{\boldsymbol{\epsilon}}}{T - K - 1},$$

and an unbiased estimator of $\mathbf{\Sigma}_{\tilde{\mathbf{b}}\tilde{\mathbf{b}}}$ is

$$\text{(4.27)} \qquad \mathbf{S}_{\tilde{\mathbf{b}}\tilde{\mathbf{b}}} = \tilde{s}^2(\mathbf{X}'\mathbf{\Omega}^{-1}\mathbf{X})^{-1}.$$

Proceeding in similar fashion we may establish further results for the generalized linear regression model corresponding to those established for the classical linear regression model—including the distributions, test procedures, and maximum likelihood properties for the case of normally distributed disturbances. We do not pursue this but do note a useful result. Consider the nonsingular matrix $\mathbf{P}$ such that $\mathbf{P}\mathbf{\Omega}\mathbf{P}' = \mathbf{I}$ and $\mathbf{P}'\mathbf{P} = \mathbf{\Omega}^{-1}$; since $\mathbf{\Omega}$ is positive definite there will be such a matrix by (2.7.11). If we premultiply through the original relation (4.4) by $\mathbf{P}$ we obtain

$$\text{(4.28)} \qquad \mathbf{y}^* = \mathbf{X}^*\boldsymbol{\beta} + \boldsymbol{\epsilon}^*,$$

where $\mathbf{y}^* = \mathbf{P}\mathbf{y}$, $\mathbf{X}^* = \mathbf{P}\mathbf{X}$, and $\boldsymbol{\epsilon}^* = \mathbf{P}\boldsymbol{\epsilon}$. Then we have

$$\text{(4.29)} \qquad E\boldsymbol{\epsilon}^*\boldsymbol{\epsilon}^{*\prime} = E\mathbf{P}\boldsymbol{\epsilon}\boldsymbol{\epsilon}'\mathbf{P}' = \sigma^2\mathbf{P}\mathbf{\Omega}\mathbf{P}' = \sigma^2\mathbf{I},$$

so that the classical model will be appropriate for (4.28). That is, the BLUE of $\boldsymbol{\beta}$ will be

$$(\mathbf{X}^{*\prime}\mathbf{X}^*)^{-1}\mathbf{X}^{*\prime}\mathbf{y}^* = (\mathbf{X}'\mathbf{P}'\mathbf{P}\mathbf{X})^{-1}\mathbf{X}'\mathbf{P}'\mathbf{P}\mathbf{y} = (\mathbf{X}'\mathbf{\Omega}^{-1}\mathbf{X})^{-1}\mathbf{X}'\mathbf{\Omega}^{-1}\mathbf{y} = \tilde{\mathbf{b}}.$$

Thus the generalized least-squares estimator may be interpreted as the classical least-squares estimator in a transformed problem, and its properties deduced therefrom.

Although we have solved in principle the problem of estimation in the generalized linear regression model, an obvious practical difficulty remains; to compute $\tilde{\mathbf{b}}$ (and $\tilde{s}^2$) we must know $\mathbf{\Omega}$. That is, knowledge of the variances and covariances of the disturbances up to a factor of proportionality is required if the BLUE of $\boldsymbol{\beta}$ is to be obtained. We might think of taking the classical regression and using the residuals to estimate $\mathbf{\Omega}$; i.e., using $\hat{\epsilon}_s\hat{\epsilon}_t$ as an estimate of $E\epsilon_s\epsilon_t$, and employing these estimates in place of $\mathbf{\Omega}$ in the formula for $\tilde{\mathbf{b}}$. This, however, will not work in general since $\hat{\boldsymbol{\epsilon}}\hat{\boldsymbol{\epsilon}}'$, being the product of a $T \times 1$ matrix with a $1 \times T$ matrix, will have rank 1 and will hence be singular. Nevertheless, the pattern of residuals from the classical regression can be suggestive as to the nature of the nonsphericalness of the disturbances. In the sequel we show how certain restrictions on $\mathbf{\Omega}$ suffice to permit its estimation from the classical regression.

So much in the way of general discussion of the generalized linear regression model; we now turn to more specific aspects.

Heteroskedastic Disturbances

If only heteroskedasticity is present, (4.2) is replaced by

$$E\epsilon_t^2 = \sigma^2 k_t, \tag{4.30}$$

say, while (4.3) remains valid. Thus $\mathbf{\Omega}$ is a diagonal matrix with the k_t's on the diagonal, so that

$$\mathbf{\Omega}^{-1} = \begin{pmatrix} 1/k_1 & 0 & \cdots & 0 \\ \cdot & & & \cdot \\ \cdot & & & \cdot \\ \cdot & & & \cdot \\ 0 & 0 & \cdots & 1/k_T \end{pmatrix}. \tag{4.31}$$

It follows that where the k's are known the generalized least-squares estimator $\tilde{\mathbf{b}}$ may be computed by dividing the tth observation on all variables by $\sqrt{k_t}$ and then computing the classical least-squares estimator on the transformed observations. In addition, the quadratic form that is minimized is simply the weighted sum of squares $\mathbf{e}'\mathbf{\Omega}^{-1}\mathbf{e} = \Sigma(e_t^2/k_t)$; heuristically, we discount disturbances whose variances are large.

Thus, when heteroskedasticity is present statisical considerations suggest transformation of the variables to obtain a relation with homoskedasticity. In the previously cited savings-income relationship

$$y_t = \alpha + \beta x_t + \epsilon_t, \tag{4.32}$$

where y = savings and x = income, it often appears that the disturbance variance is proportional to the square of income: $E\epsilon_t^2 = \sigma^2 x_t^2$, where σ^2

is the factor of proportionality. Then if we divide through by x_t, we obtain

$$(4.33) \qquad \left(\frac{y}{x}\right)_t = \alpha \frac{1}{x_t} + \beta + \left(\frac{\epsilon}{x}\right)_t,$$

in which the disturbance *is* homoskedastic, $E(\epsilon/x)_t^2 = E\epsilon_t^2/x_t^2 = \sigma^2$. Classical least squares is then applicable to the transformed relation.

Interdependent Disturbances

There are of course many ways in which the successive disturbances can be interdependent. Where the sample consists of economic time series a natural specification is that the disturbances $\epsilon_1, \ldots, \epsilon_T$ constitute a sample from a stationary stochastic process. Thus although each ϵ_t is identically distributed they are not mutually independent, and the autocovariances $E\epsilon_s\epsilon_t$ do not vanish for $s \neq t$. Indeed, it may well be appropriate to specify that the disturbances are generated by a first-order autoregressive process of the kind discussed in Section 3.8. Investigations have shown that this is a plausible description of many economic time series, which suggests that it is an appropriate specification for the disturbances, which after all, are generally taken to represent the effect of omitted unobserved variables.

We proceed to investigate the implications of this important type of interdependence. Suppose then that (4.3) is droppped and replaced by

$$(4.34) \qquad \epsilon_t = \rho\epsilon_{t-1} + u_t,$$

where the u_t ($t = \ldots, -2, -1, 0, 1, 2, \ldots$) are independent, identically distributed random variables with $Eu_t = 0$, $Eu_t^2 = \sigma_u^2$, and $|\rho| < 1$. Then as was shown in (3.8.20)–(3.8.26) the ϵ_t's constitute a sample from a stationary stochastic process with

$$(4.35) \qquad E\epsilon_t = 0, \qquad E\epsilon_t^2 = \sigma^2, \qquad E\epsilon_t\epsilon_s = \sigma^2\rho^{|t-s|},$$

where $\sigma^2 = \sigma_u^2(1 - \rho^2)^{-1}$ so that as in (3.8.27) the disturbance expectation vector and covariance matrix are

$$(4.36) \qquad E\boldsymbol{\epsilon} = \mathbf{0}, \quad E\boldsymbol{\epsilon\epsilon}' = \sigma^2\boldsymbol{\Omega} = \sigma^2 \begin{pmatrix} 1 & \rho & \rho^2 & \cdots & \rho^{T-1} \\ \rho & 1 & \rho & \cdots & \rho^{T-2} \\ \cdot & \cdot & \cdot & & \cdot \\ \cdot & \cdot & \cdot & & \cdot \\ \cdot & \cdot & \cdot & & \cdot \\ \rho^{T-1} & \rho^{T-2} & \rho^{T-3} & \cdots & 1 \end{pmatrix}.$$

It is readily confirmed that

$$\Omega^{-1} = (1-\rho^2)^{-1} \begin{pmatrix} 1 & -\rho & 0 & \cdots & 0 & 0 \\ -\rho & (1+\rho^2) & -\rho & \cdots & 0 & 0 \\ 0 & -\rho & (1+\rho^2) & \cdots & 0 & 0 \\ \cdot & \cdot & \cdot & & \cdot & \cdot \\ \cdot & \cdot & \cdot & & \cdot & \cdot \\ \cdot & \cdot & \cdot & & \cdot & \cdot \\ 0 & 0 & 0 & \cdots & (1+\rho^2) & -\rho \\ 0 & 0 & 0 & \cdots & -\rho & 1 \end{pmatrix} \tag{4.37}$$

Thus when the interdependence of the disturbance is accounted for by the first-order autoregressive specification (4.34), knowledge of the single parameter ρ suffices to enable us to obtain the BLUE $\tilde{\mathbf{b}}$. It may be recalled that in obtaining (4.36) the only properties of the u_t's that have been used are $Eu_t = 0$, $Eu_t^2 = \sigma_u^2$, and $Eu_s u_t = 0$ for $s \neq t$.

For computations in the present case the following procedure has been suggested. Transform the original variables, letting $y_t^* = y_t - \rho y_{t-1}$, $x_{t1}^* = x_{t1} - \rho x_{t-1,1}$, etc., and take the classical least-square regression in the transformed variables. Note that there will be only $T - 1$ observations. The idea of this procedure is that if

$$y_t = \beta_0 + \beta_1 x_{t1} + \cdots + \beta_K x_{tK} + \epsilon_t \tag{4.38}$$

and

$$\epsilon_t = \rho\epsilon_{t-1} + u_t, \tag{4.39}$$

with u_t spherical, then lagging (4.38) one period and premultiplying through by ρ gives

$$\rho y_{t-1} = \rho\beta_0 + \beta_1 \rho x_{t-1,1} + \cdots + \beta_K \rho x_{t-1,K} + \rho\epsilon_{t-1}, \tag{4.40}$$

which subtracted from (4.38) gives

$$\begin{aligned} y_t - \rho y_{t-1} = \beta_0(1-\rho) + \beta_1(x_{t1} - \rho x_{t-1,1}) + \cdots \\ + \beta_K(x_{tK} - \rho x_{t-1,K}) + (\epsilon_t - \rho\epsilon_{t-1}), \end{aligned} \tag{4.41}$$

with $(\epsilon_t - \rho\epsilon_{t-1}) = u_t$ being spherical. A more formal justification is that the procedure amounts to multiplying through $\mathbf{y} = \mathbf{X}\boldsymbol{\beta} + \boldsymbol{\epsilon}$ by

$$\mathbf{Q} = \begin{pmatrix} -\rho & 1 & 0 & \cdots & 0 & 0 \\ 0 & -\rho & 1 & \cdots & 0 & 0 \\ \cdot & \cdot & \cdot & & \cdot & \cdot \\ \cdot & \cdot & \cdot & & \cdot & \cdot \\ \cdot & \cdot & \cdot & & \cdot & \cdot \\ 0 & 0 & 0 & \cdots & -\rho & 1 \end{pmatrix}$$

and minimizing $\mathbf{e}'\mathbf{Q}'\mathbf{Q}\mathbf{e}$. Now the generalized least-squares procedure calls for minimization of $\mathbf{e}'\boldsymbol{\Omega}^{-1}\mathbf{e}$, but since $\mathbf{Q}'\mathbf{Q}$ is proportional to $\boldsymbol{\Omega}^{-1}$ except in the upper left-hand element, this computational procedure leads to virtually the identical estimate.

A common procedure in time series regression is to use the first differences of the variables, rather than their absolute values. We now see that this can be justified as a device to eliminate autocorrelation of the disturbances on the assumption that ρ is virtually equal to 1.

Properties of the Classical Least-Squares Estimators

What are the properties of the classical least-squares estimator $\mathbf{b} = (\mathbf{X}'\mathbf{X})^{-1}\mathbf{X}'\mathbf{y}$ applied to (4.4) when in fact the generalized linear regression model is appropriate? It is easy to see that $\mathbf{b}$ is still unbiased; we have $\mathbf{b} - \boldsymbol{\beta} = (\mathbf{X}'\mathbf{X})^{-1}\mathbf{X}'(\mathbf{X}\boldsymbol{\beta} + \boldsymbol{\epsilon}) - \boldsymbol{\beta} = (\mathbf{X}'\mathbf{X})^{-1}\mathbf{X}'\boldsymbol{\epsilon}$, whose expectation is still zero. [Alternatively we may note that $(\mathbf{X}'\mathbf{X})^{-1}\mathbf{X}'\mathbf{X} = \mathbf{I}$, which suffices for unbiasedness according to (4.9).] Of course, it no longer has minimum variance; and its covariance matrix is now

$$(4.42)\qquad \boldsymbol{\Sigma}_{\mathbf{bb}} = E(\mathbf{b} - \boldsymbol{\beta})(\mathbf{b} - \boldsymbol{\beta})' = E[(\mathbf{X}'\mathbf{X})^{-1}\mathbf{X}'\boldsymbol{\epsilon}\boldsymbol{\epsilon}'\mathbf{X}(\mathbf{X}'\mathbf{X})^{-1}]$$
$$= \sigma^2(\mathbf{X}'\mathbf{X})^{-1}(\mathbf{X}'\boldsymbol{\Omega}\mathbf{X})(\mathbf{X}'\mathbf{X})^{-1}.$$

Thus the classical formula for the covariance matrix of $\mathbf{b}$ is no longer appropriate. Furthermore, the classical estimator of σ^2 is no longer unbiased. Where $\hat{\boldsymbol{\epsilon}}$ is the residual vector from the classical regression, we still have, as in the fifth line of (4.4.27),

$$(4.43)\qquad E\hat{\boldsymbol{\epsilon}}'\hat{\boldsymbol{\epsilon}} = tr(\mathbf{M}E\boldsymbol{\epsilon}\boldsymbol{\epsilon}')$$

where $\mathbf{M} = \mathbf{I} - \mathbf{X}(\mathbf{X}'\mathbf{X})^{-1}\mathbf{X}'$, but now $E\boldsymbol{\epsilon}\boldsymbol{\epsilon}' = \sigma^2\boldsymbol{\Omega}$, so that

$$(4.44)\qquad E\hat{\boldsymbol{\epsilon}}'\hat{\boldsymbol{\epsilon}} = \sigma^2\, tr\, \mathbf{M}\boldsymbol{\Omega} = \sigma^2\, tr[\boldsymbol{\Omega} - \mathbf{X}(\mathbf{X}'\mathbf{X})^{-1}\mathbf{X}'\boldsymbol{\Omega}]$$
$$= \sigma^2[tr\,\boldsymbol{\Omega} - tr(\mathbf{X}'\mathbf{X})^{-1}(\mathbf{X}'\boldsymbol{\Omega}\mathbf{X})].$$

Then

$$(4.45)\qquad Es^2 = \frac{E\hat{\boldsymbol{\epsilon}}'\hat{\boldsymbol{\epsilon}}}{T - K - 1} = \sigma^2\,\frac{tr\boldsymbol{\Omega} - tr(\mathbf{X}'\mathbf{X})^{-1}(\mathbf{X}'\boldsymbol{\Omega}\mathbf{X})}{T - K - 1},$$

which differs from σ^2 to the extent that the difference of the traces in the numerator differs from $T - K - 1$. Taking (4.42) and (4.45) together we see that the classical estimator of the covariance matrix of **b**, $s^2(\mathbf{X}'\mathbf{X})^{-1}$, will be biased on two counts: First $Es^2 \neq \sigma^2$, and second $(\mathbf{X}'\mathbf{X})^{-1} \neq (\mathbf{X}'\mathbf{X})^{-1}(\mathbf{X}'\mathbf{\Omega}\mathbf{X})(\mathbf{X}'\mathbf{X})^{-1}$.

For further analysis it will be useful to write $\mathbf{\Omega} = \mathbf{I} - \mathbf{F}$, whence in turn

$$\mathbf{X}'\mathbf{\Omega}\mathbf{X} = \mathbf{X}'(\mathbf{I} - \mathbf{F})\mathbf{X} = \mathbf{X}'\mathbf{X} - \mathbf{X}'\mathbf{F}\mathbf{X}, \tag{4.46}$$

$$(\mathbf{X}'\mathbf{X})^{-1}\mathbf{X}'\mathbf{\Omega}\mathbf{X} = \mathbf{I} - (\mathbf{X}'\mathbf{X})^{-1}\mathbf{X}'\mathbf{F}\mathbf{X}, \tag{4.47}$$

and

$$(\mathbf{X}'\mathbf{X})^{-1}\mathbf{X}'\mathbf{\Omega}\mathbf{X}(\mathbf{X}'\mathbf{X})^{-1} = (\mathbf{X}'\mathbf{X})^{-1} - (\mathbf{X}'\mathbf{X})^{-1}\mathbf{X}'\mathbf{F}\mathbf{X}(\mathbf{X}'\mathbf{X})^{-1}. \tag{4.48}$$

From (4.47) we have

$$tr(\mathbf{X}'\mathbf{X})^{-1}\mathbf{X}'\mathbf{\Omega}\mathbf{X} = (1 + K) - tr(\mathbf{X}'\mathbf{X})^{-1}\mathbf{X}'\mathbf{F}\mathbf{X}, \tag{4.49}$$

and using the normalization rule that the sum of the diagonal elements of $\mathbf{\Omega}$ is T we have

$$tr(\mathbf{\Omega}) = T. \tag{4.50}$$

In these terms (4.42) and (4.45) become

$$\mathbf{\Sigma}_{\mathbf{bb}} = \sigma^2(\mathbf{X}'\mathbf{X})^{-1} - \sigma^2(\mathbf{X}'\mathbf{X})^{-1}\mathbf{X}'\mathbf{F}\mathbf{X}(\mathbf{X}'\mathbf{X})^{-1}, \tag{4.51}$$

$$Es^2 = \sigma^2 + \sigma^2\,\frac{tr(\mathbf{X}'\mathbf{X})^{-1}\mathbf{X}'\mathbf{F}\mathbf{X}}{T - K - 1}. \tag{4.52}$$

Then we find for the expectation of the classical estimator of the covariance matrix of **b**:

$$\begin{aligned} Es^2(\mathbf{X}'\mathbf{X})^{-1} &= \left[\sigma^2 + \sigma^2\,\frac{tr(\mathbf{X}'\mathbf{X})^{-1}\mathbf{X}'\mathbf{F}\mathbf{X}}{T - K - 1}\right](\mathbf{X}'\mathbf{X})^{-1} \\ &= \mathbf{\Sigma}_{\mathbf{bb}} + \sigma^2(\mathbf{X}'\mathbf{X})^{-1}\mathbf{X}'\mathbf{F}\mathbf{X}(\mathbf{X}'\mathbf{X})^{-1} \\ &\quad + \sigma^2\,\frac{tr(\mathbf{X}'\mathbf{X})^{-1}\mathbf{X}'\mathbf{F}\mathbf{X}}{T - K - 1}(\mathbf{X}'\mathbf{X})^{-1}. \end{aligned} \tag{4.53}$$

Let us apply our results to some special cases. First, consider the case of pure heteroskedasticity and a single regressor ($K = 1$). Without loss of generality we take $\Sigma\, x_t = 0$, and recall that by the normalization rule $\Sigma\, k_t = T$. Then we have

$$\mathbf{X}'\mathbf{X} = \begin{pmatrix} T & 0 \\ 0 & \Sigma\, x^2 \end{pmatrix}, \tag{4.54}$$

whence

$$(4.55)\qquad (\mathbf{X'X})^{-1} = \begin{pmatrix} 1/T & 0 \\ 0 & 1/\Sigma\, x^2 \end{pmatrix},$$

and

$$(4.56)\qquad \mathbf{F} = \begin{pmatrix} (1-k_1) & 0 & \cdots & 0 \\ \cdot & \cdot & & \cdot \\ \cdot & \cdot & & \cdot \\ \cdot & \cdot & & \cdot \\ 0 & 0 & \cdots & (1-k_T) \end{pmatrix},$$

whence

$$(4.57)\qquad \mathbf{X'FX} = \begin{pmatrix} \Sigma(1-k_t) & \Sigma(1-k_t)x_t \\ \Sigma(1-k_t)x_t & \Sigma(1-k_t)x_t^2 \end{pmatrix}$$

$$= \begin{pmatrix} 0 & \Sigma(1-k_t)x_t \\ \Sigma(1-k_t)x_t & \Sigma(1-k_t)x_t^2 \end{pmatrix},$$

and

$$(4.58)\qquad (\mathbf{X'X})^{-1}(\mathbf{X'FX}) = \begin{pmatrix} 0 & \Sigma(1-k_t)x_t/T \\ \Sigma(1-k_t)x_t/\Sigma x^2 & \Sigma(1-k_t)x_t^2/\Sigma x^2 \end{pmatrix}.$$

Using this in (4.52) we find that

$$(4.59)\qquad Es^2 = \sigma^2\left[1 + \frac{\Sigma(1-k_t)x_t^2/\Sigma x^2}{T-K-1}\right].$$

Using $\Sigma\, k_t = T$ and $K = 1$, this reduces to

$$(4.60)\qquad Es^2 = \sigma^2 \sum k_t\left[\frac{T-1}{T(T-2)} - \frac{x_t^2}{\Sigma x^2(T-2)}\right]$$

$$= \sum\left[\sigma^2 k_t\left(\frac{1 - x_t^2/\Sigma x^2 - 1/T}{T-2}\right)\right],$$

which, since the terms in parentheses sum to 1, shows that the expectation of the classical variance estimator is a weighted average of the individual variances $\sigma^2 k_t$. Furthermore we have

$$(4.61)\qquad (\mathbf{X'X})^{-1}\mathbf{X'FX}(\mathbf{X'X})^{-1}$$

$$= \begin{pmatrix} 0 & \Sigma(1-k_t)x_t/T\Sigma x^2 \\ \Sigma(1-k_t)x_t/T\Sigma x^2 & \Sigma(1-k_t)x_t^2/(\Sigma x^2)^2 \end{pmatrix};$$

thus from (4.53) the excess of the expectation of the classical estimator of the variance of b_1 over the true variance of b_1 is

$$(4.62) \qquad \sigma^2 \frac{\Sigma(1 - k_t)x_t^2}{(\Sigma x^2)^2} + \sigma^2 \frac{\Sigma(1 - k_t)x_t^2}{(T-2)(\Sigma x^2)^2} = \sigma^2 \frac{(T-1)\Sigma(1 - k_t)x_t^2}{(T-2)(\Sigma x^2)^2}.$$

This expression will be negative—so that the classical formula will underestimate $\sigma_{b_1}^2$—when high variances—negative $(1 - k_t)$'s—correspond to high values of x_t^2.

Second, consider the case of interdependence due to a first-order autoregressive process as in (4.34) and (4.35) with a single regressor. Without loss of generality we take $\Sigma\, x_t = 0$; we also have homoskedasticity so that each $k_t = 1$. For simplicity we obtain approximate results by ignoring powers of ρ beyond the first, taking $\mathbf{\Omega}$ to be simply

$$(4.63) \qquad \mathbf{\Omega} = \begin{pmatrix} 1 & \rho & 0 & \cdots & 0 & 0 \\ \rho & 1 & \rho & \cdots & 0 & 0 \\ \cdot & \cdot & \cdot & & \cdot & \cdot \\ \cdot & \cdot & \cdot & & \cdot & \cdot \\ \cdot & \cdot & \cdot & & \cdot & \cdot \\ 0 & 0 & 0 & \cdots & \rho & 1 \end{pmatrix},$$

and thus

$$(4.64) \qquad \mathbf{F} = \mathbf{I} - \mathbf{\Omega} = \begin{pmatrix} 0 & -\rho & 0 & \cdots & 0 & 0 \\ -\rho & 0 & -\rho & \cdots & 0 & 0 \\ \cdot & \cdot & \cdot & & \cdot & \cdot \\ \cdot & \cdot & \cdot & & \cdot & \cdot \\ \cdot & \cdot & \cdot & & \cdot & \cdot \\ 0 & 0 & 0 & \cdots & -\rho & 0 \end{pmatrix}.$$

This gives in turn

$$(4.65) \qquad \mathbf{X'FX} = \begin{pmatrix} -2(T-1)\rho & \rho(x_1 + x_T) \\ \rho(x_1 + x_T) & -2\rho \sum_{t=2}^{T} x_t x_{t-1} \end{pmatrix},$$

$$(4.66) \qquad (\mathbf{X'X})^{-1}(\mathbf{X'FX}) = \begin{pmatrix} -2(T-1)\rho/T & \rho(x_1 + x_T)/T \\ \rho(x_1 + x_T)/\Sigma x^2 & -2\rho \sum_{t=2}^{T} x_t x_{t-1}/\Sigma x^2 \end{pmatrix}.$$

Looking at the lower right-hand term, we see it is essentially $-2\rho r$ where r is the first-order autocorrelation coefficient of the regressor x:

$$(4.67)\qquad r = \sqrt{R^2_{x_t x_{t-1}}} = \frac{\sum_{t=2}^{T} x_t x_{t-1}}{\sqrt{\sum_{t=2}^{T} x_t^2}\sqrt{\sum_{t=2}^{T} x_{t-1}^2}}$$

since $\Sigma_{t=2}^{T} x_{t-1}^2 = \Sigma_{t=1}^{T-1} x_t^2 \doteq \Sigma_{t=1}^{T} x_t^2 \doteq \Sigma_{t=2}^{T} x_t^2$. Thus approximately

$$(4.68)\qquad (\mathbf{X}'\mathbf{X})^{-1}(\mathbf{X}'\mathbf{F}\mathbf{X}) = \begin{pmatrix} -2\rho & \rho(x_1 + x_T)/T \\ \rho(x_1 + x_T)/\Sigma x^2 & -2\rho r \end{pmatrix},$$

where $T - 1$ is taken as T. Using this in (4.52) we find

$$(4.69)\qquad Es^2 = \sigma^2 + \sigma^2\left[\frac{-2\rho(1 + r)}{T - 2}\right].$$

Now since $1 + r \geq 0$ the second term will be negative if $\rho > 0$ (unless $r = -1$). Since positive autocorrelation is the typical situation in economic time series, the classical variance estimator is seen to be an underestimator of σ^2. To suggest the order of magnitude suppose $T = 22$, $\rho = r = \frac{1}{2}$. Then the term in brackets is $-2(\frac{1}{2})(\frac{3}{2})/20 = -3/40$ so that σ^2 is underestimated by $7\frac{1}{2}\%$. Continuing, we have

$$(4.70)\qquad (\mathbf{X}'\mathbf{X})^{-1}\mathbf{X}'\mathbf{F}\mathbf{X}(\mathbf{X}'\mathbf{X})^{-1} = \begin{pmatrix} -2\rho/T & \rho(x_1 + x_T)/T\Sigma x^2 \\ \rho(x_1 + x_T)/T\Sigma x^2 & -2\rho r/\Sigma x^2 \end{pmatrix};$$

from (4.51) we see that the lower right element of $\sigma^2(\mathbf{X}'\mathbf{X})^{-1}$ will be less than that of $\mathbf{\Sigma}_{\mathbf{bb}}$ when ρ and r have the same sign. The typical situation in economic time series is that both ρ and r are positive, so that we may expect the classical estimator of the variance of b_1 to be an underestimator on this count too. Indeed, using (4.53), the expectation of the classical estimator of the variance of b_1 is

$$(4.71)\qquad \frac{\sigma^2\{1 - [2\rho(1 + r)/(T - 2)]\}}{\Sigma x^2}$$
$$= \frac{1 - [2\rho(1 + r)/(T - 2)]}{1 + 2\rho r}\,\frac{\sigma^2(1 + 2\rho r)}{\Sigma x^2}$$
$$= \frac{1 - [2\rho(1 + r)/(T - 2)]}{1 + 2\rho r}\,\sigma^2_{b_1}.$$

To suggest the order of magnitude again suppose $T = 22$ and $\rho = r = \frac{1}{2}$.

Then the ratio in (4.71) is

$$\frac{1 - 2(\frac{1}{2})(\frac{3}{2})/20}{1 + 2(\frac{1}{2})(\frac{1}{2})} = \frac{\frac{37}{40}}{\frac{3}{2}} = \frac{37}{60}$$

so that $\sigma^2_{b_1}$ is underestimated by 39%.

Testing for Nonsphericalness of Disturbances

We have seen that the BLUE property of the classical least-squares estimator **b** and the classical formula for its variances do not hold when the disturbances are nonspherical. Therefore, when the classical estimator is used it is desirable to test the assumption of spherical disturbances. If we are forced to reject that assumption, the classical regression results are called into question. There are of course many ways in which a series can be nonspherical; thus there is no general test of sphericalness but rather specific tests against specific nonspherical alternatives. In any event, the tests are naturally based on the residuals from the fitted classical regression. We restrict ourself to the case where ϵ is normally distributed.

First, consider the question of heteroskedasticity. If we have several observations on y for each set of values of the x's, we could compute the sample variance of the residuals at each set of values of the x's, and test for homogeneity of variances. The appropriate test procedure could be based on the classical one given in Mood (1950, pp. 269–270). In practice, of course, replication of this sort is rarely present in the sample, and we may have to resort to marking off rather arbitrary ranges of the x's, computing the sample variance of the residuals in each range, and applying the standard tests.

Next consider the question of interdependence. We restrict our attention to the leading case where the nonrandomness, if any, is generated by a first-order autoregressive process of the type of (4.34) and (4.35). Then the hypothesis to be tested is that ρ is equal to zero. Naturally, such a test is based on the first-order autocorrelation coefficient of the residuals from the classical regression,

$$\hat{\rho} = \frac{\sum_{t=2}^{T} \hat{\epsilon}_t \hat{\epsilon}_{t-1}}{\sqrt{\sum_{t=2}^{T} \hat{\epsilon}_t^2}\sqrt{\sum_{t=2}^{T} \hat{\epsilon}_{t-1}^2}}. \tag{4.72}$$

The statistic actually used is the Durbin-Watson d:

$$d = \frac{\sum_{t=2}^{T} (\hat{\epsilon}_t - \hat{\epsilon}_{t-1})^2}{\sum_{t=1}^{T} \hat{\epsilon}_t^2}. \tag{4.73}$$

Using the approximations $\Sigma_{t=1}^{T}\hat{\epsilon}_t^2 \doteq \Sigma_{t=2}^{T}\hat{\epsilon}_t^2 \doteq \Sigma_{t=2}^{T}\hat{\epsilon}_{t-1}^2$, it is seen that

$$(4.74)\qquad d = \frac{2\Sigma\hat{\epsilon}_t^2 - 2\Sigma\hat{\epsilon}_t\hat{\epsilon}_{t-1}}{\Sigma\hat{\epsilon}_t^2} = 2 - 2\hat{\rho} = 2(1 - \hat{\rho})$$

so that when $\hat{\rho} = 0$, then $d = 2$; as $\hat{\rho}$ rises from 0 to +1, then d falls from 2 to 0; and as $\hat{\rho}$ falls from 0 to −1, then d rises from 2 to 4. The distribution of d on the null hypothesis $\rho = 0$ is a function of T, K, and the autoregressive pattern of the regressors. Durbin and Watson (1950, 1951) are able to show that the distribution of d (given T and K) lies between that of two other statistics called d_L and d_U whose distributions they have tabulated. The expectations of these distributions on the null hypothesis lie around 2 as suggested; for selected values of T and K they are

(4.75)

		$K = 1$	$K = 3$		$K = 1$	$K = 3$
Ed_L	$T = 20$	1.89	1.65	$T = 40$	1.95	1.84
Ed_U		2.11	2.35		2.05	2.16

The critical values of these distributions for the one-tail 5% level of significance, appropriate where the alternative is $\rho > 0$, are, for these selected values of T and K

(4.76)

		$K = 1$	$K = 3$		$K = 1$	$K = 3$
d_L^*	$T = 20$	1.20	1.00	$T = 40$	1.44	1.34
d_U^*		1.41	1.68		1.54	1.66

The procedure for testing $\rho = 0$ against $\rho > 0$ is

$$d \geq d_U^*: \text{ accept } \rho = 0,$$
$$d_L^* < d < d_U^*: \text{ test inconclusive,}$$
$$d \leq d_L^*: \text{ reject } \rho = 0.$$

A one-tailed test of $\rho = 0$ against $\rho < 0$ is obtained by using $4 - d$ in place of d; a two-tailed test is obtained by combination of the one-tailed tests. Nonparametric tests are available for testing other types of nonrandomness in a series; but their distribution for the case of residuals from a fitted regression has not yet been derived.

Estimation of Parameters of Nonsphericalness

Suppose that the classical assumption $E\boldsymbol{\epsilon\epsilon}' = \sigma^2\mathbf{I}$ is untenable (either on a priori grounds or as a result of tests like those in the preceding subsection), and that we then adopt $E\boldsymbol{\epsilon\epsilon}' = \sigma^2\boldsymbol{\Omega}$, but that we do not know

$\mathbf{\Omega}$ and hence are unable to proceed with BLUE estimation. We may consider estimating $\mathbf{\Omega}$ from the data along with $\boldsymbol{\beta}$ and σ^2. We should not be optimistic about the possibility of estimating the $T + \frac{1}{2}T(T-1)$ distinct elements of $\mathbf{\Omega}$ with only T observations available. If we are willing, however, to put severe restrictions on $\mathbf{\Omega}$ as we did in (4.30) and (4.35), the situation becomes more favorable.

First consider the case of pure heteroskedasticity (4.30), where further (as is often reasonable) the disturbance variance is proportional to the square of the expected value of y; i.e., $k_t = (Ey_t)^2$:

$$(4.77) \qquad E\epsilon_t^2 = \sigma^2(Ey_t)^2.$$

Ey_t is of course unknown. Then a two-step procedure is proposed. In the first step obtain the classical least-squares regression and thus the calculated values $\hat{y}_t$. Let

$$(4.78) \qquad \mathbf{\Omega}_* = \begin{pmatrix} \hat{y}_1^2 & \cdots & 0 \\ \cdot & & \cdot \\ \cdot & & \cdot \\ \cdot & & \cdot \\ 0 & \cdots & \hat{y}_T^2 \end{pmatrix}.$$

Then in the second step obtain

$$(4.79) \qquad \tilde{\mathbf{b}}_* = (\mathbf{X}'\mathbf{\Omega}_*^{-1}\mathbf{X})^{-1}\mathbf{X}'\mathbf{\Omega}_*^{-1}\mathbf{y}$$

as the estimate of $\boldsymbol{\beta}$. The idea is that $\hat{y}_t$ is an (unbiased) estimate of Ey_t so that $\mathbf{\Omega}_*$ is an estimate of $\mathbf{\Omega}$. To be sure, $\tilde{\mathbf{b}}_*$ is not the BLUE of $\boldsymbol{\beta}$; but it does take account of heteroskedasticity.

Second, consider the case of interdependence attributable to a first-order autoregressive disturbance, $E\epsilon_s\epsilon_t = \sigma^2\rho^{|t-s|}$, with ρ unknown. Then a parallel two-step procedure is proposed. In the first step obtain the classical least-squares regression and then the first-order autocorrelation coefficient of the residuals $\hat{\rho}$. Let

$$(4.80) \qquad \mathbf{\Omega}_* = \begin{pmatrix} 1 & \hat{\rho} & \cdots & \hat{\rho}^{T-1} \\ \hat{\rho} & 1 & \cdots & \hat{\rho}^{T-2} \\ \cdot & \cdot & & \cdot \\ \cdot & \cdot & & \cdot \\ \cdot & \cdot & & \cdot \\ \hat{\rho}^{T-1} & \hat{\rho}^{T-2} & \cdots & 1 \end{pmatrix}.$$

Then in the second step obtain

$$\tilde{\mathbf{b}}_* = (\mathbf{X}'\mathbf{\Omega}_*^{-1}\mathbf{X})^{-1}(\mathbf{X}'\mathbf{\Omega}_*^{-1}\mathbf{y}) \tag{4.81}$$

as the estimate of $\boldsymbol{\beta}$. To be sure, $\tilde{\mathbf{b}}_*$ is not the BLUE of $\boldsymbol{\beta}$; but it does take account of interdependence. Simultaneous rather than two-step solutions to these problems have been proposed. We may minimize the generalized sum of squares $(\mathbf{y} - \mathbf{X}\boldsymbol{\beta})'\mathbf{\Omega}^{-1}(\mathbf{y} - \mathbf{X}\boldsymbol{\beta})$—which is also equivalent to maximizing the likelihood function in the case of normally distributed disturbances—with respect to both $\boldsymbol{\beta}$ and $\mathbf{\Omega}^{-1}$. The computational burdens of this approach have inhibited its use.

Finally, the presence of autocorrelation in the residuals might well be taken as an indication that a particular variable should be added to the list of regressors. For an example of this approach, see the revision of the depreciation function in Klein and Goldberger (1955, pp. 69, 90).

Best Linear Unbiased Estimation in the Multivariate Classical Linear Regression Model

In Section 4.11 we considered estimation of a set of relations embodied in the multivariate classical linear regression model. We showed that the classical least-squares estimators were unbiased but reserved judgment on their efficiency. As will be recalled we had the M relations

$$\mathbf{y}_m = \mathbf{X}\boldsymbol{\beta}_m + \boldsymbol{\epsilon}_m \qquad (m = 1, \ldots, M), \tag{4.82}$$

with

$$E\boldsymbol{\epsilon}_m = \mathbf{0},\ E\boldsymbol{\epsilon}_m\boldsymbol{\epsilon}'_{m'} = \omega_{mm'}\mathbf{I} \qquad (m, m' = 1, \ldots, M). \tag{4.83}$$

Let us write all M relations together as the single regression

$$\begin{pmatrix} \mathbf{y}_1 \\ \cdot \\ \cdot \\ \cdot \\ \mathbf{y}_M \end{pmatrix} = \begin{pmatrix} \mathbf{X} & \mathbf{0} & \cdots & \mathbf{0} \\ \cdot & \cdot & & \cdot \\ \cdot & \cdot & & \cdot \\ \cdot & \cdot & & \cdot \\ \mathbf{0} & \mathbf{0} & \cdots & \mathbf{X} \end{pmatrix} \begin{pmatrix} \boldsymbol{\beta}_1 \\ \cdot \\ \cdot \\ \cdot \\ \boldsymbol{\beta}_M \end{pmatrix} + \begin{pmatrix} \boldsymbol{\epsilon}_1 \\ \cdot \\ \cdot \\ \cdot \\ \boldsymbol{\epsilon}_M \end{pmatrix}, \tag{4.84}$$

or more compactly as

$$\mathbf{y} = \mathbf{Z}\boldsymbol{\beta} + \boldsymbol{\epsilon}, \tag{4.85}$$

where $\mathbf{y}$ is $MT \times 1$, $\mathbf{Z}$ is $MT \times MK$, $\boldsymbol{\beta}$ is $MK \times 1$, and $\boldsymbol{\epsilon}$ is $MT \times 1$. Now in view of (4.83) the covariance matrix of $\boldsymbol{\epsilon}$ is

$$(4.86)\qquad \boldsymbol{\Phi} = E\boldsymbol{\epsilon}\boldsymbol{\epsilon}' = \begin{pmatrix} E\boldsymbol{\epsilon}_1\boldsymbol{\epsilon}_1' & \cdots & E\boldsymbol{\epsilon}_1\boldsymbol{\epsilon}_M' \\ \cdot & & \cdot \\ \cdot & E\boldsymbol{\epsilon}_m\boldsymbol{\epsilon}_{m'}' & \cdot \\ \cdot & & \cdot \\ E\boldsymbol{\epsilon}_M\boldsymbol{\epsilon}_1' & \cdots & E\boldsymbol{\epsilon}_M\boldsymbol{\epsilon}_M' \end{pmatrix}$$

$$= \begin{pmatrix} \omega_{11}\mathbf{I} & \cdots & \omega_{1M}\mathbf{I} \\ \cdot & & \cdot \\ \cdot & \omega_{mm'}\mathbf{I} & \cdot \\ \cdot & & \cdot \\ \omega_{M1}\mathbf{I} & \cdots & \omega_{MM}\mathbf{I} \end{pmatrix} = \boldsymbol{\Omega} \otimes \mathbf{I}$$

where $\boldsymbol{\Omega}$ was defined in (4.11.36).

Since $\boldsymbol{\Phi}$ is not diagonal the generalized linear regression model is applicable to (4.85). Therefore the BLUE of $\boldsymbol{\beta}$ is

$$(4.87)\qquad \tilde{\mathbf{b}} = (\mathbf{Z}'\boldsymbol{\Phi}^{-1}\mathbf{Z})^{-1}(\mathbf{Z}'\boldsymbol{\Phi}^{-1}\mathbf{y})$$

It is readily confirmed that

$$(4.88)\qquad \boldsymbol{\Phi}^{-1} = \begin{pmatrix} \omega^{11}\mathbf{I} & \cdots & \omega^{1M}\mathbf{I} \\ \cdot & & \cdot \\ \cdot & \omega^{mm'}\mathbf{I} & \cdot \\ \cdot & & \cdot \\ \omega^{M1}\mathbf{I} & \cdots & \omega^{MM}\mathbf{I} \end{pmatrix} = \boldsymbol{\Omega}^{-1} \otimes \mathbf{I}$$

where $\omega^{mm'}$ is the element in the mth row and m'th column of $\boldsymbol{\Omega}^{-1}$, and then that in view of the form of $\mathbf{Z}$

$$(4.89)\qquad \mathbf{Z}'\boldsymbol{\Phi}^{-1}\mathbf{Z} = \begin{pmatrix} \omega^{11}\mathbf{X}'\mathbf{X} & \cdots & \omega^{1M}\mathbf{X}'\mathbf{X} \\ \cdot & & \cdot \\ \cdot & & \cdot \\ \cdot & & \cdot \\ \omega^{M1}\mathbf{X}'\mathbf{X} & \cdots & \omega^{MM}\mathbf{X}'\mathbf{X} \end{pmatrix} = \boldsymbol{\Omega}^{-1} \otimes \mathbf{X}'\mathbf{X},$$

and

$$(4.90)\qquad \mathbf{Z}'\boldsymbol{\Phi}^{-1}\mathbf{y} = \begin{pmatrix} \omega^{11}\mathbf{X}'\mathbf{y}_1 + \cdots + \omega^{1M}\mathbf{X}'\mathbf{y}_M \\ \cdot \qquad\qquad \cdot \\ \cdot \qquad\qquad \cdot \\ \cdot \qquad\qquad \cdot \\ \omega^{M1}\mathbf{X}'\mathbf{y}_1 + \cdots + \omega^{MM}\mathbf{X}'\mathbf{y}_M \end{pmatrix}.$$

It follows that

$$
(4.91) \qquad (\mathbf{Z}'\mathbf{\Phi}^{-1}\mathbf{Z})^{-1} = \begin{pmatrix} \omega_{11}(\mathbf{X}'\mathbf{X})^{-1} & \cdots & \omega_{1M}(\mathbf{X}'\mathbf{X})^{-1} \\ \vdots & \omega_{mm'}(\mathbf{X}'\mathbf{X})^{-1} & \vdots \\ \omega_{M1}(\mathbf{X}'\mathbf{X})^{-1} & \cdots & \omega_{MM}(\mathbf{X}'\mathbf{X})^{-1} \end{pmatrix}
$$

$$
= \mathbf{\Omega} \otimes (\mathbf{X}'\mathbf{X})^{-1}
$$

so that the mth subvector of $\tilde{\mathbf{b}} = (\mathbf{Z}'\mathbf{\Phi}^{-1}\mathbf{Z})^{-1}\mathbf{Z}'\mathbf{\Phi}^{-1}\mathbf{y}$ is

$$
(4.92) \qquad \tilde{\mathbf{b}}_m = \sum_{\mu=1}^{M} \omega_{m\mu}(\mathbf{X}'\mathbf{X})^{-1} \sum_{\mu'=1}^{M} \omega^{\mu\mu'}\mathbf{X}'\mathbf{y}_{\mu'} = \sum_{\mu'=1}^{M}\sum_{\mu=1}^{M} \omega_{m\mu}\omega^{\mu\mu'}(\mathbf{X}'\mathbf{X})^{-1}\mathbf{X}'\mathbf{y}_{\mu'}
$$

$$
= (\mathbf{X}'\mathbf{X})^{-1}\mathbf{X}'\mathbf{y}_m = \mathbf{b}_m,
$$

where $\mathbf{b}_m$ is the mth subvector of $\mathbf{b}$ and we use the fact that

$$
\sum_{\mu=1}^{M} \omega_{m\mu}\omega^{\mu\mu'} = \begin{cases} 1 & \text{if} \quad m = \mu' \\ 0 & \text{if} \quad m \neq \mu' . \end{cases}
$$

Thus $\tilde{\mathbf{b}} = \mathbf{b}$ so that the classical least-squares estimators are indeed the BLUE's of the coefficient vectors in the multivariate classical linear regression model.

5. QUALITATIVE AND LIMITED DEPENDENT VARIABLES

In the models considered up to now we placed no restrictions on the range of variation of the disturbance and hence none on the range of variation of y in its conditional distribution. In particular, when normality of the disturbance distribution is assumed, the implication is that y can take on any value between plus infinity and minus infinity. Now in many economic contexts the dependent variable is inherently limited; e.g., prices cannot be negative. In this section we are concerned with ways of handling these and related problems.

Qualitative Dependent Variables

In a variety of cases economic relationships are formulated with a dependent variable that is dichotomous. For example, a family either owns a house or it does not, it either purchases a car during the year or does not. It is natural to attempt to account for this variable by a regression equation in which the regressand can take on only two values, which without loss of generality may be designated 0 and 1:

$$
(5.1) \qquad y = \begin{cases} 1 & \text{if} \quad \text{event occurs} \\ 0 & \text{if} \quad \text{event does not occur.} \end{cases}
$$

As usual, we specify that the expected value of y is a function of the explanatory variables. This does not suffice to define a statistical model; several alternatives are available, and we discuss two of them next. For an instructive comparison of these and other approaches see Warner (1962).

The most obvious and most commonly used is the *linear probability function*. Here we treat the dichotomous regressand problem as an ordinary linear regression problem, taking the expected value of y to be a linear function of the regressors:

(5.2) $$\mathbf{y} = \mathbf{X}\boldsymbol{\beta} + \boldsymbol{\epsilon}$$

with

(5.3) $$E\boldsymbol{\epsilon} = \mathbf{0}.$$

Then classical least-squares estimators are obtained. In view of the 1, 0 nature of the regressand, the conditional expectation of y given the x's may be interpreted as the conditional probability that the event will occur given the x's. Then the calculated value of y is interpreted as an estimate of this conditional probability.

To illustrate the linear probability approach, we draw on a study of new 1952 auto purchases by de Janosi (1956). With x = disposable income in \$100 and $y = 1$ for purchasers and 0 for nonpurchasers, the function estimated by classical least squares is

(5.4) $$\hat{y} = -0.008 + 0.0022x.$$

Thus the estimate of the probability that an individual with \$10,000 disposable income will buy a new car in a year is $-0.008 + 0.0022(100) = 0.212$.

A weakness of this natural procedure is that the classical assumption of homoskedasticity is untenable. For, writing a particular set of x's—a row of $\mathbf{X}$—as $\mathbf{X}_t'$ we see $\epsilon_t = y_t - \mathbf{X}_t'\boldsymbol{\beta}$. Since y_t is either 0 or 1, ϵ_t must be either $-\mathbf{X}_t'\boldsymbol{\beta}$ or $1 - \mathbf{X}_t'\boldsymbol{\beta}$. Then if ϵ_t is to have expectation zero, its distribution must be

(5.5)

ϵ_t	$f(\epsilon_t)$
$-\mathbf{X}_t'\boldsymbol{\beta}$	$1 - \mathbf{X}_t'\boldsymbol{\beta}$
$1 - \mathbf{X}_t'\boldsymbol{\beta}$	$\mathbf{X}_t'\boldsymbol{\beta}$

with variance

(5.6) $$\begin{aligned} E\epsilon_t^2 &= (-\mathbf{X}_t'\boldsymbol{\beta})^2(1 - \mathbf{X}_t'\boldsymbol{\beta}) + (1 - \mathbf{X}_t'\boldsymbol{\beta})^2(\mathbf{X}_t'\boldsymbol{\beta}) \\ &= (\mathbf{X}_t'\boldsymbol{\beta})(1 - \mathbf{X}_t'\boldsymbol{\beta}) = Ey_t(1 - Ey_t), \end{aligned}$$

since $Ey_t = \mathbf{X}_t'\boldsymbol{\beta}$. Thus the disturbance is heteroskedastic, varying systematically with Ey_t and hence with $\mathbf{X}_t$. It is the generalized linear regression model that seems to be appropriate, which indicates that the generalized least-squares regression is appropriate. The obvious difficulty is that Ey_t is unknown. The two-step procedure of Section 4 is in order; from the classical least-squares regression obtain the calculated values $\hat{y}_t = \hat{E}y_t$, then use $\hat{y}_t(1 - \hat{y}_t)$ as the diagonal elements of an estimated disturbance covariance matrix $\mathbf{\Omega}_*$ and obtain $\mathbf{b}_* = (\mathbf{X}'\mathbf{\Omega}_*^{-1}\mathbf{X})^{-1}(\mathbf{X}'\mathbf{\Omega}_*^{-1}\mathbf{y})$ in the second step.

A distinct difficulty remains. The linear probability function formulation allows Ey_t to fall outside the interval between 0 and 1, which is inconsistent with the definition of y and with the interpretation of the expectation as a probability. Since a linear function is unbounded, there are certain sets of values of the x's for which $Ey_t = \mathbf{X}_t'\boldsymbol{\beta}$ exceeds 1, and others for which it is less than 0. Indeed within the sample there may be $\mathbf{X}_t$'s for which $\hat{y}_t$ is outside the unit interval.

In view of this problem, alternative approaches to the dichotomous regressand problem develop models in which Ey is kept within the unit interval from the start. One such alternative is the *probit analysis model*, which has a long history in biometrics. Let I be an index which is a linear function of the regressors: $I_t = \mathbf{X}_t'\boldsymbol{\beta}$, let I^* be a $\mathcal{N}(0, 1)$ variable, and let the value of y be determined as follows:

$$(5.7) \qquad y_t = \begin{cases} 1 & \text{if} \quad I_t \geq I_t^* \\ 0 & \text{if} \quad I_t < I_t^*. \end{cases}$$

Each y_t is thus a function of the x_t's (via I_t) and of I_t^*. The I_t^*'s, which play the role of disturbances, may be interpreted as critical values of the index, reflecting individual tastes. If e.g., y = car ownership and x = income, an individual with a high I^* would own a car only if his income x is so high that $I_t \geq I_t^*$.

Letting $F(z)$ = value of the standard normal cumulative distribution at z, we have

$$(5.8) \qquad \text{Prob}\,\{y = 1 \mid I\} = \text{Prob}\,\{I^* \leq I \mid I\} = F(I)$$

and

$$(5.9) \qquad \text{Prob}\,\{y = 0 \mid I\} = \text{Prob}\,\{I^* > I \mid I\} = 1 - F(I),$$

in view of the fact that I^* is $\mathcal{N}(0, 1)$. The fact that I, and hence the probabilities, is a function of the β's suggests maximum likelihood estimation of the β's. Without loss of generality, suppose the sample to be ordered so that the first S observations have $y = 1$ and the remaining $T - S$ observations have $y = 0$. Then the likelihood of the sample is

$$(5.10) \qquad \mathscr{L} = F(I_1) \cdots F(I_S) \cdot [1 - F(I_{S+1})] \cdots [1 - F(I_T)],$$

with logarithmic likelihood

$$(5.11) \qquad L = \sum_{t=1}^{S} \log F(I_t) + \sum_{t=S+1}^{T} \log [1 - F(I_t)],$$

in which each term is a function of the β's:

$$(5.12) \qquad F(I_t) = (2\pi)^{-1/2} \int_{-\infty}^{\mathbf{X}_t'\boldsymbol{\beta}} e^{-u^2/2} \, du.$$

Setting the derivatives of (5.11) with respect to the β's equal to zero gives the normal equations determining the maximum likelihood estimators, the $\hat{\beta}$'s; the normal equations are of course nonlinear.

In the probit model, the conditional expectation is given by

$$E(y_t \mid I_t) = \text{Prob}\,\{y_t = 1 \mid I_t\} = F(I_t),$$

the ordinate of the cumulative normal distribution, which necessarily falls in the unit interval, and which forms an S-shaped curve. The estimated expectation is $\hat{y}_t = F(\hat{I}_t) = F(\mathbf{X}_t'\hat{\boldsymbol{\beta}})$, which has the same properties.

To illustrate the probit method, we draw on a study of durable purchases by Tobin (1955). With x = disposable income in thousands of dollars and $y = 1$ for purchasers and 0 for nonpurchasers, the estimated index is

$$(5.13) \qquad \hat{I} = -0.64 + 0.14x.$$

More informative is this tabulation for selected values of x; $\bar{y}$ is the observed relative frequency of purchasers at each income level:

(5.14)

x	$\hat{I}$	$\hat{y}$	$\bar{y}$
0.5	−0.57	0.28	0.15
2.5	−0.29	0.39	0.37
4.5	−0.01	0.50	0.58
6.5	0.27	0.61	0.53
8.5	0.54	0.70	0.67

Limited Dependent Variables

We may of course be concerned not only with whether or not an event occurred but also the extent of occurrence. Our concern may be, e.g., with the price paid for a car if it was bought as well as with whether or not it was bought. The natural approach is simply to use the price paid as regressand in a conventional regression, recording $y = 0$ for those who did not buy. There is a weakness with the approach, however. There will be many nonpurchasers, and with a concentration of values at $y = 0$, the linear regression will often be empirically inappropriate. The absence of negative y's in the sample will tend to keep the estimated regression relation above the axis over the relevant range of the x's. But this protection is purchased at the expense of making the relation so flat that the amounts spent will be underestimated at the high end of the relation. The classical regression model appears to be inappropriate when the range of variation of the regressand is inherently bounded and there is a concentration of the regressand at its bound. We discuss several approaches to this situation, which we designate the limited dependent variable case.

The most obvious is the *twin linear probability function*, an extension of the linear probability approach. First a linear probability function is fit to the 1, 0 regressand y^*. Then, restricting the sample to those with $y^* = 1$, a classical linear regression is fit with the amount y^{**} as regressand.

To illustrate the twin linear probability approach, we draw on a study by Janet A. Fisher (1962), tabulating the least-squares regression coefficients as:

	(5.15)	(5.16)
$x_0 = 1$	0.1411	0.0224
$x_1 =$ income	0.0251	0.0789
$x_2 = x_1^2$	−0.0004	0.0005
$x_3 =$ checking deposits	−0.0051	0.0868
$x_4 =$ savings deposits	0.0013	0.0011
$x_5 =$ savings bonds	−0.0079	−0.0085
$x_6 =$ 1 if home-renter, 0 otherwise	−0.0469	0.1379
$x_7 =$ 1 if home-owner, 0 otherwise ($x_6 = x_7 = 0$ if neither owns nor rents)	0.0136	0.0889
$x_8 =$ monthly rent	−0.7540	−1.0436
$x_9 =$ monthly mortgage payments	−0.9809	−0.0745
$x_{10} =$ monthly installment debt payments	0.2182	1.5493
$x_{11} =$ personal noninstallment debt	−0.0367	−0.1013
$x_{12} =$ age in years	0.0046	0.0150
$x_{13} = x_{12}^2$	−0.0001	−0.0002
$x_{14} =$ 1 if married, 0 otherwise	0.1760	−0.1032
$x_{15} =$ number of children	0.0398	0.0502
$x_{16} = x_{15}^2$	−0.0036	−0.0174
$x_{17} =$ 1 if planned to buy, 0 otherwise	0.1760	0.0391

Here (5.15) was fit to the full sample of 762 observations, the regressand being $y^* = 1$ if the household purchased durable goods, 0 if it did not; whereas (5.16) was fit to the subsample of 359 observations who did purchase ($y^* = 1$), the regressand being $y^{**} =$ amount spent on durable goods in thousands of dollars. The regressors x_1, x_3, x_4, x_5, x_8, x_9, x_{10} and x_{11} are also in thousands of dollars.

In the twin linear probability approach, the first function estimates the probability that $y > 0$. The second function estimates the expected value of y given that $y > 0$. The two results may be combined to express the expected value of y, since

$$(5.17) \qquad \begin{aligned} Ey &= \sum y \cdot f(y) = \sum_{y=0} 0 \cdot f(0) + \sum_{y>0} y \cdot f(y) \\ &= 0 + \sum_{y>0} \{y \cdot [f(y \mid y > 0)] \cdot f(y > 0)\} \\ &= f(y > 0) \cdot \sum_{y>0} \{y \cdot [f(y \mid y > 0)]\} \\ &= \text{Prob}\,\{y > 0\} \cdot E(y \mid y > 0). \end{aligned}$$

Although this procedure is straightforward, it should be noted that the previously cited weaknesses of the linear probability function persist; thus there is nothing in the second function to keep Ey above zero outside the sample range. Furthermore, the procedure does not directly attempt to fit Ey to y, it takes no explicit account of the estimation of Ey by $\hat{y} = \hat{y}^*\hat{y}^{**}$ in accordance with (5.17).

An alternative one-step procedure is the extension of probit analysis developed by Tobin (1958) that we designate the *Tobit model.* Again I is an index which is a linear function of the regressors: $I_t = \mathbf{X}_t'\boldsymbol{\beta}$. But now individual behavior is determined by

$$(5.18) \qquad y_t = \begin{cases} 0 & \text{if} \quad I_t < I_t^* \\ I_t - I_t^* & \text{if} \quad I_t \geq I_t^*, \end{cases}$$

where y is the amount and where I^* is a $\mathcal{N}(0, \sigma^2)$ variable. Each y_t is thus a function of the x_t's (via I_t) and of I_t^*. The I_t^*'s again play the role of disturbances, and may be interpreted as critical values of the index. At any value of I there will be a concentration of $y = 0$ (those whose critical values are so high that I falls short of I^*), and there will be a distribution of positive y's (those whose critical values are exceeded by I). Letting $F(z)$ = value of the standard normal cumulative distribution at z as before, we have

$$(5.19) \qquad \text{Prob}\,\{y = 0 \mid I\} = \text{Prob}\,\{I^* > I \mid I\} = 1 - F\left(\frac{I}{\sigma}\right)$$

and

$$(5.20) \qquad \begin{aligned} \text{Prob}\,\{y > y^* \geq 0 \mid I\} &= \text{Prob}\,\{I^* < I - y^* \mid I\} \\ &= F\left(\frac{I - y^*}{\sigma}\right) \end{aligned}$$

in view of the fact that I^* is $\mathcal{N}(0, \sigma^2)$. The fact that I, and hence the probabilities, is a function of the β's suggests maximum likelihood estimation of the β's and of σ. Without loss of generality, suppose the sample to be ordered so that the first S observations have $y = 0$ and the remaining $T - S$ have $y > 0$. Then the likelihood of the sample is

$$(5.21) \qquad \mathscr{L} = \left[1 - F\left(\frac{I_1}{\sigma}\right)\right] \cdots \left[1 - F\left(\frac{I_S}{\sigma}\right)\right] \times \frac{1}{\sigma} f\left(\frac{I_{S+1} - y_{S+1}}{\sigma}\right) \cdots \frac{1}{\sigma} f\left(\frac{I_T - y_T}{\sigma}\right)$$

where $f(z)$ = value of the standard normal density distribution at z. The logarithmic likelihood is

$$(5.22) \qquad L = \sum_{t=1}^{S} \log\left[1 - F\left(\frac{I_t}{\sigma}\right)\right] - (T - S)\log\sigma + \sum_{t=S+1}^{T} \log f\left(\frac{I_t - y_t}{\sigma}\right)$$

in which each term is a function of the β's and σ:

$$(5.23) \qquad F\left(\frac{I_t}{\sigma}\right) = (2\pi)^{-1/2} \int_{-\infty}^{\mathbf{x}_t'\boldsymbol{\beta}/\sigma} e^{-u^2/2}\, du$$

and

$$(5.24) \qquad f\left(\frac{I_t - y_t}{\sigma}\right) = (2\pi)^{-1/2} e^{-1/2[\mathbf{x}_t'\boldsymbol{\beta} - y_t/\sigma]^2}.$$

Setting the derivatives of (5.22) with respect to the β's and σ equal to zero gives the normal equations determining the maximum likelihood estimators, the $\hat{\beta}$'s and $\hat{\sigma}$. The normal equations are of course nonlinear; methods for solving them, for finding standard errors, and for testing hypotheses may be found in Tobin's paper.

In the Tobit model the conditional expectation may be shown to be

$$E(y_t \mid I_t) = I_t F\left(\frac{I_t}{\sigma}\right) + \sigma f\left(\frac{I_t}{\sigma}\right),$$

which is necessarily nonnegative. The estimated expectation is

$$\hat{y}_t = \hat{I}_t F\left(\frac{\hat{I}_t}{\hat{\sigma}}\right) + \hat{\sigma} f\left(\frac{\hat{I}_t}{\hat{\sigma}}\right).$$

To illustrate the Tobit method we use a relation from Tobin's paper. With x_1 = age (coded so that it = 1 for those 18–24 years, . . . , = 6 for those over 65 years), x_2 = initial ratio of liquid assets to disposable income, and y = ratio of durable expenditures to disposable income, the estimated index is

$$(5.25) \qquad \hat{I} = 0.167 - 0.028x_1 + 0.004x_2$$

and $\hat{\sigma} = 0.124$. More informative is this tabulation for selected values of x_1 all with $x_2 = 0$—$\hat{y}$ is the calculated expected value—unfortunately the corresponding observed figures are not available.

(5.26)

x_1	$\hat{I}$	$F(\hat{I}/\hat{\sigma})$	$\hat{y}$
1	0.14	0.87	0.15
2	0.11	0.81	0.12
4	0.06	0.67	0.08
6	−0.00	0.50	0.05

6. USE OF EXTRANEOUS INFORMATION

Up to this point in our discussion of regression the a priori information of the investigator has consisted of the form of the relationship (including the list of the regressors) and of the form and some parameters of the disturbance distribution. Armed with this knowledge he turns to the sample and applies some desirable estimation procedure to obtain an estimate of $\boldsymbol{\beta}$ and of other parameters of interest. In fact, the investigator may be more heavily armed. He may have knowledge of the ratios of some coefficients, of the values of some coefficients, of the values of some linear combination of the coefficients, or perhaps of merely the signs of some coefficients. This knowledge may derive from economic theory, from earlier empirical investigations, or from other samples. We refer to this type of knowledge as extraneous information; it comes from outside the sample itself.

The desirability of exploiting this extraneous information should be clear; it is intuitive that a gain in efficiency will result. In some modern statistical theory, the Bayesian approach to statistical inference is employed: Extraneous and sample information are combined to obtain knowledge of the population parameters. We do not develop the full-fledged Bayesian approach; but we do consider several devices which have been developed to incorporate extraneous information about the coefficient vector $\boldsymbol{\beta}$ into the estimation procedure, within the framework of classical statistical inference.

Throughout this section we deal with the case in which the sample observations are generated by the classical linear regression model with

(6.1) $$\mathbf{y} = \mathbf{X}\boldsymbol{\beta} + \boldsymbol{\epsilon},$$

(6.2) $$E\boldsymbol{\epsilon} = \mathbf{0},$$

(6.3) $$E\boldsymbol{\epsilon}\boldsymbol{\epsilon}' = \sigma^2\mathbf{I},$$

with the $T \times K$ matrix $\mathbf{X}$ of rank K fixed in repeated samples (for simplicity we use K, not $1 + K$). Generalizations to the case where $E\boldsymbol{\epsilon}\boldsymbol{\epsilon}' = \sigma^2\boldsymbol{\Omega}$ are straightforward but are not undertaken here. In the final subsection we treat a multivariate case.

Exact Linear Restrictions: Restricted Least Squares

Suppose that the extraneous information consists of exact linear restrictions on the coefficients:

$$\mathbf{r} = \mathbf{R}\boldsymbol{\beta} \tag{6.4}$$

where $\mathbf{r}$ is a $J \times 1$ known vector and $\mathbf{R}$ is a $J \times K$ known matrix of rank $J < K$, so that we have J independent restrictions on the elements of $\boldsymbol{\beta}$. Special cases are: (1) knowledge of the values of some elements of $\boldsymbol{\beta}$, e.g., $\beta_1 = \beta_1^*$ with

$$\mathbf{r} = (\beta_1^*), \qquad \mathbf{R} = (1 \quad 0 \quad 0 \quad \cdots \quad 0); \tag{6.5}$$

(2) knowledge of the ratios of the values of some elements of $\boldsymbol{\beta}$, e.g., $\beta_1/\beta_2 = c_1$ and $\beta_3/\beta_2 = c_3$, with

$$\mathbf{r} = \begin{pmatrix} 0 \\ 0 \end{pmatrix}, \qquad \mathbf{R} = \begin{pmatrix} 1 & -c_1 & 0 & 0 & \cdots & 0 \\ 0 & -c_3 & 1 & 0 & \cdots & 0 \end{pmatrix}; \tag{6.6}$$

and (3) knowledge of the value of a linear combination of the values of elements of $\boldsymbol{\beta}$, e.g., $\beta_1 + \cdots + \beta_K = 1$, with

$$\mathbf{r} = (1), \qquad \mathbf{R} = (1 \quad 1 \quad 1 \quad \cdots \quad 1). \tag{6.7}$$

To incorporate this information the method of *restricted least squares* is proposed. We seek the $\boldsymbol{\beta}$ that minimizes the sum of squared residuals $(\mathbf{y} - \mathbf{X}\boldsymbol{\beta})'(\mathbf{y} - \mathbf{X}\boldsymbol{\beta})$ subject to the restriction $\mathbf{R}\boldsymbol{\beta} - \mathbf{r} = \mathbf{0}$. Therefore we minimize

$$S = (\mathbf{y} - \mathbf{X}\boldsymbol{\beta})'(\mathbf{y} - \mathbf{X}\boldsymbol{\beta}) - 2\boldsymbol{\lambda}'(\mathbf{R}\boldsymbol{\beta} - \mathbf{r}), \tag{6.8}$$

where $\boldsymbol{\lambda}$ is a $J \times 1$ vector of Lagrange multipliers, with respect to $\boldsymbol{\beta}$ and $\boldsymbol{\lambda}$. Setting the derivative of S with respect to $\boldsymbol{\beta}$ equal to zero gives for the minimizing value $\mathbf{b}^*$

$$\frac{1}{2}\frac{\partial S}{\partial \boldsymbol{\beta}} = -\mathbf{X}'\mathbf{y} + \mathbf{X}'\mathbf{X}\mathbf{b}^* - \mathbf{R}'\boldsymbol{\lambda}^* = \mathbf{0}, \tag{6.9}$$

whence

$$\mathbf{b}^* = \mathbf{b} + (\mathbf{X}'\mathbf{X})^{-1}\mathbf{R}'\boldsymbol{\lambda}^*, \tag{6.10}$$

where $\mathbf{b} = (\mathbf{X}'\mathbf{X})^{-1}\mathbf{X}'\mathbf{y}$ is the classical (unrestricted) least-squares estimator.

Premultiplying (6.10) by **R** gives

(6.11) $$\mathbf{Rb}^* = \mathbf{Rb} + \mathbf{R}(\mathbf{X}'\mathbf{X})^{-1}\mathbf{R}'\boldsymbol{\lambda}^*;$$

imposing the restriction $\mathbf{Rb}^* = \mathbf{r}$ gives

(6.12) $$\mathbf{r} = \mathbf{Rb}^* = \mathbf{Rb} + \mathbf{R}(\mathbf{X}'\mathbf{X})^{-1}\mathbf{R}'\boldsymbol{\lambda}^*,$$

whence

(6.13) $$\boldsymbol{\lambda}^* = [\mathbf{R}(\mathbf{X}'\mathbf{X})^{-1}\mathbf{R}']^{-1}(\mathbf{r} - \mathbf{Rb}).$$

Inserting this back into (6.10) gives

(6.14) $$\mathbf{b}^* = \mathbf{b} + (\mathbf{X}'\mathbf{X})^{-1}\mathbf{R}'[\mathbf{R}(\mathbf{X}'\mathbf{X})^{-1}\mathbf{R}']^{-1}(\mathbf{r} - \mathbf{Rb}).$$

It is seen that the restricted estimator $\mathbf{b}^*$ differs from the unrestricted one $\mathbf{b}$ by a linear function of the amount $\mathbf{r} - \mathbf{Rb}$ by which the unrestricted estimator fails to satisfy the restrictions. The sampling properties of $\mathbf{b}^*$ may be derived as follows. Insert the familiar $\mathbf{b} = \boldsymbol{\beta} + (\mathbf{X}'\mathbf{X})^{-1}\mathbf{X}'\boldsymbol{\epsilon}$ into (6.14):

(6.15) $$\begin{aligned}\mathbf{b}^* &= \boldsymbol{\beta} + (\mathbf{X}'\mathbf{X})^{-1}\mathbf{X}'\boldsymbol{\epsilon} + (\mathbf{X}'\mathbf{X})^{-1}\mathbf{R}'[\mathbf{R}(\mathbf{X}'\mathbf{X})^{-1}\mathbf{R}']^{-1} \\ &\quad \times [\mathbf{r} - \mathbf{R}\boldsymbol{\beta} - \mathbf{R}(\mathbf{X}'\mathbf{X})^{-1}\mathbf{X}'\boldsymbol{\epsilon}] \\ &= \boldsymbol{\beta} + \{\mathbf{I} - (\mathbf{X}'\mathbf{X})^{-1}\mathbf{R}'[\mathbf{R}(\mathbf{X}'\mathbf{X})^{-1}\mathbf{R}']^{-1}\mathbf{R}\}(\mathbf{X}'\mathbf{X})^{-1}\mathbf{X}'\boldsymbol{\epsilon},\end{aligned}$$

where we have used $\mathbf{r} - \mathbf{R}\boldsymbol{\beta} = \mathbf{0}$. The restricted least-squares estimator is clearly unbiased. Further we may derive for the covariance matrix

(6.16) $$\begin{aligned}\mathbf{V}^* = \boldsymbol{\Sigma}_{\mathbf{b}^*\mathbf{b}^*} &= E(\mathbf{b}^* - \boldsymbol{\beta})(\mathbf{b}^* - \boldsymbol{\beta})' \\ &= \sigma^2(\mathbf{X}'\mathbf{X})^{-1}\{\mathbf{I} - \mathbf{R}'[\mathbf{R}(\mathbf{X}'\mathbf{X})^{-1}\mathbf{R}']^{-1}\mathbf{R}(\mathbf{X}'\mathbf{X})^{-1}\} \\ &= \mathbf{V} - \mathbf{VR}'(\mathbf{RVR}')^{-1}\mathbf{RV}\end{aligned}$$

where $\mathbf{V} = \boldsymbol{\Sigma}_{\mathbf{bb}} = \sigma^2(\mathbf{X}'\mathbf{X})^{-1}$ is the covariance matrix of $\mathbf{b}$. It is easy to see that there has been a gain in efficiency. $\mathbf{V}$ is of course positive definite. Then since $\mathbf{R}'$ is a $K \times J$ matrix of rank J, it follows from (2.7.4) that $\mathbf{RVR}'$ is positive definite, and then it follows from (2.7.6) that $(\mathbf{RVR}')^{-1}$ is positive definite. Further, the second matrix on the right of (6.16), namely $(\mathbf{RV})'(\mathbf{RVR}')^{-1}(\mathbf{RV})$, is nonnegative definite by (2.7.14). Thus $\mathbf{V}^*$ is equal to $\mathbf{V}$ less a nonnegative definite matrix so that each diagonal element of $\mathbf{V}^*$ is less than or equal to the corresponding element of $\mathbf{V}$. We conclude that the variance of each element of $\mathbf{b}^*$ is less than or equal to the variance of the corresponding element of $\mathbf{b}$. Indeed, it can be shown that $\mathbf{b}^*$ is the BLUE of $\boldsymbol{\beta}$ in the sense that its elements have the minimum variance within the class of all unbiased estimators which are linear functions of $\mathbf{y}$ and $\mathbf{r}$. The proof is given by Theil (1961, pp. 536–538).

In practice it may be more convenient to compute $\mathbf{b}^*$ by first using the restrictions to eliminate some elements of $\boldsymbol{\beta}$, then applying classical least squares to the reduced problem, and finally imposing the restrictions to estimate the remaining elements of $\boldsymbol{\beta}$. To illustrate, suppose $y = \beta_1 x_1 + \beta_2 x_2 + \epsilon$, and let the restriction be $1 = -2\beta_1 + \beta_2$. Substitute in the restriction to obtain

$$y = \beta_1 x_1 + (2\beta_1 + 1)x_2 + \epsilon \quad \text{or} \quad y - x_2 = \beta_1(x_1 + 2x_2) + \epsilon,$$

which we write as $y^* = \beta_1 x^* + \epsilon$. Regressing y^* on x^* gives b_1^*, and then imposing the restriction gives $b_2^* = 2b_1^* + 1$.

Extraneous Unbiased Estimates: Restricted Least Squares

Now suppose that the extraneous information is not exact but rather consists of unbiased estimates of some elements of $\boldsymbol{\beta}$ obtained from another sample. Again a restricted least-squares procedure is possible. Consider the partitioned relationship:

$$\mathbf{y} = \mathbf{X}_1\boldsymbol{\beta}_1 + \mathbf{X}_2\boldsymbol{\beta}_2 + \boldsymbol{\epsilon} \tag{6.17}$$

and suppose we have $\mathbf{b}_1^*$ such that $\mathbf{b}_1^*$ is an unbiased estimate of $\boldsymbol{\beta}_1$:

$$\mathbf{b}_1^* = \boldsymbol{\beta}_1 + \mathbf{d} \tag{6.18}$$

where $E\mathbf{d} = \mathbf{0}$. Then applying the restricted least-squares procedure as suggested at the end of the previous subsection, we regress $\mathbf{y} - \mathbf{X}_1\mathbf{b}_1^*$ on $\mathbf{X}_2$ to estimate $\boldsymbol{\beta}_2$ as

$$\mathbf{b}_2^* = (\mathbf{X}_2'\mathbf{X}_2)^{-1}\mathbf{X}_2'(\mathbf{y} - \mathbf{X}_1\mathbf{b}_1^*). \tag{6.19}$$

To find the sampling properties of this estimator of $\boldsymbol{\beta}_2$ substitute (6.17) into (6.19):

$$\begin{aligned} \mathbf{b}_2^* &= (\mathbf{X}_2'\mathbf{X}_2)^{-1}\mathbf{X}_2'(\mathbf{X}_1\boldsymbol{\beta}_1 + \mathbf{X}_2\boldsymbol{\beta}_2 + \boldsymbol{\epsilon} - \mathbf{X}_1\mathbf{b}_1^*) \\ &= \boldsymbol{\beta}_2 + (\mathbf{X}_2'\mathbf{X}_2)^{-1}\mathbf{X}_2'\boldsymbol{\epsilon} - (\mathbf{X}_2'\mathbf{X}_2)^{-1}\mathbf{X}_2'\mathbf{X}_1\mathbf{d}. \end{aligned} \tag{6.20}$$

Since $E\boldsymbol{\epsilon} = \mathbf{0}$ and $E\mathbf{d} = \mathbf{0}$, $\mathbf{b}_2^*$ is unbiased. For the covariance matrix of $\mathbf{b}_2^*$, we find, assuming $E\mathbf{d}\boldsymbol{\epsilon}' = \mathbf{0}$:

$$\begin{aligned} \mathbf{V}_2^* &= E(\mathbf{b}_2^* - \boldsymbol{\beta}_2)(\mathbf{b}_2^* - \boldsymbol{\beta}_2)' \\ &= \sigma^2(\mathbf{X}_2'\mathbf{X}_2)^{-1} + (\mathbf{X}_2'\mathbf{X}_2)^{-1}\mathbf{X}_2'\mathbf{X}_1\mathbf{V}_1^*\mathbf{X}_1'\mathbf{X}_2(\mathbf{X}_2'\mathbf{X}_2)^{-1} \end{aligned} \tag{6.21}$$

where $\mathbf{V}_1^* = E\mathbf{d}\mathbf{d}'$ is the covariance matrix of the extraneous estimator $\mathbf{b}_1^*$. Now the covariance matrix of the unrestricted least-squares estimator of $\boldsymbol{\beta}_2$ may be written as

$$\begin{aligned} \mathbf{V}_2 &= E(\mathbf{b}_2 - \boldsymbol{\beta}_2)(\mathbf{b}_2 - \boldsymbol{\beta}_2)' \\ &= \sigma^2(\mathbf{X}_2'\mathbf{X}_2)^{-1} + (\mathbf{X}_2'\mathbf{X}_2)^{-1}\mathbf{X}_2'\mathbf{X}_1\mathbf{V}_1\mathbf{X}_1'\mathbf{X}_2(\mathbf{X}_2'\mathbf{X}_2)^{-1} \end{aligned} \tag{6.22}$$

where $\mathbf{V}_1 = E(\mathbf{b}_1 - \boldsymbol{\beta}_1)(\mathbf{b}_1 - \boldsymbol{\beta}_1)' = \sigma^2[\mathbf{X}_1'\mathbf{X}_1 - \mathbf{X}_1'\mathbf{X}_2(\mathbf{X}_2'\mathbf{X}_2)^{-1}\mathbf{X}_2'\mathbf{X}_1]^{-1}$

is the covariance matrix of the unrestricted least-squares estimator of $\boldsymbol{\beta}_1$. [To obtain this result we have employed the partitioned inversion procedure used in (4.7.10)-(4.7.13), but with the roles of $\mathbf{X}_1$ and $\mathbf{X}_2$ interchanged]. Then subtracting (6.21) from (6.22) gives a comparison of the covariance matrices of the restricted and unrestricted least-squares estimators of $\boldsymbol{\beta}_2$:

$$\text{(6.23)} \qquad \begin{aligned} \mathbf{V}_2 - \mathbf{V}_2^* &= (\mathbf{X}_2'\mathbf{X}_2)^{-1}\mathbf{X}_2'\mathbf{X}_1(\mathbf{V}_1 - \mathbf{V}_1^*)\mathbf{X}_1'\mathbf{X}_2(\mathbf{X}_2'\mathbf{X}_2)^{-1} \\ &= \mathbf{B}(\mathbf{V}_1 - \mathbf{V}_1^*)\mathbf{B}' \end{aligned}$$

where $\mathbf{B} = (\mathbf{X}_2'\mathbf{X}_2)^{-1}\mathbf{X}_2'\mathbf{X}_1$ is the coefficient matrix of the "auxiliary regressions" of $\mathbf{X}_1$ on $\mathbf{X}_2$. If we let $\mathbf{B}_j$ denote the jth column of $\mathbf{B}'$ we see that the variance of the unrestricted estimator of the jth element of $\boldsymbol{\beta}_2$ will exceed the variance of its restricted estimator by $\mathbf{B}_j'(\mathbf{V}_1 - \mathbf{V}_1^*)\mathbf{B}_j$. There will be a gain in efficiency in the estimation of the jth element of $\boldsymbol{\beta}_2$ when this expression is positive. This is seen to depend on whether the variances of the extraneous estimator of $\boldsymbol{\beta}_1$ are small relative to those of its unrestricted least squares estimator. Suppose, e.g., that $\mathbf{V}_1 - \mathbf{V}_1^*$ is nonnegative definite. Then $\mathbf{B}_j'(\mathbf{V}_1 - \mathbf{V}_1^*)\mathbf{B}_j \geq 0$ for all j. To illustrate for the case of just two regressors, we have var $(b_2^*) \leq$ var (b_2) if and only if var $(b_1^*) \leq$ var (b_1).

Intuitively, it is advantageous to employ extraneous estimators when their variance is relatively small. It should be clear that this development may be extended to the case of unbiased estimates of linear combinations of some elements of $\boldsymbol{\beta}$. It is also apparent that the imposition of "exact" linear restrictions may be advantageous even when the restrictions are false; the error may be handled as a sampling error.

Extraneous Unbiased Estimates: Generalized Least Squares

There is an obvious deficiency with the method of the previous subsection: It fails to utilize the sample information to improve on the estimate of $\boldsymbol{\beta}_1$. We turn now to a method that uses the extraneous unbiased estimator of $\boldsymbol{\beta}_1$ together with the sample information to estimate both $\boldsymbol{\beta}_1$ and $\boldsymbol{\beta}_2$ efficiently. Once again we have

$$\text{(6.24)} \qquad \mathbf{y} = \mathbf{X}\boldsymbol{\beta} + \boldsymbol{\epsilon},$$

$$\text{(6.25)} \qquad E\boldsymbol{\epsilon}\boldsymbol{\epsilon}' = \sigma^2\mathbf{I},$$

$$\text{(6.26)} \qquad \mathbf{b}_1^* = \boldsymbol{\beta}_1 + \mathbf{d},$$

$$\text{(6.27)} \qquad E\mathbf{d} = \mathbf{0},$$

and $E\mathbf{d}\boldsymbol{\epsilon}' = \mathbf{0}$. Further, we require knowledge of $\mathbf{W} = \mathbf{V}_1^* = E\mathbf{d}\mathbf{d}'$. We write the extraneous and sample information together as

$$\text{(6.28)} \qquad \begin{pmatrix} \mathbf{y} \\ \mathbf{b}_1^* \end{pmatrix} = \begin{pmatrix} \mathbf{X} \\ \mathbf{R} \end{pmatrix}\boldsymbol{\beta} + \begin{pmatrix} \boldsymbol{\epsilon} \\ \mathbf{d} \end{pmatrix}$$

where $\mathbf{R} = (\mathbf{I} \quad \mathbf{0})$. We have for the covariance matrix of the extended "disturbance"

$$(6.29) \qquad E\begin{pmatrix} \boldsymbol{\epsilon} \\ \mathbf{d} \end{pmatrix}(\boldsymbol{\epsilon}' \quad \mathbf{d}') = \begin{pmatrix} \sigma^2\mathbf{I} & \mathbf{0} \\ \mathbf{0} & \mathbf{W} \end{pmatrix}.$$

Therefore the BLUE of $\boldsymbol{\beta}$—in the sense of having minimum variance in the class of all unbiased estimators which are linear in $\mathbf{y}$ and $\mathbf{b}_1^*$—is the generalized least-squares estimator

$$(6.30) \qquad \mathbf{b}^{**} = \left\{(\mathbf{X}' \quad \mathbf{R}')\begin{pmatrix} \sigma^2\mathbf{I} & \mathbf{0} \\ \mathbf{0} & \mathbf{W} \end{pmatrix}^{-1}\begin{pmatrix} \mathbf{X} \\ \mathbf{R} \end{pmatrix}\right\}^{-1}(\mathbf{X}' \quad \mathbf{R}')\begin{pmatrix} \sigma^2\mathbf{I} & \mathbf{0} \\ \mathbf{0} & \mathbf{W} \end{pmatrix}^{-1}\begin{pmatrix} \mathbf{y} \\ \mathbf{b}_1^* \end{pmatrix}$$
$$= \left[\frac{1}{\sigma^2}\mathbf{X}'\mathbf{X} + \mathbf{R}'\mathbf{W}^{-1}\mathbf{R}\right]^{-1}\left[\frac{1}{\sigma^2}\mathbf{X}'\mathbf{y} + \mathbf{R}'\mathbf{W}^{-1}\mathbf{b}_1^*\right].$$

To illuminate the result consider the case where $\boldsymbol{\beta}_1$ consists of a single element, so that $\mathbf{R} = (1 \quad 0 \quad \cdots \quad 0)$. Letting σ_*^2 be the scalar $\mathbf{W}$ we have

$$(6.31) \qquad \mathbf{R}'\mathbf{W}^{-1}\mathbf{R} = \frac{1}{\sigma_*^2}\begin{pmatrix} 1 & 0 & \cdots & 0 \\ 0 & 0 & \cdots & 0 \\ \cdot & \cdot & & \cdot \\ \cdot & \cdot & & \cdot \\ \cdot & \cdot & & \cdot \\ 0 & 0 & \cdots & 0 \end{pmatrix}, \qquad \mathbf{R}'\mathbf{W}^{-1}\mathbf{b}_1^* = \frac{1}{\sigma_*^2}\begin{pmatrix} b_1^* \\ 0 \\ \cdot \\ \cdot \\ \cdot \\ 0 \end{pmatrix},$$

so that the normal equations of (6.30) are explicitly

$$(6.32) \qquad \begin{pmatrix} \Sigma x_1^2 + \lambda & \Sigma x_1x_2 & \cdots & \Sigma x_1x_K \\ \Sigma x_2x_1 & \Sigma x_2^2 & \cdots & \Sigma x_2x_K \\ \cdot & \cdot & & \cdot \\ \cdot & \cdot & & \cdot \\ \cdot & \cdot & & \cdot \\ \Sigma x_Kx_1 & \Sigma x_Kx_2 & \cdots & \Sigma x_K^2 \end{pmatrix}\begin{pmatrix} b_1^{**} \\ b_2^{**} \\ \cdot \\ \cdot \\ \cdot \\ b_K^{**} \end{pmatrix} = \begin{pmatrix} \Sigma x_1y + \lambda b_1^* \\ \Sigma x_2y \\ \cdot \\ \cdot \\ \cdot \\ \Sigma x_Ky \end{pmatrix},$$

where $\lambda = \sigma^2/\sigma_*^2$. Thus the only difference from the classical normal equations is in the upper left-hand element of $\mathbf{X}'\mathbf{X}$ and in the upper element of $\mathbf{X}'\mathbf{y}$.

This method is due to Durbin (1953). His approach was in fact to seek the best linear unbiased combination of $\mathbf{b} = (\mathbf{X}'\mathbf{X})^{-1}\mathbf{X}'\mathbf{y}$ and $\mathbf{b}_1^*$; our approach is equivalent. It should be clear that this development may be extended to the case of unbiased estimates of linear combinations of elements of $\boldsymbol{\beta}$.

Note that this method requires knowledge of σ^2 and $\mathbf{W}$, up to a factor of proportionality. An approximate use of the method is to employ unbiased estimates of these variances and covariances. For example, σ^2 may be estimated unbiasedly from the unrestricted least-squares regression, and $\mathbf{W}$ may be estimated unbiasedly from the regression that provided $\mathbf{b}_1^*$.

Extraneous Inequality Constraints: Mixed Linear Estimation

Economic theory often provides a priori bounds on the values of some coefficients. For example, the extraneous information may be that the price elasticity of supply is nonnegative or that the income elasticity of demand for an agricultural product lies between 0 and 1. A method for incorporating such inequality constraints into the estimation procedure is suggested by the method of the previous subsection. To illustrate, suppose that it is known a priori that the coefficient β_1 almost certainly lies between 0 and 1. Then this may be formulated as

$$\tfrac{1}{2} = \beta_1 + d \qquad (6.33)$$

with

$$Ed = 0, \qquad Ed^2 = \tfrac{1}{16}, \qquad (6.34)$$

capturing the idea that values of β_1 outside the two-sigma range $\frac{1}{2} \pm 2\sqrt{\frac{1}{16}}$ —which is the range 0 to 1—are virtually impossible. Then (6.33) may be employed in the generalized least-squares procedure of the preceding subsection, just as were the unbiased estimates.

This method is due to Theil and Goldberger (1961); for further results see Theil (1963). It should be clear that this development may be extended to the case of inequality constraints on linear combinations of coefficients.

Extraneous Inequality Constraints: Restricted Least Squares

There is of course some arbitrariness in the choice of Ed^2 in (6.34). A method of least squares restricted by the inequality constraints which avoids this is available. Suppose these constraints are given by

$$\mathbf{R}\boldsymbol{\beta} \leq \mathbf{r}. \qquad (6.35)$$

Then we may minimize the sum of squared deviations $(\mathbf{y} - \mathbf{X}\boldsymbol{\beta})'(\mathbf{y} - \mathbf{X}\boldsymbol{\beta})$ subject to these constraints; this is a problem in quadratic programming.

To illustrate for the case of a single regressor, suppose we have $y = \beta x + \epsilon$, with a priori information that

$$\beta_L \leq \beta \leq \beta_U \tag{6.36}$$

where the two bounds are known. It is clear that the restricted least squares estimator will be

$$\hat{\beta} = \begin{cases} \beta_L & \text{if} \quad b < \beta_L \\ b & \text{if} \quad \beta_L \leq b \leq \beta_U \\ \beta_U & \text{if} \quad \beta_U < b, \end{cases} \tag{6.37}$$

where b is the classical unrestricted least-squares estimator.

This method is presented in Zellner (1961*a*); there the sampling properties of this estimator and of related ones are developed.

Zero Restrictions in the Multivariate Model: Restricted Least Squares

Finally let us consider the use of extraneous information when we have a set of linear relationships embodied in the multivariate classical linear regression model. The set of M relationships is given by $\mathbf{Y} = \mathbf{X}\boldsymbol{\beta} + \boldsymbol{\mathcal{E}}$, and we have seen that least squares applied to each relation provided the BLUE's of the elements of $\boldsymbol{\beta}$. But now suppose that we have a priori information that certain elements of $\boldsymbol{\beta}$ are zero. An obvious way of utilizing these zero restrictions is to drop out of each relation the regressors whose coefficients are known to be zero in that relation and proceed to estimate each relation by least squares. A gain in efficiency is generally available, however, if the zero restrictions are utilized in another manner to estimate all the M relations together.

Let us rewrite the restricted relations as

$$\mathbf{y}_m = \mathbf{X}_m\boldsymbol{\beta}_m^* + \boldsymbol{\epsilon}_m \qquad (m = 1, \ldots, M) \tag{6.38}$$

where $\boldsymbol{\beta}_m^*$ is $\boldsymbol{\beta}_m$ with the zeros deleted and $\mathbf{X}_m$ is $\mathbf{X}$ after deletion of the columns referring to regressors whose coefficients in the mth relation are zero. The full system, with restrictions incorporated, may then be written as

$$\begin{pmatrix} \mathbf{y}_1 \\ \cdot \\ \cdot \\ \cdot \\ \mathbf{y}_M \end{pmatrix} = \begin{pmatrix} \mathbf{X}_1 & \mathbf{0} & \cdots & \mathbf{0} \\ \cdot & \cdot & & \cdot \\ \cdot & \cdot & & \cdot \\ \cdot & \cdot & & \cdot \\ \mathbf{0} & \mathbf{0} & \cdots & \mathbf{X}_M \end{pmatrix} \begin{pmatrix} \boldsymbol{\beta}_1^* \\ \cdot \\ \cdot \\ \cdot \\ \boldsymbol{\beta}_M^* \end{pmatrix} + \begin{pmatrix} \boldsymbol{\epsilon}_1 \\ \cdot \\ \cdot \\ \cdot \\ \boldsymbol{\epsilon}_M \end{pmatrix}, \tag{6.39}$$

or more compactly as

$$\mathbf{y} = \mathbf{Z}^*\boldsymbol{\beta}^* + \boldsymbol{\epsilon}. \tag{6.40}$$

As in (4.86) $E\boldsymbol{\epsilon\epsilon}' = \boldsymbol{\Phi} = \boldsymbol{\Omega} \otimes \mathbf{I}$, but now the BLUE of $\boldsymbol{\beta}$ using the extraneous information is

$$\tilde{\mathbf{b}}^* = (\mathbf{Z}^{*\prime}\boldsymbol{\Phi}^{-1}\mathbf{Z}^*)^{-1}(\mathbf{Z}^{*\prime}\boldsymbol{\Phi}^{-1}\mathbf{y}), \tag{6.41}$$

which is to be distinguished from (4.87) since $\mathbf{Z}^*$ is not the same as $\mathbf{Z}$. Making the appropriate changes in (4.88)–(4.92) we find for $\tilde{\mathbf{b}}^*$

$$\tilde{\mathbf{b}}^* = \begin{pmatrix} \omega^{11}\mathbf{X}_1'\mathbf{X}_1 & \cdots & \omega^{1M}\mathbf{X}_1'\mathbf{X}_M \\ \cdot & & \cdot \\ \cdot & & \cdot \\ \cdot & & \cdot \\ \omega^{M1}\mathbf{X}_M'\mathbf{X}_1 & \cdots & \omega^{MM}\mathbf{X}_M'\mathbf{X}_M \end{pmatrix}^{-1} \begin{pmatrix} \sum_{\mu'=1}^{M} \omega^{1\mu'}\mathbf{X}_1'\mathbf{y}_{\mu'} \\ \cdot \\ \cdot \\ \cdot \\ \sum_{\mu'=1}^{M} \omega^{M\mu'}\mathbf{X}_M'\mathbf{y}_{\mu'} \end{pmatrix}, \tag{6.42}$$

which in general does not reduce to the $\mathbf{b}$ of classical least-squares estimators. The covariance matrix of $\tilde{\mathbf{b}}^*$ is, as usual, the inverse matrix on the right of (6.42).

If there are no restrictions—or equivalently if the same regressors are excluded from every relation—then $\mathbf{X}_1 = \cdots = \mathbf{X}_M = \mathbf{X}$, and as we have seen in (4.92) the BLUE's are just the classical least-squares estimators: $\tilde{\mathbf{b}}^*$ reduces to $\mathbf{b}$. Alternatively, suppose that the contemporaneous disturbance covariance matrix is diagonal—i.e., $\omega_{mm'} = 0$ for all $m \neq m'$. Then $\omega^{mm'} = 0$ for all $m \neq m'$ and (6.42) reduces to

$$\tilde{\mathbf{b}}_* = \begin{pmatrix} \omega^{11}\mathbf{X}_1'\mathbf{X}_1 & \cdots & \mathbf{0} \\ \cdot & & \cdot \\ \cdot & & \cdot \\ \cdot & & \cdot \\ \mathbf{0} & \cdots & \omega^{MM}\mathbf{X}_M'\mathbf{X}_M \end{pmatrix}^{-1} \begin{pmatrix} \omega^{11}\mathbf{X}_1'\mathbf{y}_1 \\ \cdot \\ \cdot \\ \cdot \\ \omega^{MM}\mathbf{X}_M'\mathbf{y}_M \end{pmatrix} \tag{6.43}$$

$$= \begin{pmatrix} \omega_{11}(\mathbf{X}_1'\mathbf{X}_1)^{-1} & \cdots & \mathbf{0} \\ \cdot & & \cdot \\ \cdot & & \cdot \\ \cdot & & \cdot \\ \mathbf{0} & \cdots & \omega_{MM}(\mathbf{X}_M'\mathbf{X}_M)^{-1} \end{pmatrix}$$

$$\times \begin{pmatrix} \omega^{11}\mathbf{X}_1'\mathbf{y}_1 \\ \cdot \\ \cdot \\ \cdot \\ \omega^{MM}\mathbf{X}_M'\mathbf{y}_M \end{pmatrix} = \begin{pmatrix} (\mathbf{X}_1'\mathbf{X}_1)^{-1}\mathbf{X}_1'\mathbf{y}_1 \\ \cdot \\ \cdot \\ \cdot \\ (\mathbf{X}_M'\mathbf{X}_M)^{-1}\mathbf{X}_M'\mathbf{y}_M \end{pmatrix} = \mathbf{b}.$$

If, however, neither of the sufficient conditions—$\mathbf{X}_m = \mathbf{X}$ $(m = 1, \ldots, M)$ or $\omega_{mm'} = 0$ $(m, m' = 1, \ldots, M;\ m \neq m')$—holds, then $\tilde{\mathbf{b}}_* \neq \mathbf{b}$ and $\tilde{\mathbf{b}}_*$ will be more efficient than $\mathbf{b}$. Thus in general a gain in efficiency will result from imposing the zero restrictions and estimating the set of relations together rather than by estimating each relation by classical least squares.

It is instructive to examine the gain in efficiency explicitly for the two-equation case $M = 2$. The covariance matrix of the classical estimator of the coefficients of the first equation is of course

$$(6.44) \qquad \mathbf{V} = \omega_{11}(\mathbf{X}_1'\mathbf{X}_1)^{-1}$$

whereas the covariance matrix of the efficient estimator of these coefficients is the upper left-hand submatrix, call it $\mathbf{V}^*$, of

$$(6.45) \qquad \begin{pmatrix} \omega^{11}\mathbf{X}_1'\mathbf{X}_1 & \omega^{12}\mathbf{X}_1'\mathbf{X}_2 \\ \omega^{21}\mathbf{X}_2'\mathbf{X}_1 & \omega^{22}\mathbf{X}_2'\mathbf{X}_2 \end{pmatrix}^{-1}.$$

For convenience we write the disturbance covariance matrix as

$$(6.46) \qquad \mathbf{\Omega} = \begin{pmatrix} \omega_{11} & \omega_{12} \\ \omega_{21} & \omega_{22} \end{pmatrix} = \begin{pmatrix} \omega_1^2 & \rho\omega_1\omega_2 \\ \rho\omega_1\omega_2 & \omega_2^2 \end{pmatrix},$$

where $\omega_1 = \sqrt{\omega_{11}}$, $\omega_2 = \sqrt{\omega_{22}}$, and ρ is the correlation coefficient $\sqrt{\omega_{12}^2/\omega_{11}\omega_{22}}$; then

$$(6.47) \qquad \mathbf{\Omega}^{-1} = \begin{pmatrix} \omega^{11} & \omega^{12} \\ \omega^{21} & \omega^{22} \end{pmatrix} = (1 - \rho^2)^{-1}\begin{pmatrix} \omega_1^{-2} & -\rho\omega_1^{-1}\omega_2^{-1} \\ -\rho\omega_1^{-1}\omega_2^{-1} & \omega_2^{-2} \end{pmatrix}.$$

With this notation (6.44) becomes

$$(6.48) \qquad \mathbf{V} = \omega_1^2(\mathbf{X}_1'\mathbf{X}_1)^{-1}$$

and (6.45) becomes

$$(6.49) \qquad (1 - \rho^2)\begin{pmatrix} \omega_1^{-2}\mathbf{X}_1'\mathbf{X}_1 & -\rho\omega_1^{-1}\omega_2^{-1}\mathbf{X}_1'\mathbf{X}_2 \\ -\rho\omega_1^{-1}\omega_2^{-1}\mathbf{X}_2'\mathbf{X}_1 & \omega_2^{-2}\mathbf{X}_2'\mathbf{X}_2 \end{pmatrix}^{-1}.$$

Application of the rule for partitioned matrix inversion gives for the upper left-hand submatrix of (6.49)

$$\begin{aligned}(6.50) \qquad \mathbf{V}^* &= (1 - \rho^2)\{\omega_1^{-2}(\mathbf{X}_1'\mathbf{X}_1) - \rho^2\omega_1^{-2}\mathbf{X}_1'\mathbf{X}_2(\mathbf{X}_2'\mathbf{X}_2)^{-1}\mathbf{X}_2'\mathbf{X}_1\}^{-1} \\ &= \{\omega_1^{-2}\mathbf{X}_1'\mathbf{X}_1 \\ &\qquad + \rho^2(1 - \rho^2)^{-1}\omega_1^{-2}[\mathbf{X}_1'\mathbf{X}_1 - \mathbf{X}_1'\mathbf{X}_2(\mathbf{X}_2'\mathbf{X}_2)^{-1}\mathbf{X}_2'\mathbf{X}_1]\}^{-1} \\ &= (\mathbf{V}^{-1} + \mathbf{C})^{-1},\end{aligned}$$

say, where $\mathbf{C} = \rho^2(1 - \rho^2)^{-1}\omega_1^{-2}[\mathbf{X}_1'\mathbf{X}_1 - \mathbf{X}_1'\mathbf{X}_2(\mathbf{X}_2'\mathbf{X}_2)^{-1}\mathbf{X}_2'\mathbf{X}_1]$. Now $\mathbf{V}^{-1}$ is positive definite and $\mathbf{C}$ is nonnegative definite—it is a nonnegative scalar times a moment matrix of "auxiliary regression" residuals—whence by (2.7.21) $\mathbf{V} - \mathbf{V}^*$ is nonnegative definite. Note that $\mathbf{C} = \mathbf{0}$ (so that $\mathbf{V} = \mathbf{V}^*$) if $\rho = 0$ or $\mathbf{X}_1 = \mathbf{X}_2$.

A difficulty with the proposed procedure is that it requires knowledge of $\mathbf{\Omega}$. In practice, $\mathbf{\Omega}$ may be estimated as $\hat{\mathbf{\Omega}} = T^{-1}\mathbf{W}$ where $\mathbf{W}$ is the moment matrix of the residuals from the classical least-squares regression. Using $\hat{\mathbf{\Omega}}$ in place of $\mathbf{\Omega}$ gives $\hat{\hat{\mathbf{b}}}^* = (\mathbf{Z}^{*\prime}\hat{\mathbf{\Phi}}^{-1}\mathbf{Z}^*)^{-1}(\mathbf{Z}^{*\prime}\hat{\mathbf{\Phi}}^{-1}\mathbf{y})$—where $\hat{\mathbf{\Phi}} = \hat{\mathbf{\Omega}} \otimes \mathbf{I}$—as an approximation to the BLUE. This method is due to Zellner (1962*a*); its properties are also discussed in Zellner (1962*b*) and Zellner and Huang (1962). More general linear restrictions may also be utilized along the lines of (6.4).

CHAPTER 6

Linear Regression with Stochastic Regressors

1. INTRODUCTION

The classical linear regression model requires that the regressors be nonstochastic; i.e., that the regressor observation matrix $\mathbf{X}$ be fixed in repeated samples. This may be appropriate for laboratory experiments, in which the investigator has control over the explanatory variables and can conceive of keeping the values the same in repeated samples. In many economic contexts, however, the explanatory variables are themselves generated by some stochastic mechanism and they would not have the same values in repeated samples. Then the regressand vector will differ from sample to sample not only because of variation in the disturbance vector, but also because of variation in the regressor matrix.

In this chapter we begin our analysis of estimation under these circumstances. Successive samples are now generated by drawing from the joint distribution of $\mathbf{X}$ and $\boldsymbol{\epsilon}$. As might be anticipated, the properties of estimators will depend critically on the nature of this joint distribution; in particular, on whether or not $\mathbf{X}$ and $\boldsymbol{\epsilon}$ are independently distributed. We proceed in increasing order of complexity. In Section 2 we consider the case where $\mathbf{X}$ is distributed entirely independently of $\boldsymbol{\epsilon}$. In Section 3 a specific sort of partial dependence, important in time series analysis, is allowed. That analysis suggests a further weakening of the independence assumption into one of "contemporaneous uncorrelatedness"; the model incorporating this latter assumption is discussed in Section 4. Finally in Section 5 we introduce the general case of stochastic regressors, where no independence is assumed. One interpretation of this last is that there are errors of observation in measuring the variables, and this is briefly dealt with. Another interpretation is that the relationship being investigated is one of a system of simultaneous relations in which the regressors are jointly determined along with the regressand. This situation, which is naturally an important one in econometrics, is held over for Chapter 7.

2. INDEPENDENT STOCHASTIC LINEAR REGRESSION

Suppose that we modify the classical linear regression model by replacing the assumption of fixed regressors (4.3.4) with

(2.1) $\quad \mathbf{X}$ is stochastic but distributed independently of $\boldsymbol{\epsilon}$.

That is, viewing each row of $\mathbf{X}$, $\mathbf{X}_t'$ $(t = 1, \ldots, T)$ as an observation on a $(1 + K) \times 1$ random vector, the new specification is that $\mathbf{X}_t'$ and ϵ_s are independent for all t and s. This independence, taken together with the other assumptions of the model, implies that

$$E(\boldsymbol{\epsilon} \mid \mathbf{X}) = E\boldsymbol{\epsilon} = \mathbf{0}, \tag{2.2}$$

$$E(\mathbf{y} \mid \mathbf{X}) = E(\mathbf{X}\boldsymbol{\beta} + \boldsymbol{\epsilon} \mid \mathbf{X}) = \mathbf{X}\boldsymbol{\beta} + E(\boldsymbol{\epsilon} \mid \mathbf{X}) = \mathbf{X}\boldsymbol{\beta}, \tag{2.3}$$

and

$$E(\boldsymbol{\epsilon}\boldsymbol{\epsilon}' \mid \mathbf{X}) = E\boldsymbol{\epsilon}\boldsymbol{\epsilon}' = \sigma^2\mathbf{I}. \tag{2.4}$$

Thus the new specification implies that the conditional distribution of the disturbances has the classical properties for all values of $\mathbf{X}$. (If the distribution of $\mathbf{X}$ is degenerate—i.e., if the matrix $\mathbf{X}$ can take on only one value—then we are back to the fixed regressor specification.)

Let us consider applying classical least-squares estimation in the modified model. It is of course still true that

$$\mathbf{b} = (\mathbf{X}'\mathbf{X})^{-1}\mathbf{X}'\mathbf{y} = \boldsymbol{\beta} + (\mathbf{X}'\mathbf{X})^{-1}\mathbf{X}'\boldsymbol{\epsilon}. \tag{2.5}$$

Since $\boldsymbol{\epsilon}$ is independent of $\mathbf{X}$ it is also independent of $(\mathbf{X}'\mathbf{X})^{-1}\mathbf{X}'$, which is simply a nonstochastic function of $\mathbf{X}$. It follows that

$$E\mathbf{b} = \boldsymbol{\beta} + E(\mathbf{X}'\mathbf{X})^{-1}\mathbf{X}'\boldsymbol{\epsilon} = \boldsymbol{\beta} + E(\mathbf{X}'\mathbf{X})^{-1}\mathbf{X}'E\boldsymbol{\epsilon} = \boldsymbol{\beta} \tag{2.6}$$

$$\begin{aligned} \boldsymbol{\Sigma}_{\mathbf{bb}} &= E(\mathbf{b} - \boldsymbol{\beta})(\mathbf{b} - \boldsymbol{\beta})' = E[(\mathbf{X}'\mathbf{X})^{-1}\mathbf{X}'\boldsymbol{\epsilon}\boldsymbol{\epsilon}'\mathbf{X}(\mathbf{X}'\mathbf{X})^{-1}] \\ &= E\{E[(\mathbf{X}'\mathbf{X})^{-1}\mathbf{X}'\boldsymbol{\epsilon}\boldsymbol{\epsilon}'\mathbf{X}(\mathbf{X}'\mathbf{X})^{-1}] \mid \mathbf{X}\} \\ &= E[(\mathbf{X}'\mathbf{X})^{-1}\mathbf{X}'\sigma^2\mathbf{I}\mathbf{X}(\mathbf{X}'\mathbf{X})^{-1}] \\ &= \sigma^2 E(\mathbf{X}'\mathbf{X})^{-1}, \end{aligned} \tag{2.7}$$

where we have used the fact that the expectation of a random variable may be written as the expectation of its conditional expectations. Similarly for the residual sum of squares we have

$$E\hat{\boldsymbol{\epsilon}}'\hat{\boldsymbol{\epsilon}} = E[E(\hat{\boldsymbol{\epsilon}}'\hat{\boldsymbol{\epsilon}} \mid \mathbf{X})] = E[\sigma^2(T - K - 1)] = \sigma^2(T - K - 1), \tag{2.8}$$

so that for the disturbance variance estimator

$$(2.9)\qquad Es^2 = E[E(s^2 \mid \mathbf{X})] = E[E(T - K - 1)^{-1}\hat{\boldsymbol{\epsilon}}'\hat{\boldsymbol{\epsilon}} \mid \mathbf{X}] = \sigma^2$$

and for the coefficient covariance matrix estimator

$$(2.10)\qquad E\mathbf{S}_{\mathbf{bb}} = E[E(\mathbf{S}_{\mathbf{bb}} \mid \mathbf{X})] = E\{E[s^2(\mathbf{X}'\mathbf{X})^{-1}] \mid \mathbf{X}\} = \sigma^2 E(\mathbf{X}'\mathbf{X})^{-1} = \boldsymbol{\Sigma}_{\mathbf{bb}}.$$

We conclude that

(2.11) If in the classical linear regression model the specification of fixed regressors is replaced by the specification that $\mathbf{X}$ is distributed independently of $\boldsymbol{\epsilon}$, then the classical least-squares estimators of $\boldsymbol{\beta}$, σ^2, and $\boldsymbol{\Sigma}_{\mathbf{bb}}$ are unbiased.

Note that in the formula for the covariance matrix of the coefficient estimators the inverse regressor moment matrix must now be replaced by its expectation. Note too that $\mathbf{b} = (\mathbf{X}'\mathbf{X})^{-1}\mathbf{X}'\mathbf{y}$ is now a stochastic function of $\mathbf{y}$; it is strictly speaking not a linear estimator and hence not the BLUE of $\boldsymbol{\beta}$. This point aside, the desirable properties of the classical least-squares estimators do carry over to the case where the regressors are stochastic provided that they are distributed independently of the disturbances. It is readily shown that $\mathbf{b}$ is still the maximum likelihood estimator of $\boldsymbol{\beta}$ if the disturbances are normally distributed and the distribution of $\mathbf{X}$ does not involve $\boldsymbol{\beta}$ and σ^2.

Heuristically, the independence of the disturbances and the regressors ensures that the least-squares estimators have the classical properties conditional on any value of $\mathbf{X}$, and hence that they have the classical properties unconditionally over all possible values of $\mathbf{X}$. Similarly the classical interval estimation and test procedures remain valid; e.g., an interval which covers the true value of a parameter with 95% probability for every value of $\mathbf{X}$ will cover the true value with 95% probability over all possible values of $\mathbf{X}$.

At this point it is convenient to establish some asymptotic properties for the least-squares estimators when $\mathbf{X}$ and $\boldsymbol{\epsilon}$ are independent, without reliance on the maximum likelihood principle. To investigate the properties of the estimators as the sample size grows indefinitely it is of course necessary to specify how the successive sample observations are generated. Suppose then that the stochastic $T \times (1 + K)$ matrix $\mathbf{X}$ is a sample of size T from a stationary $(1 + K)$-variate stochastic process. We do not assume that the successive rows of $\mathbf{X}$ are mutually independent, but we do require that the dependence between distant rows wears off sufficiently rapidly with the distance that the general conditions discussed in Section 3.8 are satisfied. Then the sample contemporaneous "covariance" matrix

$T^{-1}\mathbf{X}'\mathbf{X}$ will have as its probability limit the population contemporaneous "covariance" matrix $\mathbf{\Sigma}_{xx}$, say. (Strictly these are second-moment matrices but for convenience we refer to them as covariance matrices.) Similarly we suppose that the $T \times 1$ vector $\boldsymbol{\epsilon}$ is a sample from a stationary univariate stochastic process. Again we do not assume that the successive elements of $\boldsymbol{\epsilon}$ are mutually independent, but we do require them to be uncorrelated and that any dependence between distant elements wears off sufficiently rapidly with the distance that the sample variance $T^{-1}\boldsymbol{\epsilon}'\boldsymbol{\epsilon}$ has as its probability limit the population variance σ^2.

Consider then the independent stochastic linear regression model defined by the following set of assumptions:

(2.12) $\mathbf{y} = \mathbf{X}\boldsymbol{\beta} + \boldsymbol{\epsilon}$,

(2.13) $\boldsymbol{\epsilon}$ is a sample from a stationary univariate stochastic process with mean 0, variance σ^2, and all lag covariances 0,

(2.14) $\mathbf{X}$ is a sample from a stationary multivariate stochastic process with contemporaneous covariance matrix $\mathbf{\Sigma}_{xx}$,

(2.15) The stochastic process generating $\mathbf{X}$ is independent of the stochastic process generating $\boldsymbol{\epsilon}$,

(2.16) $\mathbf{\Sigma}_{xx}$ is nonsingular,

it being understood that any dependence in each of the processes is sufficiently weak that sample variances and covariances have the corresponding population parameters as their probability limits.

Then from (2.13) we have

(2.17) $E\boldsymbol{\epsilon} = \mathbf{0}$,

(2.18) $E\boldsymbol{\epsilon}\boldsymbol{\epsilon}' = \sigma^2\mathbf{I}$,

(2.19) $\text{plim } T^{-1}\, \boldsymbol{\epsilon}'\boldsymbol{\epsilon} = \sigma^2$;

from (2.14) we have

(2.20) $\text{plim } T^{-1}\, \mathbf{X}'\mathbf{X} = \mathbf{\Sigma}_{xx}$;

and since independence implies zero covariances, from (2.15) we have

(2.21) $\text{plim } T^{-1}\mathbf{X}'\boldsymbol{\epsilon} = \mathbf{0}$.

It may be instructive to derive (2.21) explicitly. The sample contemporaneous covariance between a regressor x_k and the disturbance ϵ is

(2.22) $$s_{k\epsilon} = T^{-1}\sum_{t=1}^{T} x_{tk}\epsilon_t.$$

Its expectation is

$$(2.23)\qquad Es_{k\epsilon} = T^{-1}E\sum_{t=1}^{T} x_{tk}\epsilon_t = T^{-1}\sum_{t=1}^{T} Ex_{tk}\epsilon_t = 0,$$

since the independence of x_{tk} and ϵ_t for all t implies $Ex_{tk}\epsilon_t = Ex_{tk}E\epsilon_t$ while $E\epsilon_t = 0$; its variance is

$$(2.24)\qquad Es_{k\epsilon}^2 = T^{-2}E\left(\sum_{t=1}^{T} x_{tk}\epsilon_t\right)^2 = T^{-2}\sum_{t=1}^{T}\sum_{s=1}^{T} Ex_{tk}x_{sk}\epsilon_t\epsilon_s$$

$$= T^{-2}T\sigma_{kk}\sigma^2 = T^{-1}\sigma_{kk}\sigma^2,$$

(where σ_{kk} is the kth diagonal element of $\mathbf{\Sigma}_{\mathbf{xx}}$) since in the double sum, in view of the independence of $\mathbf{X}$ and $\boldsymbol{\epsilon}$,

$$Ex_{tk}x_{sk}\epsilon_t\epsilon_s = Ex_{tk}x_{sk}E\epsilon_t\epsilon_s = \begin{cases} 0 & \text{if } s \neq t. \\ \sigma_{kk}\sigma^2 & \text{if } s = t \end{cases}$$

Now $\lim_{T\to\infty} T^{-1}\sigma_{kk}\sigma^2 = 0$, so that (2.23) and (2.24) imply plim $s_{k\epsilon} = 0$. This holds for $k = 0, 1, \ldots, K$, which is (2.21).

Consider then the least-squares estimator $\mathbf{b}$ in (2.5); taking probability limits gives

$$\begin{aligned}(2.25)\qquad \text{plim } \mathbf{b} &= \boldsymbol{\beta} + \text{plim } (\mathbf{X}'\mathbf{X})^{-1}\mathbf{X}'\boldsymbol{\epsilon} \\ &= \boldsymbol{\beta} + \text{plim } (T^{-1}\mathbf{X}'\mathbf{X})^{-1}(T^{-1}\mathbf{X}'\boldsymbol{\epsilon}) \\ &= \boldsymbol{\beta} + \text{plim } (T^{-1}\mathbf{X}'\mathbf{X})^{-1} \text{ plim } (T^{-1}\mathbf{X}'\boldsymbol{\epsilon}) \\ &= \boldsymbol{\beta} + \mathbf{\Sigma}_{\mathbf{xx}}^{-1} \cdot \mathbf{0} = \boldsymbol{\beta},\end{aligned}$$

using Slutsky's theorem (3.6.15) and (3.6.16) and (2.20), (2.16), and (2.21). Further, since

$$(2.26)\qquad \hat{\boldsymbol{\epsilon}}'\hat{\boldsymbol{\epsilon}} = \boldsymbol{\epsilon}'\boldsymbol{\epsilon} - \boldsymbol{\epsilon}'\mathbf{X}(\mathbf{X}'\mathbf{X})^{-1}\mathbf{X}'\boldsymbol{\epsilon}$$

by (4.4.24) and (4.4.26), we have

$$\begin{aligned}(2.27)\qquad \text{plim } (T^{-1}\hat{\boldsymbol{\epsilon}}'\hat{\boldsymbol{\epsilon}}) &= \text{plim } (T^{-1}\boldsymbol{\epsilon}'\boldsymbol{\epsilon}) - \text{plim } (T^{-1}\boldsymbol{\epsilon}'\mathbf{X}) \\ &\qquad \times \text{plim } (T^{-1}\mathbf{X}'\mathbf{X})^{-1} \text{ plim } (T^{-1}\mathbf{X}'\boldsymbol{\epsilon}) \\ &= \sigma^2 - \mathbf{0} \cdot \mathbf{\Sigma}_{\mathbf{xx}}^{-1} \cdot \mathbf{0} = \sigma^2,\end{aligned}$$

using also (2.19). Clearly, then,

$$\begin{aligned}(2.28)\qquad \text{plim } s^2 &= \text{plim } (T - K - 1)^{-1}\hat{\boldsymbol{\epsilon}}'\hat{\boldsymbol{\epsilon}} \\ &= \text{plim } (T - K - 1)^{-1}T\, T^{-1}\hat{\boldsymbol{\epsilon}}'\hat{\boldsymbol{\epsilon}} \\ &= \text{plim } [(T - K - 1)^{-1}T] \text{ plim } (T^{-1}\hat{\boldsymbol{\epsilon}}'\hat{\boldsymbol{\epsilon}}) = 1\sigma^2 = \sigma^2.\end{aligned}$$

For the asymptotic covariance matrix of $\mathbf{b}$ we may utilize (2.7), write it as $\mathbf{\Sigma_{bb}} = T^{-1}\sigma^2 E(T^{-1}\mathbf{X}'\mathbf{X})^{-1}$, and conclude

(2.29) $$\bar{\mathbf{\Sigma}}_{\mathbf{bb}} = \bar{E}(\mathbf{b} - \boldsymbol{\beta})(\mathbf{b} - \boldsymbol{\beta})' = T^{-1}\sigma^2\bar{E}(T^{-1}\mathbf{X}'\mathbf{X})^{-1} = T^{-1}\sigma^2\mathbf{\Sigma}_{\mathbf{xx}}^{-1}$$

since $\bar{E}(T^{-1}\mathbf{X}'\mathbf{X})^{-1} = \text{plim}\,(T^{-1}\mathbf{X}'\mathbf{X})^{-1}$. The consistency of $\mathbf{b}$ is confirmed by the fact that the elements of (2.29) go to zero as T goes to infinity. Then writing the estimator of the covariance matrix as $\mathbf{S_{bb}} = s^2(\mathbf{X}'\mathbf{X})^{-1} = T^{-1}s^2(T^{-1}\mathbf{X}'\mathbf{X})^{-1}$ we conclude

(2.30) $$\text{plim}\,\mathbf{S_{bb}} = \bar{\mathbf{\Sigma}}_{\mathbf{bb}}$$

since $\text{plim}\, s^2 = \sigma^2$ and $\text{plim}\,(T^{-1}\mathbf{X}'\mathbf{X})^{-1} = \mathbf{\Sigma}_{\mathbf{xx}}^{-1}$.

To summarize,

(2.31) In the independent stochastic linear regression model, the classical least-squares estimators of $\boldsymbol{\beta}$, σ^2, and $\bar{\mathbf{\Sigma}}_{\mathbf{bb}}$ are consistent and (hence) asymptotically unbiased.

For future reference we present an alternative derivation of the asymptotic covariance matrix of $\mathbf{b}$. In view of (3.6.17) we may write

(2.32) $$\begin{aligned}\bar{\mathbf{\Sigma}}_{\mathbf{bb}} &= \bar{E}(\mathbf{b} - \boldsymbol{\beta})(\mathbf{b} - \boldsymbol{\beta})' = T^{-1}\,\text{plim}\,[\sqrt{T}(\mathbf{b} - \boldsymbol{\beta})\sqrt{T}(\mathbf{b} - \boldsymbol{\beta})']\\ &= T^{-1}\,\text{plim}\,[T(\mathbf{X}'\mathbf{X})^{-1}\mathbf{X}'\boldsymbol{\epsilon}\boldsymbol{\epsilon}'\mathbf{X}(\mathbf{X}'\mathbf{X})^{-1}]\\ &= T^{-1}\,\text{plim}\,[(T^{-1}\mathbf{X}'\mathbf{X})^{-1}T^{-1}\mathbf{X}'\boldsymbol{\epsilon}\boldsymbol{\epsilon}'\mathbf{X}(T^{-1}\mathbf{X}'\mathbf{X})^{-1}]\\ &= T^{-1}\mathbf{\Sigma}_{\mathbf{xx}}^{-1}\,\text{plim}\,(T^{-1}\mathbf{X}'\boldsymbol{\epsilon}\boldsymbol{\epsilon}'\mathbf{X})\mathbf{\Sigma}_{\mathbf{xx}}^{-1}.\end{aligned}$$

The k,lth element of $(T^{-1}\mathbf{X}'\boldsymbol{\epsilon}\boldsymbol{\epsilon}'\mathbf{X})$ is $T^{-1}(\Sigma_{t=1}^{T}x_{tk}\epsilon_t)(\Sigma_{t=1}^{T}x_{tl}\epsilon_t) = Ts_{k\epsilon}s_{l\epsilon}$; its expectation is

(2.33) $$\begin{aligned}ETs_{k\epsilon}s_{l\epsilon} &= T^{-1}E\left(\sum_{t=1}^{T}x_{tk}\epsilon_t\right)\left(\sum_{t=1}^{T}x_{tl}\epsilon_t\right) = T^{-1}\sum_{t=1}^{T}\sum_{s=1}^{T}Ex_{tk}x_{sl}\epsilon_t\epsilon_s\\ &= T^{-1}T\sigma_{kl}\sigma^2 = \sigma_{kl}\sigma^2,\end{aligned}$$

(where σ_{kl} is the k,lth element of $\mathbf{\Sigma_{xx}}$) since in the double sum, in view of the independence of $\mathbf{X}$ and $\boldsymbol{\epsilon}$,

$$Ex_{tk}x_{sl}\epsilon_t\epsilon_s = Ex_{tk}x_{sl}E\epsilon_t\epsilon_s = \begin{cases}0 & \text{if } s \neq t\\ \sigma_{kl}\sigma^2 & \text{if } s = t.\end{cases}$$

Thus

(2.34) $$E(T^{-1}\mathbf{X}'\boldsymbol{\epsilon}\boldsymbol{\epsilon}'\mathbf{X}) = \sigma^2\mathbf{\Sigma_{xx}}.$$

Further under our weak-dependence conditions the variance of $Ts_{k\epsilon}s_{l\epsilon}$ will go to zero as T goes to infinity so that $\text{plim}\,Ts_{k\epsilon}s_{l\epsilon} = \sigma_{kl}\sigma^2$; thus

(2.35) $$\text{plim}\,(T^{-1}\mathbf{X}'\boldsymbol{\epsilon}\boldsymbol{\epsilon}'\mathbf{X}) = \sigma^2\mathbf{\Sigma_{xx}}.$$

Inserting this in (2.32) gives (2.29) again.

Finally, it should be noted that if the regressors are fixed in repeated samples then the model of this section is not strictly applicable. Stationarity requires that the successive rows of $\mathbf{X}$ be identically distributed; if also each row is fixed in repeated samples, the rows will all be identical in each sample. But this would preclude estimation—$\mathbf{X}'\mathbf{X}$ would always be singular. The question of the asymptotic properties of least-squares estimation in the classical linear regression model might, therefore, appear to be unanswered. Suppose, however, that the sequence of regressor vectors $\mathbf{X}_1', \ldots, \mathbf{X}_t', \ldots, \mathbf{X}_T', \ldots$ is nonstochastic and that

$$(2.36) \qquad \boldsymbol{\Sigma}_{\mathbf{xx}} = \lim_{T \to \infty} T^{-1}\mathbf{X}'\mathbf{X} \text{ exists and is nonsingular.}$$

Then the argument of (2.17)–(2.30) goes through with a reinterpretation of "plim" as "$\lim_{T\to\infty}$" where appropriate. Thus classical least-squares estimation is consistent in the classical linear regression model provided that (2.36) holds. The extension of this result to the case where some of the regressors are nonstochastic and the others are stochastic but independent of the disturbances is similarly straightforward.

3. AUTOREGRESSIVE LINEAR REGRESSION

The Autoregressive Linear Regression Model

It is common in econometric work to formulate relationships in which lagged values of the regressand are included among the regressors. For example, a familiar version of the consumption function is

$$(3.1) \qquad C_t = \beta_0 + \beta_1 Y_t + \beta_2 C_{t-1} + \epsilon_t,$$

where C_t is consumption in period t and Y_t is income in period t. Clearly in such a case the assumption of full independence between regressors and disturbances is untenable, for C_{t-1}, having been determined by the relation in period $t - 1$, will clearly be dependent on that period's disturbance, i.e., ϵ_{t-1}. Indeed, we see that C_{t-1} was in part determined by C_{t-2} which must be dependent on ϵ_{t-2}, so that C_{t-1} will clearly be dependent on ϵ_{t-2} as well. Indeed, we see that the regressor at time t, C_{t-1}, is in general dependent on all prior disturbances $\epsilon_{t-1}, \epsilon_{t-2}, \ldots$. Nevertheless, if the disturbances are temporally independent, the assumption that C_{t-1} is independent of the contemporary disturbance ϵ_t and the succeeding disturbances $\epsilon_{t+1}, \epsilon_{t+2}, \ldots, \epsilon_T$ is tenable.

This suggests that we consider a model in which the assumption of full independence of regressors and disturbances is replaced by an assumption of partial independence. Thus we are led to formulate the autoregressive linear regression model in which (2.13) and (2.15) are respectively replaced by

(3.2) The ϵ_t $(t = 1, \ldots, T)$ are independently and identically distributed random variables with mean 0 and variance σ^2.

(3.3) Each $\mathbf{X}_t'$ is distributed independently of the contemporaneous and succeeding disturbances $\epsilon_t, \epsilon_{t+1}, \ldots, \epsilon_T$.

Again it is understood that any dependence in the **X** process is sufficiently weak that the sample variances and covariances have the corresponding population parameters as their probability limits. This will clearly be the case if the set of regressors contains, apart from the constant, only successively lagged values of the regressand. For then the relationship is $y_t = \beta_0 + \beta_1 y_{t-1} + \cdots + \beta_K y_{t-K} + \epsilon_t$, and our model amounts to specifying that the y_t's are generated by a Kth-order autoregressive process —see (3.8.30). And the elements of the regressor moment matrix are then simply sample means, variances, and autocovariances; these will indeed have the corresponding population parameters as their probability limits provided only that the process is stable—see (3.8.31).

Since **X** is no longer independent of $\boldsymbol{\epsilon}$ the development of (2.1)–(2.11) is no longer applicable, and indeed **b** is no longer unbiased. Consider the case $K = 1$—$y_t = \beta_0 + \beta_1 y_{t-1} + \epsilon_t$; here

$$b_1 = \beta_1 + \frac{\sum_{t=1}^{T} y_{t-1}(\epsilon_t - \bar{\epsilon})}{\sum_{t=1}^{T} (y_{t-1} - \tilde{y})^2} \tag{3.4}$$

where $\tilde{y} = T^{-1} \sum_{t=1}^{T} y_{t-1}$. Now the expectation of the numerator

$$E \sum_{t=1}^{T} y_{t-1}(\epsilon_t - \bar{\epsilon}) = \sum_{t=1}^{T} E y_{t-1}\epsilon_t - \sum_{t=1}^{T} E\bar{\epsilon} y_{t-1} = -\sum_{t=1}^{T} E\bar{\epsilon} y_{t-1}$$

is clearly nonzero since $\bar{\epsilon} = T^{-1} \sum_{t=1}^{T} \epsilon_t$ contains terms which are correlated with each y_{t-1}, i.e., $\epsilon_1, \ldots, \epsilon_{t-1}$. Although the expectation of the ratio in (3.4) is not the ratio of the expectations of the numerator and denominator, this at least suggests the reason for the bias. This argument is based on that of Johnston (1963, pp. 214–215). The exact bias is considered by Hurwicz (1950*b*); it naturally depends on the form of the disturbance distribution.

The least-squares estimators, however, retain desirable asymptotic properties, because (2.17)–(2.21) remain valid in the autoregressive model; $T^{-1}\boldsymbol{\epsilon}'\boldsymbol{\epsilon}$ is now a random sample variance and hence has the population variance as its probability limit; the weak dependence in the $\mathbf{X}$ process means that $T^{-1}\mathbf{X}'\mathbf{X}$ has the population covariance matrix as its probability limit; and this weak dependence means that $T^{-1}\mathbf{X}'\boldsymbol{\epsilon}$ has as its probability limit the population covariance vector, which is zero since $\mathbf{X}_t'$ and ϵ_t are independent. Again it may be instructive to derive (2.21) explicitly. The expectation of its typical element is

$$(3.5) \qquad Es_{k\epsilon} = T^{-1}E\sum_{t=1}^{T} x_{tk}\epsilon_t = T^{-1}\sum_{t=1}^{T} Ex_{tk}\epsilon_t = 0$$

since the independence of x_{tk} and ϵ_t for all t implies $Ex_{tk}\epsilon_t = Ex_{tk}E\epsilon_t$ while $E\epsilon_t = 0$; the variance of this typical element is

$$(3.6) \qquad Es_{k\epsilon}^2 = T^{-2}E\left(\sum_{t=1}^{T} x_{tk}\epsilon_t\right)^2 = T^{-2}\sum_{t=1}^{T}\sum_{s=1}^{T} Ex_{tk}x_{sk}\epsilon_t\epsilon_s$$
$$= T^{-2}T\sigma_{kk}\sigma^2 = T^{-1}\sigma_{kk}\sigma^2$$

since in the double sum when $s = t$, $Ex_{tk}x_{sk}\epsilon_t\epsilon_s = Ex_{tk}^2\epsilon_t^2 = Ex_{tk}^2E\epsilon_t^2 = \sigma_{kk}\sigma^2$ in view of the independence of x_{tk} and ϵ_t, whereas when $s \neq t$—without loss of generality taking $s > t$—$Ex_{tk}x_{sk}\epsilon_t\epsilon_s = Ex_{tk}x_{sk}\epsilon_t E\epsilon_s = 0$ in view of the independence of x_{tk}, x_{sk}, and ϵ_t from ϵ_s for $s > t$. As in Section 2, (3.5) and (3.6) imply (2.21).

Then the development of (2.25)–(2.28) goes through, and under general conditions so does that of (2.32)–(2.35). In particular, note that (2.33) now holds since, when $s = t$, $Ex_{tk}x_{sl}\epsilon_t\epsilon_s = Ex_{tk}x_{tl}E\epsilon_t^2 = \sigma_{kl}\sigma^2$ in view of the independence of x_{tk} and x_{tl} from ϵ_t, whereas when $s \neq t$—without loss of generality taking $s > t$—$Ex_{tk}x_{sl}\epsilon_t\epsilon_s = Ex_{tk}x_{sl}\epsilon_t E\epsilon_s = 0$ in view of the independence of x_{tk}, x_{sl}, and ϵ_t from ϵ_s for $s > t$. We conclude that

(3.7) In the autoregressive linear regression model the classical least-squares estimators of $\boldsymbol{\beta}$, σ^2, and $\bar{\boldsymbol{\Sigma}}_{\mathbf{bb}}$ are consistent and (hence) asymptotically unbiased.

It may also be shown that if the disturbance distribution is normal, $\mathbf{b}$ is essentially the maximum likelihood estimator of $\boldsymbol{\beta}$. A rigorous development of some of these results is given by Mann and Wald (1943); see also Koopmans and Hood (1953, pp. 147–151) and Johnston (1963, pp. 211–214).

Distributed Lag Models

It is common to find in economics the formulation in which the regressand responds to the explanatory variable with a delay. The simplest form is illustrated by the consumption function

$$(3.8) \qquad C_t = \beta Y_{t-1} + \epsilon_t,$$

where C_t = consumption in period t and Y_t = income in period t. (We omit the constant for simplicity.) The more general form allows for a *distributed lag:*

$$(3.9) \qquad y_t = \beta x_t + \beta_1 x_{t-1} + \beta_2 x_{t-2} + \cdots + \epsilon_t.$$

Let us make the classical assumptions about the disturbance, in particular:

$$(3.10) \qquad E\epsilon_t^2 = \sigma^2;\ E\epsilon_s\epsilon_t = 0 \quad \text{for} \quad s \neq t;\ \mathbf{X} \text{ and } \boldsymbol{\epsilon} \text{ independent.}$$

Although (3.9) is more general than the formulation of instantaneous response or of a single-period lag, its estimation presents obvious difficulties. Since our sample will be finite in size the infinite set of lagged regressors must be cut off at some point; even then, there is likely to be multicollinearity among the successive regressors.

Some sort of restriction is in order; a natural one is to specify a priori that the coefficients of the successive x's decline systematically as we go further back in time. This was originally suggested by Irving Fisher in 1925; more recently it has been revived and extended by Koyck (1954) and by Nerlove (1958). Koyck's specification is that the coefficients of (3.9) decline geometrically:

$$(3.11) \qquad \beta_k = \beta\lambda^k \qquad (k = 0, 1, \ldots)$$

where $0 < \lambda < 1$, so that the relationship may be written

$$(3.12) \qquad y_t = \beta x_t + \lambda\beta x_{t-1} + \lambda^2\beta x_{t-2} + \cdots + \epsilon_t.$$

The point is that if we lag (3.12) by one period and multiply through by λ we obtain

$$(3.13) \qquad \lambda y_{t-1} = \lambda\beta x_{t-1} + \lambda^2\beta x_{t-2} + \lambda^3\beta x_{t-3} + \cdots + \lambda\epsilon_{t-1},$$

which when subtracted from (3.12) gives, after rewriting,

$$(3.14) \qquad y_t = \beta x_t + \lambda y_{t-1} + \epsilon_t^*,$$

where

$$(3.15) \qquad \epsilon_t^* = \epsilon_t - \lambda\epsilon_{t-1}.$$

Thus, on Koyck's specification the distributed lag relationship may be reduced to one that involves only two variables—and only two parameters to be estimated.

Nerlove provides two alternative theories to justify the form (3.14) directly. The first is the "rigidity model." Suppose that x_t determines y_t^*, the "desired value" of y_t:

$$(3.16) \qquad y_t^* = \alpha x_t,$$

but that the adjustment to the desired value in one period is only gradual:

$$(3.17) \qquad y_t - y_{t-1} = \delta(y_t^* - y_{t-1}),$$

where $0 < \delta < 1$ is the "coefficient of adjustment." Inserting (3.16) into (3.17) and rewriting gives just the form of (3.14):

$$(3.18) \qquad y_t = \alpha\,\delta x_t + (1 - \delta)y_{t-1}.$$

An obvious economic example would be the demand for a durable good with y = stock and x = income. The second model is the "expectation model." Suppose that the expected (in the sense of anticipated) value of x_{t+1} is x_t^*, and it is this which determines y_t,

$$(3.19) \qquad y_t = \alpha x_t^*,$$

and further that expectations are formed recursively as follows:

$$(3.20) \qquad x_t^* = x_{t-1}^* + \delta(x_t - x_{t-1}^*)$$

where $0 < \delta < 1$ is the "coefficient of expectations." Inserting (3.20) into (3.19) gives just the form of (3.14):

$$(3.21) \qquad y_t = \alpha\,\delta x_t + \alpha(1 - \delta)x_{t-1}^* = \alpha\,\delta x_t + (1 - \delta)y_{t-1}$$

since $x_{t-1}^* = (1/\alpha)y_{t-1}$ from (3.19) lagged one period. An obvious economic example would be an expected income hypothesis of consumption, with y = consumption and x = income.

Now consider the problem of estimation of (3.14). At first glance it might seem that the autoregressive linear regression model is appropriate: Note that one of the regressors is the lagged value of the regressand. In fact, the situation is worse than that, for there is contemporaneous dependence between lagged y and the disturbance; y_{t-1}, being determined in part by ϵ_{t-1}, will not be independent of $\epsilon_t^* = \epsilon_t - \lambda\epsilon_{t-1}$. In fact from (3.12) lagged one period and (3.15),

$$(3.22) \qquad \begin{aligned} E\epsilon_t^* y_{t-1} &= E(\epsilon_t - \lambda\epsilon_{t-1})(\beta x_{t-1} + \lambda\beta x_{t-2} + \cdots + \epsilon_{t-1}) \\ &= E\epsilon_t\epsilon_{t-1} - \lambda E\epsilon_{t-1}^2 = 0 - \lambda\sigma^2 \\ &= -\lambda\sigma^2, \end{aligned}$$

using (3.10). For future reference we obtain the variance of ϵ^*,

$$(3.23) \qquad E\epsilon_t^{*2} = E(\epsilon_t - \lambda\epsilon_{t-1})^2 = \sigma^2 + \lambda^2\sigma^2 - 2\lambda 0 = (1 + \lambda^2)\sigma^2.$$

It is easy to see that the classical least-squares estimators of β and λ in (3.14) are not consistent. The normal equations are

$$(3.24) \qquad \begin{pmatrix} \Sigma x^2 & \Sigma xy_{-1} \\ \Sigma xy_{-1} & \Sigma y_{-1}^2 \end{pmatrix} \begin{pmatrix} b \\ l \end{pmatrix} = \begin{pmatrix} \Sigma xy \\ \Sigma y_{-1}y \end{pmatrix};$$

or, writing $\mathbf{S}_{\mathbf{xx}}$ for T^{-1} times the matrix on the left,

$$\mathbf{S}_{\mathbf{xx}}\begin{pmatrix} b \\ l \end{pmatrix} = \begin{pmatrix} \Sigma\, xy/T \\ \Sigma\, y_{-1}y/T \end{pmatrix}, \tag{3.25}$$

which gives—compare (2.25)—

$$\begin{pmatrix} \text{plim } b \\ \text{plim } l \end{pmatrix} = \begin{pmatrix} \beta \\ \lambda \end{pmatrix} + (\text{plim } \mathbf{S}_{\mathbf{xx}})^{-1}\begin{pmatrix} \text{plim } \Sigma\, x\epsilon^*/T \\ \text{plim } \Sigma\, y_{-1}\epsilon^*/T \end{pmatrix}. \tag{3.26}$$

We may again assert that plim $\mathbf{S}_{\mathbf{xx}} = \mathbf{\Sigma}_{\mathbf{xx}}$, the population covariance matrix of the regressors, and since x is independent of ϵ^* (it is independent of all ϵ's), we also have plim $(\Sigma\, x\epsilon^*/T) = 0$. But now plim $(\Sigma\, y_{-1}\epsilon^*/T) = E(\Sigma\, y_{-1}\epsilon^*/T) = \Sigma\,(Ey_{-1}\epsilon^*)/T = -\lambda\sigma^2 \neq 0$, so that the least-squares estimators are inconsistent:

$$\text{plim}\begin{pmatrix} b \\ l \end{pmatrix} = \begin{pmatrix} \beta \\ \lambda \end{pmatrix} + \mathbf{\Sigma}_{\mathbf{xx}}^{-1}\begin{pmatrix} 0 \\ -\lambda\sigma^2 \end{pmatrix}. \tag{3.27}$$

The saving grace is that plim $(\Sigma\, y_{-1}\epsilon^*/T)$ is expressed in terms of the parameters λ and σ^2; (3.27) suggests that consistent estimates would be obtained by modifying the least-squares vector by subtracting a vector whose plim is $\mathbf{\Sigma}_{\mathbf{xx}}^{-1}\begin{pmatrix} 0 \\ -\lambda\sigma^2 \end{pmatrix}$, i.e., one that is $\mathbf{S}_{\mathbf{xx}}^{-1}$ times a vector whose plim is $\begin{pmatrix} 0 \\ -\lambda\sigma^2 \end{pmatrix}$. Let us therefore consider the sum of squared residuals from the least-squares regression. In general

$$\hat{\boldsymbol{\epsilon}}'\hat{\boldsymbol{\epsilon}} = \boldsymbol{\epsilon}'\boldsymbol{\epsilon} - \boldsymbol{\epsilon}'\mathbf{X}(\mathbf{X}'\mathbf{X})^{-1}\mathbf{X}'\boldsymbol{\epsilon} = \boldsymbol{\epsilon}'\boldsymbol{\epsilon} - \boldsymbol{\epsilon}'\mathbf{X}(\mathbf{b} - \boldsymbol{\beta}); \tag{3.28}$$

specializing,

$$\frac{\Sigma\,\hat{\epsilon}^{*2}}{T} = \frac{\Sigma\,\epsilon^{*2}}{T} - \begin{pmatrix} \dfrac{\Sigma\, x\epsilon^*}{T} & \dfrac{\Sigma\, y_{-1}\epsilon^*}{T} \end{pmatrix}\begin{pmatrix} b - \beta \\ l - \lambda \end{pmatrix}, \tag{3.29}$$

whence

$$\begin{aligned} \text{plim}\frac{\Sigma\,\hat{\epsilon}^{*2}}{T} &= \text{plim}\frac{\Sigma\,\epsilon^{*2}}{T} \\ &\quad - \begin{pmatrix} \text{plim}\dfrac{\Sigma\, x\epsilon^*}{T} & \text{plim}\dfrac{\Sigma\, y_{-1}\epsilon^*}{T} \end{pmatrix}\begin{pmatrix} \text{plim } (b - \beta) \\ \text{plim } (l - \lambda) \end{pmatrix} \\ &= (1 + \lambda^2)\sigma^2 - (0 \quad -\lambda\sigma^2)\begin{pmatrix} \text{plim } (b - \beta) \\ \text{plim } (l - \lambda) \end{pmatrix} \\ &= (1 + \lambda^2)\sigma^2 + \lambda\sigma^2 \text{ plim } (l - \lambda) \\ &= \sigma^2(1 + \lambda \text{ plim } l). \end{aligned} \tag{3.30}$$

It follows that

$$\text{(3.31)} \qquad \operatorname{plim} \frac{\lambda \Sigma \hat{\epsilon}^{*2}/T}{1 + \lambda l} = \frac{\lambda \operatorname{plim} (\Sigma \hat{\epsilon}^{*2}/T)}{1 + \lambda \operatorname{plim} l} = \frac{\lambda \sigma^2 (1 + \lambda \operatorname{plim} l)}{1 + \lambda \operatorname{plim} l} = \lambda \sigma^2.$$

We then consider the estimates $\hat{\beta}$ and $\hat{\lambda}$ defined by the normal equations

$$\text{(3.32)} \qquad \begin{pmatrix} \Sigma x^2 & \Sigma x y_{-1} \\ \Sigma x y_{-1} & \Sigma y_{-1}^2 \end{pmatrix} \begin{pmatrix} \hat{\beta} \\ \hat{\lambda} \end{pmatrix} = \begin{pmatrix} \Sigma xy \\ \Sigma y_{-1} y + \dfrac{\hat{\lambda} \Sigma \hat{\epsilon}^{*2}}{1 + \hat{\lambda} l} \end{pmatrix}$$

Dividing through by T, solving, and taking probability limits

$$\text{(3.33)} \qquad \begin{pmatrix} \operatorname{plim} \hat{\beta} \\ \operatorname{plim} \hat{\lambda} \end{pmatrix} = \begin{pmatrix} \operatorname{plim} b \\ \operatorname{plim} l \end{pmatrix} + \boldsymbol{\Sigma}_{\mathbf{xx}}^{-1} \begin{pmatrix} 0 \\ \dfrac{\operatorname{plim} \hat{\lambda} \operatorname{plim} (\Sigma \hat{\epsilon}^{*2}/T)}{1 + \operatorname{plim} \hat{\lambda} \operatorname{plim} l} \end{pmatrix},$$

in view of (3.25). But from (3.26) and (3.27) we see that the parameters satisfy

$$\text{(3.34)} \qquad \begin{pmatrix} \beta \\ \lambda \end{pmatrix} = \begin{pmatrix} \operatorname{plim} b \\ \operatorname{plim} l \end{pmatrix} + \boldsymbol{\Sigma}_{\mathbf{xx}}^{-1} \begin{pmatrix} 0 \\ \dfrac{\lambda \operatorname{plim} (\Sigma \hat{\epsilon}^{*2}/T)}{1 + \lambda \operatorname{plim} l} \end{pmatrix}.$$

Comparison of (3.33) and (3.34) shows that $\operatorname{plim} \hat{\beta}$ and $\operatorname{plim} \hat{\lambda}$ satisfy the same equation system as the parameters β and λ, so that they are identical, so that $\hat{\beta}$ and $\hat{\lambda}$ are consistent. This two-step estimation procedure is due to Koyck: First compute the classical least-squares regression, finding l and $\Sigma \hat{\epsilon}^{*2}$, then insert these in (3.32) and solve for $\hat{\beta}$ and $\hat{\lambda}$. The system will be nonlinear; it involves a quadratic expression in $\hat{\lambda}$.

Extensions of this treatment to handle more explanatory variables and to the case where the ϵ's are autocorrelated are considered in the previously cited works of Koyck and Nerlove. The computations become quite cumbersome. All these difficulties may be avoided if we start from (3.14) directly assuming ϵ^* is nonautocorrelated, without deriving it from (3.9); see Klein (1958).

4. CONTEMPORANEOUSLY UNCORRELATED LINEAR REGRESSION

The Contemporaneously Uncorrelated Linear Regression Model

How much further can we weaken the assumption of independence of regressors and disturbances without destroying the consistency of the classical least-squares estimators? Referring back to the discussions of the asymptotic properties of the classical estimators in Sections 2 and 3, it will be seen that the critical requirement is that

(4.1) $$\operatorname{plim} T^{-1}\mathbf{X}'\boldsymbol{\epsilon} = \mathbf{0},$$

i.e., that

(4.2) $$\operatorname{plim} T^{-1}\sum_{t=1}^{T} x_{tk}\epsilon_t = 0 \qquad (k = 0, 1, \ldots, K).$$

Now $s_{k\epsilon} = T^{-1}\sum_{t=1}^{T} x_{tk}\epsilon_t$ is the sample contemporaneous covariance between the regressor x_k and the disturbance ϵ. In our discussion of stochastic processes in Section 3.8 we have argued that under general conditions such sample statistics have the corresponding population parameter as their probability limit. Thus the assumption (4.2) is plausible provided the population contemporaneous covariance is zero:

(4.3) $$Ex_{tk}\epsilon_t = 0 \qquad (k = 0, 1, \ldots, K;\ t = 1, \ldots, T).$$

Now (4.3) will be the case if the conditional expectation of the regressand is the specified linear function of the regressors. This is so because the conditional expectation of the regressand

$$E(y_t \mid \mathbf{X}_t') = E(\mathbf{X}_t'\boldsymbol{\beta} + \epsilon_t \mid \mathbf{X}_t') = \mathbf{X}_t'\boldsymbol{\beta} + E(\epsilon_t \mid \mathbf{X}_t')$$

will equal $\mathbf{X}_t'\boldsymbol{\beta}$ if and only if $E(\epsilon_t \mid \mathbf{X}_t') = E\epsilon_t = 0$. The condition $E(\epsilon_t \mid \mathbf{X}_t') = E\epsilon_t$ for all $\mathbf{X}_t'$ implies that $E(\epsilon_t \mid x_{tk}) = E\epsilon_t = 0$ for all k, which in turn implies that ϵ and x_k are uncorrelated random variables in which case their contemporaneous covariance vanishes. We conclude that, under general conditions, if the conditional expectation of the regressand is given by the specified linear function of the regressors—essentially, if the disturbance and the regressors are contemporaneously uncorrelated—the least-squares estimator of the regression coefficient vector $\boldsymbol{\beta}$ will be consistent.

It is useful to formalize this argument by specifying the contemporaneously uncorrelated linear regression model as follows:

(4.4) $\mathbf{y} = \mathbf{X}\boldsymbol{\beta} + \boldsymbol{\epsilon}$,

(4.5) $\boldsymbol{\epsilon}$ is a sample from a stationary univariate stochastic process with mean 0, variance σ^2, and all lag autocovariances 0,

(4.6) $\mathbf{X}$ is a sample from a stationary multivariate stochastic process with contemporaneous covariance matrix $\boldsymbol{\Sigma}_{\mathbf{xx}}$,

(4.7) The stochastic process generating $\mathbf{X}$ is contemporaneously uncorrelated with the stochastic process generating $\boldsymbol{\epsilon}$,

(4.8) $\boldsymbol{\Sigma}_{\mathbf{xx}}$ is nonsingular,

it being understood that any dependence in each of the processes is sufficiently weak that sample variances and covariances have the corresponding population parameters as their probability limits. It is readily seen that with these assumptions (2.17)–(2.21) remain valid. In particular the expectation of the typical element of $T^{-1}\mathbf{X}'\boldsymbol{\epsilon}$ is

$$(4.9) \qquad Es_{k\epsilon} = T^{-1}E\sum_{t=1}^{T} x_{tk}\epsilon_t = T^{-1}\sum_{t=1}^{T} Ex_{tk}\epsilon_t = 0,$$

since the uncorrelatedness of x_{tk} and ϵ_t for all t together with $E\epsilon_t = 0$ implies $Ex_{tk}\epsilon_t = Ex_{tk}(\epsilon_t - E\epsilon_t) = \text{cov}\,(x_{tk}, \epsilon_t) = 0$. Thus the results of (2.25)–(2.28) remain valid and under general conditions so do those of (2.32)–(2.35). We conclude that

(4.10) In the contemporaneously uncorrelated linear regression model the classical least-squares estimators of $\boldsymbol{\beta}$, σ^2, and $\bar{\boldsymbol{\Sigma}}_{\mathbf{bb}}$ are consistent and (hence) asymptotically unbiased.

It will be recognized that the independent stochastic model, where the regressors are fully independent of the disturbances, and the autoregressive model, where the regressors are independent of contemporary and succeeding disturbances, are in fact special cases of the present contemporaneously uncorrelated model. In the former two cases the critical assumption (4.1) was derived from more basic and stronger assumptions. But as we have seen it is possible for (4.1) to be satisfied without those stronger assumptions being satisfied.

The development of this subsection is suggested by Chernoff and Rubin (1953). For a further weakening of the assumptions under which the classical least-squares estimator of $\boldsymbol{\beta}$ is consistent see Wold (1961) and Lyttkens (1964) where the successive disturbances are allowed to be correlated with each other.

The Multivariate Contemporaneously Uncorrelated Linear Regression Model

A multivariate extension of these results is available. In Sections 4.11 and 5.4 we considered a system of M linear relations in which the regressor matrix was fixed in repeated samples. Now we formulate the multivariate contemporaneously uncorrelated linear regression model defined by the following assumptions:

$$(4.11) \qquad \mathbf{y}_m = \mathbf{X}\boldsymbol{\beta}_m + \boldsymbol{\epsilon}_m, \qquad (m = 1, \ldots, M)$$

(4.12) $(\boldsymbol{\epsilon}_1 \;\cdots\; \boldsymbol{\epsilon}_M)$ is a sample from a stationary multivariate stochastic process with mean vector $\mathbf{0}$, contemporaneous covariance matrix $\boldsymbol{\Omega}$, and all lag covariances 0,

(4.13) $\mathbf{X}$ is a sample from a stationary multivariate stochastic process with contemporaneous covariance matrix $\mathbf{\Sigma}_{\mathbf{xx}}$,

(4.14) The stochastic process generating $\mathbf{X}$ is contemporaneously uncorrelated with the stochastic process generating $(\boldsymbol{\epsilon}_1 \quad \cdots \quad \boldsymbol{\epsilon}_M)$,

(4.15) $\mathbf{\Sigma}_{\mathbf{xx}}$ is nonsingular.

it being understood that any dependence in each of the processes is sufficiently weak that the sample variances and covariances have the corresponding population parameters as their probability limits.

Then we have

$$E\boldsymbol{\epsilon}_m = \mathbf{0} \qquad (m = 1, \ldots, M) \tag{4.16}$$

$$E\boldsymbol{\epsilon}_m\boldsymbol{\epsilon}'_{m'} = \omega_{mm'}\mathbf{I} \qquad (m, m' = 1, \ldots, M) \tag{4.17}$$

$$\text{plim } T^{-1}\boldsymbol{\epsilon}'_m\boldsymbol{\epsilon}_{m'} = \omega_{mm'} \qquad (m, m' = 1, \ldots, M) \tag{4.18}$$

$$\text{plim } T^{-1}\mathbf{X}'\boldsymbol{\epsilon}_m = \mathbf{0} \qquad (m = 1, \ldots, M) \tag{4.19}$$

$$\text{plim } T^{-1}\mathbf{X}'\mathbf{X} = \mathbf{\Sigma}_{\mathbf{xx}} \tag{4.20}$$

$$\text{plim } (T^{-1}\mathbf{X}'\boldsymbol{\epsilon}_m\boldsymbol{\epsilon}'_{m'}\mathbf{X}) = \omega_{mm'}\mathbf{\Sigma}_{\mathbf{xx}} \qquad (m, m' = 1, \ldots, M). \tag{4.21}$$

It is a straightforward matter to show that

$$\text{plim } \mathbf{b}_m = \boldsymbol{\beta}_m \qquad (m = 1, \ldots, M) \tag{4.22}$$

$$\text{plim } \bar{w}_{mm'} = \omega_{mm'} \qquad (m, m' = 1, \ldots, M) \tag{4.23}$$

$$\begin{aligned} \bar{\mathbf{\Sigma}}_{\mathbf{b}_m\mathbf{b}_{m'}} &= \bar{E}(\mathbf{b}_m - \boldsymbol{\beta}_m)(\mathbf{b}_{m'} - \boldsymbol{\beta}_{m'})' \\ &= T^{-1}\omega_{mm'}\,\mathbf{\Sigma}_{\mathbf{xx}}^{-1} \qquad (m, m' = 1, \ldots, M) \end{aligned} \tag{4.24}$$

$$\text{plim } \mathbf{S}_{\mathbf{b}_m\mathbf{b}_{m'}} = \bar{\mathbf{\Sigma}}_{\mathbf{b}_m\mathbf{b}_{m'}} \qquad (m, m' = 1, \ldots, M), \tag{4.25}$$

where, it will be recalled,

$$\mathbf{b}_m = (\mathbf{X}'\mathbf{X})^{-1}\mathbf{X}'\mathbf{y}_m, \quad \bar{w}_{mm'} = (T - K)^{-1}(\mathbf{y}_m - \mathbf{X}\mathbf{b}_m)'(\mathbf{y}_{m'} - \mathbf{X}\mathbf{b}_{m'}),$$

and $\mathbf{S}_{\mathbf{b}_m\mathbf{b}_{m'}} = \bar{w}_{mm'}(\mathbf{X}'\mathbf{X})^{-1}$, are the classical least-squares estimators. We conclude that

(4.26) In the multivariate contemporaneously uncorrelated linear regression model, the classical least-squares estimators of the $\boldsymbol{\beta}_m$, the $\omega_{mm'}$, and the $\bar{\mathbf{\Sigma}}_{\mathbf{b}_m\mathbf{b}_{m'}}$ are consistent and (hence) asymptotically unbiased.

Of course it will be recognized that a gain in efficiency is in general obtainable if a priori restrictions on the $\boldsymbol{\beta}_m$ are available.

5. GENERAL STOCHASTIC LINEAR REGRESSION

The General Stochastic Linear Regression Model

By now we have come some distance from the classical specification that the regressors are fixed in repeated samples. In so doing we have found that classical least-squares estimation retains desirable asymptotic properties under considerably more general conditions. Nevertheless, as we shall see, in various economic contexts even these weaker conditions will not be appropriate. It remains then to consider the general stochastic linear regression model in which even the contemporaneously uncorrelated assumption (4.7) is dropped. Then since in general the regressors and the disturbances may be contemporaneously correlated, $Ex_{tk}\epsilon_t \neq 0$, and $\text{plim}\, T^{-1} \sum_{t=1}^{T} x_{tk}\epsilon_t \neq 0$, so that $\text{plim}\, \mathbf{b} = \boldsymbol{\beta} + \boldsymbol{\Sigma}_{\mathbf{xx}}^{-1} \,\text{plim}\,(T^{-1}\mathbf{X}'\boldsymbol{\epsilon}) \neq \boldsymbol{\beta}$; the least-squares estimators will not even be consistent nor asymptotically unbiased. Heuristically, if a regressor is correlated with the disturbance, then least-squares estimation—which attempts to give as much credit to regressors and as little to disturbance as possible—will give a misleading estimate of the influence of variations in the regressor on variations in the regressand.

Errors in the Variables

Until this section we have been assuming that the sample observations exactly measure what they purport to measure, i.e., the variables in the theoretically specified relationship. The essential source of random fluctuation has been the behavioral error, or "error in the equation." Although this is the scheme most generally adopted in econometrics, there is a long history of work in an alternative framework in which the source of random variation has been errors of measurement—or "errors in the variables." Here we consider a simple example to indicate that the "errors-in-the variables" framework fits into the general stochastic linear regression model.

Suppose then that our theory specifies that an exact linear relationship holds between the variables y^* and x^*,

$$(5.1) \qquad y_t^* = \beta x_t^*,$$

but that these true variables are unobserved. Our sample consists of observations on the measured variables y and x that are related to the true variables by

$$(5.2) \qquad y_t = y_t^* + y_t^{**}, \qquad x_t = x_t^* + x_t^{**}$$

where y^{**} and x^{**} are the errors of observation. Inserting (5.2) into (5.1) and rearranging gives for the relationship between the measured variables

$$(5.3) \qquad y_t = \beta(x_t - x_t^{**}) + y_t^{**} = \beta x_t + \epsilon_t$$

where

$$(5.4) \qquad \epsilon_t = y_t^{**} - \beta x_t^{**}$$

Let us specify that the measurement errors have zero means and constant variances, that they are uncorrelated, and that they are independent of the true variables so that

$$(5.5) \qquad \begin{aligned} &Ey_t^{**} = Ex_t^{**} = 0, \qquad E(y_t^{**})^2 = \sigma^2_{y^{**}}, \qquad E(x_t^{**})^2 = \sigma^2_{x^{**}}, \\ &Ey_t^{**}y_t^{*} = Ex_t^{**}x_t^{*} = Ey_t^{**}x_t^{*} = Ex_t^{**}y_t^{*} = Ex_t^{**}y_t^{**} = 0. \end{aligned}$$

Then it is clear that in the operational relationship (5.3) the regressor is contemporaneously correlated with the disturbance:

$$(5.6) \qquad \begin{aligned} Ex_t\epsilon_t &= E(x_t^{*} + x_t^{**})(y_t^{**} - \beta x_t^{**}) \\ &= Ex_t^{*}y_t^{**} - \beta Ex_t^{**}x_t^{**} - \beta Ex_t^{*}x_t^{**} + Ex_t^{**}y_t^{**} \\ &= 0 - \beta\sigma^2_{x^{**}} - \beta\cdot 0 + 0 = -\beta\sigma^2_{x^{**}}; \end{aligned}$$

after all the measured value is correlated with the error of measurement. Under general conditions on the process generating the true values of x, the general stochastic linear regression model will be applicable to (5.3) and the least-squares estimators will be inconsistent. Indeed the asymptotic bias will be

$$(5.7) \qquad \text{plim}\,(b - \beta) = \frac{\text{plim}\,(\Sigma\, x\epsilon/T)}{\text{plim}\,(\Sigma\, x^2/T)} = -\beta\,\frac{\sigma^2_{x^{**}}}{\sigma^2_{x^{**}} + \sigma^2_{x^{*}}}$$

since $Ex^2 = E(x^* + x^{**})^2 = Ex^{*2} + Ex^{**2} + 2Ex^*x^{**} = \sigma^2_{x^*} + \sigma^2_{x^{**}}$ where $\sigma^2_{x^*}$ is the variance of the true variable x^*.

An example of the "errors-in-the-variables" framework in econometric research is the permanent income hypothesis developed by Friedman (1957). Let y^* be permanent consumption and x^* be permanent income; then (5.1) is Friedman's consumption function. Further let y^{**} be transitory consumption and x^{**} be transitory income; then measured consumption y and measured income x are defined by (5.2), and (5.5) is just Friedman's specification on the transitory components. Rewriting (5.7) we obtain

$$(5.8) \qquad \text{plim}\, b = \beta - \beta\,\frac{\sigma^2_{x^{**}}}{\sigma^2_{x^{**}} + \sigma^2_{x^{*}}} = \beta\left(\frac{\sigma^2_{x^{*}}}{\sigma^2_{x^{*}} + \sigma^2_{x^{**}}}\right),$$

which is just Friedman's result that the classical least-squares estimate of the marginal propensity to consume underestimates the true marginal propensity to consume according as the variance of permanent income is small relative to the variance of total income.

It should be noted that when there is no error in measuring x^*—i.e., when $x_t^{**} = 0$ for all t so that $\sigma^2_{x^{**}} = 0$—the model (5.1)–(5.5) reduces to the classical linear regression model, provided that the x^* can be taken as fixed in repeated samples and that the y^{**} are temporally uncorrelated Thus an error in measurement of the regressand can be treated as an ordinary disturbance. Alternatively, when there is no error of measuring y^*—i.e., when $y_t^{**} = 0$ for all t so that $\sigma^2_{y^{**}} = 0$—the model may be transformed into one for which the classical model may be appropriate For then we may write

$$(5.9) \qquad x_t = \gamma y_t + u_t$$

where $\gamma = 1/\beta$, $u_t = x_t^{**}$, and the classical model is appropriate under a proviso parallel to that used before—if the x^* are fixed in repeated samples, then so are the $y^* = \beta x^*$.

For a more thorough treatment of errors of measurement in regression models see Johnston (1963, pp. 148–176.)

Returning to the more familiar "error-in-the-equation" framework, the general stochastic model plays an important role there also. If we think of the regressors in our relationship as being the regressands in other relationships that form a simultaneous system together with ours then in general in our relationship the regressors will be contemporaneously correlated with the disturbance. This topic is reserved for Chapter 7.

Instrumental Variable Estimation

We have seen that in the general stochastic linear regression model the least-squares estimator of $\boldsymbol{\beta}$ is biased, even asymptotically. The method of instrumental variables is available for obtaining consistent and (hence) asymptotically unbiased estimates of $\boldsymbol{\beta}$. We suppose that in addition to our observations $\mathbf{y}$ and $\mathbf{X}$ we have also available joint observations on a set of $1 + K$ "instrumental variables" $z_0, z_1, \ldots, z_K$ which are contemporaneously uncorrelated with the disturbances in the sense that

$$(5.10) \qquad \text{plim } T^{-1}\mathbf{Z}'\boldsymbol{\epsilon} = \mathbf{0}$$

where $\mathbf{Z}$ is the $T \times (1 + K)$ matrix of observations on the instruments. Further we require that the instruments are correlated with the regressors so that

$$(5.11) \qquad \text{plim } T^{-1}\mathbf{Z}'\mathbf{X} = \boldsymbol{\Sigma}_{zx} \text{ exists and is nonsingular.}$$

Then consider the instrumental variable estimator of $\boldsymbol{\beta}$ defined by

$$\text{(5.12)} \qquad \mathbf{b}^* = (\mathbf{Z}'\mathbf{X})^{-1}\mathbf{Z}'\mathbf{y};$$

it is readily confirmed that $\mathbf{b}^*$ is consistent. For inserting $\mathbf{y} = \mathbf{X}\boldsymbol{\beta} + \boldsymbol{\epsilon}$ in (5.12) gives

$$\text{(5.13)} \qquad \begin{aligned} \mathbf{b}^* &= (\mathbf{Z}'\mathbf{X})^{-1}\mathbf{Z}'(\mathbf{X}\boldsymbol{\beta} + \boldsymbol{\epsilon}) = \boldsymbol{\beta} + (\mathbf{Z}'\mathbf{X})^{-1}\mathbf{Z}'\boldsymbol{\epsilon} \\ &= \boldsymbol{\beta} + (T^{-1}\mathbf{Z}'\mathbf{X})^{-1}(T^{-1}\mathbf{Z}'\boldsymbol{\epsilon}), \end{aligned}$$

whence in view of (5.10) and (5.11)

$$\text{(5.14)} \qquad \text{plim}\, \mathbf{b}^* = \boldsymbol{\beta} + \boldsymbol{\Sigma}_{\mathbf{zx}}^{-1} \cdot \mathbf{0} = \boldsymbol{\beta}.$$

To rationalize this method consider the following. The instrumental variable estimator $\mathbf{b}^*$ is the solution to the normal equations $\mathbf{Z}'\mathbf{X}\mathbf{b}^* = \mathbf{Z}'\mathbf{y}$, which can be obtained by premultiplying the observational relation $\mathbf{y} = \mathbf{X}\boldsymbol{\beta} + \boldsymbol{\epsilon}$ through by $\mathbf{Z}'$, replacing $\boldsymbol{\beta}$ by $\mathbf{b}^*$, and dropping $\mathbf{Z}'\boldsymbol{\epsilon}$. This is quite parallel to the least-squares estimator $\mathbf{b} = (\mathbf{X}'\mathbf{X})^{-1}\mathbf{X}'\mathbf{y}$ which is the solution to the normal equations $\mathbf{X}'\mathbf{X}\mathbf{b} = \mathbf{X}'\mathbf{y}$ which can be obtained by premultiplying the observational relation $\mathbf{y} = \mathbf{X}\boldsymbol{\beta} + \boldsymbol{\epsilon}$ through by $\mathbf{X}'$, replacing $\boldsymbol{\beta}$ by $\mathbf{b}$ and dropping $\mathbf{X}'\boldsymbol{\epsilon}$. In each case the term dropped is essentially a vector of sample covariances; dropping is heuristically justified since the corresponding vector of population covariances is zero. There is another way of looking at the parallelism, which we illustrate for the case $K = 1$. Specializing (5.12) we see that

$$\text{(5.15)} \qquad b^* = \frac{\Sigma(z - \bar{z})(y - \bar{y})}{\Sigma(z - \bar{z})(x - \bar{x})} = \Sigma\left[\frac{(z - \bar{z})(x - \bar{x})}{\Sigma(z - \bar{z})(x - \bar{x})} \cdot \frac{y - \bar{y}}{x - \bar{x}}\right]$$

so that the instrumental variable estimator is a weighted average of the observed slopes $(y - \bar{y})/(x - \bar{x})$ with weights summing to 1. But the least-squares estimator is also a weighted average of these slopes with weights summing to 1, because

$$\text{(5.16)} \qquad b = \frac{\Sigma(x - \bar{x})(y - \bar{y})}{\Sigma(x - \bar{x})^2} = \Sigma\left[\frac{(x - \bar{x})^2}{\Sigma(x - \bar{x})^2} \cdot \frac{y - \bar{y}}{x - \bar{x}}\right].$$

Continuing our analysis we have

$$\text{(5.17)} \qquad (\mathbf{b}^* - \boldsymbol{\beta})(\mathbf{b}^* - \boldsymbol{\beta})' = (\mathbf{Z}'\mathbf{X})^{-1}\mathbf{Z}'\boldsymbol{\epsilon}\boldsymbol{\epsilon}'\mathbf{Z}(\mathbf{X}'\mathbf{Z})^{-1},$$

whence by an argument parallel to that of (2.32)–(2.35) the asymptotic covariance matrix of $\mathbf{b}^*$ is

$$\text{(5.18)} \qquad \bar{\boldsymbol{\Sigma}}_{\mathbf{b}^*\mathbf{b}^*} = \bar{E}(\mathbf{b}^* - \boldsymbol{\beta})(\mathbf{b}^* - \boldsymbol{\beta})' = T^{-1}\sigma^2\, \boldsymbol{\Sigma}_{\mathbf{zx}}^{-1}\boldsymbol{\Sigma}_{\mathbf{zz}}\boldsymbol{\Sigma}_{\mathbf{zx}}^{-1\prime}$$

provided that plim $T(T^{-1}\mathbf{Z}'\boldsymbol{\epsilon})(T^{-1}\mathbf{Z}'\boldsymbol{\epsilon})' = \sigma^2\boldsymbol{\Sigma}_{zz}$ where $\boldsymbol{\Sigma}_{zz}$ is the covariance matrix of the instrumental variables; this proviso will again be met under general conditions. Also by an argument parallel to that of (2.26)–(2.28) it can be shown that s^{*2}, the sum of squared residuals from the instrumental variable regression divided by $T - K - 1$, is a consistent estimator of the disturbance variance σ^2, and then that

$$\text{(5.19)} \qquad \mathbf{S}_{\mathbf{b}^*\mathbf{b}^*} = s^{*2}(\mathbf{Z}'\mathbf{X})^{-1}(\mathbf{Z}'\mathbf{Z})(\mathbf{Z}'\mathbf{X})^{-1'}$$

is a consistent estimator of $\bar{\boldsymbol{\Sigma}}_{\mathbf{b}^*\mathbf{b}^*}$.

Thus the instrumental variable method provides consistent estimators in circumstances where least squares fails. For the method to be appropriate, of course, the specifications (5.10) and (5.11) must be valid. It will be recognized that (5.10) will be satisfied if the instruments are fully independent of the disturbances, or if the instruments are independent of contemporary and succeeding disturbances, or in general even if the instruments are only contemporaneously uncorrelated with the disturbances. Any regressors that have the required properties will serve as their own instruments; it is also useful to note that the lagged value of a regressor may well be an appropriate instrument. Apart from this there may be a surplus of instruments available. Although any set of $1 + K$ variables that satisfy (5.10) and (5.11) will provide consistent estimators, a choice may be made on the grounds of asymptotic efficiency. A definitive analysis has been provided by Sargan (1958).

We illustrate the instrumental variables method by estimation of an inventory demand equation using annual data for the United States, 1929–1941 and 1946–1953. The relationship to be estimated is

$$\text{(5.20)} \qquad y = \beta_0 + \beta_1 x_1 + \beta_2 x_2 + \epsilon$$

where y = end of year inventory stock, x_1 = lagged end of year inventory stock, x_2 = gross national sales, and ϵ = disturbance term, with all variables measured in hundred billions of 1947 dollars. It is reasonable to specify that x_1 and ϵ are uncorrelated, but it is not reasonable to specify that x_2 and ϵ are uncorrelated; the reasons for this will become clear in Chapter 7. Observations on z_2 = government expenditures (in the same units) are also available and it may be reasonable to specify that z_2 and ϵ are uncorrelated. Hence we shall apply instrumental variable estimation with x_1 serving as its own instrument and z_2 serving as the instrument for x_2. The moments about the means are

(5.21)

	$x_1 = z_1$	x_2	z_2	y
$x_1 = z_1$	7.443	30.336	8.223	7.881
x_2		140.564	36.558	34.717
z_2			11.186	9.216
y				8.993

The instrumental variable estimates of β_1 and β_2 are computed in accordance with (5.12) as

$$(5.22)\qquad \begin{pmatrix} b_1^* \\ b_2^* \end{pmatrix} = \begin{pmatrix} 7.443 & 30.336 \\ 8.223 & 36.558 \end{pmatrix}^{-1} \begin{pmatrix} 7.881 \\ 9.216 \end{pmatrix} = \begin{pmatrix} 1.598 & -1.325 \\ -0.359 & 0.325 \end{pmatrix} \begin{pmatrix} 7.881 \\ 9.216 \end{pmatrix}$$

$$= \begin{pmatrix} 0.384 \\ 0.166 \end{pmatrix}.$$

The residual sum of squares from the estimated relation is 0.253, so that the disturbance variance is estimated as

$$(5.23)\qquad s^{*2} = (21 - 3)^{-1}(0.253) = 0.014,$$

and in accordance with (5.19) the asymptotic covariance matrix of the coefficient estimators is estimated as

$$(5.24)\qquad \mathbf{S_{b^*b^*}} = 0.014 \begin{pmatrix} 1.598 & -1.325 \\ -0.359 & 0.325 \end{pmatrix} \begin{pmatrix} 7.443 & 8.223 \\ 8.223 & 11.186 \end{pmatrix} \begin{pmatrix} 1.598 & -0.359 \\ -1.325 & 0.325 \end{pmatrix}$$

$$= \begin{pmatrix} 0.054 & 0.013 \\ 0.013 & 0.003 \end{pmatrix}.$$

Thus the instrumental variable estimated relationship (for variables measured as deviations around the sample mean) is

$$(5.25)\qquad y = \underset{(0.232)}{0.384x_1} + \underset{(0.054)}{0.166x_2}.$$

For comparison the classical least-squares estimated relationship would be

$$(5.26)\qquad y = 0.434x_1 + 0.153x_2$$

in accordance with

$$(5.27)\qquad \begin{pmatrix} b_1 \\ b_2 \end{pmatrix} = \begin{pmatrix} 7.443 & 30.336 \\ 30.336 & 140.465 \end{pmatrix}^{-1} \begin{pmatrix} 7.881 \\ 34.717 \end{pmatrix} = \begin{pmatrix} 0.434 \\ 0.153 \end{pmatrix}.$$

CHAPTER 7

Systems of Simultaneous Linear Relationships

1. INTRODUCTION

Up to this point we have been concerned almost exclusively with the estimation of single relationships among economic variables. Yet much of economic theory is cast in the form of systems of economic relationships, and it would be surprising if estimation procedures which ignored that fact were to be appropriate. Indeed, as we shall see, when a relationship is part of a system, some regressors will typically be stochastic and not independent of the disturbance. Then classical least-squares estimation will be inconsistent, and special procedures must be developed to provide consistent estimates.

This chapter is concerned with the problems of estimation and application of systems of simultaneous economic relationships. In Section 2 we illustrate the general problem with two very familiar simple economic models. Section 3 is devoted to developing the concepts and notation needed for handling the general case. The central problem of identification is analyzed in Section 4. Then in Sections 5, 6, and 7, we develop alternative methods of consistent estimation of systems of simultaneous equations. Section 8 compares these alternative methods and Section 9 discusses several applications of such systems. Finally, Section 10 discusses some deeper questions of formulation and causal interpretation of simultaneous equation systems.

2. ILLUSTRATIVE SIMULTANEOUS EQUATION SYSTEMS

Simple Keynesian Model

Perhaps the most familiar textbook model of the economy is the simple Keynesian system

(2.1) $$C = \alpha + \beta Y,$$

(2.2) $$Y = C + I,$$

where C = consumption, Y = income, I = investment. The standard textbook interpretation of the model is that (2.1) reflects the behavior of consumers, that (2.2) is an equilibrium condition equating savings $(Y - C)$ to investment, and that investment is autonomous. That is, given investment, the model determines the equilibrium values of consumption and income. The explicit dependence of C and Y on I is made clear if we solve the system into

$$C = \frac{\alpha}{1-\beta} + \frac{\beta}{1-\beta} I, \tag{2.3}$$

$$Y = \frac{\alpha}{1-\beta} + \frac{1}{1-\beta} I. \tag{2.4}$$

Thus far the model is an exact one and hence obviously unsuitable as an empirical description of the economy. A statistical formulation of the system is

$$C_t = \alpha + \beta Y_t + \epsilon_t, \tag{2.5}$$

$$Y_t = C_t + I_t, \tag{2.6}$$

where ϵ is a random disturbance with

$$E\epsilon_t = 0, \qquad E\epsilon_t^2 = \sigma^2, \qquad E\epsilon_s\epsilon_t = 0 \quad \text{for} \quad \text{all } s, t;\ s \neq t, \tag{2.7}$$

and to capture the idea that investment is autonomous—determined outside the system—it is assumed that

$$I_t \text{ and } \epsilon_s \text{ are independent } (t = 1, \ldots, T;\ s = 1, \ldots, T). \tag{2.8}$$

The explicit dependence of C and Y on I and ϵ is now given by solving the system into

$$C_t = \frac{\alpha}{1-\beta} + \frac{\beta}{1-\beta} I_t + \frac{1}{1-\beta} \epsilon_t, \tag{2.9}$$

$$Y_t = \frac{\alpha}{1-\beta} + \frac{1}{1-\beta} I_t + \frac{1}{1-\beta} \epsilon_t. \tag{2.10}$$

Given a sample of joint observations on C, Y, and I, our interest is in estimating the parameters of the consumption function (2.5). Now in that equation the regressor and the disturbance are not uncorrelated, not even contemporaneously. The covariance of Y and ϵ may be found by multiplying through (2.10) by ϵ_t and taking expectations:

$$\begin{aligned} EY_t\epsilon_t &= \frac{\alpha}{1-\beta} E\epsilon_t + \frac{\beta}{1-\beta} EI_t\epsilon_t + \frac{1}{1-\beta} E\epsilon_t^2 \\ &= \frac{1}{1-\beta} \sigma^2 \neq 0, \end{aligned} \tag{2.11}$$

using (2.7) and (2.8). Thus it is the general stochastic linear regression model that is appropriate for estimation of (2.5): classical least-squares estimates will not be consistent.

Let us consider this explicitly. The classical least-squares estimator of β in (2.5) is

$$(2.12)\qquad b = \frac{\Sigma\, C(Y-\bar{Y})}{\Sigma\,(Y-\bar{Y})^2} = \frac{\Sigma\,(\alpha+\beta Y+\epsilon)(Y-\bar{Y})}{\Sigma\,(Y-\bar{Y})^2} = \beta + \frac{\Sigma\,\epsilon(Y-\bar{Y})}{\Sigma\,(Y-\bar{Y})^2}$$

$$= \beta + \frac{\Sigma\,\epsilon(Y-\bar{Y})/T}{\Sigma\,(Y-\bar{Y})^2/T}\,.$$

Now $\Sigma\,\epsilon(Y-\bar{Y})/T$ is a sample covariance so that under general conditions

$$(2.13)\qquad \text{plim}\,\frac{\Sigma\,\epsilon(Y-\bar{Y})}{T} = \bar{E}\epsilon_t Y_t = E\epsilon_t Y_t = (1-\beta)^{-1}\sigma^2;$$

similarly $\Sigma\,(Y-\bar{Y})^2/T$ is a sample variance so that under general conditions

$$(2.14)\qquad \text{plim}\,\frac{\Sigma\,(Y-\bar{Y})^2}{T} = \bar{E}(Y-EY)^2 = E(Y-EY)^2 = \sigma_{yy},$$

say. Then

$$(2.15)\qquad \text{plim}\, b = \beta + \frac{(1-\beta)^{-1}\sigma^2}{\sigma_{yy}}\,,$$

so that the least-squares estimator will not be consistent. Indeed the direction of the asymptotic bias is clear if we employ the economic information that the marginal propensity to consume lies between zero and one: With $0 < \beta < 1$, plim $b > \beta$.

An alternative expression for the bias is also informative. Since I and ϵ are uncorrelated, (2.10) implies

$$(2.16)\qquad E(Y-EY)^2 = (1-\beta)^{-2}[E(I-EI)^2 + E\epsilon^2]$$

$$= (1-\beta)^{-2}(\sigma_{ii} + \sigma^2),$$

say. Inserting this for σ_{yy} in (2.15), we find

$$(2.17)\qquad \text{plim}\, b = \beta + \frac{(1-\beta)^{-1}\sigma^2}{(1-\beta)^{-2}(\sigma_{ii}+\sigma^2)} = \beta + (1-\beta)\frac{\sigma^2}{\sigma_{ii}+\sigma^2}\,.$$

Again with $0 < \beta < 1$, plim $b > \beta$. Further, plim $(b-\beta)$ will be large when the disturbance variance is large relative to the variance of investment.

Note the close analogy to our result in the errors-in-variables model, (6.5.8). A heuristic interpretation of the result is that the classical least-squares regression of consumption on income gives credit to income for the effect of disturbances since the disturbances are positively correlated with income. Still another way of looking at the result is the following. Classical least-squares may provide consistent estimates when the parameters in the relationship are the parameters of the conditional expectation of the regressand given the regressors. But this is not the case in (2.5):

$$(2.18) \qquad E(C_t \mid Y_t) = \alpha + \beta Y_t + E(\epsilon_t \mid Y_t),$$

but $E(\epsilon_t \mid Y_t) \neq E\epsilon_t = 0$.

This way of looking at the result reminds us that classical least-squares should be appropriate in the solved relationships (2.9) and (2.10). That is, (2.9) falls under the independent stochastic linear regression model; note

$$(2.19) \qquad E(C_t \mid I_t) = \frac{\alpha}{1-\beta} + \frac{\beta}{1-\beta} I_t + E\left(\frac{1}{1-\beta}\epsilon_t \mid I_t\right)$$
$$= \frac{\alpha}{1-\beta} + \frac{\beta}{1-\beta} I_t.$$

Suppose then that we estimate by classical least squares

$$(2.20) \qquad C_t = \pi_0 + \pi_1 I_t + v_t$$

where

$$(2.21) \qquad \pi_0 = \frac{\alpha}{1-\beta}, \qquad \pi_1 = \frac{\beta}{1-\beta}, \qquad v_t = \frac{\epsilon_t}{1-\beta},$$

and let us designate the least-squares estimates of π_0 and π_1 as p_0 and p_1 respectively. Then by (6.2.25) these are consistent:

$$(2.22) \qquad \operatorname{plim} p_0 = \pi_0 = \frac{\alpha}{1-\beta}, \qquad \operatorname{plim} p_1 = \pi_1 = \frac{\beta}{1-\beta}.$$

Now (2.21) suggests that we consider estimating β by $\hat{\beta}$, defined by $p_1 = \hat{\beta}/(1-\hat{\beta})$; i.e.,

$$(2.23) \qquad \hat{\beta} = \frac{p_1}{1+p_1}.$$

Indeed $\hat{\beta}$ is consistent:

$$(2.24) \qquad \operatorname{plim} \hat{\beta} = \frac{\operatorname{plim} p_1}{\operatorname{plim}(1+p_1)} = \frac{\beta/(1-\beta)}{1+\beta/(1-\beta)} = \beta.$$

Similarly (2.21) suggests that we consider estimating α by $\hat{\alpha}$, defined by $p_0 = \hat{\alpha}/(1 - \hat{\beta})$; i.e.,

$$\hat{\alpha} = p_0(1 - \hat{\beta}). \tag{2.25}$$

Indeed $\hat{\alpha}$ is consistent:

$$\text{plim } \hat{\alpha} = \text{plim } p_0 \text{ plim } (1 - \hat{\beta}) = \frac{\alpha}{1 - \beta}(1 - \beta) = \alpha. \tag{2.26}$$

It should be noted that although p_0 and p_1 are unbiased, $\hat{\alpha}$ and $\hat{\beta}$, which are nonlinear functions of p_0 and p_1, are not unbiased. Still, they are consistent and hence asymptotically unbiased.

To summarize: The simple Keynesian model illustrates that when a relationship is one of several in a simultaneous system, classical least-squares estimates of its coefficients will in general be inconsistent. The underlying reason is that some regressors are jointly determined with the regressand and hence are dependent on the contemporaneous disturbance. We have also seen that we may be able to obtain consistent estimates by a kind of indirect least-squares procedure. It will develop, however, that this latter alternative is not generally available.

The method of instrumental variables is of course available. Indeed it is not hard to show that our estimators $\hat{\alpha}$ and $\hat{\beta}$ are the instrumental variable estimators of α and β in (2.5) when I, which is independent of the disturbance, is used as the instrument for Y. It will not always be so simple, however, to find a legitimate instrumental variable.

We might, incidentally, have looked at (2.10), noted that

$$\begin{aligned} E(Y_t \mid I_t) &= \frac{\alpha}{1 - \beta} + \frac{1}{1 - \beta} I_t + E\left(\frac{1}{1 - \beta}\epsilon_t \mid I_t\right) \\ &= \frac{\alpha}{1 - \beta} + \frac{1}{1 - \beta} I_t \end{aligned} \tag{2.27}$$

and estimated by classical least squares

$$Y_t = \delta_0 + \delta_1 I_t + w_t \tag{2.28}$$

where

$$\delta_0 = \frac{\alpha}{1 - \beta}, \qquad \delta_1 = \frac{1}{1 - \beta}, \qquad \text{and} \qquad w_t = \frac{\epsilon_t}{1 - \beta}. \tag{2.29}$$

Then the least-squares estimates, designated by d_0 and d_1, would be consistent:

$$\text{plim } d_0 = \delta_0 = \frac{\alpha}{1 - \beta}, \qquad \text{plim } d_1 = \delta_1 = \frac{1}{1 - \beta}. \tag{2.30}$$

Then we could have considered the estimators $\tilde{\beta}$ and $\tilde{\alpha}$ defined by $d_1 = 1/(1 - \tilde{\beta})$ and $d_0 = \tilde{\alpha}/(1 - \tilde{\beta})$, i.e.,

$$(2.31) \qquad \tilde{\beta} = 1 - \frac{1}{d_1}, \qquad \tilde{\alpha} = \frac{d_0}{d_1},$$

and seen that they were consistent;

$$(2.32) \qquad \text{plim } \tilde{\beta} = \beta, \qquad \text{plim } \tilde{\alpha} = \alpha.$$

There is no point, however, in doing this in the present model; using (2.6) it can be shown that $\tilde{\beta} = \hat{\beta}$ and $\tilde{\alpha} = \hat{\alpha}$.

Simple Market Model

For a second illustration, consider the textbook model of supply and demand for a particular commodity, with allowance for disturbances (random shifts in the demand and supply curves):

$$(2.33) \qquad \text{Demand:} \quad q_t = \alpha + \beta p_t + \epsilon_t,$$

$$(2.34) \qquad \text{Supply:} \quad q_t = \gamma + \delta p_t + \epsilon_t^*.$$

If in the demand equation the regressor p_t were independent of the disturbance ϵ_t, then when the demand equation received a positive disturbance, q_t in (2.33) would have to rise by the amount of the disturbance. But then so would q_t in (2.34), which with independence of p_t and ϵ_t would imply that $\epsilon_t = \epsilon_t^*$. Although the demand and supply disturbances may well be correlated, it is nevertheless absurd to specify that they are identical. We conclude that p_t and ϵ_t are not independent, price is jointly determined with quantity and *is* influenced by random shifts in the demand equation.

Numerical illustration. We draw on some computations by Haavelmo (1953) to illustrate the discussion of estimation of the simple Keynesian model. Using annual data for the United States, 1922–1941, with variables measured in 1935–1939 dollars per capita, the following moments about the mean were computed:

(2.35)

	C	Y	I
C	35,887	47,585	11,698
Y		64,993	17,408
I			5,710

The inconsistent classical least-squares estimate of β in (2.5) is then

$$(2.36) \qquad b = \frac{m_{cy}}{m_{yy}} = \frac{47{,}585}{64{,}993} = 0.732.$$

The consistent classical least-squares estimate of π_1 in (2.20) is

$$(2.37) \qquad p_1 = \frac{m_{ci}}{m_{ii}} = \frac{11{,}698}{5{,}710} = 2.048;$$

from this we may derive a consistent estimate of β through (2.23)

$$(2.38) \qquad \hat{\beta} = \frac{p_1}{1 + p_1} = \frac{2.048}{3.048} = 0.672.$$

Note that $b > \hat{\beta}$ for this sample, which is not surprising since plim $b > \beta =$ plim $\hat{\beta}$. Alternatively we may take the consistent classical least-squares estimate of δ_1 in (2.28):

$$(2.39) \qquad d_1 = \frac{m_{yi}}{m_{ii}} = \frac{17{,}408}{5{,}710} = 3.048$$

and from this derive a consistent estimate of β through (2.31):

$$(2.40) \qquad \tilde{\beta} = 1 - \frac{1}{d_1} = 1 - \frac{1}{3.048} = 0.672 = \hat{\beta}.$$

And also for the instrumental variable estimate of β in (2.5) we see

$$(2.41) \qquad b^* = \frac{m_{ic}}{m_{iy}} = \frac{11{,}698}{17{,}408} = 0.672 = \hat{\beta}.$$

3. SIMULTANEOUS LINEAR STRUCTURAL EQUATION MODEL

We now proceed to develop a vocabulary, notation, and statistical model for the general case of a system of simultaneous linear economic relationships.

Classification of Variables

We consider an economic theory that specifies the existence of a system of simultaneous linear relationships, each of which expresses some aspect of the behavior of an individual, sector, or market. The variables of the system are classified into *endogenous variables* and *exogenous variables* according as the theory is or is not intended to account for their values. (In the simple Keynesian model I is exogenous and C and Y are endogenous.) For most statistical purposes, however, the relevant distinction is between *jointly dependent variables* and *predetermined variables.* In a dynamic model, lagged values of the endogenous variables are to be distinguished from current values of the endogenous variables. The jointly dependent variables are the current endogenous variables; the predetermined variables are the exogenous variables and the lagged endogenous variables. If no lagged endogenous variables appear, the endogenous/exogenous classification is equivalent to the jointly dependent/predetermined classification. The precise content of these terms does not become clear until we specify the statistical assumptions. To illustrate the point, however, consider the simple dynamic Keynesian model:

$$C_t = \alpha + \beta Y_{t-1}, \tag{3.1a}$$

$$Y_t = C_t + I_t, \tag{3.1b}$$

with investment taken as autonomous. Here I is exogenous and C and Y are endogenous; I_t and Y_{t-1} are predetermined and C_t and Y_t are jointly dependent. A lagged *exogenous* variable should be considered simply as a distinct exogenous variable. We often refer to jointly dependent variables as *dependent* variables.

Structural Form

We consider economic theories that have the following *structural form:*

(3.2)

$$\begin{matrix} \gamma_{11}y_1(t) + \cdots + \gamma_{M1}y_M(t) + \beta_{11}x_1(t) + \cdots + \beta_{K1}x_K(t) + u_1(t) = 0 \\ \vdots \\ \gamma_{1M}y_1(t) + \cdots + \gamma_{MM}y_M(t) + \beta_{1M}x_1(t) + \cdots + \beta_{KM}x_K(t) + u_M(t) = 0 \end{matrix}$$

for $t = 1, \ldots, T$, where

$y_{m'}(t)$ is the tth observation on the m'th jointly dependent variable $(m' = 1, \ldots, M)$;
$x_k(t)$ is the tth observation on the kth predetermined variable, $(k = 1, \ldots, K)$;
$\gamma_{m'm}$ is the coefficient in the mth structural equation, of the m'th jointly dependent variable $y_{m'}(t)$ $(m, m' = 1, \ldots, M)$;
β_{km} is the coefficient, in the mth structural equation, of the kth predetermined variable $x_k(t)$ $(k = 1, \ldots, K;\ m = 1, \ldots, M)$;
$u_m(t)$ is the unobserved disturbance at the tth observation in the mth structural equation $(m = 1, \ldots, M)$.

A matrix formulation is the following:

$$\mathbf{y}'(t)\mathbf{\Gamma} + \mathbf{x}'(t)\mathbf{B} + \mathbf{u}'(t) = \mathbf{0} \qquad (t = 1, \ldots, T), \tag{3.3}$$

where

$$\mathbf{\Gamma} = \begin{pmatrix} \gamma_{11} & \cdots & \gamma_{1M} \\ \vdots & & \vdots \\ \gamma_{M1} & \cdots & \gamma_{MM} \end{pmatrix}$$

is the $M \times M$ matrix of coefficients of the jointly dependent variables, each column of which refers to a single equation;

$$\mathbf{B} = \begin{pmatrix} \beta_{11} & \cdots & \beta_{1M} \\ \cdot & & \cdot \\ \cdot & & \cdot \\ \cdot & & \cdot \\ \beta_{K1} & \cdots & \beta_{KM} \end{pmatrix}$$

is the $K \times M$ matrix of coefficients of the predetermined variables, each column of which refers to a single equation;

$\mathbf{y}'(t) = [y_1(t) \quad \cdots \quad y_M(t)]$ is the $1 \times M$ row vector of the tth observations on the jointly dependent variables;

$\mathbf{x}'(t) = [x_1(t) \quad \ldots \quad x_K(t)]$ is the $1 \times K$ row vector of the tth observations on the predetermined variables; and

$\mathbf{u}'(t) = [u_1(t) \quad \cdots \quad u_M(t)]$ is the $1 \times M$ row vector of the tth (unobserved) values of the disturbances.

Note that (3.3) refers to only a single joint observation. To write the system in terms of all the observations, we define

$$\mathbf{Y} = \begin{pmatrix} \mathbf{y}'(1) \\ \cdot \\ \cdot \\ \cdot \\ \mathbf{y}'(T) \end{pmatrix} = \begin{pmatrix} y_1(1) & \cdots & y_M(1) \\ \cdot & & \cdot \\ \cdot & & \cdot \\ \cdot & & \cdot \\ y_1(T) & \cdots & y_M(T) \end{pmatrix},$$

the $T \times M$ matrix of observations on the jointly dependent variables;

$$\mathbf{X} = \begin{pmatrix} \mathbf{x}'(1) \\ \cdot \\ \cdot \\ \cdot \\ \mathbf{x}'(T) \end{pmatrix} = \begin{pmatrix} x_1(1) & \cdots & x_K(1) \\ \cdot & & \cdot \\ \cdot & & \cdot \\ \cdot & & \cdot \\ x_1(T) & \cdots & x_K(T) \end{pmatrix}$$

the $T \times K$ matrix of observations on the predetermined variables; and

$$\mathbf{U} = \begin{pmatrix} \mathbf{u}'(1) \\ \cdot \\ \cdot \\ \cdot \\ \mathbf{u}'(T) \end{pmatrix} = \begin{pmatrix} u_1(1) & \cdots & u_M(1) \\ \cdot & & \cdot \\ \cdot & & \cdot \\ \cdot & & \cdot \\ u_1(T) & \cdots & u_M(T) \end{pmatrix},$$

the $T \times M$ matrix of values of the disturbances. With these definitions the structural form may be written compactly as

(3.4) $$\mathbf{Y\Gamma} + \mathbf{XB} + \mathbf{U} = \mathbf{0},$$

the tth row of which is indeed (3.3).

The structural form contains as many relations as there are jointly dependent variables; from the economic point of view it is a system of M equations in M unknowns. The idea is that with fixed values of the coefficients—i.e., with $\mathbf{B}$ and $\mathbf{\Gamma}$ being population parameters—the system may be solved uniquely for the tth values of the jointly dependent variables in terms of the tth values of the predetermined variables and the disturbances. It is in this sense that the system is supposed to account for the values of the current endogenous variables. (Indeed, when the model is dynamic, the idea is that the system recursively generates the successive values of the endogenous variables in terms of initial conditions, *exogenous* variables, and disturbances. But we postpone this interpretation until Section 9.) In any event, so that the structural form makes sense as an economic theory we require it to be soluble uniquely for $\mathbf{y}(t)$ in terms of $\mathbf{x}(t)$ and $\mathbf{u}(t)$, i.e., we will assume

(3.5) $\mathbf{\Gamma}$ is nonsingular.

Reduced Form

In the structural form—(3.3) or its equivalents (3.2) and (3.4)—each equation is intended to represent the behavior of some element of the economic structure; i.e., the behavior of some unit of the economy. This is the form derived from economic theory. The interaction of the units is reflected in the set of structural equations. Nevertheless, to bring out the explicit dependence of the dependent variables on the predetermined variables and the disturbances, we should solve the structural form into the *reduced form:* Postmultiplying (3.3) through by $\mathbf{\Gamma}^{-1}$ and rearranging, we obtain

$$\text{(3.6)} \qquad \begin{aligned} \mathbf{y}'(t) &= \mathbf{x}'(t)(-\mathbf{B}\mathbf{\Gamma}^{-1}) + \mathbf{u}'(t)(-\mathbf{\Gamma}^{-1}) \\ &= \mathbf{x}'(t)\mathbf{\Pi} + \mathbf{v}'(t) \qquad (t = 1, \ldots, T), \end{aligned}$$

where

$$\mathbf{\Pi} = -\mathbf{B}\mathbf{\Gamma}^{-1} = \begin{pmatrix} \pi_{11} & \cdots & \pi_{1M} \\ \cdot & & \cdot \\ \cdot & & \cdot \\ \cdot & & \cdot \\ \pi_{K1} & \cdots & \pi_{KM} \end{pmatrix}$$

is the $K \times M$ matrix of reduced-form coefficients, each column of which refers to a single equation, and $\mathbf{v}'(t) = -\mathbf{u}'(t)\mathbf{\Gamma}^{-1} = [v_1(t) \quad \cdots \quad v_M(t)]$ is the $1 \times M$ row vector of the tth values of the reduced-form disturbances.

The distinctive feature of the reduced form is that in each of its equations only one dependent variable appears. This contrast with the structural form is made explicit if we write out (3.6) algebraically, analogously to (3.2):

$$\text{(3.7)} \qquad \begin{matrix} y_1(t) & = & \pi_{11}x_1(t) & + \cdots + & \pi_{K1}x_K(t) & + & v_1(t) \\ \cdot & & \cdot & & \cdot & & \cdot \\ \cdot & & \cdot & & \cdot & & \cdot \\ \cdot & & \cdot & & \cdot & & \cdot \\ y_M(t) & = & \pi_{1M}x_1(t) & + \cdots + & \pi_{KM}x_K(t) & + & v_M(t) \end{matrix}$$

for $t = 1, \ldots, T$. Note that (3.6) and (3.7) refer to a single joint observation. To write the system compactly in terms of all the observations we define

$$\mathbf{V} = \begin{pmatrix} \mathbf{v}'(1) \\ \cdot \\ \cdot \\ \cdot \\ \mathbf{v}'(T) \end{pmatrix} = \begin{pmatrix} v_1(1) & \cdots & v_M(1) \\ \cdot & & \cdot \\ \cdot & & \cdot \\ \cdot & & \cdot \\ v_1(T) & \cdots & v_M(T) \end{pmatrix} = -\mathbf{U}\mathbf{\Gamma}^{-1},$$

the $T \times M$ matrix of values of the reduced-form disturbances. With this definition, the reduced form may be written compactly as

$$\text{(3.8)} \qquad \mathbf{Y} = \mathbf{X}\mathbf{\Pi} + \mathbf{V},$$

the tth row of which is indeed (3.6).

It is to be noted that each reduced-form coefficient is in general a function of all the structural coefficients in $\mathbf{\Gamma}$ and in a row of $\mathbf{B}$; also each reduced-form disturbance is a linear function of all the contemporaneous structural disturbances. This is made clear if we write out $\mathbf{\Pi} = -\mathbf{B}\mathbf{\Gamma}^{-1}$:

$$\begin{pmatrix} \pi_{11} & \cdots & \pi_{1M} \\ \cdot & & \cdot \\ \cdot & & \cdot \\ \cdot & & \cdot \\ \pi_{K1} & \cdots & \pi_{KM} \end{pmatrix} = -\begin{pmatrix} \beta_{11} & \cdots & \beta_{1M} \\ \cdot & & \cdot \\ \cdot & & \cdot \\ \cdot & & \cdot \\ \beta_{K1} & \cdots & \beta_{KM} \end{pmatrix} \times \begin{pmatrix} \gamma^{11} & \cdots & \gamma^{1M} \\ \cdot & & \cdot \\ \cdot & & \cdot \\ \cdot & & \cdot \\ \gamma^{M1} & \cdots & \gamma^{MM} \end{pmatrix}, \tag{3.9}$$

where $\gamma^{m'm}$ is the element in the m'th row and mth column of $\mathbf{\Gamma}^{-1}$. Thus we see for a reduced-form coefficient

$$\pi_{km} = -\sum_{m'=1}^{M} \beta_{km'}\gamma^{m'm}, \tag{3.10}$$

and for a reduced-form disturbance:

$$v_m(t) = -\sum_{m'=1}^{M} \gamma^{m'm} u_{m'}(t). \tag{3.11}$$

Stochastic Specifications

We now turn to the stochastic specifications which are generalizations of those assumed for the stochastic regression models of Chapter 6. The structural disturbances are generated by a stationary multivariate stochastic process with:

$$\mathscr{E}\mathbf{u}(t) = \mathbf{0} \qquad (t = 1, \ldots, T) \quad \text{or} \quad \mathscr{E}\mathbf{U} = \mathbf{0}, \tag{3.12}$$

i.e., each disturbance vector has a zero expectation, or $\mathscr{E}u_m(t) = 0$ for all m and t;

$$\mathscr{E}\mathbf{u}(t)\mathbf{u}'(t) = \mathbf{\Sigma} \qquad (t = 1, \ldots, T) \tag{3.13}$$

where $\boldsymbol{\Sigma}$ is an $M \times M$ nonnegative definite matrix, i.e., the contemporaneous covariance matrix of the disturbances in the different equations is the same for all t, or $Eu_m(t)u_{m'}(t) = \sigma_{mm'}$ for all t (we do not assume that $\boldsymbol{\Sigma}$ is diagonal);

$$\text{(3.14)} \qquad E\mathbf{u}(t)\mathbf{u}'(t') = \mathbf{0} \qquad (t, t' = 1, \ldots, T;\ t \neq t'),$$

i.e., the disturbance vector is temporally uncorrelated, all lagged covariances between disturbances in the *same* or *different* equations are zero, or $Eu_m(t)u_{m'}(t') = 0$ for all m,m', t,t' with $t \neq t'$. Note that these assumptions imply, under general conditions, that the sample variances and covariances of the structural disturbances have as their probability limits the corresponding population parameters, so that

$$\text{(3.15)} \qquad \operatorname{plim} \frac{\sum_{t=1}^{T} \mathbf{u}(t)\mathbf{u}'(t)}{T} = \boldsymbol{\Sigma} \quad \text{or} \quad \operatorname{plim} T^{-1}\mathbf{U}'\mathbf{U} = \boldsymbol{\Sigma}.$$

We also assume that the predetermined variables are generated by a stationary multivariate stochastic process with *nonsingular* contemporaneous covariance matrix $\boldsymbol{\Sigma}_{\mathbf{xx}}$ and that any dependence in the process is sufficiently weak that

$$\text{(3.16)} \qquad \operatorname{plim} \frac{\sum_{t=1}^{T} \mathbf{x}(t)\mathbf{x}'(t)}{T} = \boldsymbol{\Sigma}_{\mathbf{xx}} \quad \text{or} \quad \operatorname{plim} T^{-1}\mathbf{X}'\mathbf{X} = \boldsymbol{\Sigma}_{\mathbf{xx}}.$$

Continuing, we assume that the process generating the predetermined variables is contemporaneously uncorrelated with the process generating the disturbances, so that $E\mathbf{x}(t)\mathbf{u}'(t) = E\mathbf{x}(t)E\mathbf{u}'(t) = \mathbf{0}$ and that any dependence in each of the processes is sufficiently weak that

$$\text{(3.17)} \qquad \operatorname{plim} \frac{\sum_{t=1}^{T} \mathbf{x}(t)\mathbf{u}'(t)}{T} = \mathbf{0} \quad \text{or} \quad \operatorname{plim} T^{-1}\mathbf{X}'\mathbf{U} = \mathbf{0},$$

i.e., plim $\sum_{t=1}^{T} x_k(t)u_m(t)/T = 0$ for all k and m. This specification captures the idea that the predetermined variables are not determined by the system at time t and hence are not dependent on the disturbances at time t. Exogenous variables may be distributed independently of all disturbances or simply uncorrelated with the contemporaneous disturbances; lagged endogenous variables will be distributed independently of contemporary and succeeding disturbances—in any of these events (3.17) will be justified by the discussion in Chapter 6. To be sure, when there are lagged endogenous variables among the predetermined variables, it may be necessary to assume that the successive disturbances are mutually independent (not merely uncorrelated).

In some contexts it may be appropriate to assume that the predetermined variables are fixed in repeated samples, i.e., that the sequence $\mathbf{x}(1), \ldots, \mathbf{x}(t), \ldots, \mathbf{x}(T), \ldots$ is nonstochastic. This is an acceptable alternative assumption provided that $\lim_{T\to\infty} \sum_{t=1}^{T} \mathbf{x}(t)\mathbf{x}'(t)/T$ does exist. This case may be subsumed in the present model simply by reinterpreting the probability limit in (3.16) as an ordinary limit (as T goes to infinity); clearly if the $\mathbf{x}(t)$'s are nonstochastic then (3.17) will hold as well. Indeed, some of the derivations in the sequel could be simplified if the predetermined variables were nonstochastic. In view of the prevalence of lagged endogenous variables in empirical work, however, the stationary stochastic process specification seems to be more useful. For still wider applicability, (3.16) and (3.17) may be interpreted to cover the case where some of the predetermined variables are nonstochastic and the others are stochastic. For another alternative specification see Basmann (1960*a*) where the successive $\mathbf{x}(t)$'s are assumed to be independently, but not necessarily identically, distributed.

Continuing, since the reduced-form disturbances are linear combinations of the structural disturbances, their properties may now be derived quite simply. Thus

$$(3.18)\qquad E\mathbf{v}(t) = E[-\mathbf{\Gamma}'^{-1}\mathbf{u}(t)] = -\mathbf{\Gamma}'^{-1}E\mathbf{u}(t) = \mathbf{0} \qquad (t = 1, \ldots, T)$$
$$\text{or}\quad E\mathbf{V} = \mathbf{0},$$

i.e., each reduced-form disturbance vector has a zero expectation, or $Ev_m(t) = 0$ for all m and t;

$$(3.19)\qquad \begin{aligned} E\mathbf{v}(t)\mathbf{v}'(t) &= E[(-\mathbf{\Gamma}'^{-1})\mathbf{u}(t)\cdot\mathbf{u}'(t)(-\mathbf{\Gamma}^{-1})] \\ &= \mathbf{\Gamma}'^{-1}\cdot E\mathbf{u}(t)\mathbf{u}'(t)\cdot\mathbf{\Gamma}^{-1} \\ &= \mathbf{\Gamma}'^{-1}\mathbf{\Sigma}\mathbf{\Gamma}^{-1} = \mathbf{\Omega} \qquad (t = 1, \ldots, T), \end{aligned}$$

say, where $\mathbf{\Omega}$ is an $M \times M$ nonnegative definite matrix, or the contemporaneous covariance matrix of the disturbances in the different equations is the same for all t, or $Ev_m(t)v_{m'}(t) = \omega_{mm'}$ for all t, where $\omega_{mm'} = \sum_{\mu=1}^{M} \sum_{\mu'=1}^{M} \gamma^{\mu m}\, \sigma_{\mu\mu'}\gamma^{\mu' m'}$;

$$(3.20)\qquad \begin{aligned} E\mathbf{v}(t)\mathbf{v}'(t') &= E[(-\mathbf{\Gamma}'^{-1})\mathbf{u}(t)\mathbf{u}'(t')(-\mathbf{\Gamma}^{-1})] \\ &= \mathbf{\Gamma}'^{-1}E\mathbf{u}(t)\mathbf{u}'(t')\mathbf{\Gamma}^{-1} \\ &= \mathbf{0} \qquad (t', t = 1, \ldots, T;\ t \neq t'), \end{aligned}$$

i.e., the reduced-form disturbance vector is temporally uncorrelated; all lagged covariances between disturbances in the same or different reduced-form equations are zero, or $Ev_m(t)v_{m'}(t') = 0$ for all m, m', t, t' with

$t \neq t'$. Again, this will imply under general conditions that the sample variances and covariances of the reduced-form disturbances have as their probability limits the corresponding population parameters; from (3.15)

$$\text{(3.21)} \qquad \text{plim } T^{-1}\mathbf{V}'\mathbf{V} = \text{plim } T^{-1}\mathbf{\Gamma}'^{-1}\mathbf{U}'\mathbf{U}\mathbf{\Gamma}^{-1}$$
$$= \mathbf{\Gamma}'^{-1} \text{ plim } (T^{-1}\mathbf{U}'\mathbf{U})\mathbf{\Gamma}^{-1} = \mathbf{\Gamma}'^{-1}\mathbf{\Sigma}\,\mathbf{\Gamma}^{-1} = \mathbf{\Omega}$$

$$\text{or plim } \frac{\sum_{t=1}^{T} \mathbf{v}(t)\mathbf{v}'(t)}{T} = \mathbf{\Omega}.$$

Also the predetermined variables will be contemporaneously uncorrelated with reduced-form disturbances; from (3.17)

$$\text{(3.22)} \qquad \text{plim } T^{-1}\mathbf{X}'\mathbf{V} = -\text{plim } T^{-1}\mathbf{X}'\mathbf{U}\mathbf{\Gamma}^{-1} = -\text{plim } (T^{-1}\mathbf{X}'\mathbf{U})\mathbf{\Gamma}^{-1} = \mathbf{0}$$

$$\text{or plim } \frac{\sum_{t=1}^{T} \mathbf{x}(t)\mathbf{v}'(t)}{T} = \mathbf{0},$$

i.e., $\text{plim } \Sigma_{t=1}^{T} x_k(t)v_m(t)/T = 0$ for all k and m.

Illustrative examples. At this point we should pause to illustrate the notation. First, we rewrite the simple Keynesian system of (2.5) and (2.6) as

$$\text{(3.23}a\text{)} \qquad -C_t + \beta Y_t + \alpha + \epsilon_t = 0,$$

$$\text{(3.23}b\text{)} \qquad C_t - Y_t + I_t = 0.$$

Then the structural form (3.3) reads

$$\text{(3.24)} \qquad (C_t \quad Y_t)\begin{pmatrix} -1 & 1 \\ \beta & -1 \end{pmatrix} + (1 \quad I_t)\begin{pmatrix} \alpha & 0 \\ 0 & 1 \end{pmatrix} + (\epsilon_t \quad 0) = (0 \quad 0).$$

Note that in this system it happens that $K = M = 2$. We proceed to compute

$$\mathbf{\Pi} = -\mathbf{B}\mathbf{\Gamma}^{-1} = -\begin{pmatrix} \alpha & 0 \\ 0 & 1 \end{pmatrix}\begin{pmatrix} -1 & 1 \\ \beta & -1 \end{pmatrix}^{-1}$$
$$= -\begin{pmatrix} \alpha & 0 \\ 0 & 1 \end{pmatrix}\begin{pmatrix} -1/(1-\beta) & -1/(1-\beta) \\ -\beta/(1-\beta) & -1/(1-\beta) \end{pmatrix}$$
$$= \begin{pmatrix} \alpha/(1-\beta) & \alpha/(1-\beta) \\ \beta/(1-\beta) & 1/(1-\beta) \end{pmatrix}$$

whence the reduced form (3.6) reads

$$\text{(3.25)} \qquad (C_t \quad Y_t) = (1 \quad I_t)\begin{pmatrix} \alpha/(1-\beta) & \alpha/(1-\beta) \\ \beta/(1-\beta) & 1/(1-\beta) \end{pmatrix} + (v_{1t} \quad v_{2t})$$

where $v_{1t} = \epsilon_t/(1-\beta) = v_{2t}$; as we had already found in (2.9) and (2.10).

A second system we shall use in the sequel is Tintner's model of the American meat market, presented in Tintner (1952, pp. 176–179).

$$\text{(3.26a)} \qquad \text{Demand:} \quad y_1 = a_1 y_2 + a_2 x_1 + u_1,$$

$$\text{(3.26b)} \qquad \text{Supply:} \quad y_1 = b_1 y_2 + b_2 x_2 + b_3 x_3 + u_2,$$

where the dependent variables are y_1 = meat consumption per capita (pounds), y_2 = meat price (1935–1939 = 100); and the predetermined variables are x_1 = disposable income per capita (dollars), x_2 = unit cost of meat processing (1935–1939 = 100), and x_3 = cost of agricultural production (1935–1939 = 100). Then the structural form (3.3) reads:

$$\text{(3.27)} \qquad (y_1 \quad y_2)\begin{pmatrix} -1 & -1 \\ a_1 & b_1 \end{pmatrix} + (x_1 \quad x_2 \quad x_3)\begin{pmatrix} a_2 & 0 \\ 0 & b_2 \\ 0 & b_3 \end{pmatrix} + (u_1 \quad u_2) = (0 \quad 0).$$

We have omitted the constant term and the time index for simplicity. Here $K = 3$ and $M = 2$. We proceed to compute

$$\begin{aligned} \mathbf{\Pi} = -\mathbf{B}\mathbf{\Gamma}^{-1} &= -\begin{pmatrix} a_2 & 0 \\ 0 & b_2 \\ 0 & b_3 \end{pmatrix}\begin{pmatrix} -1 & -1 \\ a_1 & b_1 \end{pmatrix}^{-1} \\ &= -\begin{pmatrix} a_2 & 0 \\ 0 & b_2 \\ 0 & b_3 \end{pmatrix}\begin{pmatrix} b_1/(a_1 - b_1) & 1/(a_1 - b_1) \\ -a_1/(a_1 - b_1) & -1/(a_1 - b_1) \end{pmatrix}, \end{aligned}$$

whence the reduced form (3.6) reads

$$\text{(3.28)} \qquad (y_1 \quad y_2) = (x_1 \quad x_2 \quad x_3)\begin{pmatrix} -a_2 b_1/(a_1 - b_1) & -a_2/(a_1 - b_1) \\ a_1 b_2/(a_1 - b_1) & b_2/(a_1 - b_1) \\ a_1 b_3/(a_1 - b_1) & b_3/(a_1 - b_1) \end{pmatrix} + (v_1 \quad v_2),$$

where $v_1 = (a_1 u_2 - b_1 u_1)/(a_1 - b_1)$ and $v_2 = (u_2 - u_1)/(a_1 - b_1)$.

A third illustrative system we shall use in the sequel is Klein's Model I of the United States economy presented in Klein (1950, pp. 58–66), which may be formulated as follows:

$$\begin{array}{lll} \text{(3.29a)} & \text{Consumption:} & C = a_0 + a_1 P + a_2 P_{-1} + a_3 W + \epsilon_1 \\ \text{(3.29b)} & \text{Investment:} & I = b_0 + b_1 P + b_2 P_{-1} + b_3 K_{-1} + \epsilon_2 \\ \text{(3.29c)} & \text{Private wages:} & W^* = c_0 + c_1 E + c_2 E_{-1} + c_3 A + \epsilon_3 \\ \text{(3.29d)} & \text{Product:} & Y + T = C + I + G \\ \text{(3.29e)} & \text{Income:} & Y = P + W \\ \text{(3.29f)} & \text{Capital:} & K = K_{-1} + I \\ \text{(3.29g)} & \text{Wages:} & W = W^* + W^{**} \\ \text{(3.29h)} & \text{Private product:} & E = Y + T - W^{**}, \end{array}$$

where the dependent variables are C = consumption, I = investment, W^* = private wage bill, P = profits, Y = national income, K = end-of-year capital stock; W = total wage bill, and E = private product, and the predetermined variables are the exogenous variables 1 = unity, W^{**} = government wage bill, T = indirect taxes, G = government expenditures, and A = time and the lagged endogenous variables P_{-1}, K_{-1}, and E_{-1}. All the variables are in billions of constant (1934) dollars, except 1, and except A, which is in years measured from 1931. We again omit the time index for simplicity. It is a useful exercise to write out the system (3.29) in the structural form (3.3) and then to derive the reduced form (3.6). Note that in this system there happen to be as many dependent as predetermined variables, $K = M = 8$.

Estimation in the Simultaneous Linear Structural Equation Model

Returning to our general analysis, it will be seen that a structural equation is not essentially altered if we multiply it through by some nonzero number, provided that we make the appropriate adjustments to $\mathbf{\Sigma}$. To avoid this trivial indeterminancy—which arose because we treated all the dependent variables symmetrically in writing the structural form—we prescribe a normalization rule:

(3.30) In each structural equation, the coefficient of one jointly dependent variable may be taken as -1, a priori, i.e., for each $m = 1, \ldots, M$, there is a known $\gamma_{0m} = -1$.

We have now built up a statistical model for handling systems of economic relationships. The set of assumptions (3.3), (3.5), (3.12), (3.13), (3.14), (3.16), (3.17), and (3.30) we designate as the simultaneous linear structural equation model. It is seen to be a natural generalization of the stochastic linear regression models which we developed in the preceding chapter.

Let us then consider the possibilities for estimation of any single structural equation in the system. The mth structural equation may be selected out of (3.4), and written as

$$\mathbf{Y}\boldsymbol{\gamma}_m + \mathbf{X}\boldsymbol{\beta}_m + \mathbf{u}_m = \mathbf{0} \tag{3.31}$$

where the $M \times 1$ vector $\boldsymbol{\gamma}_m$ is the mth column of $\mathbf{\Gamma}$, the $K \times 1$ vector $\boldsymbol{\beta}_m$ is the mth column of $\mathbf{B}$, and the $T \times 1$ vector $\mathbf{u}_m$ is the mth column of $\mathbf{U}$. In algebraic form this is

$$\begin{aligned}\gamma_{1m}y_1(t) + \cdots + \gamma_{Mm}y_M(t) + \beta_{1m}x_1(t) + \cdots \\ + \beta_{Km}x_K(t) + u_m(t) = 0 \qquad (t = 1, \ldots, T).\end{aligned} \tag{3.32}$$

Indeed, let us utilize the normalization rule (3.30). Denote by $y_0(t)$ the variable whose coefficient is set at -1 in the mth equation. Taking this variable over to the other side, we may write the mth structural equation as

$$\mathbf{y}_0 = \mathbf{Y}_{m0}\boldsymbol{\gamma}_{m0} + \mathbf{X}\boldsymbol{\beta}_m + \mathbf{u}_m \tag{3.33}$$

where

$\mathbf{y}_0$ is the $T \times 1$ vector of observations on the variable whose coefficient $\gamma_{0m} = -1$—i.e., one column of $\mathbf{Y}$;

$\mathbf{Y}_{m0}$ is the $T \times (M-1)$ matrix of observations on the remaining dependent variables—i.e., $\mathbf{Y}$ with the one column deleted; and

$\boldsymbol{\gamma}_{m0}$ is the $(M-1) \times 1$ vector of coefficients of these remaining dependent variables—i.e., $\boldsymbol{\gamma}_m$ with the one element $\gamma_{0m} = -1$ deleted.

Although (3.33) is in the form of a linear regression, least-squares estimation is not appropriate. For the dependent variables on the right-hand side are not uncorrelated with the disturbance. This is easily shown; we have

$$\text{(3.34)} \qquad \mathbf{Y}'\mathbf{U} = (\mathbf{\Pi}'\mathbf{X}' + \mathbf{V}')\mathbf{U} = \mathbf{\Pi}'\mathbf{X}'\mathbf{U} - \mathbf{\Gamma}'^{-1}\mathbf{U}'\mathbf{U}$$

using the reduced form expressions $\mathbf{Y} = \mathbf{X\Pi} + \mathbf{V}$ and $\mathbf{V} = -\mathbf{U\Gamma}^{-1}$. Then

$$\text{(3.35)} \qquad \begin{aligned} \text{plim}\,(T^{-1}\mathbf{Y}'\mathbf{U}) &= \text{plim}\, T^{-1}\mathbf{\Pi}'\mathbf{X}'\mathbf{U} - \text{plim}\, T^{-1}\mathbf{\Gamma}'^{-1}\mathbf{U}'\mathbf{U} \\ &= \mathbf{\Pi}'\,\text{plim}\,(T^{-1}\mathbf{X}'\mathbf{U}) - \mathbf{\Gamma}'^{-1}\,\text{plim}\,(T^{-1}\mathbf{U}'\mathbf{U}) \\ &= \mathbf{\Pi}' \cdot \mathbf{0} - \mathbf{\Gamma}'^{-1}\mathbf{\Sigma} = -\mathbf{\Gamma}'^{-1}\mathbf{\Sigma} \neq \mathbf{0}, \end{aligned}$$

using (3.15) and (3.17). Thus for the m'th jointly dependent variable and the mth structural disturbance,

$$\text{(3.36)} \qquad \text{plim}\,\frac{\sum_{t=1}^{T} y_{m'}(t)u_m(t)}{T} = -\sum_{\mu=1}^{M} \gamma^{\mu m'}\sigma_{\mu m},$$

which will in general be nonzero (note that the variance σ_{mm} is among the elements in the summation).

With some regressors being interdependent with the disturbance in (3.33), it is the general stochastic linear regression model which is appropriate. In that model, as we have seen, the classical least-squares estimators are not consistent.

We may check out (3.36) in the simple Keynesian model (3.23)–(3.25), which has $M = 2$. For $m' = 2$ and $m = 1$, (3.36) gives plim $(\Sigma\, y_2 u_1/T) = -\gamma^{12}\sigma_{11} - \gamma^{22}\sigma_{21}$. Inserting the values of these parameters, we find for the (asymptotic) covariance of income Y and the structural disturbance in the consumption function $(1-\beta)^{-1}E\epsilon_t^2 + (1-\beta)^{-1}E(\epsilon_t \cdot 0) = (1-\beta)^{-1}\sigma^2$, which corresponds to the result of (2.11).

On the other hand, let us consider the possibilities for estimation of any single reduced-form equation in the system. The mth reduced-form equation may be selected out of (3.8), and written as

$$\text{(3.37)} \qquad \mathbf{y}_m = \mathbf{X}\boldsymbol{\pi}_m + \mathbf{v}_m$$

where $\mathbf{y}_m$, $\boldsymbol{\pi}_m$, and $\mathbf{v}_m$ are the mth columns of $\mathbf{Y}$, $\boldsymbol{\Pi}$, and $\mathbf{V}$ respectively. Since the regressors are at least contemporaneously uncorrelated with the disturbances in this relationship—plim $(T^{-1}\mathbf{X}'\mathbf{v}_m) = \mathbf{0}$ is the mth column of (3.22)—the multivariate contemporaneously uncorrelated linear regression model is applicable, and least-squares estimates are consistent.

The situation, then, is as follows. We have developed a statistical model that seems to be appropriate for handling systems of simultaneous relationships, which are so prevalent in economics. In this model, we find that if the coefficients of individual structural relationships—which are presumably the prime focus of econometric estimation—are estimated by classical least squares, inconsistent estimators are obtained. When the reduced form of the system is estimated by classical least squares, consistent estimators of the reduced-form coefficients are obtained. The reduced-form coefficients are, in general, complicated functions of the structural coefficients. A way out of the problem suggests itself. Suppose that we proceed to estimate all the reduced-form coefficients, and then utilize the relationship between the structural and reduced-form coefficients to translate these into estimates of the structural coefficients. This is what we did in the simple Keynesian system of Section 2. If this indirect procedure were always available, we would have a consistent method of structural estimation.

As we shall see, however, the translation of reduced-form estimates into structural estimates is not always so straightforward—and it is sometimes impossible. To investigate the problem, we require a digression on a crucial nonstatistical problem known as identification.

4. IDENTIFICATION

Observationally Equivalent Structures

A familiar concept in scientific method is that two or more theories may be "observationally equivalent," i.e., they may have exactly the same implications about observable phenomena under all circumstances. If so, then no possible set of observations would enable us to choose among the theories. Any attempt to estimate the parameters of any one of the observationally equivalent theories would be doomed to failure. We would be unable to identify any function of the observations as an estimator of the parameters of one theory—it might just as well be estimating the parameters of another, observationally equivalent theory.

This problem is of concern to econometricians attempting to estimate the parameters of a relationship, and in the context of systems of simultaneous relationships has become known as the problem of *identification*.

Identification is logically prior to estimation. To investigate it, we bypass the questions associated with sampling variability and assume that we have knowledge of the population distribution of the observations—i.e., of the conditional distribution of the dependent variables for any and all values of the predetermined variables. If this knowledge enables us to deduce uniquely the value of a parameter, that parameter is identified (or equivalently, identifiable); if not, the parameter is not identified (or equivalently, not identifiable). Similarly, if all the parameters in a relationship are identified, the relationship is said to be identified; if all the parameters in a system of relationships are identified, the system is said to be identified.

The burden of this section is that without sufficient further restrictions, the structural parameters $\mathbf{B}$, $\mathbf{\Gamma}$, and $\mathbf{\Sigma}$ of our simultaneous linear structural equation model are not identified. For the present analysis, let us distinguish between a *structure* and a *model.* By a structure we mean a specific, numerical set of relationships connecting the observable variables together with a specific, numerical distribution function of the unobservable disturbances. By a model we mean merely a specification of the *form* of the relations connecting the variables and of the *form* of the distribution function of the disturbances. Thus a model can be thought of as a set of structures. For example, the specifications (3.3), (3.5), (3.12)–(3.14), (3.16), (3.17), and (3.30) define a *model.* When specific numerical values are assigned to parameters like $\mathbf{B}$, $\mathbf{\Gamma}$, and $\mathbf{\Sigma}$, we will have a *structure* (belonging to that model). The model is intended to incorporate all our a priori knowledge of the mechanism that generates our observations—in the language of statistical inference, it is the maintained hypothesis. Then the observations are in fact generated by the true structure—one of the "members" of the model. Suppose that there is another "member" of the model—another structure consistent with it—which would generate exactly the same distribution of the observations. Then the two structures would be operationally equivalent and any parameter whose value was not the same in the two structures would not be identified.

Let us illustrate these points. Consider the following simple *model*—it is a special case of our simultaneous linear structural equation model:

(4.1*a*) $$y_1(t) = \alpha y_2(t) + \beta x(t) + u_1(t),$$

(4.1*b*) $$y_1(t) = \gamma y_2(t) + \delta x(t) + u_2(t),$$

(4.1*c*) $u_1(t)$ and $u_2(t)$ are unobservable disturbances, with zero expectations, constant variances and contemporaneous covariances, and zero lagged covariances, and they are distributed independently of the fixed exogenous variable x.

One *structure* that belongs to this model is the following structure I; here and in the sequel we drop the index (t) for simplicity:

(4.2*a*) $y_1 = 2y_2 + 1x + u_1,$

(4.2*b*) $y_1 = -1y_2 + 2x + u_2,$

(4.2*c*) u_1 and u_2 have the joint distribution

(u_1, u_2)	$f(u_1, u_2)$
1, 2	$\frac{1}{4}$
1, −2	$\frac{1}{4}$
−1, 2	$\frac{1}{4}$
−1, −2	$\frac{1}{4}$

for all observations, independently of x, and successive drawings from the joint distribution are independent.

To deduce the joint distribution of y_1 and y_2 conditional on any value of x, it is clearly convenient to obtain the reduced form first, i.e.,

(4.3*a*) $y_1 = \frac{5}{3}x + \frac{1}{3}u_1 + \frac{2}{3}u_2,$

(4.3*b*) $y_2 = \frac{1}{3}x - \frac{1}{3}u_1 + \frac{1}{3}u_2.$

Then when $x = 1$, e.g., we find that when $u_1 = 1$ and $u_2 = 2$—which happens with probability $\frac{1}{4}$—$y_1 = \frac{5}{3}(1) + \frac{1}{3}(1) + \frac{2}{3}(2) = \frac{10}{3}$ and $y_2 = \frac{1}{3}(1) - \frac{1}{3}(1) + \frac{1}{3}(2) = \frac{2}{3}$.

In this manner the joint distribution of y_1 and y_2 for $x = 1$ may be generated:

(4.4)

(y_1, y_2)	$f(y_1, y_2)$
$\frac{10}{3}, \frac{2}{3}$	$\frac{1}{4}$
$\frac{2}{3}, -\frac{2}{3}$	$\frac{1}{4}$
$\frac{8}{3}, \frac{4}{3}$	$\frac{1}{4}$
0, 0	$\frac{1}{4}$

and similarly the joint distribution of y_1 and y_2 for any value of x may be generated:

(4.5)

(y_1, y_2)	$f(y_1, y_2)$
$\frac{5}{3}x + \frac{5}{3}, \frac{1}{3}x + \frac{1}{3}$	$\frac{1}{4}$
$\frac{5}{3}x - 1, \frac{1}{3}x - 1$	$\frac{1}{4}$
$\frac{5}{3}x + 1, \frac{1}{3}x + 1$	$\frac{1}{4}$
$\frac{5}{3}x - \frac{5}{3}, \frac{1}{3}x - \frac{1}{3}$	$\frac{1}{4}$

Now consider a second structure, structure II, which also belongs to the model (4.1). Note that its coefficients α, β, γ, and δ are all different from those of structure I:

(4.6a) $y_1 = 1y_2 + \frac{4}{3}x + u_1^*$,

(4.6b) $y_1 = -\frac{2}{5}y_2 + \frac{9}{5}x + u_2^*$,

(4.6c) u_1^* and u_2^* have the joint distribution

(u_1^*, u_2^*)	$f(u_1^*, u_2^*)$
$\frac{4}{3}, \frac{9}{5}$	$\frac{1}{4}$
$0, \frac{7}{5}$	$\frac{1}{4}$
$0, -\frac{7}{5}$	$\frac{1}{4}$
$-\frac{4}{3}, -\frac{9}{5}$	$\frac{1}{4}$

for all observations, independently of x, and successive drawings from this distribution are independent.

To deduce the joint distribution of y_1 and y_2 generated by this structure for any value of x, it is clearly convenient to obtain the reduced form first, i.e.,

(4.7a) $y_1 = \frac{5}{3}x + \frac{2}{7}u_1^* + \frac{5}{7}u_2^*$,

(4.7b) $y_2 = \frac{1}{3}x - \frac{5}{7}u_1^* + \frac{5}{7}u_2^*$.

Then when $x = 1$, e.g., we find that when $u_1^* = \frac{4}{3}$ and $u_2^* = \frac{9}{5}$—which happens with probability $\frac{1}{4}$—then $y_1 = \frac{5}{3}(1) + \frac{2}{7}(\frac{4}{3}) + \frac{5}{7}(\frac{9}{5}) = \frac{10}{3}$ and $y_2 = \frac{1}{3}(1) - \frac{5}{7}(\frac{4}{3}) + \frac{5}{7}(\frac{9}{5}) = \frac{2}{3}$. In this manner the joint distribution of y_1 and y_2 for $x = 1$ may be generated,

(4.8)

(y_1, y_2)	$f(y_1, y_2)$
$\frac{10}{3}, \frac{2}{3}$	$\frac{1}{4}$
$\frac{8}{3}, \frac{4}{3}$	$\frac{1}{4}$
$\frac{2}{3}, -\frac{2}{3}$	$\frac{1}{4}$
$0, 0$	$\frac{1}{4}$

and it is seen to be identical with (4.4). Indeed, the joint distribution of y_1 and y_2 for any value of x is found to be

(4.9)

(y_1, y_2)	$f(y_1, y_2)$
$\frac{5}{3}x + \frac{5}{3}, \frac{1}{3}x + \frac{1}{3}$	$\frac{1}{4}$
$\frac{5}{3}x + 1, \frac{1}{3}x + 1$	$\frac{1}{4}$
$\frac{5}{3}x - 1, \frac{1}{3}x - 1$	$\frac{1}{4}$
$\frac{5}{3}x - \frac{5}{3}, \frac{1}{3}x - \frac{1}{3}$	$\frac{1}{4}$

which is identical with (4.5).

Thus we have seen two structures consistent with the model but with different values for all the parameters, which generate the same joint distribution of the dependent variables for any value of the predetermined variable. The two structures are observationally equivalent—no possible set of observations would enable us to conclude that the true structure was structure I rather than structure II. No set of observations would lead us to conclude that the values of the coefficients α, β, γ, and δ were 2, 1, -1, and 2 rather than 1, $\frac{4}{3}$, $-\frac{2}{5}$, and $\frac{9}{5}$. None of the parameters of the model are identified; the model is not identified.

Reduced Form and Identification

Now it can be seen that structures I and II had the same reduced form, namely,

(4.10*a*) $y_1 = \frac{5}{3}x + v_1,$

(4.10*b*) $y_2 = \frac{1}{3}x + v_2,$

(4.10*c*) v_1 and v_2 have the joint distribution

(v_1, v_2)	$f(v_1, v_2)$
$\frac{5}{3}, \frac{1}{3}$	$\frac{1}{4}$
$-1, -1$	$\frac{1}{4}$
$1, 1$	$\frac{1}{4}$
$-\frac{5}{3}, -\frac{1}{3}$	$\frac{1}{4}$

for all observations, independently of x, and successive drawings from the joint distribution are independent.

To see this, consider (4.2*c*) and (4.6*c*) and note that we may write $v_1 = \frac{1}{3}u_1 + \frac{2}{3}u_2 = \frac{2}{7}u_1^* + \frac{5}{7}u_2^*$ and $v_2 = -\frac{1}{3}u_1 + \frac{1}{3}u_2 = -\frac{5}{7}u_1^* + \frac{5}{7}u_2^*$.

It is no surprise then that the two structures generated the same joint distribution of the dependent variables for all values of the predetermined variable, since in the model that joint distribution may be deduced uniquely from the reduced form. Indeed, the converse is true: The parameters of the reduced form are uniquely deducible from the joint distribution of the dependent variables conditional on the predetermined variable. Consider the joint distribution of the dependent variables—(4.5) or (4.9). The means, variances, and covariance of the conditional joint distribution are readily computed to be

$$\begin{aligned}(4.11)\quad \mu_{1|x} &\equiv E(y_1 \mid x) = \tfrac{1}{4}(\tfrac{5}{3}x + \tfrac{5}{3}) + \tfrac{1}{4}(\tfrac{5}{3}x - 1)\\ &\quad + \tfrac{1}{4}(\tfrac{5}{3}x + 1) + \tfrac{1}{4}(\tfrac{5}{3}x - \tfrac{5}{3}) = \tfrac{5}{3}x\\ \mu_{2|x} &\equiv E(y_2 \mid x) = \tfrac{1}{3}x\\ \sigma_{1|x}^2 &\equiv E(y_1 - \mu_{1|x} \mid x)^2 = \tfrac{17}{9}\\ \sigma_{2|x}^2 &\equiv E(y_2 - \mu_{2|x} \mid x)^2 = \tfrac{5}{9}\\ \sigma_{12|x} &\equiv E[(y_1 - \mu_{1|x})(y_2 - \mu_{2|x}) \mid x] = \tfrac{7}{9},\end{aligned}$$

and it is readily confirmed that these are the parameters of the reduced form; $\frac{5}{3}$ and $\frac{1}{3}$ are the coefficients of x in (4.10a) and (4.10b), and $\frac{17}{9}$, $\frac{5}{9}$, and $\frac{7}{9}$ are var (v_1), var (v_2), and cov (v_1, v_2) respectively in (4.10c). We conclude that the parameters of the reduced form may be uniquely deduced from a knowledge of the joint distribution, and hence that the reduced form is identified.

Now this conclusion is a general one. For knowledge of the joint distribution of the dependent variables for all sets of values of the predetermined variables implies knowledge of the conditional expectations of this distribution, as a function of the predetermined variables. But this function is just the reduced-form coefficient matrix $\mathbf{\Pi}$:

$$E[\mathbf{y}'(t) \mid \mathbf{x}'(t)] = E[\mathbf{x}'(t)\mathbf{\Pi} + \mathbf{v}'(t) \mid \mathbf{x}'(t)] = \mathbf{x}'(t)\mathbf{\Pi}. \tag{4.12}$$

Further, knowledge of the joint distribution of the dependent variables for all sets of values of the predetermined variables implies knowledge of the conditional covariance matrix of that distribution. But this matrix is just the reduced-form disturbance covariance matrix:

$$\begin{aligned} E\{[\mathbf{y}'(t) - E\mathbf{y}'(t) \mid \mathbf{x}'(t)]'[\mathbf{y}'(t) - E\mathbf{y}'(t) \mid \mathbf{x}'(t)]\} \\ = E[\mathbf{v}(t)\mathbf{v}'(t) \mid \mathbf{x}'(t)] = E\mathbf{v}(t)\mathbf{v}'(t) = \mathbf{\Omega}. \end{aligned} \tag{4.13}$$

Higher moments of the joint distribution of the dependent variables may similarly be identified as further parameters of the reduced form. Thus the reduced-form parameters are always identified since they are uniquely deducible from the parameters of the joint distribution of the observations. Indeed it is easily seen that knowledge of the reduced-form parameters implies knowledge of the conditional distribution of the dependent variables given the predetermined variables.

Therefore we may conclude that a structural parameter is identified if and only if it can be uniquely deduced from the reduced-form parameters. Now in our simultaneous linear structural equation model the connections between the structural parameters $\mathbf{\Gamma}$, $\mathbf{B}$, and $\mathbf{\Sigma}$ and the reduced-form parameters $\mathbf{\Pi}$ and $\mathbf{\Omega}$ are completely contained in (3.6) and (3.19), i.e., in

$$\mathbf{\Pi\Gamma} = -\mathbf{B}, \tag{4.14a}$$

$$\mathbf{\Sigma} = \mathbf{\Gamma}'\mathbf{\Omega\Gamma}. \tag{4.14b}$$

We ought not to be very optimistic about the possibilities of deducing the structural parameters from the reduced-form parameters. After all, $\mathbf{\Pi}$ has only $K \times M$ elements, whereas $\mathbf{\Gamma}$ and $\mathbf{B}$ together have $(M \times M) + (K \times M)$ elements [or rather, with the normalization rule, $M \times (M - 1)$ plus $K \times M$ unknown elements]. And indeed if the model as specified thus far really contained all our a priori information, structural estimation would be a hopeless task. As we shall see, what are required are restrictions on the structural parameters; e.g., a priori knowledge of the values of some of the coefficients.

Linear Transformations and Identification

Another way of looking at our problem is the following. Two structures are observationally equivalent if they have the same reduced form. It is easy to see, however, that any nonsingular set of linear combinations of the equations of a structure gives another structure with the same reduced form. Let one structure be

$$\text{(4.15)} \qquad \mathbf{y}'(t)\mathbf{\Gamma}_{\text{I}} + \mathbf{x}'(t)\mathbf{B}_{\text{I}} + \mathbf{u}_{\text{I}}'(t) = \mathbf{0}, \qquad E\mathbf{u}_{\text{I}}(t)\mathbf{u}_{\text{I}}'(t) = \mathbf{\Sigma}_{\text{I}};$$

its reduced form is

$$\text{(4.16)} \qquad \mathbf{y}'(t) = \mathbf{x}'(t)\mathbf{\Pi}_{\text{I}} + \mathbf{v}_{\text{I}}'(t), \qquad E\mathbf{v}_{\text{I}}(t)\mathbf{v}_{\text{I}}'(t) = \mathbf{\Omega}_{\text{I}}$$

where

$$\text{(4.17)} \qquad \mathbf{\Pi}_{\text{I}} = -\mathbf{B}_{\text{I}}\mathbf{\Gamma}_{\text{I}}^{-1}; \qquad \mathbf{\Omega}_{\text{I}} = \mathbf{\Gamma}_{\text{I}}'^{-1}\mathbf{\Sigma}_{\text{I}}\mathbf{\Gamma}_{\text{I}}^{-1}.$$

Then taking any $M \times M$ nonsingular matrix $\mathbf{T}$ and postmultiplying through (4.15) gives a second structure

$$\text{(4.18)} \qquad \mathbf{y}'(t)\mathbf{\Gamma}_{\text{II}} + \mathbf{x}'(t)\mathbf{B}_{\text{II}} + \mathbf{u}_{\text{II}}'(t) = \mathbf{0}, \qquad E\mathbf{u}_{\text{II}}(t)\mathbf{u}_{\text{II}}'(t) = \mathbf{\Sigma}_{\text{II}},$$

where

$$\text{(4.19)} \qquad \mathbf{\Gamma}_{\text{II}} = \mathbf{\Gamma}_{\text{I}}\mathbf{T}, \qquad \mathbf{B}_{\text{II}} = \mathbf{B}_{\text{I}}\mathbf{T}, \qquad \mathbf{u}_{\text{II}}'(t) = \mathbf{u}_{\text{I}}'(t)\mathbf{T},$$

whence

$$\text{(4.20)} \qquad \mathbf{\Sigma}_{\text{II}} = \mathbf{T}'\mathbf{\Sigma}_{\text{I}}\mathbf{T}.$$

Then the reduced form of the second structure will be the same as that of the first, for

$$\text{(4.21}a\text{)} \qquad \mathbf{\Pi}_{\text{II}} \equiv -\mathbf{B}_{\text{II}}\mathbf{\Gamma}_{\text{II}}^{-1} = -(\mathbf{B}_{\text{I}}\mathbf{T})(\mathbf{T}^{-1}\mathbf{\Gamma}_{\text{I}}^{-1}) = -\mathbf{B}_{\text{I}}\mathbf{\Gamma}_{\text{I}}^{-1} = \mathbf{\Pi}_{\text{I}}$$

$$\mathbf{\Omega}_{\text{II}} \equiv \mathbf{\Gamma}_{\text{II}}'^{-1}\mathbf{\Sigma}_{\text{II}}\mathbf{\Gamma}_{\text{II}}^{-1} = (\mathbf{T}'\mathbf{\Gamma}_{\text{I}}')^{-1}\mathbf{T}'\mathbf{\Sigma}_{\text{I}}\mathbf{T}(\mathbf{\Gamma}_{\text{I}}\mathbf{T})^{-1}$$

$$\text{(4.21}b\text{)} \qquad = \mathbf{\Gamma}_{\text{I}}'^{-1}\mathbf{T}'^{-1}\mathbf{T}'\mathbf{\Sigma}_{\text{I}}\mathbf{T}\mathbf{T}^{-1}\mathbf{\Gamma}_{\text{I}}^{-1} = \mathbf{\Gamma}_{\text{I}}'^{-1}\mathbf{\Sigma}_{\text{I}}\mathbf{\Gamma}_{\text{I}}^{-1} = \mathbf{\Omega}_{\text{I}},$$

(and similarly for any higher moments).

To illustrate, it is readily confirmed that structure II of (4.6) is a nonsingular linear transformation of structure I of (4.2). The $\mathbf{T}$ matrix used was

$$\text{(4.22)} \qquad \mathbf{T} = \begin{pmatrix} \frac{2}{3} & \frac{1}{5} \\ \frac{1}{3} & \frac{4}{5} \end{pmatrix},$$

i.e., (4.6a) = $\frac{2}{3}$(4.2a) + $\frac{1}{3}$(4.2b) and (4.6b) = $\frac{1}{5}$(4.2a) + $\frac{4}{5}$(4.2b).

We also have the converse: If two structures have the same reduced form, one is a nonsingular linear transformation of the other; this can be shown by taking $\mathbf{T} = \mathbf{\Gamma}_{\text{I}}^{-1}\mathbf{\Gamma}_{\text{II}}$.

This approach to the identification problem is developed with some instructive illustrations in Koopmans (1953).

Since there is an infinite number of nonsingular matrices available, given any proposed structure we can always construct an indefinite number of structures having the same reduced form, and hence operationally equivalent to it. How then can we hope to identify parameters? The saving grace will be a priori restrictions on the equations of the model. If the equations are restricted, linear combinations of the equations may violate the restrictions. Thus although a linear transformation of a proposed structure would be observationally equivalent to it, it might not be an admissible alternative, because it might be inconsistent with the a priori restrictions of the model. If we refine our specification of the model to include a priori restrictions on the parameters, the model will be identified if every linear transformation of its equations (apart from the "identity" transformation) provides a set of equations which is inconsistent with the a priori restrictions. Similarly a parameter is identified if its value is the same in all structures consistent with the model, and an equation is identified if the values of all its parameters are the same in all structures consistent with the model.

A Priori Restrictions and Identification

Fortunately for econometric model construction, economic theory generally provides a priori information beyond that incorporated thus far in our simultaneous linear structural equation model. In particular we often know that certain variables do not appear in certain equations. Thus in the simple Keynesian model it is specified that consumers react to income and not to investment in itself. In Tintner's meat market model, it is specified that cost factors like x_2 and x_3 do not enter the demand *function*. In Klein's Model I, neither the stock of capital nor the time trend appear in the consumption function, and there are similar exclusions from the other equations. In that model we see examples of other sorts of restrictions as well—indeed, in the identities all the coefficients are known a priori. It should be obvious that such restrictions help to identify the model; they reduce the number of unknown structural parameters to be deduced from the reduced-form parameters. The structural form will be identified if it is sufficiently restricted. (From this point of view the reduced form is identified because it is so strongly restricted—only one dependent variable occurs in each reduced-form equation.)

Now, as suggested, a priori restrictions can be of various kinds. It may be that two structural coefficients are known to be equal—or to have a known ratio. It may be that a coefficient in one equation is known to equal a coefficient in another equation. It may be that the covariance between two structural disturbances is known to be zero.

In practice, the most common type of a priori knowledge consists of "zero restrictions"—specifying that certain variables are absent in certain equations, i.e., that certain structural coefficients are zero. Let us limit our attention to such restrictions and to identities. Then, henceforth, by the simultaneous linear structural equation model we shall understand the specifications (3.3), (3.5), (3.12)–(3.14), (3.16), (3.17), and (3.30) together with

(4.23*a*) Certain elements of $\begin{pmatrix} \mathbf{\Gamma} \\ \mathbf{B} \end{pmatrix}$ are known to be zero.

(4.23*b*) Certain columns of $\begin{pmatrix} \mathbf{\Gamma} \\ \mathbf{B} \end{pmatrix}$ are known a priori; the corresponding rows and columns of $\mathbf{\Sigma}$ are zeros. The corresponding equations are called identities.

There is no problem in identifying an identity—since all its parameters are known a priori. We are then in a position to develop a simple rule for the identifiability of a (nonidentity) equation in the model—i.e., a necessary and sufficient condition for all the coefficients in any equation to be identified. Consider then the mth structural equation—as in (3.31)—

$$\mathbf{Y}\boldsymbol{\gamma}_m + \mathbf{X}\boldsymbol{\beta}_m + \mathbf{u}_m = \mathbf{0}. \tag{4.24}$$

Suppose the restrictions are that a certain M^{**} elements of $\boldsymbol{\gamma}_m$ and K^{**} elements of $\boldsymbol{\beta}_m$ are zero; the corresponding variables are *excluded* from the equation. Then with suitable rearrangement of the variables and partitioning, we may write this equation as

$$\mathbf{Y}_*\boldsymbol{\gamma}_* + \mathbf{Y}_{**}\boldsymbol{\gamma}_{**} + \mathbf{X}_*\boldsymbol{\beta}_* + \mathbf{X}_{**}\boldsymbol{\beta}_{**} + \mathbf{u} = \mathbf{0} \tag{4.25}$$

(dropping the subscript m for simplicity) where

$\mathbf{Y}_*$ is the $T \times M^*$ matrix of observations on the included dependent variables—$M^* = M - M^{**}$;

$\boldsymbol{\gamma}_*$ is the $M^* \times 1$ coefficient vector of these variables in this equation;

$\mathbf{Y}_{**}$ is the $T \times M^{**}$ matrix of observations on the excluded dependent variables;

$\boldsymbol{\gamma}_{**}$ is the $M^{**} \times 1$ vector of coefficients of these variables in this equation—$\boldsymbol{\gamma}_{**} = \mathbf{0}$;

$\mathbf{X}_*$ is the $T \times K^*$ matrix of observations on the included predetermined variables—$K^* = K - K^{**}$;
$\boldsymbol{\beta}_*$ is the $K^* \times 1$ coefficient vector of these variables in this equation;
$\mathbf{X}_{**}$ is the $T \times K^{**}$ matrix of observations on the excluded predetermined variables;
$\boldsymbol{\beta}_{**}$ is the $K^{**} \times 1$ vector of coefficients of these variables in this equation—$\boldsymbol{\beta}_{**} = \mathbf{0}$; and
$\mathbf{u}$ is again the $T \times 1$ disturbance vector in this equation.

Correspondingly we shall rearrange and partition the reduced-form coefficient matrix so that $\mathbf{Y} = \mathbf{X\Pi} + \mathbf{V}$ may be written as

$$(4.26) \qquad (\mathbf{Y}_* \quad \mathbf{Y}_{**}) = (\mathbf{X}_* \quad \mathbf{X}_{**})\begin{pmatrix} \mathbf{\Pi}_{*,*} & \mathbf{\Pi}_{*,**} \\ \mathbf{\Pi}_{**,*} & \mathbf{\Pi}_{**,**} \end{pmatrix} + (\mathbf{V}_* \quad \mathbf{V}_{**})$$

where, in the partitioned $\mathbf{\Pi}$ matrix, the first subscript refers to the predetermined variables and the second to the dependent variables. Thus $\mathbf{\Pi}_{*,*}$ is K^* by M^*, $\mathbf{\Pi}_{**,*}$ is K^{**} by M^*, $\mathbf{\Pi}_{*,**}$ is K^* by M^{**}, and $\mathbf{\Pi}_{**,**}$ is K^{**} by M^{**}.

Now are $\boldsymbol{\gamma}_*$ and $\boldsymbol{\beta}_*$ identifiable? That is, can they be deduced from $\mathbf{\Pi}$ and $\mathbf{\Omega}$? All the information connecting $\boldsymbol{\gamma}_*$ and $\boldsymbol{\beta}_*$ with $\mathbf{\Pi}$ is contained in the mth column of (4.14a)—$\mathbf{\Pi}\boldsymbol{\gamma}_m = -\boldsymbol{\beta}_m$—which with our partitioning and zero restrictions is

$$(4.27) \qquad \begin{pmatrix} \mathbf{\Pi}_{*,*} & \mathbf{\Pi}_{*,**} \\ \mathbf{\Pi}_{**,*} & \mathbf{\Pi}_{**,**} \end{pmatrix}\begin{pmatrix} \boldsymbol{\gamma}_* \\ \mathbf{0} \end{pmatrix} = -\begin{pmatrix} \boldsymbol{\beta}_* \\ \mathbf{0} \end{pmatrix}.$$

(It will be noted that since $\mathbf{\Sigma}$ is really unrestricted (4.14b) provides no information on $\mathbf{\Gamma}$.) Proceeding, (4.27) breaks up into two pieces:

$$(4.28a) \qquad -\mathbf{\Pi}_{*,*}\boldsymbol{\gamma}_* = \boldsymbol{\beta}_*,$$

$$(4.28b) \qquad \mathbf{\Pi}_{**,*}\boldsymbol{\gamma}_* = \mathbf{0},$$

where (4.28a) simply enables us to deduce $\boldsymbol{\beta}_*$ uniquely from $\boldsymbol{\gamma}_*$ and $\mathbf{\Pi}_{*,*}$. Thus the structural equation will be identified if and only if we can deduce $\boldsymbol{\gamma}_*$ uniquely from (4.28b) and the normalization rule (3.30). We see that (4.28b) is a system of K^{**} homogeneous equations in M^* unknowns; it has a nontrivial solution if and only if $r(\mathbf{\Pi}_{**,*}) < M^*$ by (2.4.17). Our model specifies that $\mathbf{\Pi}_{**,*}$ and $\boldsymbol{\gamma}_*$ are the true parameters, so that there must be a nontrivial solution, so that necessarily

$$(4.29) \qquad r(\mathbf{\Pi}_{**,*}) \leq M^* - 1.$$

Now (4.28b) will have a unique-up-to-a-factor-of-proportionality solution if $r(\mathbf{\Pi}_{**,*}) = M^* - 1$, by (2.4.18). Then the ratios of the elements of $\boldsymbol{\gamma}_*$ are uniquely determined—and application of the normalization rule determines their values uniquely; and then (4.28*a*) determines $\boldsymbol{\beta}_*$ uniquely. If, however, $r(\boldsymbol{\Pi}_{**,*}) < M^* - 1$, the solution to (4.28*b*) is not determined uniquely up to a factor of proportionality. In that case the ratios of the elements of $\boldsymbol{\gamma}_*$ are not uniquely determined—and even with the normalization rule $\boldsymbol{\gamma}_*$ is not uniquely determined; and then (4.28*a*) will not determine $\boldsymbol{\beta}_*$ uniquely.

We have established the

(4.30) ***Rank condition of identifiability.*** In the simultaneous linear structural equation model, the structural equation (4.25) is identified if and only if $r(\boldsymbol{\Pi}_{**,*}) = M^* - 1$.

Since the rank of a matrix can not exceed the number of rows of the matrix, this implies the

(4.31) ***Order condition of identifiability.*** In the simultaneous linear structural equation model, a necessary condition for the structural equation (4.25) to be identified is $K^{**} \geq M^* - 1$.

Although in practice $\boldsymbol{\Pi}$ will be unknown the latter condition will still be operational. It says that for an equation to be identified, the number of predetermined variables *excluded* from the equation must be at least as great as one less than the number of dependent variables *included* in the equation. Intuitively, identifiability requires restrictions. Note, however, that (4.31) is only a necessary, not a sufficient, condition.

These results hold where the only restrictions are exclusions of variables. For a discussion of other types of restrictions and derivation of the appropriate conditions see Koopmans, Rubin, and Leipnik (1950, pp. 69–110) and F. M. Fisher (1959).

Illustrative examples. We may illustrate the use of the identification rules with several simple systems.

In the model used earlier in this section—see (4.1)—there are no zero restrictions: In (4.1*a*) $K^{**} = 0$, while $M^* - 1 = 2 - 1 = 1$, so that the necessary condition for identifiability is not satisfied, and the same situation prevails in (4.1*b*). Neither equation is identified; the model is not identified, as we have indeed already seen.

Next, consider the following market model:

(4.32*a*) Demand: $q = ap + bz + u_1,$

(4.32*b*) Supply $p = cq \qquad + u_2,$

where the dependent variables are q = quantity and p = price, and the predetermined variable is z = personal income. The structural form may be written

$$(4.33) \qquad (q \quad p)\begin{pmatrix} -1 & c \\ a & -1 \end{pmatrix} + (z)(b \quad 0) + (u_1 \quad u_2) = 0$$

whence the reduced-form matrix is

$$(4.34)\qquad \mathbf{\Pi} = -(b \quad 0)\begin{pmatrix} -1 & c \\ a & -1 \end{pmatrix}^{-1} = \begin{pmatrix} \dfrac{b}{1-ac} & \dfrac{bc}{1-ac} \end{pmatrix}.$$

In the demand function q and p are included so that $M^* = 2$, no predetermined variable is excluded so that $K^{**} = 0$; since $0 < 2 - 1$, the necessary condition for identifiability is not met. For this equation $\mathbf{\Pi}_{**,*}$ is empty, so that $r(\mathbf{\Pi}_{**,*}) = 0 \neq 2 - 1$, so that the rank condition is, of course, not met. Thus the demand function is not identified. In the supply function q and p are included so that $M^* = 2$, z is excluded so that $K^{**} = 1$; since $1 \geq 2 - 1$, the necessary condition for identifiability is met. For this equation,

$$(4.35)\qquad \mathbf{\Pi}_{**,*} = \begin{pmatrix} \dfrac{b}{1-ac} & \dfrac{bc}{1-ac} \end{pmatrix}$$

has rank $= 1 = 2 - 1$; the rank condition is met. Thus the supply function is identified. Alternatively in any nontrivial linear transformation of (4.32) the first equation would be a legitimate demand equation in the model; but the second equation would also contain z and hence would not be a legitimate supply equation. This implies again that (4.32*a*) is not identified, while (4.32*b*) is.

Next, consider the Keynesian system of (3.23). In the consumption function (3.23*a*), C and Y are included so that $M^* = 2$; I is excluded, so that $K^{**} = 1$; since $1 \geq 2 - 1$, the order condition is satisfied. Further, for the consumption function

$$(4.36)\qquad \mathbf{\Pi}_{**,*} = \begin{pmatrix} \dfrac{\beta}{1-\beta} & \dfrac{1}{1-\beta} \end{pmatrix}$$

has rank $1 = 2 - 1$; the rank condition is satisfied. There are no parameters to be estimated in the other function (3.23*b*). The model is identified.

Next consider Tintner's meat market model of (3.26). In the demand function (3.26*a*), y_1 and y_2 are included so that $M^* = 2$; x_2 and x_3 are excluded so that $K^{**} = 2$; since $2 \geq 2 - 1$, the order condition is satisfied. Further for this function

$$(4.37)\qquad \mathbf{\Pi}_{**,*} = \begin{pmatrix} a_1b_2/(a_1-b_1) & b_2/(a_1-b_1) \\ a_1b_3/(a_1-b_1) & b_3/(a_1-b_1) \end{pmatrix}$$

has rank $1 = 2 - 1$ (the second column is a multiple of the first) so that the rank condition is satisfied. In the supply function (3.26*b*), y_1 and y_2 are included so that $M^* = 2$; x_1 is excluded so that $K^{**} = 1$; since $1 \geq 2 - 1$, the order condition is satisfied. Further for this function

$$(4.38)\qquad \mathbf{\Pi}_{**,*} = \begin{pmatrix} \dfrac{-a_2b_1}{a_1-b_1} & \dfrac{-a_2}{a_1-b_1} \end{pmatrix}$$

has rank $1 = 2 - 1$ so that the rank condition is satisfied. Both equations are identified, so that the model is identified.

Finally, for Klein's Model I of (3.29) we content ourselves with checking the order condition. In the consumption function (3.29*a*), C, P, and W are included, so that $M^* = 3$; W^{**}, T, G, A, K_{-1}, and E_{-1} are excluded, so that $K^{**} = 6$; since $6 \geq 3 - 1$, the order condition is satisfied.

In the investment function (3.29*b*), I and P are included so that $M^* = 2$; W^{**}, T, G, A, and E_{-1} are excluded so that $K^{**} = 5$; since $5 \geq 2 - 1$, the order condition is satisfied. In the private wages equation (3.29c), W^* and E are included so that $M^* = 2$; W^{**}, T, G, P_{-1}, and K_{-1} are excluded so that $K^{**} = 5$; since $5 \geq 2 - 1$, the order condition is satisfied. Indeed, if we examined the appropriate $\mathbf{\Pi}_{**,*}$ matrices we would find the rank condition satisfied for all three equations. There are of course, no unknown parameters in the remaining equations (3.29d)–(3.29h). The model is identified.

5. REDUCED-FORM ESTIMATION AND INDIRECT LEAST SQUARES

We now turn to consider estimation in the simultaneous linear structural equation model, keeping in mind that only identified equations can be estimated. In this section we follow up the suggestion that consistent estimates of structural parameters may be obtainable from consistent estimates of the reduced-form parameters. We begin with a presentation of reduced-form estimation and then present a method which is sometimes available for estimating a structural equation.

Reduced-Form Estimation

The parameters of the reduced form are consistently estimated by classical least squares applied to each reduced-form equation. The stochastic specification of the simultaneous linear structural equation model implies that the multivariate contemporaneously uncorrelated linear regression model is appropriate to the set of reduced forms. It is now convenient to collect some of the earlier results, bringing them into the notation of this chapter.

The mth reduced-form equation is

$$\mathbf{y}_m = \mathbf{X}\boldsymbol{\pi}_m + \mathbf{v}_m \tag{5.1}$$

where $\mathbf{y}_m$ is the $T \times 1$ vector of observations on the mth dependent variable, $\mathbf{X}$ is the $T \times K$ matrix of observations on all the predetermined variables, $\boldsymbol{\pi}_m$ is the $K \times 1$ vector of coefficients of the mth reduced-form equation—the mth column of $\mathbf{\Pi}$, and $\mathbf{v}_m$ is the $T \times 1$ vector of disturbances in the mth reduced-form equation—the mth column of $\mathbf{V}$. The classical least-squares estimator of $\boldsymbol{\pi}_m$ is

$$\mathbf{p}_m = (\mathbf{X}'\mathbf{X})^{-1}\mathbf{X}'\mathbf{y}_m \tag{5.2}$$

and its sampling error is

$$\mathbf{p}_m - \boldsymbol{\pi}_m = (\mathbf{X}'\mathbf{X})^{-1}\mathbf{X}'(\mathbf{X}\boldsymbol{\pi}_m + \mathbf{v}_m) - \boldsymbol{\pi}_m = (\mathbf{X}'\mathbf{X})^{-1}\mathbf{X}'\mathbf{v}_m. \tag{5.3}$$

Then $\mathbf{p}_m$ is consistent:

$$\begin{aligned} \text{plim}\,(\mathbf{p}_m - \boldsymbol{\pi}_m) &= \text{plim}(T^{-1}\mathbf{X}'\mathbf{X})^{-1}\,\text{plim}\,(T^{-1}\mathbf{X}'\mathbf{v}_m) \\ &= \mathbf{\Sigma}_{\mathbf{XX}}^{-1} \cdot \mathbf{0} = \mathbf{0}, \end{aligned} \tag{5.4}$$

and its asymptotic covariance matrix is

$$(5.5)\qquad \bar{\boldsymbol{\Sigma}}_{\mathbf{p}_m\mathbf{p}_m} = \bar{E}(\mathbf{p}_m - \boldsymbol{\pi}_m)(\mathbf{p}_m - \boldsymbol{\pi}_m)'$$
$$= T^{-1}\,\text{plim}\; T(\mathbf{X}'\mathbf{X})^{-1}\mathbf{X}'\mathbf{v}_m\mathbf{v}_m'\mathbf{X}(\mathbf{X}'\mathbf{X})^{-1} = T^{-1}\omega_{mm}\boldsymbol{\Sigma}_{\mathbf{xx}}^{-1}.$$

The vector of residuals from the least-squares regression is

$$(5.6)\qquad \hat{\mathbf{v}}_m = \mathbf{y}_m - \mathbf{X}\mathbf{p}_m;$$

the sum of squared residuals divided by T,

$$(5.7)\qquad \bar{w}_{mm} = T^{-1}\hat{\mathbf{v}}_m'\hat{\mathbf{v}}_m,$$

is a consistent estimator of ω_{mm}; and a consistent estimator of the asymptotic covariance matrix is

$$(5.8)\qquad \mathbf{S}_{\mathbf{p}_m\mathbf{p}_m} = \bar{w}_{mm}(\mathbf{X}'\mathbf{X})^{-1}.$$

(In our earlier work we divided the sum of squared residuals by $T - K$; obviously using T instead does not affect asymptotic results, and we now follow that convention.) Further consider the estimates of the mth and m'th equation. We have

$$(5.9)\qquad (\mathbf{p}_m - \boldsymbol{\pi}_m)(\mathbf{p}_{m'} - \boldsymbol{\pi}_{m'})' = (\mathbf{X}'\mathbf{X})^{-1}\mathbf{X}'\mathbf{v}_m\mathbf{v}_{m'}'\mathbf{X}(\mathbf{X}'\mathbf{X})^{-1},$$

$$(5.10)\qquad \bar{\boldsymbol{\Sigma}}_{\mathbf{p}_m\mathbf{p}_{m'}} = \bar{E}(\mathbf{p}_m - \boldsymbol{\pi}_m)(\mathbf{p}_{m'} - \boldsymbol{\pi}_{m'})' = T^{-1}\omega_{mm'}\boldsymbol{\Sigma}_{\mathbf{xx}}^{-1}.$$

The sum of cross products of residuals divided by T,

$$(5.11)\qquad \bar{w}_{mm'} = T^{-1}\hat{\mathbf{v}}_m'\hat{\mathbf{v}}_{m'},$$

is a consistent estimator of $\omega_{mm'}$; and a consistent estimator of the asymptotic covariance matrix is

$$(5.12)\qquad \mathbf{S}_{\mathbf{p}_m\mathbf{p}_{m'}} = \bar{w}_{mm'}(\mathbf{X}'\mathbf{X})^{-1}.$$

We also collect the results for all M reduced-form equations. The full reduced-form system is

$$(5.13)\qquad \mathbf{Y} = \mathbf{X}\boldsymbol{\Pi} + \mathbf{V}.$$

The coefficient matrix $\boldsymbol{\Pi}$ is consistently estimated by

$$(5.14)\qquad \mathbf{P} = (\mathbf{X}'\mathbf{X})^{-1}\mathbf{X}'\mathbf{Y}.$$

The matrix of residuals from the estimated reduced forms is

$$(5.15)\qquad \hat{\mathbf{V}} = \mathbf{Y} - \mathbf{XP} = \mathbf{Y} - \mathbf{X}(\mathbf{X}'\mathbf{X})^{-1}\mathbf{X}'\mathbf{Y} = [\mathbf{I} - \mathbf{X}(\mathbf{X}'\mathbf{X})^{-1}\mathbf{X}']\mathbf{Y},$$

and the matrix of their sums of squares and cross products divided by T

$$(5.16)\qquad \bar{\mathbf{W}} = T^{-1}\hat{\mathbf{V}}'\hat{\mathbf{V}},$$

is a consistent estimator of $\boldsymbol{\Omega}$. Let $\boldsymbol{\pi}$ be the $MK \times 1$ vector of the elements of $\boldsymbol{\Pi}$ arranged by columns and let $\mathbf{p}$ be the $MK \times 1$ vector of the elements of $\mathbf{P}$ arranged by columns:

$$(5.17)\qquad \boldsymbol{\pi} = \begin{pmatrix} \boldsymbol{\pi}_1 \\ \cdot \\ \cdot \\ \cdot \\ \boldsymbol{\pi}_m \\ \cdot \\ \cdot \\ \cdot \\ \boldsymbol{\pi}_M \end{pmatrix}, \qquad \mathbf{p} = \begin{pmatrix} \mathbf{p}_1 \\ \cdot \\ \cdot \\ \cdot \\ \mathbf{p}_m \\ \cdot \\ \cdot \\ \cdot \\ \mathbf{p}_M \end{pmatrix}.$$

Then the asymptotic variances and covariances of all of the elements of P are displayed in the $MK \times MK$ matrix

$$(5.18)\qquad \boldsymbol{\Psi} = \bar{E}(\mathbf{p} - \boldsymbol{\pi})(\mathbf{p} - \boldsymbol{\pi})'$$

$$= T^{-1}\begin{pmatrix} \omega_{11}\boldsymbol{\Sigma}_{\mathbf{xx}}^{-1} & \cdots & \omega_{1M}\boldsymbol{\Sigma}_{\mathbf{xx}}^{-1} \\ \cdot & & \cdot \\ \cdot & \omega_{mm'}\boldsymbol{\Sigma}_{\mathbf{xx}}^{-1} & \cdot \\ \cdot & & \cdot \\ \omega_{M1}\boldsymbol{\Sigma}_{\mathbf{xx}}^{-1} & \cdots & \omega_{MM}\boldsymbol{\Sigma}_{\mathbf{xx}}^{-1} \end{pmatrix} = T^{-1}\boldsymbol{\Omega} \otimes \boldsymbol{\Sigma}_{\mathbf{xx}}^{-1},$$

which is consistently estimated by

$$(5.19)\qquad \hat{\boldsymbol{\Psi}} = \begin{pmatrix} \bar{w}_{11}(\mathbf{X}'\mathbf{X})^{-1} & \cdots & \bar{w}_{1M}(\mathbf{X}'\mathbf{X})^{-1} \\ \cdot & & \cdot \\ \cdot & \bar{w}_{mm'}(\mathbf{X}'\mathbf{X})^{-1} & \cdot \\ \cdot & & \cdot \\ \bar{w}_{M1}(\mathbf{X}'\mathbf{X})^{-1} & \cdots & \bar{w}_{MM}(\mathbf{X}'\mathbf{X})^{-1} \end{pmatrix}$$

$$= \bar{\mathbf{W}} \otimes (\mathbf{X}'\mathbf{X})^{-1}.$$

It will be recalled from (4.11.19)–(4.11.28) that these least-squares reduced forms minimize not only the individual residual variances $\bar{w}_{mm}$, but also the *generalized residual variance* $|\bar{\mathbf{W}}|$. In addition, if the v's are normally distributed, then **P** and $\bar{\mathbf{W}}$ are maximum likelihood estimators of **Π** and **Ω**, provided that the predetermined variables are independent of contemporary and succeeding disturbances and that the initial values of the lagged endogenous variables are fixed in repeated samples; see Koopmans and Hood (1953, pp. 151–155).

We may illustrate the estimation of reduced forms by computations on our illustrative models. First, for the simple Keynes model (with variables measured as deviations about sample means and the intercept of the consumption function dropped), the matrices of moments about the mean are given in (5.20). Here and in the sequel we use row and column headings for ease of reference.

$$(5.20) \quad \begin{pmatrix} \mathbf{X'X} & \mathbf{X'Y} \\ & \mathbf{Y'Y} \end{pmatrix} = \begin{array}{c} \\ I \\ C \\ Y \end{array} \begin{pmatrix} \overset{I}{5{,}710} & \overset{C}{11{,}698} & \overset{Y}{17{,}408} \\ & 35{,}887 & 47{,}585 \\ & & 64{,}993 \end{pmatrix},$$

whence the estimated reduced-form matrix is

$$(5.21) \quad \mathbf{P} = (\mathbf{X'X})^{-1}\mathbf{X'Y} = I\begin{pmatrix} \overset{C}{2.048} & \overset{Y}{3.048} \end{pmatrix}.$$

Next for Tintner's meat market model the matrices of moments about the mean using annual observations, United States 1919–1941, are

$$(5.22) \quad \begin{pmatrix} \mathbf{X'X} & \mathbf{X'Y} \\ & \mathbf{Y'Y} \end{pmatrix}$$

$$= \begin{array}{c} \\ x_1 \\ x_2 \\ x_3 \\ y_1 \\ y_2 \end{array} \begin{pmatrix} \overset{x_1}{83{,}433.65} & \overset{x_2}{3{,}611.72} & \overset{x_3}{12{,}204.77} & \overset{y_1}{3{,}671.91} & \overset{y_2}{8{,}354.59} \\ & 2{,}534.80 & 730.78 & -536.48 & 850.33 \\ & & 2{,}626.99 & 983.86 & 1{,}235.76 \\ & & & 1{,}369.54 & -352.44 \\ & & & & 1{,}581.49 \end{pmatrix},$$

whence the estimated reduced-form matrix is

$$(5.23) \quad \mathbf{P} = (\mathbf{X'X})^{-1}\mathbf{X'Y} = \begin{array}{c} x_1 \\ x_2 \\ x_3 \end{array} \begin{pmatrix} \overset{y_1}{-0.030839} & \overset{y_2}{0.096075} \\ -0.344626 & 0.208343 \\ 0.613660 & -0.033902 \end{pmatrix}.$$

Finally, for Klein's Model I the raw moment matrices, using annual observations, United States, 1921–1941, are shown in (5.24a)–(5.24c). From these the estimated reduced-form matrix is as shown in (5.25).

(5.24*a*) $\mathbf{X'X} =$

	1	W^{**}	T	G	A	P_{-1}	K_{-1}	E_{-1}
1	21.00	107.50	142.90	208.20	0.00	343.90	4,210.40	1,217.70
W^{**}		626.87	789.27	1,200.19	238.00	1,746.22	21,683.18	6,364.43
T			1,054.95	1,546.11	176.00	2,348.48	28,766.23	8,436.53
G				2,369.94	421.70	3,451.86	42,026.14	12,473.50
A					770.00	−11.90	590.60	495.60
P_{-1}						5,956.29	69,073.54	20,542.22
K_{-1}							846,132.70	244,984.77
E_{-1}								72,200.03

(5.24b) $\mathbf{X'Y} =$

	C	I	W^*	P	Y	K	W	E
1	1,133.90	26.60	763.60	354.70	1,225.80	4,237.00	871.10	1,261.20
W^{**}	5,977.33	103.80	4,044.07	1,821.11	6,492.05	21,786.98	4,670.94	6,654.45
T	7,858.86	160.40	5,315.62	2,405.53	8,510.42	28,926.63	6,104.89	8,776.10
G	11,633.68	243.19	7,922.46	3,578.05	12,700.70	42,269.33	9,122.65	13,046.62
A	577.70	−105.60	460.90	18.90	717.80	485.00	698.90	655.80
P_{-1}	18,929.37	655.33	12,871.73	6,070.13	20,688.08	69,728.87	14,617.95	21,290.34
K_{-1}	227,767.38	5,073.25	153,470.56	70,946.78	246,100.52	851,205.95	175,153.74	253,183.59
E_{-1}	66,815.25	1,831.13	45,288.51	21,030.44	72,683.38	246,815.90	51,652.94	74,755.48

(5.24c) $\mathbf{Y'Y} =$

	C	I	W^*	P	Y	K	W	E
C	62,166.63	1,679.01	42,076.78	19,566.35	67,620.46	229,446.39	48,054.11	69,501.99
I		286.02	1,217.92	726.10	2,047.82	5,359.27	1,321.72	2,104.42
W^*			28,560.86	13,296.61	45,901.54	154,688.48	32,604.93	47,173.09
P				6,347.25	21,464.97	71,672.88	15,117.72	22,049.39
Y					73,858.56	248,148.34	52,393.59	75,876.93
K						856,565.22	176,475.46	255,288.01
W							37,275.87	53,827.54
E								77,998.58

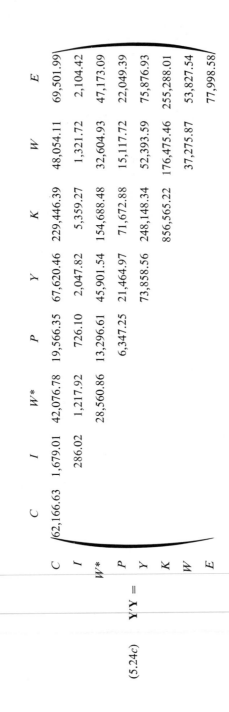

(5.25) $\mathbf{P} = (\mathbf{X}'\mathbf{X})^{-1}\mathbf{X}'\mathbf{Y} =$

	C	I	W^*	P	Y	K	W	E
1	58.3022	35.5181	43.4358	50.3661	93.8017	35.5181	43.4358	93.8197
W^{**}	−0.0117	−0.8168	−1.3100	−0.5186	−0.8286	−0.8168	−0.3100	−1.8286
T	−0.3657	−0.1615	−0.6042	−0.9231	−1.5273	−0.1615	−0.6042	−0.5273
G	0.2050	0.1002	0.8662	0.4390	1.3052	0.1002	0.8662	1.3052
A	0.7011	0.3319	0.7136	0.3194	1.0330	0.3319	0.7136	1.0330
P_{-1}	0.7480	0.9264	0.8719	0.8025	1.6744	0.9264	0.8719	1.6744
K_{-1}	−0.1465	−0.1925	−0.1230	−0.2160	−0.3390	0.8075	−0.1230	−0.3391
E_{-1}	0.2301	−0.1127	0.0953	0.0220	0.1173	−0.1127	0.0953	0.1173

Indirect Least-Squares Estimation

We now consider the possibilities of deriving structural estimators from the reduced-form estimator $\mathbf{P}$. We shall of course attempt this only when the structural equations being estimated are identified. First suppose that all of the equations of the structural model are identified. This means that sufficient restrictions have been placed on $\mathbf{\Pi}$ by the restrictions on $\mathbf{\Gamma}$ and $\mathbf{B}$ to enable us to solve $\mathbf{\Pi\Gamma} = -\mathbf{B}$ uniquely for $\mathbf{\Gamma}$ and $\mathbf{B}$ in terms of $\mathbf{\Pi}$. Naturally we consider the estimates $\hat{\mathbf{\Gamma}}$ and $\hat{\mathbf{B}}$ defined by $\mathbf{P}\hat{\mathbf{\Gamma}} = -\hat{\mathbf{B}}$. And now the difficulty in deriving structural estimates from the reduced-form estimates becomes apparent. In computing $\mathbf{P}$ we have not introduced the restrictions. Then, in general, the system $\mathbf{P}\hat{\mathbf{\Gamma}} = -\hat{\mathbf{B}}$ will not be soluble for $\hat{\mathbf{B}}$ and $\hat{\mathbf{\Gamma}}$. Thus the obvious method of deriving structural estimates from the reduced-form estimates may break down.

To investigate this more closely let us consider a single structural equation (4.25) which is identified. Omitting the two terms known to be zero we write it as

$$\text{(5.26)} \qquad \mathbf{Y}_*\boldsymbol{\gamma}_* + \mathbf{X}_*\boldsymbol{\beta}_* + \mathbf{u} = \mathbf{0}.$$

As in (4.26) we partition $\mathbf{\Pi}$ as

$$\text{(5.27)} \qquad \begin{pmatrix} \mathbf{\Pi}_{*,*} & \mathbf{\Pi}_{*,**} \\ \mathbf{\Pi}_{**,*} & \mathbf{\Pi}_{**,**} \end{pmatrix},$$

where $\mathbf{\Pi}_{*,*}$ is $K^* \times M^*$, $\mathbf{\Pi}_{**,*}$ is $K^{**} \times M^*$, $\mathbf{\Pi}_{*,**}$ is $K^* \times M^{**}$, and $\mathbf{\Pi}_{**,**}$ is $K^{**} \times M^{**}$. In (4.28) we noted that the connections between $\mathbf{\Pi}$ and $\boldsymbol{\gamma}_*$ and $\boldsymbol{\beta}_*$ are

$$\text{(5.28}a\text{)} \qquad -\mathbf{\Pi}_{*,*}\boldsymbol{\gamma}_* = \boldsymbol{\beta}_*,$$

$$\text{(5.28}b\text{)} \qquad \mathbf{\Pi}_{**,*}\boldsymbol{\gamma}_* = \mathbf{0},$$

and we have a normalization rule $\gamma_0 = -1$. We have specified that the equation is identified so that $r(\mathbf{\Pi}_{**,*}) = M^* - 1$ so (5.28) is uniquely soluble for $\boldsymbol{\gamma}_*$ and $\boldsymbol{\beta}_*$ when the normalization rule is used.

Attempting the indirect least-squares procedure we arrange and partition $\mathbf{P}$ to conform to the partitioning of $\mathbf{\Pi}$:

$$\text{(5.29)} \qquad \mathbf{P} = \begin{pmatrix} \mathbf{P}_{*,*} & \mathbf{P}_{*,**} \\ \mathbf{P}_{**,*} & \mathbf{P}_{**,**} \end{pmatrix}$$

where $\mathbf{P}_{*,*}$ is $K^* \times M^*$, $\mathbf{P}_{**,*}$ is $K^{**} \times M^*$, $\mathbf{P}_{*,**}$ is $K^* \times M^{**}$, and $\mathbf{P}_{**,**}$ is $K^{**} \times M^{**}$, and consider the estimators $\hat{\boldsymbol{\gamma}}_*$ and $\hat{\boldsymbol{\beta}}_*$ defined by

$$\text{(5.30}a\text{)} \qquad -\mathbf{P}_{*,*}\hat{\boldsymbol{\gamma}}_* = \hat{\boldsymbol{\beta}}_*,$$

$$\text{(5.30}b\text{)} \qquad \mathbf{P}_{**,*}\hat{\boldsymbol{\gamma}}_* = \mathbf{0},$$

$$\text{(5.30}c\text{)} \qquad \hat{\gamma}_0 = -1.$$

Since no restrictions were placed on $\mathbf{P}$, the $K^{**} \times M^*$ matrix $\mathbf{P}_{**,*}$ will have rank either K^{**} or M^* whichever is smaller. Now the equation is identified so $K^{**} \geq M^* - 1$. Considering (5.30*b*) it will be seen that a crucial distinction is between the case where $K^{**} = M^* - 1$ and the case where $K^{**} > M^* - 1$. In the former case we may say that we have minimum requisite information for estimation of (5.26) or that (5.26) is *just-identified.* In the latter case we say that we have extra information for estimation of (5.26) or that (5.26) is *over-identified.* Although in either case $r(\mathbf{\Pi}_{**,*}) = M^* - 1$, the rank of the estimating matrix $\mathbf{P}_{**,*}$ differs.

Suppose first that the equation is just-identified so that $K^{**} = M^* - 1$. Then the rank of the $K^{**} \times M^*$ matrix $\mathbf{P}_{**,*}$ will be $M^* - 1$. Having computed $\mathbf{P}_{**,*}$, we may use (5.30*b*) to determine elements of $\hat{\boldsymbol{\gamma}}_*$ up to a factor of proportionality; and the normalization rule (5.30*c*) to determine the elements of $\hat{\boldsymbol{\gamma}}_*$ uniquely. Then insertion of $\hat{\boldsymbol{\gamma}}_*$ into (5.30*a*) determines the elements of $\hat{\boldsymbol{\beta}}_*$ uniquely. This method of estimation is known as the *indirect least-squares* method—the structural estimates are derived indirectly from classical least-squares estimates of the reduced-form coefficients. These estimates are clearly consistent. Taking probability limits in (5.30*b*) we see, in view of the consistency of $\mathbf{P}$, plim $\mathbf{P}_{**,*} \times$ plim $\hat{\boldsymbol{\gamma}}_* = \mathbf{\Pi}_{**,*}$ plim $\hat{\boldsymbol{\gamma}}_* = \mathbf{0}$, which in view of the uniqueness of the normalized solution to (4.28*b*) implies plim $\hat{\boldsymbol{\gamma}}_* = \boldsymbol{\gamma}_*$. Then taking probability limits in (5.30*a*) and comparing with (4.28*a*) shows that plim $\hat{\boldsymbol{\beta}}_* = \boldsymbol{\beta}_*$. Further, the asymptotic covariance matrix of the structural estimates may be derived from that of the reduced-form estimates by use of the general formulas for asymptotic variances and covariances of functions of random variables (3.6.31); see also p. 334.

Suppose, however, that the equation is over-identified so that $K^{**} > M^* - 1$. Then the rank of the $K^{**} \times M^*$ matrix $\mathbf{P}_{**,*}$ will exceed $M^* - 1$—indeed since it has only M^* columns, this rank will be M^*. But then there is no nontrivial solution to (5.30*b*), and the indirect least-squares method of estimation cannot be applied. The simple straightforward method of converting reduced-form estimates into structural estimates is no longer possible.

We conclude that indirect least-squares estimation is available only when the structural equation is just-identified, in which case it provides consistent estimates. It will be seen that economic models typically have many restrictions so that the *over-identified* situation is likely to be the prevalent one. Thus the indirect least-squares method will not be generally available. Several possibilities are open. We may arbitrarily throw away enough rows of $\mathbf{P}_{**,*}$ to bring its rank down to $M^* - 1$. This amounts to throwing away over-identifying restrictions—i.e., to ignoring the information that certain predetermined variables excluded from this structural equation are indeed included elsewhere in the system. Consistent estimates are still obtained, but this procedure is not recommended since it is arbitrary and since discarding information, as usual, results in a loss of efficiency. The methods presented in the succeeding two sections are designed to avoid the arbitrariness and the efficiency loss. Effectively, they use varying amounts of restrictions in estimating the reduced form or in going from the reduced form to the structure.

We proceed to illustrate the indirect least-squares method with our examples. First, for the consumption function of the Keynes model, we have $K^{**} = 1 = 2 - 1 = M^* - 1$ so that it is just-identified. Pulling out the relevant submatrix from (5.21) and using the normalization rule we have

$$\text{(5.31)} \qquad \mathbf{P}_{**,*}\hat{\gamma}_* = (2.048 \quad 3.048)\begin{pmatrix} -1 \\ \hat{\beta} \end{pmatrix} = 0,$$

whence

$$\text{(5.32)} \qquad \hat{\beta} = 0.672.$$

There are no coefficients of predetermined variables to be estimated. It will be seen that indirect least squares is in fact the method used to obtain consistent estimates in our original discussion of this model in Section 2.

Next, for the supply function of Tintner's meat market model, we have $K^{**} = 1 = 2 - 1 = M^* - 1$ so that it is just identified. Pulling out the relevant submatrix from (5.23) and using the normalization rule we have

$$\text{(5.33)} \qquad \mathbf{P}_{**,*}\hat{\gamma}_* = (-0.030839 \quad 0.096075)\begin{pmatrix} -1 \\ \hat{b}_1 \end{pmatrix} = 0,$$

whence

$$\text{(5.34)} \qquad \hat{b}_1 = -\frac{0.030839}{0.096075} = -0.320989.$$

Then pulling out the relevant submatrix from (5.23) we have

$$\text{(5.35)} \qquad \hat{\boldsymbol{\beta}}_* = -\mathbf{P}_{*,*}\hat{\gamma}_* = -\begin{pmatrix} -0.344626 & 0.208343 \\ 0.613660 & -0.033902 \end{pmatrix}\begin{pmatrix} -1.000000 \\ -0.320989 \end{pmatrix}$$

$$= \begin{pmatrix} -0.277750 \\ 0.602778 \end{pmatrix} = \begin{pmatrix} \hat{b}_2 \\ \hat{b}_3 \end{pmatrix}$$

so that the consistent indirect least-squares estimate of the supply function is

$$\text{(5.36)} \qquad y_1 = -0.32y_2 - 0.28x_2 + 0.60x_3.$$

For comparison we give the (inconsistent) estimates obtained by regressing y_1 on y_2, x_2, and x_3:

$$\text{(5.37)} \qquad y_1 = -0.72y_2 - 0.19x_2 + 0.77x_3.$$

For the demand function of this model we have seen $K^{**} = 2 > 2 - 1 = M^* - 1$, so that this equation is over-identified. The indirect least-squares method is not available. To see this explicitly, pull out the relevant submatrix from (5.23). With the normalization rule this gives

$$(5.38) \qquad \mathbf{P}_{**,*}\hat{\Upsilon}_* = \begin{pmatrix} -0.344626 & 0.208343 \\ 0.613660 & -0.033902 \end{pmatrix} \begin{pmatrix} -1 \\ \hat{a}_1 \end{pmatrix} = \begin{pmatrix} 0 \\ 0 \end{pmatrix},$$

to which no solution exists since $r(\mathbf{P}_{**,*}) = 2$. If we arbitrarily discard the second row—ignore the fact that x_3 appears elsewhere in the model—we obtain

$$(5.39) \qquad \hat{a}_1 = -\frac{0.344626}{0.208343} = -1.65;$$

if we discard the first row—ignore the fact that x_2 appears elsewhere in the model—we obtain

$$(5.40) \qquad \hat{a}_1 = -\frac{0.613660}{0.033902} = -18.10.$$

For comparison we give the (inconsistent) estimates obtained by regressing y_1 on y_2 and x_1:

$$(5.41) \qquad y_1 = -0.97y_2 + 0.14x_1.$$

Turning to Klein's Model I we have seen that: For the consumption function $K^{**} = 6 > 3 - 1 = M^* - 1$; for the investment function $K^{**} = 5 > 2 - 1 = M^* - 1$; for the private wages equation, $K^{**} = 5 > 2 - 1 = M^* - 1$. Thus all three equations are over-identified so that indirect least-squares estimation is unavailable. This may be confirmed by pulling out from (5.25) the appropriate $\mathbf{P}_{**,*}$'s; it will be seen that for the consumption function the rank of that 6×3 matrix is 3, for the investment function the rank of that 5×2 matrix is 2, and for the private wages function, the rank of that 5×2 matrix is 2. In each case, there are more independent relations than coefficients to estimate, whence no solutions exist.

6. STRUCTURAL ESTIMATION: SINGLE-EQUATION METHODS

In this section we develop several methods that are available for consistently estimating the parameters of an over-identified structural equation.

Two-Stage Least Squares

Our first method is that of *two-stage least squares*, which is also known as the "generalized classical linear" method. It was developed by Theil (1953; 1961, pp. 225–231, 334–344) and independently by Basmann (1957).

In presenting this method, we use the normalization rule from the start, and also revise the notation. Taking the variable whose coefficient is -1 in (5.26) over to the other side, we rewrite the structural equation to be estimated as

$$(6.1) \qquad \mathbf{y} = \mathbf{Y}_1\boldsymbol{\gamma}_1 + \mathbf{X}_1\boldsymbol{\beta}_1 + \mathbf{u},$$

where

$\mathbf{y}$ is the $T \times 1$ vector of observations on the "left-hand" dependent variable—a column of $\mathbf{Y}_*$;
$\mathbf{Y}_1$ is the $T \times (M^* - 1)$ matrix of observations on the "right-hand" included dependent variables—$\mathbf{Y}_*$ with one column deleted;
$\boldsymbol{\gamma}_1$ is the $(M^* - 1) \times 1$ vector of coefficients of these right-hand dependent variables—$\boldsymbol{\gamma}_*$ with the -1 deleted;
$\mathbf{X}_1$ is the $T \times K^*$ matrix of observations on the included predetermined variables—previously denoted as $\mathbf{X}_*$;
$\boldsymbol{\beta}_1$ is the $K^* \times 1$ vector of coefficients of these included predetermined variables—previously denoted as $\boldsymbol{\beta}_*$; and
$\mathbf{u}$ is again the $T \times 1$ vector of disturbances in this structural equation.

We also refine the partitioning of $\mathbf{\Pi}$ and $\mathbf{P}$ to distinguish between the left-hand and the right-hand dependent variables, and thus revise our notation. Thus

$$(6.2) \qquad \mathbf{\Pi} = \begin{pmatrix} \mathbf{\Pi}_{10} & \mathbf{\Pi}_{11} & \mathbf{\Pi}_{12} \\ \mathbf{\Pi}_{20} & \mathbf{\Pi}_{21} & \mathbf{\Pi}_{22} \end{pmatrix} = (\mathbf{\Pi}_{X0} \quad \mathbf{\Pi}_{X1} \quad \mathbf{\Pi}_{X2}),$$

$$(6.3) \qquad \mathbf{P} = \begin{pmatrix} \mathbf{P}_{10} & \mathbf{P}_{11} & \mathbf{P}_{12} \\ \mathbf{P}_{20} & \mathbf{P}_{21} & \mathbf{P}_{22} \end{pmatrix} = (\mathbf{P}_{X0} \quad \mathbf{P}_{X1} \quad \mathbf{P}_{X2}).$$

Here the first subscript refers to the predetermined variables: 1 to the included predetermined variables, 2 to the excluded predetermined variables, and X to all of them; the second subscript refers to the dependent variables: 0 to the left-hand one, 1 to the (included) right-hand ones, and 2 to the excluded ones. (Note that the submatrices having 0 in the second subscript are in fact column vectors.) We also use a partitioning of $\mathbf{X}$ into $(\mathbf{X}_1 \quad \mathbf{X}_2)$ where $\mathbf{X}_2$ is $T \times K^{**}$.

In this notation, the portion of the reduced form $\mathbf{Y} = \mathbf{X\Pi} + \mathbf{V}$ that refers to the right-hand dependent variables is

$$(6.4) \qquad \mathbf{Y}_1 = \mathbf{X}_1\mathbf{\Pi}_{11} + \mathbf{X}_2\mathbf{\Pi}_{21} + \mathbf{V}_1 = \mathbf{X\Pi}_{X1} + \mathbf{V}_1,$$

where $\mathbf{V}_1$ is the appropriate $T \times (M^* - 1)$ submatrix of $\mathbf{V}$. Inserting (6.4) into (6.1) and rearranging,

$$(6.5) \qquad \mathbf{y} = \mathbf{X\Pi}_{X1}\boldsymbol{\gamma}_1 + \mathbf{X}_1\boldsymbol{\beta}_1 + (\mathbf{u} + \mathbf{V}_1\boldsymbol{\gamma}_1).$$

Since the predetermined variables are contemporaneously uncorrelated with all disturbances (structural and reduced form), if we took the classical least-squares regression of $\mathbf{y}$ on $\bar{\mathbf{Y}}_1 = \mathbf{X}\mathbf{\Pi}_{X1}$ and $\mathbf{X}_1$ we would obtain consistent estimates of $\boldsymbol{\gamma}_1$ and $\boldsymbol{\beta}_1$. This procedure is not available to us because we do not know $\mathbf{\Pi}_{X1}$ and hence do not have observations on $\bar{\mathbf{Y}}_1$. We can, however, consistently estimate $\mathbf{\Pi}_{X1}$ by $\mathbf{P}_{X1}$ and hence $\bar{\mathbf{Y}}_1$ by $\mathbf{X}\mathbf{P}_{X1}$.

These considerations suggest the following two-stage procedure.

Stage one: Obtain the classical least-squares estimator of $\mathbf{\Pi}_{X1}$ by regressing (each column of) $\mathbf{Y}_1$ on $\mathbf{X}$; this is the submatrix of $\mathbf{P}$:

$$\text{(6.6)} \qquad \mathbf{P}_{X1} = (\mathbf{X}'\mathbf{X})^{-1}\mathbf{X}'\mathbf{Y}_1,$$

and obtain the calculated values in these regressions:

$$\text{(6.7)} \qquad \hat{\mathbf{Y}}_1 = \mathbf{X}\mathbf{P}_{X1}.$$

Stage two: Take the classical least-squares regression of $\mathbf{y}$ on $\hat{\mathbf{Y}}_1$ and $\mathbf{X}_1$. The resulting coefficients are the two-stage least-squares estimators of $\boldsymbol{\gamma}_1$ and $\boldsymbol{\beta}_1$.

Thus the two-stage least-squares estimator of $\begin{pmatrix}\boldsymbol{\gamma}_1\\ \boldsymbol{\beta}_1\end{pmatrix}$ is the $\begin{pmatrix}\mathbf{c}\\ \mathbf{b}\end{pmatrix}$ defined by the normal equations

$$\text{(6.8)} \qquad \begin{pmatrix}\hat{\mathbf{Y}}_1'\hat{\mathbf{Y}}_1 & \hat{\mathbf{Y}}_1'\mathbf{X}_1\\ \mathbf{X}_1'\hat{\mathbf{Y}}_1 & \mathbf{X}_1'\mathbf{X}_1\end{pmatrix}\begin{pmatrix}\mathbf{c}\\ \mathbf{b}\end{pmatrix} = \begin{pmatrix}\hat{\mathbf{Y}}_1'\mathbf{y}\\ \mathbf{X}_1'\mathbf{y}\end{pmatrix},$$

a system of $M^* - 1 + K^*$ equations in $M^* - 1 + K^*$ unknowns which will, in general, have a unique solution.

To establish the consistency of the two-stage least-squares estimator we might write the structural equation as

$$\text{(6.9)} \qquad \mathbf{y} = \hat{\mathbf{Y}}_1\boldsymbol{\gamma}_1 + \mathbf{X}_1\boldsymbol{\beta}_1 + [\mathbf{u} + (\mathbf{Y}_1 - \hat{\mathbf{Y}}_1)\boldsymbol{\gamma}_1],$$

and show that $\hat{\mathbf{Y}}_1$ and $\mathbf{X}_1$ are independent of the compound disturbance term in brackets, in the sense that the probability limits of the sample covariances are zero. Alternatively, we interpret (6.8) as the normal equations of instrumental variable estimation, which will permit us to draw on the results of Section 6.5 for standard errors as well. Suppose, then, that we estimate (6.1) by the instrumental variable method with the calculated values of the right-hand dependent variables as instruments for the corresponding observed values, and with the included predetermined variables serving as their own instruments. Then the estimator of $\begin{pmatrix}\boldsymbol{\gamma}_1\\ \boldsymbol{\beta}_1\end{pmatrix}$ would be defined by

$$\text{(6.10)} \qquad \begin{pmatrix}\hat{\mathbf{Y}}_1'\mathbf{Y}_1 & \hat{\mathbf{Y}}_1'\mathbf{X}_1\\ \mathbf{X}_1'\mathbf{Y}_1 & \mathbf{X}_1'\mathbf{X}_1\end{pmatrix}\begin{pmatrix}\mathbf{c}^*\\ \mathbf{b}^*\end{pmatrix} = \begin{pmatrix}\hat{\mathbf{Y}}_1'\mathbf{y}\\ \mathbf{X}_1'\mathbf{y}\end{pmatrix},$$

and supposing that the instruments were legitimate, we see, by reference to (6.5.14)–(6.5.19), that this estimator would be consistent; that its asymptotic covariance matrix would be

$$(6.11)\qquad T^{-1}\sigma^2\left[\text{plim}\, T^{-1}\begin{pmatrix}\hat{\mathbf{Y}}_1'\mathbf{Y}_1 & \hat{\mathbf{Y}}_1'\mathbf{X}_1\\ \mathbf{X}_1'\mathbf{Y}_1 & \mathbf{X}_1'\mathbf{X}_1\end{pmatrix}\right]^{-1}\left[\text{plim}\, T^{-1}\begin{pmatrix}\hat{\mathbf{Y}}_1'\hat{\mathbf{Y}}_1 & \hat{\mathbf{Y}}_1'\mathbf{X}_1\\ \mathbf{X}_1'\hat{\mathbf{Y}}_1 & \mathbf{X}_1'\mathbf{X}_1\end{pmatrix}\right] \times\left[\text{plim}\, T^{-1}\begin{pmatrix}\mathbf{Y}_1'\hat{\mathbf{Y}}_1 & \mathbf{Y}_1'\mathbf{X}_1\\ \mathbf{X}_1'\hat{\mathbf{Y}}_1 & \mathbf{X}_1'\mathbf{X}_1\end{pmatrix}\right]^{-1}$$

where σ^2 is the structural disturbance variance; and that this matrix would be consistently estimated by

$$(6.12)\qquad s^2\begin{pmatrix}\hat{\mathbf{Y}}_1'\mathbf{Y}_1 & \hat{\mathbf{Y}}_1'\mathbf{X}_1\\ \mathbf{X}_1'\mathbf{Y}_1 & \mathbf{X}_1'\mathbf{X}_1\end{pmatrix}^{-1}\begin{pmatrix}\hat{\mathbf{Y}}_1'\hat{\mathbf{Y}}_1 & \hat{\mathbf{Y}}_1'\mathbf{X}_1\\ \mathbf{X}_1'\hat{\mathbf{Y}}_1 & \mathbf{X}_1'\mathbf{X}_1\end{pmatrix}\begin{pmatrix}\mathbf{Y}_1'\hat{\mathbf{Y}}_1 & \mathbf{Y}_1'\mathbf{X}_1\\ \mathbf{X}_1'\hat{\mathbf{Y}}_1 & \mathbf{X}_1'\mathbf{X}_1\end{pmatrix}^{-1},$$

where s^2 is the sum of squared residuals divided by T. Now the instruments are legitimate; from (3.17)

$$(6.13)\qquad \text{plim}\, T^{-1}\mathbf{X}_1'\mathbf{u} = \mathbf{0};$$

and since $\mathbf{P}$ is consistent,

$$(6.14)\qquad \text{plim}\, T^{-1}\hat{\mathbf{Y}}_1'\mathbf{u} = \text{plim}\, T^{-1}\mathbf{P}_{X1}'\mathbf{X}'\mathbf{u} = \mathbf{\Pi}_{X1}'\,\text{plim}\, T^{-1}\mathbf{X}'\mathbf{u} = \mathbf{0}.$$

Next we show the algebraic equivalence of (6.10) and (6.8). From the definition of $\hat{\mathbf{Y}}_1$ in (6.7),

$$(6.15)\qquad \begin{aligned}\hat{\mathbf{Y}}_1'\hat{\mathbf{Y}}_1 &= \mathbf{Y}_1'\mathbf{X}(\mathbf{X}'\mathbf{X})^{-1}\mathbf{X}'\cdot\mathbf{X}(\mathbf{X}'\mathbf{X})^{-1}\mathbf{X}'\mathbf{Y}_1\\ &= \mathbf{Y}_1'\mathbf{X}(\mathbf{X}'\mathbf{X})^{-1}\mathbf{X}'\cdot\mathbf{Y}_1 = \hat{\mathbf{Y}}_1'\mathbf{Y}_1 = \mathbf{Y}_1'\hat{\mathbf{Y}}_1,\end{aligned}$$

$$(6.16)\qquad \begin{aligned}\mathbf{X}_1'\hat{\mathbf{Y}}_1 &= \mathbf{X}_1'\cdot\mathbf{X}(\mathbf{X}'\mathbf{X})^{-1}\mathbf{X}'\mathbf{Y}_1\\ &= (\mathbf{X}_1'\mathbf{X}_1\quad \mathbf{X}_1'\mathbf{X}_2)\begin{pmatrix}\mathbf{X}_1'\mathbf{X}_1 & \mathbf{X}_1'\mathbf{X}_2\\ \mathbf{X}_2'\mathbf{X}_1 & \mathbf{X}_2'\mathbf{X}_2\end{pmatrix}^{-1}\begin{pmatrix}\mathbf{X}_1'\\ \mathbf{X}_2'\end{pmatrix}\mathbf{Y}_1\\ &= (\mathbf{I}\quad \mathbf{0})\begin{pmatrix}\mathbf{X}_1'\\ \mathbf{X}_2'\end{pmatrix}\mathbf{Y}_1 = \mathbf{X}_1'\mathbf{Y}_1.\end{aligned}$$

Thus we see that two-stage least squares is identical with an instrumental variable estimation—which establishes its consistency. In addition, in (6.11) and (6.12) the middle matrix has as its inverse the third matrix so that these two matrices "cancel out." We also see that there is no need to compute explicitly the individual calculated values. Rather, the computationally efficient formula for two-stage least-squares estimation (henceforth 2SLS) is given by

$$(6.17)\qquad \begin{pmatrix}\mathbf{Y}_1'\mathbf{X}(\mathbf{X}'\mathbf{X})^{-1}\mathbf{X}'\mathbf{Y}_1 & \mathbf{Y}_1'\mathbf{X}_1\\ \mathbf{X}_1'\mathbf{Y}_1 & \mathbf{X}_1'\mathbf{X}_1\end{pmatrix}\begin{pmatrix}\mathbf{c}\\ \mathbf{b}\end{pmatrix} = \begin{pmatrix}\mathbf{Y}_1'\mathbf{X}(\mathbf{X}'\mathbf{X})^{-1}\mathbf{X}'\mathbf{y}\\ \mathbf{X}_1'\mathbf{y}\end{pmatrix}.$$

The asymptotic covariance matrix may be written as

$$\bar{\boldsymbol{\Sigma}}_{\mathbf{cb,cb}} = T^{-1}\sigma^2\begin{pmatrix} \boldsymbol{\Pi}'_{\mathrm{X}1}\boldsymbol{\Sigma}_{\mathbf{xx}}\boldsymbol{\Pi}_{\mathrm{X}1} & \boldsymbol{\Pi}'_{\mathrm{X}1}\boldsymbol{\Sigma}'_{\mathbf{1x}} \\ \boldsymbol{\Sigma}_{\mathbf{1x}}\boldsymbol{\Pi}_{\mathrm{X}1} & \boldsymbol{\Sigma}_{\mathbf{11}} \end{pmatrix}^{-1} \tag{6.18}$$

where $\boldsymbol{\Sigma}_{\mathbf{1x}}$ and $\boldsymbol{\Sigma}_{\mathbf{11}}$ are submatrices of $\boldsymbol{\Sigma}_{\mathbf{xx}} = \text{plim}\,(T^{-1}\mathbf{X}'\mathbf{X})$. To see this, note that

$$\begin{aligned} \text{plim}\, T^{-1}\mathbf{X}'\mathbf{Y}_1 &= \text{plim}\, T^{-1}\mathbf{X}'(\mathbf{X}\boldsymbol{\Pi}_{\mathrm{X}1} + \mathbf{V}_1) \\ &= \text{plim}\, T^{-1}\mathbf{X}'\mathbf{X}\boldsymbol{\Pi}_{\mathrm{X}1} + \text{plim}\, T^{-1}\mathbf{X}'\mathbf{V}_1 \\ &= \boldsymbol{\Sigma}_{\mathbf{xx}}\boldsymbol{\Pi}_{\mathrm{X}1} + \mathbf{0} = \boldsymbol{\Sigma}_{\mathbf{xx}}\boldsymbol{\Pi}_{\mathrm{X}1}; \end{aligned} \tag{6.19}$$

so that

$$\begin{aligned} &\text{plim}\, T^{-1}\mathbf{Y}_1'\mathbf{X}(\mathbf{X}'\mathbf{X})^{-1}\mathbf{X}'\mathbf{Y}_1 \\ &\quad = \text{plim}\,(T^{-1}\mathbf{Y}_1'\mathbf{X})[\text{plim}\,(T^{-1}\mathbf{X}'\mathbf{X})]^{-1}\,\text{plim}\,(T^{-1}\mathbf{X}'\mathbf{Y}_1) \\ &\quad = \boldsymbol{\Pi}'_{\mathrm{X}1}\boldsymbol{\Sigma}_{\mathbf{xx}}\cdot\boldsymbol{\Sigma}_{\mathbf{xx}}^{-1}\cdot\boldsymbol{\Sigma}_{\mathbf{xx}}\boldsymbol{\Pi}_{\mathrm{X}1} = \boldsymbol{\Pi}'_{\mathrm{X}1}\boldsymbol{\Sigma}_{\mathbf{xx}}\boldsymbol{\Pi}_{\mathrm{X}1}; \end{aligned} \tag{6.20}$$

and also

$$\begin{aligned} \text{plim}\, T^{-1}\mathbf{X}_1'\mathbf{Y}_1 &= \text{plim}\, T^{-1}\mathbf{X}_1'(\mathbf{X}\boldsymbol{\Pi}_{\mathrm{X}1} + \mathbf{V}_1) \\ &= \text{plim}\, T^{-1}\mathbf{X}_1'\mathbf{X}\boldsymbol{\Pi}_{\mathrm{X}1} + \text{plim}\, T^{-1}\mathbf{X}_1'\mathbf{V}_1 \\ &= \boldsymbol{\Sigma}_{\mathbf{1x}}\boldsymbol{\Pi}_{\mathrm{X}1}. \end{aligned} \tag{6.21}$$

The estimator of (6.18) may then be written as

$$\mathbf{S}_{\mathbf{cb,cb}} = s^2\begin{pmatrix} \mathbf{Y}_1'\mathbf{X}(\mathbf{X}'\mathbf{X})^{-1}\mathbf{X}'\mathbf{Y}_1 & \mathbf{Y}_1'\mathbf{X}_1 \\ \mathbf{X}_1'\mathbf{Y}_1 & \mathbf{X}_1'\mathbf{X}_1 \end{pmatrix}^{-1}. \tag{6.22}$$

It may also be seen that s^2 may be computed, without explicit computation of the residuals, by

$$\begin{aligned} s^2 &= T^{-1}(\mathbf{y} - \mathbf{Y}_1\mathbf{c} - \mathbf{X}_1\mathbf{b})'(\mathbf{y} - \mathbf{Y}_1\mathbf{c} - \mathbf{X}_1\mathbf{b}) \\ &= T^{-1}(\mathbf{y}'\mathbf{y} - 2\mathbf{c}'\mathbf{Y}_1'\mathbf{y} - 2\mathbf{b}'\mathbf{X}_1'\mathbf{y} + 2\mathbf{c}'\mathbf{Y}_1'\mathbf{X}_1\mathbf{b} + \mathbf{c}'\mathbf{Y}_1'\mathbf{Y}_1\mathbf{c} \\ &\qquad + \mathbf{b}'\mathbf{X}_1'\mathbf{X}_1\mathbf{b}) \\ &= T^{-1}(\mathbf{y}'\mathbf{y} + \mathbf{c}'\mathbf{Y}_1'\mathbf{Y}_1\mathbf{c} - 2\mathbf{c}'\mathbf{Y}_1'\mathbf{y} - \mathbf{b}'\mathbf{X}_1'\mathbf{X}_1\mathbf{b}), \end{aligned} \tag{6.23}$$

using the second row of (6.17), namely, $\mathbf{b} = (\mathbf{X}_1'\mathbf{X}_1)^{-1}(-\mathbf{X}_1'\mathbf{Y}_1\mathbf{c} + \mathbf{X}_1'\mathbf{y})$.

From the point of view of instrumental variable estimation, the calculated values of the right-hand dependent variables are desirable instruments since they are contemporaneously uncorrelated with the disturbance and yet are correlated with the observed values of the variables for which they serve as instruments.

Finally we show that when the equation is just-identified, the 2SLS estimators are identical with the indirect least-squares estimators. Rewriting the equations of indirect least squares (5.30) in our new notation we have

$$\begin{pmatrix} \mathbf{P}_{10} & \mathbf{P}_{11} \\ \mathbf{P}_{20} & \mathbf{P}_{21} \end{pmatrix} \begin{pmatrix} -1 \\ \hat{\boldsymbol{\gamma}}_1 \end{pmatrix} = \begin{pmatrix} -\hat{\boldsymbol{\beta}}_1 \\ \mathbf{0} \end{pmatrix}, \tag{6.24}$$

which in view of the definition of $\mathbf{P}$ is

$$(\mathbf{X}'\mathbf{X})^{-1}\mathbf{X}'(\mathbf{y} \quad \mathbf{Y}_1)\begin{pmatrix} -1 \\ \hat{\boldsymbol{\gamma}}_1 \end{pmatrix} = \begin{pmatrix} -\hat{\boldsymbol{\beta}}_1 \\ \mathbf{0} \end{pmatrix}. \tag{6.25}$$

If we premultiply (6.25) by $\mathbf{Y}_1'\mathbf{X}$ we find

$$\begin{aligned} -\mathbf{Y}_1'\mathbf{X}(\mathbf{X}'\mathbf{X})^{-1}\mathbf{X}'\mathbf{y} + \mathbf{Y}_1'\mathbf{X}(\mathbf{X}'\mathbf{X})^{-1}\mathbf{X}'\mathbf{Y}_1\hat{\boldsymbol{\gamma}}_1 &= \mathbf{Y}_1'(\mathbf{X}_1 \quad \mathbf{X}_2)\begin{pmatrix} -\hat{\boldsymbol{\beta}}_1 \\ \mathbf{0} \end{pmatrix} \\ &= -\mathbf{Y}_1'\mathbf{X}_1\hat{\boldsymbol{\beta}}_1. \end{aligned} \tag{6.26}$$

If we premultiply (6.25) by $\mathbf{X}_1'\mathbf{X}$ we find

$$\begin{aligned} -\mathbf{X}_1'\mathbf{X}(\mathbf{X}'\mathbf{X})^{-1}\mathbf{X}'\mathbf{y} + \mathbf{X}_1'\mathbf{X}(\mathbf{X}'\mathbf{X})^{-1}\mathbf{X}'\mathbf{Y}_1\hat{\boldsymbol{\gamma}}_1 &= \mathbf{X}_1'(\mathbf{X}_1 \quad \mathbf{X}_2)\begin{pmatrix} -\hat{\boldsymbol{\beta}}_1 \\ \mathbf{0} \end{pmatrix} \\ &= -\mathbf{X}_1'\mathbf{X}_1\hat{\boldsymbol{\beta}}_1 \end{aligned} \tag{6.27a}$$

or

$$-(\mathbf{I} \quad \mathbf{0})\begin{pmatrix} \mathbf{X}_1' \\ \mathbf{X}_2' \end{pmatrix}\mathbf{y} + (\mathbf{I} \quad \mathbf{0})\begin{pmatrix} \mathbf{X}_1' \\ \mathbf{X}_2' \end{pmatrix}\mathbf{Y}_1\hat{\boldsymbol{\gamma}}_1 = -\mathbf{X}_1'\mathbf{X}_1\hat{\boldsymbol{\beta}}_1 \tag{6.27b}$$

or

$$-\mathbf{X}_1'\mathbf{y} + \mathbf{X}_1'\mathbf{Y}_1\hat{\boldsymbol{\gamma}}_1 = -\mathbf{X}_1'\mathbf{X}_1\hat{\boldsymbol{\beta}}_1. \tag{6.27c}$$

Now (6.26) and (6.27c) will be recognized as the first and second "rows" respectively of (6.17). Thus when they are defined the indirect least-squares estimators satisfy the same (nonsingular) system (6.17) as do the 2SLS estimators, so that they are identical with the latter.

We illustrate 2SLS estimation with computations on two over-identified equations from our illustrative models.

For Tintner's meat demand function (3.26a) we pull out from (5.22) and (5.23) the submatrices $\mathbf{Y}_1'\mathbf{X}$, $\mathbf{y}'\mathbf{X}$, and $(\mathbf{X}'\mathbf{X})^{-1}\mathbf{X}'\mathbf{Y}_1$ and compute

$$\begin{aligned} \begin{pmatrix} \mathbf{Y}_1'\mathbf{X} \\ \mathbf{y}'\mathbf{X} \end{pmatrix} \cdot (\mathbf{X}'\mathbf{X})^{-1}\mathbf{X}'\mathbf{Y}_1 &= \begin{pmatrix} 8354.59 & 850.33 & 1235.76 \\ 3671.91 & -536.48 & 983.86 \end{pmatrix} \begin{pmatrix} 0.096075 \\ 0.208343 \\ -0.033902 \end{pmatrix} \\ &= \begin{pmatrix} 937.93 \\ 207.64 \end{pmatrix}; \end{aligned} \tag{6.28}$$

using these along with the other relevant submatrices of (5.22) we set up the normal equations of (6.17):

$$(6.29)\qquad \begin{pmatrix} 937.93 & 8354.59 \\ 8354.59 & 83433.65 \end{pmatrix}\begin{pmatrix} \hat{a}_1 \\ \hat{a}_2 \end{pmatrix} = \begin{pmatrix} 207.64 \\ 3671.91 \end{pmatrix}.$$

Inverting the left-hand matrix and multiplying into the right-hand vector we find

$$(6.30)\qquad \begin{pmatrix} \hat{a}_1 \\ \hat{a}_2 \end{pmatrix} = \begin{pmatrix} 0.009867 & -0.000988 \\ -0.000988 & 0.000111 \end{pmatrix}\begin{pmatrix} 207.64 \\ 3671.91 \end{pmatrix} = \begin{pmatrix} -1.579063 \\ 0.202434 \end{pmatrix}.$$

Next pulling out the relevant submatrices from (5.22) and (6.30) we use them in (6.23) to find

$$(6.31)\qquad \begin{aligned} s^2 &= (23)^{-1}[1369.54 + (-1.579063)^2(1581.49) \\ &\qquad - 2(-1.579063)(-352.44) - (0.202434)^2(83433.65)] \\ &= (23)^{-1}(780.77) = 33.947. \end{aligned}$$

Multiplying this into the inverse matrix given in (6.30) gives the estimated covariance matrix

$$(6.32)\qquad \begin{aligned} \mathbf{S}_{\mathbf{bc},\mathbf{bc}} &= 33.947\begin{pmatrix} 0.009867 & -0.000988 \\ -0.000988 & 0.000111 \end{pmatrix} \\ &= \begin{pmatrix} 0.334955 & -0.033540 \\ -0.033540 & 0.003768 \end{pmatrix}, \end{aligned}$$

the square roots of the diagonal elements of which are the estimated asymptotic standard errors of our coefficient estimators. Thus the 2SLS estimate of Tintner's demand function is

$$(6.33)\qquad y_1 = \underset{(0.58)}{-1.58y_2} + \underset{(0.06)}{0.20x_1}.$$

For comparison, the (inconsistent) estimate obtained by regressing y_1 on y_2 and x_1 is

$$(6.34)\qquad y_1 = -0.97y_2 + 0.14x_1.$$

[It would be useful to verify the equivalence of 2SLS and indirect least squares in the just-identified case by re-estimating Tintner's meat supply function (3.26*b*).]

In similar fashion, using submatrices of (5.24) and (5.25), the normal equations for 2SLS estimation of Klein's consumption function (3.29*a*) are computed and set up to be

$$(6.35)\qquad \begin{pmatrix} 6{,}285.30 & 15{,}076.14 & 354.70 & 6{,}070.13 \\ & 37{,}235.86 & 871.10 & 14{,}617.95 \\ & & 21.00 & 343.90 \\ & & & 5{,}956.29 \end{pmatrix}\begin{pmatrix} \hat{a}_1 \\ \hat{a}_3 \\ \hat{a}_0 \\ \hat{a}_2 \end{pmatrix} = \begin{pmatrix} 19{,}507.72 \\ 48{,}010.45 \\ 1{,}133.90 \\ 18{,}929.37 \end{pmatrix},$$

and the 2SLS estimate of this function is computed to be

$$\text{(6.36)} \qquad C = \underset{(1.320)}{16.555} + \underset{(0.118)}{0.017}P + \underset{(0.107)}{0.216}P_{-1} + \underset{(0.040)}{0.810}W.$$

For comparison the (inconsistent) estimate obtained by regressing C on P, P_{-1}, and W is

$$\text{(6.37)} \qquad C = 16.299 + 0.090P + 0.913P_{-1} + 0.796W.$$

For more on computational procedure see Basmann (1959). If $K^* = 0$ so that there are no predetermined variables included in the structural equation, then the terms involving $\mathbf{X}_1$ and/or $\mathbf{b}$ in (6.17), (6.22), and (6.23) are simply deleted. If $M^* = 1$ so that there are no included right hand dependent variables in the structural equation, then the terms involving $\mathbf{Y}_1$ and/or $\mathbf{c}$ are simply deleted; note that this means that $\mathbf{b}$ is estimated by a straightforward regression of $\mathbf{y}$ on $\mathbf{X}_1$.

The (k)-Class Estimators

Theil (1961, pp. 231–237) has noted that there is a whole family of estimators of the structural equation (6.1) of which 2SLS is a special case. The family, known as the (k)-*class estimators*, is defined by the normal equations

$$\text{(6.38)} \qquad \begin{pmatrix} \mathbf{Y}_1'\mathbf{Y}_1 - k\hat{\mathbf{V}}_1'\hat{\mathbf{V}}_1 & \mathbf{Y}_1'\mathbf{X}_1 \\ \mathbf{X}_1'\mathbf{Y}_1 & \mathbf{X}_1'\mathbf{X}_1 \end{pmatrix} \begin{pmatrix} \mathbf{c}_{(k)} \\ \mathbf{b}_{(k)} \end{pmatrix} = \begin{pmatrix} \mathbf{Y}_1'\mathbf{y} - k\hat{\mathbf{V}}_1'\mathbf{y} \\ \mathbf{X}_1'\mathbf{y} \end{pmatrix},$$

where $\hat{\mathbf{V}}_1$ is the $T \times (M^* - 1)$ matrix of residuals from the estimated reduced forms of the right-hand dependent variables—$\hat{\mathbf{V}}_1 = \mathbf{Y}_1 - \hat{\mathbf{Y}}_1$, and where k is any scalar, stochastic or nonstochastic. For any choice of k, the normal equations define $\mathbf{c}_{(k)}$ and $\mathbf{b}_{(k)}$, the (k) estimators of $\boldsymbol{\gamma}_1$ and $\boldsymbol{\beta}_1$.

First we note some algebraic facts:

(6.39) Classical least squares applied to (6.1) gives the (k) estimator with $k = 0$.

Also

$$\text{(6.40)} \qquad \hat{\mathbf{V}}_1'\mathbf{y} = \mathbf{Y}_1'[\mathbf{I} - \mathbf{X}(\mathbf{X}'\mathbf{X})^{-1}\mathbf{X}']\mathbf{y} = \mathbf{Y}_1'\mathbf{y} - \hat{\mathbf{Y}}_1'\mathbf{y},$$

and since $\mathbf{I} - \mathbf{X}(\mathbf{X}'\mathbf{X})^{-1}\mathbf{X}'$ is idempotent,

$$\text{(6.41)} \qquad \hat{\mathbf{V}}_1'\hat{\mathbf{V}}_1 = \mathbf{Y}_1'[\mathbf{I} - \mathbf{X}(\mathbf{X}'\mathbf{X})^{-1}\mathbf{X}']\mathbf{Y}_1 = \mathbf{Y}_1'\mathbf{Y}_1 - \hat{\mathbf{Y}}_1'\hat{\mathbf{Y}}_1.$$

Thus if we set $k = 1$ in (6.38) and use (6.15) we obtain just the 2SLS normal equations of (6.17). Hence

(6.42) Two-stage least squares applied to (6.1) gives the (k) estimator with $k = 1$.

Suppose now k is such that $\text{plim}\,(k - 1) = 0$. Then as $T \to \infty$ the normal equations (6.38) will converge to the normal equations of 2SLS, so that the unique solution vector will converge to the solution vector of 2SLS, and the estimators will also be consistent. More formally, let us divide through (6.38) by T, solve, and write this compactly as

$$(6.43) \qquad \begin{pmatrix} \mathbf{c}_{(k)} \\ \mathbf{b}_{(k)} \end{pmatrix} = \mathbf{M}_{(k)}^{-1}\mathbf{m}_{(k)}.$$

If $\text{plim}\,(k - 1) = 0$, it is clear that $\text{plim}\,\mathbf{M}_{(k)} = \text{plim}\,\mathbf{M}_{(1)}$ where $\mathbf{M}_{(1)}$ is the moment matrix of 2SLS divided by T:

$$(6.44) \qquad \mathbf{M}_{(1)} = T^{-1}\begin{pmatrix} \mathbf{Y}_1'\mathbf{X}(\mathbf{X}'\mathbf{X})^{-1}\mathbf{X}'\mathbf{Y}_1 & \mathbf{Y}_1'\mathbf{X}_1 \\ \mathbf{X}_1'\mathbf{Y}_1 & \mathbf{X}_1'\mathbf{X}_1 \end{pmatrix},$$

and also $\text{plim}\,\mathbf{m}_{(k)} = \text{plim}\,\mathbf{m}_{(1)}$ where $\mathbf{m}_{(1)}$ is the moment vector of 2SLS divided by T

$$(6.45) \qquad \mathbf{m}_{(1)} = T^{-1}\begin{pmatrix} \mathbf{Y}_1'\mathbf{X}(\mathbf{X}'\mathbf{X})^{-1}\mathbf{X}'\mathbf{y} \\ \mathbf{X}_1'\mathbf{y} \end{pmatrix}.$$

Hence if $\text{plim}\,(k - 1) = 0$,

$$(6.46) \qquad \text{plim}\begin{pmatrix} \mathbf{c}_{(k)} \\ \mathbf{b}_{(k)} \end{pmatrix} = \text{plim}\,\mathbf{M}_{(k)}^{-1} \cdot \text{plim}\,\mathbf{m}_{(k)} = \text{plim}\,\mathbf{M}_{(1)}^{-1} \cdot \text{plim}\,\mathbf{m}_{(1)}$$
$$= \text{plim}\begin{pmatrix} \mathbf{c} \\ \mathbf{b} \end{pmatrix} = \begin{pmatrix} \boldsymbol{\gamma}_1 \\ \boldsymbol{\beta}_1 \end{pmatrix},$$

using the consistency of 2SLS. Thus, there is a whole class of estimators that share the asymptotic property of consistency with 2SLS:

(6.47) Any (k) estimator that has $\text{plim}\,(k - 1) = 0$ provides consistent estimators of $\boldsymbol{\gamma}_1$ and $\boldsymbol{\beta}_1$.

Of course $\text{plim}\,(0 - 1) \neq 0$, so we have not established that classical least squares is consistent! On the other hand, if we take $k = 1 + T^{-1}$, then $\text{plim}\,(k - 1) = \text{plim}\,(T^{-1}) = 0$, so that we have a (trivial) alternative to 2SLS. In the next subsection we discuss a more interesting alternative.

Suppose that in fact k is such that $\text{plim}\,T^{1/2}(k - 1) = 0$; this is a stricter requirement—if $\text{plim}\,T^{1/2}x = 0$, then a fortiori $\text{plim}\,x = 0$. Then it can be shown that the (k) estimator has the same asymptotic covariance matrix as 2SLS, i.e., the $\bar{\boldsymbol{\Sigma}}_{\mathbf{cb},\mathbf{cb}}$ of (6.18). Thus, there is a whole class of estimators that share the asymptotic covariance matrix of 2SLS:

(6.48) Any (k) estimator that has $\text{plim}\,T^{1/2}(k - 1) = 0$ has the same asymptotic covariance matrix as the 2SLS estimator.

On grounds of consistency and asymptotic efficiency, then, there is a whole class of estimators as desirable as 2SLS.

Limited-Information–Least Generalized Residual Variance Estimators

Another approach to consistent estimation of an over-identified structural equation is one we shall call the limited-information–least generalized residual variance method. This LI/LGRV method was developed prior to the 2SLS and (k)-class methods by Anderson and Rubin (1949, 1950). They arrived at these estimators by application of the maximum likelihood principle under the specification that the structural disturbances are normally distributed and utilizing only the restrictions on the structural equation being estimated. For this reason the method is generally known as the "limited-information maximum likelihood" method. Most of the properties of these estimators, however, do not depend on normality and maximum likelihood, and it is useful to develop and refer to the method without using those considerations. Still another derivation of these estimators, which suggests yet another name—"least variance ratio" method—is given by Koopmans and Hood (1953, pp. 166–177).

The structural equation to be estimated is again that of (6.1) or (5.26); mixing notation somewhat we write it as

$$\mathbf{Y}_* \boldsymbol{\gamma}_* + \mathbf{X}_1 \boldsymbol{\beta}_* + \mathbf{u} = \mathbf{0}, \tag{6.49}$$

where $\mathbf{Y}_* = (\mathbf{y} \quad \mathbf{Y}_1)$, $\boldsymbol{\gamma}_* = \begin{pmatrix} \gamma_0 \\ \boldsymbol{\gamma}_1 \end{pmatrix}$, $\boldsymbol{\beta}_* = \boldsymbol{\beta}_1$, and where the normalization rule $\gamma_0 = -1$ is ignored for the time being. The portion of the reduced form $\mathbf{Y} = \mathbf{X\Pi} + \mathbf{V}$ that relates to the dependent variables in (6.49) is

$$\mathbf{Y}_* = \mathbf{X}\mathbf{\Pi}_{X*} + \mathbf{V}_* = \mathbf{X}_1 \mathbf{\Pi}_{*,*} + \mathbf{X}_2 \mathbf{\Pi}_{**,*} + \mathbf{V}_*. \tag{6.50}$$

If we had a consistent estimator of $\mathbf{\Pi}_{X*}$ that satisfied the restriction $\mathbf{\Pi}_{**,*}\boldsymbol{\gamma}_* = \mathbf{0}$, consistent estimators of $\boldsymbol{\gamma}_*$ and $\boldsymbol{\beta}_*$ could be derived in accordance with (5.28). It will be recalled that the unrestricted classical least-squares estimators of a set of relations like (6.50) minimize the generalized residual variance $|T^{-1}\mathbf{V}_*'\mathbf{V}_*|$. This suggests that we minimize $|T^{-1}\mathbf{V}_*'\mathbf{V}_*|$ subject to the restriction $\mathbf{\Pi}_{**,*}\boldsymbol{\gamma}_* = \mathbf{0}$; indeed this defines the LI/LGRV method. To minimize $|T^{-1}\mathbf{V}_*'\mathbf{V}_*|$ we may as well minimize $\frac{1}{2}\log|\mathbf{W}|$ where $\mathbf{W} = \mathbf{V}_*'\mathbf{V}_*$.

Therefore we form

$$z = \tfrac{1}{2}\log|\mathbf{W}| - \boldsymbol{\mu}'\mathbf{\Pi}_{**,*}\boldsymbol{\gamma}_* \tag{6.51}$$

where $\boldsymbol{\mu}$ is a $K^{**} \times 1$ vector of Lagrange multipliers. Differentiating z with respect to $\mathbf{\Pi}_{X*}$ gives—compare (4.11.26)—

$$\frac{\partial z}{\partial \mathbf{\Pi}_{X*}} = (\mathbf{X}'\mathbf{Y}_* - \mathbf{X}'\mathbf{X}\mathbf{\Pi}_{X*})\mathbf{W}^{-1} - \frac{\partial \boldsymbol{\mu}'\mathbf{\Pi}_{**,*}\boldsymbol{\gamma}_*}{\partial \mathbf{\Pi}_{X*}}, \tag{6.52}$$

which in partitioned form is

$$(6.53)\qquad \frac{\partial z}{\partial \mathbf{\Pi}_{*,*}} = (\mathbf{X}_1'\mathbf{Y}_* - \mathbf{X}_1'\mathbf{X}_1\mathbf{\Pi}_{*,*} - \mathbf{X}_1'\mathbf{X}_2\mathbf{\Pi}_{**,*})\mathbf{W}^{-1} - \mathbf{0},$$

$$(6.54)\qquad \frac{\partial z}{\partial \mathbf{\Pi}_{**,*}} = (\mathbf{X}_2'\mathbf{Y}_* - \mathbf{X}_2'\mathbf{X}_1\mathbf{\Pi}_{*,*} - \mathbf{X}_2'\mathbf{X}_2\mathbf{\Pi}_{**,*})\mathbf{W}^{-1} - \boldsymbol{\mu}\boldsymbol{\gamma}_*';$$

whereas differentiating z with respect to $\boldsymbol{\mu}$ and $\boldsymbol{\gamma}_*$ gives

$$(6.55)\qquad \frac{\partial z}{\partial \boldsymbol{\mu}} = \mathbf{\Pi}_{**,*}\boldsymbol{\gamma}_*,$$

$$(6.56)\qquad \frac{\partial z}{\partial \boldsymbol{\gamma}_*} = \mathbf{\Pi}_{**,*}'\boldsymbol{\mu}.$$

We proceed to impose the first-order conditions for a minimum, using hats to denote that the conditions have been imposed. First setting (6.53) equal to zero, postmultiplying by $\hat{\mathbf{W}}$, and solving gives

$$(6.57)\qquad \hat{\mathbf{\Pi}}_{*,*} = (\mathbf{X}_1'\mathbf{X}_1)^{-1}\mathbf{X}_1'\mathbf{Y}_* - (\mathbf{X}_1'\mathbf{X}_1)^{-1}\mathbf{X}_1'\mathbf{X}_2\hat{\mathbf{\Pi}}_{**,*};$$

then setting (6.54) equal to zero, postmultiplying by $\hat{\mathbf{W}}$, and inserting (6.57) gives, after rearrangement,

$$(6.58)\qquad \hat{\mathbf{\Pi}}_{**,*} = (\mathbf{X}_2'\mathbf{M}_1\mathbf{X}_2)^{-1}\mathbf{X}_2'\mathbf{M}_1\mathbf{Y}_* - (\mathbf{X}_2'\mathbf{M}_1\mathbf{X}_2)^{-1}\hat{\boldsymbol{\mu}}\hat{\boldsymbol{\gamma}}_*'\hat{\mathbf{W}}$$

where $\mathbf{M}_1 = \mathbf{I} - \mathbf{X}_1(\mathbf{X}_1'\mathbf{X}_1)^{-1}\mathbf{X}_1'$ is a familiar idempotent matrix. Setting (6.55) equal to zero and inserting (6.58) gives, after rearrangement,

$$(6.59)\qquad \hat{\boldsymbol{\mu}} = (\hat{\boldsymbol{\gamma}}_*'\hat{\mathbf{W}}\hat{\boldsymbol{\gamma}}_*)^{-1}\mathbf{X}_2'\mathbf{M}_1\mathbf{Y}_*\hat{\boldsymbol{\gamma}}_*,$$

which inserted back into (6.58) gives—since $\hat{\boldsymbol{\gamma}}_*'\hat{\mathbf{W}}\hat{\boldsymbol{\gamma}}_*$ is a scalar—

$$(6.60)\qquad \hat{\mathbf{\Pi}}_{**,*} = (\mathbf{X}_2'\mathbf{M}_1\mathbf{X}_2)^{-1}\mathbf{X}_2'\mathbf{M}_1\mathbf{Y}_*[\mathbf{I} - (\hat{\boldsymbol{\gamma}}_*'\hat{\mathbf{W}}\hat{\boldsymbol{\gamma}}_*)^{-1}\hat{\boldsymbol{\gamma}}_*\hat{\boldsymbol{\gamma}}_*'\hat{\mathbf{W}}].$$

Now using (6.57) to eliminate $\hat{\mathbf{\Pi}}_{*,*}$ we may write $\hat{\mathbf{W}}$ as

$$\begin{aligned}(6.61)\qquad \hat{\mathbf{W}} &= (\mathbf{Y}_* - \mathbf{X}_1\hat{\mathbf{\Pi}}_{*,*} - \mathbf{X}_2\hat{\mathbf{\Pi}}_{**,*})'(\mathbf{Y}_* - \mathbf{X}_1\hat{\mathbf{\Pi}}_{*,*} - \mathbf{X}_2\hat{\mathbf{\Pi}}_{**,*})\\ &= [\mathbf{M}_1(\mathbf{Y}_* - \mathbf{X}_2\hat{\mathbf{\Pi}}_{**,*})]'[\mathbf{M}_1(\mathbf{Y}_* - \mathbf{X}_2\hat{\mathbf{\Pi}}_{**,*})]\\ &= \mathbf{Y}_*'\mathbf{M}_1\mathbf{Y}_* + \hat{\mathbf{\Pi}}_{**,*}'\mathbf{X}_2'\mathbf{M}_1\mathbf{X}_2\hat{\mathbf{\Pi}}_{**,*}\\ &\qquad - \hat{\mathbf{\Pi}}_{**,*}'\mathbf{X}_2'\mathbf{M}_1\mathbf{Y}_* - \mathbf{Y}_*'\mathbf{M}_1\mathbf{X}_2\hat{\mathbf{\Pi}}_{**,*}.\end{aligned}$$

Inserting (6.60) into (6.61) we find, after rearrangement,

$$\begin{aligned}(6.62)\qquad \hat{\mathbf{W}} &= \mathbf{Y}_*'\mathbf{M}_1\mathbf{Y}_* - \mathbf{Y}_*'\mathbf{M}_1\mathbf{X}_2(\mathbf{X}_2'\mathbf{M}_1\mathbf{X}_2)^{-1}\mathbf{X}_2'\mathbf{M}_1\mathbf{Y}_*\\ &\quad + (\hat{\boldsymbol{\gamma}}_*'\hat{\mathbf{W}}\hat{\boldsymbol{\gamma}}_*)^{-2}\hat{\mathbf{W}}\hat{\boldsymbol{\gamma}}_*[\hat{\boldsymbol{\gamma}}_*'\mathbf{Y}_*'\mathbf{M}_1\mathbf{X}_2(\mathbf{X}_2'\mathbf{M}_1\mathbf{X}_2)^{-1}\mathbf{X}_2'\mathbf{M}_1\mathbf{Y}_*\hat{\boldsymbol{\gamma}}_*]\hat{\boldsymbol{\gamma}}_*'\hat{\mathbf{W}}\end{aligned}$$

where we have used $\hat{\mathbf{W}}' = \hat{\mathbf{W}}$. Now it will be recognized that

$$(6.63)\qquad \mathbf{W}_{**} = \mathbf{Y}_*'\mathbf{M}_1\mathbf{Y}_* - \mathbf{Y}_*'\mathbf{M}_1\mathbf{X}_2(\mathbf{X}_2'\mathbf{M}_1\mathbf{X}_2)^{-1}\mathbf{X}_2'\mathbf{M}_1\mathbf{Y}_*$$

is T times the covariance matrix of the residuals from the least-squares fit of $\mathbf{Y}_*$ on $\mathbf{X}_1$ and $\mathbf{X}_2$; compare (4.7.21). Then we write (6.62) as

$$\hat{\mathbf{W}} = \mathbf{W}_{**} + \phi(\hat{\gamma}_*'\hat{\mathbf{W}}\hat{\gamma}_*)^{-1}\hat{\mathbf{W}}\hat{\gamma}_*\hat{\gamma}_*'\hat{\mathbf{W}} \tag{6.64}$$

where ϕ is the scalar

$$\phi = (\hat{\gamma}_*'\hat{\mathbf{W}}\hat{\gamma}_*)^{-1}\hat{\gamma}_*'\mathbf{Y}_*'\mathbf{M}_1\mathbf{X}_2(\mathbf{X}_2'\mathbf{M}_1\mathbf{X}_2)^{-1}\mathbf{X}_2'\mathbf{M}_1\mathbf{Y}_*\hat{\gamma}_*. \tag{6.65}$$

Note that the second term on the right of (6.64) is a nonnegative definite matrix, whence by (2.7.21) $|\hat{\mathbf{W}}| \geq |\mathbf{W}_{**}|$—which should come as no surprise since $|\hat{\mathbf{W}}|$ is a constrained minimum whereas $|\mathbf{W}_{**}|$ is an unconstrained minimum. Postmultiplying (6.64) by $\hat{\gamma}_*$ we find

$$\begin{aligned}\hat{\mathbf{W}}\hat{\gamma}_* &= \mathbf{W}_{**}\hat{\gamma}_* + \phi(\hat{\gamma}_*'\hat{\mathbf{W}}\hat{\gamma}_*)^{-1}\hat{\mathbf{W}}\hat{\gamma}_*\hat{\gamma}_*'\hat{\mathbf{W}}\hat{\gamma}_* \\ &= (1-\phi)^{-1}\mathbf{W}_{**}\hat{\gamma}_*,\end{aligned} \tag{6.66}$$

which inserted into (6.64) gives

$$\begin{aligned}\hat{\mathbf{W}} &= \mathbf{W}_{**} + \phi[\hat{\gamma}_*'(1-\phi)^{-1}\mathbf{W}_{**}\hat{\gamma}_*]^{-1}(1-\phi)^{-2}\mathbf{W}_{**}\hat{\gamma}_*\hat{\gamma}_*'\mathbf{W}_{**} \\ &= \mathbf{W}_{**} + \phi(1-\phi)^{-1}(\hat{\gamma}_*'\mathbf{W}_{**}\hat{\gamma}_*)^{-1}\mathbf{W}_{**}\hat{\gamma}_*\hat{\gamma}_*'\mathbf{W}_{**}.\end{aligned} \tag{6.67}$$

Now we set (6.56) equal to zero, inserting (6.60), (6.59), (6.66), and (6.65), to give

$$\begin{aligned}&[\mathbf{I} - (\hat{\gamma}_*'\hat{\mathbf{W}}\hat{\gamma}_*)^{-1}\hat{\mathbf{W}}\hat{\gamma}_*\hat{\gamma}_*']\mathbf{Y}_*'\mathbf{M}_1\mathbf{X}_2(\mathbf{X}_2'\mathbf{M}_1\mathbf{X}_2)^{-1}(\hat{\gamma}_*'\hat{\mathbf{W}}\hat{\gamma}_*)^{-1} \\ &\times \mathbf{X}_2'\mathbf{M}_1\mathbf{Y}_*\hat{\gamma}_* = [\mathbf{I} - (\hat{\gamma}_*'\hat{\mathbf{W}}\hat{\gamma}_*)^{-1}(1-\phi)^{-1}\mathbf{W}_{**}\hat{\gamma}_*\hat{\gamma}_*'] \\ &\times \mathbf{Y}_*'\mathbf{M}_1\mathbf{X}_2(\mathbf{X}_2'\mathbf{M}_1\mathbf{X}_2)^{-1}(\hat{\gamma}_*'\hat{\mathbf{W}}\hat{\gamma}_*)^{-1}\mathbf{X}_2'\mathbf{M}_1\mathbf{Y}_*\hat{\gamma}_* \\ &\qquad = (\hat{\gamma}_*'\hat{\mathbf{W}}\hat{\gamma}_*)^{-1}\mathbf{Y}_*'\mathbf{M}_1\mathbf{X}_2(\mathbf{X}_2'\mathbf{M}_1\mathbf{X}_2)^{-1}\mathbf{X}_2'\mathbf{M}_1\mathbf{Y}_*\hat{\gamma}_* \\ &\qquad\quad - \phi(1-\phi)^{-1}(\hat{\gamma}_*'\hat{\mathbf{W}}\hat{\gamma}_*)^{-1}\mathbf{W}_{**}\hat{\gamma}_* = \mathbf{0}\end{aligned}$$

or

$$[\mathbf{Y}_*'\mathbf{M}_1\mathbf{X}_2(\mathbf{X}_2'\mathbf{M}_1\mathbf{X}_2)^{-1}\mathbf{X}_2'\mathbf{M}_1\mathbf{Y}_* - \phi(1-\phi)^{-1}\mathbf{W}_{**}]\hat{\gamma}_* = \mathbf{0} \tag{6.68}$$

after multiplication by $(\hat{\gamma}_*'\hat{\mathbf{W}}\hat{\gamma}_*)$. A more convenient form for (6.68) is available if we note from (6.63) that $\mathbf{Y}_*'\mathbf{M}_1\mathbf{X}_2(\mathbf{X}_2'\mathbf{M}_1\mathbf{X}_2)^{-1}\mathbf{X}_2'\mathbf{M}_1\mathbf{Y}_* = \mathbf{W}_{**}^{(1)} - \mathbf{W}_{**}$, where $\mathbf{W}_{**}^{(1)} = \mathbf{Y}_*'\mathbf{M}_1\mathbf{Y}_* = \mathbf{Y}_*'\mathbf{Y}_* - \mathbf{Y}_*'\mathbf{X}_1(\mathbf{X}_1'\mathbf{X}_1)^{-1}\mathbf{X}_1'\mathbf{Y}_*$ will be recognized as T times the covariance matrix of the residuals from the least-squares fit of $\mathbf{Y}_*$ on $\mathbf{X}_1$ alone. Thus we write (6.68) as

$$(\mathbf{W}_{**}^{(1)} - l\mathbf{W}_{**})\hat{\gamma}_* = \mathbf{0} \tag{6.69}$$

where the scalar $l = 1 + \phi(1-\phi)^{-1} = (1-\phi)^{-1}$.

Now (6.69) is a system of M^* homogenous equations in M^* unknowns; for a nontrivial solution l must be a root of the determinantal equation

$$|\mathbf{W}_{**}^{(1)} - l\mathbf{W}_{**}| = 0. \tag{6.70}$$

Any such root determines $\hat{\gamma}_*$ up to a factor of proportionality from (6.69) and a unique $\hat{\mathbf{W}}$ from (6.67). It is not hard to show that to minimize $|\hat{\mathbf{W}}|$ we must take the smallest of the roots. For let $l_1, \ldots, l_{M^*}$ be the M^* distinct roots of (6.70) and let $\mathbf{g}_1, \ldots, \mathbf{g}_{M^*}$ be the corresponding solutions to (6.69), each normalized by $\mathbf{g}_m'\mathbf{W}_{**}\mathbf{g}_m = 1$. Then from (6.67) the $\hat{\mathbf{W}}$ that results when l_m is used is

$$(6.71)\qquad \hat{\mathbf{W}}_m = \mathbf{W}_{**} + (l_m - 1)\mathbf{W}_{**}\mathbf{g}_m\mathbf{g}_m'\mathbf{W}_{**}$$

since $\phi(1-\phi)^{-1} = l - 1$ and $(\mathbf{g}_m'\mathbf{W}_{**}\mathbf{g}_m)^{-1} = 1^{-1} = 1$. Let $\mathbf{G} = (\mathbf{g}_1 \quad \cdots \quad \mathbf{g}_m)$; then $\mathbf{G}'\mathbf{W}_{**}\mathbf{G} = \mathbf{I}$ since

$$\mathbf{g}_m'\mathbf{W}_{**}\mathbf{g}_{m'} = \begin{cases} 1 & \text{if} \quad m = m' \\ 0 & \text{if} \quad m \neq m' \end{cases}$$

by the present normalization rule and (2.6.6)—and $\mathbf{G}'\mathbf{W}_{**}\mathbf{g}_m = \mathbf{e}_m$ where $\mathbf{e}_m$ is the $M^* \times 1$ vector having 1 as its mth element and 0's elsewhere. [We rule out multiple roots; see Koopmans and Hood (1953, p. 173).] Pre- and postmultiplying (6.71) by $\mathbf{G}'$ and $\mathbf{G}$ respectively then gives

$$(6.72)\qquad \begin{aligned} \mathbf{G}'\hat{\mathbf{W}}_m\mathbf{G} &= \mathbf{G}'\mathbf{W}_{**}\mathbf{G} + (l_m - 1)\mathbf{G}'\mathbf{W}_{**}\mathbf{g}_m\mathbf{g}_m'\mathbf{W}_{**}\mathbf{G} \\ &= \mathbf{I} + (l_m - 1)\mathbf{e}_m\mathbf{e}_m', \end{aligned}$$

which is a diagonal matrix with $1 + l_m - 1 = l_m$ as the mth diagonal element and with 1's as the other diagonal elements. Then $|\mathbf{G}'\hat{\mathbf{W}}_m\mathbf{G}| = l_m$ whence $|\hat{\mathbf{W}}_m| = |\mathbf{G}|^{-2}\, l_m$; but $|\mathbf{G}|^{-2} = |\mathbf{W}_{**}|$ since $\mathbf{G}'\mathbf{W}_{**}\mathbf{G} = \mathbf{I}$; so that

$$(6.73)\qquad |\hat{\mathbf{W}}_m| = |\mathbf{W}_{**}|\, l_m.$$

Clearly to minimize $|\hat{\mathbf{W}}|$ we must take the smallest possible l_m—i.e., the smallest root of (6.70); note that $l_m \geq 1$ since as we have seen $|\hat{\mathbf{W}}| \geq |\mathbf{W}_{**}|$.

To recapitulate, the LI/LGRV method proceeds as follows. The smallest root, $\hat{l}$, of (6.70) is found, inserted in (6.69) giving $\hat{\boldsymbol{\gamma}}_*$ up to a factor of proportionality; taking $\hat{\gamma}_0 = -1$ gives $\hat{\boldsymbol{\gamma}}_*$ uniquely. Then $\hat{\boldsymbol{\beta}}_1$ is determined as

$$(6.74)\qquad \begin{aligned} \hat{\boldsymbol{\beta}}_1 &= -\hat{\boldsymbol{\Pi}}_{*,*}\hat{\boldsymbol{\gamma}}_* = -[(\mathbf{X}_1'\mathbf{X}_1)^{-1}\mathbf{X}_1'\mathbf{Y}_* - (\mathbf{X}_1'\mathbf{X}_1)^{-1}\mathbf{X}_1'\mathbf{X}_2\hat{\boldsymbol{\Pi}}_{**,*}]\hat{\boldsymbol{\gamma}}_* \\ &= -(\mathbf{X}_1'\mathbf{X}_1)^{-1}\mathbf{X}_1'\mathbf{Y}_*\hat{\boldsymbol{\gamma}}_* \end{aligned}$$

where we have used (6.57) and $\hat{\boldsymbol{\Pi}}_{**,*}\hat{\boldsymbol{\gamma}}_* = \mathbf{0}$.

It is a remarkable fact that the LI/LGRV estimator is a member of the (k)-class estimator family; it has $k = \hat{l}$. This is shown by the following algebraic manipulation. Consider the (k)-class normal equations (6.38). Note first that

$$(6.75)\qquad \begin{aligned} \hat{\mathbf{V}}_1'\mathbf{y} &= \mathbf{Y}_1'[\mathbf{I} - \mathbf{X}(\mathbf{X}'\mathbf{X})^{-1}\mathbf{X}']\mathbf{y} \\ &= \mathbf{Y}_1'[\mathbf{I} - \mathbf{X}(\mathbf{X}'\mathbf{X})^{-1}\mathbf{X}'][\mathbf{I} - \mathbf{X}(\mathbf{X}'\mathbf{X})^{-1}\mathbf{X}']\mathbf{y} = \hat{\mathbf{V}}_1'\hat{\mathbf{v}}_0 \end{aligned}$$

where $\hat{\mathbf{v}}_0$ is the $T \times 1$ vector of residuals in the reduced form of the left-hand dependent variable. Then the first "row" of (6.38) may be written

$$(\mathbf{Y}_1'\mathbf{Y}_1 - k\hat{\mathbf{V}}_1'\hat{\mathbf{V}}_1)c_{(k)} + \mathbf{Y}_1'\mathbf{X}_1 b_{(k)} - \mathbf{Y}_1'\mathbf{y} + k\hat{\mathbf{V}}_1'\hat{\mathbf{v}}_0 = \mathbf{0}$$

or

$$(\mathbf{Y}_1'\mathbf{y} - k\hat{\mathbf{V}}_1'\hat{\mathbf{v}}_0 \quad \mathbf{Y}_1'\mathbf{Y}_1 - k\hat{\mathbf{V}}_1'\hat{\mathbf{V}}_1)\begin{pmatrix} -1 \\ \mathbf{c}_{(k)} \end{pmatrix} + \mathbf{Y}_1'\mathbf{X}_1\mathbf{b}_{(k)} = \mathbf{0}$$

or more compactly as

$$(6.76) \qquad (\mathbf{Y}_1'\mathbf{Y}_* - k\hat{\mathbf{V}}_1'\hat{\mathbf{V}}_*)\begin{pmatrix} -1 \\ \mathbf{c}_{(k)} \end{pmatrix} + \mathbf{Y}_1'\mathbf{X}_1\mathbf{b}_{(k)} = \mathbf{0},$$

where $\hat{\mathbf{V}}_* = (\hat{\mathbf{v}}_0 \quad \hat{\mathbf{V}}_1)$ and again $\mathbf{Y}_* = (\mathbf{y} \quad \mathbf{Y}_1)$. Further the second "row" of (6.38) on premultiplication by $(\mathbf{X}_1'\mathbf{X}_1)^{-1}$ and rearrangement gives

$$(6.77) \qquad \begin{aligned} \mathbf{b}_{(k)} &= (\mathbf{X}_1'\mathbf{X}_1)^{-1}\mathbf{X}_1'\mathbf{y} - (\mathbf{X}_1'\mathbf{X}_1)^{-1}\mathbf{X}_1'\mathbf{Y}_1\mathbf{c}_{(k)} \\ &= -(\mathbf{X}_1'\mathbf{X}_1)^{-1}\mathbf{X}_1'\mathbf{Y}_*\begin{pmatrix} -1 \\ \mathbf{c}_{(k)} \end{pmatrix}. \end{aligned}$$

Inserting this in (6.76) and rearranging we find that $\mathbf{c}_{(k)}$ satisfies

$$(6.78) \qquad [\mathbf{Y}_1'\mathbf{Y}_* - k\hat{\mathbf{V}}_1'\hat{\mathbf{V}}_* - \mathbf{Y}_1'\mathbf{X}_1(\mathbf{X}_1'\mathbf{X}_1)^{-1}\mathbf{X}_1'\mathbf{Y}_*]\begin{pmatrix} -1 \\ \mathbf{c}_{(k)} \end{pmatrix} = \mathbf{0}.$$

But $\mathbf{Y}_1'\mathbf{Y}_* - \mathbf{Y}_1'\mathbf{X}_1(\mathbf{X}_1'\mathbf{X}_1)^{-1}\mathbf{X}_1'\mathbf{Y}_*$ is simply $\mathbf{W}_{**}^{(1)}$ with the first row deleted; let us write it as $\hat{\mathbf{V}}_1^{(1)\prime}\hat{\mathbf{V}}_*^{(1)}$. In addition, $\hat{\mathbf{V}}_1'\hat{\mathbf{V}}_*$ is $\mathbf{W}_{**}$ with the first row deleted. Thus $\mathbf{c}_{(k)}$ satisfies

$$(6.79) \qquad (\hat{\mathbf{V}}_1^{(1)\prime}\hat{\mathbf{V}}_*^{(1)} - k\hat{\mathbf{V}}_1'\hat{\mathbf{V}}_*)\begin{pmatrix} -1 \\ \mathbf{c}_{(k)} \end{pmatrix} = \mathbf{0},$$

which are just the last $M^* - 1$ rows of

$$(6.80) \qquad (\mathbf{W}_{**}^{(1)} - k\mathbf{W}_{**})\begin{pmatrix} -1 \\ \mathbf{c}_{(k)} \end{pmatrix} = \mathbf{0}.$$

Since the LI/LGRV estimator is constructed to satisfy (6.80) with $k = \hat{l}$ it certainly satisfies the last $M^* - 1$ rows of it. Thus the LI/LGRV estimator of $\boldsymbol{\gamma}_1$ is just $\mathbf{c}_{(k)}$ with $k = \hat{l}$. Comparing (6.74) with (6.77) we see that then the LI/LGRV estimator of $\boldsymbol{\beta}_1$ is just $\mathbf{b}_{(k)}$ with $k = \hat{l}$. We conclude that

(6.81) Limited information–least generalized residual variance estimation applied to (6.1) gives the (k) estimator with $k = \hat{l}$ where $\hat{l}$ is the smallest root of (6.70).

Now, as Anderson and Rubin (1950) have shown, under general conditions the asymptotic distribution of $T(\hat{l} - 1)$ is χ_k^2 where $k = K^{**} - M^* + 1$. Since a χ_k^2 variable has expectation k and variance $2k$ it follows that the asymptotic expectation of the quantity $T^{1/2}(\hat{l} - 1)$ is $T^{-1/2}(K^{**} - M^* + 1)$ and the asymptotic variance of $T^{1/2}(\hat{l} - 1)$ is $2T^{-1}(K^{**} - M^* + 1)$. Since both of these go to zero as T goes to infinity we have

$$\text{(6.82)} \qquad \text{plim } T^{1/2}(\hat{l} - 1) = 0$$

and a fortiori

$$\text{(6.83)} \qquad \text{plim } (\hat{l} - 1) = 0.$$

Then application of the general rules (6.47) and (6.48) for (k) estimators shows that the LI/LGRV estimators are consistent and have the same asymptotic covariance matrix as do the 2SLS estimators.

Here we only show that plim $(\hat{l} - 1) = 0$. Consider the population analogue of (6.70)

$$\text{(6.84)} \qquad |\mathbf{\Omega}_{**}^{(1)} - \lambda\mathbf{\Omega}_{**}| = 0;$$

where $\mathbf{\Omega}_{**}$ is the population covariance matrix of the disturbances in the reduced forms of all the included dependent variables—a submatrix of $\mathbf{\Omega}$—

$$\text{(6.85)} \qquad \mathbf{\Omega}_{**} = ET^{-1}\mathbf{V}_*'\mathbf{V}_* = \text{plim } T^{-1}\mathbf{Y}_*'\mathbf{M}\mathbf{Y}_*$$

where $\mathbf{M} = \mathbf{I} - \mathbf{X}(\mathbf{X}'\mathbf{X})^{-1}\mathbf{X}'$ is a familiar idempotent matrix; and where $\mathbf{\Omega}_{**}^{(1)}$ is the population covariance matrix of the residuals in the population regressions of all the included dependent variables on the *included* predetermined variables:

$$\text{(6.86)} \qquad \mathbf{\Omega}_{**}^{(1)} = \text{plim } T^{-1}\mathbf{Y}_*'\mathbf{M}_1\mathbf{Y}_*$$

where $\mathbf{M}_1 = \mathbf{I} - \mathbf{X}_1(\mathbf{X}_1'\mathbf{X}_1)^{-1}\mathbf{X}_1$. By use of (6.50), (3.22), and $\mathbf{M}_1\mathbf{X}_1 = \mathbf{0}$, $\mathbf{MX} = \mathbf{0}$, we find

$$\text{(6.87)} \qquad \begin{aligned} \mathbf{\Omega}_{**}^{(1)} - \mathbf{\Omega}_{**} &= \text{plim } T^{-1}\mathbf{Y}_*'(\mathbf{M}_1 - \mathbf{M})\mathbf{Y}_* \\ &= \text{plim } T^{-1}\mathbf{\Pi}_{**,*}'\mathbf{X}_2'\mathbf{M}_1\mathbf{X}_2\mathbf{\Pi}_{**,*} \\ &= \mathbf{\Pi}_{**,*}'\mathbf{\Sigma}_{22.1}\mathbf{\Pi}_{**,*} \end{aligned}$$

where $\mathbf{\Sigma}_{22.1} = \text{plim } T^{-1}\mathbf{X}_2'\mathbf{M}_1\mathbf{X}_2$ is the population covariance matrix of residuals in the auxiliary regressions of $\mathbf{X}_2$ on $\mathbf{X}_1$. Using (6.87) we may write the determinantal equation (6.84) as

$$\text{(6.88)} \qquad |\mathbf{\Pi}_{**,*}'\mathbf{\Sigma}_{22.1}\mathbf{\Pi}_{**,*} - (\lambda - 1)\mathbf{\Omega}_{**}| = 0.$$

Now $\boldsymbol{\Sigma}_{22.1}$ is nonnegative definite whence $\boldsymbol{\Pi}'_{**,*}\boldsymbol{\Sigma}_{22.1}\boldsymbol{\Pi}_{**,*}$ is nonnegative definite by (2.7.14)—but not positive definite since $r(\boldsymbol{\Pi}_{**,*}) = M^* - 1$. Application of (2.7.20) shows that the smallest root $\hat{\lambda} - 1$ of (6.88) is zero; i.e., that the smallest root $\hat{\lambda}$ of (6.84) is 1. Now the $\hat{l}$ of LI/LGRV estimation is the smallest root of (6.70) or equivalently of

$$(6.89) \qquad |T^{-1}\mathbf{W}^{(1)}_{**} - lT^{-1}\mathbf{W}_{**}| = 0.$$

Since the determinant is a continuous function of the elements of a matrix

$$(6.90) \qquad \text{plim}\,|T^{-1}\mathbf{W}^{(1)}_{**} - lT^{-1}\mathbf{W}_{**}|$$
$$= |\text{plim}\,T^{-1}\mathbf{W}^{(1)}_{**} - \text{plim}\,l\,\text{plim}\,T^{-1}\mathbf{W}_{**}| = |\boldsymbol{\Omega}^{(1)}_{**} - \text{plim}\,l\boldsymbol{\Omega}_{**}|$$

in view of the definitions in (6.85) and (6.86). Since the root of a polynomial equation is a continuous function of the coefficients of the polynomial the probability limit of the smallest root satisfies

$$(6.91) \qquad |\boldsymbol{\Omega}^{(1)}_{**} - \text{plim}\,\hat{l}\boldsymbol{\Omega}_{**}| = 0,$$

which is the same polynomial (6.84) satisfied by the smallest root $\hat{\lambda} = 1$. Thus plim $\hat{l} = \hat{\lambda} = 1$ or plim $(\hat{l} - 1) = 0$.

Finally it may be noted that when the equation is just-identified LI/LGRV estimation reduces to indirect least squares. Then the unrestricted least-squares estimators of the reduced-form portion $\mathbf{Y}_* = \mathbf{X}\boldsymbol{\Pi}_{X^*} + \mathbf{V}_*$ satisfy the restriction $\boldsymbol{\Pi}_{**,*}\boldsymbol{\gamma}_* = \mathbf{0}$ so that the constrained minimum $|\hat{\mathbf{W}}|$ equals the unconstrained minimum $|\mathbf{W}_{**}|$. Then $\hat{l} = |\hat{\mathbf{W}}|/|\mathbf{W}_{**}| = 1$ by (6.73). LI/LGRV estimation is then identical with 2SLS estimation; the latter, as we have seen, reduces to indirect least squares in the just-identified case.

We may illustrate LI/LGRV estimation with computations on equations from our illustrative models.

For Tintner's meat demand function (3.26*a*) the relevant submatrices are pulled out from (5.22) and (5.23) and the computation of coefficient estimates proceeds:

$$(6.92) \qquad \mathbf{Y}'_*\mathbf{Y}_* = \begin{pmatrix} 1369.54 & -352.44 \\ -352.44 & 1581.49 \end{pmatrix}$$

$$\mathbf{Y}'_*\mathbf{X}_1 = \begin{pmatrix} 3671.91 \\ 8354.59 \end{pmatrix} \qquad (\mathbf{X}'_1\mathbf{X}_1)^{-1} = (83433.65)^{-1}$$

$$(\mathbf{X}'_1\mathbf{X}_1)^{-1}\mathbf{X}'_1\mathbf{Y}_* = (0.044010 \quad 0.100135)$$

$$\mathbf{Y}'_*\mathbf{X}_1(\mathbf{X}'_1\mathbf{X}_1)^{-1}\mathbf{X}'_1\mathbf{Y}_* = \begin{pmatrix} 161.60 & 367.69 \\ 367.69 & 836.59 \end{pmatrix}$$

$$\mathbf{Y}'_*\mathbf{X} = \begin{pmatrix} 3671.91 & -536.48 & 983.86 \\ 8354.59 & 850.33 & 1235.76 \end{pmatrix}$$

$$(\mathbf{X}'\mathbf{X})^{-1}\mathbf{X}'\mathbf{Y}_* = \begin{pmatrix} -0.030839 & 0.096075 \\ -0.344626 & 0.208343 \\ 0.613660 & -0.033902 \end{pmatrix}$$

$$\mathbf{Y}_*'\mathbf{X}(\mathbf{X}'\mathbf{X})^{-1}\mathbf{X}'\mathbf{Y}_* = \begin{pmatrix} 675.40 & 207.69 \\ 207.69 & 937.93 \end{pmatrix}$$

$$\mathbf{W}_{**}^{(1)} = \mathbf{Y}_*'\mathbf{Y}_* - \mathbf{Y}_*'\mathbf{X}_1(\mathbf{X}_1'\mathbf{X}_1)^{-1}\mathbf{X}_1'\mathbf{Y}_* = \begin{pmatrix} 1207.94 & -720.13 \\ -720.13 & 744.90 \end{pmatrix}$$

$$\mathbf{W}_{**} = \mathbf{Y}_*'\mathbf{Y}_* - \mathbf{Y}_*'\mathbf{X}(\mathbf{X}'\mathbf{X})^{-1}\mathbf{X}'\mathbf{Y}_* = \begin{pmatrix} 694.14 & -560.13 \\ -560.13 & 643.56 \end{pmatrix}$$

$$|\mathbf{W}_{**}^{(1)} - \hat{l}\mathbf{W}_{**}| = \begin{vmatrix} 1207.94 - 694.14\hat{l} & -720.13 + 560.13\hat{l} \\ -720.13 + 560.13\hat{l} & 744.90 - 643.56\hat{l} \end{vmatrix}$$

$$= 132{,}975.12\hat{l}^2 - 487{,}713.92\hat{l} + 381{,}207.29 = 0,$$

whence $\hat{l} = 1.1294$

$$(\mathbf{W}_{**}^{(1)} - \hat{l}\mathbf{W}_{**})\hat{\gamma}_* = \begin{pmatrix} 423.98 & -87.52 \\ -87.52 & 18.06 \end{pmatrix}\begin{pmatrix} -1 \\ \hat{a}_1 \end{pmatrix} = \begin{pmatrix} 0 \\ 0 \end{pmatrix}$$

$$\hat{a}_1 = -\frac{87.52}{18.06} = -\frac{423.98}{87.52} = -4.85$$

$$\hat{\beta}_1 = -(\mathbf{X}_1'\mathbf{X}_1)^{-1}\mathbf{X}_1'\mathbf{Y}_*\hat{\gamma}_* = -(0.044010 \quad 0.100135)\begin{pmatrix} -1.00 \\ -4.85 \end{pmatrix}$$

$$= 0.53 = \hat{a}_2$$

Thus the LI/LGRV estimate of Tintner's meat demand function is

$$(6.93a) \qquad y_1 = -4.85y_2 + 0.53x_1.$$

This illustration is intended to illustrate the theory and does not represent efficient computational design. In particular, direct extraction of the smallest root of an M^*-degree polynomial will be impracticable when $M^* > 2$ or 3. For efficient computational procedures, see Chernoff and Divinsky (1953) and Klein (1953, pp. 169–184). These sources also spell out the procedure for estimating asymptotic standard errors. We do not develop the procedure here, but simply indicate results. For Tintner's meat demand function, the LI/LGRV estimate with standard errors is

$$(6.93b) \qquad y_1 = \underset{(5.69)}{-4.85y_2} + \underset{(0.58)}{0.53x_1}.$$

In similar fashion, the LI/LGRV estimate of Klein's consumption function has been found to be

$$(6.94) \qquad C = 17.15 - \underset{(0.19)}{0.22P} + \underset{(0.17)}{0.40P_{-1}} + \underset{(0.05)}{0.82W}.$$

Test of Over-Identifying Restrictions

In the preceding development we have assumed that the zero restrictions —which specify that certain variables are excluded from the structural equation—are correct. It may be desirable to treat this as a hypothesis which is subject to a statistical test. Intuitively, a high value of $\hat{l}$ would be evidence against the validity of the restrictions since it means that the restrictions substantially increase the generalized residual variance. More formally, the hypothesis that the restrictions on the structural equation are valid implies that $r(\mathbf{\Pi}_{**,*}) \leq M^* - 1$, which in turn implies that $\lambda = 1$ where $\hat{\lambda}$ is the smallest root of (6.84). As we have noted, the statistic $T(\hat{l} - 1)$ is then asymptotically distributed as $\chi^2_{K^{**}-M^*+1}$. This provides, at least asymptotically, a test procedure, with large values of $T(\hat{l} - 1)$ leading to rejection of the hypothesis that the restrictions are valid. For if the restrictions are not valid, then $r(\mathbf{\Pi}_{**,*}) = M^*$ so that

$$\mathbf{\Pi}'_{**,*}\mathbf{\Sigma}_{22.1}\mathbf{\Pi}_{**,*}$$

is positive definite; by an extension of (2.7.20) the smallest root $\hat{\lambda} - 1$ of (6.88) is positive; and $\hat{\lambda} > 1$. For further details on this test in the context of LI/LGRV estimation see Koopmans and Hood (1953, pp. 178–183) and for the corresponding test in the context of 2SLS see Basmann (1960*b*).

7. STRUCTURAL ESTIMATION: SYSTEM METHODS

In this section we develop several available methods for consistently and simultaneously estimating the parameters of all (identified) structural equations of a model. Of course, the 2SLS, (*k*)-class, and LI/LGRV methods may be, and indeed are, used to estimate each of the structural equations in turn. Nevertheless, although they do take account of the fact that each equation to be estimated is imbedded in a system of equations, they do so in only a limited way. Reviewing the methods, it will have been seen that in estimating one equation we draw on the rest of system only to tell us what are the excluded predetermined variables—i.e., only to construct $\mathbf{X}_2$. No use is made of the fact that the excluded dependent variables $\mathbf{Y}_{**}$ indeed appear in other equations in the system. No use was made of estimates of the parameters of other structural equations; nor did we use any a priori restrictions on the other structural equations. For example, in estimating Tintner's demand function, we did not use the fact that x_1 was excluded from the supply function. For these reasons, we may refer to the single equation methods of the preceding section as *limited-information* methods: In estimating any structural equation they draw on the rest of the model only to learn what predetermined variables, excluded from this equation, indeed appear in the other structural equations.

The methods to be developed in this section may be termed *full-information* methods: They make use of restrictions on the parameters of the full system in estimating each structural equation. We also refer to them as system methods; they estimate all the structural equations simultaneously. As is true in general, the introduction of further information serves to increase the efficiency of estimation. It is also true that the full-information methods require more complicated computations than did the limited-information methods.

We shall find that the system methods can utilize a priori information on $\mathbf{\Sigma}$ as well as on $\mathbf{\Gamma}$ and $\mathbf{B}$. Hence, when relevant, we extend the specifications of the model to include knowledge that certain elements of $\mathbf{\Sigma}$ are zero—i.e., that the covariances of the disturbances in certain pairs of structural equations are zero.

Three-Stage Least Squares

The *three-stage least-squares* method of consistently estimating the parameters of a structural model was developed by Zellner and Theil (1962).

We introduce the method by presenting an alternative derivation of 2SLS estimation. The structural equation to be estimated is again (6.1), which we write as

$$\text{(7.1)} \qquad \mathbf{y}_1 = \mathbf{Z}_1\boldsymbol{\alpha}_1 + \mathbf{u}_1$$

where

$$\mathbf{y}_1 = \mathbf{y}, \quad \mathbf{u}_1 = \mathbf{u}, \quad \mathbf{Z}_1 = (\mathbf{Y}_1 \quad \mathbf{X}_1), \quad \text{and} \quad \boldsymbol{\alpha}_1 = \begin{pmatrix} \boldsymbol{\gamma}_1 \\ \boldsymbol{\beta}_1 \end{pmatrix}.$$

Premultiplying through by the matrix of observations on all the predetermined variables in the system we obtain

$$\text{(7.2)} \qquad \mathbf{X}'\mathbf{y}_1 = \mathbf{X}'\mathbf{Z}_1\boldsymbol{\alpha}_1 + \mathbf{X}'\mathbf{u}_1.$$

For convenience we assume that all predetermined variables are exogenous variables distributed fully independently of the disturbances; the results however, carry over to the general case. Now let us interpret (7.2) as a regression equation $\mathbf{y}^* = \mathbf{X}^*\boldsymbol{\alpha}_1 + \mathbf{u}^*$ where $\mathbf{y}^* = \mathbf{X}'\mathbf{y}_1$, $\mathbf{X}^* = \mathbf{X}'\mathbf{Z}_1$, and $\mathbf{u}^* = \mathbf{X}'\mathbf{u}_1$. We note that the disturbance is heteroskedastic for

$$\text{(7.3)} \qquad E\mathbf{X}'\mathbf{u}_1\mathbf{u}_1'\mathbf{X} = \mathbf{X}'E(\mathbf{u}_1\mathbf{u}_1')\mathbf{X} = \mathbf{X}'\sigma^2\mathbf{I}\mathbf{X} = \sigma^2\mathbf{X}'\mathbf{X};$$

this suggests that we apply generalized least squares. That is, we estimate $\boldsymbol{\alpha}_1$ by

$$(7.4)\qquad [\mathbf{Z}_1'\mathbf{X}(\mathbf{X}'\mathbf{X})^{-1}\mathbf{X}'\mathbf{Z}_1]\mathbf{a}_1^* = \mathbf{Z}_1'\mathbf{X}(\mathbf{X}'\mathbf{X})^{-1}\mathbf{X}'\mathbf{y}_1.$$

On partitioning, (7.4) will be seen to be just the normal equations of 2SLS. [Incidentally, it will also be seen that if the equation is just-identified so that $K^{**} = M^* - 1$, then the $(K^* + M^* - 1) \times (K^* + K^{**})$ matrix $\mathbf{Z}_1'\mathbf{X}$ will be square and in general nonsingular. Upon premultiplication by $(\mathbf{X}'\mathbf{X})(\mathbf{Z}_1'\mathbf{X})^{-1}$ (7.4) then simplifies to $(\mathbf{X}'\mathbf{Z}_1)\mathbf{a}_1^* = \mathbf{X}'\mathbf{y}_1$ which is a square system with a unique solution. This solution, when written out and rearranged, will be seen to be just that of indirect least squares. This provides another proof of the coincidence of two-stage and indirect least squares in the just-identified case, and also constitutes a more efficient computational design for indirect least squares than that used in Section 5.]

Thus 2SLS may be viewed as an application of generalized least squares to a structural equation. It should be noted that whereas $\mathbf{X}$ is distributed independently of $\mathbf{u}_1$, $\mathbf{X}'\mathbf{Z}_1$ will not be distributed independently of $\mathbf{X}'\mathbf{u}_1$, so that strictly speaking generalized least squares is not applicable to (7.2). Nevertheless, the correlation between $\mathbf{X}'\mathbf{Z}_1$ and $\mathbf{X}'\mathbf{u}_1$ is sufficiently weak that what we have is an extension of generalized least squares which can be shown to be consistent and asymptotically efficient. For future reference we note that the asymptotic covariance matrix of the 2SLS estimators—developed in (6.11)—may be written as

$$(7.5)\qquad \bar{E}(\mathbf{a}_1^* - \boldsymbol{\alpha}_1)(\mathbf{a}_1^* - \boldsymbol{\alpha}_1)' = \bar{E}\sigma^2[\mathbf{Z}_1'\mathbf{X}(\mathbf{X}'\mathbf{X})^{-1}\mathbf{X}'\mathbf{Z}_1]^{-1}.$$

Now this approach to 2SLS suggests an extension to handle all equations simultaneously. We assume that under-identified equations, if there are any, have been dropped. We also assume that identities, if there are any, have been used to eliminate variables from the system. Then what we are considering is a system of M identified structural equations, each with a normalization condition and with zero restrictions on its coefficient vector. Since the identities—which have zero disturbances—have been eliminated it is now reasonable to require, and we do so, that there is no exact linear dependence among the structural disturbances; i.e.,

$$(7.6)\qquad \boldsymbol{\Sigma} \text{ is nonsingular.}$$

Then let us write each structural equation in the form (7.1):

$$(7.7)\qquad \mathbf{y}_m = \mathbf{Z}_m\boldsymbol{\alpha}_m + \mathbf{u}_m \qquad (m = 1, \ldots, M);$$

where in the mth equation $\mathbf{y}_m$ is the vector of observations on the left-hand dependent variable, $\mathbf{Z}_m = (\mathbf{X}_m \;\; \mathbf{Y}_m)$ is the matrix of observations on the included predetermined and right-hand dependent variables, $\boldsymbol{\alpha}_m$ is the coefficient vector of these variables, and $\mathbf{u}_m$ is the structural disturbance vector. These M equations may be written together as

$$\mathbf{y} = \mathbf{Z}\boldsymbol{\alpha} + \mathbf{u} \tag{7.8}$$

where

$$\mathbf{y} = \begin{pmatrix} \mathbf{y}_1 \\ \cdot \\ \cdot \\ \cdot \\ \mathbf{y}_M \end{pmatrix}, \quad \mathbf{Z} = \begin{pmatrix} \mathbf{Z}_1 & \mathbf{0} & \cdots & \mathbf{0} \\ \mathbf{0} & \mathbf{Z}_2 & \cdots & \mathbf{0} \\ \cdot & \cdot & & \cdot \\ \cdot & \cdot & & \cdot \\ \cdot & \cdot & & \cdot \\ \mathbf{0} & \mathbf{0} & \cdots & \mathbf{Z}_M \end{pmatrix} \tag{7.9}$$

$$\boldsymbol{\alpha} = \begin{pmatrix} \boldsymbol{\alpha}_1 \\ \cdot \\ \cdot \\ \cdot \\ \boldsymbol{\alpha}_M \end{pmatrix}, \quad \mathbf{u} = \begin{pmatrix} \mathbf{u}_1 \\ \cdot \\ \cdot \\ \cdot \\ \mathbf{u}_M \end{pmatrix}.$$

Premultiplying each equation of (7.7) by $\mathbf{X}'$, i.e., (7.8) by $\boldsymbol{\Xi}'$, gives

$$\boldsymbol{\Xi}'\mathbf{y} = \boldsymbol{\Xi}'\mathbf{Z}\boldsymbol{\alpha} + \boldsymbol{\Xi}'\mathbf{u} \tag{7.10}$$

where

$$\boldsymbol{\Xi}'\mathbf{y} = \begin{pmatrix} \mathbf{X}'\mathbf{y}_1 \\ \cdot \\ \cdot \\ \cdot \\ \mathbf{X}'\mathbf{y}_M \end{pmatrix}, \quad \boldsymbol{\Xi}'\mathbf{Z} = \begin{pmatrix} \mathbf{X}'\mathbf{Z}_1 & \mathbf{0} & \cdots & \mathbf{0} \\ \mathbf{0} & \mathbf{X}'\mathbf{Z}_2 & \cdots & \mathbf{0} \\ \cdot & \cdot & & \cdot \\ \cdot & \cdot & & \cdot \\ \cdot & \cdot & & \cdot \\ \mathbf{0} & \mathbf{0} & \cdots & \mathbf{X}'\mathbf{Z}_M \end{pmatrix}, \tag{7.11}$$

$$\boldsymbol{\Xi}'\mathbf{u} = \begin{pmatrix} \mathbf{X}'\mathbf{u}_1 \\ \cdot \\ \cdot \\ \cdot \\ \mathbf{X}'\mathbf{u}_M \end{pmatrix}, \quad \boldsymbol{\Xi} = \begin{pmatrix} \mathbf{X} & \mathbf{0} & \cdots & \mathbf{0} \\ \mathbf{0} & \mathbf{X} & \cdots & \mathbf{0} \\ \cdot & \cdot & & \cdot \\ \cdot & \cdot & & \cdot \\ \cdot & \cdot & & \cdot \\ \mathbf{0} & \mathbf{0} & \cdots & \mathbf{X} \end{pmatrix}.$$

Now (7.10) is in the form $\mathbf{y}^* = \mathbf{Z}^*\boldsymbol{\alpha} + \mathbf{u}^*$ and we estimate it by generalized least squares.

The covariance matrix of the disturbance vector $\boldsymbol{\Xi}'\mathbf{u}$ is

$$(7.12) \qquad E\boldsymbol{\Xi}'\mathbf{u}\mathbf{u}'\boldsymbol{\Xi} = E\begin{pmatrix} \mathbf{X}'\mathbf{u}_1 \\ \cdot \\ \cdot \\ \cdot \\ \mathbf{X}'\mathbf{u}_M \end{pmatrix}(\mathbf{u}_1'\mathbf{X} \quad \cdots \quad \mathbf{u}_M\mathbf{X})$$

$$= \begin{pmatrix} \sigma_{11}\mathbf{X}'\mathbf{X} & \cdots & \sigma_{1M}\mathbf{X}'\mathbf{X} \\ \cdot & & \cdot \\ \cdot & & \cdot \\ \cdot & & \cdot \\ \sigma_{M1}\mathbf{X}'\mathbf{X} & \cdots & \sigma_{MM}\mathbf{X}'\mathbf{X} \end{pmatrix} = \boldsymbol{\Sigma} \otimes \mathbf{X}'\mathbf{X}$$

where the $\sigma_{mm'}$ are the elements of $\boldsymbol{\Sigma}$. Direct computation shows that the inverse of this covariance matrix is

$$(7.13) \qquad \begin{pmatrix} \sigma^{11}(\mathbf{X}'\mathbf{X})^{-1} & \cdots & \sigma^{1M}(\mathbf{X}'\mathbf{X})^{-1} \\ \cdot & & \cdot \\ \cdot & & \cdot \\ \cdot & & \cdot \\ \sigma^{M1}(\mathbf{X}'\mathbf{X})^{-1} & \cdots & \sigma^{MM}(\mathbf{X}'\mathbf{X})^{-1} \end{pmatrix} = \boldsymbol{\Sigma}^{-1} \otimes (\mathbf{X}'\mathbf{X})^{-1}$$

where the $\sigma^{mm'}$ are the elements of $\boldsymbol{\Sigma}^{-1}$. Straightforward application of generalized least squares to (7.10) would then lead to estimation of $\boldsymbol{\alpha}$ as

$$(7.14) \qquad \boldsymbol{\alpha}^* = \{\mathbf{Z}'\boldsymbol{\Xi}[\boldsymbol{\Sigma}^{-1} \otimes (\mathbf{X}'\mathbf{X})^{-1}]\boldsymbol{\Xi}'\mathbf{Z}\}^{-1}\mathbf{Z}'\boldsymbol{\Xi}[\boldsymbol{\Sigma}^{-1} \otimes (\mathbf{X}'\mathbf{X})^{-1}]\boldsymbol{\Xi}'\mathbf{y}$$

i.e.,

(7.15)

$$\begin{pmatrix} \boldsymbol{\alpha}_1^* \\ \cdot \\ \cdot \\ \cdot \\ \boldsymbol{\alpha}_M^* \end{pmatrix} = \begin{pmatrix} \sigma^{11}\mathbf{Z}_1'\mathbf{X}(\mathbf{X}'\mathbf{X})^{-1}\mathbf{X}'\mathbf{Z}_1 & \cdots & \sigma^{1M}\mathbf{Z}_1'\mathbf{X}(\mathbf{X}'\mathbf{X})^{-1}\mathbf{X}'\mathbf{Z}_M \\ \cdot & & \cdot \\ \cdot & & \cdot \\ \cdot & & \cdot \\ \sigma^{M1}\mathbf{Z}_M'\mathbf{X}(\mathbf{X}'\mathbf{X})^{-1}\mathbf{X}'\mathbf{Z}_1 & \cdots & \sigma^{MM}\mathbf{Z}_M'\mathbf{X}(\mathbf{X}'\mathbf{X})^{-1}\mathbf{X}'\mathbf{Z}_M \end{pmatrix}^{-1}$$

$$\times \begin{pmatrix} \sigma^{11}\mathbf{Z}_1'\mathbf{X}(\mathbf{X}'\mathbf{X})^{-1}\mathbf{X}'\mathbf{y}_1 + \cdots + \sigma^{1M}\mathbf{Z}_1'\mathbf{X}(\mathbf{X}'\mathbf{X})^{-1}\mathbf{X}'\mathbf{y}_M \\ \cdot \\ \cdot \\ \cdot \\ \sigma^{M1}\mathbf{Z}_M'\mathbf{X}(\mathbf{X}'\mathbf{X})^{-1}\mathbf{X}'\mathbf{y}_1 + \cdots + \sigma^{MM}\mathbf{Z}_M'\mathbf{X}(\mathbf{X}'\mathbf{X})^{-1}\mathbf{X}'\mathbf{y}_M \end{pmatrix}.$$

The matrix $\boldsymbol{\Sigma}$ is unknown, however, so that this straightforward procedure is not operational. Still a consistent estimator of $\boldsymbol{\Sigma}$ is obtainable from the residuals of consistently estimated structural equations: We take

$$s_{mm'} = T^{-1}\hat{\mathbf{u}}_m'\hat{\mathbf{u}}_{m'},$$

where $\hat{\mathbf{u}}_m$ is the vector of residuals from the 2SLS estimated mth structural equation. (Of course, if it is specified a priori that some $\sigma_{mm'} = 0$, then we might take $s_{mm'} = 0$.) Then we arrange the $s_{mm'}$ into the $M \times M$ matrix $\hat{\boldsymbol{\Sigma}}$; $\hat{\boldsymbol{\Sigma}}$ is a consistent estimator of $\boldsymbol{\Sigma}$. Inverting $\hat{\boldsymbol{\Sigma}}$ we obtain $\hat{\boldsymbol{\Sigma}}^{-1}$, the elements of which we write $s^{mm'}$. Then the three-stage least-squares estimator is defined by (7.13)—or (7.14)—with the $s^{mm'}$ replacing the $\sigma^{mm'}$—or $\hat{\boldsymbol{\Sigma}}^{-1}$ replacing $\boldsymbol{\Sigma}^{-1}$. Explicitly the three-stage least-squares (3SLS) estimator is defined by

$$\hat{\boldsymbol{\alpha}} = \{\mathbf{Z}'\boldsymbol{\Xi}[\hat{\boldsymbol{\Sigma}}^{-1} \otimes (\mathbf{X}'\mathbf{X})^{-1}]\boldsymbol{\Xi}'\mathbf{Z}\}^{-1}\mathbf{Z}'\boldsymbol{\Xi}[\hat{\boldsymbol{\Sigma}}^{-1} \otimes (\mathbf{X}'\mathbf{X})^{-1}]\boldsymbol{\Xi}'\mathbf{y} \tag{7.16}$$

i.e.,

$$\begin{pmatrix} \hat{\boldsymbol{\alpha}}_1 \\ \cdot \\ \cdot \\ \cdot \\ \hat{\boldsymbol{\alpha}}_M \end{pmatrix} \tag{7.17}$$

$$= \begin{pmatrix} s^{11}\mathbf{Z}_1'\mathbf{X}(\mathbf{X}'\mathbf{X})^{-1}\mathbf{X}'\mathbf{Z}_1 & \cdots & s^{1M}\mathbf{Z}_1'\mathbf{X}(\mathbf{X}'\mathbf{X})^{-1}\mathbf{X}'\mathbf{Z}_M \\ \cdot & & \cdot \\ \cdot & & \cdot \\ \cdot & & \cdot \\ s^{M1}\mathbf{Z}_M'\mathbf{X}(\mathbf{X}'\mathbf{X})^{-1}\mathbf{X}'\mathbf{Z}_1 & \cdots & s^{MM}\mathbf{Z}_M'\mathbf{X}(\mathbf{X}'\mathbf{X})^{-1}\mathbf{X}'\mathbf{Z}_M \end{pmatrix}^{-1}$$

$$\times \begin{pmatrix} s^{11}\mathbf{Z}_1'\mathbf{X}(\mathbf{X}'\mathbf{X})^{-1}\mathbf{X}'\mathbf{y}_1 + \cdots + s^{1M}\mathbf{Z}_1'\mathbf{X}(\mathbf{X}'\mathbf{X})^{-1}\mathbf{X}'\mathbf{y}_M \\ \cdot \qquad\qquad \cdot \\ \cdot \qquad\qquad \cdot \\ \cdot \qquad\qquad \cdot \\ s^{M1}\mathbf{Z}_M'\mathbf{X}(\mathbf{X}'\mathbf{X})^{-1}\mathbf{X}'\mathbf{y}_1 + \cdots + s^{MM}\mathbf{Z}_M'\mathbf{X}(\mathbf{X}'\mathbf{X})^{-1}\mathbf{X}'\mathbf{y}_M \end{pmatrix}.$$

To repeat, 3SLS estimates of all the structural coefficients of the system are obtained as follows. *Stage one:* Estimate the full reduced-form system. *Stage two:* For each structural equation select the submatrix of the reduced form which refers to the included right-hand dependent variables of that equation, and compute the 2SLS estimates and the residuals from these estimated relations. Use the residuals from these estimated relationships to compute the $s_{mm'}$ forming $\hat{\boldsymbol{\Sigma}}$. *Stage three:* Invert $\hat{\boldsymbol{\Sigma}}$

to obtain the $s^{mm'}$ and use these in (7.16) or (7.17) to obtain the 3SLS estimates. An efficient computational design is given in the Zellner-Theil article; but see Rothenberg and Leenders (1964) for some corrections.

The following results are derived by Zellner and Theil. The asymptotic covariance matrix of the 3SLS coefficient estimators is given by the asymptotic expectation of the inverse matrix on the right of (7.14):

$$\bar{E}(\hat{\boldsymbol{\alpha}} - \boldsymbol{\alpha})(\hat{\boldsymbol{\alpha}} - \boldsymbol{\alpha})' = \bar{E}\{\mathbf{Z}'\boldsymbol{\Xi}[\boldsymbol{\Sigma}^{-1} \otimes (\mathbf{X}'\mathbf{X})^{-1}]\boldsymbol{\Xi}'\mathbf{Z}\}^{-1} \tag{7.18}$$

and is consistently estimated by the corresponding inverse matrix on the right of (7.16). The 3SLS estimators are consistent. In general the 3SLS estimators are more asymptotically efficient than the 2SLS estimators. When the disturbances in the different structural equations are uncorrelated, however, so that $\boldsymbol{\Sigma}$ and $\boldsymbol{\Sigma}^{-1}$ are diagonal, then 3SLS reduces to 2SLS, as may be seen by taking all $s^{mm'} = 0$ $(m \neq m')$ in (7.17). Further, just-identified equations do not help in improving the efficiency of estimation of the other equations. Indeed, if we drop out just-identified equations and proceed with 3SLS estimation of the remaining over-identified set, we obtain as efficient estimates of the latter as we do when all equations are included; and then the 3SLS estimators of the just-identified equations are obtainable in a separate calculation. The results are essentially consequences of the fact that 3SLS is simply an application of Zellner's method, discussed in Section 5.6, for utilizing zero restrictions in a multivariate regression model.

Finally, to illustrate the results of this subsection we present the 3SLS estimates of Klein's consumption function:

$$C = \underset{(1.134)}{16.691} + \underset{(0.108)}{0.123P} + \underset{(0.100)}{0.170P_{-1}} + \underset{(0.039)}{0.782W}. \tag{7.19}$$

Full-Information–Least Generalized Residual Variance Estimators

Another approach to consistent estimation of the parameters of a structural model is one we call the *full-information–least generalized residual variance* method. This FI/LGRV method was developed prior to the 3SLS method by Koopmans, Rubin, and Leipnik (1950). They arrived at the method by application of the maximum likelihood principle under the specification that the structural disturbances are normally distributed, utilizing all the restrictions on the structural equations. For this reason the method is generally known as the "full-information maximum likelihood" method. Most of the properties of these estimators, however, do not depend on normality and maximum likelihood, and it is useful to develop and refer to the method without using those considerations.

The structural system to be estimated is again $\mathbf{Y\Gamma} + \mathbf{XB} + \mathbf{U} = \mathbf{0}$, and we again assume that under-identified equations and identities have been eliminated and that $\boldsymbol{\Sigma}$ is nonsingular. The reduced-form system is $\mathbf{Y} = \mathbf{X}\boldsymbol{\Pi} + \mathbf{V}$; if we had a consistent estimator of $\boldsymbol{\Pi}$ which satisfied all the restrictions, we could obtain consistent estimators of $\boldsymbol{\Gamma}$ and $\mathbf{B}$ in accordance with $\mathbf{B} = -\boldsymbol{\Pi}\boldsymbol{\Gamma}$. Now it will be recalled that the unrestricted classical least-squares estimators of the reduced-form system minimize the generalized residual variance $|T^{-1}\mathbf{V}'\mathbf{V}|$. This suggests that we estimate $\boldsymbol{\Pi}$ by minimizing $|T^{-1}\mathbf{V}'\mathbf{V}|$ subject to all the restrictions; indeed, this defines the FI/LGRV method. To minimize $|T^{-1}\mathbf{V}'\mathbf{V}|$ subject to constraints we may as well minimize $\frac{1}{2}\log|\mathbf{V}'\mathbf{V}|$ subject to the same constraints. Writing the structural system as

$$\text{(7.20)} \qquad \bar{\mathbf{Z}}\mathbf{A} + \mathbf{U} = \mathbf{0}$$

where $\bar{\mathbf{Z}} = (\mathbf{X} \quad \mathbf{Y})$ is the $T \times (K + M)$ matrix of observations on all the variables and $\mathbf{A} = \begin{pmatrix} \mathbf{B} \\ \boldsymbol{\Gamma} \end{pmatrix}$ is the $(K + M) \times M$ matrix of all the structural coefficients, we note that $\mathbf{V}'\mathbf{V} = \boldsymbol{\Gamma}'^{-1}\mathbf{A}'\bar{\mathbf{Z}}'\bar{\mathbf{Z}}\mathbf{A}\boldsymbol{\Gamma}^{-1}$ since $\mathbf{V} = -\mathbf{U}\boldsymbol{\Gamma}^{-1} = \bar{\mathbf{Z}}\mathbf{A}\boldsymbol{\Gamma}^{-1}$. Then

$$\text{(7.21)} \qquad \tfrac{1}{2}\log|\mathbf{V}'\mathbf{V}| = \tfrac{1}{2}\log|\boldsymbol{\Gamma}'^{-1}\mathbf{A}'\bar{\mathbf{Z}}'\bar{\mathbf{Z}}\mathbf{A}\boldsymbol{\Gamma}^{-1}| = \tfrac{1}{2}\log|\boldsymbol{\Gamma}|^{-2}\,|\mathbf{A}'\bar{\mathbf{Z}}'\bar{\mathbf{Z}}\mathbf{A}|$$
$$= -\log|\boldsymbol{\Gamma}| + \tfrac{1}{2}\log|\mathbf{A}'\bar{\mathbf{Z}}'\bar{\mathbf{Z}}\mathbf{A}|$$

is the quantity which is minimized, subject to all the restrictions, to obtain the FI/LGRV estimator of the structural coefficient matrix $\mathbf{A}$. As might be expected the computations are complex, involving the solution of nonlinear equation systems. For computational procedure see Chernoff and Divinsky (1953), Klein (1953, pp. 160–169), and Brown (1959).

It is useful to note that for any choice of $\mathbf{A}$, say $\tilde{\mathbf{A}}$, $\tilde{\mathbf{A}}'\bar{\mathbf{Z}}'\bar{\mathbf{Z}}\tilde{\mathbf{A}}$ is the structural residual covariance matrix:

$$\text{(7.22)} \qquad \tilde{\mathbf{A}}'\bar{\mathbf{Z}}'\bar{\mathbf{Z}}\tilde{\mathbf{A}} = \tilde{\mathbf{U}}'\tilde{\mathbf{U}} = \begin{pmatrix} \tilde{\mathbf{u}}_1'\tilde{\mathbf{u}}_1 & \cdots & \tilde{\mathbf{u}}_1'\tilde{\mathbf{u}}_M \\ \cdot & & \cdot \\ \cdot & & \cdot \\ \cdot & & \cdot \\ \tilde{\mathbf{u}}_M'\tilde{\mathbf{u}}_1 & \cdots & \tilde{\mathbf{u}}_M'\tilde{\mathbf{u}}_M \end{pmatrix}.$$

The asymptotic covariance matrix of the FI/LGRV estimators and a proof of their consistency have been obtained by Koopmans, Rubin, and Leipnik (1950, pp. 133–153). Rothenberg and Leenders (1964) have obtained a very convenient form for the covariance matrix. In the notation of the preceding subsection let $\mathbf{Z}_m$ and $\boldsymbol{\alpha}_m$ be the observation matrix of the right-hand variables and coefficient vector in the mth equation, let

$$\boldsymbol{\alpha} = \begin{pmatrix} \boldsymbol{\alpha}_1 \\ \cdot \\ \cdot \\ \cdot \\ \boldsymbol{\alpha}_M \end{pmatrix}, \qquad \mathbf{Z} = \begin{pmatrix} \mathbf{Z}_1 & \mathbf{0} & \cdots & \mathbf{0} \\ \mathbf{0} & \mathbf{Z}_2 & \cdots & \mathbf{0} \\ \cdot & \cdot & & \cdot \\ \cdot & \cdot & & \cdot \\ \cdot & \cdot & & \cdot \\ \mathbf{0} & \mathbf{0} & \cdots & \mathbf{Z}_M \end{pmatrix},$$

and let $\boldsymbol{\Xi}$ be as defined in (7.11). Then the asymptotic covariance matrix of the FI/LGRV estimators is given by

$$\text{(7.23)} \qquad \bar{E}(\tilde{\boldsymbol{\alpha}} - \boldsymbol{\alpha})(\tilde{\boldsymbol{\alpha}} - \boldsymbol{\alpha})' = \bar{E}\{\mathbf{Z}'\boldsymbol{\Xi}[\boldsymbol{\Sigma}^{-1} \otimes (\mathbf{X}'\mathbf{X})^{-1}]\boldsymbol{\Xi}'\mathbf{Z}\}^{-1}.$$

Note that $\boldsymbol{\alpha}_m$ is the mth column of $\mathbf{A}$ after deletion of (a) the coefficients known to be zero and (b) the coefficient normalized at -1; these coefficients are known a priori and hence have no sampling variability. [Strictly, Rothenberg and Leenders derive (7.23) under the assumptions that the disturbances are normally distributed and that the predetermined variables are nonstochastic; their result presumably remains valid under the weaker assumptions of our model.] Now (7.23) will be recognized as the asymptotic covariance matrix of the 3SLS estimators; thus as a general result 3SLS and FI/LGRV estimators are on a par with respect to consistency and asymptotic efficiency.

It is instructive to note how (7.21) simplifies in some interesting special cases. First, consider the case where the system is *recursive*, i.e., where the structural equations may be arranged so that $\boldsymbol{\Gamma}$ is an upper triangular matrix—i.e., has only zeros below the diagonal. In such a case the normalization rule may be used to make each diagonal element of $\boldsymbol{\Gamma}$ equal to -1, so that $|\boldsymbol{\Gamma}| = \pm 1$, and we need only minimize the generalized *structural* residual variance

$$\text{(7.24)} \qquad |\mathbf{A}'\bar{\mathbf{Z}}'\bar{\mathbf{Z}}\mathbf{A}|,$$

subject of course to all the restrictions on the structural parameters. For an example consider the market model:

$$\text{(7.25}a\text{)} \qquad \text{Supply: } Q = \beta P_{-1} + u,$$

$$\text{(7.25}b\text{)} \qquad \text{Demand: } P = \gamma Q^* + u^*,$$

$$\text{(7.25}c\text{)} \qquad \text{Market clearing: } Q^* = Q,$$

where Q = quantity supplied, Q^* = quantity demanded, and P = price are the dependent variables; and P_{-1} = lagged price is predetermined.

After using the "identity" (7.25*c*) to eliminate Q^* the structural model is

$$(7.26) \qquad (Q \quad P)\begin{pmatrix} -1 & \gamma \\ 0 & -1 \end{pmatrix} + P_{-1}(\beta \quad 0) + (u \quad u^*) = 0,$$

and we see that $|\mathbf{\Gamma}| = 1$.

Next, consider the case where the system is *diagonal*, i.e., where it is known a priori that disturbances in all the structural equations are uncorrelated so that the disturbance covariance matrix $\mathbf{\Sigma}$ is a diagonal matrix—i.e., has only zeros off the diagonal. In that case this information will naturally be used to set the off-diagonal elements of $\mathbf{A}'\bar{\mathbf{Z}}'\bar{\mathbf{Z}}\mathbf{A}$ equal to zero, in which case $|\mathbf{A}'\bar{\mathbf{Z}}'\bar{\mathbf{Z}}\mathbf{A}|$ will be taken to be the product of its diagonal elements and the quantity to be minimized simplified to

$$(7.27) \qquad -\log|\mathbf{\Gamma}| + \tfrac{1}{2}\log[(\mathbf{u}_1'\mathbf{u}_1)\cdots(\mathbf{u}_M'\mathbf{u}_M)]$$
$$= -\log|\mathbf{\Gamma}| + \tfrac{1}{2}\log(\mathbf{u}_1'\mathbf{u}_1) + \cdots + \tfrac{1}{2}\log(\mathbf{u}_M'\mathbf{u}_M).$$

Finally, consider the case where the system is *diagonally recursive*, i.e., where $\mathbf{\Sigma}$ is diagonal and $\mathbf{\Gamma}$ is triangular. In that case the quantity to be minimized is reduced to

$$(7.28) \qquad \tfrac{1}{2}(\log \mathbf{u}_1'\mathbf{u}_1 + \cdots + \log \mathbf{u}_M'\mathbf{u}_M),$$

whence it is apparent that the FI/LGRV estimators may be obtained equation by equation by classical least squares applied to each structural equation individually. In each equation, as the regressand we take the dependent variable whose coefficient in that equation has been normalized as -1, and as the regressors all the other variables except those whose coefficients in that equation have been specified to be zero. The simplicity of the estimation procedure in the diagonally recursive case is attributable to the fact that despite appearances the system is a chain rather than a simultaneous system. If in the model of (7.25), e.g., it is known that $Euu^* = 0$ then the workings of the system are as follows. "First," the quantity supplied is determined by (7.25*a*); "then," this quantity is sold by (7.25*c*) at a price determined by (7.25*b*). This interpretation is not available if $Euu^* \neq 0$. Note also that although single-equation least squares is appropriate in the diagonally recursive case, an analysis of the full model was needed to discover that fact and also to tell us which variable should be the regressand in which equation. Thus in our example we found that γ should be estimated as the slope of the regression of P on Q^* and not as the reciprocal of the slope of Q^* on P.

When a priori information on the disturbance covariance matrix $\mathbf{\Sigma}$ is employed we expect a gain in efficiency. Rothenberg and Leenders have shown that this is indeed the case; so that the asymptotic covariance matrix of the estimators are given not by (7.23) but by (7.23) less a non-negative definite matrix.

Finally, for comparison with prior illustrations, we present the results of FI/LGRV estimation of Klein's consumption function obtained on the specification that $\mathbf{\Sigma}$ is diagonal:

(7.29) $$C = 16.78 + 0.02P + 0.23P_{-1} + 0.80W;$$

standard errors are not available.

Maximum Likelihood Estimation

If to the statistical specifications of our model we add the assumption that the structural disturbances are normal,

(7.30) $\mathbf{u}(t)$ is normally distributed $(t = 1, \ldots, T)$,

we have the simultaneous linear normal structural equation model. Since the reduced-form disturbance vector $\mathbf{v}(t)$ is a linear function of $\mathbf{u}(t)$, it too is normally distributed and its density is

(7.31) $$f[\mathbf{v}(t)] \doteq (2\pi)^{-M/2}\,|\mathbf{\Omega}|^{-1/2} \exp\{-\tfrac{1}{2}\mathbf{v}'(t)\mathbf{\Omega}^{-1}\mathbf{v}(t)\}.$$

Then since the disturbances are temporally independent the likelihood of the sample is

(7.32) $$\mathscr{L} = \prod_{t=1}^{T} f[\mathbf{v}(t)] = (2\pi)^{-MT/2}|\mathbf{\Omega}|^{-T/2} \exp\left\{-\tfrac{1}{2}\sum_{t=1}^{T} \mathbf{v}'(t)\mathbf{\Omega}^{-1}\mathbf{v}(t)\right\}.$$

Then we may consider estimation by the maximum likelihood principle. It can be shown that maximizing this likelihood function is equivalent to minimizing the generalized reduced-form residual variance. (We have already seen this in our discussion of the multivariate regression model in Section 4.11.) In particular, it has been shown that if we maximize the likelihood function subject to all the restrictions on the model we are led to the FI/LGRV method—see Koopmans and Hood (1953, pp. 143–162); while if we maximize the likelihood function subject only to the restrictions on a single structural equation we are led to the LI/LGRV method—see Koopmans and Hood (1953, pp. 162–177). This accounts for the usual names "full-information maximum likelihood" and "limited-information maximum likelihood" for what we have termed FI/LGRV and LI/LGRV respectively. It also indicates that when the disturbances are normally distributed the LGRV estimators are asymptotically efficient as well as consistent. Note that since it uses more a priori information FI/LGRV is more efficient asymptotically than LI/LGRV.

8. COMPARISON OF ALTERNATIVE STRUCTURAL ESTIMATION METHODS

Choice of Alternative Methods

In the preceding sections we have developed alternative methods for consistent estimation of the structural parameters in the simultaneous structural linear equation model. For estimating a single structural equation we have seen that consistent estimators are obtainable by 2SLS, by LI/LGRV, or indeed by any other (k) estimator for which $\text{plim}\,(k - 1) = 0$. (We have also seen that if the equation is just-identified, both 2SLS and LI/LGRV reduce to indirect least squares.) For estimating all the structural equations we have seen that consistent estimators are obtainable by applying any of those single-equation methods to each equation in turn, by 3SLS, or by FI/LGRV.

Now this situation is analogous to that of classical linear regression, where many unbiased estimators of the coefficient vector were available—e.g., all linear estimators $\mathbf{C}'\mathbf{y}$ for which $\mathbf{C}'\mathbf{X} = \mathbf{I}$. In that case, the *embarrass du choix* was resolved by introduction of the additional criterion of efficiency. Restricting our attention to linear estimators, we sought—and found—the unbiased estimator with minimum variance. It might be expected that the analogous approach would be taken in the simultaneous structural equation case. That is, restricting our attention to some broad class of estimators, we should seek the consistent estimator with minimum asymptotic variance.

This program has not yet been carried out, however—for several reasons. First, the mathematical complexities involved in the simultaneous structural equation model have hampered analytic work in this area. Second, the computational complexities of the estimation methods have maintained interest in methods which are computationally simpler though clearly less efficient. (In the language of statistical decision theory, computational cost has been included in the cost function.) Third, the cold comfort provided by desirable asymptotic properties when only small samples are available has stimulated interest in small-sample properties of the estimators.

Thus we are unable at present to propose a single estimation procedure as the best one. Instead, in this section we survey some of the information available on the performance of the alternative estimators of the structural parameters.

Asymptotic Efficiency

Considering first the single-equation methods, we have seen that all (k) estimators which have $\text{plim}\, T^{1/2}(k - 1) = 0$ are not only consistent and hence asymptotically unbiased but have the same asymptotic covariance matrix. In particular, then, 2SLS and LI/LGRV estimators have equal asymptotic efficiency. It has also been noted that when the disturbances are normally distributed, LI/LGRV is the maximum-likelihood estimator. This implies that in that case LI/LGRV—and of course 2SLS, which shares the same asymptotic covariance matrix—is at least as efficient asymptotically as any other estimator which uses the same amount of information.

Turning to the systems methods we have seen that 3SLS and FI/LGRV estimators have the same asymptotic covariance matrix. Thus they have equal asymptotic efficiency. It has also been noted that when the disturbances are normally distributed, FI/LGRV is the maximum likelihood estimator. This implies that in that case FI/LGRV—and of course 3SLS which shares the same asymptotic covariance matrix—is at least as efficient asymptotically as any other estimator which uses the same amount of information.

As between the systems methods and the single-equation methods we may rely on the general rule that estimators which use more information are more efficient. It may be instructive to consider explicitly the two-equation case $M = 2$. The asymptotic covariance matrix of the 2SLS (or LI/LGRV) estimator of the coefficients of the first structural equation is, from (7.5),

$$\sigma_{11}\bar{E}[\mathbf{Z}_1'\mathbf{X}(\mathbf{X}'\mathbf{X})^{-1}\mathbf{X}'\mathbf{Z}_1]^{-1} \tag{8.1}$$

while the asymptotic covariance matrix of the 3SLS (or FI/LGRV) estimator of these coefficients is, from (7.18), the upper left-hand submatrix of

$$\begin{pmatrix} \sigma^{11}\bar{E}[\mathbf{Z}_1'\mathbf{X}(\mathbf{X}'\mathbf{X})^{-1}\mathbf{X}'\mathbf{Z}_1] & \sigma^{12}\bar{E}[\mathbf{Z}_1'\mathbf{X}(\mathbf{X}'\mathbf{X})^{-1}\mathbf{X}'\mathbf{Z}_2] \\ \sigma^{21}\bar{E}[\mathbf{Z}_2'\mathbf{X}(\mathbf{X}'\mathbf{X})^{-1}\mathbf{X}'\mathbf{Z}_1] & \sigma^{22}\bar{E}[\mathbf{Z}_2'\mathbf{X}(\mathbf{X}'\mathbf{X})^{-1}\mathbf{X}'\mathbf{Z}_2] \end{pmatrix}^{-1}. \tag{8.2}$$

Then an analysis parallel to that of (5.6.44)–(5.6.50) will show that the asymptotic covariance matrix of 2SLS equals that of 3SLS plus a nonnegative definite matrix. Zellner and Theil (1962, pp. 61–63) show that that nonnegative definite matrix will be zero if the disturbances are uncorrelated or if the second equation is just-identified, which are the conditions under which 3SLS estimation of the first equation yields no gain over 2SLS estimation.

We should recall an exception to the general rule that 3SLS and FI/LGRV are equally efficient asymptotically. When a priori information on the disturbance covariance matrix $\mathbf{\Sigma}$ is available and is exploited in the FI/LGRV method, then, as noted in Section 7, the asymptotic variances of the estimators are reduced; see Rothenberg and Leenders (1964).

At present it seems that 3SLS is unable to utilize such information as adequately as FI/LGRV.

It has been argued by some that despite their inconsistency, classical least-squares estimators retain a minimum variance property. Consider again a single structural equation

$$\mathbf{y} = \mathbf{Z}_1\boldsymbol{\alpha}_1 + \mathbf{u}. \tag{8.3}$$

The classical least-squares estimator of $\boldsymbol{\alpha}_1$ is $\bar{\mathbf{a}}_1 = (\mathbf{Z}_1'\mathbf{Z}_1)^{-1}\mathbf{Z}_1'\mathbf{y}$; its asymptotic expectation is clearly

$$\text{plim}\ \bar{\mathbf{a}}_1 = \boldsymbol{\alpha}_1 + \text{plim}\ (T^{-1}\mathbf{Z}_1'\mathbf{Z}_1)^{-1}\ \text{plim}\ (T^{-1}\mathbf{Z}_1'\mathbf{u}) = \boldsymbol{\alpha}_1 + \mathbf{G}^{-1}\mathbf{g}, \tag{8.4}$$

say, where $\mathbf{G} = \text{plim}\ (T^{-1}\mathbf{Z}_1'\mathbf{Z}_1)$ and $\mathbf{g} = \text{plim}\ (T^{-1}\mathbf{Z}_1'\mathbf{u})$. Let us rewrite (8.3) as

$$\mathbf{y} = \mathbf{Z}_1(\boldsymbol{\alpha}_1 + \mathbf{G}^{-1}\mathbf{g}) + \mathbf{u} - \mathbf{Z}_1\mathbf{G}^{-1}\mathbf{g} = \mathbf{Z}_1\bar{\boldsymbol{\alpha}}_1 + \bar{\mathbf{u}}, \tag{8.5}$$

say, where $\bar{\boldsymbol{\alpha}}_1 = \boldsymbol{\alpha}_1 + \mathbf{G}^{-1}\mathbf{g}$ and $\bar{\mathbf{u}} = \mathbf{u} - \mathbf{Z}_1\mathbf{G}^{-1}\mathbf{g}$. Now by construction $\mathbf{Z}_1$ and $\bar{\mathbf{u}}$ are contemporaneously uncorrelated—

$$\begin{aligned}\text{plim}\ (T^{-1}\mathbf{Z}_1'\bar{\mathbf{u}}) &= \text{plim}\ (T^{-1}\mathbf{Z}_1'\mathbf{u}) - \text{plim}\ (T^{-1}\mathbf{Z}_1'\mathbf{Z}_1\mathbf{G}^{-1}\mathbf{g}) \\ &= \mathbf{g} - \mathbf{G}\mathbf{G}^{-1}\mathbf{g} = \mathbf{0}.\end{aligned}$$

If we assume that the predetermined variables as well as the disturbances *are temporally independent*, then the constructed disturbance $\bar{\mathbf{u}}$ will be temporally uncorrelated. It follows that the contemporaneously uncorrelated model is applicable to (8.5) so that $\bar{\mathbf{a}}_1$ is a consistent and asymptotically unbiased estimator of $\bar{\boldsymbol{\alpha}}_1$—which after all is its asymptotic expectation by construction—and the asymptotic covariance matrix of $\bar{\mathbf{a}}_1$ is given by

$$\bar{\boldsymbol{\Sigma}}_{\bar{\mathbf{a}}_1\bar{\mathbf{a}}_1} = \bar{E}(\bar{\mathbf{a}}_1 - \bar{\boldsymbol{\alpha}}_1)(\bar{\mathbf{a}}_1 - \bar{\boldsymbol{\alpha}}_1)' = T^{-1}\sigma^2_{-}\mathbf{G}^{-1} \tag{8.6}$$

where σ^2_{-} is the variance of $\bar{\mathbf{u}}$. For comparison we have the asymptotic covariance matrix of the 2SLS estimator of (8.3) which may be written as

$$\bar{\boldsymbol{\Sigma}}_{\mathbf{a}_1^*\mathbf{a}_1^*} = \bar{E}(\mathbf{a}_1^* - \boldsymbol{\alpha}_1)(\mathbf{a}_1^* - \boldsymbol{\alpha}_1)' = T^{-1}\sigma^2\mathbf{H}^{-1} \tag{8.7}$$

where $\mathbf{H} = \text{plim}\ [T^{-1}\mathbf{Z}_1'\mathbf{X}(\mathbf{X}'\mathbf{X})^{-1}\mathbf{X}'\mathbf{Z}_1]$. Let us write

$$\begin{aligned}\bar{\boldsymbol{\Sigma}}_{\mathbf{a}_1^*\mathbf{a}_1^*} &= T^{-1}[\sigma^2_{-}\mathbf{G}^{-1} + \sigma^2(\mathbf{H}^{-1} - \mathbf{G}^{-1}) + (\sigma^2 - \sigma^2_{-})\mathbf{G}^{-1}] \\ &= \bar{\boldsymbol{\Sigma}}_{\bar{\mathbf{a}}_1\bar{\mathbf{a}}_1} + T^{-1}[\sigma^2(\mathbf{H}^{-1} - \mathbf{G}^{-1}) + (\sigma^2 - \sigma^2_{-})\mathbf{G}^{-1}].\end{aligned} \tag{8.8}$$

Now $\mathbf{G}$ is positive definite and $\mathbf{G} - \mathbf{H}$ is nonnegative definite [$\mathbf{Z}_1'\mathbf{Z}_1 - \mathbf{Z}_1'\mathbf{X}(\mathbf{X}'\mathbf{X})^{-1}\mathbf{X}'\mathbf{Z}_1$ may be interpreted as the moment matrix of residuals from the least-squares regression of $\mathbf{Z}_1$ on $\mathbf{X}$]; thus

(8.9) $\mathbf{G}^{-1}$ is positive definite; $\mathbf{H}^{-1} - \mathbf{G}^{-1}$ is nonnegative definite.

But also since $\sigma^2 = \text{plim } T^{-1}\mathbf{u}'\mathbf{u}$, $\sigma^2_- = \text{plim } T^{-1}\bar{\mathbf{u}}'\bar{\mathbf{u}}$, and $\bar{\mathbf{u}} = \mathbf{u} - \mathbf{Z}_1\mathbf{G}^{-1}\mathbf{g}$ we have

$$(8.10) \qquad \begin{aligned} \sigma^2_- &= \text{plim } (T^{-1}\bar{\mathbf{u}}'\bar{\mathbf{u}}) \\ &= \text{plim } (T^{-1}\mathbf{u}'\mathbf{u}) + \mathbf{g}'\mathbf{G}^{-1} \text{ plim } (T^{-1}\mathbf{Z}_1'\mathbf{Z}_1)\mathbf{G}^{-1}\mathbf{g} \\ &\quad - \mathbf{g}'\mathbf{G}^{-1} \text{ plim } (T^{-1}\mathbf{Z}_1'\mathbf{u}) - \text{plim } (T^{-1}\mathbf{u}'\mathbf{Z}_1)\mathbf{G}^{-1}\mathbf{g} \\ &= \sigma^2 + \mathbf{g}'\mathbf{G}^{-1}\mathbf{G}\mathbf{G}^{-1}\mathbf{g} - \mathbf{g}'\mathbf{G}^{-1}\mathbf{g} - \mathbf{g}'\mathbf{G}^{-1}\mathbf{g} = \sigma^2 - \mathbf{g}'\mathbf{G}^{-1}\mathbf{g}. \end{aligned}$$

Now $\mathbf{g}'\mathbf{G}^{-1}\mathbf{g} > 0$ since $\mathbf{G}^{-1}$ is positive definite and $\mathbf{g} \neq \mathbf{0}$; thus

$$(8.11) \qquad \sigma^2 > \sigma^2_-$$

In view of (8.9) and (8.11) the term in square brackets in (8.8) must be positive definite. We conclude that at least in the case considered classical least-squares estimation retains a minimum variance property; the asymptotic variances of the classical least-squares estimators (about their expectations) are less than the asymptotic variances of the corresponding 2SLS estimators.

This analysis suggests that for small samples the second moments of the classical least-squares estimators (about the true parameter values) may be less than those of the 2SLS estimators—their variances may be sufficiently small to compensate for their bias. It should be emphasized, however, that as the sample size increases, the variances of both classical least squares and 2SLS go to zero, but the bias of classical least squares persists.

Small-Sample Properties

Little analytic work is available on the small-sample properties of structural estimators. Basmann (1961) has derived the exact density distribution of the 2SLS estimators for a special two-equation model in which the disturbances are normally distributed and are fully independent of the predetermined variables. Nagar (1959*a*) has obtained approximate means and covariance matrices of (k) estimators in more general models. His analysis suggests several other interesting members of the (k) estimator family.

Considerably more experimental or "Monte Carlo" work is available; Johnston (1963, pp. 275–295) provides a convenient survey of this research. The experimental or "Monte Carlo" approach may be described as follows. A structural model is set up with specified values of the structural coefficient matrices $\mathbf{\Gamma}$ and $\mathbf{B}$ and with a specified probability distribution of the disturbances. Values are specified for the exogenous variables. The known structure and known values of the exogenous variables, together with random drawings from the specified disturbance probability distribution, are used to generate a sample of size 20, e.g., of observations on the endogenous variables. From this sample estimates of the population parameters are obtained by several estimation methods. This procedure is replicated many times, say 100—each time consists of drawing a fresh sample of disturbances while keeping the structure and the exogenous variables fixed, generating the endogenous variables,. and estimating the parameters by alternative methods. Then the empirical frequency distributions of the estimates are tabulated and compared with the known population parameters. Taking the empirical frequency distributions (which are based on 100 samples) as approximations to the true sampling distributions (which are based on an infinity of samples) permits us to conjecture the small-sample properties of the estimators. (In this description we have treated the predetermined variables as fixed in repeated samples; alternatively, their values may be generated by random drawings from specified distributions, or, when they are lagged endogenous variables, their values are generated, observation by observation, within each sample).

The approach may be illustrated with one set of results obtained by Basmann (1958). The structure is specified to be

(8.12*a*)
$$-y_1 - 2y_2 + 1.5y_3 + 3x_1 - 0.6x_5 + 10 = u_1$$

(8.12*b*)
$$1.5y_1 - y_2 + 0.5x_1 + 1.5x_2 + 2x_3 - 2.5x_4 + 12 = u_2$$

(8.12*c*)
$$0.1y_1 - 4y_2 - y_3 + 1.6x_1 - 3.5x_2 + 1.2x_4 + 0.4x_5 - 5 = u_3$$

where the u's are normally distributed with zero expectations and covariance matrix

$$\Sigma = E\begin{pmatrix} u_1 \\ u_2 \\ u_3 \end{pmatrix}(u_1 \quad u_2 \quad u_3) \tag{8.13}$$
$$= \begin{pmatrix} 721.5315 & -199.0370 & -347.6670 \\ & 1219.7597 & 335.3136 \\ & & 507.6689 \end{pmatrix}$$

and values of the x's are specified for $t = 1, \ldots, 16$. Then 200 samples of size 16 are generated and for each sample estimates of the coefficients of the first structural equation (8.12*a*) are obtained by classical least squares [CLS in (8.14)], by 2SLS, and by LI/LGRV estimation. The summary measures of the frequency distributions of the estimates shown in (8.14) are found. There, denoting the estimate of a parameter α from

(8.14)

	True value of parameter				
	−2.00	1.50	3.00	−0.60	10.00
Mean					
CLS	−0.89	1.13	2.33	−0.59	−10.69
2SLS	−1.94	1.47	2.95	−0.65	15.28
LI/LGRV	−2.69	1.66	3.53	−0.60	−4.00
Bias					
CLS	1.11	−0.37	−0.67	0.01	−20.69
2SLS	0.06	−0.03	−0.05	−0.05	5.28
LI/LGRV	−0.69	0.16	0.53	−0.03	−14.00
Variance					
CLS	1.01	0.05	1.08	0.46	22.6×10^3
2SLS	2.43	0.14	2.10	0.63	30.3×10^3
LI/LGRV	17.39	1.08	14.97	1.74	101.6×10^3
Second moment					
CLS	2.24	0.19	1.53	0.46	23.0×10^3
2SLS	2.43	0.14	2.10	0.63	30.3×10^3
LI/LGRV	17.89	1.11	15.25	1.74	101.8×10^3

the ith sample by a_i and letting Σ denote summation over i ($i = 1, \ldots, 200$), the summary statistics are: The mean $\bar{a} = \Sigma\, a_i/200$; the bias $b = \bar{a} - \alpha$; the variance $v = \Sigma\, (a_i - \bar{a})^2/200$; and the second moment about α, $m = \Sigma\, (a_i - \alpha)^2/200 = v + b^2$. Briefly surveying these results we note that the asymptotically unbiased estimators (2SLS and LI/LGRV) generally had smaller biases than did the asymptotically biased estimator (CLS)—with 2SLS generally having the smallest; that the CLS estimator always had the smallest variance, with 2SLS having the next smallest; and that the variance of CLS was sufficiently small to give it generally the smallest second moment, with 2SLS having the next smallest.

To be sure, the quantitative results are specific to the numerical model employed. Still, some of the qualitative features of Basmann's study have been found in the other Monte Carlo studies: The consistent estimators tend to have smaller biases, classical least squares tends to have smaller variances, and on the second-moment criterion one of the consistent estimators tends to perform about as well as classical least squares. It is interesting—and encouraging—to recognize that this means that the asymptotic theory apparently provides a good guide to the small-sample theory.

The results of such Monte Carlo studies are of interest only if the specified structures capture the crucial features of the real world. It is also worthwhile to compare the estimates obtained by applying alternative methods to some set of real-world data. In such comparisons the true structure is unknown and repeated samples are rarely available. Still we may obtain some feel for the way in which the estimators differ when applied to a single sample. In the preceding sections we have presented alternative estimates for the consumption function of Klein's Model I and for Tintner's meat market model. Tabulated estimates of the other functions of Klein's Model I may be found in Nagar (1959*b*, p. 68) and in Rothenberg and Leenders (1964). Tabulated CLS and LI/LGRV estimates of the parameters of the twenty-equation Klein-Goldberger model of the United States are given in Fox (1958, pp. 264–265). Another model for which alternative estimates have been computed is the five-equation Girschik-Haavelmo model of the United States food market; Theil (1961, p. 237) gives a graphic representation of the (k) estimates of this model for all values of k between 0 and 1.5.

Computational Properties

Considering first the single-equation methods it is clear that classical least squares is the simplest from the computational point of view. In addition, 2SLS is simpler than LI/LGRV estimation; the latter involves the extraction of the smallest root of an M^*th-degree polynomial, a calculation which may be tedious for $M^* > 2$. The systems methods are more complicated than the single-equation methods. Moreover, 3SLS is simpler than FI/LGRV; the latter involves the solution of systems of nonlinear equations. Rothenberg and Leenders (1964) have proposed a modification of FI/LGRV to remove this difficulty. Their "linearized maximum likelihood" method involves solving only linear equations and, at least under the assumption that the disturbances are normally distributed, has the same asymptotic covariance matrix as does FI/LGRV.

Conclusions

Although information presently available precludes the selection of one structural estimation method as the best, it does permit the following tentative conclusions. If computational costs restrict us to single-equation methods, then 2SLS seems to be the most preferable. Otherwise 3SLS seems to be preferable; except when a priori information on the disturbance covariance matrix $\mathbf{\Sigma}$ is available, in which case FI/LGRV or its linearized version should be chosen. It should be noted that the LGRV computations treat all the included dependent variables in a structural equation symmetrically until the end, whereas 2SLS and 3SLS require that one included dependent variable be chosen as the left-hand one from the start.

9. APPLICATIONS OF STRUCTURAL ECONOMETRIC MODELS

In the preceding sections we have concentrated on the estimation of the structural parameters in the simultaneous structural linear equation model. Assuming that consistent estimates of these parameters and of the variances and covariances of the structural coefficients have been obtained, we now consider some applications.

Structural Model

An obvious application of an estimated structural model is to the testing of economic hypotheses. Where the hypothesis refers to a single structural coefficient α_i, the test will naturally be based on $t_i = (a_i - \alpha_i)/s_{a_i}$, where a_i is the estimate of α_i and where s_{a_i} is the estimated asymptotic standard error of a_i—i.e., the square root of a consistent estimate of the asymptotic variance of a_i. Under general conditions the asymptotic distribution of t_i is $\mathcal{N}(0, 1)$ so that the standard test procedure may be used as an approximation. Similarly asymptotic confidence intervals may be based on t_i. Also, where our interest is in hypothesis testing or confidence regions for sets of structural coefficients, approximate procedures will be based on those developed in the classical linear regression model.

Derived Reduced Forms

For many applications we are interested in the reduced form rather than the structural form of the model. For example, in Klein's Model I we may be interested not merely in the direct effect of "technological change" on private wages as given by the structural coefficient c_3 in (3.29c) but of its effect after taking account of the mutual interdependence of the wages and national product. Or, in that model, we may be interested in the effect of government expenditures on consumption. For such applications the reduced form is required. Now, given $\hat{\mathbf{\Gamma}}$ and $\hat{\mathbf{B}}$, estimates of the structural coefficient matrices $\mathbf{\Gamma}$ and $\mathbf{B}$, we may estimate the reduced-form coefficient matrix $\mathbf{\Pi}$ by the derived reduced-form coefficient matrix

$$\hat{\mathbf{\Pi}} = -\hat{\mathbf{B}}\hat{\mathbf{\Gamma}}^{-1}. \tag{9.1}$$

Then since $\mathbf{\Pi} = -\mathbf{B}\mathbf{\Gamma}^{-1}$ and $\text{plim}\ \hat{\mathbf{\Pi}} = -\text{plim}\ \hat{\mathbf{B}}\ \text{plim}\ \hat{\mathbf{\Gamma}}^{-1}$, $\hat{\mathbf{\Pi}}$ will be consistent if $\hat{\mathbf{\Gamma}}$ and $\hat{\mathbf{B}}$ are. Given also $\hat{\mathbf{\Sigma}}$, an estimate of the structural disturbance covariance matrix $\mathbf{\Sigma}$, we may estimate the reduced-form disturbance covariance matrix $\mathbf{\Omega}$ by the derived reduced-form residual covariance matrix

$$(9.2) \qquad \hat{\mathbf{\Omega}} = \hat{\mathbf{\Gamma}}'^{-1} \hat{\mathbf{\Sigma}} \hat{\mathbf{\Gamma}}^{-1}.$$

Again since $\mathbf{\Omega} = \mathbf{\Gamma}'^{-1} \mathbf{\Sigma} \mathbf{\Gamma}^{-1}$ and $\text{plim}\ \hat{\mathbf{\Omega}} = \text{plim}\ \hat{\mathbf{\Gamma}}'^{-1}\ \text{plim}\ \hat{\mathbf{\Sigma}}\ \text{plim}\ \hat{\mathbf{\Gamma}}^{-1}$, $\hat{\mathbf{\Omega}}$ will be consistent if $\hat{\mathbf{\Gamma}}$ and $\hat{\mathbf{\Sigma}}$ are. In addition, by the familiar invariance property these derived reduced-form estimates will be maximum-likelihood estimates if the structural estimates are.

To illustrate, the indirect least-squares estimates of the structural coefficients of the simple Keynesian model are, from (2.38), in the notation of (3.24) but omitting the constant term,

$$(9.3a) \qquad \hat{\mathbf{\Gamma}} = \begin{pmatrix} -1.000 & 1.000 \\ 0.672 & -1.000 \end{pmatrix}, \qquad \hat{\mathbf{B}} = (0 \quad 1.000),$$

so that

$$(9.3b) \qquad \hat{\mathbf{\Pi}} = -\hat{\mathbf{B}}\hat{\mathbf{\Gamma}}^{-1} = (2.048 \quad 3.048).$$

For Klein's Model I the 2SLS estimates of the three nonidentity structural relationships (3.29*a*)–(3.29*c*) are found to be

$$(9.4a) \qquad C = \underset{(1.320)}{16.555} + \underset{(0.118)}{0.017}P + \underset{(0.107)}{0.216}P_{-1} + \underset{(0.040)}{0.810}W,$$

$$(9.4b) \qquad I = \underset{(7.523)}{20.278} + \underset{(0.173)}{0.150}P + \underset{(0.162)}{0.616}P_{-1} - \underset{(0.036)}{0.158}K_{-1},$$

$$(9.4c) \qquad W^* = \underset{(1.147)}{1.500} + \underset{(0.036)}{0.439}E + \underset{(0.039)}{0.147}E_{-1} + \underset{(0.029)}{0.130}A.$$

(For future reference estimated asymptotic standard errors are given in parentheses below the coefficients.) Using these together with the identities (3.29*d*)–(3.29*h*) we may set up the estimated structural coefficients in the matrices (9.5*a*) and (9.5*b*), and derive (9.5*c*). Row and column headings have been used for ease of reference. (For future reference, estimated asymptotic standard errors are given in parentheses below the reduced-form coefficients.)

It should be noted that in general—i.e., unless all structural equations are just-identified—the derived reduced form $\hat{\mathbf{\Pi}}$ does not coincide with the direct reduced-form estimate $\mathbf{P}$ considered in Section 5; e.g., compare (9.5*c*) and (5.25). The direct reduced form $\mathbf{P}$ is obtained by regressing each current endogenous variable on all predetermined variables, without using any restrictions. In contrast, the derived reduced form $\hat{\mathbf{\Pi}}$ will clearly incorporate those restrictions which were used in estimating the structural equations. Although both $\mathbf{P}$ and $\hat{\mathbf{\Pi}}$ are consistent estimators of $\mathbf{\Pi}$, the latter incorporates more a priori information and hence will be more efficient, at least asymptotically.

In the reduced-form system each current endogenous variable is expressed in terms of only predetermined variables and a disturbance. The

$$
(9.5a) \qquad \hat{\boldsymbol{\Gamma}} = \begin{array}{c} \\ C \\ I \\ W^* \\ P \\ Y \\ K \\ W \\ E \end{array}
\begin{pmatrix}
(a) & (b) & (c) & (d) & (e) & (f) & (g) & (h) \\
-1.000 & 0 & 0 & 1.000 & 0 & 0 & 0 & 0 \\
0 & -1.000 & 0 & 1.000 & 0 & 1.000 & 0 & 0 \\
0 & 0 & -1.000 & 0 & 0 & 0 & 1.000 & 0 \\
0.017 & 0.150 & 0 & 0 & 1.000 & 0 & 0 & 0 \\
0 & 0 & 0 & -1.000 & -1.000 & 0 & 0 & 1.000 \\
0 & 0 & 0 & 0 & 0 & -1.000 & 0 & 0 \\
0.810 & 0 & 0 & 0 & 1.000 & 0 & -1.000 & 0 \\
0 & 0 & 0.439 & 0 & 0 & 0 & 0 & -1.000
\end{pmatrix}
$$

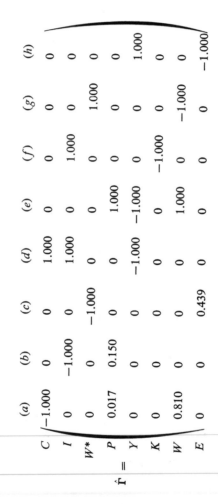

$$
(9.5b) \qquad \hat{\mathbf{B}} = \begin{array}{c} \\ 1 \\ W^{**} \\ T \\ G \\ A \\ P_{-1} \\ K_{-1} \\ E_{-1} \end{array}
\begin{array}{c} \\ \left(\begin{array}{cccccccc} (a) & (b) & (c) & (d) & (e) & (f) & (g) & (h) \\ 16.555 & 20.278 & 1.500 & 0 & 0 & 0 & 0 & 0 \\ 0 & 0 & 0 & 0 & 0 & 0 & 1.000 & -1.000 \\ 0 & 0 & 0 & -1.000 & 0 & 0 & 0 & 1.000 \\ 0 & 0 & 0 & 1.000 & 0 & 0 & 0 & 0 \\ 0 & 0 & 0.130 & 0 & 0 & 0 & 0 & 0 \\ 0.216 & 0.616 & 0 & 0 & 0 & 0 & 0 & 0 \\ 0 & -0.158 & 0 & 0 & 0 & 1.000 & 0 & 0 \\ 0 & 0 & 0.147 & 0 & 0 & 0 & 0 & 0 \end{array} \right) \end{array}
$$

(9.5c) $\hat{\mathbf{\Pi}} = -\hat{\mathbf{B}}\hat{\mathbf{\Gamma}}^{-1} =$

	C	I	W^*	P	Y	K	W	E
1	42.826 (8.619)	25.841 (7.567)	31.635 (7.240)	37.032 (8.833)	68.667 (15.303)	25.841 (7.567)	31.635 (7.240)	68.667 (15.303)
W^{**}	0.684 (0.062)	−0.029 (0.040)	−0.151 (0.054)	−0.194 (0.045)	0.655 (0.089)	−0.029 (0.040)	0.849 (0.054)	−0.345 (0.089)
T	−0.128 (0.276)	−0.176 (0.238)	−0.134 (0.214)	−1.171 (0.275)	−1.304 (0.480)	−0.176 (0.238)	−0.134 (0.214)	−0.304 (0.480)
G	0.664 (0.237)	0.153 (0.208)	0.797 (0.198)	1.019 (0.243)	1.817 (0.420)	0.153 (0.208)	0.797 (0.198)	1.817 (0.420)
A	0.159 (0.021)	−0.007 (0.009)	0.197 (0.014)	−0.045 (0.013)	0.152 (0.026)	−0.007 (0.009)	0.197 (0.014)	0.512 (0.026)
P_{-1}	0.768 (0.197)	0.743 (0.173)	0.664 (0.165)	0.848 (0.202)	1.512 (0.350)	0.743 (0.173)	0.664 (0.165)	1.512 (0.350)
K_{-1}	−0.105 (0.037)	−0.182 (0.033)	−0.126 (0.031)	−0.161 (0.038)	−0.287 (0.066)	0.818 (0.033)	−0.126 (0.031)	−0.287 (0.066)
E_{-1}	0.179 (0.024)	−0.008 (0.010)	0.222 (0.016)	−0.051 (0.015)	0.171 (0.029)	−0.008 (0.010)	0.222 (0.016)	0.171 (0.029)

disturbance is uncorrelated with the predetermined variables so that the conditional expectation of the endogenous variable is given by the linear function of the predetermined variables. A particular reduced-form coefficient π_{km} may then be interpreted as the partial derivative (of the conditional expectation) of the current endogenous variable y_{tm} with respect to the predetermined variable x_{tk}, with all other x_t's held constant. Thus the reduced-form coefficient indicates the "total" effect of a change in x_{tk} on (the conditional expectation of) y_{tm} after taking account of the interdependences among the current endogenous variables; a familiar economists' word for such a coefficient is "multiplier." In contrast, a structural coefficient indicates only a direct effect within a single sector of the economy. It is clear that economic hypotheses often refer to reduced-form, rather than structural, coefficients, so that $\hat{\mathbf{\Pi}}$ will be of interest. In Klein's Model I, e.g., government expenditures G_t do not directly influence consumer expenditures C_t—see (9.4*a*)—but the total effect (through income) is estimated to be 0.664 per unit change in G_t—see (9.5*c*). Also in that model the direct effect of the time trend on private wages is estimated to be 0.130—see (9.4*c*)—but the total effect (taking into account the fact that an increase in W^* raises Y, which raises W^*, etc.) is estimated to be 0.197—see (9.5*c*).

Each derived reduced-form coefficient is in general a nonlinear function of many structural coefficients—see (3.10). The method of Section 3.6 is available for obtaining the asymptotic variances and covariances of the derived reduced-form coefficient estimates in terms of the asymptotic variances and covariances of the structural coefficient estimates. Let

$$\mathbf{A} = \begin{pmatrix} \mathbf{\Gamma} \\ \mathbf{B} \end{pmatrix}$$

be the $(M + K) \times M$ matrix of structural coefficients and let

$$\hat{\mathbf{A}} = \begin{pmatrix} \hat{\mathbf{\Gamma}} \\ \hat{\mathbf{B}} \end{pmatrix}$$

be the $(M + K) \times M$ matrix of consistent estimates. Then we define $\boldsymbol{\alpha}$ to be the $M(M + K) \times 1$ vector of structural coefficients arranged by equations (i.e., by columns of $\mathbf{A}$) and $\hat{\boldsymbol{\alpha}}$ to be the $M(M + K) \times 1$ vector of structural coefficient estimates correspondingly arranged (i.e., by columns of $\hat{\mathbf{A}}$). Then

$$\bar{E}\hat{\boldsymbol{\alpha}} = \boldsymbol{\alpha}, \tag{9.6}$$

and the asymptotic variances and covariances of the structural coefficient estimates are given in the $M(M + K) \times M(M + K)$ matrix

$$\boldsymbol{\Delta} = \bar{E}(\hat{\boldsymbol{\alpha}} - \boldsymbol{\alpha})(\hat{\boldsymbol{\alpha}} - \boldsymbol{\alpha})'. \tag{9.7}$$

For the systems methods formulas for all such variances and covariances have been given in Section 7. For the single-equation methods we have given formulas only for the variances and covariances of the coefficients in each structural equation—but not for covariances of coefficients in different structural equations. When single-equation methods have been applied to each structural equation these covariances are also defined—see Theil (1961, p. 342).

Now let $\mathbf{\Pi}$ be the $K \times M$ matrix of reduced-form coefficients and let $\hat{\mathbf{\Pi}}$ be the $K \times M$ consistent derived reduced-form coefficient matrix. Then we define $\boldsymbol{\pi}$ to be the $MK \times 1$ vector of reduced-form coefficients arranged by equations (i.e., by columns of $\mathbf{\Pi}$) and $\hat{\boldsymbol{\pi}}$ to be the $MK \times 1$ vector of consistent derived reduced-form coefficients correspondingly arranged (i.e., by columns of $\hat{\mathbf{\Pi}}$). Then

$$\bar{E}\hat{\boldsymbol{\pi}} = \boldsymbol{\pi}, \tag{9.8}$$

and the asymptotic variances of the derived reduced-form coefficients are given in the $MK \times MK$ matrix

$$\mathbf{\Psi} = \bar{E}(\hat{\boldsymbol{\pi}} - \boldsymbol{\pi})(\hat{\boldsymbol{\pi}} - \boldsymbol{\pi})'. \tag{9.9}$$

Then by (3.6.32)

$$\mathbf{\Psi} = \mathbf{J}'\mathbf{\Delta}\mathbf{J} \tag{9.10}$$

where $\mathbf{J} = \partial\boldsymbol{\pi}/\partial\boldsymbol{\alpha}$ is the $M(M + K) \times MK$ matrix of partial derivatives of the elements of $\boldsymbol{\pi}$ with respect to the elements of $\boldsymbol{\alpha}$.

Goldberger, Nagar, and Odeh (1961) have derived an expression for $\mathbf{J}$ as follows. From (3.10) we see that

$$\pi_{km} = -\sum_{m'=1}^{M} \beta_{km'}\gamma^{m'm} \tag{9.11}$$

where $\gamma^{m'm}$ is the m',mth element of $\mathbf{\Gamma}^{-1}$. Differentiating (9.11) with respect to $\gamma_{\mu'\mu}$ we have

$$\frac{\partial\pi_{km}}{\partial\gamma_{\mu'\mu}} = -\sum_{m'=1}^{M} \beta_{km}\frac{\partial\gamma^{m'm}}{\partial\gamma_{\mu'\mu}} = \gamma^{\mu m}\sum_{m'=1}^{M} \beta_{km'}\gamma^{m'\mu'} = -\gamma^{\mu m}\pi_{k\mu'} \tag{9.12}$$

where use is made of the fact that

$$\frac{\partial\gamma^{m'm}}{\partial\gamma_{\mu'\mu}} = -\gamma^{m'\mu'}\gamma^{\mu m} \tag{9.13}$$

by (2.8.14). Differentiating (9.11) with respect to $\beta_{\kappa'\kappa}$ we have

$$\frac{\partial\pi_{km}}{\partial\beta_{\kappa'\kappa}} = \begin{cases} -\gamma^{\kappa m} & \text{if } \kappa' = k \\ 0 & \text{otherwise.} \end{cases} \tag{9.14}$$

It is readily confirmed that these partial derivatives are properly arranged in the matrix

$$(9.15)\qquad \mathbf{J} = \frac{\partial \boldsymbol{\pi}}{\partial \boldsymbol{\alpha}} = -\begin{pmatrix} \gamma^{11}\begin{pmatrix}\boldsymbol{\Pi}'\\ \mathbf{I}\end{pmatrix} & \cdots & \gamma^{1M}\begin{pmatrix}\boldsymbol{\Pi}'\\ \mathbf{I}\end{pmatrix} \\ \cdot & & \cdot \\ \cdot & & \cdot \\ \cdot & & \cdot \\ \gamma^{M1}\begin{pmatrix}\boldsymbol{\Pi}'\\ \mathbf{I}\end{pmatrix} & \cdots & \gamma^{MM}\begin{pmatrix}\boldsymbol{\Pi}'\\ \mathbf{I}\end{pmatrix} \end{pmatrix}.$$

In practice, of course, $\mathbf{J}$ will be unknown (since $\boldsymbol{\Gamma}^{-1}$ and $\boldsymbol{\Pi}$ are unknown), and $\boldsymbol{\Delta}$ will also be unknown. But using $\hat{\boldsymbol{\Gamma}}^{-1}$ and $\hat{\boldsymbol{\Pi}}$ in place of $\boldsymbol{\Gamma}^{-1}$ and $\boldsymbol{\Pi}$ gives $\hat{\mathbf{J}}$, a consistent estimate of $\mathbf{J}$, so that

$$(9.16)\qquad \hat{\boldsymbol{\Psi}} = \hat{\mathbf{J}}'\hat{\boldsymbol{\Delta}}\hat{\mathbf{J}},$$

where $\hat{\boldsymbol{\Delta}}$ is a consistent estimate of $\boldsymbol{\Delta}$, will be a consistent estimate of $\boldsymbol{\Psi}$. The diagonal elements of $\hat{\boldsymbol{\Psi}}$ will be the estimated asymptotic variances of the derived reduced-form coefficients, and their square roots will be the estimated asymptotic standard errors. Again hypothesis testing and interval estimation may be carried out by the standard procedures. Goldberger, Nagar, and Odeh provide a numerical illustration, computing $\hat{\boldsymbol{\Psi}}$ for Klein's Model I; the standard errors were reproduced in (9.5*c*).

Forecasting

Another important application of an estimated structural model is to economic forecasting. Given the $K \times 1$ vector $\mathbf{x}(*)$ of values of the predetermined variables for a forecast period, the $M \times 1$ vector $\mathbf{y}(*)$ of values of the endogenous variables will be determined by

$$(9.17)\qquad \mathbf{y}'(*) = \mathbf{x}'(*)\boldsymbol{\Pi} + \mathbf{v}'(*)$$

where $\mathbf{v}(*)$ is the $M \times 1$ vector of reduced-form disturbances for the forecast period. Defining the $MK \times M$ matrix

$$(9.18)\qquad \mathbf{F} = \begin{pmatrix} \mathbf{x}(*) & \mathbf{0} & \cdots & \mathbf{0} \\ \mathbf{0} & \mathbf{x}(*) & \cdots & \mathbf{0} \\ \cdot & \cdot & & \cdot \\ \cdot & \cdot & & \cdot \\ \cdot & \cdot & & \cdot \\ \mathbf{0} & \mathbf{0} & \cdots & \mathbf{x}(*) \end{pmatrix},$$

we may transpose (9.17) and write it as

$$\text{(9.19)} \qquad \mathbf{y}(*) = \mathbf{F}'\boldsymbol{\pi} + \mathbf{v}(*),$$

where the $MK \times 1$ vector $\boldsymbol{\pi}$ was defined in the preceding subsection. Our forecast $\hat{\mathbf{y}}(*)$ will be determined by

$$\text{(9.20)} \qquad \hat{\mathbf{y}}'(*) = \mathbf{x}'(*)\hat{\boldsymbol{\Pi}};$$

i.e.,

$$\text{(9.21)} \qquad \hat{\mathbf{y}}(*) = \mathbf{F}'\hat{\boldsymbol{\pi}}.$$

Then the vector of forecast errors is

$$\text{(9.22)} \qquad \mathbf{f} = \mathbf{y}(*) - \hat{\mathbf{y}}(*) = (\boldsymbol{\Pi} - \hat{\boldsymbol{\Pi}})'\mathbf{x}(*) + \mathbf{v}(*) = \mathbf{F}'(\boldsymbol{\pi} - \hat{\boldsymbol{\pi}}) + \mathbf{v}(*).$$

If we treat $\mathbf{x}(*)$ as fixed we find that the asymptotic expectation of the forecast error is zero for $\bar{E}(\boldsymbol{\pi} - \hat{\boldsymbol{\pi}}) = \mathbf{0}$ and $E\mathbf{v}(*) = \mathbf{0}$, and then for the asymptotic forecast covariance matrix

$$\begin{aligned} \text{(9.23)} \qquad \boldsymbol{\Phi} &= \bar{E}\mathbf{f}\mathbf{f}' \\ &= \mathbf{F}'\bar{E}(\boldsymbol{\pi} - \hat{\boldsymbol{\pi}})(\boldsymbol{\pi} - \hat{\boldsymbol{\pi}})'\mathbf{F} + E\mathbf{v}(*)\mathbf{v}'(*) \\ &\quad + \mathbf{F}'\bar{E}(\boldsymbol{\pi} - \hat{\boldsymbol{\pi}})\mathbf{v}'(*) + \bar{E}\mathbf{v}(*)(\boldsymbol{\pi} - \hat{\boldsymbol{\pi}})'\mathbf{F} \\ &= \mathbf{F}'\boldsymbol{\Psi}\mathbf{F} + \boldsymbol{\Omega}, \end{aligned}$$

assuming $\hat{\boldsymbol{\pi}}$ is uncorrelated with $\mathbf{v}(*)$ and $\mathbf{v}(*)$ is distributed just as $\mathbf{v}(t)$ $(t = 1, \ldots, T)$. In practice $\boldsymbol{\Phi}$ will be unknown (since $\boldsymbol{\Psi}$ and $\boldsymbol{\Omega}$ are unknown) but

$$\text{(9.24)} \qquad \hat{\boldsymbol{\Phi}} = \mathbf{F}'\hat{\boldsymbol{\Psi}}\mathbf{F} + \hat{\boldsymbol{\Omega}}$$

will be a consistent estimate of $\boldsymbol{\Phi}$.

Forecasting undertaken in realistic contexts with an estimated structural model, and the related application to policy formation, is illustrated in Klein and Goldberger (1955, pp. 95–114), Goldberger, (1959, pp. 4–13), and Suits (1962). For a numerical illustration we use Klein's Model I. For 1947 the values of the predetermined variables were

$$\text{(9.25)} \qquad \mathbf{x}'(*) = \begin{pmatrix} \scriptstyle 1 & \scriptstyle W^{**} & \scriptstyle T & \scriptstyle G & \scriptstyle A & \scriptstyle P_{-1} & \scriptstyle K_{-1} & \scriptstyle E_{-1} \\ 1.0 & 8.7 & 9.2 & 17.4 & 17.0 & 26.2 & 197.7 & 94.8 \end{pmatrix}.$$

Applying the $\hat{\boldsymbol{\Pi}}$ of (9.5*c*) to this $\mathbf{x}(*)$ gave the forecast values of the current endogenous variables for 1947 as

$$\text{(9.26)} \qquad \hat{\mathbf{y}}'(*) \quad \begin{pmatrix} \scriptstyle C & \scriptstyle I & \scriptstyle W^{*} & \scriptstyle P & \scriptstyle Y & \scriptstyle K & \scriptstyle W & \scriptstyle E \\ 78.2 & 9.3 & 59.9 & 27.2 & 95.7 & 207.0 & 68.6 & 96.2 \end{pmatrix}.$$

Using the $\hat{\Psi}$ and $\hat{\Omega}$ referred to, the asymptotic covariance matrix of forecast errors was estimated as

$$
(9.27)\qquad \mathbf{G} = \begin{array}{c} \\ C \\ I \\ W^* \\ P \\ Y \\ K \\ W \\ E \end{array}
\begin{array}{c} \begin{array}{cccccccc} C & I & W^* & P & Y & K & W & E \end{array} \\
\begin{pmatrix}
57.58 & 33.40 & 47.83 & 43.15 & 90.98 & 33.40 & 47.83 & 90.98 \\
 & 33.31 & 29.88 & 36.84 & 66.72 & 33.32 & 29.88 & 66.72 \\
 & & 49.93 & 27.77 & 77.71 & 29.88 & 49.93 & 77.71 \\
 & & & 52.22 & 79.99 & 36.84 & 27.77 & 79.99 \\
 & & & & 157.70 & 66.72 & 77.71 & 157.70 \\
 & & & & & 33.31 & 29.88 & 66.72 \\
 & & & & & & 49.93 & 77.71 \\
 & & & & & & & 157.70
\end{pmatrix} \end{array}
$$

The square roots of the diagonal elements of (9.27) are the estimated asymptotic standard errors of the forecasts:

$$
(9.28)\qquad \begin{array}{cccccccc} C & I & W^* & P & Y & K & W & E \end{array} \\
\mathbf{s}_{\mathbf{f}}' = (7.6 \quad 5.8 \quad 7.1 \quad 7.2 \quad 12.6 \quad 5.8 \quad 7.1 \quad 12.6).
$$

In fact, the actual 1947 values of the current endogenous variables were

$$
(9.29)\qquad \begin{array}{cccccccc} C & I & W^* & P & Y & K & W & E \end{array} \\
\mathbf{y}'(*) = (82.8 \quad 6.4 \quad 60.7 \quad 27.9 \quad 97.4 \quad 204.1 \quad 69.4 \quad 97.9),
$$

so that subtracting (9.26) from (9.29) gave for the vector of forecast errors (after rounding)

$$
(9.30)\qquad \begin{array}{cccccccc} C & I & W^* & P & Y & K & W & E \end{array} \\
\mathbf{f}' = (4.6 \quad -2.9 \quad 0.8 \quad 0.8 \quad 1.7 \quad -2.9 \quad 0.8 \quad 1.7).
$$

Dynamic Models

Some of the most interesting applications of estimated structural models are concerned with their dynamic aspects. As indicated in Section 3, a structural model may do more than specify how the predetermined variables at a point in time generate the dependent variables at that point. When the predetermined variables include lagged endogenous variables—so that the model is dynamic—then the model also specifies how the time path of the *exogenous* variables generates the time path of the *endogenous* variables over a span of time.

Consider the reduced form of the model:

$$
(9.31)\qquad \mathbf{y}'(t) = \mathbf{x}'(t)\mathbf{\Pi} + \mathbf{v}'(t)
$$

and suppose that of the K predetermined variables, M are the endogenous variables lagged one period while the remaining $K - M$ are exogenous variables. (The extension to include higher-order lags is straightforward but is not pursued here.) Then after partitioning and rearranging, the reduced form may be written as

$$\text{(9.32)} \qquad \mathbf{y}_t = \mathbf{A}\mathbf{y}_{t-1} + \mathbf{B}\mathbf{z}_t + \mathbf{v}_t$$

where $\mathbf{y}_t$ is the $M \times 1$ vector of current endogenous variables;
- $\mathbf{y}_{t-1}$ is the $M \times 1$ vector of endogenous variables lagged one period [a subvector of $\mathbf{x}(t)$];
- $\mathbf{z}_t$ is the $(K - M) \times 1$ vector of exogenous variables [the remaining subvector of $\mathbf{x}(t)$];
- $\mathbf{v}_t$ is the $M \times 1$ vector of reduced-form disturbances;
- $\mathbf{A}$ is the $M \times M$ matrix of reduced-form coefficients of $\mathbf{y}_{t-1}$ (a submatrix of $\mathbf{\Pi}'$), and
- $\mathbf{B}$ is the $M \times (K - M)$ matrix of reduced-form coefficients of $\mathbf{z}_t$ (the remaining submatrix of $\mathbf{\Pi}'$).

This notation deviates from that used in the rest of this chapter but is convenient for present purposes.

Lagging (9.32) one period and substituting back in we have

$$\begin{aligned}\text{(9.33)} \qquad \mathbf{y}_t &= \mathbf{A}(\mathbf{A}y_{t-2} + \mathbf{B}\mathbf{z}_{t-1} + \mathbf{v}_{t-1}) + \mathbf{B}\mathbf{z}_t + \mathbf{v}_t \\ &= \mathbf{A}^2\mathbf{y}_{t-2} + \mathbf{B}\mathbf{z}_t + \mathbf{A}\mathbf{B}\mathbf{z}_{t-1} + \mathbf{v}_t + \mathbf{A}\mathbf{v}_{t-1}.\end{aligned}$$

Applying this procedure s times we find

$$\text{(9.34)} \qquad \mathbf{y}_t = \mathbf{A}^{s+1}\mathbf{y}_{t-s-1} + \sum_{\tau=0}^{s} \mathbf{C}_\tau \mathbf{z}_{t-\tau} + \sum_{\tau=0}^{s} \mathbf{A}^\tau \mathbf{v}_{t-\tau}$$

where

$$\text{(9.35)} \qquad \mathbf{C}_\tau = \mathbf{A}^\tau\mathbf{B}.$$

Letting s go to infinity we find the *final form* of the model:

$$\text{(9.36)} \qquad \mathbf{y}_t = \sum_{\tau=0}^{\infty} \mathbf{C}_\tau \mathbf{z}_{t-\tau} + \sum_{\tau=0}^{\infty} \mathbf{A}^\tau \mathbf{v}_{t-\tau}$$

assuming that $\lim_{\tau\to\infty} \mathbf{A}^\tau = \mathbf{0}$, in which case the system is said to be stable.

It will be recalled that the elements of $\mathbf{C}_0 = \mathbf{A}^0\mathbf{B} = \mathbf{B}$ are elements of $\mathbf{\Pi}'$. We have already referred to such elements as multipliers: $c_{0,mk}$ gives the effect of a unit change in z_{tk} on the expectation of y_{tm}, with all other exogenous variables held constant. In the same way, the elements of $\mathbf{C}_\tau = \mathbf{A}^\tau\mathbf{B}$ for $\tau > 0$ are multipliers: $c_{\tau,mk}$ gives the effect of a unit change in $z_{t-\tau,k}$ on the expectation of y_{tm}, with the rest of the exogenous time path constant. All this is readily confirmed by partial differentiation in (9.34). To distinguish these multipliers, we may refer to $\mathbf{C}_0$ as the *impact* multiplier matrix—its elements give the contemporaneous response to an exogenous change—and to $\mathbf{C}_\tau$ for $\tau > 0$ as the *delay-τ* multiplier matrix—its elements give the delayed response to an exogenous change. The contemporaneous response involves the contemporaneous feedbacks among the endogenous variables while the delayed response involves the cross-temporal feedbacks among them. Such delayed responses may be of extreme importance in dynamic models.

Now both impact and delay multipliers refer to "one-shot" or impulse exogenous changes; they answer the question, "If an exogenous variable is raised by one unit in a period and then restored to its original level, what will happen to the current and future values of an endogenous variable?" In many cases we are in fact interested in another question, "If an exogenous variable is raised by one unit in a period and then sustained at its new level, what will happen to the current and future values of an endogenous variable?" It is clear that the answer to this question is given by elements of the *cumulated* multiplier matrices

$$(9.37)\qquad \mathbf{D}_\tau = \sum_{v=0}^{\tau} \mathbf{C}_v = \sum_{v=0}^{\tau} \mathbf{A}^v\mathbf{B} = (\mathbf{I} + \mathbf{A} + \cdots + \mathbf{A}^\tau)\mathbf{B} \qquad (\tau = 1, \ldots);$$

the elements of which, $d_{\tau,mk} = \Sigma_{v=0}^{\tau} c_{v,mk}$, give the response to such a sustained unit change. Finally, if $\lim_{v\to\infty} \mathbf{A}^v = \mathbf{0}$, we may define the *equilibrium* multiplier matrix

$$(9.38)\qquad \bar{\mathbf{D}} = \mathbf{D}_\infty = \sum_{v=0}^{\infty} \mathbf{C}_v = \sum_{v=0}^{\infty} \mathbf{A}^v\mathbf{B} = (\mathbf{I} + \mathbf{A} + \mathbf{A}^2 + \cdots)\mathbf{B},$$

the elements of which give the ultimate or equilibrium response to such a sustained unit change: $\bar{d}_{mk} = \Sigma_{v=0}^{\infty} c_{v,mk}$. All this is readily confirmed by partial differentiation in (9.36). If the exogenous variable vector is indefinitely sustained at some value $\bar{\mathbf{z}}$, then the endogenous variable vector approaches the equilibrium value

$$(9.39)\qquad \bar{\mathbf{y}} = \bar{\mathbf{D}}\bar{\mathbf{z}}.$$

It is useful to note that $(\mathbf{I} + \mathbf{A} + \mathbf{A}^2 + \cdots)$ may be interpreted as the series expansion of $(\mathbf{I} - \mathbf{A})^{-1}$ so that we may rewrite (9.38) as

$$(9.40)\qquad \bar{\mathbf{D}} = (\mathbf{I} - \mathbf{A})^{-1}\mathbf{B}$$

and then rewrite (9.37) as

$$(9.41)\qquad \mathbf{D}_\tau = (\mathbf{I} - \mathbf{A}^{\tau+1})\bar{\mathbf{D}}$$

using $(\mathbf{I} - \mathbf{A})(\mathbf{I} + \mathbf{A} + \cdots + \mathbf{A}^\tau) = (\mathbf{I} - \mathbf{A}^{\tau+1}) = (\mathbf{I} + \mathbf{A} + \cdots + \mathbf{A}^\tau) \times (\mathbf{I} - \mathbf{A})$.

Theil and Boot (1962) have computed these multipliers for Klein's Model I, using the FI/LGRV structural estimates. To illustrate their results we give the estimates of the various multipliers of government expenditures on consumption:

$$\begin{array}{llllllll} \tau = 0 & 1 & 2 & 3 & 4 & \cdots & \infty \\ c_\tau = 0.671 & 1.170 & 0.859 & 0.396 & -0.031 & \cdots & 0 \\ d_\tau = 0.671 & 1.841 & 2.700 & 3.096 & 3.065 & \cdots & 1.323. \end{array} \tag{9.42}$$

Goldberger (1959, Chapters 3, 5, 6) investigates some similar multipliers in the Klein-Goldberger model.

Other applications are concerned with the inherent dynamic properties of the model. To investigate these it is convenient to take $s = t - 1$ in (9.34):

$$\mathbf{y}_t = \mathbf{A}^t\mathbf{y}_0 + \sum_{\tau=0}^{t-1} \mathbf{C}_\tau \mathbf{z}_{t-\tau} + \sum_{\tau=0}^{t-1} \mathbf{A}^\tau \mathbf{v}_{t-\tau}, \tag{9.43}$$

rewrite (9.39) as

$$\begin{aligned} \bar{\mathbf{y}} = \sum_{\tau=0}^{\infty} \mathbf{C}_\tau \bar{\mathbf{z}} &= \sum_{\tau=0}^{t-1} \mathbf{C}_\tau \bar{\mathbf{z}} + \sum_{\tau=t}^{\infty} \mathbf{C}_\tau \bar{\mathbf{z}} = \sum_{\tau=0}^{t-1} \mathbf{C}_\tau \bar{\mathbf{z}} + \mathbf{A}^t \sum_{\tau=0}^{\infty} \mathbf{C}_\tau \bar{\mathbf{z}} \\ &= \sum_{\tau=0}^{t-1} \mathbf{C}_\tau \bar{\mathbf{z}} + \mathbf{A}^t \bar{\mathbf{y}}, \end{aligned} \tag{9.44}$$

and subtract (9.44) from (9.43) to obtain

$$\mathbf{y}_t^* = \mathbf{A}^t\mathbf{y}_0^* + \sum_{\tau=0}^{t-1} \mathbf{C}_\tau \mathbf{z}_{t-\tau}^* + \sum_{\tau=0}^{t-1} \mathbf{A}^\tau \mathbf{v}_{t-\tau}, \tag{9.45}$$

where $\mathbf{z}^* = \mathbf{z} - \bar{\mathbf{z}}$ is the deviation from the constant vector $\bar{\mathbf{z}}$ and $\mathbf{y}^* = \mathbf{y} - \bar{\mathbf{y}}$ is the deviation from the corresponding equilibrium value $\bar{\mathbf{y}}$. Either (9.45) or (9.43) expresses the time path of the endogenous variables in terms of three components: initial conditions ($\mathbf{y}_0$ or $\mathbf{y}_0^*$), the time path of the exogenous variables ($\mathbf{z}_{t-\tau}$ or $\mathbf{z}_{t-\tau}^*$ for $\tau = 0, \ldots, t-1$), and the time path of the disturbances ($\mathbf{v}_{t-\tau}$ for $\tau = 0, \ldots, t-1$). The inherent dynamic properties refer to the characteristics of the time path undertaken by the endogenous variables following an initial displacement from equilibrium without further exogenous changes or disturbances. Therefore let us take both $\mathbf{z}_{t-\tau}^* = \mathbf{0}$ and $\mathbf{v}_{t-\tau} = \mathbf{0}$ for all $\tau \geq 0$ in (9.45); this leaves

$$\mathbf{y}_t^* = \mathbf{A}^t\mathbf{y}_0^*. \tag{9.46}$$

It is a theorem in matrix algebra that a square matrix $\mathbf{A}$ may be expressed as

$$\mathbf{A} = \mathbf{P}\mathbf{\Lambda}\mathbf{Q} \tag{9.47}$$

where

$$\Lambda = \begin{pmatrix} \lambda_1 & 0 & \cdots & 0 \\ 0 & \lambda_2 & \cdots & 0 \\ \cdot & \cdot & & \cdot \\ \cdot & \cdot & & \cdot \\ \cdot & \cdot & & \cdot \\ 0 & 0 & \cdots & \lambda_M \end{pmatrix} \tag{9.48}$$

is the diagonal matrix containing the characteristic roots of **A** and where $\mathbf{Q} = \mathbf{P}^{-1}$, provided that **A** has no multiple characteristic roots—see Hadley (1961, pp. 249–251); our diagonalization theorem for symmetric matrices is a special case of this result. Then $\mathbf{A}^2 = \mathbf{P\Lambda QP\Lambda Q} = \mathbf{P\Lambda P^{-1}P\Lambda Q} = \mathbf{P\Lambda^2Q}$ and similarly

$$\mathbf{A}^t = \mathbf{P\Lambda}^t\mathbf{Q}. \tag{9.49}$$

It is readily confirmed that

$$\Lambda^t = \begin{pmatrix} \lambda_1^t & 0 & \cdots & 0 \\ 0 & \lambda_2^t & \cdots & 0 \\ \cdot & \cdot & & \cdot \\ \cdot & \cdot & & \cdot \\ \cdot & \cdot & & \cdot \\ 0 & 0 & \cdots & \lambda_M^t \end{pmatrix}, \tag{9.50}$$

whence $\mathbf{A}^t$ may be written as

$$\mathbf{A}^t = \sum_{m=1}^{M} \lambda_m^t \mathbf{R}_m \tag{9.51}$$

where $\mathbf{R}_m = \mathbf{p}_m\mathbf{q}_m'$ is the product of the mth column of **P** by the mth row of **Q**. Indeed $\mathbf{A}^t$ may be written in a form like (9.51) with summation running from $m = 1$ to $m = r$ where $r = r(\mathbf{A})$ provided only that **A** has no multiple *nonzero* roots—see Zurmühl (1958, p. 181).

Inserting (9.51) into (9.46) gives

$$\mathbf{y}_t^* = \sum_{m=1}^{M} \lambda_m^t \mathbf{R}_m \mathbf{y}_0^*, \tag{9.52}$$

whence it is clear that the inherent dynamic properties of the model are determined by the characteristic roots of **A**. First from (9.51) the stability condition $\lim_{\tau\to\infty} \mathbf{A}^\tau = \lim_{\tau\to\infty} \sum_{m=1}^{M} \lambda_m^\tau \mathbf{R}_m = \mathbf{0}$ requires that each characteristic root of **A** be less than 1 in absolute value. Then from (9.52) each positive real root a introduces a monotonic component $(a)^t$, each negative real root $-a$ introduces a sawtooth component $(-a)^t$, and each pair of conjugate complex roots $a(\cos b \pm i \sin b)$ introduces a sinusoidal component with period $2\pi/b$ and amplitude a^t into the time path of the endogenous variables. For a discussion of these results see Baumol (1959, pp. 197–201).

The inherent dynamic properties naturally play an important role in econometric investigations of business cycles. Theil and Boot (1962), using the FI/LGRV structural estimates, find the estimates of the nonzero characteristic roots in Klein's Model I to be

$$(9.53) \qquad \lambda_1 = 0.334; \qquad \lambda_2, \lambda_3 = 0.838(\cos 0.435 \pm i \sin 0.435);$$

the complex roots implying a cycle with period of 14.4 ($= 2\pi/0.435$) years. Goldberger (1959, Chapter 6) investigates the dynamic properties of the Klein-Goldberger model.

It should be recognized that estimates of characteristic roots are sample statistics—they are after all ultimately derived from the estimates of the structural parameters—and hence subject to sampling error. Theil and Boot (1962) derive a general expression for the asymptotic variance of the absolute value of the largest root in terms of the asymptotic covariance matrix of the structural coefficient estimates. For Klein's Model I they estimate this variance to be 0.05; so that the standard error associated with the point estimate 0.838 is 0.22 ($= \sqrt{0.05}$). Finally it should be noted that the time path of economic variables may well be dominated not by inherent dynamic properties, but rather by exogenous shifts and random disturbances.

Structural Form and Reduced Form

We have seen that the reduced form rather than the structural form is relevant for several important applications. This suggests that the choice among alternative methods of estimation might be made on the basis of the properties of the resulting derived reduced-form estimates rather than on the properties of the structural estimates themselves. The following points may be noted. The invariance property of maximum likelihood implies that reduced-form estimates derived from maximum likelihood structural estimates will also be maximum likelihood estimates, and hence will be at least as asymptotically efficient as reduced-form estimates derived from any other structural estimates (using the same amount of a priori information). More generally, reduced-form estimates derived from any consistent structural estimates will also be consistent while there is also an invariance property associated with asymptotic efficiency, which may be seen as follows. Suppose that a method of structural estimation is asymptotically efficient so that $\tilde{\mathbf{\Delta}} - \mathbf{\Delta}$ is nonnegative definite where $\mathbf{\Delta}$ is the asymptotic covariance matrix of the structural coefficient estimates of the efficient method and $\tilde{\mathbf{\Delta}}$ is the asymptotic covariance matrix of the structural coefficient estimates of any other consistent method. Now let $\mathbf{\Psi}$ be the asymptotic covariance matrix of the reduced-form coefficient estimates derived from the efficient structural estimates; by (9.10) $\mathbf{\Psi} = \mathbf{J}'\mathbf{\Delta}\mathbf{J}$ where $\mathbf{J}$ is the partial derivative matrix defined in (9.15). Similarly let $\tilde{\mathbf{\Psi}}$ be the asymptotic covariance matrix of the reduced-form coefficient estimates derived from any other consistent structural estimates; $\tilde{\mathbf{\Psi}} = \mathbf{J}'\tilde{\mathbf{\Delta}}\mathbf{J}$. Then

$$\tilde{\mathbf{\Psi}} - \mathbf{\Psi} = \mathbf{J}'\tilde{\mathbf{\Delta}}\mathbf{J} - \mathbf{J}'\mathbf{\Delta}\mathbf{J} = \mathbf{J}'(\tilde{\mathbf{\Delta}} - \mathbf{\Delta})\mathbf{J}$$

is nonnegative definite by (2.7.14) so that the reduced-form estimates derived from the efficient structural estimates are also efficient.

Focusing on the reduced form rather than the structural form does tend to undercut the argument in favor of classical least-squares structural estimation given in Section 8. It was indicated there that the bias of classical least-squares structural estimators might be sufficiently small to be compensated for by their minimum variance property. Nevertheless, (*a*) small sampling errors in individual structural coefficients may build up into large sampling errors in the derived reduced-form coefficients, and (*b*) the minimum variance property does not carry over from the structural to the derived reduced-form coefficients. This counterargument is due to Klein (1960), who illustrates the points with the simple Keynesian model.

In view of the fact that the reduced form suffices for several important applications, it might be argued that structural estimation is not necessary. Thus some have proposed that we need only fit the unrestricted reduced-form system by classical least squares to obtain consistent estimates of $\mathbf{\Pi}$ (and $\mathbf{\Omega}$), thus avoiding the complexities involved first in estimating the structural parameters and then in deriving reduced-form estimates from them. The counterargument to this has two main strands. First, as we have seen, the derived reduced form estimates, incorporating restrictions, will be more efficient—at least asymptotically—than the unrestricted estimates; Klein (1960) formalizes this in the context of forecasting. Second, in realistic applications, knowledge of the reduced form will not in fact suffice. True, if the structure of the economy is the same in the forecast period as it was in the sample period, the estimated reduced form will be adequate for forecasting. Suppose, however, that some structural change is known to have occurred. If structural estimates are available, they may be modified appropriately and revised reduced-form estimates derived from them. If only reduced-form estimates are available, however, we will in general be unable to make the appropriate modifications; the derivative of a reduced-form coefficient with respect to a structural parameter will in general be a function of structural parameters. For illustrations, see Marschak (1953). A related point is that extraneous information on structural parameters may become available; without structural estimates this information may be useless. For examples, see Klein and Goldberger (1955, pp. 82–88, 104–109).

10. FORMULATION AND INTERPRETATION OF ECONOMETRIC MODELS

To sharpen our understanding of structural equation models, it is useful to consider alternative formulations of econometric models. In these alternative formulations, as in the structural equation formulation, the underlying view of the economic mechanism is as follows. At each point of time, the current endogenous vector $\mathbf{y}'(t) = [y_1(t) \quad \cdots \quad y_M(t)]$ is determined by the predetermined vector $\mathbf{x}'(t) = [x_1(t) \quad \cdots \quad x_K(t)]$ in the sense that its probability distribution is so determined. Thus there is a joint conditional probability distribution of the current endogenous variables conditional on the values of the predetermined variables; we may write this underlying distribution as

$$(10.1) \qquad f[\mathbf{y}(t) \mid \mathbf{x}(t)] = f[y_1(t), \ldots, y_M(t) \mid x_1(t), \ldots, x_K(t)].$$

In formulating a model a basic concern of the econometrician is to characterize this joint conditional distribution using what a priori information he has. It will be recognized that there are alternative ways of characterizing such a joint distribution; associated with these are alternative approaches to formulating an econometric model.

To simplify the discussion we make the following assumptions, which are really not essential to the argument: The joint conditional distribution of (10.1) is multivariate normal with expectation vector linear in, and covariance matrix independent of, the predetermined variables:

$$(10.2) \qquad f[\mathbf{y}(t) \mid \mathbf{x}(t)] = \mathcal{N}[\mathbf{\Pi}'\mathbf{x}(t), \mathbf{\Omega}];$$

and the set of T observations $\{\mathbf{y}(1), \mathbf{x}(1); \ldots; \mathbf{y}(T), \mathbf{x}(T)\}$ are T independent drawings from $f[\mathbf{y}(t) \mid \mathbf{x}(t)]$ with the values $\mathbf{x}(1), \ldots, \mathbf{x}(T)$ being nonstochastic. (We are ruling out the presence of lagged endogenous variables.) In the sequel we omit the time index, writing $f(\mathbf{y} \mid \mathbf{x}) = \mathcal{N}(\mathbf{\Pi}'\mathbf{x}, \mathbf{\Omega})$ for simplicity.

The *reduced-form* approach to formulating an econometric model is perhaps the most direct one. If, conditional on **x**, **y** has a joint normal distribution with expectation linear in, and covariance matrix independent of, the conditioning vector **x**, then the distribution of an element of **y** conditional on **x** is univariate normal with expectation linear in, and variance independent of, the conditioning vector. More specifically,

(10.3) Let the conditional distribution of **y** given **x** be $\mathcal{N}(\mathbf{\Pi}'\mathbf{x}, \mathbf{\Omega})$. Then the conditional distribution of y_m given **x** is $\mathcal{N}(\boldsymbol{\pi}_m'\mathbf{x}, \omega_{mm})$ where y_m is the *m*th element of **y**, $\boldsymbol{\pi}_m'$ the *m*th row of $\mathbf{\Pi}'$, and ω_{mm} the *m*th diagonal element of $\mathbf{\Omega}$;

this is a straightforward application of (3.5.11). If then we write $y_m = \boldsymbol{\pi}_m'\mathbf{x} + v_m$, v_m will be distributed $\mathcal{N}(0, \omega_{mm})$ independently of **x**; and indeed the joint distribution of $v_1, \ldots, v_M$ will be normal with

$$Ev_m = 0, \quad Ev_m v_{m'} = \begin{cases} \omega_{mm}, & m' = m \\ \omega_{mm'}, & m' \neq m, \end{cases}$$

independently of $x_1, \ldots, x_K$, where $\omega_{mm'}$ is the m,m'th element of $\mathbf{\Omega}$.

Consider then the reduced-form model consisting of M equations in which each endogenous variable is expressed as a linear function of all the predetermined variables and a disturbance:

$$\begin{aligned} y_1 &= \pi_{11}x_1 + \cdots + \pi_{K1}x_K + v_1 \\ y_2 &= \pi_{12}x_1 + \cdots + \pi_{K2}x_K + v_2 \\ &\;\;\vdots \\ y_M &= \pi_{1M}x_1 + \cdots + \pi_{KM}x_K + v_M \end{aligned} \tag{10.4}$$

in which the v_m's are jointly normally distributed with

$$Ev_m = 0, \quad Ev_m v_{m'} = \begin{cases} \omega_{mm}, & m' = m \\ \omega_{mm'}, & m' \neq m, \end{cases}$$

independently of $x_1, \ldots, x_K$. In this formulation the joint distribution of **y** (conditional on **x**) is characterized directly: Each relationship of (10.4) refers to the distribution of a y_m (conditional on **x**). Clearly the reduced-form parameters suffice to define the joint distribution of **y** (conditional on **x**) completely. Note that in each relationship of (10.4) the right-hand side with the disturbance suppressed gives the conditional expectation of the left-hand variable as a linear function of the conditioning variables. Then unbiased estimates of the reduced-form parameters are obtainable by classical least-squares regression applied to each equation of (10.4). Note also that the reduced-form parameters are identified in the sense that they may be uniquely deduced from the parameters of the joint distribution of $\mathbf{y}$ (conditional on $\mathbf{x}$).

A second approach to formulating an econometric model may be termed the *recursive-form* approach. If, conditional on $\mathbf{x}$, $\mathbf{y}$ has a joint normal distribution with expectation linear in, and covariance matrix independent of, the conditioning vector $\mathbf{x}$, then the distribution of an element of $\mathbf{y}$ conditional on $\mathbf{x}$ and on the remaining elements of $\mathbf{y}$ is univariate normal with expectation linear in, and variance independent of, all the conditioning variables. More specifically,

(10.5) Let the conditional distribution of $\mathbf{y}$ given $\mathbf{x}$ be $\mathcal{N}(\mathbf{\Pi}'\mathbf{x}, \mathbf{\Omega})$; let $\mathbf{y}$ be partitioned as $\begin{pmatrix} \mathbf{y}_* \\ y_m \end{pmatrix}$, and correspondingly let $\mathbf{\Pi}'$ and $\mathbf{\Omega}$ be partitioned as

$$\begin{pmatrix} \mathbf{\Pi}'_* \\ \boldsymbol{\pi}'_m \end{pmatrix} \quad \text{and} \quad \begin{pmatrix} \mathbf{\Omega}_{**} & \boldsymbol{\omega}_{*m} \\ \boldsymbol{\omega}'_{*m} & \omega_{mm} \end{pmatrix}.$$

Then the conditional distribution of y_m given $\mathbf{y}_*$ and $\mathbf{x}$ is

$$\mathcal{N}(\boldsymbol{\eta}'_m \mathbf{y}_* + \boldsymbol{\theta}'_m \mathbf{x}, \phi_{mm})$$

where $\boldsymbol{\eta}'_m = \boldsymbol{\omega}'_{*m}\mathbf{\Omega}^{-1}_{**}$, $\boldsymbol{\theta}'_m = \boldsymbol{\pi}'_m - \boldsymbol{\omega}'_{*m}\mathbf{\Omega}^{-1}_{**}\mathbf{\Pi}'_*$,

and $\phi_{mm} = \omega_{mm} - \boldsymbol{\omega}'_{*m}\mathbf{\Omega}^{-1}_{**}\boldsymbol{\omega}_{*m}$;

this is a straightforward application of (3.5.12). If then we select an appropriate subvector of $\mathbf{y}$ and write $y_m = \boldsymbol{\eta}'_m \mathbf{y}_{\bar{m}} + \boldsymbol{\theta}'_m \mathbf{x} + w_m$, where

$$\mathbf{y}_{\bar{m}} = \begin{pmatrix} y_1 \\ \cdot \\ \cdot \\ \cdot \\ y_{m-1} \end{pmatrix},$$

w_m will be distributed $\mathcal{N}(0, \phi_{mm})$ independently of $\mathbf{y}_{\bar{m}}$ and $\mathbf{x}$. Doing this for each $m = 1, \ldots, M$, we may note that $Ew_m w_{m'} = 0$ $(m' \neq m)$: without loss of generality taking $m' < m$, since w_m is independent of the variables $y_1, \ldots, y_{m-1}, \mathbf{x}$ it is independent of $w_{m'}$ which is simply a linear combination of a subset of those variables (i.e., $y_1, \ldots, y_{m'}, \mathbf{x}$).

Consider then the recursive-form model in which each endogenous variable is expressed as a linear function of all the "preceding" endogenous variables, all predetermined variables, and a disturbance:

(10.6)

$$
\begin{aligned}
y_1 &= && \theta_{11}x_1 + \cdots + \theta_{K1}x_K + w_1 \\
y_2 &= \eta_{12}y_1 && + \theta_{12}x_1 + \cdots + \theta_{K2}x_K + w_2 \\
&\vdots && \vdots \\
y_M &= \eta_{1M}y_1 + \cdots + \eta_{M-1,M}y_{M-1} && + \theta_{1M}x_1 + \cdots + \theta_{KM}x_K + w_M
\end{aligned}
$$

in which the w_m's are normally distributed with

$$Ew_m = 0, \quad Ew_m w_{m'} = \begin{cases} \phi_{mm}, & m' = m \\ 0, & m' \neq m, \end{cases}$$

and each w_m is independent of $y_1, \ldots, y_{m-1}, x_1, \ldots, x_K$. In this formulation the joint distribution of $\mathbf{y}$ (conditional on $\mathbf{x}$) is characterized indirectly through a sequence of "nested" univariate distributions; each relationship in (10.6) refers to the distribution of a y_m (conditional on $y_1, \ldots, y_{m-1}$, and $\mathbf{x}$). Clearly, using the relationships in (10.5) recursively for $m = M$, $M - 1, \ldots, 1$ we can deduce the reduced-form parameters from the recursive-form parameters; since the former suffice to completely define the joint distribution of $\mathbf{y}$ (conditional on $\mathbf{x}$), so do the latter. [More generally, if we know $f(y_m \mid y_1, \ldots, y_{m-1}, \mathbf{x})$ for $m = 1, \ldots, M$, then we know $f(y_1, \ldots, y_M \mid \mathbf{x}) = \Pi_{m=1}^{M} f(y_m \mid y_1, \ldots, y_{m-1}, \mathbf{x})$.] Note that in each relationship of (10.6) the right-hand side with the disturbance suppressed gives the conditional expectation of the left-hand variable as a linear function of the conditioning variables. Then unbiased estimates of the recursive-form parameters are obtainable by classical least-squares regression applied to each equation of (10.6). Note also that the recursive-form parameters are identified—using the relationships in (10.5) we can deduce them from the reduced-form parameters and hence from the parameters of the joint distribution of $\mathbf{y}$ (conditional on $\mathbf{x}$). Finally note that the order in which the endogenous variables are arranged is quite arbitrary so that there are in fact many alternative recursive decompositions.

A third approach to formulating an econometric model is the *structural-form* approach taken in the previous sections of this chapter. In the present context this may be viewed as follows. If, conditional on $\mathbf{x}$, $\mathbf{y}$ has a joint normal distribution with expectation linear in, and covariance matrix independent of, the conditioning vector $\mathbf{x}$, then the distribution of a linear combination of elements of $\mathbf{y}$, conditional on $\mathbf{x}$, is univariate normal with expectation linear in, and variance independent of, the conditioning vector. More specifically,

(10.7) Let the conditional distribution of $\mathbf{y}$ given $\mathbf{x}$ be $\mathcal{N}(\mathbf{\Pi}'\mathbf{x}, \mathbf{\Omega})$ and let $\tilde{y}_m = -\boldsymbol{\gamma}_m' \mathbf{y}$ where $\boldsymbol{\gamma}_m'$ is a $1 \times M$ vector of constants. Then the conditional distribution of $\tilde{y}_m$ given $\mathbf{x}$ is $\mathcal{N}(\boldsymbol{\beta}_m'\mathbf{x}, \sigma_{mm})$ where $\boldsymbol{\beta}_m' = -\boldsymbol{\gamma}_m' \mathbf{\Pi}'$ and $\sigma_{mm} = \boldsymbol{\gamma}_m'\mathbf{\Omega}\boldsymbol{\gamma}_m$;

this is a straightforward extension of (3.5.8). If then we write $\tilde{y}_m = \boldsymbol{\beta}_m'\mathbf{x} + u_m$, u_m will be distributed $\mathcal{N}(0, \sigma_{mm})$ independently of $\mathbf{x}$. If we take M independent linear combinations of the elements of $\mathbf{y}$—$\tilde{y}_{m'} = -\boldsymbol{\gamma}_{m'}' \mathbf{y}$ $(m' = 1, \ldots, M)$—and write $\tilde{y}_{m'} = \boldsymbol{\beta}_{m'}'\mathbf{x} + u_{m'}$ where $\boldsymbol{\beta}_{m'}' = -\boldsymbol{\gamma}_{m'}'\mathbf{\Pi}'$ and $\sigma_{m'm'} = \boldsymbol{\gamma}_{m'}'\mathbf{\Omega}\boldsymbol{\gamma}_{m'}$ $(m' = 1, \ldots, M)$, then the joint distribution of $u_1, \ldots, u_M$ will be normal with

$$Eu_m = 0, \quad Eu_m u_{m'} = \begin{cases} \sigma_{mm}, & m' = m \\ \sigma_{mm'}, & m' \neq m, \end{cases}$$

independently of $\mathbf{x}$, where $\sigma_{mm'}$ is the m,m'th element of $\mathbf{\Sigma} = \mathbf{\Gamma}'\mathbf{\Omega}\mathbf{\Gamma}$, in which $\mathbf{\Gamma}$ is the $M \times M$ nonsingular matrix $\mathbf{\Gamma} = (\boldsymbol{\gamma}_1 \ \cdots \ \boldsymbol{\gamma}_M)$.

Consider then the structural-form model in which linear combinations of endogenous variables (with one coefficient equal to -1 in each combination) are expressed as linear functions of predetermined variables and a disturbance:

$$(10.8)\qquad \begin{array}{rcl} -y_1 - \cdots - \gamma_{M1}y_M &=& \beta_{11}x_1 + \cdots + \beta_{K1}x_K + u_1 \\ -\gamma_{12}y_1 - \cdots - \gamma_{M2}y_M &=& \beta_{12}x_1 + \cdots + \beta_{K2}x_K + u_2 \\ \vdots & & \vdots \\ -\gamma_{1M}y_1 - \cdots - y_M &=& \beta_{1M}x_1 + \cdots + \beta_{KM}x_K + u_M \end{array}$$

in which the u_m's are jointly normally distributed with

$$Eu_m = 0, \quad Eu_m u_{m'} = \begin{cases} \sigma_{mm}, & m' = m \\ \sigma_{mm'}, & m' \neq m, \end{cases}$$

independently of $x_1, \ldots, x_K$, and for simplicity each $\gamma_{mm} = -1$. In this formulation the joint distribution of $\mathbf{y}$ (conditional on $\mathbf{x}$) is characterized indirectly by way of a set of univariate distributions: Each relationship in (10.8) refers to the distribution of a $\tilde{y}_m$ (conditional on $\mathbf{x}$). Clearly, using the relationships in (10.7) we can deduce the reduced-form parameters from the structural-form parameters; since the former suffice to completely define the joint distribution of $\mathbf{y}$ (conditional on $\mathbf{x}$), so do the latter. Note that in each relationship of (10.8) the right-hand side with the disturbance suppressed gives the conditional expectation of the left-hand *combination* of variables as a linear function of the conditioning variables. Then if we knew the coefficients of the left-hand combination (the γ's), unbiased estimates of the remaining structural-form parameters would be obtainable by classical least-squares regression ($\tilde{y}_m$ on $\mathbf{x}$) applied to each equation of (10.8).

Of course this estimation procedure is not available in practice where the γ's are not known. We may take to the right-hand side of each structural-form equation all terms except the endogenous variable with coefficient 1 in (10.8), thus obtaining the M equations

$$\text{(10.9)} \quad y_m = \gamma_{1m}y_1 + \cdots + \gamma_{m-1,m}y_{m-1} + \gamma_{m+1,m}y_{m+1} + \cdots + \gamma_{M,m}y_M + \beta_{1m}x_1 + \cdots + \beta_{Km}x_K + u_m \qquad (m = 1, \ldots, M).$$

Now the right-hand side of these relations with the disturbance suppressed does *not* give the conditional expectation of the left hand variable as a function of the conditioning variables. This is so because in general $E(u_m \mid y_1, \ldots, y_{m-1}, y_{m+1}, \ldots, y_M, x_1, \ldots, x_K) \neq 0$; for

$$u_m = \tilde{y}_m - \boldsymbol{\beta}'_m\mathbf{x} = -\boldsymbol{\gamma}'_m\mathbf{y} - \boldsymbol{\beta}'_m\mathbf{x} = -\boldsymbol{\gamma}'_m(\boldsymbol{\Pi}'\mathbf{x} + \mathbf{v} - \boldsymbol{\Pi}'\mathbf{x})$$
$$= -\boldsymbol{\gamma}'_m\mathbf{v}$$

will in general be correlated with $y_{m'} = \boldsymbol{\pi}'_{m'}\mathbf{x} + v_{m'}$, where

$$\mathbf{v} = \begin{pmatrix} v_1 \\ \cdot \\ \cdot \\ \cdot \\ v_M \end{pmatrix}$$

is the reduced-form disturbance vector. Then unbiased estimates of the structural-form parameters are *not* obtainable by classical least-squares regression applied to each of the equations (10.9). Note also that without sufficient a priori restrictions the structural-form parameters will not be identified—compare our discussion in Section 4.

It will be recognized that this structural-form approach corresponds to the one we have taken in our simultaneous linear structural equation model. After all, the system (10.8) is that of (3.2)—with some terms transferred to the other side of the equation and the normalization rule imposed—while the present stochastic specifications also satisfy those of Section 3. We have surely seen that classical least-squares applied to the individual structural equations yields biased estimates of their parameters.

Now in comparison with the reduced-form and recursive-form approaches, the structural-form approach might seem to be an unnecessarily roundabout method for characterizing the joint distribution of the endogenous variables given the predetermined variables. Its linear combinations of endogenous variables appear artificial, its individual relationships do not give conditional expectations of individual endogenous variables, consistent estimation of its parameters generally requires computations which are considerably more complex than those of classical least squares, and problems of identifiability arise. Therefore it is not surprising to find that some theorists have argued for the use of alternative formulations of econometric models. Liu (1960) has made a case for the reduced-form approach. Wold has vigorously argued for a recursive-form approach—see Wold and Jureen (1953, pp. 48–53), Wold (1959, 1960), and Strotz and Wold (1960).

Nevertheless, the structural-form approach remains attractive for reasons which are indeed implicit in the discussion of the earlier sections of this chapter. If we are simply interested in describing the joint distribution of **y** (conditional on **x**) which generated the sample observations, then the reduced-form (or the recursive-form) approach may well be simpler and more direct. (Even then, as we have seen, the use of a priori information—as in the structural-form approach—can contribute to greater efficiency of estimation). If, however, we are interested in describing this joint distribution in terms of components which are likely to remain invariant under changed circumstances, then the structural-form approach may be seen to have important advantages over its rivals.

In formulating a structural model, the econometrician, after all, does not take arbitrary linear combinations of endogenous variables. Rather he attempts to construct operational counterparts of the behavioral and technological equations of economic theory. As was indicated in Section 3, each structural equation is intended to represent the behavior (or some aspect of the behavior) of an economic unit, such as an individual, a firm, a sector, or a market. If this intention is realized, a change in "circumstances"—e.g., in consumer tastes, in industrial technology, in government tax rates, in market procedures—should imply a change in a single structural equation (perhaps only in a few parameters thereof), the other structural equations remaining valid. Such a change in the economic mechanism will indeed imply a change in the joint distribution of the endogenous variables (conditional on the predetermined variables). And in general it will imply a change in all the reduced-form coefficients—each of which, as we have seen, is comprised of the net result of interactions among the economic units—and similarly in all the recursive-form parameters—which are similarly comprised. When such a change occurs, the econometrician who has estimated a structural model may still be able to make inferences about the new joint distribution of **y**, given **x**.

Typically he will have some "extraneous" information on the nature of the change and so will be able to modify the appropriate structural equation and then deduce the new joint distribution of **y**, given **x**. If he has estimated only a reduced-form or recursive-form model he will, in general, not know what modifications are called for—compare our discussion at the end of Section 9.

Elaboration and illustration of this classical case for the structural-form approach may be found in Haavelmo (1943), Hurwicz (1950*a*), and Marschak (1953). That the approach is a natural one in economics is demonstrated repeatedly, if implicitly, in the large body of empirical literature in which models are built up equation by equation, unit by unit; see, e.g., Klein (1950). The complexities associated with the structural-form approach are then seen to be consequences of its more ambitious objective of seeking "autonomous" relationships. It should be noted, however, that some of Wold's argument may be read as claiming autonomy for the recursive-form relations.

Finally let us note that embedded in this classical case—see especially Haavelmo (1943, pp. 3–5)—is a conditional expectation interpretation of structural coefficients. Consider for example the consumption function (3.29*a*) of Klein's Model I:

$$(10.10) \qquad C = a_0 + a_1 P + a_2 P_{-1} + a_3 W + \epsilon_1.$$

We may interpret this relation as follows. Consider the series of experiments in which consumers are repeatedly furnished a preassigned package of values of the right-hand variables W, P, and P_{-1}. Then on the average they would spend an amount $a_0 + a_1 P + a_2 P_{-1} + a_3 W$ on consumption goods, deviating from this amount by random amounts ϵ_1 in the successive runs of the experiment. This specification—that

$$E(C \mid P, P_{-1}, W) = a_0 + a_1 P + a_2 P_{-1} + a_3 W$$

when P, P_{-1}, W are fixed in repeated samples is perfectly consistent with the specification that

$$E(C \mid P, P_{-1}, W) \neq a_0 + a_1 P + a_2 P_{-1} + a_3 W$$

when W, P, and P_{-1} are determined jointly with C as in the real-world sample to which the model was in fact applied.

To conclude our survey of econometric theory, let us note a general issue raised by the analysis of Chapters 5–7. We have considered problems that arise when the classical linear regression assumptions are untenable, developing estimation procedures that handle such complicating factors as temporally dependent disturbances, heteroskedastic disturbances, errors of observation, or simultaneous determination. But each of the procedures typically takes account of a single complicating factor, and we have not presented a model and procedure appropriate to the situation where several or all the complications are present. This limitation may, with some justification, be attributed to the current state of econometric theory; the researcher may well have to decide which complicating factor is most important in his data and adopt the model and procedure that would be appropriate if the others were absent. Considerable work is now under way on these problems, however, and it is reasonable to expect that more adequate tools will become available. Indeed, a start has been made on simultaneous models with autocorrelated disturbances—see Sargan (1961) and Zellner (1961*b*).

Bibliography

Aitchison, J. and J. A. C. Brown (1957), *The Lognormal Distribution*, Cambridge: Cambridge University Press, 1957.

Anderson, T. W. (1958), *An Introduction to Multivariate Statistical Analysis*, New York: John Wiley and Sons, 1958.

Anderson, T. W. and H. Rubin (1949), "Estimation of the parameters of a single equation in a complete system of stochastic equations," *Annals of Mathematical Statistics*, Vol. 20, March 1949, pp. 46–63.

Anderson, T. W. and H. Rubin (1950), "The asymptotic properties of estimates of the parameters of a single equation in a complete system of stochastic equations," *Annals of Mathematical Statistics*, Vol. 21, December 1950, pp. 570–582.

Barten, A. P. (1962), "Note on unbiased estimation of the squared multiple correlation coefficient," *Statistica Neerlandica*, Vol. 16, 1962, pp. 151–163.

Basmann, R. L. (1957), "A generalized classical method of linear estimation of coefficients in a structural equation," *Econometrica*, Vol. 25, January 1957, pp. 77–83.

Basmann, R. L. (1958), "An experimental investigation of some small sample properties of (GCL) estimators of structural equations: some preliminary results," Richland: General Electric Company, 1958.

Basmann, R. L. (1959), "The computation of generalized classical estimates of coefficients in a structural equation," *Econometrica*, Vol. 27, January 1959, pp. 72–81; "Errata," *Econometrica*, Vol. 28, January 1960, p. 170.

Basmann, R. L. (1960*a*), "On the asymptotic distribution of generalized linear estimators," *Econometrica*, Vol. 28, January 1960, pp. 97–107.

Basmann, R. L. (1960*b*), "On finite sample distributions of generalized classical linear identifiability test statistics," *Journal of the American Statistical Association*, Vol. 55, December 1960, pp. 650–659.

Basmann, R. L. (1961), "A note on the exact finite sample frequency functions of generalized classical linear estimators in two leading over-identified cases," *Journal of the American Statistical Association*, Vol. 56, September 1961, pp. 619–636.

Baumol, W. (1959), *Economic Dynamics*, second edition, New York: Macmillan, 1959.

Brown, T. M. (1959), "Simplified full maximum likelihood and comparative structural estimates," *Econometrica*, Vol. 27, October 1959, pp. 638–653.

Chernoff, H. and N. Divinsky (1953), "The computation of maximum-likelihood estimates of linear structural equations," Chapter 10 in *Studies in Econometric Method*, Cowles Commission Monograph 14, W. C. Hood and T. C. Koopmans, editors, New York: John Wiley and Sons, 1953, pp. 236–269.

Chernoff, H. and H. Rubin (1953), "Asymptotic properties of limited-information estimates under generalized conditions," Chapter 7 in *Studies in Econometric Method*, Cowles Commission Monograph 14, W. C. Hood and T. C. Koopmans, editors, New York: John Wiley and Sons, 1953, pp. 200–212.

de Janosi, P. E. (1956), *Factors Influencing the Demand for New Automobiles: A Cross-section Analysis*, doctoral dissertation, University of Michigan, 1956.

Durbin, J. (1953), "A note on regression when there is extraneous information about one of the coefficients," *Journal of the American Statistical Association*, Vol. 48, December 1953, pp. 799–808.

Durbin, J. and G. S. Watson (1950), "Testing for serial correlation in least squares regression I," *Biometrika*, Vol. 37, December 1950, pp. 409–428.

Durbin, J. and G. S. Watson (1951), "Testing for serial correlation in least squares regression II," *Biometrika*, Vol. 38, June 1951, pp. 159–178.

Dwyer, P. (1951), *Linear Computations*, New York: John Wiley and Sons, 1951.

Fisher, F. M. (1959), "Generalization of the rank and order conditions for identifiability," *Econometrica*, Vol. 27, July 1959, pp. 431–447.

Fisher, Janet A. (1962), "An analysis of consumer durable goods expenditures in 1957," *Review of Economics and Statistics*, Vol. 44, February 1962, pp. 64–71.

Fox, K. A. (1958), *Econometric Analysis for Public Policy*, Ames: Iowa State University, 1958.

Friedman, M. (1957), *A Theory of the Consumption Function*, Princeton: Princeton University Press, 1957.

Goldberger, A. S. (1959), *Impact Multipliers and Dynamic Properties of the Klein-Goldberger Model*, Amsterdam: North-Holland, 1959.

Goldberger, A. S., A. L. Nagar, and H. S. Odeh (1961), "The covariance matrices of reduced-form coefficients and of forecasts for a structural econometric model," *Econometrica*, Vol. 29, October 1961, pp. 556–573.

Haavelmo, T. (1943), "The statistical implications of a system of simultaneous equations," *Econometrica*, Vol. 11, January 1943, pp. 1–12.

Haavelmo, T. (1953), "Methods of measuring the marginal propensity to consume," Chapter 4 in *Studies in Econometric Method*, Cowles Commission Monograph 14, W. C. Hood and T. C. Koopmans, editors, New York: John Wiley and Sons, 1953, pp. 75–91.

Hadley, G. (1961), *Linear Algebra*, Reading: Addison-Wesley, 1961.

Hannan, E. J. (1960), *Time Series Analysis*, London: Methuen, 1960.

Hurwicz, L. (1950*a*), "Prediction and least squares," Chapter 6 in *Statistical Inference in Dynamic Economic Models*, Cowles Commission Monograph 10, T. C. Koopmans, editor, New York: John Wiley and Sons, 1950, pp. 266–300.

Hurwicz, L. (1950*b*), "Least-squares bias in time series," Chapter 15 in *Statistical Inference in Dynamic Economic Models*, Cowles Commission Monograph 10, T. C. Koopmans, editor, New York: John Wiley and Sons, 1950, pp. 365–383.

Johnston, J. (1963), *Econometric Methods*, New York: McGraw-Hill, 1963.

Kendall, M. G. and A. Stuart (1958, 1961), *The Advanced Theory of Statistics*, Volumes I, II, London: Charles Griffin, 1958, 1961.

Klein, L. R. (1950), *Economic Fluctuations in the United States, 1921–1941*, Cowles Commission Monograph 11, New York: John Wiley and Sons, 1950.

Klein, L. R. (1951), "Estimating patterns of savings behavior from sample survey data," *Econometrica*, Vol. 19, October 1951, pp. 438–454.

Klein, L. R. (1953), *A Textbook of Econometrics*, Evanston: Row, Peterson, 1953.

Klein, L. R. (1958), "The estimation of distributed lags," *Econometrica*, Vol. 26, October 1958, pp. 553–565.

Klein, L. R. (1960), "The efficiency of estimation in econometric models," in *Essays in Economics and Econometrics*, Chapel Hill: University of North Carolina, 1960, pp. 216–232.

Klein, L. R. (1962), *An Introduction to Econometrics*, Englewood Cliffs: Prentice-Hall, 1962.

Klein, L. R. and A. S. Goldberger (1955), *An Econometric Model of the United States 1929–1952*, Amsterdam: North-Holland, 1955.

Kloek, T. (1961), "Note on convenient matrix notations in multivariate statistical analysis and in the theory of linear aggregation," *International Economic Review*, Vol. 2, September 1961, pp. 351–360.

Koopmans, T. C. (1953), "Identification problems in economic model construction," Chapter 2 in *Studies in Econometric Method*, Cowles Commission Monograph 14, W. C. Hood and T. C. Koopmans, editors, New York: John Wiley and Sons, 1953, pp. 27–48.

Koopmans, T. C. and W. C. Hood (1953), "The estimation of simultaneous linear economic relationships," Chapter 6 in *Studies in Econometric Method*, Cowles Commission Monograph 14, W. C. Hood and T. C. Koopmans, editors, New York: John Wiley and Sons, 1953, pp. 112–199.

Koopmans, T. C., H. Rubin, and R. B. Leipnik (1950), "Measuring the equation systems of dynamic economics," Chapter 2 in *Statistical Inference in Dynamic Economic Models*, Cowles Commission Monograph 10, T. C. Koopmans, editor, New York: John Wiley and Sons, 1950, pp. 53–237.

Koyck, L. (1954), *Distributed Lags and Investment Analysis*, Amsterdam: North-Holland, 1954.

Lee, Tong Hun (1963), "Demand for housing: a cross-section analysis," *Review of Economics and Statistics*, Vol. 45, May 1963, pp. 190–196.

Liu, Ta-Chung (1960), "Underidentification, structural estimation, and forecasting," *Econometrica*, Vol. 28, October 1960, pp. 855–865.

Lyttkens, E. (1964), "Standard errors of regression coefficients by autocorrelated residuals," Chapter 4 in *Econometric Model Building*, H. O. A. Wold, editor, Amsterdam: North-Holland, 1964, pp. 169–228.

Mann, H. B. and A. Wald (1943), "On the statistical treatment of linear stochastic difference equations," *Econometrica*, Vol. 11, July–October 1943, pp. 173–220.

Marschak, J. (1953), "Economic measurements for policy and prediction," Chapter 1 in *Studies in Econometric Method*, Cowles Commission Monograph 14, W. C. Hood and T. C. Koopmans, editors, New York: John Wiley and Sons, 1953, pp. 1–26.

Mood, A. M. (1950), *Introduction to the Theory of Statistics*, New York: McGraw-Hill, 1950.

Nagar, A. L. (1959*a*), "The bias and moment matrix of the general *k*-class estimators of the parameters in simultaneous equations," *Econometrica*, Vol. 27, October 1959, pp. 575–595.

Nagar, A. L. (1959*b*), *Statistical Estimation of Simultaneous Economic Relationships*, doctoral dissertation, Netherlands School of Economics, 1960.

Nerlove, M. (1958), *Distributed Lags and Demand Analysis for Agricultural and Other Commodities*, Washington: U.S. Department of Agriculture, 1958.

Parzen, E. (1960), *Modern Probability Theory and Its Applications*, New York: John Wiley and Sons, 1960.

Rothenberg, T. J. and C. T. Leenders (1964), "Efficient estimation of simultaneous equation systems," *Econometrica*, Vol. 32, January–April 1964, pp. 57–76.

Sargan, J. D. (1958), "The estimation of economic relationships using instrumental variables," *Econometrica*, Vol. 26, July 1958, pp. 393–415.

Sargan, J. D. (1961), "The maximum likelihood estimation of economic relationships with autoregressive residuals," *Econometrica*, Vol. 29, July 1961, pp. 414–426.

Scheffé, H. (1959), *The Analysis of Variance*, New York: John Wiley and Sons, 1959.

Strotz, R. H. and H. O. A. Wold (1960), "Recursive vs. nonrecursive systems: an attempt at synthesis," *Econometrica*, Vol. 28, April 1960, pp. 417–427.

Suits, D. B. (1962), "Forecasting and analysis with an econometric model," *American Economic Review*, Vol. 52, March 1962, pp. 104–132.

Theil, H. (1953), "Estimation and simultaneous correlation in complete equation systems," The Hague: Centraal Planbureau, 1953.

Theil, H. (1961), *Economic Forecasts and Policy*, second revised edition, Amsterdam: North-Holland, 1961.

Theil, H. (1963), "On the use of incomplete prior information in regression analysis," *Journal of the American Statistical Association*, Vol. 58, June 1963, pp. 401–414.

Theil, H. and J. C. G. Boot (1962), "The final form of econometric equation systems," *Review of the International Statistical Institute*, Vol. 30, 1962, pp. 136–152.

Theil, H. and A. S. Goldberger (1961), "On pure and mixed statistical estimation in economics," *International Economic Review*, Vol. 2, January 1961, pp. 65–78.

Tintner, G. (1952), *Econometrics*, New York: John Wiley and Sons, 1952.

Tobin, J. (1955), "The application of multivariate probit analysis to economic survey data," Cowles Foundation Discussion Paper 1, 1955.

Tobin, J. (1958), "Estimation of relationships for limited dependent variables," *Econometrica*, Vol. 26, January 1958, pp. 24–36.

Warner, S. L. (1962), *Stochastic Choice of Mode in Urban Travel: A Study in Binary Choice*, Evanston: Northwestern University, 1962.

Wilks, S. S. (1962), *Mathematical Statistics*, New York: John Wiley and Sons, 1962

Wold, H. O. A. (1959), "Ends and means in econometric model building," pp. 355–434 in *Probability and Statistics*, U. Grenander, editor, New York: John Wiley and Sons, 1959.

Wold, H. O. A. (1960), "A generalization of causal chain models," *Econometrica*, Vol. 28, April 1960, pp. 443–463.

Wold, H. O. A. (1961), "Unbiased predictors," pp. 719–761 in *Proceedings of the Fourth Berkeley Symposium on Mathematical Statistics and Probability, Volume I*, J. Neyman, editor, Berkeley and Los Angeles: University of California, 1961.

Wold, H. O. A. and L. Jureen (1953), *Demand Analysis*, New York: John Wiley and Sons, 1953.

Yaglom, A. M. (1962), *An Introduction to the Theory of Stationary Random Functions*, Englewood Cliffs: Prentice-Hall, 1962.

Zellner, A. (1961*a*), "Linear regression with inequality constraints on the coefficients: an application of quadratic programming and linear decision rules," International Center for Management Science, Report 6109 (MS No. 9), 1961.

Zellner, A. (1961*b*), "Econometric estimation with temporally dependent disturbance terms," *International Economic Review*, Vol. 2, May 1961, pp. 164–178.

Zellner, A. (1962*a*), "An efficient method of estimating seemingly unrelated regressions and tests for aggregation bias," *Journal of the American Statistical Association*, Vol. 57, June 1962, pp. 348–368.

Zellner, A. (1962*b*), "Estimators for seemingly unrelated regression equations: some exact finite sample results," Systems Formulation and Methodology Workshop Paper 6205, Social Systems Research Institute, University of Wisconsin, 1962.

Zellner, A. and D. S. Huang (1962), "Further properties of efficient estimators for seemingly unrelated regression equations," *International Economic Review*, Vol. 3, September 1962, pp. 300–313.

Zellner, A. and H. Theil (1962), "Three-stage least-squares: simultaneous estimation of simultaneous equations," *Econometrica*, Vol. 30, January 1962, pp. 54–78.

Zurmühl, R. (1958), *Matrizen*, Berlin: Springer, 1958.

Index